A GRAMMAR OF MOTIVES

Ad bellum purificandum

A GRAMMAR
OF MOTIVES

by

KENNETH BURKE

UNIVERSITY OF CALIFORNIA PRESS

Berkeley, Los Angeles, London

University of California Press
Berkeley and Los Angeles, California
University of California Press, Ltd.
London, England
Copyright 1945 by Prentice-Hall, Inc.
First paperback edition copyright © 1962 by The World Publishing Company

California edition © Kenneth Burke, 1969

ISBN: 0–520–01544–4
Library of Congress Catalog Card Number: 69–16741
Manufactured in the United States of America

5 6 7 8 9 0

To ELIZABETH
WITHOUT WHOM NOT

Synecdoche — form of metaphor —
a part signifies the whole or the
whole signifies the part.
motor —> automobiles

ACKNOWLEDGMENTS

Portions of *A Grammar of Motives* have previously been published in *Accent, Chimera, The Kenyon Review, The Sewanee Review,* and *View.* And I wish to acknowledge here my indebtedness to the editors of these magazines. I also wish to state my indebtedness to various publishers, editors, and authors for permission to quote from certain copyrighted material; thus: International Publishers, V. I. Lenin's *What Is To Be Done?;* The Macmillan Company, Marianne Moore's *Selected Poems* and *What Are Years?,* and Herbert Read's *Poetry and Anarchism;* The University of Chicago Press, George Herbert Mead's *The Philosophy of the Act* and Otto Neurath's *Foundations of the Social Sciences;* Little, Brown and Company, Ralph Barton Perry's *The Thought and Character of William James;* the University of California Press, Josephine Miles's *Pathetic Fallacy in the Nineteenth Century;* Harcourt, Brace and Company, Inc., I. A. Richards' *Principles of Literary Criticism* and Matthew Josephson's *Jean-Jacques Rousseau;* Peter Smith, Publisher, *Baldwin's Dictionary of Philosophy and Psychology;* the Houghton Mifflin Company, *The Education of Henry Adams,* by Henry Adams; Randon House, Inc., Eugene O'Neill's *Mourning Becomes Electra;* Mr. Yvor Winters, *Primitivism and Decadence,* published by Arrow Editions; Mr. Allen Tate, *Reason in Madness,* published by G. P. Putnam's Sons; Mr. Edgar Johnson, *One Mighty Torrent: The Drama of Biography,* published by Stackpole Sons; *The New Republic,* Stark Young's review of Clifford Odets' *Night Music; Partisan Review,* the essay by John Dewey that appeared in the "Failure of Nerve" controversy; *Science & Society,* an article by Lewis S. Feuer on "logical empiricism" and one by K. Ostrovitianov on principles of the Russian economy; *View,* for permission to quote from Parker Tyler; *The New York Times* and Mr. Arthur Krock, for permission to quote a column by Mr. Krock entitled: "Is There a Way to Dispense with Elections?"; *The Virginia Quarterly Review* and M. Denis de Rougemont, for permission to quote from his essay, "The Idea of a Federation," appearing in the Autumn 1941 issue; *The University Review* and the authors, for permission to quote from a series of essays on the theory and practice of literary criticism by R. S. Crane, Norman Maclean, and Elder Olson.

The opening pages of *A Rhetoric of Motives* were previously published in *The Hudson Review,* and some remarks on science and magic are taken from my review of Ernst Cassirer's *The Myth of the State* that appeared in *The Nation*. Otherwise, to my recollection, no portions of the work have been previously published.

I wish to thank the members of my classes at Bennington College, who with charming patience participated in the working-out of the ideas here presented.

And I wish to thank Dr. J. Robert Oppenheimer for the opportunity to spend some very helpful months at the Institute for Advanced Study in Princeton, while making a final revision of the manuscript. Also, during this time, I was fortunate in being able to discuss many of these theories and analyses at the Princeton Seminars in Literary Criticism, then in process of formation.

I regret that I did not have an opportunity to incorporate additions suggested by a six-month sojourn at the University of Chicago where, under the auspices of the College, I presented some of this material.

Many authors of the past and present have contributed to the notions herein considered, in this project for "carving out a rhetoric," often from materials not generally thought to fall under the head. And I wish to make special acknowledgment for permission to quote from the following works still in copyright: Harcourt, Brace and Company, Inc., *Collected Poems* and *Four Quartets* by T. S. Eliot, and *The Meaning of Meaning* by C. K. Ogden and I. A. Richards; Charles Scribner's Sons, George Santayana's *Realms of Being,* and *The Prefaces of Henry James,* edited by Richard Blackmur; Dr. Clyde Kluckhohn, Director of the Russian Research Center, Harvard University, for permission to quote from his pamphlet, *Navaho Witchcraft;* Harvard University Press, the *Loeb Classical Library* translation (by H. Rackham) of Cicero's *De Oratore;* Princeton University Press, Walter Lowrie's translation of Kierkegaard's *Fear and Trembling;* The University of Chicago Press, Austin Warren's *Rage for Order; Modern Philology,* Richard McKeon's essay, "Poetry and Philosophy in the Twelfth Century," which appeared in the May 1946 issue. And to The Mediaeval Academy of America for permission to quote from an essay by the same author, "Rhetoric in the Middle Ages," published in the January 1942 issue of *Speculum;* Longmans, Green and Co., *The Varieties of Religious Experience,* by William James; Schocken Books, Inc., Franz Kafka's *The Castle,* copyright 1946, and Max Brod's *Kafka: A Biography,* copyright 1947; the Oxford University Press, a poem by Gerard Manley Hopkins; The Viking Press, Thorstein Veblen's *The Theory of the Leisure Class;* The Macmillan Company, W. B. Yeats' "Byzantium" in *Winding Stair,* copyright 1933.

K. B.

CONTENTS

PART TWO—THE PHILOSOPHIC SCHOOLS

PART THREE—ON DIALECTIC

APPENDIX

INTRODUCTION: THE FIVE KEY TERMS
OF DRAMATISM

WHAT is involved, when we say what people are doing and why they are doing it? An answer to that question is the subject of this book. The book is concerned with the basic forms of thought which, in accordance with the nature of the world as all men necessarily experience it, are exemplified in the attributing of motives. These forms of thought can be embodied profoundly or trivially, truthfully or falsely. They are equally present in systematically elaborated metaphysical structures, in legal judgments, in poetry and fiction, in political and scientific works, in news and in bits of gossip offered at random.

We shall use five terms as generating principle of our investigation. They are: Act, Scene, Agent, Agency, Purpose. In a rounded statement about motives, you must have some word that names the *act* (names what took place, in thought or deed), and another that names the *scene* (the background of the act, the situation in which it occurred); also, you must indicate what person or kind of person (*agent*) performed the act, what means or instruments he used (*agency*), and the *purpose*. Men may violently disagree about the purposes behind a given act, or about the character of the person who did it, or how he did it, or in what kind of situation he acted; or they may even insist upon totally different words to name the act itself. But be that as it may, any complete statement about motives will offer *some kind of* answers to these five questions: what was done (act), when or where it was done (scene), who did it (agent), how he did it (agency), and why (purpose).

If you ask why, with a whole world of terms to choose from, we select these rather than some others as basic, our book itself is offered as the answer. For, to explain our position, we shall show how it can be applied.

Act, Scene, Agent, Agency, Purpose. Although, over the centuries, men have shown great enterprise and inventiveness in pondering matters of human motivation, one can simplify the subject by this pentad of key terms, which are understandable almost at a glance. They need never to be abandoned, since all statements that assign motives can be shown to arise out of them and to terminate in them. By examining them quizzically, we can range far; yet the terms are always there for us to reclaim, in their everyday simplicity, their almost miraculous easiness, thus enabling us constantly to begin afresh. When they might become difficult, when we can hardly see them, through having stared at them too intensely, we can of a sudden relax, to look at them as we always have, lightly, glancingly. And having reassured ourselves, we can start out again, once more daring to let them look strange and difficult for a time.

In an exhibit of photographic murals (*Road to Victory*) at the Museum of Modern Art, there was an aerial photograph of two launches, proceeding side by side on a tranquil sea. Their wakes crossed and recrossed each other in almost an infinity of lines. Yet despite the intricateness of this tracery, the picture gave an impression of great simplicity, because one could quickly perceive the generating principle of its design. Such, ideally, is the case with our pentad of terms, used as generating principle. It should provide us with a kind of simplicity that can be developed into considerable complexity, and yet can be discovered beneath its elaborations.

We want to inquire into the purely internal relationships which the five terms bear to one another, considering their possibilities of transformation, their range of permutations and combinations—and then to see how these various resources figure in actual statements about human motives. Strictly speaking, we mean by a Grammar of motives a concern with the terms alone, without reference to the ways in which their potentialities have been or can be utilized in actual statements about motives. Speaking broadly we could designate as "philosophies" any statements in which these grammatical resources are specifically utilized. Random or unsystematic statements about motives could be considered as fragments of a philosophy.

One could think of the Grammatical resources as *principles,* and of the various philosophies as *casuistries* which apply these principles to temporal situations. For instance, we may examine the term Scene simply as a blanket term for the concept of background or setting *in general,* a name for *any* situation in which acts or agents are placed. In our usage, this concern would be "grammatical." And we move into matters of "philosophy" when we note that one thinker uses "God" as his term for the ultimate ground or scene of human action, another uses "nature," a third uses "environment," or "history," or "means of production," etc. And whereas a statement about the grammatical principles of motivation might lay claim to a universal validity, or complete certainty, the choice of any one philosophic idiom embodying these principles is much more open to question. Even before we know what act is to be discussed, we can say with confidence that a rounded discussion of its motives must contain a reference to *some kind of* background. But since each philosophic idiom will characterize this background differently, there will remain the question as to which characterization is "right" or "more nearly right."

It is even likely that, whereas one philosophic idiom offers the best calculus for one case, another case answers best to a totally different calculus. However, we should not think of "cases" in too restricted a sense. Although, from the standpoint of the grammatical principles inherent in the internal relationships prevailing among our five terms, any given philosophy is to be considered as a casuistry, even a cultural situation extending over centuries is a "case," and would probably require a much different philosophic idiom as its temporizing calculus of motives than would be required in the case of other cultural situations.

In our original plans for this project, we had no notion of writing a "Grammar" at all. We began with a theory of comedy, applied to a treatise on human relations. Feeling that competitive ambition is a drastically over-developed motive in the modern world, we thought this motive might be transcended if men devoted themselves not so much to "excoriating" it as to "appreciating" it. Accordingly, we began taking notes on the foibles and antics of what we tended to think of as "the Human Barnyard."

We sought to formulate the basic stratagems which people employ, in endless variations, and consciously or unconsciously, for the outwitting or cajoling of one another. Since all these devices had a "you and me" quality about them, being "addressed" to some person or to some advantage, we classed them broadly under the heading of a Rhetoric. There were other notes, concerned with modes of expression and appeal in the fine arts, and with purely psychological or psychoanalytic matters. These we classed under the heading of Symbolic.

We had made still further observations, which we at first strove uneasily to class under one or the other of these two heads, but which we were eventually able to distinguish as the makings of a Grammar. For we found in the course of writing that our project needed a grounding in formal considerations logically prior to both the rhetorical and the psychological. And as we proceeded with this introductory ground-work, it kept extending its claims until it had spun itself from an intended few hundred words into nearly 200,000, of which the present book is revision and abridgement.

Theological, metaphysical, and juridical doctrines offer the best illus-tration of the concerns we place under the heading of Grammar; the forms and methods of art best illustrate the concerns of Symbolic; and the ideal material to reveal the nature of Rhetoric comprises observa-tions on parliamentary and diplomatic devices, editorial bias, sales methods and incidents of social sparring. However, the three fields overlap considerably. And we shall note, in passing, how the Rhetoric and the Symbolic hover about the edges of our central theme, the Grammar.

A perfectionist might seek to evolve terms free of ambiguity and in-consistency (as with the terministic ideals of symbolic logic and logical positivism). But we have a different purpose in view, one that prob-ably retains traces of its "comic" origin. We take it for granted that, insofar as men cannot themselves create the universe, there must re-main something essentially enigmatic about the problem of motives, and that this underlying enigma will manifest itself in inevitable ambiguities and inconsistencies among the terms for motives. Accordingly, what we want is *not terms that avoid ambiguity,* but *terms that clearly reveal the strategic spots at which ambiguities necessarily arise.*

Occasionally, you will encounter a writer who seems to get great exal-tation out of proving, with an air of much relentlessness, that some phil-osophic term or other has been used to cover a variety of meanings, and who would smash and abolish this idol. As a general rule, when a term is singled out for such harsh treatment, if you look closer you will find that it happens to be associated with some cultural or political trend from which the writer would dissociate himself; hence there is a certain notable ambiguity in this very charge of ambiguity, since he presumably feels purged and strengthened by bringing to bear upon this particular term a kind of attack that could, with as much justice, be brought to bear upon any other term (or "title") in philosophy, includ-ing of course the alternative term, or "title," that the writer would

swear by. Since no two things or acts or situations are exactly alike,
you cannot apply the same term to both of them without thereby introducing a certain margin of ambiguity, an ambiguity as great as the
difference between the two subjects that are given the identical title.
And all the more may you expect to find ambiguity in terms so "titular"
as to become the marks of a philosophic school, or even several philosophic schools. Hence, instead of considering it our task to "dispose of"
any ambiguity by merely disclosing the fact that it is an ambiguity, we
rather consider it our task to study and clarify the *resources* of ambiguity. For in the course of this work, we shall deal with many kinds
of *transformation*—and it is in the areas of ambiguity that transformations take place; in fact, without such areas, transformation would be
impossible. Distinctions, we might say, arise out of a great central
moltenness, where all is merged. They have been thrown from a liquid center to the surface, where they have congealed. Let one of these
crusted distinctions return to its source, and in this alchemic center it
may be remade, again becoming molten liquid, and may enter into
new combinations, whereat it may be again thrown forth as a new
crust, a different distinction. So that A may become non-A. But not
merely by a leap from one state to the other. Rather, we must take A
back into the ground of its existence, the logical substance that is its
causal ancestor, and on to a point where it is consubstantial with
non-A; then we may return, this time emerging with non-A instead.

And so with our five terms: certain formal interrelationships prevail
among these terms, by reason of their role as attributes of a common
ground or substance. Their participation in a common ground makes
for transformability. At every point where the field covered by any one
of these terms overlaps upon the field covered by any other, there is an
alchemic opportunity, whereby we can put one philosophy or doctrine
of motivation into the alembic, make the appropriate passes, and take
out another. From the central moltenness, where all the elements are
fused into one togetherness, there are thrown forth, in separate crusts,
such distinctions as those between freedom and necessity, activity and
passiveness, coöperation and competition, cause and effect, mechanism
and teleology.

Our term, "Agent," for instance, is a general heading that might, in
a given case, require further subdivision, as an agent might have his act
modified (hence partly motivated) by friends (co-agents) or enemies

(counter-agents). Again, under "Agent" one could place any personal properties that are assigned a motivational value, such as "ideas," "the will," "fear," "malice," "intuition," "the creative imagination." A portrait painter may treat the body as a property of the agent (an expression of personality), whereas materialistic medicine would treat it as "scenic," a purely "objective material"; and from another point of view it could be classed as an agency, a means by which one gets reports of the world at large. Machines are obviously instruments (that is, Agencies); yet in their vast accumulation they constitute the industrial scene, with its own peculiar set of motivational properties. War may be treated as an Agency, insofar as it is a means to an end; as a collective Act, subdivisible into many individual acts; as a Purpose, in schemes proclaiming a cult of war. For the man inducted into the army, war is a Scene, a situation that motivates the nature of his training; and in mythologies war is an Agent, or perhaps better a super-agent, in the figure of the war god. We may think of voting as an act, and of the voter as an agent; yet votes and voters both are hardly other than a politician's medium or agency; or from another point of view, they are a part of his scene. And insofar as a vote is cast without adequate knowledge of its consequences, one might even question whether it should be classed as an activity at all; one might rather call it passive, or perhaps sheer motion (what the behaviorists would call a Response to a Stimulus).

Or imagine that one were to manipulate the terms, for the imputing of motives, in such a case as this: The hero (agent) with the help of a friend (co-agent) outwits the villain (counter-agent) by using a file (agency) that enables him to break his bonds (act) in order to escape (purpose) from the room where he has been confined (scene). In selecting a casuistry here, we might locate the motive in the agent, as were we to credit his escape to some trait integral to his personality, such as "love of freedom." Or we might stress the motivational force of the scene, since nothing is surer to awaken thoughts of escape in a man than a condition of imprisonment. Or we might note the essential part played by the *co-agent,* in assisting our hero to escape—and, with such thoughts as our point of departure, we might conclude that the motivations of this act should be reduced to social origins.

Or if one were given to the brand of speculative enterprise exemplified by certain Christian heretics (for instance, those who worshipped

Judas as a saint, on the grounds that his betrayal of Christ, in leading to the Crucifixion, so brought about the opportunity for mankind's redemption) one might locate the necessary motivational origin of the act in the *counter-agent*. For the hero would not have been prodded to escape if there had been no villain to imprison him. Inasmuch as the escape could be called a "good" act, we might find in such motivational reduction to the counter-agent a compensatory transformation whereby a bitter fountain may give forth sweet waters. In his *Anti-Dühring* Engels gives us a secular variant which no one could reasonably call outlandish or excessive:

> It was slavery that first made possible the division of labour between agriculture and industry on a considerable scale, and along with this, the flower of the ancient world, Hellenism. Without slavery, no Greek state, no Greek art and science; without slavery, no Roman Empire. But without Hellenism and the Roman Empire as a basis, also no modern Europe.
>
> We should never forget that our whole economic, political and intellectual development has as its presupposition a state of things in which slavery was as necessary as it was universally recognized. In this sense we are entitled to say: Without the slavery of antiquity, no modern socialism.

Pragmatists would probably have referred the motivation back to a source in *agency*. They would have noted that our hero escaped by using an *instrument,* the file by which he severed his bonds; then in this same line of thought, they would have observed that the hand holding the file was also an instrument; and by the same token the brain that guided the hand would be an instrument, and so likewise the educational system that taught the methods and shaped the values involved in the incident.

True, if you reduce the terms to any one of them, you will find them branching out again; for no one of them is enough. Thus, Mead called his pragmatism a philosophy of the *act*. And though Dewey stresses the value of "intelligence" as an instrument (agency, embodied in "scientific method"), the other key terms in his casuistry, "experience" and "nature," would be the equivalents of act and scene respectively. We must add, however, that Dewey is given to stressing the *overlap* of these two terms, rather than the respects in which they are distinct, as he proposes to "replace the traditional separation of nature and experience with the idea of continuity." (The quotation is from *Intelligence and the Modern World.*)

As we shall see later, it is by reason of the pliancy among our terms that philosophic systems can pull one way and another. The margins of overlap provide opportunities whereby a thinker can go without a leap from any one of the terms to any of its fellows. (We have also likened the terms to the fingers, which in their extremities are distinct from one another, but merge in the palm of the hand. If you would go from one finger to another without a leap, you need but trace the tendon down into the palm of the hand, and then trace a new course along another tendon.) Hence, no great dialectical enterprise is necessary if you would merge the terms, reducing them even to as few as one; and then, treating this as the "essential" term, the "causal ancestor" of the lot, you can proceed in the reverse direction across the margins of overlap, "deducing" the other terms from it as its logical descendants.

This is the method, explicitly and in the grand style, of metaphysics which brings its doctrines to a head in some over-all title, a word for being in general, or action in general, or motion in general, or development in general, or experience in general, etc., with all its other terms distributed about this titular term in positions leading up to it and away from it. There is also an implicit kind of metaphysics, that often goes by the name of No Metaphysics, and aims at reduction not to an over-all title but to some presumably underlying atomic constituent. Its vulgar variant is to be found in techniques of "unmasking," which would make for progress and emancipation by applying materialistic terms to immaterial subjects (the pattern here being, "X is nothing but Y," where X designates a higher value and Y a lower one, the higher value being thereby reduced to the lower one).

The titular word for our own method is "dramatism," since it invites one to consider the matter of motives in a perspective that, being developed from the analysis of drama, treats language and thought primarily as modes of action. The method is synoptic, though not in the historical sense. A purely historical survey would require no less than a universal history of human culture; for every judgment, exhortation, or admonition, every view of natural or supernatural reality, every intention or expectation involves assumptions about motive, or cause. Our work must be synoptic in a different sense: in the sense that it offers a system of placement, and should enable us, by the systematic manipulation of the terms, to "generate," or "anticipate" the various classes of motivational theory. And a treatment in these terms, we hope to show, reduces the subject synoptically while still permitting us to appreciate its scope and complexity.

It is not our purpose to import dialectical and metaphysical concerns into a subject that might otherwise be free of them. On the contrary, we hope to make clear the ways in which dialectical and metaphysical issues *necessarily* figure in the subject of motivation. Our speculations, as we interpret them, should show that the subject of motivation is a philosophic one, not ultimately to be solved in terms of empirical science.

PART ONE

WAYS OF PLACEMENT

I

CONTAINER AND THING CONTAINED

The Scene–Act Ratio

U SING "scene" in the sense of setting, or background, and "act" in the sense of action, one could say that "the scene contains the act." And using "agents" in the sense of actors, or acters, one could say that "the scene contains the agents."

It is a principle of drama that the nature of acts and agents should be consistent with the nature of the scene. And whereas comic and grotesque works may deliberately set these elements at odds with one another, audiences make allowance for such liberty, which reaffirms the same principle of consistency in its very violation.

The nature of the scene may be conveyed primarily by suggestions built into the lines of the verbal action itself, as with the imagery in the dialogue of Elizabethan drama and with the descriptive passages of novels; or it may be conveyed by non-linguistic properties, as with the materials of naturalistic stage-sets. In any case, examining first the relation between scene and act, all we need note here is the principle whereby the scene is a fit "container" for the act, expressing in fixed properties the same quality that the action expresses in terms of development.

Ibsen's *An Enemy of the People* is a good instance of the scene-act ratio, since the correlations between scene and act are readily observable, beginning with the fact that this representative middle-class drama is enacted against a typical middle-class setting. Indeed, in this work written at the very height of Ibsen's realistic period, we can see how readily realism leads into symbolism. For the succession of scenes both *realistically reflects* the course of the action and *symbolizes* it.

The first act (we are now using the word "act" in the purely technical sense, to designate the major division of a play, a sense in which we could even reverse our formula and say that "the act contains its scenes")—the first act takes place in Dr. Stockmann's sitting room, a

3

background perfectly suited to the thoroughly bourgeois story that is to unfold from these beginnings. In the course of this act, we learn of a scene, or situation, prior to the opening of the play, but central to its motivation. Dr. Stockmann refers to an earlier period of withdrawal, spent alone in the far North. During his isolation, he had conceived of his plan for the public Baths. This plan may be considered either realistically or symbolically; it is the dramatist's device for materializing, or objectifying, a purely spiritual process, since the plot has to do with pollution and purification on a moral level, which has its scenic counterpart in the topic of the Baths.

Act II. Still in Dr. Stockmann's sitting room. Dr. Stockmann has learned that the Baths, the vessels of purification, are themselves polluted, and that prominent business and professional men would suppress this fact for financial reasons. This opposition is epitomized in the figure of Peter Stockmann, the Doctor's brother. The intimate, familial quality of the setting thus has its counterpart in the quality of the action, which involves the struggle of two social principles, the conservative and the progressive, as objectified and personalized in the struggle of the two brothers.

Act III takes place in the editorial office of the People's Messenger, a local newspaper in which Dr. Stockmann had hoped to publish his evidence that the water supply was contaminated. The action takes on a more forensic reference, in keeping with the nature of the place. In this Act we have the peripety of the drama, as Dr. Stockmann's expectations are reversed. For he learns that the personal and financial influence of his enemies prevents the publication of the article. This turn of the plot has its scenic replica in mimicry involving Peter Stockmann's hat and stick, properties that symbolize his identity as mayor. In false hope of victory, Dr. Stockmann had taken them up, and strutted about burlesquing his brother. But when Dr. Stockmann learns that the editor, in response to the pressure of the conservatives, will not publish the article, it is Peter Stockmann's turn to exult. This reversal of the action is materialized (made scenic) thus:

> PETER STOCKMANN. My hat and stick, if you please. (Dr. Stockmann *takes off the hat and lays it on the table with the stick*. Peter Stockmann *takes them up*.) Your authority as mayor has come to an untimely end.

In the next Act Dr. Stockmann does contrive to lay his case before a public tribunal of a sort: a gathering of fellow-townsmen, assembled in "a big old-fashioned room," in the house of a friend. His appeal is unsuccessful; his neighbors vote overwhelmingly against him, and the scene ends in turbulence. As regards the scene-act ratio, note that the semi-public, semi-intimate setting reflects perfectly the quality of Dr. Stockmann's appeal.

In Act V, the stage directions tell us that the hero's clothes are torn, and the room is in disorder, with broken windows. You may consider these details either as properties of the scene or as a reflection of the hero's condition after his recent struggle with the forces of reaction. The scene is laid in Dr. Stockmann's *study,* a setting so symbolic of the direction taken by the plot that the play ends with Dr. Stockmann announcing his plan to enroll twelve young *disciples* and with them to found a *school* in which he will work for the *education* of society.

The whole plot is that of an internality directed outwards. We progress by stages from a scene (reported) wherein the plan of social purification was conceived in loneliness, to the scene in his study where the hero announces in the exaltation of a dramatic finale: "The strongest man in the world is he who stands most alone." The pronouncement is modified by the situation in which it is uttered: as Dr. Stockmann speaks, he is surrounded by a loyal and admiring family circle, and his educational plan calls not for complete independence, but for coöperation. He is not setting himself up as the strongest man in the world, but merely as one headed in the same direction. And, with the exception of his brother Peter, we may consider his family circle as aspects of his own identity, being under the aegis of "loneliness" since it began so and retains the quality of its ancestry.

The end of the third play in O'Neill's trilogy, *Mourning Becomes Electra,* presents a contrasting instance of the scene-act ratio:

> LAVINIA. (*turns to him sharply*) You go now and close the shutters and nail them tight.
> SETH. Ayeh.
> LAVINIA. And tell Hannah to throw out all the flowers.
> SETH. Ayeh. (*He goes past her up the steps and into the house. She ascends to the portico—and then turns and stands for a while, stiff and square-shouldered, staring into the sunlight with frozen*

eyes. Seth *leans out of the window at the right of the door and pulls the shutters closed with a decisive bang. As if this were a word of command,* Lavinia *pivots sharply on her heel and marches woodenly into the house, closing the door behind her.*)

CURTAIN

We end here on the motif of the shut-in personality, quite literally objectified. And the closing, novelistic stage-directions are beautifully suited to our purpose; for note how, once the shutters have been closed, thereby placing before our eyes the scenic replica of Lavinia's mental state, this scene in turn becomes the motivation of her next act. For we are told that she walks like an automaton in response to the closing of the shutter, "as if this were a word of command."

Hamlet contains a direct reference to the motivational aspect of the scene-act ratio. In an early scene, when Hamlet is about to follow the Ghost, Horatio warns:

> What if it tempt you toward the flood, my lord,
> Or to the dreadful summit of the cliff
> That beetles o'er his base into the sea,
> And there assume some other horrible form,
> Which might deprive your sovereignty of reason
> And draw you into madness? Think of it;
> The very place puts toys of desperation,
> Without more motive, into every brain
> That looks so many fathoms to the sea
> And hears it roar beneath.

In the last four lines of this speech, Horatio is saying that the sheer natural surroundings might be enough to provide a man with a motive for an act as desperate and absolute as suicide. This notion (of the natural scene as sufficient motivation for an act) was to reappear, in many transformations, during the subsequent centuries. We find a variant of it in the novels of Thomas Hardy, and in other regionalists who derive motivations for their characters from what Virgil would have called the *genius loci.* There are unmistakable vestiges of it in scientific theories (of Darwinian cast) according to which men's behavior and development are explained in terms of environment. Geopolitics is a contemporary variant.

From the motivational point of view, there is implicit in the quality

Genius loci (Virgil)

of a scene the quality of the action that is to take place within it. This would be another way of saying that the act will be consistent with the scene. Thus, when the curtain rises to disclose a given stage-set, this stage-set contains, simultaneously, implicitly, all that the narrative is to draw out as a sequence, explicitly. Or, if you will, the stage-set contains the action *ambiguously* (as regards the norms of action)—and in the course of the play's development this ambiguity is converted into a corresponding *articulacy*. The proportion would be: scene is to act as implicit is to explicit. One could not deduce the details of the action from the details of the setting, but one could deduce the quality of the action from the quality of the setting. An extreme illustration would be an Expressionistic drama, having for its scenic reflex such abstract properties as lines askew, grotesque lighting, sinister color, and odd objects.

We have, of course, chosen examples particularly suited to reveal the distinction between act and scene as well as their interdependence. The matter is obscured when we are dealing with scene in the sense of the relationships prevailing among the various *dramatis personae*. For the characters, by being in interaction, could be treated as scenic conditions or "environment," of one another; and any act could be treated as part of the context that modifies (hence, to a degree motivates) the subsequent acts. The principles of dramatic consistency would lead one to expect such cases of overlap among the terms; but while being aware of them we should firmly fix in our minds such cases as afford a clear differentiation. Our terms lending themselves to both merger and division, we are here trying to divide two of them while recognizing their possibilities of merger.   *cf. Hegel*

The Scene–Agent Ratio

The scene-agent ratio, where the synecdochic relation is between person and place, is partly exemplified in this citation from Carlyle's *Heroes and Hero-Worship*:

> These Arabs Mohammed was born among are certainly a notable people. Their country itself is notable; the fit habitation for such a race. Savage inaccessible rock-mountains, great grim deserts, alternating with beautiful strips of verdure; wherever water is, there is greenness, beauty; odoriferous balm-shrubs, date-trees, frankincense-trees. Consider that wide waste horizon of sand, empty, silent,

like a sand-sea, dividing habitable place from habitable place. You
are all alone there, left alone with the universe; by day a fierce sun
blazing down on it with intolerable radiance; by night the great deep
heaven with its stars. Such a country is fit for a swift-handed, deep-
hearted race of men.

The correlation between the quality of the country and the quality of
its inhabitants is here presented in quite secular terms. There is a sonnet by Wordsworth that is a perfect instance of the scene-agent ratio
treated theologically:

Scene

It is a beauteous evening, calm and free,
The holy time is quiet as a Nun
Breathless with adoration; the broad sun
Is sinking down in its tranquillity;
The gentleness of heaven broods o'er the Sea;
Listen! the mighty Being is awake,
And doth with his eternal motion make
A sound like thunder—everlastingly.

Agent

Dear Child! Dear Girl! that walkest with me here,
If thou appear untouched by solemn thought,
Thy nature is not therefore less divine:
Thou liest in Abraham's bosom all the year;
And worship'st at the Temple's inner shrine,
God being with thee when we know it not.

By selecting a religious image in which to convey the purely naturalistic sense of hush, the octave infuses the natural scene with hints of a
wider circumference, supernatural in scope. The sestet turns from
scene to agent; indeed, the octave is all scene, the sestet all agent. But
by the logic of the scene-agent ratio, if the scene is supernatural in quality, the agent contained by this scene will partake of the same supernatural quality. And so, spontaneously, purely by being the kind of
agent that is at one with this kind of scene, the child is "divine." The
contents of a divine container will synecdochically share in its divinity.

Swift's satire on philosophers and mathematicians, the Laputans in
the third book of *Gulliver's Travels,* offers a good instance of the way
in which the scene-agent ratio can be used for the depiction of character. To suggest that the Laputans are, we might say, "up in the air,"

he portrays them as living on an island that floats in space. Here the nature of the inhabitants is translated into terms of their habitation.

Variants of the scene-agent ratio abound in typical nineteenth-century thought, so strongly given to the study of motives by the dialectic pairing of people and things (man and nature, agent and scene). The ratio figures characteristically in the idealist's concern with the *Einklang zwischen Innen- und Aussenwelt*. The paintings of the pointillist Seurat carry the sense of consistency between scene and agent to such lengths that his human figures seem on the point of dissolving into their background. However, we here move beyond strictly scene-agent matters into the area better covered by our term, agency, since the extreme impression of consistency between scene and agent is here conveyed by stressing the distinctive terms of the method, or medium (that is, agency), which serves as an element common to both scene and agents.

The logic of the scene-agent ratio has often served as an embarrassment to the naturalistic novelist. He may choose to "indict" some scene (such as bad working conditions under capitalism) by showing that it has a "brutalizing" effect upon the people who are indigenous to this scene. But the scene-agent ratio, if strictly observed here, would require that the "brutalizing" situation contain "brutalized" characters as its dialectical counterpart. And thereby, in his humanitarian zeal to save mankind, the novelist portrays characters which, in being as brutal as their scene, are not worth saving. We could phrase this dilemma in another way: our novelist points up his thesis by too narrow a conception of scene as the motive-force behind his characters; and this restricting of the scene calls in turn for a corresponding restriction upon personality, or rôle.

Further Instances of These Ratios

The principles of consistency binding scene, act, and agent also lead to reverse applications. That is, the scene-act ratio either calls for acts in keeping with scenes or scenes in keeping with acts—and similarly with the scene-agent ratio. When Lavinia instructs Seth to nail fast the shutters and throw out the flowers, by her command (an act) she brings it about that the scene corresponds to her state of mind. But as soon as these scenic changes have taken place, they in turn become the motivating principle of her subsequent conduct. For the complete embodiment of her purposes functions as a "command" to her; and she obeys it as a response to a stimulus, like a pure automaton moved by the sheer disposition of material factors.

In behavioristic metaphysics (behaviorists would call it No Metaphysics) you radically truncate the possibilities of drama by eliminating action, reducing action to sheer motion. The close of the O'Neill play follows this same development from action to motion, a kind of inverted transcendence. Because of this change, Lavinia's last moments must be relegated to stage directions alone. She does not *act,* she is automatically *moved.* The trilogy did not end a moment too soon; for its close represented not only the end of Lavinia, but the end of the motivating principle of drama itself. The playwright had here obviously come to the end of a line. In his next plays he would have to "turn back." For he could have "gone on" only by abandoning drama for some more "scientific" form. (He might have transcended drama scientifically, for instance, by a collating of sociological observations designed to classify different types of motorist and to correlate them with different types of response to traffic signals.)

We noted how, in Ibsen's drama, the hero's state of mind after his conflict with the townspeople was objectified in such scenic properties as his torn clothing, and the broken windows and general disorder of his study. It is obvious that one might have carried this consistency further in either direction (for instance, spreading it more environmentally, as were we to enlist turbulent weather as an aspect of the scene, or more personally, as were we to enlist facial expressions and postures of the body, which of course the actor does, in interpreting his rôle, regardless of the playwright's omissions). If you took the hero's state of mind as your point of departure here, you could say that the whole scene becomes a mere aspect of the rôle, or person ("agent")— or that the physical body of the agent is itself but "scenic," to be listed among the person's "properties," as with a dwelling that a man had ordered built in strict accordance with his own private specifications, or as theologians see in "body" the dwelling-place of "soul." We observe the same ratio in Swift's account of his Laputans when, to suggest that in their thinking they could be transcendental, or introvert, or extremely biased, but never well balanced, he writes: "Their heads were all inclined, either to the right or to the left; one of their eyes turned inward, and the other directly up to the zenith." But lest our speculations seem too arbitrary, let us cite one more anecdote, this time from a tiny drama enacted in real life, and here reported to illustrate how, when a state of mind is pronounced in quality, the agent may be observed arranging a corresponding pattern in the very properties of the scene.

The occasion: a committee meeting. The setting: a group of committee members bunched about a desk in an office, after hours. Not far from the desk was a railing; but despite the crowding, all the members were bunched about the chairman at the desk, inside the railing. However, they had piled their hats and coats on chairs and tables outside the pale. General engrossment in the discussion. But as the discussion continued, one member quietly arose, and opened the gate in the railing. As unnoticeably as possible, she stepped outside and closed the gate. She picked up her coat, laid it across her arm, and stood waiting. A few moments later, when there was a pause in the discussion, she asked for the floor. After being recognized by the chairman, she very haltingly, in embarrassment, announced with regret that she would have to resign from the committee.

Consider with what fidelity she had set the scene for this pattern of severance as she stepped beyond the railing to make her announcement. Design: chairman and fellow members within the pale, sitting, without hats and overcoats—she outside the pale, standing, with coat over her arm preparatory to departure. She had strategically modified the arrangement of the scene in such a way that it implicitly (ambiguously) contained the quality of her act.

Ubiquity of the Ratios

If we but look about us, we find examples of the two ratios everywhere; for they are at the very centre of motivational assumptions. But to discern them in their ubiquity, we must remain aware of the many guises which the five terms may assume in the various casuistries. In the introduction to his *Discourses,* for instance, Machiavelli complains that people read history without applying its lessons, "as though heaven, the sun, the elements, and men had changed the order of their motions and power, and were different from what they were in ancient times." For our purposes, the quotation could be translated, "as though human agents and both the supernatural and the natural scenes had changed, with a corresponding change in the nature of motives."

Besides general synonyms for scene that are obviously of a background character, such as "society," or "environment," we often encounter quite specific localizations, words for particular places, situations, or eras. "It is 12:20 P.M." is a "scenic" statement. Milton's *L'Allegro* and *Il Penseroso* are formed about a scenic contrast between morning and night, with a corresponding contrast of actions. Terms for historical epochs, cultural movements, social institutions (such as "Elizabethan period," "romanticism," "capitalism") are scenic, though often with an admixture of properties overlapping upon the areas covered by the term, agent. If we recall that "ideas" are a property of agents, we can detect this strategic overlap in Locke's expression, "the scene of ideas," the form of which Carl Becker exactly reproduces when referring to "climates of opinion," in *The Heavenly City of the Eighteenth-Century Philosophers.*

The word "ground," much used in both formal philosophy and everyday speech when discussing motives, is likewise scenic, though readily encroaching upon the areas more directly covered by "agent" and "purpose." We can discern the scenic reference if the question, "On what grounds did he do this?" is translated: "What kind of scene did he say it was, that called for such an act?" Hegelian idealism exploits the double usage (ground as "background" and ground as "reason") by positing "Reason" as the ultimate ground, the *Grundprinzip,* of all history. Thus, whereas historicism regularly treats historical scenes as the background, or motive, of individual developments, Hegel would treat Reason as the background, or motive, of historical sequence in general. Let us not worry, at this point, what it may "mean" to say that "Reason" is at once the mover of history and the substance of which history is made. It is sufficient here to note that such terministic resources were utilized, and to detect the logic of the pentad behind them.

The maxim, "terrain determines tactics," is a strict localization of the scene-act ratio, with "terrain" as the casuistic equivalent for "scene" in a military calculus of motives, and "tactics" as the corresponding "act."

Political commentators now generally use the word "situation" as their synonym for scene, though often without any clear concept of its function as a statement about motives. Many social psychologists consciously use the term for its motivational bearing (it has a range extending from the broadest concepts of historical setting down to the simplified, controlled conditions which the animal experimenter imposes upon his rats in a maze). The Marxist reference to "the objective situation" is explicitly motivational, and the theorists who use this formula discuss "policies" as political acts enacted in conformity with the nature of scenes. However, the scene-act ratio can be applied in two ways. It can be applied deterministically in statements that a certain policy *had* to be adopted in a certain situation, or it may be applied in hortatory statements to the effect that a certain policy *should be* adopted in conformity with the situation. The deterministic usage (in scene-agent form) was exemplified in the statement of a traveller who, on arriving from France under German domination, characterized the politicians as "prisoners of the situation." And the hortatory usage was exemplified when a speaker said that President Roosevelt should be granted "unusual powers" because our country was in an "unusual international situation." In a judgment written by Justice Hugo L. Black, the Supreme Court ruled that it was not "beyond the war powers of Congress and the Executive to exclude those of Japanese ancestry from the West Coast area at the time they did." And by implication, the scene-act ratio was invoked to substantiate this judgment:

> When under conditions of modern warfare our shores are threatened by hostile forces, the power to protect must be commensurate with the threatened danger.

Among the most succinct instances of the scene-act ratio in dialectical materialism is Marx's assertion (cited also by Lenin in *The State and Revolution*), that "Justice can never rise superior to the economic conditions of society and the cultural development conditioned by them." That is, in contrast with those who would place justice as a property of personality (an attribute purely of the *agent*), the dialectical materialist would place it as a property of the *material situation* ("economic conditions"), the scene in which justice is to be enacted. He would say that no higher quality of justice can be enacted than the nature of the scenic properties permits. Trotsky gave the same form an ironic turn when he treated Stalinist policies as the inevitable result of the attempt to establish socialism under the given conditions. That is, you can't get a fully socialist *act* unless you have a fully socialist *scene,* and for the dialectical materialist such a scene requires a high stage of industrial development.

And there is a variant of the usage in Coleridge (in his early libertarian and "necessitarian" period, when he was exalted with thoughts of "aspheterism"). Concerning "Pantisocracy" (the plan of Coleridge, Southey, and their associates to found a communistic colony on the banks of the Susquehanna), he wrote that it would "make virtue inevitable." That is, the colonists were to arrange a social situation of such a sort that virtuous acts would be the logical and spontaneous result of conditions.

As for "act, " any verb, no matter how specific or how general, that has connotations of consciousness or purpose falls under this category. If one happened to stumble over an obstruction, that would be not an act, but a mere motion. However, one could convert even this sheer accident into something of an act if, in the course of falling, one suddenly *willed* his fall (as a rebuke, for instance, to the negligence of the person who had left the obstruction in the way). "Dramatistically," the basic unit of action would be defined as "the human body in conscious or purposive motion." Hence we are admonished that people often speak of action in a purely figurative sense when they have only motion in mind, as with reference to the action of a motor, or the interaction of forces. Terms like "adjustment" and "adaptation" are ambiguously suited to cover both action and sheer motion, so that it is usually difficut to decide in just which sense a thinker is using them, when he applies them to social motives. This ambiguity may put them in good favor with those who would deal with the human realm in a calculus patterned after the vocabularies of the physical sciences, and yet would not wholly abandon vestiges of "animism." Profession, vocation, policy, strategy, tactics are all concepts of action, as are any words for specific vocations. Our words "position," "occupation," and "office" indicate the scenic overtones in action. Our words for particular "jobs" under capitalist industrialism refer to acts, but often the element of action is reduced to a minimum and the element of sheer motion raised to a maximum. (We here have in mind not only certain near-automatic tasks performed to the timing of the conveyor belt, but also many of the purely clerical operations, filing, bookkeeping, recording, accounting, and the like, necessary to the present state of technology.)

When Christ said, "I am the way" (*hodos*), we could translate, "I am the act," or more fully, "I represent a system, or synthesis, of the right acts." *Tao* and *yoga* are similar words for act. And we see how readily act in this sense can overlap upon agency when we consider our ordinary attitude towards scientific method (*met-hodos*), which we think of pragmatically, not as a way of life, or *act* of *being,* but as a *means* of *doing.*

The Greek word for justice (*diké*) was in its beginnings as thoroughly an "act" word as *tao, yoga,* and *hodos.* Originally it meant *custom, usage, manner, fashion.* It also meant *right.* The connection between these two orders of meaning is revealed in our expression, "That sort of thing just isn't done," and in the fact that our word "morality" comes from a Latin word for "custom." Liddell and Scott's lexicon notes that in the *Odyssey* the word is used of mortals, gods, kings, and suitors, referring to their *custom, way of acting, law of being.* After the homogeneous tribal pattern of Greek life (with its one "way" or "justice" shared by all) had dissolved into a political state, with its typical conflicts of property interests, *diké* became a word of the law courts. Hence, in post-Homeric usage, it refers to *legal justice,* the *right* which is presumed to be the object of law. In this form, it could represent a Platonic ideal, that might prevail over and above the real ways of the different social classes. This is the kind of justice that Marx was refuting by a sophisticated reversion to a more "Homeric" usage.

Range of All the Ratios

Though we have inspected two ratios, the five terms would allow for ten (scene-act, scene-agent, scene-agency, scene-purpose, act-purpose, act-agent, act-agency, agent-purpose, agent-agency, and agency-purpose). The ratios are principles of determination. Elsewhere in the Grammar we shall examine two of these (scene-purpose and agency-purpose) in other connections; and the rest will figure in passing. But the consideration of words for "ways" calls for special attention to the *act-agent* ratio.

Both act and agent require scenes that "contain" them. Hence the scene-act and scene-agent ratios are in the fullest sense positive (or "positional"). But the relation between act and agent is not quite the same. The agent does not "contain" the act, though its results might be said to "pre-exist virtually" within him. And the act does not "synecdochically share" in the agent, though certain ways of acting may be said to induce corresponding moods or traits of character. To this writer, at least, the act-agent ratio more strongly suggests a temporal or sequential relationship than a purely positional or geometric one. The agent is an author of his acts, which are descended from him, being good progeny if he is good, or bad progeny if he is bad, wise progeny if he is wise, silly progeny if he is silly. And, conversely, his acts can make him or remake him in accordance with their nature. They would be his product and/or he would be theirs. Similarly, when we use the scene-act and scene-agent ratios in reverse (as with the sequence from act or agent to corresponding scene) the image of derivation is stronger than the image of position.

One discerns the workings of the act-agent ratio in the statement of a former cabinet member to the effect that "you can safely lodge responsibility with the President of the United States," owing to "the tremendously sobering influence of the Presidency on any man, especially in foreign affairs." Here, the sheer nature of an office, or position, is said to produce important modifications in a man's character. Even a purely symbolic act, such as the donning of priestly vestments, is often credited with such a result. And I have elsewhere quoted a remark by a political commentator: "There seems to be something about the judicial robes that not only hypnotizes the beholder but transforms the wearer."

Ordinarily, the scene-act and scene-agent ratios can be extended to cover such cases. Thus, the office of the Presidency may be treated as a "situation" affecting the agent who occupies it. And the donning of vestments brings about a symbolic situation that can likewise be treated in terms of the scene-agent ratio. But there are cases where a finer discrimination is needed. For instance, the resistance of the Russian armies to the Nazi invasion could be explained "scenically" in terms of the Soviet political and economic structure; or one could use the act-agent ratio, attributing the power and tenacity to "Russian" traits of character. However, in deriving the act from the scene, one would have to credit socialism as a major scenic factor, whereas a derivation of the act from the agents would allow for a much more felicitous explanation from the standpoint of capitalist apologetics.

Thus, one of our leading newspapers asked itself whether Hitler failed "to evaluate a force older than communism, more instinctive than the mumbling cult of Stalin—the attachment of the peasant masses to 'Mother Russia,' the incoherent but cohesive force of Russian patriotism." And it concluded that "the Russian soldier has proved the depth of his devotion to the Russian soil." Patriotism, attachment to the "mother," devotion to the soil—these are essentially motives located in the agent, hence requiring no acknowledgement of socialist motives.

There is, of course, scenic reference in the offing; but the stress upon the term, agent, encourages one to be content with a very vague treatment of scene, with no mention of the political and economic factors that form a major aspect of national scenes. Indeed, though our concern here is with the Grammar of Motives, we may note a related resource of Rhetoric: one may deflect attention from scenic matters by situating the motives of an act in the agent (as were one to account for wars purely on the basis of a "warlike instinct" in people): or conversely, one may deflect attention from the criticism of personal motives by deriving an act or attitude not from traits of the agent but from the nature of the situation.

The difference between the use of the scene-act and act-agent ratios can also be seen in the motivations of "democracy." Many people in Great Britain and the United States think of these nations as "vessels" of democracy. And democracy is felt to reside in us, intrinsically, because we are "a democratic people." Democratic acts are, in this mode of thought, derived from democratic agents, agents who would remain democratic in character even though conditions required the temporary curtailment or abrogation of basic democratic rights. But if one employed, instead, the scene-act ratio, one might hold that there are certain "democratic situations" and certain "situations favorable to dictatorship, or requiring dictatorship." The technological scene itself, which requires the planning of a world order, might be thought such as to favor a large measure of "dictatorship" in our political ways (at least as contrasted with the past norms of democracy). By the act-agent ratio, a "democratic people" would continue to perform "democratic acts"; and to do so they would even, if necessary, go to the extent of restoring former conditions most favorable to democracy. By the scene-act ratio, if the "situation" itself is no longer a "democratic" one, even an "essentially democratic" people will abandon democratic ways.

A picturesque effect can be got in imaginative writings by the conflicting use of the scene-act and act-agent ratios. One may place "fools" in "wise situations," so that in their acts they are "wiser than they know." Children are often "wise" in this sense. It is a principle of incongruity that Chaplin has built upon. Empson would call it an aspect of "pastoral."

Here is an interesting shift of ratios in a citation from an address by Francis Biddle when he was Attorney General:

> The change of the world in terms of time and space in the past hundred years—railroad, telegraph, telephone, automobile, movie, airplane, radio—has hardly found an echo in our political growth, except in the necessary patches and arrangements which have made it so extraordinarily complex without making it more responsive to our needs.

Note first that all the changes listed here refer to *agencies* of communication (the pragmatist emphasis). Then, having in their accumulation become scenic, they are said to have had a motivating effect upon our political acts ("growth"). But though the complexity of the scene has called forth "the necessary patches and arrangements" (another expression for "acts"), we are told that there are still unsatisfied "needs." Now, "needs" are a property of agents; hence an act designed to produce a situation "more responsive to our needs" would have its most direct locus of motivation under the heading of agent, particularly if these were said to be "primal needs" rather than "new needs," since "new needs" might best be treated as "a function of the situation." I borrow the expression from a prominent educator, Eduard C. Lindeman, who shortly after the Japanese attack at Pearl Harbor complained of a tendency "to believe that morale will now become a function of the situation and that hence it is less important to plan for education."

The ratios may often be interpreted as principles of selectivity rather than as thoroughly causal relationships. That is, in any given historical situation, there are persons of many sorts, with a corresponding variety in the kinds of acts that would be most representative of them. Thus, a given political situation may be said not to change people in their essential character, but rather to favor, or bring to the fore (to "vote for"), certain kinds of agents (with their appropriate actions) rather than others. Quick shifts in political exigencies do not of a sudden make all men "fundamentally" daring, or all men "fundamentally" cautious, in keeping with the nature of the scene; but rather, one situation calls for cautious men as its appropriate "voice," another for daring men, one for traditionalists, another for innovators. And the inappropriate acts and temperaments simply do not "count for" so much as they would in situations for which they are a better fit. One set of scenic conditions will "implement" and "amplify" given ways and temperaments which, in other situations would remain mere potentialities, unplanted seeds, "mute inglorious Miltons." Indeed, there are times when out-and-out materialistic philosophies, which are usually thought of as "tough," can be of great solace to us precisely because they encourage us to believe in the ratios as a selective principle. For we may tell ourselves that the very nature of the materials with which men deal will not permit men to fall below a certain level of sloth, error, greed, and dishonesty in their relations with one another, as the coöperative necessities of the situation implement and amplify only those traits of character and action that serve the ends of progress.

There is, of course, a circular possibility in the terms. If an agent acts in keeping with his nature as an agent (act-agent ratio), he may change the nature of the scene accordingly (scene-act ratio), and thereby establish a state of unity between himself and his world (scene-agent ratio). Or the scene may call for a certain kind of act, which makes for a corresponding kind of agent, thereby likening agent to scene. Or our act may change us and our scene, producing a mutual conformity. Such would be the Edenic paradigm, applicable if we were capable of total acts that produce total transformations. In reality, we are capable of but partial acts, acts that but partially represent us and that produce but partial transformations. Indeed, if all the ratios were adjusted to one another with perfect Edenic symmetry, they would be immutable in one unending "moment."

Theological notions of creation and re-creation bring us nearest to the concept of total acts. Among the controversies that centered around Lutheranism, for instance, there was a doctrine, put forward by the theologian Striegel, who held that Christ's work on the Cross had the effect of changing God's attitude towards mankind, and that men born after the historical Christ can take advantage of this change.

Here we have something like the conversion of God himself, brought about by Christ's sacrifice (a total action, a total passion). From the godlike nature came a godlike act that acted upon God himself. And as regards mankind, it amounts to a radical change in the very structure of the Universe, since it changed God's attitude towards men, and in God's attitude towards men resides the ultimate ground of human action.

A similar pattern is implicated in the close of Aeschylus's trilogy, the *Oresteia,* where the sufferings of Orestes terminate in the changed identity of the Furies, signalized by their change of name from Erinyes to Eumenides. Under the influence of the "new gods," their nature as motives takes on a totally different accent; for whereas it was their previous concern to avenge evil, it will henceforth be their concern to reward the good. An *inner* goad has thus been cast forth, externalized; whereby, as Athena says, men may be at peace within, their "dread passion for renown" thereafter being motivated solely by "war from without."

Only the scene-act and scene-agent ratios fit with complete comfort in this chapter on the relation between container and contained. The act-agent ratio tugs at its edges; and we shall close noting concerns that move us still farther afield. In the last example, we referred to God's *attitude.* Where would attitude fall within our pattern? Often it is the *preparation* for an act, which would make it a kind of symbolic act, or incipient act. But in its character as a state of *mind* that may or may not lead to an act, it is quite clearly to be classed under the head of *agent.* We also spoke of Christ's sacrifice as "a total action, a total passion." This suggests other "grammatical" possibilities that involve a dialectic pairing of "active" and "passive." And in the reference to a *state* of mind, we casually invite a dialectic pairing of "actus" and "status."

This group of concerns will be examined in due course. Meanwhile, we should be reminded that the term *agent* embraces not only all words general or specific for person, actor, character, individual, hero, villain, father, doctor, engineer, but also any words, moral or functional, for *patient,* and words for the motivational properties or agents, such as "drives," "instincts," "states of mind." We may also have collective words for agent, such as nation, group, the Freudian "super-ego," Rousseau's *"volonté générale,"* the Fichtean "generalized I."

II

ANTINOMIES OF DEFINITION

Paradox of Substance

THERE is a set of words comprising what we might call the Stance family, for they all derive from a concept of place, or placement. In the Indo-Germanic languages the root for this family is *stā,* to stand (Sanscrit, *sthā*). And out of it there has developed this essential family, comprising such members as: consist, constancy, constitution, contrast, destiny, ecstasy, existence, hypostatize, obstacle, stage, state, status, statute, stead, subsist, and system. In German, an important member of the Stance family is *stellen,* to place, a root that figures in *Vorstellung,* a philosopher's and psychologist's word for representation, conception, idea, image.

Surely, one could build a whole philosophic universe by tracking down the ramifications of this one root. It would be "implemented" too, for it would have stables, staffs, staves, stalls, stamens, stamina, stanchions, stanzas, steeds, stools, and studs. It would be a quite regional world, in which our Southern Agrarians might take their stand.

Unquestionably, the most prominent philosophic member of this family is "substance." Or at least it used to be, before John Locke greatly impaired its prestige, so that many thinkers today explicitly banish the term from their vocabularies. But there is cause to believe that, in banishing the *term,* far from banishing its *functions* one merely conceals them. Hence, from the dramatistic point of view, we are admonished to dwell upon the word, considering its embarrassments and its potentialities of transformation, so that we may detect its covert influence even in cases where it is overtly absent. Its relation to our five terms will become apparent as we proceed.

First we should note that there is, etymologically, a pun lurking behind the Latin roots. The word is often used to designate what some thing or agent intrinsically *is,* as *per* these meanings in Webster's: "the most important element in any existence; the characteristic and essential

21

components of anything; the main part; essential import; purport."
Yet etymologically "substance" is a scenic word. Literally, a person's
or a thing's sub-stance would be something that stands beneath or supports the person or thing.

Let us cite a relevant passage in *An Essay Concerning Human Understanding* (Chapter XXIII, "Of Our Complex Ideas of Substances"):

> 1. *Ideas of particular substances, how made.* The mind being,
> as I have declared, furnished with a great number of the simple ideas
> conveyed in by the senses, as they are found in exterior things, or by
> reflection on its own operations, takes notice, also, that a certain
> number of these simple ideas go constantly together; which being
> presumed to belong to one thing, and words being suited to common
> apprehensions, and made use of for quick despatch, are called, so
> united in one subject, by one name; which, by inadvertency, we are
> apt afterward to talk of and consider as one simple idea, which in-
> deed is a complication of many ideas together; because, as I have
> said, not imagining how these simple ideas can subsist by themselves,
> we accustom ourselves to suppose some *substratum* wherein they do
> subsist, and from which they do result; which therefore we call
> *substance.*

> 2. *Our obscure idea of substance in general.*—So that if anyone
> will examine himself concerning his notion of pure substance in
> general, he will find he has no other idea of it at all, but only a sup-
> position of he knows not what support of such qualities which are
> capable of producing simple ideas in us; which qualities are com-
> monly called accidents. If anyone should be asked, what is the
> subject wherein color or weight inheres, he would have nothing to
> say but, the solid extended parts. And if he were demanded, what is
> it that solidity and extension inhere in, he would not be in a much
> better case than the Indian before mentioned, who, saying that the
> world was supported by a great elephant, was asked, what the ele-
> phant rested on; to which his answer was, a great tortoise; but being
> again pressed to know what gave support to the broad-backed tor-
> toise, replied—something, he knew not what. And thus here, as in
> all other cases where we use words without having clear and distinct
> ideas, we talk like children: who, being questioned what such a
> thing is which they know not, readily give this satisfactory answer,
> that it is *something;* which in truth signifies no more, when so used,
> either by children or men, but that they know not what; and that the
> thing they pretend to know and talk of, is what they have no distinct
> idea of at all, and so are perfectly ignorant of it, and in the dark.

The idea, then, we have, to which we give the *general* name substance, being nothing but the supposed, but unknown support of those qualities we find existing, which we imagine cannot subsist *sine re substante,* "without something to support them," we call that support *substantia;* which according to the true import of the word, is, in plain English, standing under, or upholding.

The same structure is present in the corresponding Greek word, *hypostasis,* literally, a standing under: hence anything set under, such as stand, base, bottom, prop, support, stay; hence metaphorically, that which lies at the bottom of a thing, as the groundwork, subject-matter, argument of a narrative, speech, poem; a starting point, a beginning. And then come the metaphysical meanings (we are consulting Liddell and Scott): subsistence, reality, real being (as applied to mere appearance), nature, essence. In ecclesiastical Greek, the word corresponds to the Latin *Persona,* a Person of the Trinity (which leads us back into the old argument between the homoousians and the homoiousians, as to whether the three persons were of the same or similar substance). Medically, the word can designate a suppression, as of humours that ought to come to the surface; also matter deposited in the urine; and of liquids generally, the sediment, lees, dregs, grounds. When we are examining, from the standpoint of Symbolic, metaphysical tracts that would deal with "fundamentals" and get to the "bottom" of things, this last set of meanings can admonish us to be on the look-out for what Freud might call "cloacal" motives, furtively interwoven with speculations that may on the surface seem wholly abstract. An "acceptance" of the universe on this plane may also be a roundabout way of "making peace with the faeces."

But returning to the pun as it figures in the citation from Locke, we might point up the pattern as sharply as possible by observing that the word "substance," used to designate what a thing *is,* derives from a word designating something that a thing *is not.* That is, though used to designate something *within* the thing, *intrinsic* to it, the word etymologically refers to something *outside* the thing, *extrinsic* to it. Or otherwise put: the word in its etymological origins would refer to an attribute of the thing's *context,* since that which supports or underlies a thing would be a part of the thing's context. And a thing's context, being outside or beyond the thing, would be something that the thing is *not.*

Contextual Definition

Here obviously is a strategic moment, an alchemic moment, wherein momentous miracles of transformation can take place. For here the intrinsic and the extrinsic can change places. To tell what a thing is, you place it in terms of something else. This idea of locating, or placing, is implicit in our very word for definition itself: to *define,* or *determine* a thing, is to mark its boundaries, hence to use terms that possess, implicitly at least, contextual reference. We here take the pun seriously because we believe it to reveal an *inevitable* paradox of definition, an antinomy that must endow the concept of substance with unresolvable ambiguity, and that will be discovered lurking beneath any vocabulary designed to treat of motivation by the deliberate outlawing of the *word* for substance.

Nor is the perplexity confined to abstruse metaphysical theorizing. Note the Tory usage, for instance, in the expression, "a man of substance," or a man of "standing." Note how readily we shunt here between an intrinsic and an extrinsic reference. For those who admire someone as a man of substance, or standing, have in mind not only his personal traits of character, but also the resources that spring from his environmental connections, the external powers that his position, income, status put at his command, the outside factors that, in backing or supporting him, enable him to make his personal characteristics count. (Another meaning for the Greek *hypostasis,* incidentally, was steadfastness, endurance, firmness.) And when our Southern Agrarians issue a volume entitled *I'll Take My Stand* (their "stand in Dixie"), their claims as to what they *are* get definition in terms of scene, environment, situation, context, ground. Indeed, in the title we can also see another important ambiguity of motive emerging. When taking their stand *in* Dixie, they are also taking their stand *for* Dixie. Their stand *in* Dixie would be a "conditioning" kind of cause; but a corresponding stand *for* Dixie would be a teleological or purposive kind of cause.

In Spinoza we confront the full intensity of the contextual paradox. Indeed, from our point of view, we might translate both his concept of "God" and his concept of "nature" as "the total, or ultimate scene," since he pantheistically held that God and nature are identical. In the Judaic and Christian theologies, since nature was said to have its ultimate ground in God as a person, God was a context for nature, as nature-and-God was the context for man. But Spinoza, in equating God and nature, gave us a concept of nature that could have no scene beyond it. For nature was *everything*—and beyond *everything,* considered as a totality, there could be nothing to serve as its context.

Hence, starting from the Aristotelian notion that a substance, or being, is to be considered "in itself" (*kath auto,* which Spinoza rendered *id quod per se concipitur*), Spinoza went on to observe that nothing less than the *totality of all that exists* can meet this requirement. In Aristotle, each stone, or tree, or man, or animal, could be a substance, capable of being considered "in itself." But Spinoza held that no single thing could be considered "by itself." A distinction between "in itself" and "by itself" might be made here, but the Spinozistic calculus is designed rather to work in the area where the two meanings overlap. Thinking contextually, Spinoza held that each single object in the universe is "defined" (determined, limited, bounded) by the other things that surround it. And in calling upon men to see things "in terms of eternity" (*sub specie aeternitatis*) Spinoza meant precisely that we should consider each thing in terms of its total context, the universal scene as a whole. Only when considering the universe as a whole, and its parts in terms of the whole, would we be making an "intrinsic" statement about substance, since there was but one substance, the universal totality.

And thoroughly in keeping with his contextual strategy of definition, Spinoza explicitly held that all definition is "negation," which is another way of saying that, to define a thing in terms of its context, we must define it in terms of what it is not. And with scholastic succinctness, he formulated the paradox of contextual definition in four words: "all determination is negation; *omnis determinatio est negatio."* Since determined things are "positive," we might point up the paradox as harshly as possible by translating it, "Every positive is negative."

When we refer to "everything," our reference is indefinite, infinite, undetermined, indeterminate. Hence, to treat of things in terms of "everything" is to treat of them in terms of the infinite. Indeed, since "everything" is the "absolute" (that is, unloosed, absolved, "freed," for I think it is good to remind ourselves of the dramatic meanings lurking behind that strategic metaphysical term) we have here a variant of the so-called "negative theology," which conceived of God as the absence of all qualities; and to see things as contextually "determined" by the "absolute" is thus to see them simultaneously in terms of "necessity" and "freedom." For Spinoza, says Windelband, "the deity is all and thus—nothing." But we should also remember that the deity is equated with nature. Hence, though Spinoza's pantheism was an important step towards naturalism, in itself it had strongly mystical ingredients.

Contextual definition might also be called "positional," or "geometric," or "definition by location." The embarrassments are often revealed with particular clarity when a thinker has moved to a high level of generalization, as when motivational matters are discussed in terms of "heredity and environment," or "man and nature," or "mind and matter," or "mechanism and teleology," where each of the paired terms is the other's "context" in the universe of discourse. To define or locate "man" in terms of "nature," for instance, is to "dissolve" man "into" nature. Hence, the more thorough one is in carrying out his enterprise, the more surely he opens himself to the charge of failing to discuss man "in himself." Historicists who deal with art in terms of its background are continually suffering from the paradox of contextual definition, as their opponents accuse them of slighting the work of art in its esthetic aspects; and on the other hand, critics who would center their attention upon the work "in itself" must wince when it is made apparent that their inquiries, in ignoring contextual reference, frustrate our desire to see the products of artistic action treated in terms of the scene-act, scene-agent, and agent-act ratios.

Familial Definition

However, there is another strategy of definition, usually interwoven with the contextual sort, yet susceptible of separate observation. This is the "tribal" or "familial" sort, the definition of a substance in terms of ancestral cause. Under the head of "tribal" definition would fall any variant of the idea of biological descent, with the substance of the offspring being derived from the substance of the parents or family.

The Christian notion that the most important fact about mankind and the world is their derivation from God is an instance of "ancestral" definition on the grand scale. We find bastardized variants in political doctrines of race supremacy, such as the Nazi "blood" philosophy. The Latin word *natura*, like its Greek equivalent *physis*, has a root signifying to become, to grow, to be born. And the Aristotelian *genus* is originally not a logical, but a biological, concept. We can discern the tribal pattern behind the notion, so characteristic of Greek nationalism, that like causes like or that like recognizes like, as with Democritus' theory of perception. Similarly, there was an *ancestral* notion behind the Platonic theory of forms; in fact, it was this tribal ingredient that recommended it so strongly to the ages of Western feudalism. Each thing in this world had, as it were, an eponym in heaven, a perfect form from which it was derived—and it shared this derivation with all the other members of its class, or genus. And I think we might most quickly understand the mediaeval speculations as to whether universals were "before the thing, in the thing, or after the thing" if we first tried a dramatist translation of the three formulae respectively thus: "Does the tribe give birth to its members (universal *ante rem*), or does the tribe exist in its members (universal *in re*), or is the tribe merely a name for the sum of its members (universal *post rem*)?"

To say yes to the first would make you an extreme mediaeval realist. A realism of this sort was well attuned to feudal collectivism. To say yes to the third would make you a thorough-going nominalist, who treated general terms as mere *flatus vocis,* conventions of speech, and thus moved towards the disintegration of tribal thinking. To say yes to the second would make you an Aristotelian. The motives would be situated in the individual, yet they would be motives common to the species, or tribe, of which it was a member. That is, an individual stone would have motives proper to stones as a class, an individual man motives proper to men as a class, etc. This doctrine came to a head in the Aristotelian concept of the "entelechy," which we might call the individual's potentialities for becoming a fully representative member of its class. However, we need not here give more than a cursory glance at any particular use of the ancestral method. It is sufficient if we can indicate its range.

All told, perhaps the quickest and surest way to find oneself at the centre of the subject would be to ponder the four words, "general," "generic," "genetic," "genitive." Though they are all from the same root, only the third *unambiguously* reveals ancestral connotations. Next removed is "genitive," which refers to either source or possession. But to say that nature is "a part of" God or that man is "a part of" nature would be to use a genitive construction in which one could clearly discern ancestral reference. When we come to "generic," the tribal connotations are beginning more noticeably to fade, as purely biological

concepts can be replaced by logical notions of classification.   And with
"general'," this extinction of the familial can be complete.   A "family of
right-angled triangles in general," for instance, would just about have
lost the notion of generation, although we can still, with a little effort,
look upon them as a family in the sense that a common set of principles
is required for the generating of them.

Similarly, the members of a class derive their *generic* nature from
the "idea" of the class in which they are placed.   If I make up a classification, for instance, such as "bald-headed carpenters under forty," I
shall have "generated" a corresponding class of "objects."   These objects (the people who fit the requirements of the class) will be "imperfect copies" of my "idea" or "pure form," since they will all possess
other attributes that lie outside the strict definition of the class.   This
would be the strictly methodological equivalent for Plato's doctrine of
archetypes.   Thinking in familial terms, Plato looked upon the objects
of this world as imperfect replicas of their pure "forms" or "ideas" in
heaven.

In sum, contextual definition stresses *placement,* ancestral definition
stresses derivation.   But in any sustained discussion of motives, the two
become interwoven, as with theologies which treat God both as "causal
ancestor" of mankind and as the ultimate ground or context of mankind.

And if we were to extend the Stance family by including different
roots similar in meaning, we would promptly move into a set of live
and dead metaphors ("abstractions") where our five terms, our ratios,
and our strategies of definition could be seen emerging in all sorts of
places.

For instance, the key philosophic term, sub-ject (in Latin, thrown
under) is the companion to the Greek *hypokeimenon* (underlying), a
word that can refer to the subject of a sentence, or to the "sub-strate" of
the world (the essential constitution of things, hence indeterminately a
kind of basis or a kind of causal ancestor).   The word can also refer to
what is assumed as a ground of argument, in which capacity it serves as
a passive for *hypotithemi* (to place or put under, as a base or foundation,
to assume as a principle, take for granted, suppose, from the root of
which we get such words as theme, thesis, antithesis, synthesis, while a
similar development in Latin, from *pono,* to place, gives us position,
proposition, opposition, composition, positive, and that neat now-you-

sub-ject — GR. hypokeimenon (underlying)
hypotithemi — To put under " Thrown-under "
ANTINOMIES OF DEFINITION   29

see-me-and-now-you-don't metaphysical nuance, "posit," whereby the metaphysician is enabled to discuss the "positing" of principles without being too clear as to what kind of base they are being *placed* upon).

The mention of "substrates" brings us close to a third aspect of definition, the kind we get in projects that discuss the world in terms of the "building blocks" of which it is thought to be composed, as were one to define a kind of house in terms of the materials and operations needed for its construction, or to define an action by reducing it to terms of its necessary motions.   But from the dramatistic point of view, we can best observe this strategy later, when we consider the subject of "circumference" (in the sense that the location, or definition, of an act with reference to "the Mississippi valley" as its motivating scene could be said to involve a narrower circumference than its definition in terms of "the United States").   And we shall here pause to survey characteristic forms which the grammar of substance may embody in particular calculi:

Survey of Terms for Substance

Geometric substance.   An object placed in its setting, existing both in itself and as part of its background.   Participation in a context.   Embodied most completely in Spinoza's cult of "Euclidean" relations, logically ("necessarily") derivable from one another.   These relations exist all at once, implicitly, though they may manifest themselves, or be made manifest, in various *sequences*.   (As soon as certain antecedent steps are taken in the demonstration, certain consequent steps are "inevitable.")   The plastic connotations can lead readily into strictly materialistic notions of determinism, as with the novelist, Theodore Dreiser, who professes to view all ultimate motives in terms of "chemism."

Familial substance.   In its purity, this concept stresses common ancestry in the strictly biological sense, as literal descent from maternal or paternal sources.   But the concept of family is usually "spiritualized," so that it includes merely social groups, comprising persons of the same nationality or beliefs.   Most often, in such cases, there is the notion of some founder shared in common, or some covenant or constitution or historical act from which the consubstantiality of the group is derived.   Doctrines of creation extend the concept of familial descent to cover the relationship between the craftsman and his product ("the potter and the pot," as with the agent-act ratio).

This in turn moves us closer to purely logical derivations, of actualities from potentialities, of the explicit from the implicit, of conclusions from principles (that is, "firsts"). Plotinus' characterization of God as *to proton* would be a case in point, or Bonaventura's notion of the world's development from *rationes seminales,* an expression clearly combining the ideas of logical and biological descent. The stress upon the informative nature of beginnings can in turn lead us to treat christenings, inaugurations, and the like as aspects of familial substance. There is the girl of high spirits, for instance, who says of herself that she was born during a hurricane, as though the quality of her temper in later life were derived from the quality of the scene prevailing at her birth.

Biologists, in their concern with vital reproduction, necessarily give prominence to concepts of familial substance, in terms for genus and species, cellular structure, and the like. Often they study the responses of organisms at various levels of development, in the expectation that laws of behavior discovered at one level will apply to levels far higher in the scale of complexity. They expect differences, of course, but they also expect the processes at both the higher and lower levels to be "substantially" the same. Thus in an article of biological vulgarization published in one of the "cultural" magazines, a writer observed that, though we may lose confidence in the brotherhood of man, we can still be sure of our consubstantiality in a more inclusive concept of family: "protoplasm" (incidentally, another "first").

Since the taking of nourishment involves a *transubstantiation* of external elements into elements within, we might treat nutritive substance as a combination of the contextual and familial sufficiently notable to deserve a separate designation. Just as the organism dies when deprived of all food, so it will die in part when certain strategic ingredients are absent from its food. Thus, though one might not want to contend that a sufficiency of iodine will make men wise, we can say that a deficiency of iodine will greatly prod them to be stupid. And manganese has been called the chemical of "mother love" because, without manganese, hens won't set. (Similarly, the pituitary has been called the "mother love" gland, since a deficiency of the pituitary hormone in the female is accompanied by "lack of devotion to its offspring.") Modern chemistry prompts us to stress the scenic aspect of the nutritional motive, as the chemist would seek to reduce the efficient principle in both manganese and the pituitary hormone to a common basis. Even a stock to which a scion has been grafted may be considered, from this point of view, as a part of the scion's environment, hence an environmental control upon food supply. For any motivational special factor which is theoretically assigned to the organism (in the sense that a horse and a tiger, a dandelion and a daisy, exemplify in their behavior and development different loci of motion), can be theoretically dissolved into the environmental. If you put a hungry horse and a hungry tiger in a cage together, for instance, you would thereby get not one environment but two, since the tiger would be so drastically momentous an aspect of the horse's environment, and the horse would be a nutrient aspect of the tiger's environment. And any change of nutritive elements such as accompanies glandular transplantations or the injection of hormones is analyzable as a "new physical situation." Dr. Andras Angyal observes in his *Foundations for a Science of Personality,* "A *morphological* distinction between organism and environment is impossible." He also reminds us, "The blood has been called 'internal environment' by Claude Bernard." Accordingly, he employs the concept of a "biosphere" in which "subject (organism)" and "object (environment)" are merged as a single process.

The title of Robert M. Coates's fantasy, *Eater of Darkness,* could be translated: "The agent whose substance is one with the substance of darkness" (though we should next have to make an inquiry into the author's use of "darkness" to discover the special attributes of the term in his particular thesaurus). Totemic rites and the sacrament of the Eucharist are instances where the nutritive emphasis becomes submerged in the notion of familial consubstantiality. "Tell me what you eat, and I'll tell you what you are."

Directional substance. Doubtless biologically derived from the experience of free motion, since man is an organism that lives by locomotion. Frequently, with metaphors of "the way," the directional stresses the sense of motivation from within. Often strongly futuristic, purposive, its slogan might be: Not "Who are you?" or "Where are you from?" but "Where are you going?" Thought in terms of directional substance gained many fresh motives since the Renaissance, and the greater mobility that went with the development from status to contract, alienation of property, the growth of the monetary rationale, and revolutionary innovations in the means of transportation and communication. The directional is also susceptible of conversion from "free" motion into the "determined." Thus, one may "freely" answer a call, yet the call may be so imperious that one could not ignore it without disaster. And statistical treatment of supposedly "free" choices may disclose a uniform response prevailing among the lot.

The directional has encouraged much sociological speculation in terms of "tendencies" or "trends." With such terms, the substantial paradox is not far in the offing. If a man did *not* make a certain decision, for instance, we might nonetheless choose to say that he had a "tendency towards" the decision. Indeed, any tendency *to* do something is, by the same token, a tendency *not* to do it.

The directional is embedded in the very word, "motivation." And we may note four related nuances, or perhaps puns, with corresponding philosophies. Doctrines that reduce mental states to materialistic terms treat *motion* as motive. When an individual's acts are referred to some larger curve, we get *movement* as motive. For instance, individual immigrants came to America as part of a general movement westward. "Movement" in such cases can be either purposive or necessitarian, since one's place in a "movement" is like one's enlistment in a "cause" (and Latin *causa* is defined as: *that by, on account of, or through which anything takes place or is done; a cause, reason, motive, inducement*). Terminologies that situate the driving force of human action in human passion treat *emotion* as motive. (In his *Principles of Literary Criticism*, I. A. Richards offers a good pun for reducing *emotion* in turn to *motion*, when he proposes that we speak not of the *emotions* aroused in us by art but of the *commotions*.) And one can mystically select the *moment* as motive. Such "moments" are directional in that, being led up to and away from, they summarize the foregoing and seminally contain the subsequent. But in themselves they "just are," being an "eternal present" that has wound up the past and has the future wound up.

All metaphors or generalizations, such as *homo homini lupus,* or "life a pilgrimage," or "the economic man," that treat one order of motivation in terms of a higher order or lower order, are examples of substantiation; and they reveal the paradox of substance in that the given subject both is and is not the same as the character with which and by which it is identified. Such statements about motivating essence, often made in passing and sometimes serving as the midrib of a work, are the stock in trade of imaginative literature. As such, they can be most fully studied under the heading of Symbolic. And much that we have written in *Permanence and Change, Attitudes Toward History,* and *The Philosophy of Literary Form* could be read as an elaboration of this paragraph. The name of any well-developed character in a fiction is the term for a peculiar complexity of motives.

Dialectic Substance

From the standpoint of our present study, all the foregoing types could be considered as special cases of a more inclusive category: dialectic substance. Dialectically considered (that is, "dramatistically" considered) men are not only *in nature.* The cultural accretions made possible by the language motive become a "second nature" with them. Here again we confront the ambiguities of substance, since symbolic communication is not a merely external instrument, but also intrinsic to men as agents. Its motivational properties characterize both "the human situation" and what men are "in themselves."

Whereas there is an implicit irony in the other notions of substance, with the dialectic substance the irony is explicit. For it derives its character from the systematic contemplation of the antinomies attendant upon the fact that we necessarily define a thing in terms of something else. "Dialectic substance" would thus be the over-all category of dramatism, which treats of human motives in the terms of verbal action. By this statement we most decidedly do not mean that human motives are confined to the realm of verbal action. We mean rather that the dramatistic analysis of motives has its *point of departure* in the subject of verbal action (in thought, speech, and document).

A poem, by shifting the imagery of its metaphors, permits us to contemplate the subject from the standpoint of various objects. This effect is dialectical in the sense that we see something in terms of some other. In a more restricted sense, however, the dialectical considers things in terms not of *some* other, but of *the* other. The sharpest instance of this is an *agon* wherein the protagonist is motivated by the nature of the antagonist, as with the situating of socialist motives in resistance to capitalism, or the unifying effect of the Allied Nations' joint opposition to Hitler. There is a grim pleasantry that runs, "Of course we're

Christians—but what are we being Christians *against?*" In earlier days, when the devil enjoyed great personal prominence, he could perform this noteworthy role of agonistic unification which, in our era of humanistic progress, we generally assign exclusively to human vessels.

The ambiguity of external and internal motivation has recently plagued some enemies of Fascism who saw that an effective war against the Fascist nations would require many "Fascist" measures on the part of the Anti-Fascists. As the Irish poet, George Russell, once stated the form of their predicament: "We become the image of the thing we hate." And the great dialectician, Coleridge, has observed that *rivales* are the opposite banks of the *same* stream. And it was dialectically, or dramatically, necessary that the *devil* should be an *angel;* for were he of any less noble substance, the Christian *agonia* would to that degree have fallen short of thoroughness in imagining a common ground on which the two great conflicting motives, good and evil, can join battle.

The most thoroughgoing dialectical opposition, however, centers in that key pair: Being and Not-Being. For the contextual approach to substance, by inducing men to postulate a ground or context in which everything that is, is placed, led thinkers "by dialectical necessity" to affirm that the only ground of "Being" is "Not-Being" (for "Being" is so comprehensive a category that its dialectical opposite, "Not-Being," is the only term that would be left to designate its ground). The Neo-Platonist, Plotinus, carried such thinking to its ultimate limits, in the direction of that "negative theology" whereby the divine substance, as the ground of all that we experience in the material world, could be designated only by the absence of any attributes such as we in our material existence can conceive of. He would evolve a dialectical process that, beginning with material things, in the end had completely transcended its beginnings, thus arriving at a totally immaterial vision of God as an abstract Oneness. Accordingly, in his belief that material existence is estrangement from God, he is said to have been unwilling to name either his parents or his birthplace (the abstract concept of dialectical substance here leading him to proclaim his identity by a *negative* reference to the familial and the geometric).

The process of transcendence may, of course, be reversed. Then the ultimate abstract Oneness is taken as a source, a "first"; and the steps leading up to it are interpreted as stages emanating from it. Or terms that are contextual to each other (such as Being and Not-Being, Action and Rest, Mechanism and Purpose, the One and the Many) can be treated as familially related (as were Being to be derived from Not-Being, Action from Rest, Mechanism from Purpose, the Many from the One). Or, in general, actualities may be derived from potentialities that are in a different realm than the actualities. The most obvious instance of such a derivation would be a naturalistic assertion that the "conscious" is derived from a "pre-Conscious," or that the state of life is derived from a condition of "pre-life." However, many less apparent variants are possible. The human person, for instance, may be derived from God as a "super-person." Or human purpose may be derived from an All Purpose, or Cosmic Purpose, or Universal Purpose, or Absolute Purpose, or Pure Purpose, or Inner Purpose, etc. And instead of a "pre-conscious" as the source or latent form of consciousness, we may have a subconscious or unconscious or "collective unconscious," etc.

The Paradox of Purity

Such pairs are in contrasted orders, with one a transcendence of the other, the one latent or covert, the other patent or overt. And the ambiguities of substance here take a form that we would call the "paradox of purity," or "paradox of the absolute." We confront this paradox when deriving the nature of the human person from God as "super-person," as "pure," or "absolute" person, since God as a super-person would be impersonal—and the impersonal would be synonymous with the *negation* of personality. Hence, Pure Personality would be the same as No Personality: and the derivation of the personal principle from God as pure person would amount to its derivation from an impersonal principle. Similarly, a point that Hegel made much of, Pure Being would be the same as Not-Being; and in Aristotle, God can be defined either as "Pure Act" or as complete repose, a rest that is "eternal, unchangeable, immovable." And Leibniz was able to propose something pretty much like unconscious ideas in his doctrine of the "virtual innateness of ideas." (We might point up the oxymoron here by translating "unconscious ideas" as "unaware awarenesses.")

The painter Kandinsky illustrates our subject when, on the subject of Schönberg's esthetic, he says that, to the uninitiate, the "inner beauty" of music must seem like ugliness. And when discussing Julien Gracq's *Chateau d'Argol,* Parker Tyler comes upon the paradox of the absolute thus:

> In the eighth chapter of the book, Albert and Heide, the woman, follow a road which is said to "symbolize *pure direction.* But looking back, they realize that behind them the avenue seems to peter out and to be blocked by thicket and underbrush. It is a blind alley . . ." Like passage through water, passage through this Hegelian reality is pure direction, meaning that, wherever you turn in it, the way must be created, because behind you, the way has *ceased to be.*

The citation is from the surrealist magazine, *View,* in another copy of which Harold Rosenberg, writing on "the art of escape," says that "in democratic society, this art tends, like all the other arts, to become *Pure.*" And if the fugitive "can combine within himself perfectly all the elements of the art, he will be able to free himself perpetually." The thought suggests the element of "pure escape" that lies at the roots of liberalism. And it suggests the paradox of "pure escape." For in freeing oneself *perpetually,* one would in a sense remain perpetually a prisoner, since one would never have definitively escaped.

With regard to Symbolic, one may expect to encounter the paradox of purity whenever he finds what we have called elsewhere the "withinness of withinness," or the "atop the atop," as when Melville writes in *Moby Dick*: "It was a negro church; and the preacher's text was about the blackness of darkness," or as with the pattern in "The Garden," by Andrew Marvell, when the poet speaks of the mind as

> . . . that ocean where each kind
> Does streight its own resemblance find;
>
> .   .   .
>
> Annihilating all that's made
> To a green thought in a green shade.

And in another issue of *View,* when Parker Tyler is reviewing a manual of judo as though this kind of combat were simply a kind of dance, a "pure" art done for love of the figures involved, not for the utilitarian purpose of victory over an adversary, he states his position in a similar "atop the atop" kind of image. For he sums up his thesis in an image by observing that the high-speed camera has shown us how "a drop of milk falling into a mass of milk creates at the moment a perfectly symmetrical crown, with several points suspended in the air like jewels." His article concludes:

> In the largest sense, Mars is an enemy of Apollo. It is only on the esthetic grounds of fantasy that they may meet and fraternize with each other. So, beyond our capacity to discipline our thoughts in relation to "realities," the instinct of free movement typified by Isadora's dance asserts itself, and we may imagine as eternal, if we like, a drop of American blood being poured into its own mass, and erecting over that precious surface a fragile crown of rubies.

In theological and metaphysical works, we can recognize the paradox of the absolute readily enough. Often, in fact, it is explicitly discussed. But in historicist writings it more easily goes unnoticed. Yet the paradox may be implicit in any term for a *collective* motivation, such as a concept of class, nation, the "general will," and the like. Technically, it becomes a "pure" motive when matched against some individual locus of motivation. And it may thus be the *negation* of an individual motive. Yet despite this position as dialectical antithesis of the individual motive, the collective motive may be treated as the source or principle from which the individual motive is familially or "substantially" derived in a "like begets like" manner. That is, to derive the individual motive from the collective motive would be like deriving the personal principle familially from the super-personal principle, whereas contextually the "super-personal" principle would be the *other* of the personal.

What we are here considering formally, as a paradox of substance, can be illustrated quickly enough by example. A soldier may be *nationally* motivated to kill the enemies of his country, whereas *individually* he is motivated by a horror of killing his own enemies. Or conversely, as a patriot he may act by the motive of sacrifice in behalf of his country, but as an individual he may want to profit. Or a man's business code may differ so greatly from his private code that we can even think of him as a "split personality" (that is, a man of "two substances," or "divided substance"). Or one will find a resistance to people in particular "balanced by" a humanitarian sympathy for mankind in general.

Such histories can be imagined in an endless variety of details. What we are suggesting here is that they all embody a *grammatical form* in accordance with which we should not expect a dualism of motives to be automatically dissolved, as with those apologists of science who believe that in a scientific world ethics become unnecessary. However, to consider these possibilities further, we should move into the areas of Symbolic, involving modes of transubstantiation, rituals of rebirth, whereby the individual identifies himself in terms of the collective motive (an identification by which he both is and is not one with that with which and by which he is identified). At present it is enough to note in a general way how the paradox of the absolute figures grammatically in the dialectic, making for a transcending of one term by its other, and for the reversed ambiguous derivation of the term from its other as ancestral principle.

Dialectic of Tragedy

When things are treated in terms of other things, men may even be said to speak for the dumb objects of nature. Nor are the pronouncements assigned on a purely arbitrary basis. The use of scales, meters, controlled laboratory conditions, and the like, can set up situations in which speechless things can hand down accurate judgments. Men can so arrange it that nature gives clear, though impartial and impersonal, answers to their questions. The dialectical motives behind such methods usually escape our detection, though we get a glimpse of them when Galileo speaks of experimental testing as an "ordeal." Stated broadly the dialectical (agonistic) approach to knowledge is through the *act* of assertion, whereby one "suffers" the kind of knowledge that is the reciprocal of his act.

This is the process embodied in tragedy, where the agent's action involves a corresponding passion, and from the sufferance of the passion there arises an understanding of the act, an understanding that transcends the act. The act, in being an assertion, has called forth a counter-assertion in the elements that compose its context. And when the agent is enabled to see in terms of this counter-assertion, he has transcended the state that characterized him at the start. In this final state of tragic vision, intrinsic and extrinsic motivations are merged. That is, although purely circumstantial factors participate in his tragic destiny, these are not felt as exclusively external, or scenic; for they bring about a *representative* kind of accident, the kind of accident that belongs with the agent's particular kind of character.

It is deplorable, but not tragic, simply to be a victim of circumstance, for there is an important distinction between destiny and sheer victimization. Sheer victimization is not an assertion—and it naturally makes not for vision but for frustration. The victimizing circumstances, or accidents, seem arbitrary and exorbitant, even "silly." But at the moment of tragic vision, the fatal accidents are felt to bear fully upon the act, while the act itself is felt to have summed up the character of the agent. Nor is this vision a sense of cosmic persecution; for in seeing the self in terms of the situation which the act has brought about, the agent transcends the self. And whereas the finality and solemnity of death often leads to the assumption that the tragic vision is possible only at the point of death, we must recognize that dialectically one may die many times (in fact, each time an assertion leads beyond itself to a new birth) and that tragedy is but a special case of the dialectical process in general. In the Hegelian dialectic, for instance, the series of dyings is presented as a gradual progress towards greater and greater self-realization. For spirit has its counterpart in objectification; and by seeing himself in terms of objects, "from them the individual proceeds to the contemplation of his own inner being." (*Philosophy of History*).

We can discern something of the "tragic" grammar behind the Greek proverb's way of saying "one learns by experience"; "*ta pathemata mathemata,*" the suffered is the learned. We can also catch glimpses of a relation between dialectic and mathematics (a kind that might have figured in Plato's stress upon mathematics) in the fact that *mathemata* means both things learned in general, and the mathematical sciences (arithmetic, geometry, astronomy) in particular. A *pathema* (of the same root as our word, "passive") is the opposite of a *poiema* (a deed, doing, action, act; anything done; a poem). A *pathema* can refer variously to a suffering, misfortune, passive condition, situation, state of mind. The initial requirement for a tragedy, however, is an *action*. Hence, by our interpretation, if the proverb were to be complete at the risk of redundance, it would have three terms: *poiemata, pathemata, mathemata,* suggesting that the act organizes the opposition (brings to the fore whatever factors resist or modify the act), that the agent thus "suffers" this opposition, and as he learns to take the oppositional motives into account, widening his terminology accordingly, he has arrived at a higher order of understanding. However, this statement may indicate more of a temporal sequence than is usually the case. The three distinctions can be collapsed into a single "moment," so that we could proceed from one to the others in any order.

A similar grammar (with a similar attenuation of the tragic) may be discerned beneath the scholastic formula, *intelligere est pati,* which we might translate broadly as, "to understand is to be affected by," while remembering however that the deponent verb *pati* contains the following range of meanings: to bear, support, suffer, endure, be afflicted with, pass a life of suffering or privation, permit, experience, undergo, be in a certain state of mind or temper, (and in grammar) to be passive, to have a passive sense, a passive nature. Understanding would be "passive" in the sense that it allowed its way of sizing up things to be moulded by the actual state of affairs. We can best appreciate the dramatistic nature of this realistic formula, which treats of *knowledge* in terms of *action and passion,* by contrasting it with Berkeley's subsequent idealist formula, "to be is to be perceived" (*esse est percipi*) which reverses the direction by treating of *actuality* in terms of *knowledge.*

We may discern a dramatistic pun, involving a merger of active and passive in the expression, "the motivation of an act." Strictly speaking, the act of an agent would be the movement not of one *moved* but of a *mover* (a mover of the self or of something else by the self). For an act is by definition active, whereas to be moved (or motivated) is by definition passive. Thus, if we quizzically scrutinize the expression, "the motivating of an act," we note that it implicitly contains the paradox of substance. Grammatically, if a construction is active, it is not passive; and if it is passive, it is not active. But to consider an *act* in terms of its *grounds* is to consider it in terms of what it is not, namely, in terms of motives that, in acting upon the active, would make it a passive. We could state the paradox another way by saying that the concept of activation implies a kind of passive-behind-the-passive; for an agent who is "motivated by his passions" would be "moved by his being-movedness," or "acted upon by his state of being acted upon."

The Greek verb corresponding to *pati* is *paschein.* Among its more philosophic meanings are: to be actuated by a feeling or impulse, to be influenced by a passion; (and as a technical term of the Stoic school) to be acted upon by outward objects, or to take impressions from them. When Lear complains that he is "more sinned against than sinning," we see the two integral aspects of tragedy, the action and the passion, being dissociated.

Actus and Status

We considered the three Greek words, *poiema, pathema, mathema* (the act, the sufferance or state, the thing learned) because they are at the very center of dialectical motivation. The Greek proverb (*ta pathemata mathemata*) might be said to have merged *poiema* and *pathema* (if, for instance, we translated *ta pathemata* as "the things undergone," an expression that could embrace both the sort of things a person actively encountered and the sort of things that simply befell him). But there is also a way of bringing out *poiema* by itself and merging *pathema* and *mathema*. For *pathema* means not only suffering, but state of mind, condition—and knowledge is a state. Hence, reduced to a dichotomy, the relation could be formalized in terms of "act" and "state" (*actus* and *status*).

The actus-status pair has many possibilities. Often it quite coincides with the action-passion alignment. At other points it diverges from common usage. For though a "passion" and a "state of mind" are much the same, we strongly distinguish between a "political state" and a "political passion." The basic contrast between "motion" and "rest" is a variant of the actus-status pair. The contrast between the dramatic and the lyrical would be another variant (since drama centers in an action, whereas the lyric aims to arrest some one mood or moment). Often the traditional "faith" and "knowledge" pair (*pistis* and *gnosis; fides* and *intellectus*) can be treated as an instance of the same grammatical form, with faith as the act (cf. "an act of faith") and knowledge as the state derived from the act, quite as the tragic hero's *action*, involving his passion, attains its *rest* and *summation* in his *understanding*. From here it is but a brief step to our act-scene pair, inasmuch as the knowledge derived from the act is a knowledge of the act's context, or motivational ground.[1]

---

[1] Though faith is an act, it is faith in the nature of God as man's ground; hence it also has a strongly scenic reference.

Philologically, the actus-status pair can be used to characterize a major historical development. Consider, for instance, the Greek word for "virtue" (*arete*), and the corresponding Latin, *virtus*. Originally, these words had intensely active meanings. Indeed, *arete* is from the same root as *Ares*, the god of war, and as the Latin words for *art* and military *arms*. "Prowess" would be a good translation for the word in its origins. Gradually the concept of virtue came to place less stress upon action per se, and more stress upon the *potentialities* of action.

We can appreciate the transformation in a word of probably the same etymological origins, "hero." A hero is first of all a man who does heroic things; and his "heroism" resides in his acts. But next, a hero can be a man with the potentialities of heroic action. Soldiers on the way to the wars are heroes in this sense. Their heroism resides in their status as soldiers. Or a man may be considered a hero because he *had done* heroic acts, whereas in his present *state* as a hero he may be too old or weak to do such acts at all. And similarly, the "virtues" may become in the end purely states of mind; or proper attitudes toward God, things, and people; or *not* killing, *not* stealing, *not* coveting, etc.

Sociologically, this movement from actus to status involves *class* substance. It centers about the fact that the different occupational *acts* each have their corresponding *properties*, and out of these differences in properties there develop in time corresponding differences of *status*. Though the spread of occupational classification breaks down the purely tribal nature of a culture, notions of familial substance remain prominent.

Because occupational action requires properties, and because property is not an act but a state, in the social field we can readily observe how a ruling class develops from a stage wherein actus and status are of corresponding importance to a stage wherein the sense of position as an act is slighted and position as a traditional or inherited state is stressed. (Or sometimes we get a new kind of act, not germane to the originating state, as when a nobility, whose privileges grew out of horsemanship in war, turns to pageantry and sport, and may even employ its inherited privileges to hire or command others to fight in its place.) Kingship is originally an act, like heroism. But gradually, as inherited, it becomes a sheer state, the nature of the king's *extrinsic* properties enabling him to be a king by reason of their substantiality alone. He can *be* a king, while commissioning ministers to perform in his stead the kingly acts. (In the mediaeval frame, the primary act, the act of God, is *to be*.) Indeed, the king's holdings may retain him his position as king, investing him with their substance, long after his acts, or his failures to act, have endangered his kingdom. And may we not discern some such grammar behind the Roi Soleil's pronouncement: *"L'état, c'est moi"?* Louis's conception of being, or substance, made it quite natural for him to merge the two meanings of state: the state as a governmental property and the state or property of kingship. The administrative and tax-gathering machinery and the royal domains, we can imagine, could thus be looked upon as an extension of the king's person, a property of his character, like facial traits. In proportion as the quality of a ruling class becomes thus transformed from act to state, we may look for the emergence of a class whose substance centers in a new act.

The actus-status alignment lends itself to another sort of treatment, whereby status is considered as *potentiality* and actus as its *actualization*. That is, in a state there are implicit possibilities, and in action these possibilities are made explicit. But we shall treat of these resources when discussing the potentiality-actuality and implicit-explicit pairs.

Universal Motives as Substance

All gods are "substances," and as such are names for motives or combinations of motives. Polytheistic divinities, besides their personalistic aspects, often represent decidedly geometric, or scenic, kinds of motivation. Indeed, we may even think of local divinities as theological prototypes of contemporary environmentalist, or geographic motives. For to say that a river is a different "god" than a mountain is to say, within the rules of a polytheistic nomenclature, that a river calls for a different set of human actions than a mountain. Whereas the "enlightened" have too often been content to dismiss the pagan gods merely as instances of animistic superstition, the fact is that the complex of social behavior centering about a given "god" was often quite *correct*, in the most realistically biological sense. Thus, insofar as adequate modes of planting and harvesting and distribution are connected with the rites of a given divinity, its name would be the title for a correct summation of motives. However, such concepts of motivation are usually developed to the point where their original reference is obscured, being replaced by motivational concepts peculiar to a specialized priesthood and to the needs of class domination.

Universal religions, proclaiming some one principle of divinity as the ground of being, have assisted the development of world-wide commerce by enabling the believers, who share in this over-all substance, to retain a sense of one master motive prevailing throughout the world. For the believer in such a universal scheme of motives may go to many different scenes, each with its own peculiar motivational texture, without losing his "hypostasis," the sense of his personal identity and of one "real" motivational substratum underlying it. Scientific rationalism can also serve this end, as with the Stoic cosmopolitanism that contributed so signally to the intellectual side of Christianity. Romantic stories of the Westerner, drinking himself to death at some outpost in the tropics, indicate that there *are* local gods (local motives), and that, whereas neither his vestiges of the Christian religion nor his sense of caste permit him to do them formal obeisance, in his dissipation he reveals a distorted response to them. The British official's habit, in the Empire's remotest spots, of dressing for dinner is in effect the transporting of an idol, the vessel of a motive that has its sanctuary in the homeland.

Of course, by the time the monotheistic motive has become embodied in a structure of world empire, it has usually been transformed into its secular analogue, the monetary motive. For the incentive of monetary profit, like the One God, can be felt to prevail as a global source of action, over and above any motivations peculiar to the locale. And it serves the needs of empire precisely because it "transcends" religious motives, hence making for a "tolerant" commerce among men whose religious vocabularies of motivation differ widely.

Nonetheless, the greater the diffusion of a motive (be it the One God or the Gold Standard and its later variants) the greater its need to adopt modifications peculiar to specific local scenes. For though a doctrine proclaims a universal scene that is the motivation common to all men whatever their diversities, this "substantial" term must also have "adjectival" terms that adapt it to more restricted purposes. We would class as "polytheisms" all terminologies stressing localness of motive (such as nationalism). But we would also recognize that monotheisms (in which we would include any secular title for a universal spring of action, such as "nature" or "the profit motive") can prevail only insofar as they are "incipiently" polytheistic, containing motivational terms ("saints") that break down the universality of the motive into narrower reference.

According to the Marxist calculus, insofar as the world becomes industrialized under capitalism, workers everywhere share the same social motives, since they all have the "factory situation" in common. This is the scene that shapes the workers' acts, and their nature as agents, in conformity with it. Stated in terms of money (the capitalist god, from which are derived men's freedom and their necessity) the motive common to the workers is "wage slavery." It is universal as a motive whenever the means of production are private property, with wages and taxes being paid in symbols rather than in kind. But it divides the over-all capitalist motive into two broad economic classifications, the possessors and the dispossessed, with each status analyzable as a different substance, or contrasting bundle of motives.

Translated dramatistically: the sheer *work* in a factory would not be an *act*. It would be little more than *motion*. And this motion becomes actus only when the workers' status is understood in terms of socialist organization. This act is of revolutionary import since the sheer ownership of the factories is a *state:* hence the property relation becomes increasingly passive, while the proletarian relation becomes increasingly active. However, reversals in keeping with the antinomies of substance complicate the pattern. For the owners' state, in its governmental aspects, is anything but passive. Indeed, the property structure automatically contains an act of expropriation, since the workers receive much less than they produce; and the structure of the state is designed to keep this act of expropriation in force. From this point of view, it is the state that is active, while the workers suffer its action.

The socialist revolution is designed first to reverse the state (during the "dictatorship of the proletariat") and next to abolish it, or let it "wither away." But our grammar would lead us to doubt whether a "state" can ever really "wither away," and least of all in a complex industrial society. Though it may take strategically new forms, we expect the logic of the actus-status pair to continue manifesting itself. The selection of the proletariat as the vessel of the new act that transcends the bourgeois state may or may not be correct as a casuistry, but it violates no law of "grammar." The belief in the withering away of the state, however, does seem to violate a law of grammar. For no continuity of social act is possible without a corresponding social status; and the many different kinds of act required in an industrial state, with its high degree of specialization, make for corresponding *classifications* of status.

Intrinsic and Extrinsic

The treatment of material properties as a "state" brings the actus-status pair in line with the distinction between intrinsic and extrinsic substance, or between motivations within the agent and motivations derived from scenic sources that "support" (or "sub-stand") the agent. In the introduction to his *Philosophy of History*, where Hegel places Matter in dialectical opposition to Spirit, he clearly begins by equating Matter with the extrinsic aspect of substance and Spirit with its intrinsic aspect:

> As the essence of Matter is Gravity, so, on the other hand, we may affirm that the substance, the essence of Spirit is Freedom. . . . Matter possesses gravity in virtue of its tendency toward a central point. It is essentially composite; consisting of parts that *exclude* each other. It seeks its Unity; and therefore exhibits itself as self-destructive, as verging toward its opposite (an indivisible point). If it could attain this, it would be Matter no longer, it would have perished. It strives after the realization of its Idea; for in Unity it exists *ideally*. Spirit, on the contrary, may be defined as that which has its centre in itself. It has not a unity outside itself, but has already found it; it exists *in* and *with itself*. Matter has its essence out of itself; Spirit is *self-contained existence* (Bei-sich-selbst-sein). Now this is freedom, exactly. For if I am dependent, my being is referred to something else which I am not; I cannot exist independently of something external. I am free, on the contrary, when my existence depends upon myself.

However, before he has proceeded very far, remarks on the relation between the potential and the actual lead into the peculiarly Hegelian theory of the State as the vessel of freedom. For the Spirit is free, we are told, and the State is "the perfect embodiment of Spirit." But by the time we arrive at this point, the intrinsic and the extrinsic have begun subtly to change places. One can discern the ambiguity by experimentally shifting the accent in Hegel's formula for the nature of the State. We may say either "embodiment of *Spirit*" or "*embodiment* of Spirit." Or, since "embodiment" is here a synonym for "materialization," we could make the ambiguity still more apparent by rephrasing it as a choice between "materialization of *Spirit*" and "*materialization* of Spirit." For the expression itself is got by the merging of antithetical terms. Hence, when you have put them together, by shifting the stress you can proclaim one or the other as the essence of the pair. Accepting Hegel's definition of Matter, only a State that is the "materialization of *Spirit*" would be "essentially" free. But a State that is the "*materialization* of Spirit" would be the very *antithesis* of freedom (and this was precisely the interpretation given by the Marxist reversal of the Hegelian dialectic).

Indeed, we can take it as a reliable rule of thumb that, whenever we find a distinction between the internal and the external, the intrinsic and the extrinsic, the within and the without, (as with Korzybski's distinction between happenings "inside the skin" and happenings "outside the skin") we can expect to encounter the paradoxes of substance.

Recently, for instance, a "gerontologist," whose specialty is the study of "aging as a physiological process," is reported to have said in an address to a body of chemists:

> Aging, like life in general, is a chemical process, and just as chemistry has been able to improve on nature in many respects, virtually creating a new world by reshuffling nature's molecules, so it may be expected that eventually chemistry will learn to stimulate artificially those powers of "intrinsic resistance" to disease with which man is born.

"Intrinsic resistance," you will note, is a concept that situates a motivational source within the body as agent. But the use of chemical means to stimulate this internal motive would involve the transformation of this "intrinsic" motive into an "extrinsic" motive, since it would become but the channel or vessel through which the chemical materials ("scenic," administered "from without") would affect the chemistry of the body. Indeed, since the body is but chemistry, and all outside the body is but chemistry, the very mode of thought that forms a concept of the "intrinsic" in these terms must also by the same terms dissolve it. Everything being chemical, the physiological center of "intrinsic resistance" is but a function of the chemical scene. In fact, insofar as chemical stimulants of the required sort were found, a dependence upon them would be a dependence upon purely *external* agencies. And far from "stimulating" intrinsic resistance, the chemicals should be expected to cause a *weakening* of it, to the extent that the economy of the body grew to require these chemicals. The only place where an intrinsic motive, as a genuinely internal activation, could be said to figure in materialistic medicology is on the occasions when physicians come upon illnesses in which the chances of recovery are felt to depend upon the *mental attitude* of the patient (whether he "wants" to recover). Here one has an intrinsic motive (involving an action) in contrast with such a motive as is supplied by the administering of chemicals (involving sheer motion).[2]

One of the most common fallacies in the attempt to determine the intrinsic is the equating of the intrinsic with the unique. We recall an instance of this nominalist extreme in an essay by a literary critic who exhorted his fellows to discern the quality of a given poet's lines by finding in exactly what way they were distinct from the lines of every other poet (somewhat as advertisements recommending rival brands of the same product play up some one "talking point" that is said to distinguish this brand from all its competitors). Yet the intrinsic value of a poet's lines must also reside, to a very great degree, in attributes that his work shares with many other poets. We cannot define by differentia alone; the differentiated also has significant attributes as members of its class. The heresy that would define human nature solely in terms of some more inclusive category, such as chemistry, or protoplasm, or colloids, has as its over-compensatory counterpart the heresy that would define solely in terms of distinctive traits, actual or imputed. Thus, an article in one of our best magazines is recommended on the grounds that it "applies anthropological method to the diagnosis of our distinctive cultural traits." This is, to be sure, a legitimate limitation of subject-matter for treatment within the scope of one article; but we should be admonished against the assumption that even a wholly accurate description of our culture in terms of its distinctive traits alone could possibly give us a just interpretation of its motives. Indeed, we can discern a variant of the same error in

[2] See in appendix, "The Problem of the Intrinsic," as indication of the way in which the quandaries of substance figure in literary criticism.

nationalist and regionalist concepts of motivation as we get in the over-simplifications of literature: the treatment of motivational parts as though they were the motivational whole.

The search for the intrinsic frequently leads to the selection of calculi postulating various assortments of "instincts," "drives," "urges," etc. as the motivational springs of biologic organisms in general and of human organisms in particular. Materialistic science prefers this style of vocabulary because it assigns *scenic* terms to motives situated in the *agent;* and scenic words generally seem so much more "real" than other words, even though such lists can be expanded or contracted *ad lib.,* quite as suits one's dialectical preferences. Though the treatment of intrinsic motivation in such terms is usually made in good faith, it can also well serve as a rhetorical deflection of social criticism. For instance, if a reformer would advocate important political or social changes on the ground that the present state of affairs stimulates wars, he can be "scientifically refuted" by a calculus which postulates a "combative instinct," or "drive towards aggression," or "natural urge to kill" in all people or certain types of people. For if such motives are intrinsic to human agents, they may be expected to demand expression whatever the social and political structure may be.

When a person has his mind set upon the interpreting of human motivation in a calculus that features an innate "combative instinct" or "natural urge to kill," one may as well accept his decision as a stubborn fact of nature; instead of trying to dispel it, one should try to get around it. Recalling the paradox of substance, for instance, we are reminded that such "drives" or "urges" are like "tendencies" or "trends," which we discussed when on the subject of "directional" substance. And the man who would postulate an "instinct to kill" can be asked to round out his dialectic by postulating a contrary "instinct not to kill." For there is certainly as much empirical evidence that men let one another live as there is evidence that they kill one another. Hence, whenever such words designate motives that may or may not prevail, we can at least insist that they be balanced with their dialectical counterpart. And once the pattern is thus completed, we are able to see beyond these peculiarly "intrinsic" motives to "extrinsic" or "scenic" motives, in the sense of situations which stimulate one rather than the other of the paired motives, as some situations call forth a greater amount of combativeness and destructiveness, whereas other situations call forth a greater amount of coöperation and construction. (There are, of course, complications here that require much more discriminatory calculation than could be got by confinement to such pairings. A certain kind of coöperation is stimulated by war, for instance, both at the time and as the result of new methods which, originally designed for military aggression, can later be adapted for peaceful commercial exchange.)

Spinoza defines substance as "the cause of itself" (*causa sui*). And we can see how this formulation applies to the search for the intrinsic when we contrast supernaturalist and humanist strategies of motivation. Supernaturalist strategies derive the attributes of human substance and motive from God as their ancestral source, whereas humanistic strategies situate the motivational principles within human agents themselves. In brief, humanists assign to man an *inherent* or *intrinsic* dignity, whereas supernaturalists assign to man a *derived* dignity. Any motive humanistically postulated in the agent would be a *causa sui* insofar as it is not deduced from any cause outside itself.

Since agents require placement in scenes, humanism gets its scenic counterpart in naturalism. There is also, of course, a "supernaturalist humanism," but it would be exactly the same as the kind of doctrine we here call simply supernaturalism. And similarly what we here call humanism could be characterized more fully as "naturalistic humanism," or simply "naturalism," as in the following citation from an essay by John Dewey, assigning an intrinsic motive to human nature:

> Naturalism finds the values in question, the worth and dignity of men and women, founded in human nature itself, in the connections, actual and potential, of human beings with one another in their natural social relationships. Not only that, but it is ready at any time to maintain the thesis that a foundation within man and nature is a much sounder one than is one alleged to exist outside the constitution of man and nature.

By placing man and nature together, in dialectical opposition to the supernatural, Dr. Dewey's remarks here somewhat conceal from us the fact that we are shifting between a scenic location for motives and a location within the agent. Only the second kind would be "intrinsic" to people; the other kind would be "derivative" from nature as scene instead of from super-nature as scene. (Both "foundation" and "constitution" are "stance" words, hence capable of merging intrinsic and extrinsic reference.)

It is possible that the reverse perspective so characteristic of Russian ikons may have originated in a theory of the intrinsic, as is indicated in this citation from *The Burlington Magazine* for October 1929 ("Greco: the Epilogue to Byzantine Culture," by Robert Byron):

> It has been suggested that the habit of inverted perspective which the Greeks perpetuated in Duccio and Giotto, derived from the artist's imagining himself within the object portrayed; so that as it progressed in the direction of the beholder it necessarily diminished. Such indeed was the Byzantine vision of form as expressed in terms of light and dark. The head, the arm, was conceived primarily as a dark mass, instead of as a given space to be invested with form by the application of shadow. This principle is explicitly stated in Denys of Fourna's "Guide to Painting" in relation to flesh depiction; and the interest of this instruction lies in the fact that it exhibits the exact converse of the rules for the same process prescribed in mediaeval western manuals such as that of Cennino Cennini.

The notion of "the artist's imagining himself within the object portrayed" would seem to carry the cult of the intrinsic to the point where it exemplifies the paradox of purity, as with the wag who said that only the homosexual man can be the true admirer of women, since he carries his admiration to such an extent that, identifying himself with them, he adopts their very point of view, and thus falls in love with men. For an "intrinsic" observation of women would look, not towards women, but towards men.

The Rhetoric of Substance

The ambiguity of substance affords, as one might expect, a major resource of rhetoric. We can appreciate this by referring again to the citation from Locke, when he says that in speaking of substance "we talk like children: who, being questioned what such a thing is which they know not, readily give this satisfactory answer, that it is *something;* which in truth signifies no more, when so used, either by children or men, but that they know not what; and that the thing they pretend to know and talk of, is what they have no distinct idea of at all, and so are perfectly ignorant of it, and in the dark." For "the *general* name substance" is "nothing but the supposed, but unknown, support of those qualities we find existing." The most clear-sounding of words can thus be used for the vaguest of reference, quite as we speak of "a certain thing" when we have no particular thing in mind. And so rock-bottom a study as a treatise on the nature of substance might, from this point of view, more accurately be entitled, "A Treatise on the Nature of I-don't-know-what." One might thus express a state of considerable vagueness in the imposing accents of a juridic solidity.

We may even go a step further and note that one may say "it is *substantially* true" precisely at a time when on the basis of the evidence, it would be much more accurate to say, "it is not true." And even a human slave could be defined in Christian doctrine as "substantially" free, by reason of qualities which he had inherited "substantially" from his creator. Even in cases where the nature of the case does not justify the usage grammatically, it can be used without strain for rhetorical purposes. What handier linguistic resource could a rhetorician want than an ambiguity whereby he can say "The state of affairs is substantially such-and-such," instead of having to say "The state of affairs *is* and/or *is not* such-and-such"?

There is a similar usage in the expression, "in principle" (a word furthermore that is literally a "first," as we realize when we recall its etymological descent from a word meaning: beginning, commencement, origin). So diplomats can skirt some commendable but embarrassing proposal by accepting it "in principle," a stylistic nicety that was once very popular with the League of Nations. Positivists who would discard the category of substance assert that the only meaningful propositions are those which are capable of scientific proof; and having thus outlawed the conveniences of a substantive rhetoric, they next blandly concede that the scientific proof is not always possible *actually*, but must be possible "in principle"—which would leave them pretty much where they began, except that their doctrine won't allow them to admit it. By this device, we can even characterize as "universally valid" a proposition that may in fact be denied by whole classes of people. As one controversialist has phrased it: "To say that a proposition is valid is to say that *in principle* it can secure the universal agreement of all who abide by scientific method."

Often, of course, this function of language is preserved when there are no such telltale expressions (such as "substantially," "essentially," "in principle," or "in the long run") to make it quickly apparent. For instance, a list of citizens' signatures had been collected for a petition asking that a certain politician's name be placed on the ballot. In court it was shown that some of these signatures were genuine, but that a great many others were false. Thereupon the judge invalidated the lot on the grounds that, the whole list being a mixture of the false and the genuine, it was "saturated" with fraud. He here ruled in effect that the list was substantially or essentially fraudulent. The judgment was reversed by a higher court which ruled that, since the required number of genuine signatures had been obtained, the false signatures should be simply ignored. That is, the genuine signatures should be considered in themselves, not contextually.

Two Kinds of Departure

Since the five key terms can be considered as "principles," and since the margins of overlap among them permit a thinker to consider the genius of one term as "substantially" participant in the genius of another, the ambiguity of the substantial makes it possible to use terms as points of departure in two senses. Thus we may speak in the name of God because this expression is the summation of our thinking. Or precisely because we speak in the name of God, we may be freed to develop modes of thought that lead away from supernaturalism, since absolute conviction about religion might serve as ground for a study of nature. And whereas "naturalism" in its beginnings was a consistent title, referring to man in *nature*, it gradually became transformed into a surreptitiously compensatory title, referring to technological methods and ideals that are almost the antithesis of nature, with nature itself seen in terms of technology and the monetary. Thus, ironically, though much of the resonance in the term "nature" derives from the supernaturalist attitude, which thought of natural law as derivative from the divine, in time the *distinction* between the natural and the divine became transformed into a *contrast* between the natural and the divine. Or, if we think of "God" as the whole and "nature" as a part, we could say that the supernaturalist treated nature as a part *synecdochically* related to the whole, whereas in time naturalism treated this as a *divisive* relation. Or, to adopt a very suggestive usage in Charles M. Perry's *Toward a Dimensional Realism*, the notion of nature as *a part of* God could be converted into the notion of nature as *apart from* God.

But insofar as this divisive emphasis developed, and the secular appeal of "nature" relied less and less upon connotations of the supernatural, "nature" gained resonance from a new source, the romantic reaction against the "unnatural" world progressively created by the technological "conquest" of nature. In this way the selection of "naturalism" as the name for a philosophy of applied science may be *compensatory* rather than *consistent* (somewhat as though one were to call a philosophy "humanistic" because it aimed at the systematic elimination of traits that were formerly considered characteristically human, or as religious doctrines of "personalism" may be formulated, not because the individual person really is in a position of paramount importance, but precisely because he is *not*).

Such tactics of entitling are as legitimate as any other, once the irony has been made explicit. Indeed, philosophies are never quite "consistent" in this sense. All thought tends to name things not because they are precisely as named, but because they are not quite as named, and the name is designated as a somewhat hortatory device, to take up the slack. As others have pointed out, for instance, if the philosophy of "utilitarianism" were wholly correct, there would be no need for the philosophy. For men would spontaneously and inevitably follow the dictates of utility; whereas in actuality the doctrine proclaiming the ubiquity of the utilitarian motive was formulated to serve as a *plea* for the deliberate consulting of the utilitarian motive.

From such ambiguity is derived that irony of historical development whereby the very strength in the affirming of a given term may the better enable men to make a world that departs from it. For the affirming of the term as their god-term enables men to go far afield without sensing a loss of orientation. And by the time the extent of their departure is enough to become generally obvious, the stability of the new order they have built in the name of the old order gives them the strength to abandon their old god-term and adopt another. Hence, noting that something so highly unnatural as technology developed under the name of naturalism, we might ironically expect that, were "technologism" to become the name for "naturalism," the philosophy would be the first step towards a development *away from* technology. And as indication that this is no mere improvising, the philosophy of "operationalism," modeled after technological procedures, embodies a totally different concept of meaning than the one which, we know as a historical fact, figured as an incentive in the *invention* of technological devices and their corresponding mathematical formulae. Hence, if carried out rigorously, it would lead to the *stabilization* of technological operations rather than to the development of new ones. As "naturalism" would lead us, via technology, away from nature, so perhaps "operationalism" might be a way of leading us, in the name of technological operations, away from technology.

It has been said by one of Descartes' editors, John Veitch, that when Descartes questioned an old dogma, rather than attacking it head on, he aimed at "sapping its foundations." And he got rid of traditional principles "not so much by direct attack as by substituting for them new proofs and grounds of reasoning." Veitch also quotes a defender of Descartes who says ironically that his enemies called him an atheist "apparently because he had given new proofs of the existence of God." But these new proofs were in effect new qualifications of God. And in this capacity they subtly changed the nature of "God" as a term for motives, so that those who understood by a God only the character possessing the attributes of the old proofs were justified in calling Descartes an "atheist." Here, subtly, the ambiguous resources in the point of departure were being utilized.

As regards the principles of humanism, we may note that a supernatural grounding of humanism is "consistent" in the sense that a personal principle is ascribed to the ultimate ground of human action. And having thus been put in, it is there for the philosopher to take out, when deriving the principles of specifically human action by deduction from the nature of the universal ground. A naturalistic grounding of humanism, on the other hand, is "compensatory," in that personal agents are placed in a non-personal scene. The first strategy reasons by a "therefore," the second by a "however."

The Centrality of Substance

Contemporary scientific theory, in proposing to abandon the categories of substance and causality, has done speculation a good turn. For it has made clear wherein the difference between philosophic and scientific terminologies of motivation resides. Philosophy, like common sense, must think of human motivation dramatistically, in terms of action and its ends.   But a science is freed of philosophic taints only insofar as it confines itself to terms of motion and arrested motion (figure, structure).   This convention, almost Puritanical in its severity (surely we should not be far wrong in calling it a secularized variant of Puritanism) has brought about such magnification of human powers that any "objection" to it would have about as much force as an attempt to "refute" Niagara Falls.   But such results, however spectacular, do not justify an attempt to abide by the same terminological conventions when treating of human motives.   For one could confine the study of action within the terms of motion only by resigning oneself to gross misrepresentations of life as we normally experience it.

Though we here lay great stress upon the puns and other word play in men's ideas of motivation, we do not thereby conclude that such linguistic tactics are "nothing but" puns and word play.   Rather, we take it that men's linguistic behavior here reflects real paradoxes in the nature of the world itself—antinomies that could be resolved only if men were able, not in thought, as with the program of Hegelian idealism, but in actual concrete operations, to create an entire universe.

However, strictly for the purposes of our Grammar, we need not defend as much.   One might hypothetically grant that the treatment of motives in terms of "action" and "substance" is wholly fallacious, yet defend it as central to the placement of statements about motives. Relinquishing all claims for it as a "philosopher's stone," we might then make claims for it secondarily, as "a philosopher's stone for the synopsis of writings that have sought the philosopher's stone."   Men have talked about things in many ways, but the pentad offers a synoptic way to talk about their talk-about.   For the resources of the five terms figure in the utterances about motives, throughout all human history.   And even the most modern of scientific tracts can be adequately placed only as a development in this long line.   From this point of view, terminologies of motion and "conditioning" are to be treated as *dialectical* enterprises designed to *transcend* terminologies of action and substance.

At the very best, we admit, each time you scrutinize a concept of substance, it dissolves into thin air.   But conversely, the moment you relax your gaze a bit, it re-forms again.   For things *do* have intrinsic natures, whatever may be the quandaries that crowd upon us as soon as we attempt to decide definitively what these intrinsic natures are. And only by systematically dwelling upon the paradoxes of substance could we possibly equip ourselves to guard against the concealment of "substantialist" thought in schemes overtly designed to avoid it. Yet these schemes are usually constructed by men who contemn dialectical operations so thoroughly that, in their aversion, they cannot adequately observe them, and are accordingly prompt to persuade themselves that *their* terminology is not dialectical, whereas every terminology is dialectical by sheer reason of the fact that it is a terminology. If you will, call the category of substance sheer error. Yet it is so fertile a source of error, that only by learning to recognize its nature *from within* could we hope to detect its many disguises from without. Such thoughts apply particularly to Alfred Korzybski's admonitions against Aristotelian "elementalism"; for his aversion leads to so evasive a treatment of the subject that in a very long book he contrives to convey little more than a *negative attitude* towards it.

So, in sum: The transformations which we here study as a Grammar are not "illusions," but citable realities. The structural relations involved are observable realities. Nothing is more imperiously there for observation and study than the tactics people employ when they would injure or gratify one another—and one can readily demonstrate the role of substantiation in such tactics. To call a man a friend or brother is to proclaim him consubstantial with oneself, one's values or purposes. To call a man a bastard is to attack him by attacking his whole line, his "authorship," his "principle" or "motive" (as expressed in terms of the familial). An epithet assigns substance doubly, for in stating the character of the object it at the same time contains an implicit program of action with regard to the object, thus serving as motive.

So, one could, if he wished, maintain that all theology, metaphysics, philosophy, criticism, poetry, drama, fiction, political exhortation, historical interpretation, and personal statements about the lovable and the hateful—one could if he wanted to be as drastically thorough as some of our positivists now seem to want to be—maintain that every bit of this is nonsense. Yet these words of nonsense would themselves be real words, involving real tactics, having real demonstrable relationships, and demonstrably affecting relationships. And as such, a study of their opportunities, necessities, and embarrassments would be central to the study of human motives.

The design on a piece of primitive pottery may be wholly symbolic or allegorical. But a drawing that accurately reproduces this design in a scientific treatise would be not symbolic or allegorical, but realistic. And similarly, even when statements about the *nature of the world* are abstractly metaphysical, statements about the *nature of these statements* can be as empirical as the statement, "This is Mr. Smith," made when introducing Mr. Smith in the accepted manner.

III

SCOPE AND REDUCTION

The Representative Anecdote

MEN seek for vocabularies that will be faithful *reflections* of reality. To this end, they must develop vocabularies that are *selections* of reality. And any selection of reality must, in certain circumstances, function as a *deflection* of reality. Insofar as the vocabulary meets the needs of reflection, we can say that it has the necessary scope. In its selectivity, it is a reduction. Its scope and reduction become a deflection when the given terminology, or calculus, is not suited to the subject matter which it is designed to calculate.

Dramatism suggests a procedure to be followed in the development of a given calculus, or terminology. It involves the search for a "representative anecdote," to be used as a form in conformity with which the vocabulary is constructed. For instance, the behaviorist uses his experiments with the conditioned reflex as the anecdote about which to form his vocabulary for the discussion of human motives; but this anecdote, though notably *informative,* is not *representative,* since one cannot find a representative case of human motivation in animals, if only because animals lack that property of linguistic rationalization which is so typical of human motives. A representative case of human motivation must have a strongly linguistic bias, whereas animal experimentation necessarily neglects this.

If the originating anecdote is not representative, a vocabulary developed in strict conformity with it will not be representative. This embarrassment is usually avoided in practice by a break in the conformity at some crucial point; this means in effect that the vocabulary ceases to have the basis which is claimed for it. The very man who, with a chemical experiment as his informing anecdote, or point of departure, might tell you that people are but chemicals, will induce responses in people by talking to them, whereas he would not try to make chemicals behave by linguistic inducement. And to say that people are "chemicals that talk" is the same thing as saying that people aren't "just chemicals," since chemicals don't talk. It is to confront the paradox of substance in a terminology unsuited to the illumination of this paradox.

Conversely, the notion of chemical affinity about which Goethe organizes his novel of sorrowing love, *Die Wahlverwandtschaften,* is not really the chemicalizing of human substance, but rather the humanizing of chemical substance. For the motive is defined by the action of the characters in a way totally unrepresentative of chemicals; and the situation is not chemical, but thoroughly social. Nothing makes this more quickly apparent than the closing paragraph, where the dead lovers lie buried side by side, surely their nearest approach to a purely chemical condition. Yet the novelist refers to a "peace that hovers over them" and to "the kindred images of angels looking upon them." And what a "gracious moment" it will be, he says, when in the future (*dereinst*) the lovers awaken together.

Subsequently we shall consider at some length this question of the "representative anecdote," itself so dramatistic a conception that we might call it the dramatistic approach to dramatism: an *introduction to* dramatism that is *deduced from* dramatism, and hence gains plausibility in proportion as dramatism itself is more fully developed. For the present it is enough to observe that the issue arises as soon as one considers the relation between representation and reduction in the choice and development of a motivational calculus. A given calculus must be supple and complex enough to be representative of the subject-matter it is designed to calculate. It must have scope. Yet it must also possess simplicity, in that it is broadly a reduction of the subject-matter. And by selecting drama as our representative, or informative anecdote, we meet these requirements. For the vocabulary developed in conformity with this form can possess a systematically interrelated structure, while at the same time allowing for the discussion of human affairs and the placement of cultural expressions in such typically human terms as personality and action (two terms that might be merged in the one term, "role").

The informative anecdote, we could say, contains *in nuce* the terminological structure that is evolved in conformity with it. Such a terminology is a "conclusion" that follows from the selection of a given anecdote. Thus the anecdote is in a sense a *summation,* containing implicitly what the system that is developed from it contains explicitly.

Once we have set seriously to work developing a systematic terminology out of our anecdote, another kind of summation looms up. We might call it the "paradigm" or "prototype."

In selecting drama as our anecdote, for instance, we discover that we have made a selection in the realm of *action,* as against scientific reduction to sheer *motion.* And we thereupon begin to ask ourselves: What would be "the ultimate act," or "the most complete act"? That is, what would be the "pure" act, an act so thoroughly an act that it could be considered the form or prototype of all acts? For if we could have a conception of a consummate act, any less thorough acts could be seen as departures from it, as but partial exemplifications of it. But whatever qualities it possessed clearly, by reason of its nature as an absolute summation, we could then discern dimly in all lesser acts.

What then would be the "pure act" or "pure drama" that one might use as the paradigm of action in general? Such a paradigm or prototype of action, the concept of an ultimate or consummate act, is found in the theologians' concern with the Act of Creation. It "sums up" action quite as the theory of evolution sums up motion, but with one notable difference: whereas one must believe in evolution literally, one can discuss the Act of Creation "substantially," or "in principle."

We shall, then, examine the resources and embarrassments involved in The Creation. And if this seems like a round-about approach to the subject of our chapter, let one ask himself if he could possibly get a more advantageous position from which to observe the aspects of scope and reduction than by beginning with a subject of such comprehensive scope and reducing it.

Before going further, however, we should note that still another kind of reduction (different from both informative anecdote and paradigmatic summation) arises in the dramatist perspective. This is contained in our formula: the basic unit of action is the human body in purposive motion. We have here a kind of "lowest common denominator" of action, a minimal requirement that should appear in every act, however many more and greater are the attributes of a complex act. This is the nearest approach which dramatism affords to the "building block" kind of reduction in materialistic philosophies.

The Way of Creation

In *The Thought and Character of William James,* by Ralph Perry (Vol. II, p. 711) among the letters written by William James to his father there is one in which William is replying to some of his father's theological and ontological speculations. He raises an objection to something his father had written. This objection, he says, "refers to the whole conception of creation, from which you would exclude all arbitrariness or magic." And he continues:

> Now I don't see what the word "creation" can mean if this be totally excluded, or what there is to justify its discrimination from pantheism. Creation, emanation, have at all times been opposed to pantheism, immanence; and it is evident from the scorn with which you always mention pantheism that you, too, place a broad gulf between them. The essence of the pantheistic conception, if I understand it, consists in there being a necessary relation between Creator and creature, so that both are the same fact viewed from opposite sides, and their duality as Creator and creature becomes merged in a higher unity as Being. Consequently a conception really opposed to pantheism must necessarily refuse to admit any such ratio as this,—any such external ratio,—so to speak, between them; must deny that each term exists only by virtue of the equation to which it belongs; the Creator must be the all, and the act by which the creature is set over against him has its motive within the creative circumference. The act must therefore necessarily contain an arbitrary and magical element—that is, if I attach the right meaning to those words—undetermined by anything external to the agent. Of course it is impossible to attempt to imagine the *way* of creation, but wherever from an absolute first a second appears, *there* it must be;—and it must be magical, for if in the second there be anything coequal or coeval with the first, it becomes pantheism.[3]

[3] In the immediately following pages we shall have to mull over this passage at considerable length, perhaps even to an extent that will strike the reader as quibbling. These speculations are necessary to the ultimate rounding-out of our position; but they are not necessary to the characterizing and application of the dramatist perspective in general. After the twists and turns which begin at this point, our main line of speculation emerges again on page 74. The reader may have this thought as solace, if these intervening pages greatly worry him. Or he may even skip to page 74.

The pages deal with the halfway stage between doctrines of "the Creation" and doctrines of "Evolution," a stage that is generally called "pantheism," and that marks the area of strategic overlap between terminologies of action and terminologies of motion.

We should not be disturbed if we find this paragraph difficult to follow. After all, the philosopher is here discussing something which he was in no position to report on. Hence, if we attempt to understand his words as information, narration, exposition, we must necessarily find them incomprehensible. For there is nothing here to be understood in the sense in which one might try to understand a report about some event in history. James's discussion of the Creation is not "archaeological." He is not offering a "historical reconstruction." As he himself observes, "It is impossible to attempt to imagine the way of creation," or as some contemporary advocates of physicalist vocabularies might put it: It is impossible to explain the meaning of "the act of Creation" in terms of concrete operations.

Dramatistically considered, there is a tremendous difference between "the Creation" and "the process of Evolution" as motivational summations. One sums up in terms of action, the other in terms of motion. A statement about Evolutionary motion is "true" only if it names events that literally take place. But "the Creation" is "true," as a prototype of action, if it has *the form of the most complete act*. We can come nearest to its kind of "truth," in terms of science, when we think of a composite photograph, which is got by superimposing the portraits of many individuals upon one another. In being a likeness of their "average," it is not literally a likeness of any. The analogy is not quite satisfactory, however, since a concept of "the Creation," as the prototype of action designates not the "average" act, but the logical conclusion of the concept of action (an opponent might rather call it the *reductio ad absurdum* of the concept of action).

Statements about both "Evolution" and "the Creation" are alike in this: despite their reference to matters of sequence, to "befores" and "afters," they are *ontological* statements, statements about *being,* about what *is*. That is, the laws of Evolution *are* such-and-such; and the structure of the Creation *is* such-and-such. For even a fundamentalist who would treat the Creation as an act that *was* would have to agree that the *principles* involved in the act *are*.

We here stand at a moment of great indeterminacy, the watershed moment that slopes down to "being" on one side and "becoming" on the other. It is the ambiguity etymologically present in the Latin, *natura* (and its Greek counterpart, *physis*). For though we came to speak of a thing's "nature" as its essence, the word originally had a genetic or developmental meaning, a reference to *growth* and *birth*.

True, some terminologists would even hold that the laws of becoming themselves become. And this is true in the sense that a new species exemplifies new laws of motion: the particles of matter contained in it behave differently than the particles of matter contained in other species; hence, when this species arises, certain peculiar laws of motion are born, and these laws of motion cease to be when this species becomes extinct. But any such statement about the becoming of becoming ("emergent evolution") can be rephrased as a statement about the "laws" of the becoming of becoming, or as "generalizations" about the becoming of becoming—and this brings us back to the ontological level.

And if even a concept so super-genetic as the evolution of evolution forces us back to an ontological level as soon as we make generalizations about this process of processes, all the more clearly are we found shuttling between being and becoming in the concept of Creation. The shift is between temporal priority and logical priority. The Creation, considered as a prototype of action in our paradigmatic, or summational sense, involves "principles," and these are not historical or temporal "firsts," but logical firsts. They are the kind of "beginnings" that are always. James speaks of an "absolute first," which admonishes us that we here touch upon the paradox of purity. An "absolute" first is the kind of first that both is and is not followed by a second.

In sum: we are discussing the Creation not as a temporal event, but as the logical prototype of an act. Indeed, even if one believed it literally, one would hardly be justified in treating it as a temporal event, since it was itself the positing of time; it was the act that set up the conditions of temporal development; hence a terminology that reduced it to terms of time would lack sufficient scope. Thus, even a literal believer would have to treat it in terms that placed it, rather, at an intersection of time and the timeless—a point at which we place ourselves when we discuss it in terms of those non-temporal firsts called "principles."

Act as Locus of Motives

If one would deny pantheism, James had said, "the Creator must be the all, and the act by which the creature is set over against him has its motive within the creative circumference." And the act must "necessarily contain an arbitrary and magical element . . . undetermined by anything external to the agent." Further, we should note that arbitrariness and magic are equated with novelty, as when James says: "It is impossible to attempt to imagine the *way* of creation, but wherever from an absolute first a second appears, *there* it must be;—and it must be magical, for if in the second there be anything coequal or coeval with the first, it becomes pantheism." Indeed, the Creation as an act of God was a total novelty; and it was magic because, just as the magician would make it seem that he pulls a live rabbit out of an empty hat, so God made *everything* out of *nothing*.

The magician would have us think that he suspends the laws of motion. And God's act likewise "suspended" the laws of motion, though in an absolute sense: that is, upon his originating act depend all the laws of motion which men necessarily accept as the *conditions* of action. Indeed, the analogy suggests the thought that "true" magic prevails *outside* the strict realm of motion, in the area of more-than-motion that we call *action*. The demand for a kind of human magic that violates natural law is then revealed as a superstitious, quasi-scientific ideal. But magic, in the sense of novelty, is seen to exist normally, in some degree, as an ingredient of every human act; for each act contains some measure of motivation that cannot be explained simply in terms of the past, being to an extent, however tiny, a *new thing*.

This consideration could be approached in another way. We have said that a fully-rounded vocabulary of motives will locate motives under all five aspects of our pentad. Yet there is a paradoxical tendency to slight the term, *act,* in the very featuring of it. For we may even favor it enough to select it as our point of departure (point of departure in the sense of an ancestral term from which all the others are derived, sharing its quality "substantially"); but by the same token it may come to be a point of departure in the sense of the term that is "left behind." We see this temptation in the search for an act's motives, which one spontaneously thinks of locating under the heading of *scene, agent, agency,* or *purpose,* but hardly under the heading of *act*.

But if the scene of action is there already, and if the nature of the agent is also given, along with the instrumental conditions and the purposes of action, then there could be *novelty* only if there were likewise a locus of motivation within the act itself, a newness not already present in elements classifiable under any of the other four headings. And in this sense an act has an element of "arbitrariness" or "magic" insofar as it contains a motivational element requiring location under the heading of the term *act* itself.

At this point, we grant, our thinking departs somewhat from that in the James citation. Or rather, there is a strategic ambiguity in the James passage, as when he writes that, if one would avoid pantheism, "the creator must be the all, and the act by which the creature is set over against him has its motive within the creative circumference." If we think of "the Creator" as an "agent," we might contend that the motives of the act are here situated outside the locus of the term *act* and within the locus of the term *agent*. Yet the statement that God's creative act "has its motive within the creative circumference" comes quite close to satisfying our notion that "magic" or "novelty" arises by reason of the motive assignable under the heading of *act* itself. And the requirement is still more fully met if we recall the scholastic definition of God as "pure act."

But what precisely is our point? What are we trying to prove by an example that, we freely grant, cannot be adduced as the literal foundation of an argument? We are reasoning as follows: We are saying that, to study the nature of the term, *act,* one must select a prototype, or paradigm of action. This prototype we find in the conception of a perfect or total act, such as the act of "the Creation." Examining this concept, we find that it is "magic," for it produces something out of nothing. This enables us to equate magic with novelty—and leads us to look for a modicum of magic in every act to the extent that the act possesses a modicum of novelty. This consideration also admonishes us, however, to make a distinction between "true" and "false" magic. "False" magic is a quasi-scientific ideal that would suspend the laws of *motion,* as in the attempt to coerce natural forces by purely ritualistic means. "True" magic is an aspect not of motion but of *action.* And if the motives properly assignable to *scene, agent, agency,* and *purpose* are already given, there could be novelty only if we could also assign motives under the heading of *act* itself. That is, there would be something new intrinsic to the act; and this novelty would be the modicum of motivation assignable under the heading of act rather than under the heading of the other four terms, singly or in combination. There must, in brief, be some respect in which the act is a *causa sui,* a motive of itself.

Up to this point, we have simply followed the implications of the prototype. We have found out something about the term, *act,* as "revealed" by the contemplation of "the Creation." Next we must look about, in the world of experience, to see whether our conclusions make sense. Proverbs in particular might help us; for surely they are in the flatlands, safely distant from the magic mountain (though often we may best understand them if we think of them not just as isolated observations, but as fragments of a vast and complex dialectic structure which the proverbialist discerns not sustainedly and systematically, but in glimpses and inklings).

Proverbs such as *l'appétit vient en mangeant* or *Uebung macht den Meister* seem well suited to our purposes. Skill and habit are derived from the very acts in which they are practiced. Or let us consider some protracted act, such as the writing of a long book, where the act of the writing brings up problems and discoveries intrinsic to the act, leading to developments that derive not from the scene, or agent, or agency, or extrinsic purposes, but purely from the foregoing aspects of the act itself. That is, there is nothing present in the agent or his situation that could have led to the *final* stages of this act, except the *prior* stages of the act itself, and the logic which gradually takes form as the result of the enactment. Or, recalling our *poiemata, pathemata, mathemata* alignment, we can generalize this consideration by noting that, when an act is performed, it entails new sufferances, which in turn entail new insights. Our act itself alters the conditions of action, as "one thing leads to another" in an order that would not have occurred had we not acted.

The mediaeval schoolmen would probably object that we are here confusing "creation" with "generation." In their terminology, only God can create, while his creatures can but generate, as with the parents' generation of offspring or the artist's generation of his art work. However, it is not the purpose of our Dramatism to abide strictly by any one system of philosophic terms that happens to exemplify the dramatist pattern. Rather, it is our purpose to show that the explicit and systematic use of the dramatist pentad is best designed to bring out the strategic moments of motivational theory. Accordingly, at this point, we are more concerned to illustrate the Grammatical scruples than to select one particular casuistry as our choice among them. Philosophies again and again have got their point of departure precisely by treating as a distinction in kind what other philosophies have treated as a distinction in degree, or *v.v.* And we here come upon considerations that permit us to discern a novel ingredient in action, while this ingredient in turn can be equated with the creative.

The Aristotelian God, considered as universal motive, acted upon nature neither as creator nor as generator, but as a motionless inducement to development. The world and its genera and species were considered as eternal, hence not as derivations from God as "pure act." God acted upon nature solely as a goal, somewhat as a desired food might, by lying west of a rational and hungry man, induce him to move towards the west; or as the principles of a perfect art might lead the knowing artist to shape his work as nearly as possible in accordance with them.

The Christian merging of Aristotle's self-enwrapt *eromenon* with the Creator Jehovah (a tribal, tutelary deity made universal), necessarily calls for a drawing of the lines at a different place. In this scheme, stressing plenitude and fertility, God creates and creatures generate. But the Christian terminology also took over the concept of *hexis* (Latin, *habitus;* trained disposition), the term Aristotle uses in his Ethics to name that aptitude in virtues which is acquired by the practice of virtues. And we believe that we are but coming upon the function of this term by a different route when we recognize that the resources of the pentad invite us to locate some motives of action under the heading of Act itself.

There would thus be a modicum of novelty in the act, to the extent that the act could be said to have an ingredient not derivable from any other of the terms. And insofar as the act was derivable from the other terms, it would not possess novelty, but would be a mere unfolding of the implicit into the explicit.

The modicum of novelty in the act would seem to be the element that justified Coleridge's view of poetry as a "dim analogue of Creation." However, that formula was obscured by the idealist stress upon *agent,* as locus of the "shaping spirit of Imagination" by which we give forth that which we receive, since "in our life alone does Nature live." And to glimpse more clearly the independent claims of the term, act, we might better go back to Spinoza who, mediating between the mediaeval and the modern, defined the universal Substance as the "cause of itself." God would thus be perfect action, in that there would be no motivating principle beyond his own nature (a consideration, incidentally, that enables us to see why Spinoza would equate God and Nature).

All told, contemplating the Grammar in its simplest aspect, we are admonished to expect occasions when, in seeking for the motives of an act, the thinker will in effect locate the motive under the head of Act itself. However confusing the subject may become in the alembications of theology and metaphysics, it is at least obvious enough on this first level: That among the resources of the pentad is the invitation to locate the motives of an act under the head of Act (as with Faust's formula, *Im Anfang war die That*).

Do we not see a scruple of this sort behind the Augustinian claim that God's act of Creation must be wholly without motives? For any motivation, however slight, would be to that extent a constraint upon God's will—hence his act would not be wholly free.

But though there are ultimate moments when the substantial, all-inclusive act, as it were, is derived out of itself, as regards the pentadic resources generally we must consider rather the transformations whereby we may deal with this motivational locus in terms of the other loci. In particular, one might ask, what has become of our scene-act ratio? And that question will be the subject of our next section.

The "Grounds" of Creation

The Creation, as the ground or scene of human acts, provides the basic conditions utilized by human agents in the motions by which they act. In this sense, it represents an ultimate source of motives, though human agents by their acts may pile up lesser novelties, partial creations which they interpose between themselves and the ultimate ground, and which become a "second nature" with them, a scene having motivational properties in its own right.

Dramatistically, however, there is an embarrassment as regards God's constitutive act. James touches upon it somewhat when saying that it is impossible to imagine the "way" of creation. And we see it more clearly when we reflect that a "way" is literally a path across some *ground*. The symmetry of the pentad requires that even a "first act" must have been enacted in some kind of "scene" (could we call it a "pre-first" scene?). If "the Creation" marks the establishment of time and motion, as conditions that followed from the act, we are prompted to look contextually for a counterpart in timelessness and rest, or familially for some magnitude great enough to produce the universe as its lineal descendant. The concept of God as an agent doesn't quite satisfy the dramatistic necessities, for an agent, like an act, must be placed in some scene.

It has been said of Kant that realistic assumptions were necessary as a way into his system, but once you entered it, you had to abandon them if you would stay there. For, as Windelband puts it, "the conception of the sensibility introduced at the beginning involves the causal relation of being affected by things-in-themselves," yet causality is a category, and according to the doctrine of the Analytic, "categories must not be applied to things-in-themselves." We see here the evidences of a dialectic whereby the point arrived at transcended the point of departure. But one may well expect to find such transformations in a work which was, after all, designed to duplicate the total act of creation itself (except that there would be no operationalist account of the "way," which is an important exception).

Perhaps we should always look for "ladders" of this sort when we are on the subject of "everything," ladders that are used only to attain another level of discourse and that would be an encumbrance if one continued to carry them about with him after he had attained this level. In any case, we might detect the vestiges of such a ladder in the notion of a monotheistic God, which developed out of polytheistic thinking. Polytheistic gods usually did not make "everything." Rather, there was usually some primeval scene, more or less chaotic, that provided the materials out of which the god shaped the motivating conditions of human life. Or rather, he shaped *some* of the motivating conditions, others being supplied by other powers and natures more or less at variance with the purposes of the tutelary deity.

But when one god has risen to such prominence among the gods that he becomes "the" god (taking over, among other things, the role of *destiny* that serves, in polytheistic schemes, as a kind of over-all motivation summing up, or mediating among, the disparate motives of the various gods), theologians attempt to *start* their speculations on this *final* level, abandoning the dialectical ladder by which this level was attained. And here is where the dramatistic embarrassments arise. For whereas the divine agents of polytheism had a scene to contain them and their acts, what are we to do with a god who is himself the ground of everything? When he acts, in what scene does he act?

We may treat the matter summarily by saying simply that he is super-scene, super-act, and super-agent all in one. But in doing so, we thereby fail to appreciate the full pressure of the dramatistic logic. For Christian theology *did* speculate about the "grounds" of God's act, as in the scholastics' argument whether God willed the good because it is good or the good is good because God willed it. The first of these is obviously the more symmetrical from the dramatistic point of view, since it does in effect furnish a scene for the act of the Creation. It was the position upheld by Aquinas, the doctrine of the *perseïtas boni* (the "by-itselfness of the good") to which Scotists are said to have objected because it imposed limits upon the freedom of the divine will. We can discern the "scenic" nature of the good, as the principle of God's creation, in Bréhier's statement that Duns Scotus "would avoid the need to admit that there existed outside of God, eternal like him and imposing itself upon him, a sort of *fatum* by which his intelligence and will were guided. (*La Philosophie du Moyen Âge*, p. 387.)

The doctrine that "the good is good because God willed it" points away from dramatistic symmetry and towards the modern centuries of subjectivism and idealism, with their great stress upon the "ego," the "will," and finally the "libido." Among the scholastic upholders of this position, Occam went so far in behalf of God's freedom as to maintain that God might have willed a quite different set of moral laws, even proclaiming as bad what he did in fact proclaim as good, and *v. v.* In effect such doctrines ground the act of the Creation in the term *agent* rather than the term *scene,* for it is derived directly from the will of God, and will is a property of agents.

In contrast, the scenic emphasis in the Thomist doctrine is further revealed by the fact that the Thomists placed the "true" as of higher rank than the "good." This was managed by proclaiming the *rationality* of the good. (That is, as God willed the good because it is good, the good in turn is good because it is rational.) And we can discern the *scenic* factor behind such a concept of rationality if we consider such equations as these: what is, is true; what is true, is rational; what is, is rational. In keeping with such equations the principles of goodness, by having an eternal existence in their own right, would be scenic; and a statement about them, in being a statement about what is, would be a statement about the rational and the true, hence a statement about the scenic.

Sociologically, we may note that the pattern of the controversy corresponded to a poignant political issue of those times. The proposition that God willed the good because it was good represented the mediaeval theory of sovereignty, according to which even the sovereign *obeyed* the laws. And the proposition that the good is good because God willed it represented the newer political theories that were arising with the trend towards absolute central authority. This centralizing trend was marked by great legalistic innovation, in contrast with the former appeal to custom as the arbiter of law. The new methods of production and distribution favored and required this stress upon legalistic innovation, such as could be quickly standardized over comparatively wide areas only if it emanated from a central authority. And in such a state of affairs, since the monarch decreed the laws, the lawful was lawful because the monarch so willed it.

Pantheism and Ontology

We have now discussed three important aspects of "the Creation." We have considered the ambiguity of being and becoming, the equating of "magic" with novelty, and the dramatistic pressure for the formulation of a scene in which Creation, as an act, would be situated. We would now consider the relation between the two alternatives which James mentions: "magic" and "pantheism."

Pantheism is defined in Webster as "the doctrine that the universe, taken or conceived of as a whole, is God; the doctrine that there is no God but the combined forces and laws which are manifested in the existing universe." Its most succinct description is to be found in Spinoza's expression, "God or Nature" (*Deus sive Natura*). In doctrines of "creation, emanation," nature possesses attributes derived from its divine origin, but it is less than God. God does not *need* nature. But in doctrines of pantheism, or immanence, "God" and "Nature" are interchangeable terms. James thus situates the essence of the pantheistic conception "in there being a necessary relation between Creator and creature." In pantheism, he says, both the Creator and the created "are the same fact viewed from opposite sides." And "their duality as Creator and creature becomes merged in a higher unity as Being."

This last word, "Being," gives us our cue. For ontology, according to the dictionary, investigates "the principles and causes of being" (the Greek *onta* means the "things that are"). We may thus readily discern a "pantheistic temptation" in the very nature of ontology as a subject. For if one would treat of "everything" in terms of "being," "being" would then be the over-all concept, the summarizing "god-term," since the word that summed up "everything" would certainly be the god-term, the universal title or all-inclusive epithet to which any less generalized terms would be related as parts to whole. This is how we should interpret James's remark that in pantheism the duality of Creator and creature "becomes merged in a higher unity as Being."

Or we could state it thus: James said of the Creation, "Whenever from an absolute first a second appears, *there* it must be." But to treat of a relation between a first and a second in terms of *being* is to make one step *collapse* into the other, so that one has instead a *simultaneity,* in adopting a point of view whereby the two steps can be treated as "coeval." "The Creation" is not exactly an historical process, since it is not just *in* time and motion, but must be *outside* to the extent that it is the establishment or inauguration of time and motion. But even if one were dealing with a characteristically historical process, one could view it ontologically, or in terms of *being,* only insofar as one viewed it in terms of permanent principles that underlie the process of becoming.

"Principles" are "firsts," but they are "absolute" firsts, not the kind of firsts that require a temporal succession as we go from a first to a second. They just *are*. They have logical, rather than temporal, priority. Hence, to treat of things in terms of their relation to underlying principles is to translate historical sequence into terms of logical sequence (whereby things can "precede" and "follow" one another in a kind of succession that requires no time coördinate). This is why Spinoza's ontology proposes to treat of things *sub specie aeternitatis,* which is to say, in terms of timelessness, or being. But if a first and a second are related "logically," they are by the same token related "necessarily." For a logical relationship, or principle of being, always was, is, and will be; and what always was, is, and will be, *must* be. Whereby ontology merges the "is," the "must be," and the rational.

No aim could be more rational than the desire to find a philosophic language whose order would correspond with the order of things as they are and must be—somewhat as the sequence of letters in a phonetic alphabet corresponds with the sequence of verbal sounds of which these letters are the signs, for though the letters are transposed continually to signalize different sequences of sound, the *relation* between sound and sign is permanent, involving fixed *principles;* and when the notation is adequate, the relation between the sign and the signified is "rational."

But if a first and a second are "necessarily" related, James reminds us, we cannot have arbitrariness and magic. Creator (the first) and creature (the second) thus become "coequal and coeval," in being *ontologically* related (that is, *logically* related in terms of *being*). The second is then related to the first somewhat as conclusions are implicit in premises and premises are implicit in conclusions.

Pantheism would result whenever we went about it thoroughly to translate the "historical" account of the Creation in the book of Genesis (or Becoming) into a "flat," or "simultaneous" equivalent (conceived in terms of ontology, or Being). "In the beginning God created the heaven and the earth" would thus be ontologically translated: "God created the heaven and the earth substantially, in principle."

Grammatical Steps to Naturalism

There are two primary generalizations that characterize the quality of motives: freedom and necessity. And whenever they appear, we may know that we are in the presence of "God-terms," or names for the ultimates of motivation. Doctrines wherein Creator and Creation are not ontologically collapsed into a unity give us a kind of double genesis for motives. Consideration in terms of the *Creation* leads to "necessity" when, in accordance with the logic of geometric substance, all the parts of nature are treated as necessarily related to one another in their necessary relationship to the whole. For "necessity" names the extrinsic conditions that determine a motion and must be taken into account when one is planning an action. And consideration in terms of the *Creator* leads to "freedom" when, in accordance with the logic of tribal substance, men "substantially" derive freedom (or self-movement) from God as its ancestral source. This double genesis allows for free will *and* determinism simultaneously, rather than requiring a flat choice between them. Also, owing to the ambiguity of substance, it permits men to be "substantially" free even when, as regards their natural conditions, they are actually enslaved or imprisoned.

An ancestral source of freedom is in one sense extrinsic to the individual, inasmuch as progenitor is distinct from offspring. Yet origin is intrinsic to the individual in the sense that this genetic or generic fact about his nature is also possessed *within* him (just as members of a given biological species each possess within them, genitively, the substance or motives proper to the species generally). And as regards the geometric logic, when a thing's intrinsic nature is defined as part of a universal whole, the reference here is to a context, hence extrinsic. Formally, the issue figures in metaphysical speculations as to whether relations are internal or external, an ambiguity which, from the dramatist point of view, is implicit in the fact that one can shift between familial and geometric definition, stressing either person (agent) or ground (scene) as a locus of motives.

In pantheistic schemes, the principles of personal (intrinsic) freedom and scenic (extrinsic) determination must collapse into a unity that corresponds to the ontological merging of Creator and Creation. That is, "freedom" and "necessity" become identical, with each definable in terms of the other. Spinoza's pantheism meets this requirement in defining substance as *causa sui,* whereby the concepts of freedom and necessity are merged grammatically in the *reflexive.* The reflexive form satisfies the requirement, putting active and passive together, since one can be simultaneously free and constrained if the constraints are those of one's own choosing, an identification of scene and philosopher-agent that is possible inasmuch as both nature and the philosophy are rational.

Spinoza likewise adopts the expressions, *natura naturans* and *natura naturata* (or "naturing nature" and "natured nature"). Grammatically, we could thus treat the ground term, "nature," (which equals "God") as reflexive in form (though one usually reserves the designation for verbs) having active and passive (the *-ans* and the *-ata*) as its dual attributes. And we note a corresponding grammar in his Cartesian expressions, *res cogitans* and *res extensa,* where "thing" *(res)* would be the reflexive ground, with "thinking" *(cogitans)* as its active voice and "extended" *(extensa)* as its passive voice. So we could speak of nature, or thing, naturing, or thinking—and of nature, or thing, natured or extended. One can discern here the beginnings of the alignment that was to prevail in modern idealism, as the active participle becomes the "subjective" and the passive participle the "objective" (a grammar that is precisely reversed in materialism, where nature in *extension* is treated as the motivational source, while subjective motives are treated as either illusions or reflections).

Or, consider the passages in Aristotle's Physics where he is seeking to establish the number of principles required to account for the changes that take place in the natural world. Here we find a paradigm of grammar in his concern with the reduction of such principles to a pair of opposites, with a possible third term that would be their common ground. Grammatically, these principles are reducible to active, passive, and middle, the concept of self-movement containing active and passive ambiguously in one. Nature, Aristotle says at one point, is like a doctor doctoring himself (a figure that could, if we wanted to translate the universal into medical terms, then give us: doctor doctoring and doctor doctored).

The pantheistic moment in philosophy, by producing a merger of personal and impersonal principles (a merger of personal agent and impersonal scene), can serve well as a bridge leading from theology to naturalism. For theologies are "dramatistic" in their stress upon the personalistic, whereas the terminologies typical of natural science would eliminate the concept of the person, in reducing it to purely scenic terms. Hence, a pantheistic merging of person and scene can add up to the dissolution of the personal into the impersonal along naturalistic lines.

We might sum up the matter thus: *Theologically,* nature has attributes derived from its origin in an act of God (the Creation), but God is more than nature. *Dramatistically,* motion involves action, but action is more than motion. Hence, theologically and/or dramatistically, nature (in the sense of God's Creation) is to nature (in the sense of naturalistic science) as action is to motion, since God's Creation is an *enactment,* whereas nature as conceived in terms of naturalistic science is a sheer concatenation of motions. But inasmuch as the theological ratio between God (Creator) and Nature (Creation) is the same as the dramatistic ratio between action and motion, the *pantheistic* equating of God and Nature would be paralleled by the equating of action and motion. And since action is a personal principle while motion is an impersonal principle, the pantheistic equation leads into the *naturalistic* position which reduces personalistic concepts to depersonalized terms.

If these steps seem to have been too quickly arrived at, let us try approaching the matter from another angle. Indeed, we need not even hang on, but can almost begin anew.

Circumference

This time all we need for our text is a single word from James, his word "circumference," as when he says that, if one would avoid pantheism, "the Creator must be the all, and the act by which the creature is set over against him has its motive within the creative circumference." The word reminds us that, when "defining by location," one may place the object of one's definition in contexts of varying scope. And our remarks on the scene-act ratio, for instance, suggest that the choice of circumference for the scene in terms of which a given act is to be located will have a corresponding effect upon the interpretation of the act itself. Similarly, the logic of the scene-agent ratio will figure in our definition of the individual, insofar as principles of dramatic consistency are maintained.

That is, if we locate the human agent and his act in terms of a scene whose orbit is broad enough to include the concept of a supernatural Creator, we get a different kind of definition than if our location were confined to a narrower circumference that eliminated reference to the "supernatural" as a motivating element in the scene, and did not permit the scenic scope to extend beyond the outer limits of "nature." Or we may reduce the circumference still further, as when we define motivations in terms of the temporally or geographically local scenes that become a "second nature" to us, scenes that may themselves vary in circumference from broad historical situations to the minutely particularized situations of back-stairs gossip.

Now, it seems undeniable, by the very nature of the case, that in definition, or systematic placement, one must see things "in terms of . . ." And implicit in the terms chosen, there are "circumferences" of varying scope. Motivationally, they involve such relationships as are revealed in the analysis of the scene-act and scene-agent ratios whereby the quality of the context in which a subject is placed will affect the quality of the subject placed in that context. And since one must implicitly or explicitly select a circumference (except insofar as he can seem to avoid the predicament by adopting a slung-together terminology that contains a muddle of different circumferences) we are properly admonished to be on the look-out for these terministic relationships between the circumference and the "circumfered," even on occasions that may on the surface seem to be of a purely empirical nature.

Thus, when the behaviorist experiments with animals to discover, under "controlled laboratory conditions," the springs of conduct that operate also in human beings, we consider his experiment fully as important as he does, though for a totally different reason. For we take it to indicate, with the utmost clarity possible, the terministic relationship between the circumscription and the circumscribed. For no matter how much a matter of purely empirical observation it may seem to be, it actually is a very distinct choice of circumference for the placement of human motives. By the very nature of the case it chooses to consider human motives in terms of an animal circumference, an acutely terministic matter, not a matter of merely "empirical observation." And, ironically enough, it is most likely to reveal something about human motives distinctively, only insofar as the conditions established by the laboratory place the animals in a "human" circumference. But though nothing is more distinctly "human" than a scientific laboratory in one sense (for no other species but man is known ever to have made and used one), it is the kind of "humanity" we get in mechanization (a "part of" man that became so poignantly, in industrial routines, "apart from" man). And by the logic of the scene-act ratio, the study of conduct in terms of so mechanistic a scene led to a correspondingly mechanistic interpretation of the act.

This would probably be a good place to repeat that we do not deny the importance of seeking always for "controlled" cases, as anecdotes in conformity with which to form one's terminology for the analysis of human motives. But we maintain that one can avoid the bias of his instruments (that is, the bias of terms too simplist) only if he chooses a *representative* example of an act. Animal experiments have taught us however (we should at least grant them this) that school-teachers like to send animals to school, that physical sadists who have mastered scientific method like to torture animals methodically, and that those whose ingenuity is more psychiatrically inclined like to go on giving the poor little devils mental breakdowns, ostensibly to prove over and over again that it can be done (though this has already been amply proved to everybody's satisfaction but that of the experimenters).

We cherish the behaviorist experiment precisely because it illustrates the relation between the circumference and the circumscribed in mechanistic terms; and because the sharpest instance of the way in which the altering of the scenic scope affects the interpretation of the act is to be found in the shift from teleological to mechanistic philosophies. Christian theology, in stressing the rational, personal, and purposive aspects of the Creation as the embodiment of the Creator's pervasive will, had treated such principles as *scenic*. That is, they were not merely traits of human beings, but extended to the outer circumference of the ultimate ground. Hence, by the logic of the scene-act ratio, they were taken as basic to the constitution of human motives, and could be "deduced" from the nature of God as an objective, extrinsic principle defining the nature of human acts. But when the circumference was narrowed to naturalistic limits, the "Creator" was left out of account, and only the "Creation" remained (remained not as an "act," however, but as a concatenation of motions).

The narrowing of the circumference thus encouraged a shift from the stress upon "final cause" to the stress upon "efficient cause," the kind of cause that would reside not in a "prime mover," but in a "last mover" (as the lever with which a man moves a stone could be called the "last mover" of the stone). We are here in the orbit of the *vis a tergo* kind of cause, prominent in all theories of motivation that stress "instincts," "drives," or other sheerly compulsive properties. Such terminologies attain a particularly thorough form in behaviorism, with its stress upon reflex action and the conditioned reflex, and its treatment of motivation in terms of Stimulus and Response.

Ironically, the dramatistic logic (that is, the logic of the scene-act and scene-agent ratios) here invokes a non-dramatic mode of analysis. For the naturalistic terminology, in eliminating the principles of personality and action from the ultimate ground of motives, leads consistently to ideals of definition that dissolve the personality and its actions into depersonalization and motion respectively. In naturalism there is no Creator; and nature is not an act, but simply "the given."

However, we should add several important modifications to our notions of the movement towards the dissolution of drama. In the first place, we should note that in proportion as Naturalism dropped the principles of personality and action from the *scene,* Humanism compensatorily stressed their presence in men as *agents.* Human personality was not "deduced"; it was simply postulated in men, as part of "the given," quite as the records of our senses are "data." This humanistic stress upon the principle of personality as peculiar to people (who are conceived as set in dialectical opposition to an "impersonal" nature) could lead to a cult of "pure" personality (particularly as an over-compensation for the increasing depersonalization brought about by industrialism, and as a direct response to the vagueness of role that went with the spread of leisure and unemployment). This cult of "pure" personality could in turn attain a "counter-over-compensation" on the part of the materialists, who emphasized the importance of the scenic factor in human personality (since one is a person not "absolutely," but by reason of a *role,* and such a role involves a *situation*). But in materialism the concept of role was narrowed in scope from *acting* to *doing,* until the idea of "vocation" was no wider in scope than the idea of "job." In theories of meaning the movement probably reaches its culmination in Bridgman's "operationalism."

Note that, dialectically, the concept of the "pure" personality itself contained its dissolution as its ultimate destiny. For, by the paradox of the absolute, a "pure" person would be an "im-person." This same paradox is latent even in the theological concept of personality; for God as a super-person is also, by the same token, "impersonal." Hence the monotheistic concept of an all-inclusive God was itself an ambiguous preparation for naturalism, once the circumference was narrowed to omit "God" as a necessary term in motivational statements. And the orbit could be narrowed by reason of a readily understandable procedure in language. For if nature was deemed, as it was by many of the devout, to be a perfect exemplification of God's will, then *nature's* design would accurately represent the design of *God.* Hence, reference to God as a locus of motives would involve an unnecessary duplication of terms—since a statement of motivation in terms of natural structure alone should be sufficient.

That is, if natural structure was the visible, tangible, commensurable embodiment of God's will, one would simply be duplicating his terms if his accounts of motivation had both natural and supernatural terms. The natural terms should be enough, in accordance with the Occamite principle (the keystone of scientific terminologies) that "entities should not be multiplied beyond necessity." And this naturalistic side of the equation had the further advantage of opening the way to test by experiment, as against demonstration by purely verbal manipulation. What was a narrowing of the circumference, as considered from one point of view, was a widening, as considered from another point of view. For naturalistic experimentation was a way of giving Nature itself an articulate voice in the dialectic. When properly used, it could so put questions to Nature that Nature was able to give very definite answers. The strong dramatistic feeling behind such procedures at their inception can be glimpsed in Galileo's reference to the experiment as the "ordeal," a significance that is also in our word "trial," whose bearing upon the attenuated drama of education can be glimpsed somewhat in the expression, "trial and error," as applied to the learning of animals in a maze.

We have spoken of Spinoza's explicit equation, "God or Nature." Note that there was also an implicit equation lurking in the word "design," as when we speak of "God's design" and "Nature's design." In the first case, "design" means "intention." In the second case, it can mean simply "structure"; we could even speak of a "design produced by accident." In this pun there is, accordingly, much the same equation as that explicitly put forward by Spinoza. To make the two meanings explicitly synonymous, as they are allowed to be synonymous in the original ambiguity of the word, we might phrase the corresponding equation thus: "intention or absence of intention," where the "or" means not "the alternative to" but "the same as." Stating the matter with reference to the genitive, Nature's design as "a part of" God's design becomes available to treatment as "apart from" God's design (or otherwise put: the *synecdochically* related part of the divine whole becomes the *divisively* related part).

Such implicit or explicit equations in which distinctions are merged serve historically as bridges from one terminology to another, precisely by reason of the Occamite principle. For if the two terms, or the two aspects of the one term, are taken as synonymous, then one side of the equation can be dropped as "unnecessary." If you say that the laws of electro-chemical transformation are exactly as God would have them, then it follows that their structure represents the will of God. Whereupon, you are invited to treat of motives in terms of these electro-chemical transformations. For why shouldn't you, if their design is to be equated with God's design, plus the fact that their design lends itself to empirical study in the scientific laboratory? Thereupon, almost imperceptibly, the terministic logic has taken you from supernaturalism to "chemism."

Hence, in the course of time, it becomes clear that we have gone from one bank to the other, by reason of an expression that bridged the gulf between them. Often the given writer who first gave vigor to the equation did not, however, intend it as a "bridge" in this historical sense, as a way of abandoning one position and taking up its opposite. Rather he cherished it precisely because this midway quality itself was *his* position, as with that motionless crossing expressed by Wordsworth in his sonnet "Composed upon Westminster Bridge," where the significance of his vision lies in the very fact that he is placed midway between the City of the Living and the City of the Dead, as he sees London transfigured in the early dawn:

> Dear God! the very houses seem asleep;
> And all that mighty heart is lying still!

An equation of two terms hitherto considered unequal can, of course, lead two ways. We can make the "wider" circle of the same circumference as the "narrower" circle either by narrowing the wider, or by widening the narrower. At the close of the middle ages, such equations, or bridging terms, would generally lead from supernaturalism towards naturalism, rather than *vice versa,* precisely because their role as a point of departure came at a time when it was only the supernatural vocabulary that was sufficiently developed to be departed from.

Earlier in this book, we observed that "if all the ten ratios were adjusted to one another with perfect Edenic symmetry, they would be immutable in one unending 'moment.'" That is, the quality of scene, act, agent, agency, and purpose would be all the same, all of one piece; hence there would be no opportunity for a new "beginning" whereby the agent would undertake a different quality of act that might change the quality of himself or of his scene, etc. Thus, there could be no becoming, but only unending being; there could be no *"alloiosis,"* or qualitative change, no development, no origin and destination, no whence and whither, for all the terms would contain what all the other terms contained. We suggested an answer in the consideration that men are capable of but *partial* acts, acts that but partially represent themselves and but partially conform to their scenes. We might now expand our statement in the light of our remarks on the subject of "circumferences."

If the scene-act ratio prevails, for instance, how would it be possible for a man to perform a "good" act in a "bad" situation? Or, by reason of the scene-agent ratio, how could a man be "good" in a "bad" situation? Or, to take a specific case, here is a statement by Stark Young, made in a discussion of Clifford Odets' *Night Music:*

> Can we demand from a dramatist, in an age like ours, scattered, distracted, surging, wide, chopped-up and skimmy, that he provide his play with a background of social conceptions that are basic, sound, organized, prophetic, deep-rooted? Shall he, in sum, be asked to draw the hare of heaven from a shallow cap?

And to this, Mr. Young, in keeping with the genius of the scene-act ratio (and who should implicitly abide by it, if not a dramatic critic?) makes answer:

> The answer is no, we can scarcely demand that. In general we should remind ourselves that there is no reason to ask any theatre to surpass its epoch in solidity, depth or philosophic summation.

There are all sorts of tricks lurking in that one. When we were young, we used to ask one another whether, since we were living in a boring age, it would be possible to write works of art that were not themselves boring or that were not exclusively concerned with boring people in boring situations. Later we found that, whatever the bad character of our age might be, it was not boring. This interpretation of the scene had evidently been a function of our situation as adolescents. Indeed, we discovered that, if no better motives came along, merely the attempt to work one's way out of fear and anger was enough to stave off boredom.

There are all sorts of modifications possible when considering Mr. Young's statement. Surely the dramatic work of Shakespeare, for instance, can be said to "surpass its epoch in solidity, depth or philosophic summation," except insofar as we define the nature of the epoch itself in terms of Shakespeare. But as a matter of fact, Shakespeare has not only "surpassed his epoch" in such properties, but he has surpassed whole centuries, whole populations, whole cultures.

However, it is not our intention here to bring up the many quibbles which Mr. Young's brief statement can invite. We would say only enough to point up the fact that, when confronting such issues, one has *a great variety of circumferences* to select as characterizations of a given agent's scene. For a man is not only in the situation peculiar to his era or to his particular place in that era (even if we could agree on the traits that characterize his era). He is also in a situation extending through centuries; he is in a "generically human" situation; and he is in a "universal" situation. Who is to say, once and for all, which of these circumferences is to be selected as the motivation of his act, insofar as the act is to be defined in scenic terms?

In confronting this wide range in the choice of a circumference for the location of an act, men confront what is distinctively the human freedom and the human necessity. This necessity is a freedom insofar as the choice of circumference leads to an adequate interpretation of motives; and it is an enslavement insofar as the interpretation is inadequate. We might exploit the conveniences of "substance" by saying that, in necessarily confronting such a range of choices, men are "substantially" free.

The contracting and expanding of scene is rooted in the very nature of linguistic placement. And a selection of circumference from among this range is in itself an act, an "act of faith," with the definition or interpretation of the act taking shape accordingly. In times of adversity one can readily note the workings of the "circumferential" logic, in that men choose to define their acts in terms of much wider orbits than the orbit of the adversity itself. The "solace of religion," for instance, may have its roots not in a mere self-deception, whereby one can buoy himself up with false promises or persuade himself that the situation is not bad when it is so palpably bad; but it may stem from an accurate awareness that one can define human nature and human actions in much wider terms than the particularities of his immediate circumstances would permit; and this option is not an "illusion," but a fact, and as true a fact as any fact in his immediate circumstances.

In *The Brothers Karamazov,* Dostoevsky tells how Mitya dreams of a new life with Grushenka, who had "loved him for one hour":

With a sinking heart he was expecting every moment Grushenka's decision, always believing that it would come suddenly, on the impulse of the moment. All of a sudden she would say to him: "Take me, I'm yours for ever," and it would all be over. He would seize her and bear her away at once to the ends of the earth. Oh, then he would bear her away at once, as far, far away as possible; to the furthest end of Russia, if not of the earth, then he would marry her, and settle down with her incognito, so that no one would know anything about them, there, here, or anywhere else. Then, oh then, a new life would begin at once!

Of this different, reformed and "virtuous" life ("it must, it must be virtuous") he dreamed feverishly at every moment. He thirsted for that reformation and renewal. The filthy morass, in which he had sunk of his own free will, was too revolting to him, and, like very many men in such cases, he put faith above all else in change of place. If only it were not for these people, if only it were not for these circumstances, if only he could fly away from this accursed place—he would be altogether regenerated, would enter on a new path.

In brief, he trusted that a new scene would make possible a new act, by reason of the scene-act ratio, and the new act would make a new man, by reason of the act-agent ratio.   And he hoped to attain this new structure of motivation by sheer locomotion.   Maybe he could have—for the changes he thinks of might very well be sufficiently different in their circumstances to produce in him a correspondingly new bundle of motives.   But the mystic Alyosha, we may recall, was in the same scene as his elder brother Mitya; and for him its motivations were entirely different, and precisely because for him it had a different circumference, so that all actions were interpreted in greatly different terms.   His terms amounted to a migration in a subtler sense: by a "transcendence," a "higher synthesis," that in effect "negates" the terms of the scene as Mitya interpreted it.   For Alyosha's terms implied a wider *circumference*.

Monographic Terms of Placement

Though we have stressed the contrast between theology and behaviorism because it so readily illustrates the "circumferential logic" (that is, the effect of *scope* in a given terminology of motives), we should note that a writer's vocabulary is usually set somewhere between these two extremes. His aims are usually less thoroughgoing, more "monographic," as with the selection of some "thesis." Consider, for instance, the difference between Dante's version of the human drama in *The Divine Comedy,* and a specialized study on *Imperialism, in Relation to the Cult of "Fair Play" and the "Gentleman",* a treatise which, to our knowledge and to our great regret, has been written by nobody. In such partial tracts, for instance, one man may confine himself to a treatment of the climatic factors in motivation, another may focus upon the effects that some drug has upon the body, another will chart the curve of business cycles, etc.

Any such placement, by the selection of some specialized theme ("theme" is also a member of the Stance family), is a kind of "partial Creation." On a minor scale, and almost imperceptibly, it too is substantive, "constitutive," quite as was God's creative Act. For its terms, in being restricted to the nature of the thesis, will thereby establish a circumference, marking the outer boundaries of the ground that is to be covered. As agent, the writer will have acted creatively—and the motives and motifs featured by his terminology will fix the nature of the constitution which he has enacted.

Thus we may see, in our world of great occupational diversity, even a purely technical or "disciplinary" reason why we should have so much disrelated featuring of motives, ranging from the smallest circumference, local in time, place and purpose (such as, "The man who wrote the letter today in such-and-such a manner in order to get so-and-so to do such-and-such tomorrow") to circumferences marking off all sorts of permanent scenic or materialistic properties (such as planetary influences, hormones, or the means of production), the disposition of which may be continually changing, though the motivational relationships between mover and moved may be said to remain constant if they are stated in terms sufficiently broad.

However, though the great variety of modern instruments provides a special reason for "monographic" treatment of motivational factors, it is true that in any world there will be many and good reasons why we should want, on occasion, to discuss motives in terms of greatly narrowed scope. Ironically, a reference to "man's universal situation" would be too generalized to serve as an explanation of motives for all purposes. Ideally, we might locate an act in a set of widening circles, ranging from the uniquely particularized, through placement in terms of broad cultural developments, to absolute concepts of relationship or ground. It was thus with the eight whorls in the "spindle of Necessity" that, as we are told in the tenth book of *The Republic,* Er saw during his journey beyond the grave; for they were the celestial orbits, and were scooped out and fitted inside one another, like a nest of bowls. But in actuality, such a graduated table of circumferences would be cumbersome and unmanageable. Most circumferences are felt to be, not so much wider or narrower than one another, as merely *different.* We might say that they mark out a circumference by spotlight, while the rest of the stage is left dark.

It may often be the works of wider circumference that give us the faultiest interpretation of a particular motivational cluster. People tend to think that when they speak of "the Universe," they are actually speaking of the Universe—yet "world views" can easily be the narrowest of all in circumference, possibly (to borrow from Windelband) in accordance with a law of formal logic whereby "concepts become poorer in contents or intension in proportion as their extension increases, so that the content *zero* must correspond to the extension *infinity.*" This law also operates in "negative theology," which finds it necessary to define the "Allness" of God in terms synonymous with "nothing" ("infinite," "unending," "incomprehensible," "inexpressible," "invisible," "unknowable," and the like). We must leave for another place (notably our Symbolic) a discussion of the ways whereby such "Allness" or "Nothingness" can nonetheless manage to take on empirical reference, as a stylized replica of the Self. The possibility in its most obvious aspects is indicated by an observation about "man" in *The Education of Henry Adams:* "The universe that had formed him took shape in his mind as a reflection of his own unity."

However, there are respects in which the "monographic" study likewise can lead to a faulty interpretation of motives. Consider, for instance, a well-written little book, *Swords and Symbols, the Technique of Sovereignty,* by James Marshall. Being in the Machiavelli line, in the best sense of the word, it deals with the philosophy of political power, and with the many kinds of disequilibrium that constantly disturb the maintenance of such power. The "motive" of the study dictates its confinement to a circle characterized by such key terms as force, power, threat, police, appetite, fraud, enslavement—concepts that cluster "logically" and "necessarily" about the theme. It is a book that any student of politics could read with attention and respect. Yet, paradoxically, the very limitations inherent in the terms proper to the subject serve to give the thesis an appearance of too great scope. For though the "technique of sovereignty" is in one sense a very narrow theme, in another sense it could be said to embrace the whole world. And whereas the book's universe of discourse quite reasonably and properly invites us to consider only those aspects of power that bear centrally upon the theme, one can derive from the book the feeling that he has been contemplating the very essence of political relations.

The author's genealogy is, briefly: (a) Material needs give rise to ethical values; (b) ethical values give rise to ideologies; (c) out of ideologies, laws are constructed; (d) the sovereign wields these laws (as the principal symbol of political force and power).

The nature of the subject and the method makes it fitting that values and ideas and laws be considered *in terms of* material needs. Indeed, even if we knew it for a fact that ideas and laws and ethical values were derived from heaven, it would still remain proper to the author's universe of discourse that they be discussed in terms of material needs; for the value of such tracts resides precisely in their ability to teach us what important facts can be learned about human motives when considered from the standpoint of such terms.

To be sure, being admonished that there are ways in which temporal priority and logical priority can change places with each other, we should not, for our purposes, want to put a wholly evolutionary interpretation upon the notion that material needs give rise to ethical values. We should say, rather, that in accordance with the structure of the author's terms, the concept of "material needs" is *logically prior* to the concept of "ethical values." That is, whereas the author's position is stated in terms of *historical* sequence, we should want to read the statement more *terministically*—for the relation between material needs and ethical values is not the same kind of purely historicist matter as the mailing of a letter on the fourth and its arrival on the fifth.

No purely temporal sequence can be established here. Obviously, for instance, there is some kind of "prior" ethical faculty in people (even if we would but reduce it to an aspect of language, as were we to agree that the "ethical sense" is but the manipulation of verbal counters). And this potentiality, or latency, or ability to respond to material needs in ethical terms, must be there if the material needs are to have such a formative effect. Hence, for our purposes, we might want to rephrase the concept of genesis here, stating the causal ancestry in accordance with the paradox of substance, thus: "Material needs give rise to ethical values, *in principle*" (and that would be quite accurate, for in some respects they do, and in some respects they don't).

Let us put it this way: let us suppose that one held unquestioningly to a belief in the divine origin of the ethical. Let us further suppose that one considered material needs simply as conditions determining the constantly changing structure of the ethical in different periods of history. Even so, there would be plenty of room for a book such as this, which proposes to make such significant observations about ethical values as can be made when they are seen *in terms of*, or *from the standpoint of*, material needs. Dialectically considered, it is as though the author were at this point to write a dialogue containing a voice, or character, named "Material Needs"—and this fellow, Material Needs, would say the things about ethical values that he can see from his particular position, or point of view, or in his particular perspective (necessarily a restricted perspective, since it represents but one voice in the dialogue, and not the perspective-of-perspectives that arises from the coöperative competition of *all* the voices as they modify one another's assertions, so that the whole transcends the partiality of its parts).

Even if we were to ascribe a supernatural origin to ethics, it would still remain true that one should give Material Needs as accurate a voice as one can, for he has a major contribution to make in any discussion of human relations. And it is quite proper to such a "scientific monograph" as Mr. Marshall's that the ethical should be considered simply in material terms. For the empirical concern with *temporal conditions* is nothing other than a concern with *material de-terminations* (that is, treatment contextually in terms of scene, with scene itself narrowed to a naturalistic circumference).

But there are now many naïve readers of such scientific tracts. And it does not occur to them that a treatment of ethics, sovereignty, power in such terms is, by the very logic of its form, a *partial* treatment. A portion of the dialectic having been "monographically" selected, and made into a monologue that takes up the entire universe of discourse, the reader is prone to take this as a statement covering the essentials of the entire field. That is, instead of reading it as a statement about *ethics as considered in terms of material needs,* it is taken as a statement about *the ultimate origin of the ethical.*

It is when so misread that the very excellence of such a monograph (and we consider this one quite good) can lead to a faulty interpretation of motives. And the area "spotlighted" comes to seem like the entire world, so that what seems like a circumference with wide scope is actually the reduction to a very narrow one.

So far as we can see, this matter of circumference is imbedded in the very nature of terms, and men are continually performing "new acts," in that they are continually making judgments as to the scope of the context which they implicitly or explicitly impute in their interpretations of motives. To select a set of terms is, by the same token, to select a circumference.

The thought suggests a technical reason why one could not "rationally" demonstrate the existence of a personal God, if by "rational demonstration" one means the use of evidence derived solely from examination of the natural scene, rather than an appeal to some kind of "revelation" or "intuition." For one would be required to "demonstrate" the existence of a personal God in terms of an impersonal scene with a circumference that has, by definition, been narrowed to a point where the personal principle has been eliminated. The scene as thus restricted would become, from the thematic or terministic point of view, the "logical ground" of God's existence. God's existence as a person would thus be "grounded" in a scene of naturalistic limits. Nature would in effect be the ground of God, whereas the exactly opposite position was what was to be proved.

On a lesser scale, one may discern the same pattern of embarrassment behind the contemporary ideal of a language that will best promote good action by entirely eliminating the element of exhortation or "command." Insofar as such a project succeeded, its terms would involve a narrowing of circumference to the point where the principle of personal action is eliminated from language, so that an act could follow from it only as a non-sequitur, a kind of humanitarian after-thought. For the principle of personal action would lie completely outside the circumference of the terms. And whatever value such vocabularies may have (as in their possible service to technological development) one could not place great hope in them as an ideal for the definition of human motives. We here observe, as the theologians complain, a linguistic line which, beginning with an ideal that involved the elimination of the super-personal principle, eventually led by the same token to the elimination of the personal principle. Of course, one can always restore the personal principle by a kind of "tiny intuition," in simply proclaiming it as part of the empirically given. But this blanket restitution is not enough in itself, so long as the entire logic and structure of the vocabulary is directed differently.

Monetary Reduction

The concept of scope, or circumference, is particularly relevant as regards the sociology of motives. It is obvious, for instance, that a narrowing of circumference was involved when the rise of industrialism had its reflex in a shift from emphasis upon the rationality of the Good to emphasis upon the regularity of Nature. Or otherwise put, in both monetary and technological rationalisms (the two major interwoven strands of industrial rationalism), we see an "heretically efficient" overstressing of the rationalistic element that was in Christian theology. And this rational element underwent a progressive narrowing of circumference, in proportion as men became more exacting in their attempts to be "empirical," and developed the information and the concepts with which to be "empirical" in this sense.

As the concept of reason in God's order (and note that "order" has much the same ambiguity as we found in "design") could be narrowed, or made more precise, in terms of natural law, so the concern with natural law could become materialism; materialism in turn could be made more circumstantial in evolutionary or historicist ways by a narrowing of the motivational context to various concepts of environment; the general notion of environment, or situation, could be further narrowed to stress specifically the "economic factors"; and by many apologists of capitalist rationalism the orbit of the economic was restricted in turn to the monetary and financial. If one were feeling ironical, he could at this point adapt to his purposes a couplet from *The Dunciad*:

> When reason doubtful, like the Samian letter,
> Points him two ways, the narrower is the better.

And when we have arrived at the stage where the sheer symbols of exchange are treated as the basic motives of human relations, when we have gone from "God's law" to "natural law," and thence to the "market law" that had become a "second nature" with those raised in a fully developed capitalist ethic, we find many pious apologists of the *status quo* who would deduce human freedom itself from the free market, as the only scene from which a free social act could be drawn. They thus attribute to the mechanics of price the position in the genealogy of action once held by no less distinguished a Personage than God Himself, formerly defined as the ground of all possibility.

This narrower, more "humanistic" or "social" genealogy of freedom seemed all the more plausible in proportion as the money motive itself gained poignancy—which it did, not in the sense that men became any more greedy for treasure than they had ever been, but in the sense that the increased use of monetary symbolism as an integral part of the economic process led nations to develop their productive and distributive systems in accordance with the money motive as a rational test. This necessarily meant a "transubstantiation" of money, from its function as an *agency* of economic action into a function as the *ground* or *purpose* of economic action. That is, instead of *using* money as a medium to facilitate the production and distribution of goods, men were moved to produce and distribute goods in response to money as motive.

In proportion as the monetary motivation became a "second nature" to modern man, one was guilty of no mere rhetorical misnomer in proclaiming money the source of freedom. Such a position was a grammatically correct deduction from the conception of scene as narrowed to the circumference of the "monetary situation." The evidence of freedom was obvious. We have in mind not only the liberties available to persons of wealth, but rather a more prevalent condition, a development from that ironical kind of freedom the serf obtained in being freed of his bonds to the land and by the same token being deprived of his rights in the land.

Once the capitalist motive had become the norm, men could "of their own volition" compete with one another for monetary wages; thus they could "freely" perform all sorts of necessary acts, many of which were so new and alien to the traditions of Western culture that they would have seemed wholly irrational as judged by the norms of custom alone. They were equally irrational as judged by the tests of intrinsic satisfaction in the work, and could be rationalized *solely* in terms of the money they earned, however little that might be. Thus, we had the spectacle of free men vying with one another to get work that was intrinsically very unpleasant, with little in its favor but the extrinsic monetary reward; they *volunteered* for tasks that, in previous economic scenes, men could have been induced to perform only by compulsion, as with slaves or convicts, or by such rare motives of voluntary service as are found in personal, familial fealties.

In sum, if you have an unpleasant piece of work to be done, and don't want to do it yourself, in a slave culture you may get this done by force, compulsion, threat. Or in a pious culture you may get it done "religiously," if those who are asked to do the work are moved by such motives as devotion, admiration, sense of duty. But in a capitalist labor market, all that is necessary is for you to say, "Who'll do this for five dollars?"—and men press forward "independently," of their "own free will," under orders from no one, to "voluntarily" enlist for the work.

The money motive also had the advantage of being more nearly neutral than the motives of slavery and religion. For instead of drawing upon feelings so strong as those of fear or devotion, it could motivate merely by presenting an "opportunity." And though the work might "in itself" be drudgery, in time this shortcoming was rectified by the growth of the "amusement industry" to the point where it formed one of the biggest investments in our entire culture. And by going where one chose to be amused, one could enjoy for almost nothing such a wealth of performers, avid to entertain, as was never available to the most jaded of Oriental potentates, however vast his revenues.

Under such conditions the monetary motive, or "market law," really could with some justice replace the reference to God's law as the repository of men's "substantial" freedom, since men could be "substantially" free in willing to obey the necessities of monetary wage and monetary tax (or "price"), *wanting* to do what they *had* to do, uniting "I must," "I ought," and "I will." The noun for this union of necessity, duty, and volition was "ambition." Another such was "enterprise."

Since the religious circumference traditionally provides the basic terms for the tribal or collective motives of a culture ("God" being felt to be "real" insofar as these unifying motives really do make up the most extensive and intensive aspects of men's consciousness) the spread of secularization and rationalistic individualism is "normally" a sure sign of cultural disintegration. But the combination of technological and monetary rationalism transformed these "signs of decay" into trends wholly "progressive." For the fact is that the monetary motive, which stimulated the high development of machinery and was in turn "backed" by the new kinds of production it had so significantly helped to rationalize, could provide an effective technical substitute for the religious motive, as a "symbolic" or "spiritual" ground of social cohesion, a means of "keeping body and soul together."

For if religion is by definition a sort of Rome towards which all roads lead, money likewise has this unifying attribute. As early as Plato, the value of monetary symbolism in promoting the division of labor was recognized, as the hypothetical society in Book II of *The Republic* is soon found to need buying and selling, with "a market-place, and a money-token for purposes of exchange." Dialectically, it is the "homogenizing" principle that, in compensating for heterogeneity, so permits much heterogeneity to arise without disaster. As such it is a kind of lowest common denominator, a public or civic medium that can mediate among an infinity of private motives. We might say that it allows for much heterogeneity without disintegration.

As an abstraction into the terms of which *all* communicative acts could be translated (though not all with equal felicity, the price of a can of beans "translating" better than the price of affection) monetary symbolism provided the equivalent of a rational, monistic, universal centre of reference, such as "God." And as the communion service, wherein men make themselves one by partaking of a substance in common, contains a dialectic of the one and the many, since the rite is social in its emphasis but permits individual appropriation of the sacramental substance, so the philosophy of the market points to the public benefits that follow from individual acquisition. And private appropriation inevitably had social reference: business men could continue "making money" only insofar as they continued to sell goods—and "selling" goods meant *distributing* goods.

The analogy may be pursued even to the extent that the reference to money, like the reference to God, entails a special rationality. Many acts that would be "rational," as tested by the rationality peculiar to the monetary motive, would be "irrational" in its absence. Quite obviously, for instance, it is only by a peculiarly monetary logic that men could have called it a "favorable balance of trade" when they were shipping out of their country goods of greater cost than they were getting back. And consider the many gadgets that it would be irrational for mature men to spend their intensest efforts and the best years of their lives in planning, manufacturing, and selling, if any other but the monetary motive were the standard of judgment. Likewise many acts that might be rational enough if there is no God would be irrational if there is one.

After a society has thoroughly adapted its ways to an economy in which money figures as end rather than means, you may expect its members to carry on a maximum percentage of activities that would seem irrational in any other context. Hence, there must be an increase of occupational anguish (as revealed in suicide, war, and their attenuated variants), not only at the times when, by reason of monetary disorders, economic action is impeded, but also at the times when the money motive is attaining free expression. For at the times of free expression, the over-simplification or rational efficiency of money as motive would frustrate those sides of the human personality or organism adapted to very different tests of value.

The efficiency of money as a rationale of conduct makes it a scientific idiom of reduction which, in the realm of social motives, corresponds to the ideal of Occam's Razor in the realm of physical motives. And this very efficiency would probably be enough to make it self-perpetuating as a motive (in that men who remained discontented with large salaries would seek contentment by still larger salaries); but such self-perpetuation is threatened by problems intrinsic to the nature of money itself, and in response to which money continues to change its nature, regardless of human wishes. And many a legislative act specifically designed to maintain the financial *status quo* serves ironically to hasten its transformations.

For the moment endowing money with a personality, treating it metaphorically as an agent, we could say: Since money acts in a technological scene, by reason of the scene-act ratio, the quality of its action must change with the changing quality of that scene. And by reason of the scene-agent ratio, its nature must change *pari passu* with the nature of the industrial plant that "backs" it; for not rare metals, but economic functions, are the real backing of money. Or considering our paradox of the absolute we could say: Insofar as the monetary motive attains the state of "purity" (as it does in banking and investment, where money is derived from purely symbolic manipulations) we may expect it to become something else as a locus of motives.

Kinds of Reduction

Integral to the concept of scope is the concept of *reduction*. In a sense, every circumference, no matter how far-reaching its reference, is a reduction. A cosmology, for instance, is a reduction of the world to the dimensions of words; it is the world *in terms of* words. The reductive factor becomes quite obvious when we pause to realize that any terminology of motives reduces the vast complexity of life by reduction to principles, laws, sequences, classifications, correlations, in brief, abstractions or generalizations of one sort or another. And any generalization is necessarily a reduction in that it selects a *group* of things and gives them a property which makes it possible to consider them as a *single entity*. Thus, the general concept of "man" neglects an infinite number of particular differences in order to stress certain properties which many distinct individual entities have in common. Indeed, any characterization of any sort is a reduction. To give a proper name to one person, or to name a thing, is to recognize some principle of identity or continuity running through the discontinuities that, of themselves, would make the world sheer chaos. To note any order whatever is to "reduce." To divide experience into hungry and sated moments, into the pleasant and unpleasant, into the before and after, into here and there—even distinctions as broad as these translate the world's infinite particulars into terms that are a reduction of the world; in fact, as per the equating of infinity and zero, terms of such broad scope are perhaps the most drastically reductive of all.

In sum, we have first the reduction of the non-verbal to the verbal.

Next, within the verbal, there is the reduction of one terminology to another. Any word or concept considered from the point of view of any other word or concept is a reduction in this sense. One reduces this to that by discussing this *in terms of* that. In this sense, such expressions as "reduced to . . .," "in terms of . . .," and "with reference to . . .," are synonymous. An idealist "reduces the world to ideas" when talking of it *in terms of* mind as its underlying substance. Titles composed of two nouns connected by "and" can quite commonly be read in this light. A title like "Art and Politics," for instance, could be translated, "Art Reduced to Politics," or "Art in Terms of Politics," or "Art with Reference to Politics." Any metaphor is in this broad sense reductive, as it enables us to see one thing in terms of something else (as though we were to give the object a voice, and let it tell what a thing of its nature, and in its position, could observe about the subject). Philosophic equations are in this broad sense reductive, as Berkeley's equating of the "intelligible" with the "sensible" proposes to treat thought in terms of sensation, hence serving as a bridge from rationalism to empiricism (an idealistic bridge, in that sensation in turn was said to be composed of "ideas" grounded in the mind of God).

In this second sense, one can even be said to reduce a "lower" subject to a "higher" one, as Bonaventura, who rated theology as much higher than art, could write "On the Reduction of the Arts to Theology," which we could paraphrase, "The Arts in terms of Theology." But this brings us to the third sense of reduction, as a lowering, a lessening, a narrowing—the difficult spot today, since purely technical conceptions of lowering, lessening, and narrowing can here easily become confused with moral ones.

In recent years, the most drastic manifestation of reduction in this third sense (the sense in which "scope" and "reduction" are flatly contrasted) has been the "debunking" movement, which could be said in general to treat "higher" concepts in terms of "lower" ones, though the pattern is clearly established as far back as the maxims of La Rochefoucauld, which treat "virtues" in terms of "vices" (or what Bentham would call the "extra-regarding" motives in terms of the "self-regarding" motives). Any treatment of a "wider" circumference in terms of a "narrower" circumference would fall generally under the head of reduction in this third sense, as with the location of "consciousness" in terms of "matter," or any other "scientific" metonymies that would define the incorporeal in terms of the corporeal, the intangible in terms of the tangible, and the like. All physicalist, behaviorist, positivist, operationalist ideals of language would be classifiable here, in the technical sense (and some of their opponents would also class them here in the moral sense, on the grounds that the reduction of "spirit" to "matter" is a lowering of caste).

Variants of reduction in this sense are the atomistic vocabularies that would account for entities in terms of the particles of which they are thought to be composed, as one might account for a building in terms of the materials used in its construction. Such atomistic search for the "building blocks" of the universe stresses material cause to the exclusion of final cause. It is somewhat as though one were to "reduce" a game of football to a set of observations about the distribution and movement of masses upon a field, but without any reference whatsoever to such principles of play as one learns from reading the book of rules. The atomistic philosopher's justification would be his contention that there is no cosmic book of rules to read.

We may also note that atomistic reduction is the search for "design" in the narrower sense of that term. And this brings us again to the Occam's Razor, or the "law of parsimony," which plays a central role in the narrowing of circumference. For when two circumferences are matched, it is usually the wider set of terms that will be found to have "multiplied entities beyond necessity." If we say, for instance, that the weight fell because God willed laws according to which the weight would fall when we pushed it, and the wood burned because God willed laws according to which wood burns when we light it, we can quickly become parsimonious enough to say that the weight fell because we pushed it and the fire burned because we lit it. And thereby we have significantly reduced the scope of our motivational terminology.

Or we could state the matter this way: "God" can be omitted from our calculations since it is an invariant term, present as the ground of *all* motives. And we can concentrate upon the search for terms that help us to detect concomitant variations, for it is by the discovery of these that we shall learn how to produce or avoid the specific contexts that serve as de-terminations.

A scientist might happen to believe in a personal God, and might even pray to God for the success of his experiments. In such an act of prayer, of course, he would be treating God as a *variable*. Yet, when his prayer was finished, and he began his experiments, he would now, *qua* scientist, treat "God" as an *invariant* term, as being at most but the over-all name for the ultimate ground of all experience and all experiments, and not a name for the particularities of local context with which the scientific study of conditions, or correlations, is concerned. For scientific experiment would eliminate the personal in every respect in which the concept of the personal means an instance that can be *appealed* to as a variable. That is, the scientist might appeal to God for the *success* of his experiment, but he would not pray to have his experiment prove that the laws of nature had changed since yesterday. Even if God continually changed his mind, the scientist *qua* scientist would aim to discover the *regularities* of each new dispensation. The Marquis de Laplace, whose formulation of the *Mécanique céleste* established the stability of the solar system just about the time of the French Revolution, is said to have told Napoleon that there was no need for a divine agency as an "hypothesis" in his system. The anecdote is at least true "in principle," for it is obvious that "God" would not figure as a term in his equations for the charting of the astronomical motions.

Considered from the strictly logical point of view, to locate the motive of an act by reference to the immediate conditions of the act rather than by reference to the act's motivation "in God," is much the same as to tell a man, who had asked for directions, that Hoboken is across the Hudson from New York City instead of telling him that Hoboken is "in the solar system." Thus, to omit a term from one's calculus of motives because, as an invariant, it can be ignored, is hardly an unreasonable thing to do. But in any case it is clearly a kind of parsimony that automatically reduces the circumference of one's terms. And it can lead to terms that keep getting narrower and narrower, until every term for a state of consciousness has been replaced by a term for the conditions contextual to such a state. The consideration of reduction in this light brings us nearer to such transformations as we described when discussing the antinomies of substance. For instance, because of the fact that an invariant term can readily be omitted from one's calculus, we can begin like the eighteenth-century *philosophes* by postulating certain "constant and universal principles of human nature." Then, precisely because they are everywhere the same, we can drop them from our discussion, and devote ourselves instead to a search for the ways in which these "unchanging principles of human nature" reacted under changing historical conditions. Thereupon, lo! we shall find that we have subtly crossed from one realm into another, in having reduced our universal man to terms of the endlessly shifting historical situations that determine his behavior.

Theological vocabularies of motivation are rarely "perfectionist." Their very stress upon ideals of absolute goodness requires them to be "realistic" in acknowledging the vast number of ways whereby men can fall short of this ideal. The more exacting they are in their concepts of virtue, the more profuse they must be in terms that designate varieties and gradations of vice. However, such vocabularies do provide rich opportunities for rhetorical misnomers that can provide sanctions for iniquity (or, reversing La Rochefoucauld's formula, they can offer ample opportunity to present vices in terms of virtues, as with Molière's religious hypocrite, Tartuffe).

As an attenuated secular variant of this same relation, we have idealizing vocabularies that serve as "eulogistic coverings" for "material interests" (according to Bentham's analysis in his *Tables of the Springs of Action*). And the various "debunking" techniques regularly aim at reductions along Benthamite lines, in disclosing the "material interests" that may lie concealed beneath moralistic euphemisms.

Ironically enough, however, it is reductions of this sort that may be most open to the charge of "perfectionism," albeit a kind of "perfectionism in reverse." For when one puts forward "tough-minded" vocabularies that reduce all motives to pejorative terms (as when a "thinker" appears who tells you that "all men are motivated by nothing but greed and fear," or by "lust for power," etc.), one implies that men can be "perfect exemplars" of some vice or weakness. But human agents cannot be perfect, not even with that inverted perfectionism they might have as total vessels of some weakness or as devotees of some vice, since the scene of their acts is too complex for such ideal simplicity of motivation. The same observation applies, in a lesser degree, with any reduction to simple motives (such as "utility," "comfort," "sex," "hunger," "fear," "wonder," "climate").

At a time when the liars, the stupid, and the greedy seem too greatly in control of a society's policies, philosophies of materialistic reduction may bring us much solace in reminding us that *the very nature of the materials* out of which a civilization is constructed, or in which it is grounded, will not permit such *perfection* of lies, stupidity, and greed to prevail as some men might cause to prevail if they could have their way. For obstructive policies are self-defeating, often ironically hastening the very reforms that these policies were designed to prevent. Sinister interests may have so strong a hold upon the channels of authority, that the people will try their utmost to do what is asked of them, even to the point of destitution, perplexity, and suicide. Yet, even though the people would obey, there is materialistic solace in the thought that the sheer brute materials of the world as it is will disobey. For there are properties of the material order that are grounded in a more basic constitution than any that men can write. These material properties will produce the effects that go with their nature, regardless of how thoroughly the apologists of an outdated order may be equipped to deny this nature, and to so miseducate and misinform that men are trained to draw the lines at the wrong places, interpreting both private and social situations in woefully inaccurate terms. Then it is not by the Courts, but by the constitution of the materials themselves, that false measures will be invalidated.

Complexity of a Simple Motive

In keeping with our distrust of both "perfectionist" and "invertedly perfectionist" motivations, we should feel justified in *never* taking at its face value any motivational reduction to a "simple." As soon as we encounter, verbally or thematically, a motivational simplicity, we must assume as a matter of course that it contains a diversity. Let us consider a "pure" or paradigmatic illustration. Let us set up a hypothetical model of a universe, thus:

The universe, let us say, is a structure of ideas, all interrelated by reason of their common grounding in the mind of God. Though these ideas are distinct, they are all aspects of "the same philosophy," hence they are capable of division into the many while being at the same time consubstantial with the One. In their distinctness, they may be conceived in terms of one another (which they are not), or in terms of their common ground (which they are not). And the attempt to consider them in terms of what they are (namely themselves) is troublesome because they are not wholes, but parts, so that their intrinsic nature depends upon their role in a larger organism. In their distinctness they appear to one another, let us say, as "external" to one another, hence as "objects." Yet we might postulate a simple "motive" common to them all, since they are all parts of one total context. This common motive would be, let us say, their desire to transcend the limits of their distinctness (and the limited points of view that go with it) and to realize that they are all integrally interrelated aspects of the same position. They would recognize that they are all parts of the same sentence, so that the same "meaning" pervades them all.

Yet insofar as the "ideas" were diverse, and perceived one another as different "objects" in different relationship to one another, though they possessed familial consubstantiality by reason of their descent from a common ancestor (or their place in a common context), there would be a very real sense in which they were motivated not identically but diversely. Different things could not be identically motivated, for the differences in their intrinsic nature would involve corresponding differences in relationship to the motivating ground; and this would amount to a difference in the activating properties of the ground itself.

A man cannot be in the same situation as a stone, or even in exactly the same situation as another man—a line of thought which Thomism uses to reconcile the concept of individual free will with the concept of God as universal motive, as per the form translated from Aquinas in Émile Bréhier's *La Philosophie du Moyen Âge,* p. 331: *"Dieu meut tous les êtres selon le mode de chacun."* As regards the imputation of some one *motive* generic to all mankind, the logic of the scene-act relationship would require us to show that all men are in identically the same *situation.* For instance, a reduction of motivation to one essential motive such as "love of power" would require one to show that there is nothing but a "power situation" observable in the human scene. The usual procedure, however, is to acknowledge the existence of other *motives,* but to treat them as in some way derivative, accidental, or unsubstantial, a tactic that would seem less plausible if the speculator were required to show that the corresponding *situations* are similarly derivative from the situation corresponding with the motive he has featured.

Furthermore, although for the purposes of illustration we assume that our hypothetical model of the universe is "correct," even with such "correct" knowledge about these ultimate matters there is room for many different versions of motivation. We have postulated that the "ideas" or parts are motivated by a desire to transcend the limits of their distinctness (and the limited points of view that go with it) and to realize that they are all integrally interrelated aspects of the same position. But there are many ambiguities in this statement, allowing for many different schools of motivational theory, even though there was general agreement on our hypothetical model. One school might stress the ultimate state of consubstantiality as the "significant" feature of the motivation. Another might stress the state of division. A third might situate the strategic factor of motivation in the epistemological miracle whereby the intrinsically related "ideas" appeared to one another as externally juxtaposed "objects." Another might locate the causal ancestry in the dialectical relation between the one and the many, or the quality and the quantity. Another might situate the motivation in some logic of developmental *stages* in the progress towards realization. Others might debate as to whether the desire for realization itself involved intellectual or intuitive methods, or both. Others might attribute different scope or quality to the circumference, or differ as to the hierarchy of circumferences, and so on.

Next let us assume some body of men living in a complex but relatively stable political and economic order. And let us suppose that the philosophy advocated by one of the schools became "implemented" as the authoritative vocabulary for rationalizing this culture's acts, institutions, relationships, and expectancies. Here a new kind of ambiguity would arise. For the vocabulary of the unofficial schools would implicitly or explicitly contain different programs of action with respect to political and economic issues than would the official vocabulary. (In brief, the grammatical resources would take on rhetorical implications.) And such doctrinal differences, when sharpened by their direct or indirect bearing upon the political and economic *agon,* would in time come to be felt not simply as differences, but as antitheses.

We have now carried our hypothetical model of the universe to the point where we confront such motivational ambiguities as are treated particularly in dialectical materialism. Dialectically, the context or ground of the *verbal in general* must be the *non-verbal in general.* But the ground of any particular verbal action must be a complex of verbal and non-verbal factors that can be defined in terms of varying circumference. Hence, more schools may arise, that haggle as to the particular circumference to be selected for particular instances of interpretation. For purely thematic reasons, the analysis may be confined to the verbal alone. But dialectical materialism (like psychologies of the unconscious) may often suggest convincing reasons why apparently thematic limitations are grounded in extrinsic motives.

But surely we have by now traced the matter far enough to suggest why simple vocabularies of motivation can but leave a complexity in the offing, for the diversity of the materials that compose the human situation necessarily involves a corresponding diversity of motives. In this sense, each man's motivation is unique, since his situation is unique, which is particularly obvious when you recall that his situation also reflects the unique sequence of his past. However, for all this uniqueness of the individual, there are motives and relations generic to all mankind—and these are intrinsic to human agents as a class, in that such motives and relations will be different in quality from the motives and relations of any other natures.   Motives in this generic sense are titular; that is, they are "single" or "simple" in the way that chapter headings would be, or as is the case with our five terms.   And the contents of the chapters which would fill them out by making explicit what the speaker finds implicit in them are "demonstrations" not in the sense of *proof,* but in the sense of *illustrations,* or tautological re-statements having corrective modifiers that indicate the directions which one must take for converting the simplicity back into a complexity.

So, when confronting naturalistic attempts to arrive at intrinsic motivations by reduction to "instincts" or "drives" or "urges" within the organism as a species, upon close analysis you will invariably find that all sorts of "complicating factors" (including external, environmentalist motivations) are referred to, usually without the full awareness of the theorist, who is so intent upon introducing all aspects of his subject *in the name of* his titular terms, that to him all incidental modifiers seem infused by the spirit of their godhead.   And since these modifications of his thesis are like adjectives attached to a noun, you can with some justice adopt here a policy of either goodwill or illwill.   For it is always a matter of casuistry to decide whether you will treat the modification of a principle as an "extension of" the principle or a "deviation from" it— and so you may decide to treat the modifiers as either "constitutional" or "unconstitutional" variants of the nouns.

Motivations dialectically paired (such as "egoism and altruism," "war and peace," "domination and submission," "experience and nature," "skepticism and animal faith") are to be similarly treated, as titular simplicities which in the writing may become thoroughly and adequately complex, as each of the terms is modified by extensions until sufficient richness is attained.   Essentially, the tactics behind all such terms must be referred back to the matter of circumference—for if the substance of the terms is to descend "substantially" through all the line of modifications, it makes a strategic difference what the quality of this original constitutional act may be: whether it be supernatural, naturalistic, or referred to the broader or the narrower aspects of our "second nature."   Many a term may be chosen or rejected as titular in

the imputing of motives because of the political or programmatic quality which the term happens to possess at the given time and place in
history. That is, there may be Rhetorical motives behind the manipulations of the grammar. Similarly, the grammar may be shaped to meet
the needs of Symbolic, as were purely philosophic theories of power
affected by personal problems of potency.

In sum: In any term we can posit a world, in the sense that we can
treat the world *in terms of* it, seeing all as emanations, near or far, of
its light. Such reduction to a simplicity being technically reduction to
a summarizing title or "God term," when we confront a simplicity we
must forthwith ask ourselves what complexities are subsumed beneath
it. For a simplicity of motive being a perfection or purity of motive,
the paradox of the absolute would admonish us that it cannot prevail in
the "imperfect world" of everyday experience. It can exist not actually,
but only "in principle," "substantially."

The foregoing considerations suggest a sense in which any over-all
motive (such as is contained in the formulae, *"ad majorem gloriam
Dei"* or *"amor intellectualis Dei"* or *"homo homini lupus"*) could be
omitted when imputing the motive of a particular case. When you
have a "Rome" term to which all roads lead, you thereby have as many
different variants of the motive as there are roads. Besides, if you *start*
with your Rome term, the process of tracking down the roads that lead
to it will in effect take you *from* it. This variant of the substantial paradox (whereby the point of departure in the sense of the inaugurating
spirit that will pervade whatever follows becomes the point of departure
in the sense of the abandoned) was exemplified by Coleridge in reverse,
when he made plans for a poem that was to be called "The Brook" and
was to follow the course of a stream from its source to its mouth where,
as a broad river, it empties into the sea. In taking notes for the poem
he became interested in writings about the sources of the Nile. And in
meditating upon these he was moved by the imagery not of a forward-
flowing but of a backward-turning, or "introversion." And when he
had used the image of a stream in *Biographia Literaria,* he later persuaded himself that it must be flowing uphill.

This is, of course, but another way of coming upon our paradox of
substance. In specifically conceptual terms, the featuring of a single
motive will quickly require one to grant that its simplicity operates
but "in principle." Where it is treated simply as an "ideal" the

paradox enters at the point where the ideal turns back upon itself. Thus, were we to feature "freedom" or "tolerance," we should eventually have to ask ourselves, as with Mill, whether it would be in conformity with this ideal for us to "force freedom" upon those who resist it (as with "backward peoples" who, having a satisfactory non-monetary economy of their own, resisted the great gift of freedom that the White men brought them, in the form of money and the "free market" and the hut tax that destroyed the primitive economy by requiring the natives to work for money in the White plantations). Similarly the man who would judge by the ideal of "tolerance" alone must confront the embarrassments of trying to decide whether he must by the same token tolerate views that lead to the establishment of intolerance.

Often, however, the aspect of the substantial paradox, whereby the point of departure becomes translated into its betrayal, can lead to more felicitous results. Thus, two men may select totally different points of departure—yet both may, in the course of time, become concerned with modifications of their thought that add up to the abandonment of their starting points. And both may have come upon the *same* roads in the course of their journeys. Still other thinkers, setting out from other points, may come upon this same area of overlap. And so in time, we can build up a realm of reality shared in common, each of us having thus allowed his private point of view to be replaced by a public point of view (which is to say, in effect, that each will have "died" to his private self and been "born into" a public self). Yet whatever may be the degree of alienation that accompanies this development, we can expect to find that the point of departure, in the sense of inaugurating and pervasive spirit, still figures. For the area that all men share in common will be shared by each in accordance with his nature (the nature he expressed in his point of departure), so that the common motive can be again analyzed into different individual motives. (We here have a terministic translation of the Thomist doctrine that God moves all things, but each thing in accordance with its nature.)

Operationalist reductions would abandon over-all points of departure (titles, or "god-terms") so thoroughly as not even to begin with them. Suppose, for instance, that certain of the "ideas" in our hypothetical model of the universe ("ideas" that had the appearance of "objects") were embodied in the materials and operations necessary to the running of an elevator. You might radically change the universal motivation you attributed to these "ideas" in their relation to a common ground, yet you would not have to change your instructions for the running of the car. The instruction reads, let us say: "To move the car forward, place lever 1 in position A." And as related to different titular motivations, we could imagine the instruction figuring thus: "The significant motivating feature of the universe is the ultimate state of consubstantiality among the ideas; 'therefore,' to move the car forward, place lever 1 in position A." Or: "The significant motivating feature of the universe is the state of division among the ideas; 'therefore,' to move the car forward, place lever 1 at position A." Or: "The significant motivating feature . . . etc. is the epistemological miracle whereby the intrinsically related 'ideas' appear to one another as externally juxtaposed 'objects'; 'therefore,' to move the car . . . etc."

Nor is this simply a matter of the shift from a metaphysical to a physical circumference. You may imagine a purely physicalist frame, for instance, such as two different over-all theories as to the nature of electricity, yet along with either of them we could have the instruction: "To light the light, give the knob one half-turn to the right." We are here likewise confronting the Occamite law of parsimony. For even in secular vocabularies one finds statements that are too general for the purpose at hand. Paraphrasing Galileo, we could say that they are "god-terms" which explain too little by explaining too much.

We have spoken previously of respects in which an appositional relationship between the general and the particular, or the collective and the individual, or the "one" and the "many," can become an oppositional relationship. Or, otherwise put, the synecdochic relationship whereby a part can be taken as consistent with the whole (the principle of *omnia ubique* according to which the microcosm is a representative replica of the microcosm) is no longer felt to apply; and instead we encounter the divisive relationship, the genitive transformation of something which is "a part of" a larger context into something which is "apart from" this context. We can see the same conversion in the relation between the terms "genus" and "species." For in the consistent relationship, "species" is a subdivision of "genus"; yet one can see the concepts becoming antithetical when a speaker says: "Don't be so general, be specific."

Applying the same mode of thought to the analysis of personal motives, we often find that the meanings of titular words cannot be accepted at their face value. For every atheist who explicitly denies God, there are a thousand atheists who are church-goers in good standing. The man who will tell you that God is "all-powerful" can also be the man who gives this statement body in not one single sincere act or vigorous image or matured thought throughout his life. Indeed, in the middle ages, when men laid much more stress upon the power of God than we do in an age of technology, philosophers were much given to drawing the line between the things that God could and could not do. Close analysis of contexts would often reveal specific meanings totally at odds with one's catechistic avowals. Such considerations we should consider the equivalent of "operationalist" meanings, when applied to the sphere of personality. We should note, however, that a much wider circumference is involved in the concept of "operations" here. Two men, for instance, may be standing side by side performing the same "operations," so far as the carrying out of instructions is concerned. Yet they are performing radically different acts if one is working for charitable purposes and the other to the ends of vengeance. They are performing the same *motions* but different *acts*.

We have discussed elsewhere (notably in *The Philosophy of Literary Form*) the ways in which such motivational "clusters" can be found in the structure of literary works. They should also be present as equations intrinsic to the structure of any act. That is, as motives behind the structure of either an esthetic or a practical act, there must be an implicit set of evaluations: assumptions as to what kind of act equals heroism, what kind equals villainy, what kind contains the likelihood of reward, of punishment, etc. Such matters are to be treated at some length in the aspect of our study we call the Symbolic.

Money as Substitute for God

Reverting to our hypothetical model of the universe: whatever our philosophy of God and Nature may be, there is the temporal world of a "second nature" that calls for a reduction of circumference to the limits imposed by the "materials." We might still cling to our hypothetical somewhat Berkeleyan model of the world as a structure of "ideas" joined by their common grounding in the mind of God. Yet, within this *total* ideality, we should have to distinguish between the kind of "ideas" that seem like ideas to us and the kind that seem like "objects." And to define situations in terms of such objects would be in effect a reduction to a materialist circumference, as regards "operational" matters, though we still defined the "ultimate reality" as "ideal."

There is one notable difference between the materials of nature and the materials of our "second nature." The materials of our second nature are largely man-made. These accumulations of properties and methods have culminated in the complex of technological inventions that mothered their own peculiar kinds of necessity. And though men have been undergoing fantastic hardships in order to develop and retain these "conveniences," the fact remains that their "materiality" is at the same time an "ideality," in that every invention has been the emanation of some human mind. Nature is "given," but the environments to which we adapt ourselves as to a second nature are the creations of agents. In adapting ourselves to machinery, we are adapting ourselves to an aspect of ourselves. This would be reduction to a higher or a lower circumference, as you prefer, but in either case a reduction.

Since technology, as the primary characterizing feature of our second nature today, is "substantially" human, in accordance with the paradox of substance it can become quite "inhuman." For while the accumulations of the industrial plant are "in principle" the externalization or alienation of intrinsically human virtues, there are many unintended by-products. Many people would vote for cities—but only a few real estate men would vote *explicitly* for slums. (We are not talking of the millions who regularly vote *implicitly* for slums.) The carrying out of any human purpose can be expected to reveal the kind of alienation that accompanies any act of generating or creating, which is an embodiment from within the self, and as such is a representative part that can, by the fact of division, become an antithetical part.

For this externalization of internal aptitudes is different in its state of *being* than in its *becoming*. It is in its *becoming* that technology most fully represents the human agent, since his inventing of it is an *act,* and a rational act. In its state of *being* (or perhaps we might better say its state of *having become*) it can change from a *purpose* into a *problem*. And surely much of the anguish in the modern world derives from the paradoxical fact that machinery, as the embodiment of rationality in its most rational moments, has in effect translated rationality itself from the realm of ideal aims to the realm of material requirements. Few ironies are richer in complexities than the irony of man's servitude to his mechanical servants.   For though it is nothing less than an act of genius to *invent* a machine, it is the nagging drudgery of mere motion to *feed* one.

Occupational *diversification* equals by definition occupational *classification,* a splitting of mankind into *classes* that are separated from one another with varying degrees of distinctness and fixity at different periods in history, and with varying degrees of felicity or infelicity in their relationships to one another.   And occupational diversity signifies a corresponding motivational diversity.   The reader may ask: "Do you mean that, because of occupational classification, all plumbers have a set of social values distinct from those of carpenters, clerks, farmers, teachers, etc., all of which are equally demarcated from one another?"

Perhaps in the early days of the guilds something of this sort could have been noted, though the sense of a common membership in a single Church with a single body of tradition would presumably have supplied the common ground of mediation among the diversity of group motives, with heresy, sect, and schism as evidence of a divisive motivation.   But in recent history, with the great occupational fluidity that has accompanied industrial innovation, it would be absurd to look for the most significant aspect of motivation in occupational diversity *per se*.   For such a great diversity and fluidity of occupational classifications made it impossible to develop such distinctness of classes as we find, for instance, in the caste system of India.   In fact, the present-day jurisdictional disputes among the unions in the United States reveals that the constantly changing methods of technology are continually making new cuts on the bias across the traditional classifications, so that it would be hard for any one to say for a certainty whether a certain new material should be applied by masons, plasterers, or carpenters, and so with a great number of other new products and processes.

Confronting such a state of affairs, we should seek for the significant over-all motivating factor in the nature of the medium by which this great occupational diversity and fluidity, with its almost infinite variety of motives, is "reduced" to a common rationale.   And this reduction is made, of course, in terms of money.   Monetary symbolism is the "simple," the "god-term," in terms of which all this great complexity attains a unity transcending distinctions of climate, class, nation, cultural traditions, etc.

But reduction to money, we have said, is reduction to a simple, thus to a purity or absolute—and we have said that things in their "pure" state are something else. Hence, in reducing the subject of motivation to a "pure" state, we must warn ourselves against the risk of falling into our own variant of "inverted perfectionism." No human being could be a "perfect" capitalist, since no human being could be motivated by the rationale of money alone.

We may note, however, that the monetary reference is the over-all *public* motive for mediating among the endless diversity of occupational and private (or "preoccupational") motives. We thus encounter from another angle our notion that the monetary motive can be a "technical substitute for God," in that "God" represented the unitary substance in which all human diversity of motives was grounded. And we thus see why it was "grammatically correct" that the religious should fear the problem of money.

Usually this notion of money as the "root of all evil" is taken in a very superficial sense, to indicate the power of money as a "temptation" to dishonest dealings. On the contrary, it is more likely that the diabolic role of money as "tempter" has helped to call forth a whole new gamut of scrupulosities here; and for every ethical defeat in the way of theft or "graft," etc. there must be countless moral victories on the part of men who resisted such temptation. No, any "diabolical" effect in this sense would be a "moralizing" effect, the devil being the dialectical counterpart of God.

Money, as active temptation, could be expected to perform the dialectical role of all such counter-agents in provoking the agent to active combat, hence increasing the realm of scrupulosity (hence leading us from the simplicity of *innocence* into the complexity of *virtue*). And it could probably be said, in this respect, that pecuniary civilizations show a greater range of scruples or "tender-mindedness" (in the way of idealistic, humanitarian attitudes) than is usually the case with realistic "tough-mindedness" of more primitive cultures. Such humanitarian scruples are made possible also by reason of the fact that money, in promoting great *indirectness* or *vicariousness,* has made it possible for great numbers of people to avoid many of the harsher realities entirely. For one need simply pay to have "insensitive" things done by others instead of doing them oneself. Nor is this expedient possible only to the rich. Think how many people eat meat, and how few work in slaughter-houses.

No, where religion is tested by "ethical sensitiveness" and "humanitarianism," the monetary motive has probably added to it rather than subtracted from it. Rather, money endangers religion in that money can serve as universal symbol, the unitary ground of all action. And it endangers religion not in the dramatic, agonistic way of a "tempter," but in its quiet, rational way as a *substitute* that performs its mediatory role more "efficiently," more "parsimoniously," with less "waste motion" as regards the religious or ritualistic conception of "works." And since money thus substitutes technically or scientifically for the godhead as a *public* principle, do we not see the results of this substitution in the fact that Protestantism, arising in response to the growth of occupational diversity, trade, and the necessarily increased dependence upon the use of money, stressed on the contrary the function of the godhead as a *private* principle? For where monetary symbolism does the work of religious symbolism (as a lowest common denominator for mediating among many motives could more efficiently replace a "highest common denomination") the locus of this titular role would have to be placed elsewhere than at the point of public mediation. This was found in the doctrine of communication directly with God.

The humanistic emphasis that arose with the secularization of middle class culture was new not in the sense that humanism itself was new but in the sense that humanism began to undergo a strategic transformation. We might describe this as a change from a "consistent" humanism to a "compensatory" humanism. "Consistent" humanism had placed human personality as the lineal descendant of a "principle of personality" felt to be present in the universal ground. But with the increasingly secular emphasis, the motivations of the universal ground were viewed not in terms of a superhuman personality but in terms of naturalistic impersonality. And human personality was affirmed in dialectical opposition to the quality of the ground. For when the scene was narrowed to a secular circumference, human personality could no longer be "logically *de*duced" familially from the divine personality. But it might be vigorously affirmed simply as an "empirical fact," as part of "the given," in contrast with any new calculus in which the personality was "logically *re*duced" to atomistic, naturalistic terms of impersonality.

At this point a calculus of "therefore" was supplanted by a calculus of "nevertheless." By a change in the tactics of grammar, men ceased to think, "God's personality, *therefore* human personality" and began to think, "nature's impersonality, *nevertheless* human personality," the first pair being related consistently, the second oppositionally. And the experience of an *impersonal* motive was empirically intensified in proportion as the rationale of the monetary motive gained greater authority and organization within the realm of men's "second nature." We may discern these transformations behind the shift from "consistent" religious humanism to the "compensatory" secular humanitarianism of science and money.

The Nature of Monetary "Reality"

Where are we now? We must consider the possible charge that in our discussion of the monetary motive we have ourselves been guilty of "inverted perfectionism." For if money is viewed as a *medium* of exchange, then we have reduced our field of discussion to terms of *agency,* from which we would in turn derive all else as though it were pervaded by the same ancestral spirit.

In the first place, as we noted previously, money is *not a mere agency,* in our civilization, but is a *rationalizing ground* of action. In contrast with the psychosis that would accompany a barter economy, for instance, our monetary economy must be accompanied by a distinctive "capitalist" psychosis. For any important motivational emphasis must have its corresponding emphasis in the thinking of those whose efforts and expectancies are formed with reference to its motivating powers, resources and risks. And we could speak of a "capitalist psychosis" not in the sense of one who thinks that by eliminating capitalism one would eliminate psychosis, but in the sense of one who thinks that, given any pronounced social structure, there will be a "psychosis" corresponding to it. That is, there will be a particular recipe of overstressings and understressings peculiar to the given institutional structure. And the tendency of the culture will be to see everything in terms of this particular recipe of emphases, as the typical apologist of ideal *laissez-faire* capitalism would think "freedom" itself lost if we lost "free market freedom," since he conceived of freedom in these terms.

In this sense, we may legitimately isolate the monetary motive as an essence and may treat many apparently disrelated manifestations as its accidents. It would not be a primary motive in the sense that it "gave rise to" ethics, philosophy, art, etc. But we could feature it in the sense that its effects could be seen as a significant influence in the ethics, philosophy, art that flourished at a time when it had to be so significantly taken into account (at a time when it rationalized the adoption of new methods, for instance, in contrast with times when the norms of tradition were taken as the major rationalizing test of "right" ways).

In its nature as a "purity" or "simplicity," however, it cannot prevail in this imperfect world. Hence we must recognize that, even in the heyday of capitalism, the monetary motive is but one member of the "power" family. And the possible transformations here are many. As early as the Calvinistic sanctioning of "usury," it was apparent that a primary aspect of our monetary economy was its stress upon *credit*— and the receiving of credit is *indebtedness*. Thus, in addition to its strongly *futuristic* nature as investment, in its connotations of *owing* it provides a technical normalization of "guilt" or "sin" by converting a religious psychology of "retribution" or "penance" into a commercialist psychology of "ambition." The fact that the symbolism of debt itself can be manipulated by the resources of accountancy adds further notable convertibilities. For instance the nature of nationalist integers, formed of abstract relations in keeping with the abstractions of money, makes it readily possible for men to carry out projects that privately enrich themselves while publicly adding to the national debt, as when a "national's" interests abroad are protected by government agencies supported by a tax upon the people as a whole. We here have simultaneously an apposition of individual and collectivity on the "spiritual" level and an opposition on the practical level. When "we" get air bases, who is this "we"?

The relations of any one individual to the public medium can be understood only by examining the "clusters" or "equations" in his particular "psychic economy." In the economy of one man, monetary power may be *compensatory* to some other kind of power (physical, sexual, moral, stylistic, intellectual, etc.). That is, he may seek by the vicarage of money to "add a cubit to his stature." But in the economy of another man, monetary power may be *consistent* with one or all of these. A sense of moral guilt, for instance, or a sense of social inferiority, may "compensatorily" incite one man to seek a fortune, while the same motives may "consistently" prevent another from demanding what his services are worth. Paradoxically, an "anti-social" attitude may sometimes reach expression through the prompt paying of debts, since by the payment one's bonds or obligations would be severed. And the shady promoter may be motivated by a genuine sense of "sociality," to which men instinctively respond in letting themselves be taken in by his "cordiality," a "sociality" and "cordiality" which are not "in principle" dishonest at all, but which he finally "reduces" to the simplified idiom by leaving debts unpaid (that is, by keeping bonds of attachment between him and his creditors).

A wider circle, culminating in thoughts of life and death, may be matched by a narrower circle, culminating in thoughts of solvency and poverty. The two may be so related that each can stand for the other. And so one can seek more and more money, as a symbolic way of attaining immortality. That is, one may thus vicariously seek "more and more life," in the attempt to attain a higher *quality* in terms of a higher *quantity,* for it is easy to think of a "more intense" life in quantitative terms. Conversely, the religious injunction to "live a dying life" can be followed, in an unconscious secular translation, by systematically keeping oneself poor (thus "going to meet" death).

Obviously we could not chart here the many private roads that lead up to, or away from, the monetary Rome. And besides, this phase of our subject more properly falls under the heading of Symbolic. We might in passing, however, refer the reader to André Gide's novel, *The Counterfeiters*. Gide is very discriminating in his ironic appreciation of the ways in which the patterns of religion survive in ingenious secular distortions. He is profoundly, if perversely, a Protestant. In *The Counterfeiters,* the relationships among the important characters are symbolized in monetary terms, as with the lad of homosexual bent, who also ambiguously loves a girl, and as a memento gives her a coin that is counterfeit.

We have said that the rationale of money had much to do with the innovation, specialization, diversification, partialization, and classification of economic motives. For the great changes that the rationale of technological processes and products effected in our "second nature" could not have taken place without a universal idiom to the terms of which all the diversity could be reduced. But clearly we could with as much justice state this ratio the other way round, saying that monetary symbolism could not assume so dominant a role in the rationalization of motives without technological diversity as a ground. Various kinds of occupational diversity (or classification of status) in the past have given us the lineaments of capitalism—but only when symbiotic with applied science could it produce the peculiar kind of motivation that we know as modern capitalism.

This symbiosis of money and technology has made a "double genesis" possible in the imputing of motives, as the thinker may attribute to "capitalism" the aspects of our civilization he dislikes and to "technology" the aspects in which he places his hopes, or *vice versa*. Since both money and technology are objective "powers" existing in history, we might properly expect them to manifest the ambivalence of such powers. Either, that is, should be capable of acting favorably or unfavorably, favorably if properly "discounted," unfavorably when its workings are protected from criticism, as the money motive is piously protected in some quarters by being made synonymous with the national godhead of patriotism, and as the technological motive is protected in other quarters where it is granted immunity in the name of "science" as an absolute good. Also, our very aversion to "talking about money matters" has done much to conceal our understanding of it as a motive, though it is worth noting that this aversion in itself indicates the "godhead" of money, since in formal religions men fear to behold or name lightly their God, or motivational center.

There is an ironic possibility that orthodox capitalism, Fascism, and Communism may all three be variants of the "monetary psychosis" insofar as all three are grounded in the occupational diversity (classification) of technology. In any case Russian Communism was the most "idealistic" of the three, since technology was *willed* there in accordance with Marxist values, rather than being the material ground out of which such values arise. Voluntaristic philosophies would find nothing unusual in this sequence, but it would seem to be a paradox from the standpoint of dialectical materialism.

Though Communist industrialism relies upon financial accountancy, neither Communism nor Fascism will accord to money the primary order of "reality" it possessed for, say, the financial priesthood of capitalism. Shortly after a disastrous hurricane had swept through several northern states, destroying houses, uprooting forests, undermining railroads, and doing much other damage, all "to the value of hundreds of millions of dollars," we recall an article on the stock market page of a New York City newspaper which remarked that, great as the "losses" had been, they were much less than the shrinkage of stock values in a recent market "recession." The whole point of this article was the author's implicit assumption that the two cases were essentially analogous. Note that in the case of the *symbolic* losses of stock market value, the aggregate material wealth of the world had not been diminished one particle. The railroad that had shrunk so in value was exactly the same railroad, with the same equipment, the same trained personnel, the same physical ability to perform useful services. But in the case of the hurricane, much real material wealth had been destroyed. Yet so "instinctively" did this writer think "in terms of" the monetary idiom of reduction, so thoroughly had it become a "second nature" with him, that he made no differentiation whatsoever between these two kinds of "losses." "Spirituality" of this particular sort is lessened under either the explicitly materialist coördinates of Marxism or the realism implicit in the national barter projects of Fascism. Also, the Fascists are able to have a less pious attitude towards monetary symbolism because of their cynical attitude towards the manipulation of symbols in general. And we should note how German Fascism, by centering its attention about industrial empire, was fast approaching a position where it could have destroyed the empire of Britain, which was coming more and more to think of rule in the pure financial terms of The City.

Love, Knowledge, and Authority

It is not a part of our contract here to make final decisions on these many matters. It is enough for the purposes of our Grammar that, when on the subject of reduction in general, we consider the important respects in which both monetary and technological circumferences are themselves reductions and have provoked reductions.

All terminological reductions, when they gain sufficient adherence to form a cultural trend, should probably be ascribed to the stimulating effect which some order of power exerted upon the human imagination during the eras when men first came to recognize and appreciate and develop the resources of this particular power.

There is a sense in which powers are everywhere. According to

Aristotle, Thales believed that "all things are full of Gods." For our purposes this could be interpreted as a recognition of the fact that in everything there is a power, or motive, of some sort. That is, we would interpret it in a broader sense than the notion that "soul is intermingled in the whole universe," though Aristotle in his *De Anima* says this is what Thales "probably" meant.

The cult of Prometheus and the rites of the Vestal Virgins must stem from a time when fire was the power, the "new power," that had caught men's fancy, so that they were prompted to construct a whole system of terms about fire as a motive. At this time presumably there came to the fore the vocabularies that treat of motives in terms of fire.

When a weapon or implement or art was said to possess a divine or heroic origin, we would consider this simply as a way of characterizing it as a power or motive in keeping with the terms of definition then available. Thinkers at first would not presumably make up new words for such purposes; they would not proceed like some modern chemist naming some new drug that he had synthesized, or like a manufacturer giving his product a trade name. But they would seek to adapt the tribal terms already in use, perhaps not even being sure themselves to what extent they were giving the term new meanings.

And particularly in view of what we have already noted about the ambiguities whereby concepts of temporal priority and concepts of logical priority can change places, we should propose to translate the statement that a certain implement *came from* a power into a statement that this implement was *essentially* a power. That is, we should translate the notion of origin from terms of time to terms of timelessness (terms that consider it *sub specie aeternitatis*). And we should be all the more ready to do this because of the observations we have made about the word "genus," the etymology of which so clearly suggests that even purely logical classes were originally conceived in purely tribal terms, as derivative from ancestral principles. In sum, a statement that an art was descended from a God would be interpretable as a statement that the art was in its nature a power, or motive.

And we should infer that the original conception of the powers or motives in things is not exactly animistic. The evidences of animism which nineteenth-century anthropologists found so profusely among primitive tribes are, to our way of thinking, mainly indications of how thoroughly most of such anthropologists were imbued with the terms typical of nineteenth-century idealist philosophy, so that they *saw* things in these terms.

We should expect, rather, that the basic perception of motives is a perception of things not as possessing the souls and personalities of *agents,* but as being essentially *active.* That is, they were not felt to be *people;* they were felt to be *actions.* If one walks determinedly against a bitter wind, for instance, he feels very definitely that this wind is an *act* against which he is acting, but he does not necessarily feel that the wind is a *person.* The step from thinking of things as powers, or potential actions, to thinking of them as imbued with souls, would seem to come much later, and very probably not until a considerable degree of personal property had arisen, and men could differentiate individual identity from the tribal identity in terms of such "personalty."

Such thoughts would suggest a slight reinterpretation of the "hylozoism" that characterized the Greek "nature philosophers" of the pre-Socratic era. Would it not be more direct to say that these early thinkers saw in nature a *principle of action* rather than "souls" such as post-Christian anthropologists have in mind when they refer to animism. True, the Ionian *"physikoi"* lived in cities stimulated by the commercial enterprise of the Persian Empire; but their way of living was "primitive" as compared with the unnatural ways of modern industrialism. And much later the realism of Plato, in *The Sophist,* brings out the same *activist* rather than *animist* emphasis in the definition of Being as "that which has the power to act or be acted upon."

We can but get glimpses around the corner of the "capitalist psychosis," with its strongly futuristic emphasis, an emphasis so pronounced that an anthropologist (and a very good one) who is himself in the insurance business has made an analysis (and a very good one) of a primitive American Indian language in futuristic terms, stressing the *preparatory* ingredient in the tribal rituals rather than their nature as a mode of *action now.* Ironically, it was our monetary individualism that both invented "animism" and destroyed it (in first attributing to savages the belief in *spirits* rather than the belief in *powers,* and then proving the absurdity of the belief, since a monetary attitude towards manufactured objects transcends their fetishistic nature as aspects of the person).

What we are trying to bring out is this: we do not think merely of a step from the animistic to a conception of an inanimate nature. Instead, we would postulate first a sense of things as *powers* or *acts* (acts potentially or actually). The next stage would be a differentiation into agent and act, so that natural phenomena could come to be divided into two aspects, an invisible soul or agent and a visible material process. Then, when this stage is reached, the world is ready for an enlightened law of parsimony, as men discover that the terms for the agent behind the natural phenomenon duplicate the terms for the natural phenomenon itself. Whereupon the terms for *agent* can be dropped, and the motivational circumference can be reduced simply to terms for the *motion*. For though the original ambiguity could be felt as an act, once agent has been explicitly distinguished and then explicitly eliminated, the orbit of action is thereby reduced to terms of sheer motion. The principle of parsimony, by the way, can be quite clearly discerned in the ancient Greek's ways of saying "It is raining," "It is snowing," etc. Originally he said "the God is raining," or "Zeus is raining." Later he omitted the name for the divine agent (quite as though he had been admonished by Occam not to multiply entities beyond necessity), saying simply, "rains."

Henry Adams' pairing of Virgin and Dynamo clearly suggests two contrasting orders of power. We refer not so much to the contrast between "thirteenth-century unity" and "nineteenth-century multiplicity." Rather, we consider the important matter to be the contrast beween the natural powers and the industrial powers. Ironically, the "supernatural" vocabularies flourished when men's imagination was most powerfully stimulated by the powers of *nature,* while the philosophies that would today label themselves "naturalistic" favor terms taken from the wholly artificial and *unnatural* realm of technological invention and laboratory method.

Is not Adams' pair basic in the sense that it contrasts an order of powers centered about biological generation and an order of powers centered about technological motion? This is, we grant, not quite the way Adams himself draws the line. Rather, his *Education* seems to be a rebirth ritual whereby the author would finally bring himself to see himself in terms of impersonal "force," while renouncing the strongly *familial* sense of his identity (the "eighteenth-century" self) with which his life began. His book traces a kind of attenuated self-immolation. For few people in America could begin life with so pronounced a label of tribal identity as could a member of the Adams family. Yet he describes his quest as the search for a father. And though he was so clearly placed in an heraldic line, he was also the end of a line, for he died childless, the kind of power in terms of which he finally proclaimed his identity being not the powers of generation but the powers of the machine.

Yet, though we would perhaps place a somewhat different interpretation upon Henry Adams' quest than he would have placed upon it himself, is our interpretation of his Virgin and Dynamo pair much different from his? Except for the poignant paragraphs on the death of his sister, when "for the first time in his life, Mont Blanc for a moment looked to him what it was—a chaos of anarchic and purposeless forces," it is not in "nature" that he finds the new powers with whose terms he would identify himself. Rather, it is at the successive world's fairs and international expositions that Adams gets his "education." Of the Chicago Exposition in 1893, we are told that "education ran riot" there. And it is the machinery that impresses him. As he expresses it, "The historical mind can think only in terms of historical processes, and probably this was the first time since historians existed, that any of them had sat down helpless before a mechanical sequence."

And it is in the "great gallery of machines" at the Paris Exposition of 1900, that he found "his historical neck broken by the sudden irruption of forces totally new," forces which he compares and contrasts with the forces of the Christian Cross, on the grounds that both kinds, in their way, have been revolutionary. And while remarking that the historian "cared nothing for the sex of the dynamo until he could measure its energy," he observes:

> Every one, even among Puritans, knew that neither Diana of the Ephesians nor any of the Oriental goddesses was worshipped for her beauty. She was goddess because of her force; she was the animated dynamo; she was reproduction—the greatest and most mysterious of all energies; all she needed was to be fecund.

And so we may say that the Dynamo stands for the man-made forces of *production,* and the Virgin for the natural forces of *reproduction.* The forces of reproduction proceed by growth and decay, the forces of production proceed by the acceleration and deceleration of motion. Growth is by the assimilation of food, motion is by the consumption of fuel.

As regards human motives, the natural, biological, tribal order of food and growth would seem to culminate in the emotion of love. It is the realm of appetites generally, the whole range of desires encompassed by the psychoanalyst's concept of eros or libido. It is the realm of the nursing child, the nursing mother, the cat purring affectionately at the promise of food, sexual coupling, parental affection, feasts, harvests, trodden grapes, spilled cornucopias, the realm of *ubertas*. It is the realm of seasons and of climates. It is the realm that is expressed in the figures of Madonna and Child. But it is also to be seen, say, in the elder Breughel's engraving of Summer, with its avidity of plenty, the many acts and postures of food gathering, the seated peasant guzzling from a jug, his legs sprawling, his codpiece prominent, the woman bearing a laden basket on her head, her face obliterated, as though she were so harvest-minded that her very head had been transformed into the substance of the bounty she was carrying—a fullness everywhere: of generation the generosity.

The technological order of power would seem to represent all that attains its culmination in the faculty of intellection. In its noblest aspects, it is wisdom, reason: *veritas*. But as now reduced to a more restricted realm, it is the order of powers we encounter in the laboratory, the factory, the clinic, the draughting room, the broadcasting studio, the bank vault, the telephone exchange, the department store, the railway terminal, the files and archives. In its nobler aspects, it gives the realm of appetite its true maturity and control.

Yet would not our pair profit much by conversion into a triad? For surely there has been at least one other great order of power that has greatly stimulated men's terminologies of motives: the power of authority, *auctoritas*. Or, seen from another point of view, we could situate this motivational factor in the experience of *slavery*. Though we should want to put a different interpretation than Nietzsche upon the Nietzschean insights, surely we should agree that he is correct in stressing the part played by the motive of servitude in the shaping of the Christian ethic.

Indeed, might we not rightfully say that a most significant feature of the Christian terminology, developed probably from Stoicism, is its way of so merging concepts of servitude and freedom, of obligation and privilege, of obedience and rule, that the free man can be defined in terms of service, and the servant in terms of liberty?

Hence, lying across the order of production and of reproduction (intellection and love), and overlapping upon both, there is the order of authority, stimulating the imagination to think of motives in terms of law, tyranny, freedom, duty, inducement, compulsion, petition, obedience, submission and revolt. And as a term for an order that draws heavily upon the other two orders and is in turn drawn upon by it, "authority" designates it quite well, since the concept of the *auctor* includes both senses of originator, either as progenitor, father, ancestor, and the like, or as inventor, creator, maker, and the like, while out of both senses grows the third sense, the sense of the *auctor* as head or leader, from which we derive our usual meaning for "authority." It is the principle of group cohesion, and of cohesion among groups pitted against the group.

These overlapping areas covered by the terms can unquestionably become areas of conflict. Thus, whereas the contemporary scientific stress upon scenic terminologies of reduced circumference is an embodiment of *veritas,* the resultant cult of sheer correlation, in adding up to a dissolution of act, substance, person, becomes ultimately the antithesis of "love." The powers of fertility are replaced by the technological powers, which are devoid of natural appetite and sexual potency; they have in fact taught us all we know of sterilization.

There is perhaps no strictly logical reason why such an opposition should be felt. In strict logic, perhaps, the "love" and "knowledge" are simply in different planes, rather than being in opposition to each other. But as regards matters of Symbolic, since words have also incantatory effects, inviting men to make themselves over in the image of their imagery, the purely logical implications of reductionist terminologies take on new attributes, when translated into their equivalents in the realm of the imagination. Thus today the conception of man's consciousness as the battleground of supernatural struggles has been typically reduced to the conception of the brain as a battleground of the great motivational struggle between Microbes and Machines (with technology as a pattern for the macroscopic view, and protoplasm for the microscopic). And the cult of authority thus too often becomes an almost hysterical compensation for actual and impending impoverishments.

Indeed, looking back now upon the early theological controversy over the relation between faith and knowledge (*pistis* and *gnosis*), do we not, in the light of our present position in the long historical development from theology to science, begin to see how the Gnostics had triumphed, by implication, in the very setting of the issue? For both "faith" and "knowledge" are kinds of *knowledge;* both are thus strongly scenic in their emphasis. It requires no great gifts of prophecy now to see that the sloganizing of the controversy in terms of a relation between *pistis* and *gnosis* was implicitly a weighting on the side of *gnosis.* We grant, however, that this "prophecy" would be too tenuous if we could not refer to the course of events themselves as our corroboration.

Likewise when considering *justice,* we can readily see a conflict among the terms. Justice is properly under the sign of *veritas,* yet is forever in danger of being lost to a hysterically misused *auctoritas,* as with appeals to nation, class, and race. Or we could say that a truly personal principle is needed in justice, as with the conditions of family authority; but the vast texture of impersonal relations typical of our change from tribal living to the abstractions of the modern state make such conditions impossible. There is little reason to believe that justice is happily apportioned even in primitive clans, though we do find, as in the *Iliad,* much evidence of a pre-political equality, or sense of *personal* equality, which was familial in its origins, with authority vested in the ways of the clan as a whole, and "obeyed" by even the kings. "Justice" under conditions of economic inequality necessarily gravitates between an "ideal" and a rhetorical compensation, since it is not "substantiated" or grounded in the nature of the scene. The *Aeneid* ushers in the period of the Roman emperors by piously thinking of Roman motives in paternal terms *after* the business culture of the expanding Republic had quite obliterated the tribal culture, though the retention of the tribal terminology, throughout the days of the Republic, is clear enough in the name, Conscript Fathers, for the Roman Senate.

Love, Knowledge, Authority: three basic ideals, variously embodied in structures of power, and all liable to such transformations as make of them a mockery. As translated into the terms of social organization, they are necessarily somewhat at odds. But in moments of exaltation, ideally, we may think of them as a trinity, standing to one another in a relation of mutual reënforcement.

PART TWO

THE PHILOSOPHIC SCHOOLS

I

SCENE

The Featuring of the Terms

OUR program in this section is to consider seven primary philosophic languages in terms of the pentad, used as a generating principle that should enable us to "anticipate" these different idioms. In treating the various schools as languages, we may define their substantial relationship to one another by deriving them from a common terminological ancestor. This ancestor would be a kind of *lingua Adamica,* an Edenic "pre-language," in which the seeds of all philosophic languages would be implicit, as in the *panspermia* (or confusion of all future possibilities) that, according to some mystics, prevailed at the beginnings of the world.

In our introduction we noted that the areas covered by our five terms overlap upon one another. And because of this overlap, it is possible for a thinker to make his way continuously from any one of them to any of the others. Or he may use terms in which several of the areas are merged. For any of the terms may be seen in terms of any of the others. And we may even treat all five in terms of one, by "reducing" them all to the one or (what amounts to the same thing) "deducing" them all from the one as their common terminal ancestor. This relation we could express in temporal terms by saying that the term selected as ancestor "came first"; and in timeless or logical terms we could say that the term selected is the "essential," "basic," "logically prior" or "ultimate" term, or the "term of terms," etc.

Dramatistically, the different philosophic schools are to be distinguished by the fact that each school features a different one of the five terms, in developing a vocabulary designed to allow this one term full expression (as regards its resources and its temptations) with the other terms being comparatively slighted or being placed in the perspective of the featured term. Think, for instance, of a philosophy that had been established "in the sign of the agent." It must develop coördinates particularly suited to treat of substance and motive in "subjective," or "psychological" terms (since such terms deal most directly with the attributes of agents). Then think of that stage where the philosopher, proud in the full possession of his coördinates for featuring the realm of the *agent,* turned to consider the areas that fall most directly under the heading of *scene.* Instead of beginning over again, and seeking to analyze the realm of scene in terms that had no relation to the terms he had developed when considering the realm of agent, he might proceed to derive the nature of his terms for the discussion of scene from the nature of his terms for agent. This might well, in fact, be the procedure of a thinker who, instead of using a terminology that was merely slung together, felt the logical and aesthetic (and moral!) desire for an internal consistency among his terms. And it would amount to an "agentification" of scene even though the terms for scene were placed in dialectical opposition to the terms for agent. For a scene conceived antithetically to *agent* would differ from a scene conceived, let us say, antithetically to *act* or *purpose,* the genius of the ancestral term surviving even in its negation.

A rival philosophic terminology might propose to abandon this particular system of terms derived from agent, and to feature instead the area of motives covered by our term, scene. Its propounder could maintain that the terms imported from the area of agent were irrelevant or unwieldy as scenic references. However, principles of internal consistency might lead him to undertake imperialist expansions of his own, as were he to treat in scenic terms the areas directly covered by our terms agent or purpose.

These general examples should be enough, for the time being, to indicate what we mean by the featuring of a term. In this section we shall deal with the subject in some detail. But first surveying the entire field at a glance, let us state simply as propositions:

For the featuring of *scene,* the corresponding philosophic terminology is *materialism.*

For the featuring of *agent,* the corresponding terminology is *idealism.*

For the featuring of *agency,* the corresponding terminology is *pragmatism.*

For the featuring of *purpose,* the corresponding terminology is *mysticism.*

For the featuring of *act,* the corresponding terminology is *realism.*

Nominalism and *rationalism* increase the kinds of terminology to seven. But since we have used up all our terms, we must account for them indirectly.

Historically, nominalism stood in opposition to mediaeval realism. It was the individualistic counterpart of realism's "tribal" or "generic" emphasis. We would here widen the concept so as to include a corresponding "atomistic" movement in any of the other philosophies.

Rationalism is, in one sense, intrinsic to philosophy as a medium, since every philosophy attempts to propound a rationale of its position, even if it is a philosophy of the irrational. But more restrictedly, the term can be applied only to philosophies that treat reason as the very ground and substance of reality, somewhat as though, instead of saying, "a philosophy is a universe," one were to say, "the universe is a philosophy." The fact that rationalism, as a special philosophic strain, converts a *method* (i.e., agency) into a substance might well be the "grammatical reason" why our pragmatists descend from Hegel, who treated reason and world substance as so thoroughly identical that he proposed to recreate all history "in principle" by the sheer exercise of his philosophic method.

The addition of *nominalism* and *rationalism* to our list spoils the symmetry somewhat, for the first (as we extend its meaning) applies to all the other six schools insofar as each of them can have either a collectivistic or an individualistic ("nominalist") emphasis; and the second applies to all in the sense that it is the perfection, or logical conclusion, or *reductio ad absurdum* of the philosophic *métier*. One should also note that a philosophy may be "nominalist" or "rationalist" in one realm without necessarily being so in another—as materialism is usually atomistic in the physical realm, but may be quite collectivistic in the ethical or political realm. Similarly the mystic's merging of the One with the All would often make it difficult to say whether we should call his doctrine collectivistic or atomistic, if we stopped at this point; but there is clearly a great distinction between mystics whose doctrines lead to permanent isolation from other men, and those whose doctrines lead to the founding of religious orders.

The symmetry is also impaired by the fact that there has been much borrowing of terms among the various philosophic schools, so that one cannot always take even key terms at their face value. For instance, we have previously observed that "situation" is a synonym for "scene."

Hence one might take it as a rule that philosophies which account for motivations in terms of "the situation" are "materialistic." But the current prestige of the "situational" approach has led to the term's adoption by other schools. A literary critic who spoke of "the literary situation," for instance, meant not the "objective conditions" under which a writer writes, but the motives peculiar to a writer's medium. What looked "scenic" was here actually "pragmatic," since the writer's medium is an *agency*. And similarly, essayists now often speak of "the human situation" when they seem to have in mind the *motives peculiar to men as men,* a usage that would call for the classifying of the expression under the heading of *agent,* hence giving the *apparently* materialistic usage an *essentially* idealistic application (since, as we have said, idealism features the term agent).

Besides the concealments of misnomer and those due to mutual borrowings among the philosophic schools, there is an internal development that causes the nature of philosophy as an assertion to be lost in the problems of demonstration. That is, as soon as a philosopher has begun to investigate the possibilities in whatever term he has selected as his *Ausgangspunkt,* he finds that the term does not merely create other terms in its image. Also, it generates a particular set of *problems* —and the attempt to solve these problems may lead the philosopher far from his beginnings. It is somewhat, alas! as with the design for a perpetual motion machine. Such a design may have been quite simple in its original conception, but it becomes fantastically complex as the inventor finds that each new wheel or trip or pin or cam which he added to solve his problem gave rise to a new problem, and this in turn suggested the need of some other contrivance, which relieves his former embarrassments only by introducing a new embarrassment of its own.

Indeed, since all the terms of the pentad continually press for consideration, and since it is not possible for us, without contradiction, to recreate in words a world which is itself not verbal at all, we can safely accept it as an axiom that the mere attempt to contemplate persistently the resources of any one term will lead to the discovery of many problems the answers to which will *transcend* the genius of this term. And if a reader comes upon a philosophy after it has been thus sophisticated, he may find himself so caught up in its problems-atop-problems-atop-problems and problems-within-problems-within-problems that he cannot sense the principle of generation behind them. For usually the thinker himself has become similarly intricated.

But with the pentad as a generating principle, we may extricate ourselves from these intricacies, by discovering the kinds of *assertion* which the different schools would exemplify in a hypothetical state of purity. Once this approach is established, problems are much less likely to conceal the underlying design of assertion, or may even serve to assist in the characterizing of a given philosophic work.

Scene in General

In Baldwin's *Dictionary of Philosophy and Psychology,* materialism is defined as "that metaphysical theory which regards all the facts of the universe as sufficiently explained by the assumption of body or matter, conceived as extended, impenetrable, eternally existent, and susceptible of movement or change of relative position." The article also cites Hobbes: "All that exists is body, all that occurs motion." And Paulsen: "The reduction of psychical processes to physical is the special thesis of materialism." Similarly, the *Encyclopaedia Britannica* defines materialism as "the theory which regards all the facts of the universe as explainable in terms of matter and motion, and in particular explains all psychical processes by physical and chemical changes in the nervous system."

These citations make it obvious why one gets a materialistic philosophy by the featuring of our term, scene. We should add, however, that with materialism the circumference of scene is so narrowed as to involve the reduction of action to motion. That is, whether the materialist happens to believe in the existence of a personal God or not, he will employ a materialist vocabulary of motivation insofar as such a personal principle is omitted from the scope of the circumference. Thus the *Encyclopaedia Britannica* remarks: "It may perhaps be fairly said that materialism is at present a necessary methodological postulate of natural-scientific inquiry. The business of the scientist is to explain everything by the physical causes which are comparatively well understood and to exclude the interference of spiritual causes."

In his excellent pamphlet, *Aspects of Scientific Rationalism in the Nineteenth Century,* George de Santillana sums up the situation thus:

In the end, if we want to build up a science and not an animism, we are left with only one choice, which is the historical one: the atom must be quite dead, its substance devoid of all spontaneity.

Hobbes

With Democritus surviving only in fragments (an atomist philosopher who has left us but atoms of his philosophy), perhaps the most thorough and picturesque exemplar of a vocabulary conceived systematically in terms of "extension" is the philosophy of Hobbes, who sums up his materialism vigorously in the opening chapters of his *Leviathan:*

> Nature, the art whereby God hath made and governs the world, is by the *art* of man, as in many other things, so in this also imitated, that it can make an artificial animal. For seeing life is but a motion of limbs, the beginning whereof is in some principal part within; why may we not say, that all *automata* (engines that move themselves by springs and wheels as doth a watch) have an artificial life? For what is the heart, but a spring; and the nerves, but so many strings, and the joints, but so many wheels, giving motion to the whole body, such as was intended by the artificer?

Ironically, though Hobbes warns heatedly against the deceptions of metaphor, he is here in effect announcing that his book is to be organized about the metaphor of the machine, in taking it as the *Ausgangspunkt* of his vocabulary. Next he expands his figure into a proportion: as man is a machine, so the State is a gigantic man.

> Art goes yet further, imitating that rational and most excellent work of nature, man. For by art is created that great *Leviathan* called a *Commonwealth,* or *State,* in Latin *Civitas,* which is but an artificial man; though of greater stature and strength than the natural, for whose protection and defense it was intended—

whereupon he proceeds to trace such analogies between the human body and the body politic as recall the passages in the opening scene of *Coriolanus,* where Menenius Agrippa tells his parable of "a time when all the body's members / Rebell'd against the belly," and the belly answered its "incorporate friends," the other bodily parts, by showing how they profited in allowing it to remain "idle and unactive" instead of "bearing like labour" with the "other instruments."

That is, like the passage in Shakespeare, Hobbes' comparing of the sovereignty to an "artificial soul," of the magistrates to "artificial joints," of reward and punishment to the nerves, etc. is a figure of speech. But unlike Shakespeare's passage, it is at the same time meant to be taken literally. Or perhaps we should allow for a certain looseness of correspondence between the human body's parts and the political body's parts—but we are certainly meant to interpret the mechanistic vocabulary of human motives literally, as a few more examples can make clear beyond all question.

In the first chapter, "Of Sense," we are told that "The cause of sense is the external body, or object, which presseth the organ proper to each sense." The scenic emphasis is obvious in this reference to "external body, or object," as the motivational source. For the sensory qualities that objects seem to possess "are, in the object that causeth them, but so many several motions of the matter, by which it presseth our organs diversely. Neither in us that are pressed, are they anything else but diverse motions; for motion produceth nothing but motion."

We have cited Mr. De Santillana's reference to the scientific ideal of a "dead" atom. May we not discern a similar motive behind Hobbes' definition of imagination as "decaying sense"? That is, the imagining of things is a *weaker motion* than the sensing of things. "This decaying sense, when we would express the thing itself, I mean fancy itself, we call *imagination,* as I said before: but when we would express the decay, and signify that the thing is fading, old, and past, it is called *memory."*

Thoughts succeed one another because they are "motions within us," and motions lead into one another. "A *sign* is the evident antecedent of the consequent; and contrarily, the consequent of the antecedent, when like consequences have been observed before; and the oftener they have been observed, the less uncertain is the sign." This statement is meant to offer a mechanistic interpretation of learning and skill. "Besides sense, and thoughts, and the train of thoughts, the mind of man has no other motion; though by the help of speech, and method, the same faculties may be improved to such a height, as to distinguish men from all other living creatures."

In Chapter V he defines reason in terms of addition and subtraction. "When a man *reasoneth,* he does nothing else but conceive a sum total, from *addition* of parcels; or conceive a remainder, from subtraction of one sum from another; which, if it be done by words, is conceiving of the consequence of the names of all the parts, to the name of the whole; or from the names of the whole and one part, to the name of the other part." It is not necessary here to review his arguments for this proposition. For our purposes it is enough to discern the mechanistic genius in such definition, the reduction of reason itself to motion—and we can grasp the full significance of such reduction if we think of a comptometer not as the *product* of a rational man but as a *complete model* of reason itself.

Next, in contrast with the theological grammar of actions and passions, Hobbes undertakes to treat "the passions" themselves in terms of motion. He first distinguishes between "vital" motion (such as the processes of metabolism) and "animal" or "voluntary" motion, "as to go, to speak, to move any of our limbs in such manner as is first fancied in our minds." Since these latter motions "depend always upon a precedent thought of *whither, which way,* and *what,*" Hobbes locates their "first internal beginning" in the *imagination*. And imagination, we must remember, is "but the relics" of motion, "remaining after sense"; it is the kind of motion that, being weaker than the motions of sense, he has called "decaying sense." Such motion of the imagination is imperceptible as motion; "unstudied men do not consider any motion at all to be there"; nonetheless it is there—and "these small beginnings of motion, within the body of man, before they appear in walking, speaking, striking, and other visible actions, are called *endeavor.*"

He next subdivides endeavor into *appetite* and *aversion,* words which "we have from the Latins; and they both of them signify the motions, one of approaching, the other of retiring." He notes the same of the corresponding Greek words *hormē* and *aphormē.* In brief, he contends that we come closer to the real situation here by interpreting such words literally rather than by considering them simply as abstractions or dead metaphors. The appetites and aversions that characterize our endeavors are thus to be considered as real motions toward and "fromward" something. And the chapter proceeds to derive the various passions in terms of these "motions."

There is another passage which illustrates with special clarity the way in which materialism, or reduction to motion, is a treatment of personal motivations in terms of the *scenic,* explaining the *internal* in terms of *external* conditions:

As, in sense, that which is really within us, is, as I have said before, only motion, caused by the action of external objects; but in appearance—to the sight, light and color; to the ear, sound; to the nostril, odor, etc.: so, when the action of the same object is continued from the eyes, ears, and other organs to the heart, the real effect there is nothing but motion, or endeavor; which consisteth in *appetite* or *aversion,* to or from the object moving. But the appearance, or sense, of that motion is that we either call *delight* or *trouble* of mind.

This "motion" of delight, he says, seems to be "a corroboration of vital motion"; and things are called offensive, "from hindering and troubling the motion vital."

From this point on, I must admit, the perfect symmetry of our case is impaired. However, Hobbes's intention is clear enough; namely: the reduction of the will itself to terms of a scene mechanically determined. For he defines will as "the last appetite in deliberating." As I understand his position, one might illustrate it thus: Imagine trying to make a decision in a situation where one felt a conflict of appetite and aversion. If one put his appetite on one side of the balance and his aversion on the other, the balance would tip to whichever side was the heavier. The resulting "decision" would thus follow mechanically from the disproportion in the weight of the conflicting motives. And what we interpreted as an act of the free will would be in reality but the necessary triumph of a stronger motion over a weaker motion. I speak of the symmetry being impaired, however, because precisely at this point we find Hobbes speaking not of "motion" but of "action":

In deliberation, the last appetite or aversion immediately adhering to the action, or to the omission thereof, is that we call the *will,*—the act, not the faculty, of willing. And beasts that have deliberation, must necessarily also have will. The definition of the will given commonly by the Schools, that it is a *rational appetite,* is not good. For if it were, then could there be no voluntary act against reason. For a *voluntary act* is that which proceedeth from the will, and no other. But if instead of a rational appetite, we shall say an appetite resulting from a precedent deliberation, then the definition is the same that I have given here. *Will,* therefore, *is the last appetite in deliberating.* And though we say in common discourse, a man had a will once to do a thing, that nevertheless he forbore to do; yet that is properly but an inclination, which makes no action voluntary; because the action depends not of it, but of the last inclination or appetite.

To some extent, Hobbes here speaks of "action" rather than "motion" simply as a way of avoiding confusion. He is aiming to place a new interpretation upon a subject traditionally discussed in theological rather than mechanistic terms—and he uses the traditional expression as a convenience of discourse. That is, he is talking about a subject that usually goes by the name of "voluntary action," and he designates it accordingly. And if, as we have noted, even mechanics several centuries after Hobbes would speak of a motor's "action" without having the full significance of the term act in mind, we might well expect that Hobbes, so close to the heyday of the dramatistic vocabulary employed by the scholastics, and so close to its esthetic secularization in Elizabethan poetry, would speak now and then of human "actions," particularly in a chapter on human "passions." In any case, the whole point of his philosophy is the explanation of such actions in terms of motion. And even though he refers to the consequences of the will as "acts," his mechanistic reduction of the will itself brings his whole conception quite close to the metaphysics of modern behaviorist psychology (which has likewise literally interpreted the concept of *hormē,* as evident in its term, "hormone," to name the factors affecting what Hobbes would probably have called "vital motion").

There is another reason for the partial break in symmetry here. We have said that, when a philosopher would feature one of the terms, recreating the others in its image, the original claims of these other terms are nonetheless still in the offing. Now, when one talks of the will, one is necessarily in the field of the *moral;* and the field of the moral is, by definition, the field of *action.* A billiard ball is neither moral nor immoral, for it cannot act, it can only move, or be moved. We shall return to the matter when we consider the philosophy of Emmanuel Kant, who expended vast ingenuity upon precisely this problem of allowing personal action (moral freedom) in a world of mechanical motion. At the moment it is enough to note that Hobbes, by carrying his theories of mechanism into the moral realm, is necessarily treading upon domains more directly governed by our terms act and agent.

Indeed, he is to go even farther in this direction, for he is to tell us of salvation, "Of What Is Necessary for Man's Reception into the Kingdom of God," a naturally dramatistic concern, as we realize when we recall the Church's drama of salvation. True, he says that "perfect obedience would be enough because the kingdom of heaven is shut to none but sinners; that is to say, to the disobedient, or transgressors of the law." Not even faith in Christ would be necessary, if our obedience were perfect. So we could get to heaven purely by obeying the moral and civil laws with the mechanical accuracy that natural objects exemplify in obeying the laws of motion. Thus the scenic genius is maintained to the end, with as near a symmetry as the pressure of the other terms will permit.

Be that as it may, it was our purpose here to account for the presence of the term action in a philosophy of motion. In part, we say, it was but a loose usage, to designate kinds of "motion" that were traditionally called "actions." And in part it may have been a response to the pressure of the moral category itself, which is essentially dramatic, and may be expected to make its dramatic genius felt even in a philosophy that aims programmatically to transform the dramatic into the mechanical. In brief, there is a purely technical reason why the term, act, should encroach here. For at this point Hobbes is turning from the realm of metaphysics to the realm of politics and ethics. And even were it established that men are pure automata, one might still contend that the realm of political and ethical relations calls "naturally" for treatment in terms of *action*. That is, insofar as ethics is treated *in its own terms,* as a special context of inquiry, rather than being reduced to nonethical terms, one is pledged in advance to discourse on the subject of action and passion. For that is what the study of ethics is.

Spinoza

Spinoza's naturalistic *Ethics* is central, as seen from this point of view. For could not his basic synonymy, "God equals Nature" (*Deus sive Natura*) be with justice ambiguously translated as "action equals motion"? Again, our translating of God as an "action" word will seem obvious when one considers Kant, who grounds morality (i.e., action) on the three terms, God, freedom, and immortality. Of these three, "immortality" would stand for the nature of the soul, hence serving as a high word for *agent;* and "God" names the kind of scene in which, by the logic of the scene-act ratio, an action would be possible; namely: a scene allowing for human *freedom*. The empirical realm, on the other hand, is for Kant the realm of causality in keeping with the laws of physical motion as defined in Newton's celestial mechanics, in brief the realm of strict *necessity*.

More directly, we could get God as a scenic word for action by re-calling again the scholastic formula for God as the ground of all pos-sibility. As for the Spinozist equating of God and Nature, we might best see beyond our contemporary over-naturalistic usage by thinking of "Nature" also in the sense we have in mind when we speak of a person's or a poem's nature. A thing's "nature" is thus necessarily one with the thing. We have found Spinozistic naturalism particularly engrossing, from the dramatistic point of view. For it characterizes to perfection the great watershed moment in Western thought when men were narrowing the scope of their terminologies as *per* the Oc-camite law of parsimony. Theologically, this amounted to the narrow-ing of the circumference from a scene comprising both creation and creator to a scene comprising creation alone. And since the creation had already been enacted, such a narrowing of the scenic frame meant in turn simply an examination of the world's *constitution,* a constitu-tion which was just what it was, regardless of whether it had originally been enacted by a divine superagent or was the result of cosmic accident, or was a mere set of *relations without substance.* In other words, even if one still chose to think of it as having originally been *enacted,* it was now to be studied, from without, as a regular concatenation of *events.* Dramatistically this narrowing meant the shift from a poetic or moral-istic vocabulary of action and passion to a scientific or mechanistic vocabulary of motion.

The exquisiteness of the Spinozistic terms resides in the fact that his key equation, by our interpretation, serves as a bridge across this gap. In effect, it equates a wider frame with a narrower one. For tradi-tionally "God" is a wider term than "Nature," being the metaphysical scene or ground of Nature's existence. But by proclaiming the two circumferences to be identical in scope, Spinoza leaves you somewhat undecided whether he has naturalized God or deified Nature. The thought readily suggests why pantheism provides a perfect transition from theistic to naturalistic vocabularies of motives. And we can also see why materialists could claim Spinoza as one of themselves, by stressing the Nature side of the equation (as Western thought itself was to do progressively in the following centuries). For "God" as so conceived is a scenic term *par excellence,* and a scenic term of narrowed circumference.

On the other hand, the very fact that Spinoza's naturalism is primarily *ethical* in its stress (in contrast, for instance, with the Galilean physics) invited him to use the vocabulary of action and passion, and not glancingly as with Hobbes at moments when his strict reduction to motion became unwieldy, but formally and systematically, with a whole structure of terms developed in accordance with such dramatistic logic. In fact, one might well derive the entire alignment of terms in Spinoza by putting his word "action" on one side of the ledger and his word "passion" on the other, and treating the doctrines in his *Ethics* as a noble philosophic accountancy whereby, through the cultivation of "adequate ideas," one could transform the passives (of human bondage) into the actives (of human freedom).

Unfortunately, almost as soon as we say this, we must retract somewhat. For if Spinoza would not, like Hobbes, reduce action to motion, he has a non-dramatic ideal of his own, conceived after the analogy of geometry, as in his famous remark at the opening of Book III, where he pledges himself to treat of human actions and appetites as though it were a matter of lines, planes, and solids. This, as he says elsewhere, admonishes us to drop the concept of *purpose* from the philosophy of Nature, since mathematics is concerned not with final causes, but solely with the essences and properties of figures, thereby showing men a different standard of truth than is got by the treatment of the world as an instance of divine purpose. Thus "the reason or cause why God or nature exists, and the reason why he acts, are one and the same"; whereby the concept of *purpose* retreats behind the concept of *rational necessity.* But though action in the full sense of the term is impossible without purpose, leave me the term *Reason* in a philosophy, and you can have *purpose,* so far as the needs of a terminology of action are concerned. For there is purpose enough implicit in the very concept of Reason. Indeed, Reason is as essentially dramatistic a term as Substance, the key word of the entire Spinozistic terminology. Thus, "Reason" too is as transitional a term in Spinoza as is the God-Nature equation itself, and allows for a devoutly purposive surrender to a God whose acts are not *purposive,* but *inevitable.*

Spinoza's opening definitions, defining God or Substance as the *self-caused,* could be said to contain, in telescoped form, what is stated analytically in the *Deus sive Natura* equation. The Latin is *causa sui,* "cause of itself"—and you will note that in this key expression there is both an active and a passive significance. As *cause* it is active. But the self that is thus caused is the object or result or recipient of the cause, hence passive. Hence, God-and-Nature in the totality has, from the purely grammatical point of view, an active and a passive meaning rolled into one.

We encounter the form again in Spinoza's use of the distinction between *natura naturans* and *natura naturata* ("naturing nature" and "natured nature"—or perhaps we could say "the producer" and "the product," though remembering that in Spinoza they are one and the same). If "naturing" is active and "natured" is passive, what grammatically is the third, or ground terms of this expression, "nature"?

When confronting such dialectical embarrassments, I always like to recall a treaty which Fascist Italy made with some of the small neighboring countries. By the fictions of national sovereignty, all the signatories to this treaty were equal in their rights and dignity. By the realities of the political and economic situation, Italy was much the strongest of the signatories, hence able to make her voice heard above the others. And this state of affairs was expressed by the decision that all the signatories were equal, but Italy was "foremost among the equals" (*primus inter pares*). And so, whenever in philosophy I see two terms, of opposite and equal importance, being merged into a third term that will somehow contain the nature of both, I always ask myself: "Which of the two equal terms was foremost?" For I will expect the genius of this term to weight the third term (as Schelling's third term, "subject-object," supposedly "indifferent" to the two terms "subject" and "object" which it combines, is more "subjective" than "objective," even though he would further complicate matters by distinguishing between a "subjective subject-object" and an "objective subject-object").

In Spinoza's case, I would say that, at least as far as human limitations are concerned, though "God" is "active nature" (*natura naturans,* Spinoza's equivalent of the Creator) and God's *modes* (the concatenation of particular things and events we encounter in the vicissitude of history) are "passive nature" (*natura naturata,* his equivalent of the Creation) the essence of this active-passive pair is *active*. The world of God's *modes* (the *substantiae affectiones*) is none other than the world of Hobbes's *motions* (as see Book I, Prop. XXXII, where will and intellect are specifically placed in the category of motion. Hence we see that, at the strategic moment in his God-Nature, or action-motion equation, Spinoza differs from Hobbes in shifting to the *action* side of the pair.

We should here note a further important change which one can arrive at quickly and crudely, in a non-Spinozistic kind of dialectic, in observing that the expression, "causa sui," can be stressed two ways: either *"causa* sui" or "causa *sui."* The first gives us the active interpretation: we act, or are free "insofar as we are the adequate cause of what takes place either within us or outside us." The stress upon *sui* gives us the passive interpretation, of the self as caused—and we are constrained insofar as we are affected by other causes. (*At contra nos pati dico, cum in nobis aliquid fit, vel extra nostra natura aliquid sequitur, cujus nos non nisi partialis sumus causa.*) That is, if we are but the *partial* cause of something, we are constrained or passive to the extent of this partiality. It has already been noted how by putting the active and passive together, Spinoza gets an *active* significance for the over-all concept of Substance or the Absolute Being that embraces all passives as well (the passives or modes being, in fact, but the *parts* of the whole; for Spinoza considers the whole as logically prior to its parts, hence as their cause). But if one thinks simply of the cause and the caused in general, he will quickly see that of the two the term "cause" would contain connotations of action and freedom, while "caused" would contain the connotations of passivity and constraint.

The seventh definition of Book I gives us explicit justification for equating action with freedom and passion with necessity, since Spinoza there defines "free" things and "necessary" or "determined" things quite as he defines active and passive in the above citations from Book III, on the human "affections." Or we might state the matter somewhat non-Spinozistically by saying that the relation of part to whole is always *necessary,* but the necessary can take either "benign" or "malign" forms. We are "free" insofar as our understanding of natural (= rational) necessity leads us to greater virtue (in effect making natural law "benign").

The philosophy as a whole could thus be considered as an enterprise for so changing our attitude towards the world that we can be in the direction of peace rather than in the direction of war. The change is to be prepared by vigorous intellectual means rather than by a mere "change of heart." And to grasp the quality of the freedom of action aimed at, I think it relevant to remember that in the mediaeval terminologies of motives *contemplation* is an act. And although Spinoza's ideas of action are close to the Baconian knowledge-power equation, they are much nearer to the mediaeval ideals of contemplation than to the notions of action that go with our current political, commercial, and technological pragmatisms. The situation of which he considered himself necessarily a part was metaphysical, even theological, transcending the view of motives one gets by consideration merely of contingencies.

The point we were trying to make by our rough shifting of stress might be made still clearer if, instead of *causa sui* as the definition of God ("that whose essence involves its existence"), we used the equivalent expression, "cause of the caused." If then "God" is made to equal *everything* (as the term is treated in Spinoza's pantheistic concept of the universal scene) the "cause" and the "caused" are all *"necessarily"* bound up together, and God's "freedom" as *cause* is one with his *necessary* relation to the *caused*. For, grammatically at least, a cause needs a caused as truly as a caused needs a cause. Hence, we get the equating of freedom and necessity, *God's freedom* being synonymous with the strict *regularity of Nature,* an equation that has given much trouble to those who would use it empirically, without concern for its metaphysical, dialectical, grammatical origins. If God is everything, he both *is free* to be what he is and *must be* what he is. He is free since there is no other cause to constrain him, but by reason of this very freedom he must *necessarily* be himself. In his freedom he is perfect, and what else can the perfect or ultimate be but perfect or ultimate? For that is inevitably its Nature.

However, recalling our earlier concerns with the tactics of the Creation, we might refer again to a passage in Prof. Lovejoy's *The Great Chain of Being*, discussing St. Augustine's reasons for locating the point of origin in God's *will*. Augustine considered as impious any attempt to state God's motives: for if the act of creation had been determined by any motive, even if it but had its ground in the "divine essence," to this extent it would not have been free. To be free, the act must be ab-

solutely unmotivated. Prof. Lovejoy cites from Augustine a sorites
that runs:

> Where there is no insufficiency (need, want, lack, *indigentia*),
> there is no necessity; where there is no defect, there is no insuf-
> ficiency; but in God there is no defect, hence no necessity.

The whole matter looks so different in Spinoza because of the pantheistic merger whereby he puts God and Nature together in a "necessary"
relation. And though he treats God as "logically prior" to the Creation
(or in Spinoza's term, the *modes*), opponents of Spinoza have claimed
that such strict necessity is really a two-way relationship, so that God's
existence as a perfect whole depends upon any single one of the parts.

"Determination" in Spinoza can be best grasped by thinking of it in
the most literal sense. A thing is determined insofar as it is limited
by the boundaries of other things, determined by whatever outside itself marks its terminations. Spinoza's concern with geometry goes
much deeper than the mere borrowing of Euclid's stylistic devices, as
when he presents his philosophy *more geometrico* by the use of axioms,
propositions, demonstrations, corollaries, scholia, and the like. It is
geometrical also in the sense that it is essentially scenic or contextual; indeed, from the terministic point of view, his word for "God" might
well be translated "total context." And the world of our everyday
finite experience, the world of *positive* things like apples, houses, people,
is in the Spinozistic vocabulary a world of "negations," because each
such positive thing is *determined,* and the determined is that which has
its boundaries marked by other things, in brief by things that this
particular thing is *not*. Hence his formula, "all determination is negation." And as an interesting variant of the "negative theology" stemming from the Neo-Platonists, he attributes the use of negative names
for God to weaknesses of intelligence and the resultant errors of imagination (for Spinoza, like most philosophers prior to romanticism,
placed imagination, and its partner, memory, much closer to sheer
brute sensation than to insight or vision). To quote from his treatise
On the Improvement of the Understanding:

> Since words are a part of the imagination—that is, since we form
> many conceptions in accordance with confused arrangements of
> words in the memory, dependent on particular bodily conditions—

there is no doubt that words may, equally with the imagination, be the cause of many and great errors, unless we keep strictly on our guard. Moreover, words are formed according to popular fancy and intelligence, and are, therefore, signs of things as existing in the imagination, not as existing in the understanding. This is evident from the fact that to all such things as exist only in the understanding, not in the imagination, negative names are often given, such as incorporeal, infinite, etc. So, also, many conceptions really affirmative are expressed negatively, and *vice versa,* such as uncreate, independent, infinite, immortal, etc., inasmuch as their contraries are much more easily imagined, and, therefore, occurred first to men, and usurped positive names.

But though finite beings are ultimately to be located in terms of their total context (a context that, being conceived as positive, gives the corresponding conception of finite, determinate things as negative) there is also a device in Spinoza whereby their individual natures can be accounted for. This is the *conatus in suo esse perseverandi,* the endeavor of each being to continue being. Just as the Infinite Substance goes on forever, so every finite or determinate mode of Substance would forever persist in its nature, if its existence were not terminated by the boundaries imposed upon it by other determinate things. In brief, each part would be as eternal as the whole, if it were not for the encroachments of the other parts. Accordingly, insofar as it can be considered in itself, each determinate part seeks by its very nature as a being to endure for ever. We might translate this metaphysical principle into a blunt biological equivalent, thus: Each thing will seek to preserve its nature as long as it can, and will succeed until it is destroyed by factors beyond its control. But though this is the implication of the Spinozist *conatus,* we must remember that he modifies it by placing it in a much wider circumference than a strictly naturalistic reduction of a Darwinian sort.

This concept of the *conatus* performs the function regularly covered by our term *agent.* That is, it gives us the equivalent of a motivational locus situated *within* the individual person or thing, since a thing's being or essence is intrinsic to it. However, the principle is scenically derived, in the sense that it is but a limited application of his definition for the total context, God, Nature, Substance, the Self-Caused, whose essence is identical with its existence (*cujus essentia involvit existentiam*), which is to say that by its very nature it goes on existing.

Thus, we have observed the *scene* function modified first to account for the functions of *act* (in being treated in terms of action and passion), and next to account for the functions of *agent*. Shifting the stress, as a rough approximate we could say that individual things would go on forever in their capacity as parts of the *whole*, but they are restricted in their capacity as *parts* of the whole. The essay *On the Improvement of the Understanding* perhaps, best brings out the conversion of scenic resources to cover the functions of *agency*, as it is concerned with the ways in which the intellect, influenced by *external* causes, "makes for itself intellectual instruments"—and the essay treats of *methods* for improving these instruments. Also, his treatment of good and evil in terms of utility and hindrance respectively has a strongly pragmatist possibility. In the preface to Book IV, he calls good an agency (*medium*); and elsewhere he says that nothing is more "useful" to a man who would live rationally than his fellow-men who are guided by reason. The non-pragmatist nature of the philosophy as a whole, however, is seen in the closing proposition, which defines blessedness (*beatitudo*) not as the reward of virtue (*virtutis praemium*), but as virtue itself. As for *purpose:* it is apparent that the endeavor towards self-preservation provides at least for a stimulus in the purely biological sense, and we shall see that the equating of self-preservation with action and the development of adequate ideas gives us purpose in the rational sense, though the concept of a cosmic purpose is dissolved in the concept of rational *necessity* (as against its reduction to mechanical necessity in Hobbes).

Leibniz, confronting this same embarrassment whereby the notion of a completely rational relation between Creator and Creation dissolves purpose into rational necessity, solved the problem by introducing, along with his *principe de nécessité,* a *principe de convenance,* postulating ideas of *fitness* on the part of God which made God more of a creative agent than a necessary scene, and hence would move us into the areas of idealism proper. But in the preface and seventh definition of Book IV, Spinoza explains how he would reduce even individual human purpose to purely necessitarian terms: for he treats human *ends,* or final causes, simply as *necessary* human *desires.* This formulation, you will note, leads quite readily into the pragmatist interpretation of purpose in terms of *agency,* the recognition of *ends* being in pragmatism but a *means* for man's social and biological adjustment to his needs.

As the concept of the *conatus* is modified by the other aspects of Spinoza's terminology, it has in it something of Stoic grandeur, a high ethical quality that stresses the moral value of *endurance*. Indeed, "endurance" is quite an apt synonym for the Spinozistic *conatus* or "endeavor"; for it possesses both biological and moral meanings, as a term typical of the God-Nature equation should. The Stoics brought out more the idea of *sufferance,* Spinoza suggests rather the will to *survive* one's sufferings, the Stoics thus stressing the *passive* aspect of endurance while Spinoza stresses its nature as *activity*.

Again, we may see how Spinoza's term stands at a watershed moment, for in keeping with his emphasis, "virtue" in Spinoza is equated with *power of action*. His usage does not take us back as far as its original reference (previously discussed) to the power of the warrior; but he does sufficiently redefine the term to conclude from his definition that neither humility nor repentance are virtues, since neither of them is rational, for both involve situations wherein our power of activity is checked. Deprived of its modifiers, such a concept of virtue might be successively transformed until we come to extreme transvaluations of value, as with cults of naturalist expansion, or the characteristically modern impatience with "frustration." But, as modified by all the other key terms in Spinoza's philosophy, the concept leads to the very opposite of the militant: a philosophy of exceptional tolerance, peace, and moderation. And our concern with circumferences of placement should admonish us always to watch, in a given writer, the full orbit of his terms.

Alignment of Terms in Spinoza

Before closing our remarks on Spinoza, we should comment on the fact that, after all these pages, we have hardly mentioned what people seem to note most of all in Spinoza; namely: his relation to the Cartesian dualism, as shown in the distinction between *thought* and *extension*. According to Spinoza, God has infinite attributes; but only two of them are mentioned, the Cartesian mind-body pair. But Spinoza's position at a watershed moment is to be interpreted not merely in terms of the historical streams that have followed him. Admittedly, if we look only at this latter side of the watershed, his reconversion of Descartes' dualism into a monism of one Substance looks central. Leibniz has said: "No substance without action, no body without motion," a formula made to order for our purposes. And the Cartesian dualism was certainly the future in the sense that it led eventually into the subject-object pair of German idealism, and so finally to Hegel's programmatic replacement of "substance" by "Subject." But in its actual proportions his *Ethics,* just as this work is in itself, considered without reference to subsequent developments in history, is as much a *theology* as it is an instance of naturalism; and herein resides its dramatistic stress upon problems of action and passion, rather than the scientist stress upon knower and known (subject and object).

Indeed, if you start trying to trace the alignments in Spinoza's philosophy from the scientist point of view, rather than from the dramatist point of view, thus starting from the mind-body pair rather than the action-passion pair, you will find yourself quickly involved in confusion. Later in the history of philosophy, the problem becomes simple, as mind is flatly equated with the active and body flatly equated with the passive. But Spinoza's philosophic enterprise (in equating *idea* with *ideatum,* the "order and connection of ideas" with the "order and connection of things," and in treating both thought and extension as attributes of God) cuts across this on the bias. The mind, he tells us at the beginning of Book III, is more passive in proportion as it possesses inadequate ideas, and more active in proportion as it possesses adequate ideas. There is in us exactly as much mental activity as there is bodily activity, and exactly as much mental passivity as bodily passivity. Desire is simply the consciousness of bodily appetite. It is man's essence to desire, hence the striving for self-preservation is simultaneously physical and mental. Pleasure is as truly a passive in his system as is pain, the difference being that pleasure accompanies a transition towards greater perfection (it is in the direction of greater reality, or power of action) and pain accompanies a transition towards less perfection. Intellect and will are both passive.

Consequently, there can be no alignment of terms constructed by derivation from the quasi-scientific Cartesian pair (thought and extension). But the alignment constructed about the "pre-scientific" (or "extra-scientific") pair, the alignment sought in accordance with dramatistic admonitions, is almost pat. For instance:

ACTIVE	PASSIVE
self-caused	externally caused
infinite (positive)	finite (negative)
God (Substance)	modes
natura naturans	*natura naturata*
freedom	bondage
(that is free which exists solely by the necessity of its own nature; its actions are determined by itself alone)	(that is constrained which is determined by something external to itself to a fixed and definite kind of existence or action)
existence in itself (eternity)	existence in something else
conceived through itself *	conceived through something else
indivisibility (the whole, One)	division (the parts)
intrinsic	extrinsic
reason and intuition	intellect (except the absolute intellect), will, opinion, imagination
perfection	imperfection (but see qualifying remarks in preface to Book IV)
virtue (= power)	infirmity
good (in harmony with our nature)	bad (contrary to our nature)
useful to man	hurtful to man
determined to actions by reason	determined to actions by emotion
adequate ideas**	inadequate ideas

The list is not exhaustive. And it fails to indicate the third element in the design, the bridging devices for translating us from the bondage of the passions to the sovereignty of action. For such a function there is necessarily an ambiguous term that pontificates by leading into both realms. This function is performed in human agents by the *conatus,* the endeavor (and its corresponding desires) of each man to survive. Since men are necessarily but *parts* of the total divine Substance, the human essence is limited, and our desires are beset by confused and inadequate ideas. To this extent, the desires that characterize our nature

---

* The stress upon the self, once Spinoza's theological qualifications have been dropped away, can lead into ideals of independence individualistically conceived, and thus eventually into the "self-expression" movements of modern art.

** The mediaeval "principle of generation" is familial in its thinking; the "principle of adequation" is contextual, and as eventually simplified can be seen to lead into the Semanticist ideal of a naming adequate to the named. Spinoza's notion of the adequate, however, is ethical (and with placement in a total context of action), whereas the Semanticist version of the adequate is empirical (as with the word "house" when applied to something that really is a house).

fall on the side of the passions. But insofar as we do acquire adequate ideas, our endeavor can lead to action, power, virtue, perfection, the rational way of life. The terminology pontificates here by allowing for varying proportions of activity and passivity, whereby the human nature can pass from one side of our ledger to the other *paulatim et gradatim*. This locus of transition is, fittingly, treated in the third part of the five-part work. With parts I and II having defined the universal ground out of which this principle of individual conversion is derived, we encounter the derivation itself in the middle part; whereupon we are equipped to consider in parts IV and V its application in transforming bondage into freedom.

Here occurs that remarkable list, "Definitions of the Emotions," (or "affections"), beginning with the statement that "desire is the very essence of man," and constructed about three primary emotions: desire, pleasure, and pain. Here is the most ingeniously scholastic of all scholasticisms: "Love is pleasure, accompanied by the idea of an external cause." The list with its comments contains in itself a whole moral philosophy. The pleasant emotions are treated as transitions towards greater perfection (greater activity), the painful ones as transitions towards less perfection (greater passivity). All told, they are such as Wonder, Contempt, Love, Hate, Aversion, Devotion, Hope, Fear, Confidence, Despair, Joy, Disappointment, Pity, Indignation, Envy, Sympathy.

Only emotions of pleasure can be attributable to the mind as wholly active, and these are summed up as Strength of Character (*Fortitudo*). This is subdivided into Spirit (*Animositas*) and Generosity or group-mindedness (*Generositas*), each of which acts solely in accordance with Reason, the first being directed towards the preservation of one's own being (hence embracing such traits as temperance, sobriety, and presence of mind), while the second aims at the good of others (as with courtesy and mercy). Action, as so conceived, involving as it does the rational consideration of all human necessities in terms of the divine totality, is for Spinoza the same as Piety and Religion.

However, in our zeal to show that the action-passion pair is better able to reveal the structure of Spinoza's thought than the mind-body (*cogitatio-extensio*) pair, we must not go too far. For it is quite true that, in merging the Cartesian dualism back into a monism, Spinoza encountered the *primus inter pares* pattern, and as a result, although he would programmatically treat mind and body as equals, mind comes out with two votes to body's one. For body but represents itself, whereas mind can represent both body and itself. Or otherwise put, there are bodies, ideas of bodies, and ideas of ideas. Or in Spinoza's terms: "In God there is necessarily an idea which expresses the essence of this or that human body *sub aeternitatis specie.*" And though we question the value of the mind-body pair in revealing the basic outline of Spinoza's thought, we willingly grant that it must always be considered as the important complicating factor.

Particularly as we move towards the close of the Ethics, we encounter an exaltation much like the Platonist *transcendence* of body. Thus we are told in Prop. XXIII of Book V that "The human mind cannot be destroyed absolutely with the body, but there remains of it something which is eternal." This clearly moves us in the direction of idealism.

However, when we turn to idealism proper, and consider how thorough and strategic the stress upon the function of agent can be, I think we shall see that, by comparison, Spinoza even here is *scenic.* For he is saying always that we have eternity by reason of our natures as parts of a non-personal *whole* (just as, shifting the stress, we perish by reason of our natures as *parts* of a whole). This *contextual* emphasis is always uppermost. His formula for the highest kind of action, the "intellectual love of God," might be grammatically defined as "seeing particulars in their particularity, but remembering always that this particularity is grounded in a total context, and thus is to be understood in terms of this total context." Stated in Spinoza's theological terms it runs: (Book V. Prop. XXIV) "The more we understand particular things, the more we understand God." For (I, XXV, corollary) individual things are nothing but the modes (*modi*) in which God's attributes are expressed in a particular and determinate manner (*certo et determinato modo*).

Perhaps we can appreciate how the scenic emphasis is maintained, even towards the idealistic close of the *Ethics,* if we consider Spinoza's notion of "intuitive knowledge"; for the concept of "intuition" is especially rich in idealistic possibilities. (In fact, the changing values of this word, as we move into romantic philosophy, are as responsive as the changing values of "imagination.") Spinoza distinguished three kinds of knowledge. The first is that of opinion, or imagination, and is inadequate. The second kind is Reason—but higher than Reason stands Intuition, which "proceeds from an adequate idea of the absolute essence of certain attributes of God to the adequate knowledge of the essence of things." (Book II, Prop. XL. Note II). To understand things by this third kind of knowledge is the "highest endeavor of the mind and the highest virtue." Spinoza refers to it as the "eyes of the mind." And it is the kind of knowledge that leads to Spinoza's crowning motive, the intellectual love of God.

Spinoza illustrates the difference in the three forms of knowledge by taking the proportion "1:2::3: ? ." A tradesman, he says, multiplies the second number by the third and divides the product by the first, thus getting 6 as his answer, because he remembers being told to proceed in this way. This would be the lowest form of knowledge, and is the source of error. Or one might proceed in accordance with the demonstration in "the nineteenth proposition of the seventh book of Euclid," concerning the general property of proportionals. This would be the way of Reason. Or we may see the answer at a glance (*uno intuitu*), from the sheer nature of the relation itself (*ex ipsa ratione*).

We shall appreciate the full idealistic possibilities in the concept of intuition when we come to consider the Kantian treatment of knowledge. But note that in Spinoza intuition is derived from *Reason,* the third kind of knowledge being in his system acquired through perfection in the second kind of knowledge—and this second kind of knowledge, or Reason, is thoroughly *scenic.* The first meaning for *ratio* given in Harper's dictionary refers to the reckoning, calculating, and computing of things. Derivatively it came to signify business matters, transactions, affairs. Then respect, regard, consideration for things. Then course, conduct, procedure, manner, method. The conditions or nature of something could be called its *ratio.* Finally we move into such meanings as the faculty of mental action, judgment, understanding, reason. Thence to reasonableness, law, rule, order. And finally, theory, doctrine, system *based* on reason, science, knowledge.

Some of the meanings in the Du Cange *Glossarium Mediae et Infimae Latinitatis* are: thing, authority (*ditio*), ownership, goods, faculties, genus, offspring.

But most important of all for our purposes, one can appreciate the strongly *scenic* significance of Spinoza's usage in particular, by recalling that he equates the *logically* necessary with the *naturally* necessary. Similarly, Spinoza says that God is "naturally prior" (*prior natura*) to his modes where we today would say "logically prior." And though, by the time we reach Rousseau's *Emile,* "nature" itself is transformed from a scene word to an agent word (referring to the principles of growth inherent in human nature), it is obvious that in Spinoza's monistic ways human nature is treated simply as a special case of nature in general, hence a function of scene.

To be sure, when we say that Spinoza derives Intuition from Reason, the dramatistic grammar warns us that any derivation itself is open to two interpretations. As per the paradox of substance, a derivative may be treated as either consistently or divisively derived from its source. By the time we get to Bergson, for instance, it is hard to distinguish a super-rational "intuition" from a sub-rational "instinct." And recall the many early theological battles about the rival claims of "faith" and "knowledge," battles due to a distrust of rational knowledge as being directly inimical to religious insight. Similarly, in contrast with the rationalist claim that intuitive knowledge is the ultimate reward of rational knowledge, we encounter in esthetic theory the "instinctual" artist who, naturally expressive in some medium, resolutely refuses to look a gift horse in the mouth by the study of his craft in conceptual terms. And the psychology books tell of a prodigy who, able to extract cube roots spontaneously (*uno intuitu*) without knowing how he arrived at his results, lost this ability when a kind and helpful savant taught him how to extract cube roots methodically. But any readers sharing the Bergsonian fear that the rational may be the very death of the intuitive are invited at this point to use these very misgivings as an aid toward seeing that Spinoza's position is exactly the opposite of this, though Bergson himself did not think so. The intuition that in his terminology transcends reason is considered not as negating the source which it transcends, but as the ultimate completion or fulfilment of reason.

Darwin

We have observed in Hobbes a nearly symmetrical instance of *scenic* featuring. We could have brought out the encroachment of the *agent* function by examining his theories of monarchy, though he keeps his politics quite scenically infused by defining liberty as "external impediments of motion"; and his famous scenic formula, "the condition of man . . . is a condition of war of everyone against everyone," is stressed as basis of the covenant whereby men submit to a sovereign as a way of getting peace. We have considered Spinoza as a scenic philosopher more ambiguously placed because of the action-motion equation underlying the God-Nature equation.

At first glance, one finds in the doctrines of Darwin a fairly simple instance of the scenic principle, as with this statement at the close of Chapter VI, in *The Origin of Species:*

> It is generally acknowledged that all organic beings have been formed on two great laws—Unity of Type, and the Conditions of Existence. By unity of type is meant that fundamental agreement in structure which we see in organic beings of the same class, and which is quite independent of their habits of life. On my theory, unity of type is explained by unity of descent. The expression of conditions of existence, so often insisted on by the illustrious Cuvier, is fully embraced by the principle of natural selection. For natural selection acts by either now adapting the varying parts of each being to its organic and inorganic conditions of life; or by having adapted them during past periods of time: the adaptations being aided in many cases by the increased use or disuse of parts, being affected by the direct action of the external conditions of life, and subjected in all cases to the several laws of growth and variation. Hence, in fact, the law of the Conditions of Existence is the higher law; as it includes, through the inheritance of former variations and adaptations, that of Unity of Type.

The last sentence here is as nearly perfect an instance of materialism, or reduction to scene, as one could hope for. And Darwin's term, frequently used elsewhere, "accidental variation," is as scenic as is "conditions of existence." Yet it is worth noting, at least, that many of the key terms in Darwin lend themselves readily to appeal by ambiguities of the pathetic fallacy, (an ambiguous personalizing of impersonal events, whereby even so apparently scientific a concept as "adjustment" can refer indeterminately to both actions and motions, as a person may "adjust himself" to a situation by deliberate effort on his part, or the accommodations may be automatic, as with a thermometer's adjustment to a change in temperature). For instance, "adaptation," "competition," "struggle for life," "natural selection," and "survival of the fittest" can all be read and felt as *action* words. Or consider the almost "dramatist" mode of expression in his reference to "one general law leading to the advancement of all organic beings,—namely, multiply, vary, let the strongest live and the weakest die."

Indeed, perhaps in response to the agency-purpose pair which makes readily for a shuttling between *means* and *ends,* we even find him, in explaining his "Natural System" that is "utterly inexplicable in the theory of creation," slipping into references to *purpose.* Thus, when trying to explain why "there is so much beauty throughout nature," and attributing this largely "to the agency of selection," he goes on to say: "Fruit and flowers have been rendered conspicuous by brilliant colors in contrast with the green foliage, in order that the flowers may be readily seen, visited and fertilized by insects, and the seeds disseminated by birds." Yet if I understand his doctrines in their literal application, the flower's use of colors in attracting insects must arise as the result of purely accidental variations, which survived because they happened to attract insects, which in turn happened to make the species more prolific by aiding in the distribution of the pollen.

But, whatever may be the effect of this ambiguity in shaping the appeal of his doctrines on the emotional level, his conscious intention seems purely materialistic: The motions or changes of "conditions" are to be taken as the source of selection among the biologically conditioned motions that make for continuity of type. Some pages later, in answering "miscellaneous objections" to his doctrine, Darwin specifies how very little he would concede to an opponent who was, by our standard, idealistically inclined, and thus wanted to place a strong motivation at the spot covered by the term, agent. Thus:

> Mr. Mivart believes that species change through "an internal force or tendency," about which it is not pretended that anything is known. That species have a capacity for change will be admitted by all evolutionists; but there is no need, as it seems to me, to invoke any internal force beyond the tendency to ordinary variability, which through the aid of selection by man has given rise to many well-adapted domestic races, and which through the aid of natural selection would equally well give rise by graduated steps to natural races of species. The final result will generally have been, as already explained, an advance, but in some few cases a retrogression, in organisation.

Here we see the claims of agent in the offing. Mr. Mivart would obviously make much of them, as in contending that species change their natures through "an internal force or tendency." But Darwin would allow the barest minimum of such internal origination, a mere "tendency to ordinary variability," though even in this slight concession, we see the pressure of *agent*.

In one notable respect, however, the very nature of his subject matter invites a featuring of *agent*, just as we have said that the nature of ethics as a subject matter called for a featuring of *act*. I have in mind the dynastic or heraldic element in his biology itself, as when he considers the future of his evolutionism:

> Our classifications will come to be, as far as they can be so made, genealogies; and will then truly give what may be called the plan of creation. The rules for classifying will no doubt become simpler when we have a definite object in view. We possess no pedigrees or armorial bearings; and we have to discover and trace the many diverging lines of descent in our natural genealogies, by characters of any kind which have long been inherited.

His biology, in brief, invited him to concern himself with *families*. Indeed, his concern even has an "Adamic" pattern, as when he finds cause to assume "that the innumerable species, genera and families, with which this world is peopled, are all descended, each within its own class or group, from common parents." If these families were all families of people, they would be purely and simply *agents*. A biologist's families, however, are families of *organisms*—and organisms might be called a kind of "agent-minus." They might be classed under the term agent to the extent that their behavior has to be accounted for, at least in part, by some purely internal principle of motivation (even though it be but a "tendency to ordinary variability," or a mere power of self-movement on the part of animals). Our Grammar requires this distinction between a motive in some measure intrinsic to living things and the purely scenic explanation for the motions of a bubble rising to the surface. Yet such organisms reflect the same reduction of circumference as we have previously observed with respect to scene. In fact, as per the scene-agent ratio, the turn from agent to organism corresponds to the turn from "Creation" to "Evolution." And by contrast with religions believing in transmigration, orthodox Christianity was always "incipiently evolutionary" because, in addition to the historical elements in the very idea of The Creation itself, Christianity could readily allow that all living things but man be classed as mere automata or organisms, since they were denied the character of agents through being denied the moral freedom that goes with reason.

There is thus a kind of "quasi-idealistic" biology (such as we encounter in much modern genetics, which seeks to control the development of a species by the laws of breeding alone, as with the selecting of seeds from the sturdiest members of a given crop, or by experiments with cross-fertilization). We can detect the idealistic feature here, if we contrast such methods with the materialistic, or scenic methods of those who seek to develop new types by experimenting primarily with changes in external conditions, as with changes in the foods on which the organisms are fed, or the modification of genes by radiation, and the like. There is opportunity for a subtle Grammatical scruple here in looking upon experiments with grafting as materialistic, since the stock may be considered as a kind of environmental condition affecting the nutriment received by the scion grafted upon it. All such lines of effort are obviously scenic in their emphasis, as contrasted with the "idealoid" nature of Mendel's researches into the laws governing the inheritance of "dominant" and "recessive" characters. And laws of inherited characters obviously apply to agents or "agents-minus," practically to the total exclusion of scenic concerns.

Darwin's *Origin of Species* was published in 1859; Mendel published the account of his experiments in 1865. Thus both men wrote midway in the Century of Idealism *par excellence*. All other things being equal, we might expect their biology to be as "idealoid" as the nature of the subject matter permitted. That it would permit a great deal, is evident in the primary stress upon the *familial*, in the work of both the secular Englishman and the Austrian monk. To be sure, Darwin was typical of nineteenth-century English liberalism, in stressing the selective factor of *competition* (which the cloistered priest noticed not at all), and in deriving new species from *individual* variations. The sexual-familial emphasis in Mendel could be treated as the impersonal equivalent of Catholic personalism (one kind of sexual speculation and experiment available to those vowed to chastity and to a sacramental attitude as regards human sexuality).

In keeping with the categorical encouragement which the very nature of biology as a subject holds for the featuring of an "agent-minus," we find Darwin, despite his earlier statement that "Conditions of Existence" is the "higher law," writing in his Conclusion: "The most important of all causes of organic change is one which is almost independent of altered and perhaps suddenly altered physical conditions, namely, the mutual relation of organism to organism." A few pages earlier, in his Recapitulation, he had similarly stated that "the relation of organism to organism is the most important of all relations." And in his first chapter, on "Variation Under Domestication," he had written, "We clearly see that the nature of the conditions is of subordinate importance in comparison with the nature of the organism in determining each particular form of variation;—perhaps of not more importance than the nature of the spark, by which a mass of combustible matter is ignited, has in determining the nature of the flames." But in his later Recapitulation of this same matter, he writes:

> Under domestication we see much variability, caused, or at least excited, by changed conditions of life; but often in so obscure a manner, that we are tempted to consider the variations as spontaneous. Variability is governed by many complex laws,—by correlated growth, compensation, the increased use and disuse of parts, and the definite action of the surrounding conditions.

All told, what is our point? We are trying to specify the exact nature of a great biologist's Grammar, when the nature of the experimental sciences in general calls for a *scenic* stress, yet the study of lineal descent almost inevitably shifts the stress to the motivational functions covered by our term *agent*. Or we might put it this way: In reducing all phenomena to terms of motion, biology is as unambiguously scenic as physics. But as soon as it encounters the subject of *self*-movement, it makes claims upon the areas covered by our term *agent*. We have improvised a solution, for our purposes, by deciding that the biologist's word, "organism," is Grammatically the equivalent of "agent-minus."

As regards Darwin, we have been pointing out how, despite the passages wherein he refers ultimately to "conditions" as the locus of motives, we find in his doctrines an idealistic stress. And we should say that this ambiguity comes to an exquisite focus in his key term, "variability." To illustrate:

Suppose that I wanted to write a work on the filling of vessels. The capacity of vessels to be filled I called their "fillability." My researches would soon convince me that, aside from the mere fact of the containing walls, "fillability" could be explained entirely by *external conditions*.

When it rained, the "fillability" of the vessels was manifest in a rise of their liquid content; in dry weather, there was a cessation of the fill-activity, and a diminution.   But now suppose a new situation began to present itself.   Suppose I found that sometimes the "fillability" could not be correlated with rainfall.   Sometimes there was more fill-activity at times when there had been less rain.   So that the contents of the vessels sometimes rose, each at a different rate, even under conditions of drought.   That is, suppose they also became filled somewhat independently of conditions.   And suppose that I also used my term "fillability" to explain this phenomenon.

I am suggesting that "variability" allows for two quite different meanings, as with the two meanings for "fillability," one referring to a cause *ab extra* and the other to some internal principle of motion.   It stands pliantly at the point where scene overlaps upon agent.   Because of its affinities with scene, Darwin can use it to explain cases where changing conditions can be correlated with changes in organic structure.   But because of its affinities with agent, he can use it to explain cases where variations occur without change of conditions.   And particularly when buttressed with his principle of Continuity of Type, it serves this Janus function.   For the Conditions of Existence may explain the presence of varieties with functions better suited to conditions prevailing elsewhere.

But we have considered Darwin at sufficient length to show both the scenic logic and the threats to its symmetry in this system which, at first glance, is almost perfectly materialistic.   In closing, let us note that a die-hard scenist might save the day for total materialism, by contending that even two daisies living side by side may be living under quite different "external conditions," so that variations in one not found in its brother might be at least hypothetically referrable to external causes.   Indeed, the scenic strategy may be applied even *within* the organism itself, since a changed habit on the part of the organism as a whole may be treated as an environmental factor affecting the function of some particular organ, and so leading to its disuse and consequent atrophy.   That is, the whole organism can be treated as "environment" for any of its parts.[3]

---

[3] As for the word "environment" itself, I doubt whether this term, now so characteristic of evolutionary thought, occurs in *The Origin of Species* at all. Various Darwinian terms, in one respect or another its equivalent, are: region, physical conditions, climatal conditions, areas, geographical provinces of the world, period of time, conditions of life or existence, climatal and geographical changes,

The Two Great Hellenistic Materialisms

Of the two great Hellenistic materialisms, each features scene in considering mind as but a finer kind of body, and in contending that as with the body, at death the particles of the soul disintegrate, being scattered among the universal motions. Nevertheless, each of these philosophies has its own particular way of endowing the scene with properties of agent, properties that can then, in accordance with the logic of the scene-agent ratio, be imputed to human agents as deductions from the quality of the ground out of which they arise.

This strategic "pre-agentification" of scene is much less obvious with Epicureanism than with Stoicism; yet it can be found here too, in a term that does for the Epicurean genealogy of motives what "variability" does for Darwinism. I refer to one important trait possessed by the infinite atoms of which the Epicurean universe is said to be composed.

These atoms account for the rise of worlds and of animal forms much as with Darwinian evolution. That is, out of chance atomic combinations many forms arose that could not survive their monstrous unsuitability for the conditions of existence in which they happened to find themselves. But from the atomic seeds many other forms arose that were suited to grow and multiply, the seasonality of their development happening to correspond with the march of the seasons themselves. The stress is upon the accidental here; and in contrast with the Stoic stress upon the action of divine purpose in the creation of the world, Lucretius holds: "Nothing was born in the body that we might use it; but that which is born begets for itself a use."

But from the standpoint of our Grammar it is notable that, although Lucretius thinks of the atomic bodies as possessing different weights and as forever falling through the void, he specifically denies that they could ever have come into contact with one another, were it not for the action of another principle. For he argues that, regardless of their differences in weight, the particles would all fall through empty space at the same rate of speed, and so would remain forever out of touch with one another, except for the presence, within the atomic seeds, of a slight tendency to *swerve*. And in thus swerving, they collide, rebound, and

range, range of time, habitat, surrounding physical conditions, and scenic terms less general in meaning, such as Plutonic rocks, sedimentary formation, Laurentian, littoral.

variously combine, to cause the endless evolution and destruction of worlds, things, and beings.

This slight tendency to swerve or deviate, (L. *clinamen;* Gr. *pareg-klisis*) this *inclination* arising as a principle of motion *within* the atom, has been looked upon as a break in the symmetry of the atomic scheme. And I guess it is, if we judge it purely from the standpoint of a terminology designed to account for evolution in terms of motion. But the Epicurean physics is the basis for an *ethics.* Hence we are dramatistically admonished to look for the "seeds" of an ethical principle in the physical terminology itself. Or, otherwise stated, we are admonished to examine this "inclination" of the atoms on the possibility that it is a device for transcending sheer motion, and opening towards the wider realm of action and agenthood. Lucretius himself is quite explicit on the subject, when discussing the conclusion that would follow the denial that the atoms swerve of themselves:

> If all motions involve one another, each leading inevitably into the next, and if the first-beginnings of motion do not, by swerving (*declinando*) introduce some new principle to break the bonds of destiny and to keep causes from following causes endlessly, how, I ask, do all living things snatch from fate the power to advance according to the dictates of the will, regulating (*declinamus*) our movements not merely in set response to time and place, but as the mind directs? For unquestionably in these matters the point of origin is in the will, and movements are conveyed from it to other parts of the body. . . . The fact that the mind does not feel an inner compulsion in all its actions, and is not forced to bear and suffer as if in defeat, is due to a tiny swerving (*clinamen*) of the first-principles, not to the set requirements of time and place.

Employing our shift of emphasis as a first rough approximate, we might note that such "clinaminous" or "parenclitic" atoms have this advantage: In their role as *"swerving atoms"* they give us a scenic derivation for human freedom, thereby maintaining the symmetry of the scene-act and scene-agent ratios. But in their role as "swerving *atoms,"* they account for the world on a purely evolutionary basis, without derivation from the divine act of a divine agent. As a result, the terminology is suited to allay the terrors of superstition, by interpreting "acts of God" in terms of sheer motion, and thereby freeing men of the belief that storms, floods, plagues, earthquakes and other natural cataclysms and calamities both public and private are visited upon them by vengeful deities.

The Stoic dialectic, looking upon Nature as the process that giveth and taketh away, pantheistically equates Nature itself with Providence (*pronoia*), and so with Reason, the Will of God, and strict logical Necessity. The principle of moral action is introduced into a universe of necessary motions by an ambiguously "naturalistic" device, in that each thing is required to live according to its nature, and man is by nature rational. This rationality in turn is conceived in political or social terms, all men being intended to serve one another, and all things inferior to man being for the use of man.

As we read Marcus Aurelius from the standpoint of the Grammar, one of the most striking things we notice is the kind of "moral utilitarianism" that arises from the great stress upon the *purposive* factor in the Stoic conception of Nature as a divine plan. The agency-purpose ratio is the same as the integral Grammatical relation between means and ends; and the Stoic teleology clearly shows how this ratio provides a bridge "from Providence to pragmatism," in admonishing the philosopher to ask himself first of all to what use each thing, person, or act should be put. For to say that all things are brought about by God for a purpose, is to say that all things have a *use*. However, such moral pragmatism is still a long way from modern pragmatism as developed under the combined impetus of business and technology. Indeed, we see the Stoic philosopher in the process of *coming upon* the function of agency, but still expressing the position primarily in terms of the starting point, purpose ("Providence"). Marcus Aurelius' role as administrator doubtless had much to do with the incipient pragmatism here, while the condition of the governmental bureaucracy in a time so long prior to modern technology would call for a moral pragmatism rather than for the typical modern intellectualistic brand centering in the philosophy of scientific method.

Rhetorical and Symbolic Levels

Though these Grammatical observations should be enough for our present purposes, they leave unconsidered many important matters that would require examination and demonstration rather in terms of Rhetoric and Symbolic. Simply to illustrate how the other levels impinge upon the Grammatical, I shall add a few observations in the form of mere hypotheses, problems, or undemonstrated propositions:

(1) Note the evidence of working at cross-purposes in Lucretius' *De Rerum Natura*. A poem designed to establish the aloofness of the gods from human affairs begins with a magnificent invocation to Venus, as the all-mother. Though the poem is thus significantly offered in the name of Venus, in one book it strikingly caricatures the effects of love, particularly the errors of judgment provoked by love (in spirit somewhat as the treatment of love in the *Phaedrus* might be if it lacked the second, pious speech on love which Socrates remorsefully offered to make amends for his first impious burlesque).

The theme develops from that of the divine fertility (as exemplified in Venus and her replica, the maternal Earth), to the explanation of all evolution in terms of the seminal principle; but it *ends* when the theme has taken on a sinister quality. For just as there are atomic seeds of things good for man, so there are seeds of disease and death—and the poem closes on a scene of carnage, with a population dying hideously in a plague, and rioting amidst the rites of burial. Something seems to have gone wrong with the *direction* of this poem, at least as regards the philosophic ends of solace. The intention of showing that calamities are not acts of gods leads not to a *medical* treatment of symptoms, but to a *poetic* one, seeking to make the plague as vivid and picturesque as possible, and so building up in one way the disturbing thoughts it is designed to remove in another.

(2) Also, there is much evidence in this poem that the author is in some way goaded. Indeed, on the Symbolic plane, as a likely hunch that may or may not be verified on closer examination, I think one is always justified in looking for tender apprehensions behind the apparent toughnesses of materialist debunking, as Bentham in his childhood had an abnormally intense fear of ghosts, and in adult life developed a critique of language particularly zealous in disclosing kinds of words that named merely fabulous or fictitious entities having but the semblance of reality; or as he aimed to dispel the moral pretense in idealistic words, by treating them in terms of the material interests they cloak, thus translating spirit back into body, which as regards the childhood pattern equalled the transformation of ghosts back into corpses. And similarly, if Lucretius was not goaded, why so monumental an attempt to assure men that the wrath of the gods will pursue them neither in

this life nor in the life hereafter? What unresolved guilt may perhaps reside in this attack upon religions that believe in the punishments of heaven? What was it that would make an Epicurean find in the thought of the soul's mortality the very solace that Christians seek in the thought of immortality?

For one thing, when we contrast the Epicurean ideal of individual aloofness with the Stoic social-mindedness ("Imagine a whole city of Epicureans!" the Stoic Epictetus exclaims incredulously), we see reasons to believe that the Epicurean individualism (which began with the breakdown of the Greek *polis*) did not completely satisfy the needs of justification by socialization. Or better, put it this way: the concept of an aloofness that neither touched worldly things nor could be touched by them attributed to the gods the Epicureans' own ideal way of life. Hence, insofar as the ideal in its human aspect did invite to twinges of conscience (in the avoidance of *civic* responsibilities) the same ideal as a description of the gods assured one that these twinges of conscience were not called for by the *universal* situation.

(A page of Stoicism selected almost at random will be enough to show that the equating of the *civic* and the *universal* was very much in the air, the Stoic preparation for Christianity residing precisely in widening the concept of citizenship from *local* to *metaphysical* dimensions. On the other hand, I most decidedly do not mean to suggest that there was any cause for guilt in the Epicurean doctrine as an invitation to sensual pleasures. Such an interpretation of Epicureanism can be found only in the writings of its opponents. The guilt and sensuality rather would be that of one who thought of his private comfort while there was public work to be done. For the Epicurean ideal was of a pleasant slumber one might enjoy if at the same time he were *thoroughly aware* that he was sleeping. This would be in contrast with the Stoic ideal of a painless insomnia, moral vigilance, a constant watching and waiting which might nonetheless, with the help of rational doctrine, combine universal sympathy and individual apathy—and this moral firmness required of the virtuous was scenically grounded in the Stoics' concept of a universal tension which they name not neutrally but ethically or eulogistically: *"eutonia,"* a "good" tension, which may alas! find its modern equivalent in "hypertension," when the Stoic patience has been made impatient by conditions inviting us to experience in terms of "progress" and "frustration.")

(3) In the case of Lucretius, who was an Epicurean not in the dis-integrated culture of a Greek *polis* but in Rome at the time of Cicero, the possibilities of a secret "Epicurean guilt" seem particularly strong, in that Rome was so intensely civic-minded.   Besides, there seems to be some basic "problem of the mother" involved in his version of the fertile atoms, as though these uterine principles, from which all living things are derived and to which at death they return, constituted a *philosophic* matrix alternative to that of some *poetic* parent vaguely comprising, all in one: Mother Venus, Mother Earth, and the human mother.   (Imag-istic bridges are there aplenty for anyone who would show first that fertile Venus and the fertile Earth can be equated, and next that the human body and the earth's body can be equated.)   As regards the medium of expression: the opposition shows in his treatment of poetry itself, which he equates with childish things (saying that he writes his doctrine in verse as one uses honey to disguise bitter medicine for chil-dren).   And when he is on the subject of propitiation rites invented by humans who believe that they have defiled Mother Earth, he calls them mistaken but *beautiful*.   (Surely we should not be overstraining mat-ters here to translate: *philosophically* bad but *poetically* good.)

All told, then, there seems to be some clash between the philosophic identity and the poetic one, as exemplified in the change from the Venus-fertility to the fertility of the seminal atoms (the first involving such gods as require propitiation, the second involving such gods as leave men unpersecuted, and the conception of whom invites men to live in their image).   And as evidence that the attempted transforma-tion is incomplete, we have the direction of the work itself, ending on the imagery of plague.   One might think this an accident, except that it seems such a *fit* ending, powerful and resonant.

It is just possible that the unresolved guilt in this poem has given rise to a remarkable pun, a pun that might go far to explain why, of all Roman battles, the battles with the Carthaginians continued to assume such importance in the popular imagination, long after Carthage was destroyed in the struggles with Rome for economic control of the Medi-terranean.   I refer to a passage in Book III where Lucretius is explain-ing how, in accordance with his doctrine, we need worry no more about doom after death than we worried, before our birth, about the possible outcome of the wars with Carthage.   The editor of my school text thinks this a particularly effective statement at the time when it was written, since the Punic wars were just beyond the lifetime of Lucretius and his contemporaries, "and marked the most critical period of the Roman state up to his time." But there may be a still deeper linguistic process operating here. I refer to the fact that the Latin word for the Carthaginians is *Poeni,* while the Latin word for the goddesses of vengeance is *Poenae.* In the dative and ablative forms, the two would be exactly the same, *Poenis.* And the word is thus used in Lucretius:

ad confligendum venientibus undique Poenis,

a line which, taken in itself, could be translated, with equal justice, either as "when the Carthaginians were coming to the attack from all sides" or as "when the goddesses of Vengeance were coming to the attack from all sides." There is no doubt that literally the reference is to the Carthaginians. But if we consider it in keeping with such studies of ambiguity as Empson has given us, may we not legitimately hear effects even more resonant than the literal meaning itself? The design in Lucretius' doctrine, deriving life from seeds to which at death it returns, equates the state before birth with the state after death—and the essence of the latter (without Poenae) must well be stated ambiguously as the essence of the former (without fear of Poeni).

(4) As for Stoicism, with such profound sense of civic responsibility as we find in the Meditations of Aurelius, the burden seems to derive from a different source. One could hardly ask for a more thorough attempt at justification by socialization than shows in the diary of this conscientious emperor. Why, then, such down-turning? Why, intermingled with such a profound philosophy of acceptance, affirming so devoutly that the world and all its properties and accidents manifest the nature, will, and reason of God—why of a sudden the almost brutal hatred of the flesh? Why such sudden bursts of impatience in this austere philosophy of patience? All nature being divine, it cannot be purely doctrinal motives that prompts these sudden outcries.

Grammatically, the furthest we need go is this: the *distinction* between the finer rational matter of which mind is composed and the coarser matter of which body is composed may be heightened into a *contrast.* At least, there is always this dialectical possibility of converting the hierarchically related (one term "higher" than another) into the oppositionally related (one term *vs.* the other). But Stoic monism, on purely doctrinal grounds, would seem to require the hierarchic interpretation of the natural order.   And I would seek to account for the sudden bursts of fury against the body as resulting, on the Symbolic plane, from the fact that Stoic acceptance was aimed at the *transubstantiation of the excremental,* in attempting to proclaim even the repugnant aspects of the world as essentially divine.   As strict an exemplar of the scene-agent ratio as is to be found in all philosophy, equating the human body, the civic body, and the universal body in ways that promote a constant shuttling back and forth among the three, the Stoic burden, the doing of one's duty, seems, on the purely Symbolic plane, to derive from the necessary befouling of the nest implicit in the pantheistic doctrine.   Applying shift of accent, we could state the matter thus: in moments of moral exaltation, the result is a scrupulous *"transcendence* of offal."   But in moments of misgiving, when the exaltation has collapsed, the result is a "transcendence of *offal."*

(5) Stoicism, of course, covers quite a range of Stoics. And the Stoicism of Epictetus, the manumitted slave, differs greatly in its tone from that of Marcus Aurelius, the ruler of an empire beset by war and decay.   And just as in reading the *Meditations* we read the thoughts of a man who, writing in private, never forgot for a moment that he was an emperor, experiencing bondage only in the deeply moral sense of willingly dutiful service in the administering of the commonwealth, so in reading the *Discourses* we read the thoughts of a man who, dictating to a disciple and probably in the presence of many others, never forgot that he was a manumitted slave; or, if he did forget, he forgot only in the sense that he generalized and moralized his change of condition, and so talked always in terms of the Progress (*prokope*) from spiritual slavery to spiritual freedom.   In Epictetus, accordingly, there is a kind of lift that one will encounter not at all in the solemn emperor. To hold the highest rank in the world, and to have that rank a burden, is hardly to find much cause for talk of "progress," even in its spiritual translation—and Epictetus' stress upon the ways and means of emancipation becomes, in Marcus Aurelius, an emperor's doctrinal subjection to a political community which he secretly despised, though he repeatedly admonished that any separation from nature or society was an "abscess."

We must remember, however, that the freedman's conception of "progress" differed essentially from its modern pragmatist replica.

when "Providence" has become secularized in terms of investment and utility. The improvement of status that the freedman had in mind was quite alien to the modern "higher standard of living" based upon the acquisition of new commodities, the satisfying of "new needs," by an improvement in one's earning power and buying power. Epictetus laid great stress upon property as the very ground of freedom: but this property was in the possession of Reason and Will, inner powers that are free beyond any tyrant's control. That which is wholly "mine," that in which I am not *subject*, is my power to deal with "impressions" (that is, to philosophically discount any evidences of my misfortune). "Every man's body is a measure for his property, as the foot is the measure for his shoe," said this frail and sickly man who, by reason of the scene-agent ratio, might thus be expected to ask for little. But in the personal power of philosophic deliberation and resignation, every man was a "Senator" (Stoics always being prompt to moralize their politics and politicalize their ethics).

As for the emperor, Matthew Arnold has commented on his struggles against the "feeling of discontent, so natural to the great for whom there seems nothing left to desire or strive for." He then cites the list of indebtednesses with which the diary significantly begins: "I have to thank Heaven that I was subjected to a ruler and a father (Antoninus Pius) who was able to take away all pride from me" . . . etc. But Arnold does not relate this to a previous observation he had made about the dignity of the Stoic ethic, when noting that, as contrasted with the bribes to virtue which Christianity offered by its promises of heavenly reward, Aurelius nobly proclaimed the value of moral service in itself:

> What more dost thou want when thou hast done a man a service? Art thou not content that thou hast done something conformable to thy nature, and dost thou seek to be paid for it, just as if the eye demanded a recompense for seeing, or the feet for walking?

Might not Arnold also have related this superior ethic to his remarks on the "enfeebling" and "deteriorating" effects which the imperial status had upon Aurelius, depriving him of ambitions? The only two ambitions open to a great ruler would be the paranoiac extension of his realm into still wider regions (whereas in actuality the circumference of Roman dominion was contracting), or the improvement of the conditions of his subject. The second course, however, could only amount to service without reward, as administrator, as commander, and as secret moral exhorter.   Thus the same imperial conditions apparently offer the same contributions to the concept of virtue without heavenly bribes as to the dispiriting clamps upon ambition.[4]

(6) The spectacle of an emperor's voluntary subjection to the thought of his elders, of his family, of his intimates, and of society, and his pious gratification in the fact that he had so long preserved his sexual purity, recalls a theory that sex repression protects capitalism by serving as a device to dispirit the working classes so that their assertiveness and aggressiveness are inhibited.   I know this theory (of Wilhelm Reich) only by hearsay, so I do not know in what ways it is modified and protectively buttressed.   But in studying the diary of Aurelius, one does indeed find what is, as judged by modern romantic standards of freedom from "frustration," a ruler who obeys the code of sex repression as devotedly and devoutly and implicitly as he could ever have wished his subjects to do, had he known and subscribed to the Reich theory. Much depends upon the nature of the "equations" here.   With a person who treats sexual potency and political power as consistently related, a sexual inhibition would doubtless lead to a political dispiriting. And I would assume that Reich himself shared this equation.   But another temperament may be differently organized, treating the cause of political emancipation as a kind of secular religion, for which he might symbolically and sacrificially fit himself by an attitude of chastity, or priestliness, however tough the terms in which this might be conceived.   And while it is true that Friedrich Engels had a mistress, it is equally true that Karl Marx disapproved with an almost Puritanic vigor.

However, if you will grant me sufficient reservations, I think that the Reichian doctrine could be applied to this ruler who was, from the moral point of view, as thoroughly subject, and a worker, as an artisan could be.   For if you will read his diary carefully, I think you will agree that it is not addressed simply to "himself."   We should question whether it is addressed to any one audience, however vague or hypo-

---

[4] As for the purely family motives involved here, it is notable that Arnold subjected himself as resolutely to a father-principle as we see Aurelius doing in his opening list of indebtednesses, the pattern showing to perfection in Arnold's "Sohrab and Rustum" where, instead of dreaming the typical nineteenth-century dream of Jack the Giant-Killer, the poet dreams of a son slain in combat with a father.

thetical that audience might be. And we should do so for this reason: Stoicism was a highly alembicated dialectic. In its early stages (which survive but in fragments) it seems to have made important contributions to dialectical analysis. And the least we can expect of a dialectician, as of a dramatist, is that he speak in several voices. But the diary being all written in one voice, the variety would show more subtly, in the fact that this voice could address itself to several auditors, more or less distinct from one another, though they all be but private sub-personalities combined in the public office of the one imperial person. Each of these sub-personalities would have its own concerns, hence to an extent its own manner of speech. And one of such nameless and unplaced auditors to whom Marcus Aurelius sometimes addressed himself was a kind of *ideal, philosophy-minded subject* who could, when properly admonished by the diarist, be induced to see things in Stoic terms, yet did not share the social status, political power, and material privileges of the emperor; in fact he was often inclined to grumble at being placed in an inferior and near-destitute condition. Speaking in the firmest Stoic terms, the philosopher-king bade this grumbling subject be content with his lot, on the grounds that the assigning of a lowly position to some men was part of the divine plan, the Providential design of a natural but rational order in which no individual could really suffer so long as his deprivations served the needs of the entire community.

And that he might address this lowly citizen persuasively, thus secretly in his diary, the conscientious emperor gladly imposed upon himself all manner of dispiriting deprivations, seeking to live a kind of life that would be magically an inducement to this other self, himself not as imperial ruler, but as imperial subject. And if the subject could thus by these secret exhortations be persuaded to live accordingly, the prevailing structure of material privileges might be expected to continue. As so modified, I believe I could subscribe to the Reichian theory.

But we have said enough to indicate, even with readers who might disagree with these particular propositions, how the Grammatical area impinges upon the areas of Rhetoric and Symbolic. And though our discussion of the scenic Grammar aims to be representative rather than exhaustive, we should like to end this section by comparing and contrasting two other materialisms, both modern, one powerfully public, the other serenely private, one aggressive, the other retiring, and the two so different from one another that the adherents of either would be scandalized to hear the other mentioned in the same breath. I refer to the philosophies of Marx and Santayana. But the fact that each was strongly affected by German transcendentalism requires that we postpone their consideration until we have examined the functions of the term, *agent.*

II

AGENT IN GENERAL

IDEALISM, in the Baldwin dictionary, is described thus: "In meta-physics, any theory which maintains the universe to be throughout the work of reason and mind." And elsewhere: "Any theory which seeks the explanation, or ultimate *raison d'être*, of the cosmic evolution in the realization of reason, self-consciousness, or spirit, may fairly claim to be included under this designation. For the end in such a system is not only the result, but—is also the true world-building power." In the *Encyclopaedia Britannica*, an epistemological factor is considered uppermost, as idealism is said to hold that "Apart from the activity of the self or subject in sensory reaction, memory and association, imag-ination, judgment and inference, there can be no world of objects."

The traits here mentioned are enough to indicate that the unadulter-atedly idealistic philosophy starts and ends in the featuring of properties belonging to the term, *agent*. Idealistic philosophies think in terms of the "ego," the "self," the "super-ego," "consciousness," "will," the "generalized I," the "subjective," "mind," "spirit," the "oversoul," and any such "super-persons" as church, race, nation, etc. Historical peri-ods, cultural movements, and the like, when treated as "personalities," are usually indications of idealism.

The variants in esthetic theory stress such terms as "sensibility," "ex-pression," "self-expression," "consciousness" and the "unconscious." The Crocean philosophy has been prominent as a bridge between meta-physical and esthetic idealism. In his preface to *The Portrait of a Lady*, Henry James gives us a characteristically idealistic statement when re-ferring to "the artist's prime sensibility" as the "soil out of which his subject springs" and which "grows" the work of art. Here a book is treated as an act grounded in the author's mind as its motivating scene. The same idealistic pattern is carried into his methods as a novelist, when he selects some "sensibility" who will serve as the appreciative "centre" of his story, and lets the reader follow the story *in terms of* this single consciousness.

Because of its stress upon agent, idealism leads readily into both individual and group psychology. Its close connection with epistemology, or the problem of knowledge, is due to this same bias. For to approach the universe by asking ourselves how knowledge is possible is to ground our speculations psychologistically, in the nature of the *knower*.

Idealization

Sociologically there is an invitation to an idealistic philosophy whenever important human economic relations have become "idealized" or "spiritualized." The Greek word "Moira" is a case in point. It is defined in a modern English dictionary as "the ancient deity who assigns to every man his lot." In this sense it meant Destiny, and was associated with the Three Fates. Consulting a Greek dictionary, however, we find that the word also had a much more realistic significance: a *part* (as opposed to the whole); that which is one's due; a share, or portion (as of a meal). In short, we note the same range between realistic and idealistic senses that we find in our English word "lot" itself.

In its realistic sense, *moira* had a very explicit reference. It referred to the amount that an individual member of the tribe got when things were divided up. "Destiny" or Chance was involved, in that goods incapable of division into exactly equivalent parts were distributed by the drawing of lots, as with the rotation of public office in the Athenian democracy. Hence, one's *moira* was one's proper portion. It was probably never wholly equal, since a man's portion would differ from a child's, etc.; but in the early states of the tribal culture it was relatively near to equality; or inequalities were settled by accident as in a lottery (though the designs of Chance could themselves be felt as "meaningful," a motive in the category not of "motion" but of "action").

In time, however, the development of class distinctions within the tribe subtilized or rarified the concept of lot. Members of different classes would be allotted different *portions*. Such inequalities of portion came to be fixed by tradition rather than being decided anew on each occasion (as with the taking of booty in battle). Hence one's "lot" was decided when he was born into one social class rather than another, a peasant's lot being traditionally different from the king's, etc. In time, therefore, one's "lot" or "portion" might even come to reside in his receiving nothing at all.

In proportion as the word lost its original realistic reference to visible, tangible divisions, we should consider it to have become idealized, or spiritualized. Words of this sort are particularly serviceable when, *unity* having given way to *disunity,* there is a call for *unification.* Hence the idealistic ingredient in Plato's *Republic,* which aims at a *unified* State, founded upon a vision of absolute Good, as a reaction to the individualistic and relativistic teachings of the Sophists.

For the Sophists, defining justice in a more realistic sense, observed that there was a different justice for the rich than for the poor. Etymologically, as we have observed before, the Sophists had the better of the argument, since the Greek word for justice, *dike,* referred originally to a *way of life;* and manifestly there were different ways of life, with correspondingly different values, for the different social classes.

But Plato sought for a "higher" concept of justice, an "ideal" justice that could be conceived as transcending all these different justices. The nature of language, in allowing readily for what Korzybski would call "higher levels of generalization," encourages this search for an "idea" of justice prevailing above and despite the many different "justices," or ways, necessarily embodied in a society that had developed quite a range of economic classes, each with its own properties and proprieties. Dialectically, any conflict between two concepts of justice can be removed by the adoption of a remoter term broad enough to encompass both, as a distinction between farmhouse and palace can be resolved in classing them both as "dwellings."

Justice in such an over-all sense would obviously serve the ends of unification. And insofar as the law courts would "ideally" serve this same role, in aiming at a kind of justice that mediated among the differing ways of differing classes, we can see how the profuse development of law invites to idealistic philosophy. Materialist "debunkers" of such legal idealism can then interpret the "ideal" in terms of its "betrayal"; for "unification" is not unity, but a *compensation for disunity*—hence, any term for "ideal" justice can be interpreted as a rhetorical concealment for *material injustice,* particularly when the actual history of legal decisions over a long period can be shown to have favored class justice *in the name of* ideal justice.

The thought suggests an ironic connection between idealism and the written contract. For before the spread of literacy, a man could break his promise simply by forgetting exactly what he had promised. After the spread of literacy, however, since promises are put unchangeably into writing, the man who would break his promise must hire lawyers to prove that his words no longer mean what they were obviously meant to mean. Such enterprise often requires great "idealization" or "spiritualization," quite as your opponent in a game, if he is neither wrong nor a liar, yet would call your shot "out" when it was *in*, can do so only by being a profound idealist. The courts themselves often come to accept the ingenious misinterpretations proposed by our corporation lawyers such as the legal fiction that financial corporations are persons (thereby deserving the freedom granted to human beings by divine, natural, or Constitutional law). For the judges talk the same language, usually having been corporation lawyers themselves. Hence in time our very notions of reality are affected, since the idealistic fictions have been written into the very law of the land, and the law is our "reality" insofar as it is a public structure of *motives*.

If deception were the only result of the relation between the ideal and the real, ideas would long ago have ceased to deceive. But just as a lie is "creative" in the sense that it *adds* to reality, so there is the powerfully and nobly creative aspect of idealism, since an ideal may serve as standard, guide, incentive—hence may lead to new real conditions. The power of ideas, in such respects, is in the visionary futurism of a Washington or Lenin and their followers, of a Shelley and his public, of a promoter and his investors. And so an *idea* of justice may make possible some measure of its *embodiment* in material situations.

This side of idealism, in fitting it especially to stress the aspect of the agent as *creator,* accounts for the strong idealistic bias in esthetic theories, as with the idealistic Coleridge's view of poetry as a "dim analogue of Creation." True, esthetics came to have as its essential rule the treatment of art in terms of "uselessness." But this seems explainable rather by reason of the fact that the esthetic was conceived in direct opposition to the utilitarianism of business and applied science. And despite the opposition between philosophies of art and the philosophies of the practical, both could be idealistic insofar as business, science, and art all stressed the *innovative*.

Despite their apparent materialism, theories of positive law would likewise fall under the head of idealism. This becomes apparent when we consider that, in accordance with the theory of positive law, constitutions and similar legal enactments are to be taken as the ground by reference to which judgments of legality are substantiated. Such laws and constitutions derive from assemblies whose enactments are taken to represent "the will of the people"—and of course all variants of Rousseau's *volonté générale* are idealistic. The idealistic perspective is further accentuated, in the United States, by the fiction that the will of the people today is consubstantial with the will of the Founding Fathers. Those who established the Constitution are co-agents with those who perpetuate it—and the document itself, considered as a structure of motivations, is a creature of the human will. Hence, though it is a *ground* of action, its essential feature is in its derivation from the attitudes of human *agents*.

When we introduce materialistic considerations, we readily see how idealistic the doctrines of positive law really are. For scenic tests make it apparent that no ground resting in the human will alone can possibly have sufficient circumference to name the important conditions of legality. Any man-made constitution is itself an enactment that takes place in a constitution of a much wider orbit—and a document whose terminology of motives greatly narrows its circumference, as is necessarily the case with a Constitution adopted by some human assembly, repeatedly requires judicial decisions that press for the addition of new terms. These terms are in effect "amendments" to the Constitution, amendments made by "extra-Constitutional" procedures. They are not voted upon by the people or by the legislatures, but are introduced by the Courts. Insofar as they are new terms they introduce new coördinates of motivation. And any judgment which in effect introduces a new *motive* into the Constitution has, to that extent, amended the document. (These remarks, however, anticipate a subject that we shall consider at length in a later chapter.)

Unification

Sociologically, we can also relate the historical development from realism (and its opponent nominalism) to idealism (and its opponent materialism) as a response to the modern proliferations of finance. Indeed, we might almost state it as a cultural law that "realism plus money equals idealism." That is, the tribal pattern of thinking, when broken by the new ways that money promotes, calls for such "unification" as we find in nationalism. The introduction of money as a new term in effect gives to the act of barter a new dimension. And the greater the development of the financial rationale, the greater is the "spirituality" in man's relations to material goods, which he sees less in terms of their actual nature as goods, and more in the "ideal" terms of the future and of monetary (symbolic) profit. And any actual divisiveness in the social body which the inequalities of money intensify, is one more call upon idealistic philosophies of "unification," which can set up group "ideals" (embodied in "laws") to protect private wealth in the name of the commonwealth.

In Emerson's *Nature* there is a passage clearly indicating how the separations of private property are matched by the unifying idealism of country (here esthetically combining connotations of nature, region, and nation):

> The charming landscape which I saw this morning is indubitably made up of some twenty or thirty farms. Miller owns this field, Locke that, and Manning the woodland beyond. But none of them owns the landscape. There is a property in the horizon which no man has but he whose eye can integrate all the parts, that is, the poet. This is the best part of these men's farms, yet to this their warranty-deeds give no title.

It is a type of thinking capable of organizing mighty powers, as men materially in different worlds can be spiritually one.

Technology invites idealistic unification on two major counts. First, like money and in conjunction with money, it makes for diversity and unequal rates of change that require as social corrective the unifying function of ideas and ideals "creatively" at odds with conditions as they look when seen without the idealistic exaltation. And a more technical incentive to idealism derives from the fact that technology, as applied science, invites us to put the major stress upon knowledge. And the problem of knowledge is the epistemological problem, a psychologistic emphasis that falls directly under the head of agent.

Berkeley

But turning now to purely intrinsic considerations, let us examine a representative idealistic philosopher, George Berkeley. For though modern idealist trends emerge with Descartes and Leibniz, and eventually lead into the Big Four of German romanticism (Kant, Fichte, Schelling, and Hegel) it is through the English empiricists Locke, Berkeley, and Hume that the intermediate development is to be traced. Before Berkeley, the doctrines are still largely in formation. After him came Hume, whose brilliant skepticism saddled the school with such burdensome problems that the German Big Four all write like the shifting of cars in a freight yard. But in Berkeley's *Treatise Concerning the Principles of Human Knowledge,* we find the idealistic terminology put forward with as much clarity and directness as in the Hobbesian use of the materialist terminology. And to trace some of its major steps is to see beyond a doubt why idealism is to be considered as a featuring of the term agent, a mode of discourse that gives voice to this term, permitting the term in effect to make an address, with only occasional heckling from the other terms that stand in the offing.

The inquiry begins psychologistically, hence in terms of agent, by questioning the possibility of "abstract ideas," as Locke had defined them in his *Essay Concerning Human Understanding.* Berkeley maintains, for instance, that one cannot conceive of a triangle in the abstract, but must have a picture, more or less accurate, of some visible or tangible triangle. One may, of course, become so familiar with the *word* triangle that he can use it without pausing to imagine some empirical context for the word. But when he pauses and tries to conceive the meaning of which the word may be a sign, he must think of some particular triangle and let it serve as a reference for all triangles. The mere conception of a triangle in the abstract, with no visible or tangible shape whatever, Berkeley asserts to be an impossibility. So similarly with abstract ideas such as extension, color, animal, body.

> And it is equally impossible for me to form the abstract idea of motion distinct from the body moving, and which is neither swift nor slow, curvilinear nor rectilinear; and the like may be said of all other abstract general ideas whatsoever.

Whether or not the reader agrees with this empiricist position, he must grant it is a perfect starting-point for a philosophy that would confront the Known in terms of the *Knower*.

By thus reducing abstract ideas to mere *words*, however, Berkeley is, surprisingly, able to reduce all sensory experience to *ideas*. Or as he puts it:

> It is indeed an opinion strangely prevailing amongst men, that houses, mountains, rivers, and in a word all sensible objects, have an existence, natural or real, distinct from their being perceived by the understanding. But with how great an assurance and acquiescence soever this principle may be entertained in the world, yet whoever shall find in his heart to call it in question may, if I mistake not, perceive it to involve a manifest contradiction. For what are the fore-mentioned objects but the things we perceive by sense? and what do we perceive *besides our own ideas or sensations?* and is it not plainly repugnant that any one of these, or any combination of them, should exist unperceived?

Note that he here makes "ideas" and "sensations" synonymous. Hence the basic Berkeleian equation: To be is to be perceived, *"esse is percipi."* And everything that makes up the "real" world for us must meet this test. We make our way among "ideas." And we learn how to deal with other "ideas," that we can bring about desired situations, which are themselves "ideas," insofar as they are perceived; and insofar as they are not perceived, they don't exist.

Ingeniously reversing the usual application of the Occamite law of parsimony, he points out that no hypothesis of "matter" is necessary to account for experience. *"It is possible we might be affected with all the ideas we have now, though there were no bodies existing without, resembling them.* Hence, it is evident the supposition of external bodies is not necessary for the producing our ideas." Matter, "or the absolute existence of corporeal objects," would "be not even missed in the world, but everything as well, may much easier be conceived without it." With the help of our senses we learn how to vary the sets of "ideas" which we experience, so that we can encounter the desired sensations, or ideas, say, of buying a ticket and taking a train to a particular destination, where, if true sensations or ideas of a successful trip occur, we may expect to encounter the true sensations or ideas of arriving at our desired destination, with its appropriate set of sensations or ideas.

We here sum up briefly a position for which Berkeley argues with considerable thoroughness. One must consult the original if he would do justice to the various steps in the exposition. But whether or not one is convinced by Berkeley's arguments, one must agree that they are statements saying what can be said about "matter" (that is, *scene*) when considered in terms of "ideas" (that is, *agent*). For our purposes here, it is not necessary to review all the stages in Berkeley's argument. What we need is enough to show clearly a functioning of the term agent.

We referred to the creative emphasis in idealism. Though this creative element is often called "the Idea," in the Berkeleian system "ideas" are called inactive; for the active principle is said to reside in a more direct term for agent. "This perceiving, active being is what I call *mind, spirit, soul,* or *myself.*" And "there is not any other substance than *spirit,* or that which perceives." In contrast with materialist reduction to terms of motion, Berkeley holds that "motion is not without the mind." The "ideas" are "unthinking" things, since they are the things that the agent *thinks.* "The very being of an idea implies passiveness and inertness in it, insomuch that it is impossible for an idea to do anything." Thoughts themselves, don't think—hence the thinker is active, the thought is passive. "Things" in the everyday sense, are "collections of ideas," the scenic here clearly being seen in terms of agent:

> Thus, for example, a certain color, taste, smell, figure, and consistence, having been observed to go together, are accounted one distinct thing, signified by the name "apple." Other collections of ideas constitute a stone, a tree, a book, and the like sensible things; which, as they are pleasing or disagreeable, excite the passions of love, hatred, joy, grief, and so forth.

His position is summed up in paragraph 26:

> We perceive a continual succession of ideas, some are anew excited, others are changed or totally disappear. There is therefore some cause of these ideas, whereon they depend, and which produces and changes them. That this cause cannot be any equality or

idea or combination of ideas, is clear from the preceding section. It must therefore be a substance; but it has been shown that there is no corporeal or material substance; it remains therefore that the cause of ideas is an incorporeal active substance or Spirit.

He then proceeds to define a spirit as "one simple, undivided, active being." But though undivided, "as it perceives ideas it is called the *understanding*, and as it produces or otherwise operates about them it is called the *will*." There cannot be any ideas of soul or spirit. For ideas are inactive; hence they could not possibly represent something so different from themselves as the principle of action:

> The words *will, soul, spirit,* do not stand for different ideas, or, in truth, for any idea at all, but for something which is very different from ideas, and which, being an agent, cannot be like unto, or represented by, any idea whatsoever. Though it must be owned at the same time that we have some *notion* of soul, spirit, and the operations of the mind such as willing, loving, hating; inasmuch as we know or understand the meaning of these words.

The distinction between an "idea" and a "notion" may seem a bit tenuous. It depends upon whether one is willing to accept a distinction between the feeling that other *persons* besides oneself exist and the feeling that merely other *bodies* besides one's own exist. For "ideas or sensations" would, by this terminology, be the words for what, in everyday speech, we might call bodies; whereas our conviction that in addition to these bodies there are persons would be a "notion."

Spirit can be perceived, in the empirical sense (not as "notions" but as "ideas or sensations") only in terms of the effects it produces. This formulation allows for empirical evidence of the existence of God, who happily for our purposes is called the "Almighty Agent." In studying the laws of Nature, says Berkeley, we discover that the ideas composing our experience proceed "in a regular train or series, the admirable connection whereof sufficiently testifies the wisdom and benevolence of its Author." What we experience as "things" are to be "considered only as marks or signs for our information." And the natural philosopher should seek "to understand these signs instituted by the Author of Nature." Ideas, spirits, and relations are "all in their respective kinds the object of human knowledge."

"God," then, is Berkeley's equivalent for the ultimate scene, scene as translated into terms of agent. What we experience as "things" are "ideas" which do not cease to be when we cease to think of them, since they are maintained in the mind of God. Though his opponents accuse him of solipsism, this aspect of Berkeley's doctrine would in a Berkeleian's eyes invalidate the charge. *"Esse* is *percipi"* could thus be translated for our purposes: "To be is to be grounded in the term, super-agent." But though the lawfulness of nature is taken as the evidence of God in nature, Berkeley recognizes how his position can lead to a narrowing of circumference:

> And yet this insistent uniform working, which so evidently displays the goodness and wisdom of that governing Spirit whose will constitutes the laws of nature, is so far from leading our thoughts to Him, that it rather sends them wandering after second causes. For, when we perceive certain ideas of sense constantly followed by other ideas and we know this is not of our own doing, we forthwith attribute power and agency to the ideas themselves [that is, to the effects that the "things" of our sensory experience are thought to have upon one another] and make one the cause of another, than which nothing could be more absurd and unintelligible. Thus, for example, having observed that when we perceive by sight a certain round luminous figure we at the same time perceive by touch the idea of sensation called heat, we do from thence conclude the sun to be the cause of heat. And in like manner perceiving the motion and collision of bodies to be attended with sound, we are inclined to think the latter the effect of the former.

Hume

The strategic equating of ideas with sensations naturally leads to a narrowing of circumference. For it invites us to drop the stress upon action and the rational, and to stress rather such mental functionings as fall under the head of motion. Otherwise stated: The Berkeleian idealism served as an important step from rationalism to empiricism by equating "the intelligible" with "the sensible," whereupon in accordance with the law of parsimony the "intelligible" side of the equation could be dropped as an unnecessary duplication, the attention being focused upon the side that lent itself the better to laboratory investigation. Ironically, Berkeley prophesies this very trend in admonishing against it.

In the realm of psychology, the narrowing took place by the development of the empiricist element in Berkeley's doctrine: namely, the study of "ideas" in terms of "sensations." And the narrowing was accomplished in the realm of metaphysics by the great skeptic David Hume, with his critique of metaphysics that strongly affected the idealistic system of Emmanuel Kant.

Hume's skepticism was particularly drastic, not in the questioning of God, but in the questioning of a *God-term* as basic to secular science as it had been to religion: the concept of *causality.* Let us inspect his *Inquiry Concerning Human Understanding* just enough to specify how he went about this, in following the logic of Locke's and Berkeley's empiricism.

Beginning psychologistically, he divided "all the perceptions of the mind into two classes or species, which are distinguished by their different degrees of force and vivacity." The "less forcible and lively" he called *"thoughts* or *ideas."* And "all our more lively perceptions, when we hear, or see, or feel, or love, or hate, or desire, or will" he called "impressions." Similarly, the apparently creative power of our mind "amounts to no more than the faculty of compounding, transposing, augmenting, or diminishing the materials afforded us by the senses and experience." Our idea of God, for instance, as infinitely intelligent, wise, and good "arises from reflecting on the operations of our own mind, and augmenting, without limit, those qualities of goodness and wisdom." And where a sense is defective, one can have no idea, as a man born blind can have no idea of colors. In this way, Hume derives ideas from purely sensory impressions. And when we suspect that some term in philosophy is meaningless, for a test "we need but inquire, *from what impression is that supposed idea derived?"*

Applying this test, Hume observes that our idea of cause and effect "is not, in any instance, attained by reasonings *a priori,* but arises entirely from experience." Whereas we can advance by pure reasoning from one proposition to another in geometry, we cannot similarly anticipate what effects will follow a given cause, "for the effect is totally different from the cause, and consequently can never be discovered in it." We learn from experience that an unsupported stone will fall. There is no logical way of anticipating such an effect. (Indeed, Hume might have cited here the fact that Galileo's experiments with falling bodies discredited beliefs about motion that had previously been assumed on the basis of reason alone, and by some expert reasoners at that.)

If we were to come into the world with fully developed powers of reason, yet without experiences of fact, we should not know what to anticipate, Hume says. The principle directing our expectations is a psychological one: *"custom* or *habit."* "All inferences from experience . . . are effects of custom, not of reasoning." As a result of custom, the order of our ideas follows the order of nature. (We can get the point here by contrasting Hume's position with Spinoza's view of a *rationally necessary* connection between the *ordo idearum* and the *ordo rerum.*) "We only learn by experience the frequent *conjunction* of objects, without ever being able to comprehend anything like *connection* between them." Habit or custom thus gives rise to a scene-agent ratio on a purely experiential basis, in contrast with the Stoic doctrine of a universal rationality similarly pervading both natural scene and human agents.

In Hume's skepticism the great dramatist cluster of terms (reason, substance, cause, necessity, action, idea, God, Nature, generation, power) is beginning to fall apart. On the purely Symbolic plane, one might well be justified in examining this placid bachelor's theories as a metaphysical questioning of potency and progeny (dissolving the reality of power and cause by subjecting them to the terms of his empirical quizzicality), as we might similarly examine the theories of that placid bachelor Bentham, who put forward his ideal of a neutral vocabulary. The ideal of "sterilization" may be indigenous to the patterns of technology. In any event, at the very least the dethronement of "causality" is the rejection of a term essentially *ancestral* or *parental,* as is similarly the case with the dethronement of reason and the strong stress upon *derivation* that goes with it. On the Symbolic level, there is a pattern of "race suicide" implicit in the turn from "causality" to the cult of sheer "correlation." But be that as it may, Hume was certainly correct in contending that there is no purely empirical evidence for concepts like causality, power, necessary connection. You can observe factual sequences which you choose to interpret as an indication of causality; but you may with as much justice interpret them as indications of a Divine Purpose, so far as the evidence of the senses is concerned. "Causality" or "power" themselves are not empirically observable, any more than God is. By examining the "impression" of such ideas, we find that it arises merely "from reflecting on the operations of our own minds."

Leibniz

It was this vigilant criticism that awoke Kant from his "dogmatic," or rationalist slumbers. In Germany at that time philosophizing was done mainly under the aegis of Leibniz, whose system still placed great stress upon Substance and necessary logical connection. It was a rationalism of *idealist* cast, however, in that it stressed in substance a psychologistic factor, the nature of entities as *perceptive*, or as endowed with the power to *represent*. The Leibnizian universe was a world of individuals ("monads"), each with its own particular point of view, and "realizing itself" to the extent that the limits of its nature permitted. Indeed, Leibniz' system falls so well under the head of agent that we can clearly see in him the beginnings of our modern psychologies of the unconscious. His "monads" were atom-agents, each developing its own inner potentialities, its own particular range of growth (widest in the case of man) from the implicit to the explicit.

The famous concept of "pre-established harmony" was invented by Leibniz as *deus ex machina* to bring it about that the principle of self-development activating each of the monadic substances does not interfere with the self-development of its fellows. That is, God so adjusted the monads to one another that their development would have the same effect as if they were all mutually constraining or influencing one another. By this pre-established harmony, says Leibniz, it is as though the world were composed of infinite voices, each singing its own particular song, unaware of any other, yet if you could hear them all, you would hear the song of a choir singing in perfect time with all parts in perfect polyphonic relation to one another. Leibniz thus stressed the plurality side of the plurality-unity pair as strongly as Spinoza had stressed the unity side. But God, as the *Monas Monadum*, brought the plurality to a unified head.

This concept also provided for a difference in *degree* rather than in *kind* between God and the lesser monads. And though the infinity of monads represented a corresponding infinity of points of view, these monads were "without windows"—a device that enabled Leibniz to treat them as substances with internal principles of action proper to "things in themselves."

The Kantian idealism, then, encounters the two aspects of the idealist incentive. In the Leibnizian strain were the principles of unification, the powers of the Idea needed for service in the German community of small states, that were separated from one another by cultural traditions and tariff barriers, were feeling the individualism of the rising capitalist tradition, and were accordingly moving in the direction of national union. The Leibnizian idealizing of substance, allowing for a strong individualist emphasis along with an over-all principle of unity, gave exactly the pattern of agent and super-agent that we find in enterprisers and nation. Similarly, the stress upon the Idea allowed for the optimistically developmental, or creatively anticipatory, in short a *futuristic* emphasis (for "unification" implies a gerundive, a "to be unified").

The scientist emphasis is emergent in Leibniz, in that he slants his conception of substance towards *perception* (whereas in its pure scholastic form its primary slant was towards *action*). But it was among the British bourgeois philosophers that the insights provided by the application of science were most clearly perceived. And in Hume Kant encountered the development of idealism in direct response to scientism. (Hume's *Inquiry* opened significantly with a distinction between a philosophy that "considers man chiefly as born for action" and one that considers man "in the light of a reasonable rather than an active being" receiving "from science his proper food and nourishment.") Idealism here had stressed psychology to the point where it came upon a *"problem* of knowledge," leading us to doubt the possibilities of "necessary" truth as regards the world of facts.

Kant

In trying here to consider the complexities of Kant's philosophy, we encounter two difficulties. First we must manage somehow to review it briefly for persons who may not know it at all (so that our review is in danger of being either superficial or confusing). And we may irritate those who do know Kant's philosophy already, but have not approached it from the standpoint of the dramatist Grammar.

We may get around our difficulties somewhat by a subterfuge. Let us imagine ourselves trying to work up a Kantian vocabulary in accordance with the linguistic resources, temptations, and embarrassments we have been studying in these pages.

First, since our system is to show the influence of science, and was written at a time when science was identical with the celestial mechanics of Newton, our terminology must recognize all claims made by a terminology laying down strict laws of *motion*. Yet we are not merely to write a philosophy of physical science. We have also been thinking in the tradition of Leibniz, so we shall want a principle of *action*, an ethical principle wider in scope than the laws of sheer motion. We shall want something to take the place of Leibniz' *principle of sufficient reason*, by which he allowed for *final* causes (*purpose*), in contending that the world of factual experience could only be accounted for if we derived it from God. For no less a cause than God could be great enough to be the source or ground of the creation. However, we shall want our substitute for Leibniz' finalism to be as "scientific" as possible.

We have just been awakened with a jolt. This jolt at first seemed menacing, but on second thought was found to be just what we needed. It was in Hume, and I shall quote it because it significantly introduces one more term than we have watched in Hume so far:

> The bread, which I formerly eat, nourished me; that is, a body of such sensible qualities was, at that time, endued with such secret powers: but does it follow, that other bread must also nourish me at another time, and that like sensible qualities must always be attended with like secret powers? The consequence seems no wise necessary. At least, it must be acknowledged that there is here a consequence drawn by the mind; that there is a certain step taken; a process of thought, and an inference, which wants to be explained. These two propositions are far from being the same, *I have found that such an object has always been attended with such an effect,* and *I foresee, that other objects, which are, in appearance, similar, will be attended with similar effects.* I shall allow, if you please, that the one proposition may justly be inferred from the other; I know, in fact, that it always is inferred. But if you insist that the inference is made by a chain of reasoning, I desire you to produce that reasoning. The connection between these propositions is not intuitive. There is required a medium, which may enable the mind to draw such an inference, if indeed it be drawn by reasoning and argument. What that medium is, I must confess, passes my comprehension; and it is

incumbent on those to produce it, who assert that it really exists, and is the origin of all our conclusions concerning matter of fact.

That request for a "medium" is our cue. Suppose we provide such a medium—and do so in keeping with the genius of our term *agent*. One usually thinks of a medium as something in which an agent acts (scene) or something which an agent uses (agency). But what if we equated it with *the very nature of the agent itself?* Hume has been saying in effect that we can't *see* "causality" or "power" or "necessary connection." How, then, can we arrive at such concepts?

By utilizing a function of our term *agent*, we can transform this problem into a solution. Namely: we can say that people interpret natural sequences in terms of cause and effect not because of something in the natural scene requiring this interpretation, but *because they are the sort of agents that see things in terms of necessary relations.* In this view we do not derive our ideas of cause and effect from experience; all that we can derive from experience is the observation that certain happenings seem likely to follow certain happenings. But our ideas of cause and effect are derived *from the nature of the mind.* You must at least grant that this view would meet Hume's demand for a "medium," and would do so by equating medium with agent.

Another important linguistic resource enters at this point, however. In deriving causality from the realm covered by our term *agent* (whereas heretofore it was considered so thoroughly a property of *scene*), we need not mean *individual* agents. For if we did, the causal principle would still lack universality. That is, it would lack objective reality, being at best like the kind of general opinion that prevailed when all men thought the world was flat. The causal principle need not be assigned to the agent in this sense. Instead, we can *universalize* our concept of agent. We can say that such a way of seeing is not the property of just *your* understanding or *my* understanding but of *"the understanding"* in general.

We have now set ourselves some rich linguistic possibilities, which we shall develop as follows:

First, there is our old action-passion pair. We shall begin with this, dividing our universal agent into two aspects. The "passive" we shall assign to the *sensibility.* Abiding by the grammar of the word "data" (*the given*), we shall view the senses as passive, since they *receive* representations of objects. If only as a grammatical reflex, we shall next look for an "active." And we find it in the *understanding*, which is active in that it performs the act of unification. The senses, for instance, may passively receive a manifold of sense data, a confusion of colors, textures, shapes, etc.—and the understanding may unify all this by a concept, as when, considering that manifold, we say, "It is a house." So we have our first grammatical pair, the senses passively receiving what is "given" to them, and the understanding actively uniting this manifold by a concept. The representations of sense are, in the Kantian terminology, called *intuitions*. As Kant puts it: "Objects are *given* to us by means of sensibility, and it alone yields us *intuitions;* they are *thought* through the understanding, and from the understanding arise *concepts*." But all thought must relate ultimately to the intuitions of sensibility, "because in no other way can an object be given to us." By this last statement we take care of the demands made by empirical science, which must be grounded in the evidence of the senses.

But though we have begun with an active and a passive principle here, we should be disastrously misled if we attempted to characterize our alignment of terms with reference to it as we did in the case of Spinoza. For this philosophy takes its beginning in a *scientist* problem, not the problem of *action*, but the problem of *knowledge*. The vital concern here is with "the object," as perceived through intuition and conceived by the understanding. Let us accordingly center our attention upon the object, to see what momentous linguistic resources we may have for application here.

First, just as we universalized the function of agent, so we shall raise our concern with objects to a high level of generalization. And we shall not inquire into the conditions that make possible our knowledge of this object or that object, but of the "object in general."

Now, the surprising thing about an *object in general* is that you can't distinguish it from *no object at all*. For it is not this object or that object or any other object that you could actually point to in all the world. I realized this when contemplating a chart designed to show the interrelations among the key terms in Kant's *Critique of Pure Reason*. The attempt to represent the appearance of an object in general, in order to show how it was related eventually to an unseen thing-in-itself, led to the embarrassing discovery that such an object in general would be as impossible to represent as would the unseen thing-in-itself that by definition lies beyond the realm of sense relationships.

(Incidentally, lest the reader misinterpret my attitude here, let me add: I believe the true mettle of a philosopher is shown in what he can say about nothing. Any tyro can talk about something. But it takes a really profound thinker to say profound things about nothing. And I hasten to admit that my own five terms are all about nothing, since they designate not this scene, or that agent, etc. but scene, agent, etc. in general.)

If, then, you would talk profoundly and intelligently about the conditions of the possibility of the knowledge of nothing, what *do* you have that you can talk about? You have the *knower*. You can say, for instance, "Whatever an object in general may or may not look like, you can be sure that when you do come across one you are going to have to encounter it in terms of space and/or time." And since you can't here be talking about an object (if you are, what is it?) what you *must* be talking about is the *nature of your own mind*. Your mind is prepared to encounter this object, whatever it may be, in spatial and/or temporal terms. Furthermore, the mind is prepared to expect that the object will be a quantity of some sort (as were it single or plural), that it will have some kind of quality (it will be hard, or light, or sweet, or evanescent, or *something*), that it will be in some relation to other objects in general, etc. These are all requirements that you are mentally prepared in advance to make of the object. Thus they are in the mind, *a priori;* and the object will *necessarily* meet these requirements, since they are the requirements the mind makes of every experienced object. They are *conditions* that the object must meet; and being *mental* conditions, they reside in the *agent* rather than in the *object*. And the locating of such conditions in the agent as medium Kant calls "transcendental." Thus, the difference between "formal" and "transcendental" logic is generated by the fact that the Kantian logic takes its start in a question with which formal logic is not concerned at all. Formal logic deals with *internal* consistency. Transcendental logic, paradoxically enough, arrives at its stress upon agent through a question about scene ("conditions" of knowing).

Still using our readily available linguistic resources, we could put this in another way. We have discussed a tribal, or familial, or parental principle whereby the nature of a thing may be grounded in the nature of the source from which it is derived. Hence, one point of departure will lead to different conclusions than another. And so we can get around the thorough-going empiricist position by distinguishing two starting points, one empirical and the other transcendental.

Thus Kant distinguishes "what begins with" from "what arises out of." "There can be no doubt," he says, "that all knowledge begins with experience," for we can know nothing until we have had experience. "But though all our knowledge begins *with* experience, it does not thereby arise wholly *out of* experience." (*Wenn aber gleich alle unsere Erkenntniss* mit *der Erfahrung anhebt, so entspringt sie darum doch nicht eben alle* aus *der Erfahrung*.) For besides the knowledge we get from impressions, there may be something "which our own faculty of knowledge . . . supplies from itself." Applying the ancestral principle here in ways of our own, you will note that our Kantian structure has contrived to infuse the empirical world with "transcendental" attributes. One can glimpse the kind of resonance this grammar gives us on the Symbolic level, by recalling a recent critic's remark that Carlyle borrowed the vocabulary of transcendentalism to "poetize" the pragmatic and empirical (and though one must admit that Kant's "poetry" here is quite cumbersome, one would be wrong in allowing the occasional scientific pretenses of philosophers to conceal the fact that their basic ways and aims are to be viewed in terms of poetic action).

But look where we now are. We have described intellectual synthesis as "active." Yet what kind of "act" is this? The empirical scene has derived its character from the nature of the agent; but though we have called this action of the mind "spontaneous" and "original," we might just as well have called it "inevitable." It is *compulsory*, lacking the elements of freedom necessary for action. The mind cannot see otherwise than in terms of the categories. To observe is an act, in that one can choose either to observe it or not to observe it. But to observe *in terms of the categories* is not an act in this sense, since we *must* consider it in such terms, whether we choose to observe it or not. Conversely, though the sensibility is "passive," we find space and time called the "forms" of sensibility. And in the tradition from which Western philosophy stems, "form" is the act word par excellence. So the "passive" begins to look as active as the avowedly active. In brief, even though our construction of a Kantian system leads us to conclude that experience derives its appearance from the nature of consciousness (the "I think," or "transcendental synthesis of apperception") this is hardly origination in the moral sense of the term.

Then where are we? Putting together the sensibility (treated in the "Transcendental Aesthetic") and the understanding (treated in the "Transcendental Analytic"), we have encompassed but the world of Newtonian motion, the world of physical science as then conceived in terms of mechanistic determination. There are no "wills," "oughts," "shoulds," or "thou shalt nots" here. There is nothing but an inevitable *is,* a description of conditions as they necessarily *are* for human experience, so that Kant calls them "constitutive," which we could translate "scenic, with circumference narrowed to the scope of motion." It is not materialism, since the scene itself is said to derive its character from a function of the term agent (whereas in pure materialism agent would be derived from scene). And at this stage it is not supernaturalism, since the agent from which the nature of the scene is derived is not a divine super-agent but a kind of universalized human (we might call it a *human mind in general*).

We still have to introduce a principle of action, in the full moral sense of the term. But note that we have not yet drawn upon the resources of two master terms for philosophies of action, "idea" and "reason." So our third section (the "Transcendental Dialectic") will enable us to transcend the empirical-transcendental realm of motion (the "constitutive") by a concern with "ideas of reason," which allow for moral acts (the "regulative").

All told, then, we have:

(a) Intuitions of sensibility (which attain their maximum generalization as pure space and pure time, the two conditions necessary for any sensory representation);

(b) Concepts of understanding (which attain their maximum generalization in the categories, categories we might think of as a questionnaire with a set of blanket questions to be filled in differently in the case of each object, but with the whole set of questions requiring some kind of answer in every case);

(These two together comprise the realm of experience investigated by scientific empiricism, a world conditioned "transcendentally," which is to say conditioned by the conditions of

the mind. The forms of sensibility and categories of understanding, taken together, comprise the scene of narrowed circumference Kant calls the "constitutive.")

(c) Ideas of reason (allowing for the introduction of another principle, the "regulative," that will if properly manipulated permit
us to introduce principles of action into a world of motion).

Moral Transcendence in Kant

It is our job now to place this third step (c) in accordance with the
Grammatical tests of consistency. If ideas are active, the logic of the
scene-act ratio would require that they be derived from a different
scene than the combined empirical-transcendental structure called the
"constitutive." And this we might get by introducing a distinction,
making two meanings grow where but one had grown before. We
might "Desynonymize."

I borrow the word from Coleridge, whose *Biographia Litteraria* is
concerned with desynonymizing two words previously considered synonymous. For *imaginatio* had regularly been taken as Latin equivalent for the Greek *phantasia*. Hence the tendency had been to treat
our derivatives, *imagination* and *fancy*, as synonymous. And Coleridge set about to make a distinction in kind between them. The great
departures in human thought can be eventually reduced to a moment
where the thinker treats as *opposite*, key terms formerly considered *ap-
posite*, or *v.v.* So we are admonished to be on the look-out for those
moments when strategic synonymizings or desynonymizings occur.
And, in accordance with the logic of our ratios, when they do occur, we
are further admonished to be on the look-out for a shift in the source
of derivation, as terms formally derived from different sources are
now derived from a common source, or *v.v.* In the present case, let
us see what we can do if we strategically desynonymize "transcendental" and "transcendent," at the same time remembering grammatical scruples about a corresponding split in derivation. And it would
be all the better if, at the same time as our desynonymizing enabled us
to provide a fitting ground for moral action, it likewise solved a metaphysical problem left by our account of the world of empirical motion.

For according to our account, the world as we experience it is but
a world of *appearances*. The objects of experience, we have said, derive
their appearance from the nature of our minds (as all colors will seem

like shades of but one color if we observe them through colored glasses).
But if they are *appearances*, what are they appearances of? Our desynonymizing here will lead us to the answer. The *empirical* realm is
the realm of appearances. The *transcendental* realm is the realm that
gives things the nature they seem to have in the empirical realm. And
the *transcendent* realm will be the realm of things as they are "in themselves," not as empirically conditioned by the conditions of the transcendental.

We have thus arrived at the transcendent realm as a realm of things
"in themselves" (that is, with whatever nature they may have intrinsically, not as they are determined by the terms in which we see them).
Whereat we might profitably pause to consider the grammar of the intrinsic. It is the puzzle we encountered when discussing the paradox
of substance. As soon as one considers things in relation to other
things, one is uncomfortably on the way to dissolving them into their
context, since their relations lead beyond them. A thing in itself for
instance can't be "higher" or "heavier" than something or "inside" or
"outside" something, or "derived from" something, etc. For though
such descriptions may apply to it, they do not apply to it purely as a
thing *in itself;* rather, they are *contextual* references, pointing beyond
the thing.

Though Leibniz' notion of "pre-established harmony" among the
infinite monads may seem arbitrary, it was designed precisely as a metaphysical solution for the problem of the intrinsic. By means of this
invention, he was able to maintain that each monad was a unique substance (hence, capable of treatment in itself, whereas we will recall that
Spinoza, noting how each thing was limited by other things, contended
that nothing short of *everything considered in its totality* could be
treated as substance; for only the universal whole could have no context outside itself to which it would be externally related).

Personally, I do not see that, even if we granted Leibniz his formula,
it would wholly solve the problem. For the principle of harmonization
derived from God obviously leaves the created substances with a most
important external relation, perhaps the most important of all. But in
any case, we can know what he was driving at, which is enough for
our purpose. If God by a principle of pre-established harmony had so
brought it about that every monad could go on realizing its own intrinsic possibilities without reference to any other monad (indeed, if

its soul was "windowless" so that it could not even perceive other monads relationally, but represented them intrinsically by representing its own particular point of view), one might treat the monads as independent individuals, each with its own intrinsic principles of self-development, hence each in itself a substance, thereby avoiding the Spinozist merger of the part into the whole.

Be that as it may, I think we may now realize the Grammatical opportunities and embarrassments we encounter as we arrive in our Kantian system at a *transcendent* realm composed of things-in-themselves. Whatever it may be cosmologically, a thing in itself is Grammatically a thing without reference to context. And for our purposes, that is as far as we need go. Grammatically, then, the transcendent realm is a realm of things-without-context, or things-without-relation.

What does that give us? First, note that relations are "determinations." They assign borders (termini) to a thing. A synonym is "conditions," since "conditions" are likewise contextual, as with the conditions of an organism's existence. Without worrying greatly what it may mean in the literal sense, but merely considering the Grammatical resources available here, let us note that, as the empirical realm is the realm of the determined or conditioned, and the transcendental realm is the realm of the conditions that provided the terms (determinations), so the transcendent realm of things-in-themselves would be the realm of the undetermined or unconditioned. Whereupon, lo! we find ourselves in a realm of *freedom!* And so, we have come upon a scene that allows for the possibility of *action.*

The transcendental had transcended the empirical; it had raised us to a level of generalization that "necessarily" unified the world of particulars, infusing the world of particulars with its spirit. And so now in turn the transcendent has transcended the transcendental, thereby infusing the world of determinism with the spirit of freedom (which is another way of saying that we have added to the world of physical motion the possibilities of moral action).

However, since we began our enterprise with all respect for the requirements of empirical science, we have defined knowledge by empirical tests. Knowledge by definition, then, is the knowledge of conditions and relations. It is the knowledge of *appearances*, the knowledge of objects as they necessarily appear when seen in terms of our human categories (the categories of the mind in general). So, by defi-

nition, the transcendent realm of the unconditoned things-
selves (the scene that contains the possibilities of freedom) canne.
known. Hence, we must restrict the claims we can make about it.
But whereas it can't be *known,* it can be *thought about,* for we are now
thinking about it.

Modern positivists would question whether this statement has meaning; it is certainly "non-sense" if we interpret that word literally, for it
is a statement about a realm *outside* the realm of sensory experience.
But if you consider it purely from the standpoint of Grammatical resources, it is obvious that a word as highly generalized as "the conditioned" leaves us with "the unconditioned" as its dialectical opposite,
hence as the only term left to be the *ground* or context of the conditioned. And though we certainly cannot *know* this ground, in the
scientific meaning which we have given to "knowledge," we can
"think" it in recognizing that, *so far as the patterns of human thought
are concerned,* the only term that could antithetically match the "conditioned" would be the "unconditioned." And the *unknown* to which
we thus refer in so basic a pattern of human thought might be characterized as "thought of."

It is an important spot to haggle over, however, if you are going to
haggle at all. For once you let this point go by unquestioned, you
give Kant some important advantages. If this realm of the things-in-
themselves can be *thought* though not *known,* this limitation upon
our claims to knowledge about them applies in reverse to science.
Science compels us to admit that things-in-themselves can't be known;
but in putting them outside the area of scientific *knowledge,* by the
same token we put them outside the area of scientific *refutation* or
denial. The sources of morality thus lie beyond the reach of the
terms proper to the physical sciences (which is but another way of
saying that, in this terminology, action cannot be reduced to motion).
In his preface to the second edition Kant said: "I must abolish *knowledge,* to make room for *belief."* In taking the action out of the scene
which he equated with knowledge, he had to make sure that there was
still room for an act of faith.

To grant that these unknowns can be thought of, however, is further
to allow for a very ingenious verbalism. If they can be thought of, if
we can employ our intelligence on them, let us call them the "intelligible." Whereupon, lo! whereas empiricism took its start in equating

the intelligible with the sensible, the intelligible is now so named precisely because it *can't* be sensed. Beginning in empiricism, making a line-up that will permit the pursuit of each empirical science in its own terms, we have nonetheless managed to so wangle things that we make allowance for terms beyond the scope of empirical science.

And so, in sum, we have phenomena (appearances, objects as we encounter them in everyday experience) and noumena (the undefined somethings that must lie behind appearances, hence cannot be sensed, but can be considered mentally—*noumena* being a present passive participle from the same root as the Greek *nous*). Such a step from conditioned to the unconditioned, or from things in relation to things-in-themselves, or from the determinate to the indeterminate (in brief, from necessity to freedom) Kant frankly calls "dialectical." With this all would agree. But in so frankly labelling his third section dialectical, he tends to conceal from both us and himself the equally dialectical ingredients in the first two sections. All three involve linguistic operations which, by the very nature of language, transcend the terminology of the senses.

Kant began his inquiry (in the *Critique of Pure Reason*) by considering the "conditions of the possibility" of *knowledge*. But by the end of the book he is concerned with the conditions of the possibility of *action*. Hence his conditional principle of the "as if" (*Als ob*). We cannot *know* that there are God, freedom, and immortality; but we should act *as if* there were. Hence, moral action is rooted in the *ideas* of God, freedom, and immortality. (Unlike sensations and concepts, ideas can have no *empirical* reference. As the understanding uses the materials of sense, so reason uses the materials of the understanding). These ideas thus refer back to the transcendent realm. The moral motive is thus our bond between the realm of necessity (the caused) and the realm of freedom (first causes). We can then round out matters neatly by considering the world of nature as an example of *purpose,* while looking for signs of this purpose not mystically, but scientifically, in the study of natural law. In brief, to find indications of *purpose* behind nature, we shall look for *mechanism* in nature.

Introducing our Grammar here, in a non-Kantian but not anti-Kantian way, I would propose to consider this freedom-necessity, or teleology-mechanism manoeuver thus: Think of an enactment, as with the enacting of a constitution. The enacting is the forming of the constitution, the constitution is the permanent form left by the enactment. Let us say that men came together *of their own free will* to enact the constitution. The resulting document, however, is *not free*. It must be just what it is. The clauses are necessarily related to one another in certain ways. (We need not complicate matters by considering amendments. To a degree, an amendment simply gives us a new constitution, which is to say, a new enactment.) But insofar as we have one enactment and its corresponding form as a constitution, once the constitution has been enacted, all the relations among its parts are *necessary*. Or we could think of a poem: the freer and more perfect the poet was in his craftsmanship, the more "inevitable" would be the relationships that the parts of his poem bear to one another. It would be in this sense that signs of necessity in the phenomenal realm could be interpreted as signs of freedom in the transcendent or noumenal realm.

And perhaps the quickest way to indicate how "ideals" of action can be said to transcend empirical conditions would be by a citation from Book V of Plato's *Republic:*

> The city will be courageous because some of its members maintain under all conditions the opinions our legislator taught them about the nature of things to be feared and not to be feared.
> And by the words "under all conditions" I mean to suggest that in pleasure or in pain, or under the influence of desire or fear, a man preserves and does not lose that opinion.

And as for Kant's formula indicating how his principle of action bridges the two realms of conditioned and unconditioned:

> It does not involve a contradiction to assert on the one hand that the will, in the phenomenal realm (of visible action) necessarily obeys the laws of nature, and to this extent is *not free;* and on the other hand that, as belonging to a thing-in-itself, it is not subject to such laws and accordingly *is* free.*

* The entire pattern of thought in the *Critique of Pure Reason* stresses unification. Even the variety of data available to the intuitions of sense has an "affinity" in its manifoldness. This "affinity" I would translate Grammatically as a gerundive: for if the manifold of sense can be unified by the concepts of understanding, then there is in this manifold a kind of "to-be-unifiedness" that one could call an "affinity" among the components of the manifold. Reason aims finally at the most unified principle of all, the idea of God as the total unity that is the ground of all existence.

Idealism after Kant

The thinkable but unknowable noumenal realm, then, was taken as the ground of the phenomenal realm. But we slid over a Grammatical embarrassment. If the phenomenal is the realm of *relationships*, and the noumenal is the realm of things-*in-themselves* (i.e., *without* relationships), just how could there be a bond between the two realms? Otherwise put: If the noumenal is the realm of *freedom* and the phenomenal is the realm of *necessity*, is the connection between the two realms "free" or "necessary"? Kant compromised on a weasel word, saying that the noumenal "influences" the phenomenal. But Fichte grounded his system *wholly* in agent, maintaining that the Kantian thing-in-itself was not necessary. Kant himself had called apperception, or consciousness in general, "the highest principle in the whole

---

But there is another important unifying principle in Kant: the transcendental imagination, that stands like the keystone in an arch having sensibility at one end and understanding at the other. And in keeping with this, there is an ingenious device called the "schema," which can enable us to shuttle back and forth between intuitions and concepts. For, like intuitions it partakes of the particular; yet like the concept it has generality.

One can expect it to be ambiguous, for it has an ambiguous role to perform, since it must contrive to be homogeneous with two heterogeneous fields. This is managed thus: Suppose I put five dots in a row to represent the concept of "five"; and then seven dots in a row to represent the concept of "seven"; and then, to represent 1,000, instead of going on to make a thousand dots, I say, "You get the idea." That is, you would understand the general rule that you would follow in arriving at the proper image. Because of its function as thus *mediating* between the particular and the general, some commentators have considered imagination in Kant the principle of unification *par excellence*.

And as regards Kant's detailed analysis of the schema, since it does lie in the opposite fields of particularity and generality, would one not be entitled to expect in advance that it itself would have to split into two aspects, each aspect gravitating towards one of the sides? This embarrassment shows up, I think, in the Kantian distinction between "schemata" and "schematism," the "schemata" leaning to the side of the particular, the "schematism" leaning to the side of the general. And, as with the endless subdividing of the atom into ever smaller particles, I am sure that, if we could make our critical instruments sharp enough, we should find it necessary to subdivide "schemata" and "schematism" in turn, finding that each contained in it a particularizing aspect and a generalizing aspect, the "schemata" giving two votes for particular and one for general, the "schematism" giving two votes for general and one for particular.

At least, I offer this hypothesis as solace to the reader for whom Kant's analysis of the schema is alternately revealing and puzzling.

sphere of human knowledge." This placed a high value on the function of agent, but Fichte gave a still higher one, in reducing everything to the Ego and a Non-Ego *derived from* it. In this respect, the pattern is obviously closer to Berkeley than to Kant.

On the Symbolic level, the Nature side of the Spirit-Nature pair in Fichte was born under bad auspices. He apparently evolved his system while contemplating a career alternative to marriage. Fichte is noted for the austerity and consciousness of his doctrines. But his distinction between the I and the Not-I, which gives us in German the *Ich* and the *Nichtich*, happens to produce, for the Not-I, a word pronounced exactly like *nichtig,* the meanings of which are listed in Muret-Sanders as: *unreal, vain, frivolous, empty, hollow, futile, flimsy, transitory, ineffectual, invalid, void,* the adjective itself being derived from the word for nothing, quite like the English *naughty*. We may remember these matters, when reading in an editor of Hegel, Georg Lasson, the complaint that the Ego claims too much in Fichte's scheme, so that too little is left for the Not-Ego.

Since Fichte stressed such thought as would identify the individual ego with the communal ego, we might relevantly cite from Andrew Seth, *The Development from Kant to Hegel:* "In Fichte's own language, everything must 'hang firmly in a single ring, which is fastened to nothing, but maintains itself and the whole system by its own power.'" And Fichte's political theories were presented in the name of a "closed" commercial state (*geschlossener Handelsstaat*), the beginnings of the "autarchic" principle. And in general, there are symbolic ambiguities (or *double-entendres*) in the idealist pattern of externalization, due to the fact that it represents a movement from "inner" to "outer," as from implicit to explicit, from unconscious to conscious, from magma to lava, and thus from visceral to excretory.

In any event, from the time of Fichte the pattern of idealism pure and simple was set. With varying terms, such philosophers as Schelling, Hegel, and Schopenhauer traced the genealogy of the objective world from the subjective, treating nature as an externalization or expression of spirit somewhat as a poem may be called an externalization of the poet. Nature being thus viewed as the incarnation or embodiment of mind, the pattern was edifying in Fichte, esthetic in Schelling, optimistic in Hegel, and pessimistic in Schopenhauer (where the externalizations of the universal *will* are treated not as *assertions* of the agent, but rather like those *involuntary* expressions that the post-Schopenhauer psychologies would call "compulsion neuroses").

Marxism

The Marxian dialectical materialism grows out of idealism by antithesis. Hegel had strongly stressed a *developmental* feature in the expression, externalization, embodiment, or "utterance" (*Äusserung*) of the spirit. The development of the spirit was viewed as objectified through the medium of nature and history. And this process of mediation (*Vermittlung*) led to a much more concrete view of "conditions" than did the high levels of generalization in Kant. Though Hegel constructed an elaborate metaphysical framework for the placement of his historical stages, the stages themselves had to be portrayed by the use of historical detail. And so we got, in effect, a superagent (Spirit) manifesting itself in progressively changing historical conditions (scenes of narrowed circumference). In his *Philosophy of History,* equating World History with Reason, he defines Reason as "Thought conditioning itself with perfect freedom."

Marx materialistically reversed the genealogy here, by deriving the character of human consciousness in different historical periods from the character of the material conditions prevailing at the time. And though I have said that Hegel's treatment of "conditions" is concrete as compared with Kant's, the Marxist treatment of conditions is dazzlingly concrete; and once we look at it we are blinded to any difference between Kant and Hegel in this respect.

Perhaps the change of genealogy is best shown, in its metaphysical proportions, where Lenin, in his *Materialism and Empirio-Criticism* detects the idealistic bias in Machian post-Kantian empiricism, which took its start from the data of *sensation,* a property of agent. In idealism, he says, "sensation is taken as the primary entity." But materialistic science "takes matter as the *prius,* regarding consciousness, reason and sensation as derivative, because in a well expressed form it is connected only with the higher forms of matter (organic matter)."

Up to this point, we have obviously made a simple shift from agent to scene as point of origin. Marxists, however, are not "vulgar materialists," or "mechanical materialists," but *dialectical* materialists. And we might well translate this term as "idealistic materialist." Marx and Engels were "neo-Hegelians" before setting up their philosophic branch as a separate establishment. Hence, if one is to trace his key terms from an heraldic source in scene, and is to do so with good Grammar, there must be some quality of agenthood permeating the scene itself. This is provided clearly enough when Lenin adds to his above remarks: "It becomes possible, therefore, to assume the existence of a property similar to sensation 'in the foundation stones of the structure of matter itself.'"

The metaphysical problem of knowledge retreats into the background, to be replaced by the social problem of action in a society so much of whose resources are both consciously and unconsciously pitted against the fair presentation and examination of the Marxist doctrines. On the metaphysical plane the solution offered is antithetical to that of idealism. Idealism had decided that knowledge was possible because Nature is of the same substance as Thought, hence Thought is able to think it. Dialectical materialism reverses the relation by saying that thought is of the same substance as nature, hence can be a reflection of nature. In Engels' terms: thought and consciousness "are the products of the human brain," and "man himself is a product of Nature." Hence "the products of the human brain, being in the last analysis also products of Nature, do not contradict the rest of Nature but are in correspondence with it."

But though such a doctrine of correspondence allows for the gradual accumulation and perfection of *natural* knowledge, Marxists detect a radical obstruction to *moral* knowledge (an obstruction which can extend also to the realm of natural knowledge). I am aware that I am here presenting the Marxist position in somewhat non-Marxist terms; but to account objectively for the Marxist modifications of idealism, this method is inevitable. In this chapter it is not my purpose at this late date merely to summarize and report on past philosophies. Rather, I am trying to show how certain key terms might be used to "call the plays" in any and all philosophies. My problem at this point is to characterize as accurately as possible the strategy involved in the dialectical-materialist rejection of idealism. And the problem is obviously much more difficult than it would be to characterize an out-and-out shift from idealism to materialism. But dialectical materialism, in its constant call upon human agents, and above all its futuristic stress upon kinds of social *unification,* is intensely idealistic. And it is our task to characterize this *from without,* in over-all terms, rather than in specifically Marxist terms, as a factual report would call for.

In particular, we would consider the role of the "idea" in the Marxist genealogy. We would consider it with relation to the detailed stress upon "conditions" by which Marxists strategically alter the traditional idealistic use of that term. And for the purposes of our Grammar, we must speculate on the exact relation between ideas and the conditions *out of which they arise*—or the other way round, the relation between ideas and the conditions *which they help to bring about,* when acted upon by human agents.

Let us, then, turn to the *Communist Manifesto,* where the symbolic action of ideas is obviously intense. To realize how vigorous this document is as a pronunciamento, one might recall the typical party platform, a hodgepodge of vote-getting devices, as architecturally solid as a false front, slung together by a batch of well-meaning (or at least socially-minded, since politically-minded) party hacks, assembling in back rooms to horse-trade in behalf of the special interests they represent in the name of the national welfare. Let one then turn by contrast to this sturdy Manifesto.

Here are not merely the unsigned I.O.U.'s of the typical sales talk. This document is a *constitution.* For not only is it *regulative,* saying what may be on condition that its offer is accepted. It is soundly *constitutive,* grounding its statement of political principles in statements about the nature of the universal scene (a scene narrowed to naturalistic limits, and defined in particular with relation to the laws and directions of human history). Over and above his fears and prejudices, the true Grammarian should take great delight in the contemplation of this strong document, even though he believed that general adherence to it might entail the loss of all that he holds dear (or at least the loss of all that he holds). But perhaps the handiest way to point it up is to contrast it with the dialectic used by Hegel in his *Philosophy of History.*

Hegel

History, according to Hegel, is the development of Spirit from a state of potentiality to a state of realization, this realization being complete when it has been embodied in concrete details that lead to complete self-consciousness. This historical process is also equated with the process of Reason, and Reason is equated with Freedom. The development of World History itself (its gradual progress from nature to the freedom of self-consciousness) is conceived after a biographical analogy, with Oriental culture corresponding to childhood, Greek culture to adolescence, Roman culture to manhood, and German culture to old age (whereupon the philosopher warns that, although "the Old Age of *Nature* is weakness," that of Spirit is "perfect maturity and *strength*").

Each stage contains inherent contradictions that, as they gradually develop, lead first to great activity and attainment in the forming of a State by which these contradictions are contained. But the State in its vigor expands, and so comes into contact with external factors that lead to the betrayal of its own internal principles. It then begins to disintegrate, though not before having made its contribution to the new culture into contact with which it had been brought by its expansion. Hence with the decay of each stage there emerges the growth of the succeeding stage, which takes place in a different geographical theatre. The dying stage implicitly hands on its degree of spiritual progress to the succeeding stages, until we finally arrive at the culmination and totality of the German stage, as embodied in the German monarchic State. Here secularity, in "gaining a consciousness of its intrinsic worth, becomes aware of having a value of its own, in the morality, rectitude, probity, and activity of man."

Hegel's theory lays quite some stress on the part that human ambitions play in the realizing of World History's "Idea." The subjectivity of human passions is the material which the Spirit uses as means in the enacting of its Universal design. Spirit's way of thus acting through the passions Hegel calls "the cunning of Reason." Individual men do not aim to further the ends of World History. They aim passionately to attain their own private ends, as determined by their own special interests; but in this effort they unconsciously carry out the Will of Providence. "Secular pursuits are a spiritual occupation." In their attempt to further their interests, they develop the State, which is the highest embodiment of *Spirit,* "the Divine Idea as it exists on earth." And since the State's laws are "the objectification of Spirit," one is free in obeying the law (for the will, as Spirit, in changing the law, as Spirit, is obeying itself, hence is independent, hence free). The

State is strongest when conditions are such that private and public interests coincide. A great "World-Historical" Hero, such as Alexander, Caesar, Napoleon, consciously aims only to further his own designs. But being close to the fountainhead of Spirit, he acts when the time is ripe—and in this perfect timing resides his contribution to the development of World History over and above his conscious intentions. The people follow such a leader because they too unconsciously respond to the inner logic of historical development. Spirit is its own aim; World History is the progress of Spirit towards complete self-consciousness, which equals freedom. In sum: "The History of the world is none other than the progress of the consciousness of Freedom." This progress involves an advance to "the *intellectual* comprehension of what was presented in the first instance to *feeling* and *imagination*."

"By the close of day," Hegel says, "man has erected a building constructed from his own inner Sun; and when in the evening he contemplates this, he esteems it more highly than the original external Sun. For now he stands in a *conscious relation* to his Spirit, and therefore a *free* relation." This image symbolizes "the course of History, the great Day's work of Spirit."

Communist Manifesto

The Marxist revision of this dialectic unction opens, with admonitory clangor, in a burlesque of *spirit,* presenting Communism as a *spectre* haunting Europe. (Looking at it thus, I think we can see here something a bit more pointed than a not very fanciful figure of speech. The materialist doctrine that is to be the vessel antithetic to dialectical idealism enters with a mockery of idealism.) Next, the principle of division that for Hegel was benignly contained within the structure of the State is dramatically reinterpreted: "The history of all hitherto existing society is the history of class struggles." Whereupon we confront *conditions,* conceived in terms of reduced temporal circumference:

> Freeman and slave, patrician and plebeian, lord and serf, guild-master and journeyman, in a word, oppressor and oppressed, stood in constant opposition to one another, carried on an uninterrupted, now hidden, now open fight, a fight that each time ended, either in a revolutionary reconstitution of society at large, or in the common ruin of the contending classes.

Thus, where Hegel had said that "Society and the State are the very conditions in which freedom is realized," the materialist revision of Hegel will define the State as a means of coercion, arising in response to a deep social cleavage, and used by a dominant class to maintain the conditions of its domination. It attributes to the *class* structure of society the *bellum omnium contra omnes* which according to Hobbesian materialism, the State is designed to control. And its promise resides in the fact that the dialectic process of class antagonism must be followed through to the point where it leads to its own termination:

> When, in the course of development, class distinctions have disappeared, and all production has been concentrated in the hands of a vast association of the whole nation, the public power will lose its political character. Political power, properly so called, is merely the organized power of one class for oppressing another. If the proletariat during its contest with the bourgeoisie is compelled, by the force of circumstances, to organize itself as a class; if, by means of a revolution, it makes itself the ruling class, and, as such sweeps away by force the old conditions of production, then it will, along with these conditions, have swept away the conditions for the existence of class antagonisms and of class generally, and will thereby have abolished its own supremacy as a class.
>
> In place of the old bourgeois society, with its classes and class antagonisms, we shall have an association in which the free development of each class is the condition for the free development of all.

The entire dialectic thus traces a series of steps whereby each class produces the conditions leading to its overthrow by the class that is to succeed it, until the proletariat, as the ultimate class, produces conditions that lead to its own dissolution as a class. This last step marks the "withering away of the State" that Lenin discusses at some length in *The State and Revolution,* since Marxism agrees with orthodox Christianity, laissez-faire capitalism, and anarchism in its distrust of the State, though for reasons shared mainly by anarchism. The vigorous exertions of Marxist manhood hold out for society the promise of a benign senescence (if we think in sexual terms of this conditioned development from proletarian Dictatorship to a "withering away," a subsidence of the patriarchal State into a non-political state of total freedom).

The Manifesto uses the scene-agent ratio materialistically when asserting that "every change in the conditions" of man's material existence is accompanied by a change in "man's ideas, views, and conceptions, in one word, man's consciousness." In such passages, the idealistic stress upon consciousness or "the Idea" as "creative" gives way to the notion of consciousness as a mere reflection of conditions. "When people speak of ideas that revolutionize society," that is, ideas that act upon society in the idealistic sense of creating important changes in the social structure, "they do but express the fact, that within the old society the elements of a new one have been created, and that the dissolution of the old ideas keeps even pace with the dissolution of the old conditions of existence." Similarly, "the ideas of religious liberty and freedom of conscience merely gave expression to the sway of free competition within the domain of knowledge," an observation similar in spirit to a passage in *Capital,* where Marx refers ironically to "the 'eternal laws of Nature' of the capitalist mode of production."

The Manifesto contains about fifteen references to the role played by "conditions" in the motivating of social change. And the treatment seems to be uniformly scenic. Yet one should also note the tendency to treat cultural expressions in terms of concomitant variation (varying *"pari passu"* with variations in conditions) rather than as an out-and-out *result* of conditions. There is room for ambiguity here, if you want to be especially exacting. Also, the area covered by the term "conditions" can shift considerably, as one might expect of so crucial a concept. Sometimes it applies purely to material things or operations, sometimes to matters more symbolic, such as money and the terms of ownership. But the fact remains that, by and large, the typical idealistic genealogy is slighted. At one point polemically apostrophizing the bourgeois opposition, the Manifesto declares, "Your very ideas are but the outgrowth of the conditions of your bourgeois production and bourgeois property, just as your jurisprudence is but the will of your class made into a law for all, a will whose essential character and direction are determined by the economic conditions of your class." And there is certainly no celebrating of the "creative" factor in Communist doctrine. It is not put forward as "idea," "ideal," or "vision." Indeed, there is a direct attempt to define the doctrine in ways exactly contrary to this:

The theoretical conclusions of the Communists are in no way based on ideas or principles that have been invented, or discovered, by this or that would-be universal reformer.

They merely express, in general terms, actual relations springing from an existing class struggle, from a historical movement going on under our very eyes. The abolition of existing property relations is not at all a distinctive feature of Communism.

All property relations in the past have continually been subject to historical change consequent upon the change in historical conditions.

On the other hand, what are we to make of the fact that the Manifesto itself is an act of propaganda? Implicit in such an act there is certainly the assumption that the ideas contained in it are social *forces,* and that the course of human action, hence the course of human destiny, will be in some degree altered by the diffusion of these ideas. Thus, in the Manifesto's closing challenge, we see what "views and aims" may do, not simply as reflecting conditions, but as guides for the *changing* of conditions: "The Communists disdain to conceal their views and aims. They openly declare that their ends can be attained only by the forcible overthrow of all existing social conditions."

We have still to quote one important reference to our subject. The Manifesto tells of early Utopian socialists who were primarily humanitarian in their concern with the proletariat. "Only from the point of view of being the most suffering class does the proletariat exist for them." So they made plans for improving the lot of the workers, at a time when the economic situation did not as yet provide "the material conditions for the emancipation of the proletariat." For according to the Manifesto, bourgeois methods of production must attain a high degree of development before the political revolution is possible. This is the Marxist equivalent for the Hegelian concern with that critical moment in the development of Spirit when the times are ripe for a great "World-Historical" act. And Lenin's power as a leader resided in his learning to gauge still more accurately just what were the conditions of a "revolutionary situation."

But the Utopians did not think in such terms. So, hoping for conditions that would improve the workers' welfare, they sought "a new social science . . . new social laws . . . to create these conditions." The authors then proceed to comment on these Utopians as follows:

Historical action is to yield to their personal inventive action; historically created conditions of emancipation to imaginary ones; and the gradual, spontaneous class organization of the proletariat to an organization of society specially contrived by these inventors. Future history resolves itself, in their ideas, into the propaganda and the practical carrying out of their social plans.

Surely, here our concerns come to a head. These Utopians are obviously idealists, in relying upon the creative power of the idea to bring about the desired improvements. Their error, we are told, was in ignoring the fact that the class organization of the proletariat must be *spontaneous*. The movement must arise, as our politicians would put it, "from the grass-roots."

But matters are subtler than that. For in his *What Is to Be Done?* Lenin, though against all revision of Marxist doctrine, found it necessary to attack those who would put too much faith in "spontaneity." This greatest of the "professional revolutionaries" said that the task of preparing for the revolution required a triple struggle, "theoretical, political, and economic," under the leadership of a centralized revolutionary party. And against those who relied on "spontaneity" he wrote (International Publishers translation, footnote, p. 71):

> The tasks of the Social-Democrats [at that time the name of the Marxist faction in Russia] are not exhausted by political agitation on the economic field; their task is to *convert* trade-union politics into the Social-Democratic political struggle, to *utilize* the flashes of political consciousness which gleam in the minds of the workers during their economic struggles for the purpose of *raising* them to the level of *Social-Democratic* political consciousness. The Martynovs, however, instead of raising and stimulating the spontaneously awakening political consciousness of the workers, *bow down before spontaneity* and repeat over and over again, until one is sick and tired of hearing it, that the economic struggle "stimulates" in the workers' minds thoughts about their own lack of political rights. It is unfortunate, gentlemen, that the spontaneously awakening trade-union political consciousness does not *"stimulate"* in your minds thoughts about your Social-Democratic tasks!

Here, then, we would seem to confront the "critical moment" in the dialectical materialist theories of motivation. We might now attempt characterizing the motivational structure as a whole.

The scientist stress, of course, adds to Rhetorical effectiveness insofar as the great growth of *technological* power makes science today the best name to conjure with, when invoking *social* powers. The mingling of idealistic and materialistic ingredients due to the fact that this materialistic dialectic was derived from a philosophy of "Spirit" serves well the double purpose of exhortation and polemic; for the idealistic aspects assist party unification, and the materialistic aspects serve well as a critical instrument for disclosing the special interests that underlie bourgeois pretenses to disinterested idealism, impartial justice, and similar universal motives. (Hegel would doubtless have called the brilliant Marxist invective "Thersitism," after Homer's ungainly Thersites who reviled the king.) The patterns of communion, sacrifice, and transcendence involved in party loyalty give Marxism, on the Symbolic level, the great value of a profound social drama, quite as Christianity was formed about the patterns of drama, though the typical Marxist prefers to stress the rational elements of Marxism, while discountenancing explicit recognition of the dramatic rituals implicit in the Marxist eschatology.

From the standpoint of our Grammar, the whole philosophy is essentially ethical rather than scientist, in that its entire logic is centered about an act, a social or political act, the act of revolution, an act so critical and momentous as to produce a "rupture" of cultural traditions:

> The Communist revolution is the most radical rupture with traditional property relations; no wonder that its development involves the most radical rupture with traditional ideas.

A Dramatist Grammar for Marxism

Since the entire concern of Marxist politics prior to the success of the Russian Revolution was with the ways of action necessary to prepare for this culminating act of revolution, I must always see in Marxist terminology Grammatical conditions calling for a rounded terminology of *action,* though the formal development of such a vocabulary was stifled by scientist adherence to a terminology of motion and by the Rhetorical advantages of a vocabulary essentially different from the vocabularies of scholasticism. Marxism here was but continuing the tradition of secular bourgeois philosophers like Locke and Hume, and was in this respect an ironic turning of bourgeois thought against itself.

With the success of the Revolution in Russia, Marxism there becomes an orthodox doctrine, aiming not at revolutionary rejection of an old political structure, but at the acceptance of a new political structure. The change of political conditions put it in a new role; and though its role in other countries is ambiguous, its role in Russia is clearly conservative, aiming at the maintenance of the new State. And even if one still expects the eventual "withering away" of the State, by Marxist doctrine this could not be expected to occur until all varieties of capitalist State had become socialized, and then the change would take place as a simple and gradual cessation of State functioning, not as a revolutionary act.

Already, in Russia prior to the war, the name for the leading post-revolutionary esthetic movement was "Socialist *realism*"—and we take this itself to be evidence of a tendency towards the featuring of *act*, though necessarily an act different from the act of the Communist Manifesto to the extent of the great change in political conditions following the Revolution.

Let us, then, put the matter this way: So far as our dramatistic terminology is concerned, the Marxist philosophy began by grounding *agent* in *scene*, but by reason of its poignant concern with the ethical, it requires the systematic featuring of *act*. On the Symbolic level, it does feature act implicitly but intensely, in having so dramatic a pattern. On the Rhetorical level, its scientist and anti-scholastic vocabulary is needed for purposes of political dynamism (for the use of an ethical terminology would fail to differentiate the doctrine sufficiently from non-secular ways of salvation). But if, as an experiment, you try a systematic development of terms generated from *act*, the entire system falls quickly into place.

So we offer such a tentative restatement of the Marxist doctrine, as formed about the act of class struggle. We are following no particular text, but are trying to restate the Marxist position in general, as it appears when translated into the terms of characterization employed in this book. We freely grant, however, that such a mode of summarization, characterization, and placement is almost ludicrously inapposite, when considered from the Rhetorical point of view. For though we manipulate our terms in keeping with the all important

Marxist emphasis upon class antagonism as the locus of motives, our vocabulary necessarily lacks the partisan vigor that infuses the Marxist rhetoric, and makes the *Communist Manifesto* a masterpiece of challenge. (And as regards rare literary criticism thus rhetorically infused, I submit that the third section of the Manifesto is a masterpiece within a masterpiece.)

> Each social class, insofar as it has a way of life distinct from that of other classes, is distinct in *actus*, hence in *status*.
>
> Its distinctness in status involves a corresponding distinctness in *properties*. ("Properties" here comprising any kind of characteristics: A house is a property, a way of speaking or thinking is a property, even a condition of total impoverishment is, in this usage, a property.)
>
> The properties of a class may become relatively unsuited to the productive forces of the society in which that class is a part.
>
> Yet that class may be a ruling class, and in this capacity may be able to use the State (the status of the society as a whole) to maintain the dominance of its properties. (Insofar as it conceives of reality in terms of its status as a class, rather than in terms of the society as a whole, it will both consciously and unconsciously use the legislative, educational, and constabulary agencies of the State to perpetuate the ways and ideas deemed beneficial to its class.)
>
> From the standpoint of society as a whole, an idea is "active" insofar as it is "adequate" (that is, insofar as it does accurately name the benign and malign properties of that society).
>
> The society must suffer social "passions" insofar as its ideas are "inadequate."
>
> Insofar as any class of that society holds inadequate ideas, the entire society must suffer social passions. But in particular, the society suffers from inadequate ideas of the ruling class, since these are especially reenforced by all the resources of the State.
>
> Insofar as a class maintains inadequate ideas, it has a false view of "reality."
>
> A class's image of reality is false insofar as it is *partial*, representing only the properties peculiar to that class.
>
> A class suffering visible tangible deprivation has a proportionately greater incentive to question the structure of the State than does a class not so suffering.
>
> The agencies of the State, insofar as they represent the properties of a ruling class, prevent the transformation of such passion into action (guided by adequate ideas).

The class thus suffering visible tangible deprivation may transform its passion into action by a revolutionary act designed to change the nature of the State.

In the acts preparatory to this revolutionary act the revolutionary class is guided and represented by a party (a class within a class) whose ideas are active insofar as they are adequate, and are adequate insofar as they correctly name the malign and benign properties of that society.

Insofar as the changes of property relations would produce the desired betterment of society as a whole, the revolutionary effort is rational, hence active.

But the revolutionary act (and its preparation) is irrational, hence a passion, to the extent of the confusions resulting from the real or imaginary dislocations of society involved in revolution.

The revolutionary body can transcend these passions insofar as its ideas are adequate and lead to the success of the revolutionary act.

Insofar as the act succeeds, a new status is established.

Insofar as the new status is common to all members of the society, the society enjoys properties in common.

During the early stages of the new status, it may be necessary to protect by force the new structure of properties, until those who conceive of reality in terms of other properties have changed their ideas or lost their powers of dominion.

The properties of a State are active insofar as the ideas, in being adequate, make possible the desired operation of the society's means of material production and distribution.

Insofar as all members of a society profit by the new status, the passion of class antagonism is transformed into the action of general coöperation.

Insofar as the properties of this new status are named by adequate ideas, there is a common actus, hence a common status.

Insofar as the new properties are inadequately named, conditions are set for the rise of new conflicts.

As regards the requirements of a dramatistic Grammar, we have thus tried to characterize the Marxist doctrine in a somewhat Spinozist fashion, with two notable exceptions. We have "class-angled" [5] Spi-

[5] There is an important ambiguity in the concept of "class-consciousness" itself, with one of the meanings much more active than the other. The member of a class may share the thinking (or "consciousness") of his class without awareness that his thoughts have a class character. "Class consciousness" in this sense might, after psychoanalysis, be more aptly termed "class unconsciousness." As Marx has shown, class consciousness in this sense is so unconscious that it inter-

noza's solution of the problem as to when ideas are "active." This gives us a kind of "social realism," as against the treatment suggested by the materialist reversal of idealism. And we have used the notion of property and status in such a way as to modify one's views of the social state following the Revolution. By this usage, one would expect neither the withering away of the State nor the abolition of private property. One would expect merely a change in the nature of State and private property. Orthodox Marxism would, I believe, itself agree with the point about property. In fact, I believe it always has, though the pressures of dialectic opposition have frequently led to an over-statement of the Marxist position in this respect, hence causing undue resistance, both theological and secular, on the part of those who put a "broad interpretation" on the concept of "personal properties." [6]

prets class values as "universal" and "eternal" values. On the other hand, class consciousness may be a deliberately cultivated attitude of class partisanship, as when the proletarian is exhorted to serve his interests as a member of the proletariat. Class consciousness in this second sense involves the rationale of Marxist propaganda. Capitalist propaganda has in turn given the concept of consciousness a further twist, as with advertising campaigns to make the public "frigidaire-conscious," or "two-car conscious," and the like. Here the aim is to use words that impose upon the consciousness (the critical faculty) an automatic (uncritical) response.

[6] Since these pages were set into type, I have read the translation of a Russian essay that bears directly upon our present discussion. It is "Basic Laws of Development of Socialist Economy," by K. Ostrovitianov, and appeared in the Summer 1945 issue of the Marxist quarterly, *Science and Society*.

The author explicitly acknowledges the existence of classes in the present state of Russian socialism: "Our socialist society consists of two basic, non-antagonistic, friendly classes—the working class and the kolkhoz farmers, along with the Soviet intelligentsia."

This would seem implicitly to acknowledge at least three classes. But in any case, class distinctions are here stated as a fact; and to this extent our proposed dramatist revision of Marxism's abolitionist rhetoric would seem corroborated.

As regards the dialectical resources whereby one may stress either the element of competition in coöperation or the element of coöperation in competition, the author's choice is clear. Whereas the basis of capitalist competition is "the savage law of the struggle of one against the other," he says, "the basis of socialist rivalry is the principle of comradely coöperation and socialist mutual aid on the part of the toilers." And "in contradistinction to the politics of bourgeois states, which expresses the interests of the bourgeoisie, which are profoundly contradictory to the interests of the working mass," the Soviet state "expresses the interests of the working class, the farmers and the intelligentsia, the interests of our whole people."

As regards our previous suggestion that even socialist technology requires an over-all monetary motivation, the author recognizes "the need for an accounting of work, which at the stage of socialism is carried out in money form." And he

One ironic misunderstanding (insofar as it is not intentional misrepresentation) on the part of anti-Marxists is the complaint against Marxist "materialism." If you genuinely want to grasp the point of Marxism here, you must add another step. And when you add this step, you find that, precisely where Marxism is most often damned as *materialistic*, is precisely where it is most characteristically idealistic. Marx's most imaginative criticism is directed against the false idealism derived from the concealed protection of materialistic interests. His chapter on "The Fetishism of Commodities and the Secret Thereof," shows how the human personality itself comes to be conceived in the abstract terms of impersonal commodities. And the whole purpose of such materialist criticism is to bring about such material conditions as are thought capable of releasing men from their false bondage to materials.

Irony of ironies, this observation serves well as a transition to the elegant philosophy of George Santayana. For this brand of materialism also grew antithetically out of German transcendentalism. And it was even more explicit than Marxism in stressing the material basis of man's spiritual fulfilment.

Santayana

All told, throughout these pages we have been considering five major aspects of science:

(1) high development of technological specialization
(2) involvement with rationale of money (accountancy)
(3) progressive departure from natural conditions, usually saluted in the name of "naturalism"

---

quotes Stalin: "Money will be with us for a long time, up to the completion of the first stage of communism—the socialist stage of development."

We have also previously spoken of a possible dissociation between "capitalism" and "technology" whereby an anti-capitalist rhetoric can attribute the vices of the money-machine combination to capitalism and the virtues to technology. In internal Soviet apologetics, this pattern is transformed by the use of the distinction between socialism and communism. Socialism thus becomes a comparatively benign monetary system, as contrasted with a malign monetary motive under capitalism. And the elimination of this motive entirely is left to the future (communism, and the withering away of the State). But the article does not discuss the means whereby technology might be managed, at any stage, without monetary accountancy.

(4) reduction of scenic circumference to empirical limits (the reason why the technological powers that take us farthest from natural conditions have been called "naturalistic")

(5) stress upon the "problem of knowledge" as the point of departure for philosophic speculation

The modern stress upon the utility of business and science, with a compensatory counter-stress upon an esthetic of uselessness, was the analogue, in our wage-society, to Aristotle's stress upon the uselessness of the higher intellectual activities (which were equated with the free, the "liberal," in contrast with the utility of slaves). Marxism avoided the invitations to pragmatism in this situation by the strategic role it assigned to the class concept. Grammatically, this concept is interesting precisely because we can see its function in making a doctrine of *substance* out of a philosophy that would otherwise be purely a doctrine of *means*.

By the class concept, precisely those members of society who might consider themselves as having nothing but "jobs" at best and often not even that, are invested with a vocation. In their very deprivation there is a *status*, made manifest in properties of consciousness pregnant with futurity. We get here a variant of tribal substance, with the contents of class consciousness comprising a property shared by all members of the class. Social status is not a mere means to an end; it is a *way of life*, hence a *substantial* activity.

Turning from Marx to Santayana with the scientist emphasis in mind, we miss the tremendous moral admonition of the class concept. Though you may think that this term played too basic a role in the structure of the Manifesto, no vocabulary of social temptations is complete without it. But Santayana's great gifts as a moralist take another shape. And the human relation to material substance is conceived in universalizing or idealizing terms (as regards problems of class relationship), though Santayana's great stress upon the relation between spirit and nature is likewise an admonition without which no moral philosophy can be complete. For moral criticism in its totality, I should think, we should do justice to both the Marxist heckling and Santayana's cult of contemplation.

Though both of these materialists have their beginnings in the idealist problem of knowledge, there was an urgency in Marx that Santayana deliberately sought to dispel. Whatever speculation and investigation may precede Marxist assertions, there is the pressure to make them serviceable as a Rhetorical inducement to action on the part of people who have slight interest in speculation and investigation *per se*. Santayana, on the other hand, cultivates a *leisurely* approach—and nothing makes one feel this more poignantly than to consider him after Marx. His philosophy of serenity and retirement sounds expensive. As an adolescent, when I first read Santayana, I dreamed of a tourist life in white flannels along the Mediterranean. He still means to me something like that, though more circumstantially accurate: reading in the country, on a mild afternoon, after a bit of gardening, or a slow walk in the woods, perhaps with the sound of friends playing tennis in the distance. (Should the garden not be economically necessary, then it is cultivated on principle.)

Both Marx and Santayana are keen, Marx with the sharpness of a fighter, Santayana with the most astonishing niceties. And his point of departure in the problem of knowledge is not such as one abandons, but the kind that inaugurates. It is an initial spirit pervading all that follows. It takes the form of a systematically cultivated skepticism which is made an integral part of his philosophy.

The scrupulous show of doubt with which many thinkers (particularly since Descartes) begin their essays is usually but an ambiguous way of introducing new assertions under disarming guise. But Santayana undertakes to carry skepticism to the most exacting lengths possible. This is his response to the key scientist question, the problem of knowledge. And it results in his peculiar doctrine of essence (the ideality in his materiality).

The main obstacle to understanding Santayana's doctrine of essence is its simplicity. It is so simple, we are afraid we must have got it wrong. Having extended the areas of doubt as far as possible, he is left with one unquestionable knowledge: that we see what we see. From this point of view, there is no "illusion" in appearances. Appearances are exactly what they are. If equidistant tracks seem to approach each other in the distance, this is the way they really look.

Such perceiving of appearances he calls "intuition." The appearances themselves he calls "essences." These essences are so thoroughly in keeping with the genius of our term *agent*, that they could, if you insist, be the contents of a solipsistic consciousness. There is no device in the realm of immediate, unquestionable knowledge whereby I could prove them otherwise. For if I offer proofs that the world is not my dream, there is no way to prove that I am not dreaming the proofs. Surely skepticism could go no farther. And it does yield a kind of rock-bottom (or rather, airy) certainty: the certainty that appearances are exactly as they appear, that if I think I hear a certain sound I think I hear that sound.

Having thus theoretically restricted knowledge to the idealistic extreme, Santayana turns materialist. He does not propose to leave us thus uncomfortably suspended. He likens his skepticism to the perfect balance that a pendulum might have if it were poised exactly *above* its centre of gravity. And he contrasts it with "animal faith," which he likens to the normal position of a pendulum at rest. This animal faith "posits" the existence of the material world.

We might get the point more easily by putting "supposes" for "posits." The notion of the Ego "positing" a world is a favorite with the German idealists. This Stance word (*setzen*) gains further linguistic effectiveness in German because the word for law (*Gesetz*) so closely resembles the past particle (*gesetzt*). In English we should note the grammatical significance of the direction, from agent to scene. As Santayana uses the concept, we "posit" the existence of the external material world in taking it on *faith*.

This produces an ingenious reversal. The objects of the material world are thus found to *transcend* our knowledge. All we can immediately *know* is that we see what we see. If we assume that there are real objects behind these appearances, and that intuition itself is a material process, we do so by reason of the faith that we have as natural organisms. And we regularly *act* on this faith, in taking measures to attain or to avoid the things we assume to exist outside us and independently of us.

This reversal adds an important qualification to empiricism. For inasmuch as faith is traditionally an *act* word par excellence, at the very start it imbues the world of matter with the connotations of action. Matter, or nature, is thus the world of existence, of the flux, of constant motion; but also it is the world of power, generation, substance; it is the "field of action." For in saying that we must take the existence of matter on faith, Santayana is not questioning its existence. The belief in the reality of matter as a scene external to the self is such an act of faith as biological organisms implicitly exemplify. This material realm, which we thus take on faith, is the realm of rational, scientific knowledge (in contrast with the intuitive or transcendental knowledge in which his skepticism begins). Though truths are essences, they are embodied in this factual world of nature.

Santayana's word for thought or consciousness is "spirit." Hence, in all, he designates four realms of being: matter, essence, spirit, and truth. The significant thing about spirit in his scheme is that he grounds it materialistically, yet locates its actuality in its freedom from material conditions. Using our rough-and-ready shift of emphasis, we might explain the relation thus: One of his definitions of spirit is "the moral fruition of physical life." One could stress the transcendence of the physical in *fruition;* or one could stress the ground of this fruition in the *physical.* I think one will be less bewildered if he keeps this shift in mind; for Santayana celebrates in spirit (and its variant, imagination) its ability to transcend the mechanical flux of nature; yet at the same time he stresses its location in an animal psyche, which depends upon the conditions of material existence. It is by natural order or organization that spirit attains its opportunities for fulfilment. (And I think the same pattern of thought underlies the idealistic ingredient in Marxist materialism, despite the great difference in application.)

We have noted how Marx avoided pragmatism by the concept of class action. Santayana, who was at Harvard at the time when German idealism was being transformed into American pragmatism, clearly shows the pragmatist influence upon his doctrines. Yet he too submerges the pragmatist strain beneath strongly dramatistic patterns. Indeed, his great gifts as ironist, moralist, and literary psychologist are rooted in his explicit and systematic concern with the terminology of action, notably his application of theological thought to the realm of poetic imagination and intuition.

He shows the pragmatist strain in two ways: in equating the realm of matter with utility, and in compensatorily equating the realms of spirit and essence with a meaning directly the opposite. Though the spirit can contemplate essences for themselves alone, and loves to dwell in the realm of essence, the material interests of the organism require it to use its intuitions of essence as *signs.* The animal in the jungle, for instance, catching a sound or scent, interprets it as a sign of food or danger, thereby turning its intuition of essence to use. But the pure intuitions come first—and similarly pure art comes before the conversion of the arts to practical ends (hence the typical idealistic equating of the esthetic with "play," as with Kant's concern with the "free play of the imagination").

It is interesting to observe how, though matter is the scene in which the process of intuition is grounded, the essences which are the content of our intuitions become a kind of scene-behind-a-scene—and we shall try to trace this development, because it is characteristic of the ultimate form which Santayana's dramatism seems to have taken.

Santayana uses the traditional pair of terms: essence and existence. But he gives it elusive twists all his own. Thus, if we flatly contrast existence with essence, it follows by the sheer dialectics of the case that "essences" do not "exist." Nor can existence as such be an essence. In Plato, the world of being (that is, essence) was more real than the world of our everyday experience (which was for Plato the world of appearance). But Santayana has synonymized appearances and essences to the extent that all appearances are essences, though there are many more essences than there are appearances.

While I was puzzling over Santayana's way of distinguishing essence from existence, a six-year-old solved the problem for me when he explained, "There *is* an Easter bunny, but he isn't *real.*" I saw the application immediately: the Easter bunny has a *being*, or *essence*, but he does not *exist.* Or put it this way: there is a *character* called the Easter bunny, since it is distinguished from all other characters; yet the Easter bunny is nowhere to be found in all the realm of material substances. Here clearly is an essence that does not exist.

If it did exist, it would be subject to the flux of existence. It would thus be involved in the world of *relationships,* and of *processes* that require a constant commingling with the particles of matter surrounding it. But in its sheer *character* as Easter bunny it can be contemplated *in itself.* And so similarly, when the essences that we intuit are not interpreted as signs, we consider them *in themselves, immediately.*

Or we may think of the matter this way: Imagine a history of all that ever happened in this world since the beginning of time. Here would certainly be a history of "existence." But in the course of writing this history, let us say that you divided it into periods which you named according to the different stages the world has gone through. Let us assume that you had been quite accurate in thus listing "essences" or characters of each successive stage. Could we say that these characters exist, or ever did exist? What existed at any given time was the particular arrangement of particles comprising the historical flux at that time. It was only these infinite details that existed. The over-all "characters" that they added up to would be "essences" that never existed, hence they are as much characters now as then.

Indeed, whatever character a given stage was to exemplify was that same character even before the existence of the particular combination of particles of which it is the essence. So similarly, whereas Napoleon has ceased to exist, this fact is but an *accident* of Napoleon's essence, which is what it is, just as the character of tomorrow is already "eternal," once we think of eternity as a quality of *being*, in contrast with a quality of *existence*. Then, carrying such thought one step farther, we can people the realm of essence with an infinity of eternal beings that may never have their substantial moment in the fluctuant accidents of existence.

At this final step we suddenly discover that we have come upon a new kind of scene. For the essences are a realm of eternal "possibilities," only a small fraction of which are ever embodied in natural existence. The Easter bunny, for instance, is such a possibility, a universal (since a unique whole), eternally distinct in the realm of essence, though he may never attain embodiment in the flux of nature. And existence itself proceeds by embodying an endless succession of essences (like discrete points on a continuous line), advancing at each moment from character to character. And these successive characters are things-in-themselves, in the sense that each is what it is, without regard for relationships. Similarly, a continuity of flux can be continuity only insofar as it exemplifies the same essence throughout its existence—and this essence would be uniquely itself.

There is an infinity of such essences, and Santayana calls them the "indelible background" for all the transitory facts of nature. He uses the figure of an infinite Koran, prophesying all possible Being, while existence is like an eye that, reading, follows a thin stream of script, as "re-agent" thus selecting one line of possibilities from among the infinite number inscribed in the totality of the eternal essences. Here we find a significant variant of the scribe-script-scroll pattern, as exemplified in Avicebron's *Fons Vitae*. With Avicebron, the scene is matter (the scroll), the act is form (the script), and the agent (the scribe) is will. In Santayana's variant, the scroll corresponds to the entire immaterial realm of essence; and script and scribe combined equal the narrow bit of text selected by existence as "re-agent."

Though Santayana is usually classed as a Platonist, his essences have undergone one notable change from the Forms or Ideas of Plato. These Platonic essences were above all else *familial*, the principles of *generation*. Their very capacity to unify the world of multiplicity resides in their role as ancestral prototypes, as pure sources from which all members of their kind are descended, thereby possessing a common tribal nature. But Santayana's essences are uncompromisingly individual, even individualistic—and without progeny. He explicitly assures us that they are not "seeds." Even the philosophic way of arriving at them is by a discipline that he likens to a state of chastity prolonged until late in youth. Their relation to a vocabulary of action is arrived at by a less "substantial" route than tribal derivation. As matter is the realm of flux, or motion, the corresponding dialectical role of essence is that of *rest*. And since this orbit of mechanical motion is also ambiguously called the "field of action," the kind of rest here indicated is ambiguously both the cessation of motion and the end of action.

Let us at this point consider the subject purely in itself, regardless of Santayana. Suppose that you had called the world of mechanical motion the "field of action." You had given an initial plausibility to your position, since you had introduced this world of motion under the aegis of "faith," a term essentially active, as in the expression, "an act of faith." Obviously, you would not thereby get the full value for your term "action," since it would be confined rather to the limits of purely biological intention, as with the "action" of a hungry animal stalking game. If, then, you set up against this pole, as dialectical opposite, a concept of rest, it would be such rest as equalled the cessation of motion, and it would ambiguously be such rest as equalled the end of action (where "end" in turn can refer ambiguously to an ultimate destination of action either as the point at which action subsides or as the point at which action attains its purpose).

Let us further suppose that your field of biological action was interpreted pragmatically, as the realm in which the organism puts its awarenesses to *use*. And you want a wider concept of action, that will allow for the areas of "free play," where awareness transcends its purely utilitarian function. How might you proceed, within the usual limits of the dramatist grammar? Or, to put it bluntly, what key dramatist *words* have you left unexploited?

Santayana, at this point, exploits two such words. He calls the area of pure awareness the "actuality" of spirit; and he salutes it for having added a new dimension, that of *the passions*, to the realm of natural mechanisms.

So, all told, we have: (1) an area of the mechanical flux ambiguously called the "field of action"; (2) a correspondingly ambiguous world of rest, that serves as the ground of motion in marking successive stations in the processes of change; (3) an "actuality" of spirit that adds the dimensions of "the passions" to the natural world. Since the ambiguously active area was equated with utility, this second level of activity, the "actuality" of spirit, can thus transcend biological utility at the same time as it introduces the fully dramatic term, *passion*.

What, then, can be the final "end" in such a view? Passion for passion's sake? There is in Santayana's pages much appreciation of the passions that might lead a patchy reader to this conclusion. But there is another, more classically philosophical conclusion available. Recall that we already have an ambiguous concept of end, in our realm of essence. Centering upon this, in the light of spiritual actuality and passion, we can add the fourth step to our alignment of the previous paragraph. We can add to step (2) the qualification that makes it *unambiguously* such kind of rest as is the end of *action*. Thus our line-up would be:

(1)   motion (ambiguously "biological action")
(2)   essence (as its corresponding stasis)
(3)   spirit (dramatic: actuality and passion)
(4)   essence (as end of spirit)

Since biological action was here equated with utility, spiritual action will transcend utility. Being itself a fulfilment, it will love to dwell upon fulfilments. And so, its ultimate delight is in the contemplation of essence, which in the last analysis is a *benign* contemplation of death. The realm of essence is thus ultimately a thanatopsis. And though Santayana draws back at times from the full implications of his doctrine, reminding himself and us that he belongs to the world of rational Greek materialism, it is his serene doctrine of essence that seems most distinctive of him, particularly when we contrast his brand of dramatism with the dramatistic ingredients in Marx. Reading him, we do feel that it might be enough to cultivate the contemplation of essences, simply through love of dwelling in the vicinity of terms at rest and at peace, terms that would serve as much as terms can to guide us through a long life of euthanasia.

The pious Christian was exhorted to "live a dying life." And Santayana, whose skepticism was at every turn able to reproduce religious thought with a difference, finds ways of transforming mortification into an amenity. Though he would present the spiritual delight in essence as a transcending of utility, it seems to have done well by him, even on the purely biological level, attending him from youth into an advanced old age. His philosophy is, however, the exact opposite of a patriarchal one. In his scheme, spirit is powerless. All power is in nature. Nature is to spirit as mother is to child. He thinks as one who is the end of a line; his concern is with culminations; in applying the Aristotelian concept of the entelechy as summational, he eliminates its tribal ingredients as thoroughly as he did in the case of Plato's ideas. Whatever essences in general may be, the essence of his own thought is of a culmination that is a termination. His estheticizing of essence is, in its own way, as pronounced a step away from the familial substance as is the trend of science. But whereas science takes this step by renouncing dramatist terms, Santayana retains them and ingeniously perverts them, while at the same time his romantic cult of neo-classic calm enables him to avoid the agonies of Satanism.

Imagination

In the course of showing how and why idealism is identical with the featuring of the term *agent*, we have incidentally shown how deeply "scientism" has permeated modern thought. One is well advised to look for scientist stress in any terminology that has its start in modern idealism. Thus, although the cult of the "imagination" is usually urged today by those who champion poetry as a field *opposed* to science, our investigations would suggest the ironic possibility that they exemplify an aspect of precisely the thinking they would reject. For our modern views of the imagination come to us *via* the idealist Coleridge from the idealist Kant—and we have already seen the strong scientist bias in the Kantian doctrines.

The autumn, 1944 issue of *The Sewanee Review* contains an essay by Wallace Stevens that is quite to our purposes. Written with all the deftness and subtlety of Stevens' poetry, it speaks of poetry in precisely the idealist cluster of terms we have been examining in this section. The importance of "personality" is stressed. Poetry is derived from an "indirect egotism." "Nervous sensitiveness" is basic, for the poet's morality is "the morality of the right sensation." Poetry is the "spirit out of its own self." There are citations stressing the importance of "temperament." "Kant says that the objects of perception are conditioned by the nature of the mind as to their form." And Mr. Stevens cites a statement by Henri Focillon: "The chief characteristic of the mind is to be constantly describing *itself.*"

And the summarizing word for all this typical idealistic cluster is "imagination." The essay places it in dialectical opposition to "reason," thereby going a step beyond Coleridge, whose proportion "imagination: fancy : : reason : understanding," aligned imagination and reason together as against fancy and understanding (while imagination itself was more active, by reason of its *unifying* role). Poetry gives us "an unofficial view of being"; "philosophic truth may be said to be the official view." On the Symbolic level, philosophy and reason here seem equated with the vocational (with office hours), poetry and imagination seem equated with the vacational (after hours). Accordingly, when Mr. Stevens tries to illustrate what he means by poetic imagination, he begins: "If we close our eyes and think of a place where it would be pleasant to spend a holiday . . ."

There are subtle steps in the essay to which I cannot here do justice. In the end, for instance, the poet seems to arrive at a merger of imagination and reason; but not until important changes have been made in both terms by a strategic reference to the Minotaur. This fabulous hybrid apparently represents a joined duality of motives, and here apparently symbolizes the union of a labyrinthine imagination (the "unconscious") with the rationality of a poetic medium developed by deliberate conscious sophistication. The very title gives us further significant data, were it our task here to search for equations on the Symbolic level: "The Figure of the Youth as Virile Poet." This vacational poetry will be a *young* poetry (incidentally, apparently a dangerous ideal for some poets, however great the attainments it stimulated in Mr. Stevens, for elsewhere in the same number of *The Sewanee Review*

Horace Gregory observes: "What American poetry needs most . . . is the courage . . . to mature").

The important point for our present purposes is to note that the key term "imagination" here figures in a theory of poetry that is basically scientist. For poetry is here approached in terms of its search for "truth," as a "view" of reality, as a kind of "knowledge." Thus, Stevens quotes with approval another writer quoting Descartes:

> There are in us, as in a flint, seeds of knowledge. Philosophers adduce them through the reason; poets strike them out from the imagination, and these are the brighter.

Recall that Descartes was as influential as any philosopher in directing the turn from dramatist to scientist terminologies.

Mr. Stevens also quotes from Shelley, whose "Defence of Poetry" is itself interesting in its vacillations between dramatist realism and idealist scientism. There are strong realist ingredients, for instance, in Shelley's concern with the relation between drama and morality. But when Mr. Stevens neared such a subject, as in his remark on the morality of the poet, he ended on the most scientist term of all: "sensation." And the Shelley to whom he refers is the idealist scientist Shelley:

> He says that a poem is the very image of life expressed in its eternal truth. It is "indeed something divine. It is at once the centre and circumference of knowledge."

The figure itself is interesting, for a glance at its past enables us to see it turning scientist. In his *Principles of Nature and Grace*, Leibniz writes:

> God alone has a distinct knowledge of all, for He is the source of all. It has been very well said that as a centre He is everywhere, but his circumference is nowhere, for everything is immediately present to Him without any distance from this centre.

The editor of the Oxford edition (*The Monadology, Etc.*) reminds us that Pascal said the same of the world, while Pascal's editor traces the phrase to Rabelais and earlier writers. Pascal's version was not scientist at all: he simply calls the world an infinite sphere, with its centre everywhere and its circumference nowhere. Leibniz gives it the beginnings of a scientist turn; for though he applies it to God, the remark occurs when he is on the subject of God's *knowledge*. But Shelley, pantheistically merging divinity and poetry into one, similarly brings the poetry and the knowledge together. The next step is to drop from pantheism the *theos*, whereupon, imagination equalling knowledge, one is left with the *pan:* Mr. Stevens' *"mundo* of the imagination."

However, we must watch lest the reader mistake the eagerness of our pursuit for an "indictment" of either Mr. Stevens or of the "scientist" traces in his essay.   Indeed, we are hardly in a position to attack "scientism" per se, inasmuch as the present book itself is wholly scientist in its aims.   But high among science's obligations is the obligation to recognize its own presence, and to note as far as possible the "perturbations" of its influence upon the orbits of our thoughts.   And a notable perturbation of this sort occurs when scientist influences operate undetected in theories of poetic action as is the case with theories of moral action.   Indeed, from this point of view, "esthetics" itself is seen to have been predominantly idealist, laying major stress either upon the *expression of the subject* or upon the "object of the imagination," or upon mergers of subject and object.   And the Stevens essay, by reason of its very depth and accuracy, enables us to see how such idealist emphasis carries with it a scientist emphasis.

It is particularly important to keep the scientist "heresy" in mind when we are reading so good a statement, by so good a poet, on his own theories of poetry.   Insofar as these are expressed scientistically, in terms of *knowledge*, rather than in terms of *action*, dramatism admonishes us that they are to be discounted.   The irony is that, whereas the study of esthetics was a typical product of the modern idealistic philosophies, and although, with the weakening of religious certainties, art was often made the very basis of evaluation for all human ways, the typical idealist vocabularies were essentially scientist in their approach to artistic innovation.   Precisely at the time when the term "imagination" gained greatly in prestige (in contrast with its low rating in writers as diverse as St. Teresa, Spinoza, and Pascal) theories of art took a momentous step away from the understanding of art as action and towards a lame attempt to pit art against science as a "truer kind of truth."   The correct controversy here should not have been at all a pitting of art against science: it should have been a pitting of one view of science against another.

III

ACT

Aristotle and Aquinas

SINCE our entire book illustrates the featuring of act, there is less call for a special section on it. But let us cite a few passages from the Baldwin dictionary that will sufficiently indicate why scholastic realism should be treated as a speculative enterprise constructed about action as the basic concept.

In Aristotle "things are more or less real according as they are more or less *energeia* (*actu,* from which our 'actuality' is derived)." In scholastic realism "form is the *actus*, the attainment, which realizes the matter." "As Saint Thomas says, and as the whole Peripatetic doctrine teaches, *forma per se ipsam facit rem esse in actu* (or, as it is often expressed, *a form is an act*)." And when discussing the characteristic distinction between existence and essence, the article on Aquinas defines existence as "the act of essence." Similarly in his comments on Aristotle's *Metaphysics,* Aquinas refers to the soul as the "act of an organic physical body capable of life." Etienne Gilson's *God and Philosophy* states the matter succinctly in observing that for the scholastics existence is "an act, not a thing."[7] And when discussing the "Likeness of Creatures" in the *Summa Contra Gentiles,* Aquinas brings out a similar stress, in keeping with the agent-act ratio: "It is of the nature of action that a like agent should produce a like action, since every thing acts according as it is in act" (though he is here using the principle to distinguish between God as cause and human agents as effect, a disproportion whereby "the form of the effect is found in its transcendent cause somewhat, but in another way and another ratio").

The most convenient place I know for directly observing the essentially dramatist nature of both Aristotle and Aquinas is in Aquinas' com-

---

[7] However, *to be* is the act of acts. Gilson makes much of the fact that the copulative verb is grammatically in the active voice. Sociologically, we may note how well this identification between act and being served a feudal society built upon the maintenance of fixed social status.

ments on Aristotle's four causes (in pp. 154-163 of the *Everyman's Library* edition). In the opening citation from Aristotle, you will observe that the "material" cause, "that from which (as immanent material) a thing comes into being, e.g. the bronze of the statue and the silver of the dish," would correspond fairly closely to our term, *scene*. Corresponding to *agent* we have "efficient" cause: "the initial origin of change or rest; e.g. the adviser is the cause of the action, and the father a cause of the child, and in general the agent the cause of the deed." "Final" cause, "the end, i.e. that for the sake of which a thing is," is obviously our "purpose." "Formal" cause ("the form or pattern, i.e. the formula of the essence") is the equivalent of our term *act*. This correspondence is more clearly revealed in the earlier dictionary citation that "a form is an act"). We can approximate the equation closely enough if we think of a thing not simply as existing, but rather as "taking form," or as the record of an act which gave it form. Or one may also think of "actualities" legalistically, as the "form" of a constitution is equivalent to the principles involved in its *enactment*.

There is also a negative way of establishing the correspondence between form and act. Recall the scholastic hexameter listing the questions to be answered in the treatment of a topic: Who, what, where, by what means, why, how, when: *quis, quid, ubi, quibus auxiliis, cur, quo modo, quando*. The "who" is obviously covered by *agent*. *Scene* covers the "where" and the "when." The "why" is *purpose*. "How" and "by what means" fall under *agency*. All that is left to take care of is *act* in our terms and "what" in the scholastic formula. Also, the form of a thing was called its "whatness," or *quidditas*.

As for *agency*, Aristotle has this "fifth" cause also in his list; but in accordance with the imperative genius of the purpose-agency (or end-means) ratio, instead of dealing with agency as a special kind of cause, (say, an "instrumental cause") he introduces it incidentally to his discussion of "final" cause. Thus, after the Peripatetic has said that the desire for health may be the end, or final cause, of walking, he goes on to say: "The same is true of all the means that intervene before the end," as "purging, drugs, or instruments" may also be used for the sake of the same end. Thus, though this thinker, whose studies of logic traditionally go under the name of the *Organon* (that is, tool or instrument) omits agency as a fifth kind of cause, he clearly enough takes it into account.

In this brief reference to agency, he also indicates how it overlaps upon our term act. For distinguishing between medicines and walking as the means of health, he says that some means "are instruments and others are actions." One can see the overlap today in our references to scientific "method," which is treated sometimes as a means and sometimes more substantially, as a way of life.

Perhaps a faint indication that Aquinas' "dramatism" is farther along the road towards modern bourgeois idealism than Aristotle's was, is to be seen in Aquinas' tendency to discover the respects in which means might fall under agent as a kind of efficient cause. He here quotes "the theory of Ibn-Sina," according to which there are four varieties of efficient cause. I think one might fairly sum up the lot by saying that they deal with various kinds of "co-agent." But among these four is an *"auxiliary* efficient cause" that differs from the principal agent "in not acting for its own but another's ends":

> Thus, whoever helps a king in war, acts for that which the king intends. This same relation holds between a secondary and a primary cause; for among agents whose nature is to be in a certain order among themselves, the secondary cause acts for the ends proper to the primary cause. The action of a soldier, for instance, is directed to the aims intended by the statesman. An *adviser* differs from a principal agent by laying down the scope and manner of the action. This same relation obtains between the primary agent, acting through his intellect, and the secondary agent—whether this be a physical body or another intelligent being.

This "auxiliary" or "secondary" kind of efficient cause (or co-agent) obviously marks an overlap of agent and agency. And Aquinas leaves it thus wavering, applying either to physical instruments or to persons used as instrumentalities in carrying out the primary intentions of others. Similarly, he applies it either to the partial efficiencies of human beings using means to an end, or to the "universe of nature" as a "secondary agent" that accepts the purpose and manner of its action "from the supreme mind" as "primary agent."

But though the scholastic vocabulary is *essentially* dramatic, I doubt whether we could say that it is *consciously* so. The *direction* was scientist, in moving from the act of faith to the conditions of knowledge. The dramatism was in the *point of departure:* in the Homeric epics and Dionysian dramas that underlay the patterns of Greek thought, and in the drama of salvation that Christianity had constructed about the Bible. Socrates, approaching the world as a moralist, necessarily considered it in terms of action. Reality, he said, was the power to act and to be acted upon. And he was primarily concerned to perfect his "knowledge of the Good"—but though in Plato we may still hear this as "knowledge of the *Good*," even in Aristotle we move towards the alternate emphasis: "*knowledge* of the Good."

Every philosophy is in some respect or other a *step away from* drama. But to understand its structure, we must remember always that it is, by the same token, a step away from *drama*. In Aristotle, the dramatist nature of his vocabulary is well revealed in the fact that it was so well suited to the discussion of drama (in contrast, for instance, with the terminologies of modern science which can at best illuminate drama by their sheer incongruity, as with vocabularies that "debunk" the dramatic elements in men's social and political relations).

Thus, it was not by an added step, but in keeping with the nature of his terminology in general, that Aristotle designated the plot or *action* as the foremost among the six elements of tragedy. For he had written of the physical world itself in terms of active and passive principles, and of natural beings that develop in accordance with the ends proper to their kind. His God, the origin of all motion, was conceived dramatistically, as the *end* of action. By the paradox of the absolute, such "pure act" is like no act at all, being that of an "unmoved mover" in perfect *repose*. Also, in accordance with that same paradox, this "pure act" motivates as a *passive*. For Aristotle's God is not a creator of the world, which has existed from eternity. But he is the goal towards which all worldly forms strive, as the *loved* or *desired* (*eromenon*). But either as pure motionless act or as the loved, God is conceived in terms of action—and this is the perspective that equipped Aristotle to write:

> Tragedy is essentially an imitation not of persons but of action and life, of happiness and misery. All human happiness or misery takes the form of action; the end for which we live is a certain kind of activity, not a quality. Character gives us qualities, but it is in our actions—what we do—that we are happy or the reverse. In a play accordingly they do not act in order to portray the Characters; they include the Characters for the sake of the action. So that it is the action in it, i.e. its Fable or Plot, that is the end and purpose of the

tragedy; and the end is everywhere the chief thing. . . . A tragedy is impossible without action, but there may be one without Character.

Aligning the six elements with our five terms:

Plot would correspond to *act.* *Character* would correspond to *agent* (it is "what makes us ascribe certain moral qualities to the agents"). Whereas the action is the purpose of the play from the standpoint of the audience, *within* the play we should probably assign *purpose* to the third element, Thought (which is shown in all that the characters say "when proving a particular point or . . . enunciating a general truth"). Since Aristotle himself calls Melody and Diction "the means of imitation," they would obviously fall under *agency.* The sixth element, Spectacle, he assigns to "manner" (presumably the *quo modo* of the Latin hexameter quoted above), a kind of modality that we should want to class under *scene,* though Aristotle's view of it as accessory would seem to make it rather a kind of *scenic agency.* It was not until modern naturalism in drama that scene gained its full independence, with the "property man" giving the environmental placement that was regularly suggested in Elizabethan drama, for instance, by the use of verbal imagery. Perhaps "Spectacle" had something of the significance we associate with "sheer pageantry." Aristotle says that the Spectacle, though an attraction, "is the least artistic of all the parts, and has least to do with the art of poetry." We can be affected by a tragedy without a public performance at all; and "the getting-up of the Spectacle is more a matter for the costumer than the poet."

It is obviously the dramatist ingredient in Aristotle's science that makes it unpalatable to the norms of modern technology. His great stress upon the all-importance of "knowledge" we might interpret as a striving *towards* a scene-agent view of the world (a world of lyric agents and impersonal scene). But this striving was either hampered or corrected (depending on your point of view) by the essential featuring of act he had inherited from the Platonist dialectic, which set up a universal motivation of purposive action by deriving all from a *One* that was equated with the *Good.* (The point at which Platonist idealism and Platonist realism overlap.)

Aristotle "neutralized" this doctrine. For he denied to both the Platonist Ideas and his own God any generative function. And the kind of purpose he assigned to natural entities was hardly purpose in the Providential sense of the term. Though all motion and action are ultimately guided by a desire for the perfection of God, each kind of thing is conceived as striving to be perfectly the kind of thing it is. Teleology as thus modified allowed for much purely inductive study of genera and species.

In his *Psychology* he clearly distinguishes between philosophic and behavioristic definition, noting that we may define anger either as the "desire for vengeance" or in terms of bodily symptoms. But typically, instead of choosing between them, he favors the kind of inquiry that embraces both. In our terms, he proposes to keep the terminologies of both motion and action, though his system as a whole gives the preference to action, as revealed in his *Metaphysics,* the field where such choices are brought to a final reckoning. And it was this stress upon action, of course, that fitted his thought for adaptation by Aquinas, as rationalizer of the Christian drama.

The "Pathetic Fallacy"

As we have said before, however, our difficulties are increased by the fact that motion and action themselves are readily confounded, unless we make an especial effort to distinguish between them. Aristotle himself, in Book IX of the *Metaphysics,* remarks that "actuality" (*energeia*) in the strict sense "is thought to be identical with movement" and that whereas he equates it with "complete reality," it has "in the main been extended from movements to other things." If, however, you examine in the Greek dictionaries such root words as *ergon,* you find that the movements signified are clearly those of a *purposive* sort, such as *work* or *deed,* with connotations of *thing* here deriving from the thought of some piece of work fulfilled. (Similarly two other Greek words for thing, *pragma* and *chrema,* are implicated in verbal roots signifying *to accomplish* and *to use* respectively. Indeed, viewed from the standpoint of the pentad, "pragmatism" might better have been named "chrematism.") Only the modern concept of the "erg" can be said to belong unequivocally in the realm of motion alone.

In our passing references to the "pathetic fallacy" as a factor in the motion-action ambiguity, we have somewhat stretched the usual application of the term. The device in its pure form is considered in a discerning and suggestive little book (*Pathetic Fallacy in the Nineteenth*

Century, by Josephine Miles) which charts the incidence of this figure in representative English poets from Collins to Eliot.

Concerning her inquiry into "the attribution of feelings to things, which Ruskin called pathetic fallacy," Miss Miles defines her subject as follows:

> Since the "powers of human nature" which may be attributed to objects are so varied, I arbitrarily limit them here to the powers of emotion and passion, which are most central to the "pathetic." That is, I count as an instance of the pathetic fallacy every attribution of a named emotion to an object; and the regular signs of emotion, such as tears and laughter, are included. Thus *the trees were gay, the mountains mourned, the proud fields laughed, the hills sadly slept* are all examples.

The device as so defined well illustrates the kind of consistency between "subject" and "object" we would call the scene-agent (or lyric) ratio. We would consider it an instance of the scene-agent ratio because the stress is upon the attribution of personal *feelings,* or *attitudes* (which are properties of *agents*). The moment she thus restricted her inquiry, it was a foregone conclusion that she would slight the more distinctively dramatic ratio, involving consistency of scene and *act.*

Not that we would object to the limitations she has imposed. On the contrary, her very precision in thus defining a standard serves to illumine the area of the action-motion ambiguity lying just beyond the range of her inquiry. Once you include also, for instance, the personalizing of impersonal motions, you have no clear way of knowing when a given motion is personalized and when it is not. By her rules, *the proud fields laughed* is clearly an instance of pathetic fallacy. But if we widened the scope of personalization to include the "actualizing of motion," we might find ourselves ruling, for instance, that *the wheat tossed in the wind* refers to motion, whereas *the wheat tossed its head in the wind* refers to action.

Consider, for instance, the lines which Coleridge quotes from *Venus and Adonis* as an instance of what he means by imagination:

> Look, how a bright star shooteth from the sky,
> So glides he in the night from Venus eye.

Do shooting stars "move" or "act"? The theory of empathy suggests that even though we might, when asked, say that they simply "move," we attribute action to them when we em-pathetically move with them in our imagination.   And this particular star can make a further claim to act, since in its motion across the sky it represents Adonis in his act of departure.

If, in the light of Miss Miles's investigation, you glance through English poetry prior to the era she has charted, you will find a surprising paucity of pathetic fallacies in her restricted sense of the term.   Ironically, such formal assigning of human sentiments to the non-human realm seems to have come into prominence precisely at the time when the breach between man and nature was being intensified.   But if you examine the poetry prior to this period for examples of the action-motion ambiguity, you will find the incidence quite high indeed.   Similarly, Miss Miles finds a notable avoidance of the pathetic fallacy in Eliot.   Yet there are many lines such as the reference to "yellow smoke that slides along the street," or "the windings of the violins," or the light that "crept up between the shutters"—and these are indebted to the action-motion ambiguity for much of their power as what Aristotle would call "actualizations."

But it may be asked: Why make so much of the turn from action to motion in the vocabularies of human motivation when in the same breath we testify to the ways in which the distinction is continually being obliterated or obscured?

In the first place, it is important to note any source of ambiguity that has great bearing upon the structure of language in all its levels: Grammatical, Rhetorical, and Symbolic.   Thus our concern with the ways of characterization, summarization, and placement requires us to note a point so critical as that watershed moment dividing the dramatistic from the operationalist.   The realm of motion is now *par excellence* the realm of instruments.   No instrument can record or gauge *anything* in the realm of action ("ideas"), except insofar as the subject-matter can be reduced to the realm of motion.

Our approach forces us to face again the philosophic issue that arose with Cartesian dualism.   Many of our best naturalist philosophers seem to be drawing doctrinal sustenance from unrecognized effects of the pathetic fallacy as we have here extended it to cover the action-motion ambiguity.   Hence, condemning materialistic reduction, they can speak hopefully of a vocabulary midway between "mind" and "body" (or midway between the terms for the act of "consciousness" and the terms

for the scenic "conditions" of those manifestations we call consciousness). We need not dare to say that such a vocabulary cannot be found.
We need only say that, whenever it *seems* to be found, you are admonished to be on the look-out for the covert workings of the action-
motion ambiguity.

We may finally be forced to recognize, as integral to vocabularies of
human motivation, an active or "policy-making" function that is
necessarily "nonsense" as tested by our purely technological vocabularies
(scenic, scientist, shaped to conform with knowledge of natural behavior—for even if every atom were proved indubitably to possess a
"soul," the technologist would have use for it only insofar as it were
inanimate, quite as the sales promoter looks for techniques that induce
us mechanically and unthinkingly to buy his product). Such a "policy-
making" function would be *realistic* when it arises out of tribal experience (as with proverbs). But it tends towards *idealism* in proportion
as the derivation is from managerial agents (such as government func-
tionaries); and may often require the correctives of a materialist
criticism.

Above all, by sharpening the issue, and thus admonishing ourselves
lest *apparently* operationalist vocabularies derive appeal from ingredients *surreptitiously* dramatistic, we prepare the way for the mature development of the dramatistic itself. A slight but undetected ingredient
of action can go a long way towards making a flimsy vocabulary of motivation palatable (as is evident from the popularity enjoyed by quasi-
scientific "debunkers" in recent years). But once the requirements of
linguistic action are contemplated systematically, we become more exacting. We demand a fully worked-out version of the ways of *homo
dialecticus,* in contrast with the scraps of dialectical lore now scattered
about the literary landscape, with each typical modern verbalizer dig-
ging in some one thin vein as though it were a bonanza.

"Incipient" and "Delayed" Action

In his chapter on "Attitudes" in *The Principles of Literary Criticism,*
I. A. Richards writes:

> Every perception probably includes a response in the form of in-
> cipient action. We constantly overlook the extent to which all the
> while we are making preliminary adjustments, getting ready to act

in one way or another. Reading Captain Slocum's account of the centipede which bit him on the head when alone in the middle of the Atlantic, the writer has been caused to leap right out of his chair by a leaf which fell upon his face from a tree.

The importance of Mr. Richards' book as a contribution to the analysis of poetry unquestionably centers in his speculations as to how our responses as readers or audience involve such attitudes (which he also calls "imaginal" activities and "tendencies to action"). The symbolic representation of some object or event in art can arouse an added complexity of response in us, he suggests, because it invites us to feel such emotions as would be associated with the actual object or event, while at the same time we make allowance for it as a fiction.

And since we are not called upon to act, no *"overt* action" need take place. In fact, Mr. Richards considers it the sign of intelligence and refinement that we are able thus to leave our impulses in abeyance, at the incipient stage, where they can be contemplated and can thus enrich our consciousness. It is the "stupid or cross person" who habitually responds to his impulses by overt action.

Note, however, that the concept of *incipient* acts is ambiguous. As an attitude can be the *substitute* for an act, it can likewise be the *first step towards* an act. Thus, if we arouse in someone an attitude of sympathy towards something, we may be starting him on the road towards overtly sympathetic action with regard to it—hence the rhetoric of advertisers and propagandists who would induce action in behalf of their commodities or their causes by the formation of appropriate attitudes.

In the sphere of social relations generally, the work of George Herbert Mead has developed with great subtlety and thoroughness this alternative aspect of the incipient. As he puts it in *Mind, Self, and Society,* attitudes are "the beginnings of acts." Indeed, we should not be straining matters greatly if we read his other major work, *The Philosophy of the Act,* as if it were entitled *The Philosophy of the Attitude,* if only we remember that his concern is primarily with the incipient as the *introductory* rather than with the incipient as the *substitutive.* Thus similarly, we would place his valuable treatment of language as "vocal gestures." By such "gestures," he says, we arouse in ourselves the attitudes that language serves to arouse in others; and thereby we adopt the "attitude of the other" in the formation of our moral consciousness.

"I am going on the assumption," he writes, "that action is distinguish-
able from motion," though action as here conceived does not involve
rationality, or even "consciousness of action," but is equated with the
internal motivations of an organism which, confronting reality from its
own special point of view or biological interests, encounters "resistance"
in the external world. And this external resistance to its internal
principle of action defines the organism's action. Such a conception,
somewhat analogous to Santayana's view of the "field of action," would
give us a concept halfway between motion and action. Perhaps, as with
our previous improvisation to do with agent, we might call it action-
minus. Or rather, "attitude-minus." For when we turn to the higher
levels of consciousness we find, according to Mead, that the sense of
"self" is developed as the individual learns to foresee the kinds of resistance which external things will put forward if he acts in certain ways.
Stating the dialectics of the case in its simplest form, Mead says: "The
essential thing is that the individual, in preparing to grasp the distant
object, himself takes the attitude of resisting his own attitude in grasp-
ing." That is, the individual learns to recognize whether the object
will have an elusive or slippery or light or heavy attitude towards his
grasp. And "the attained preparation for the manipulation is the
result of this co-operation or conversation of attitudes." In studying
the nature of the object, we can in effect speak for it; and in adjusting
our conduct to its nature as revealed in the light of our interests, we in
effect modify our own assertion in reply to its assertion.

A social relation is established between the individual and external
things or other people, since the individual learns to anticipate their
attitudes toward him. He thus, to a degree, becomes aware of *himself*
in terms of *them* (or generally, in terms of the "other"). And *his*
attitudes, being shaped by their attitudes as reflected in him, modify his
ways of action. Hence, in proportion as he widens his social relations
with persons and things outside him, in learning how to anticipate their
attitudes he builds within himself a more complex set of attitudes, thoroughly social. This complexity of social attitudes comprises the "self"
(thus complexly erected atop the purely biological motives, and in particular modified by the formative effects of language, or "vocal gesture,"
which invites the individual to form himself in keeping with its social
directives). Mead is here applying in ways of his own the pattern of
the Hegelian dialectic whereby Spirit is alienated as Nature, and then

attains a higher stage of self-consciousness by seeing itself in terms of its Natural other.

In sum: "We are ready to grasp the hammer before we reach it, and the attitude of manipulatory response directs the approach." But the whole situation is complicated by an "arrest" which allows us to take "competing tendencies" into account—as an animal's attitude of desire towards its prey might yet be modified or arrested by an attitude that takes the prey's own resources of defence or escape into account. But however complicated our attitudes may thus finally become, they add up to an attitude that leads to a way of acting. They are but highly alembicated variants of the simple situation wherein "we are ready to grasp the hammer before we reach it, and the attitude of manipulatory response directs the approach."

Alfred Korzybski, in *Science and Sanity,* is concerned with another aspect of the "delayed action." Mead has said:

> The attitude which we, and all forms called intelligent, take towards things is that of overt or delayed response. The attitude which we take towards the contents of mind in their relation to the world is that of explanation.

Korzybski would offer a technique for encouraging the "delayed response." He does not go so far as Richards, who was dealing with a realm of the imagination naturally distinct from the realm of "overt response" (as even when we witness a propaganda play, that might enhearten us to go forth and join some political party, within the conditions of the performance our action is held in abeyance).

Korzybski's concern is primarily with the criticism of man's major social instrument, language. He would agree with Mead that self is largely formed by the effects of society's attitudes in general and our response to "vocal gestures" in particular. He would merely add: "Alas!" He would have it as a rule that we delay every response; and as for our attitudes of explanation, he would advocate the attitude of delayed action precisely because our explanations are askew.

I have made the suggestion that the Marxist Rhetoric, in adopting and adapting the idealistic terminology by which the bourgeoisie had effectively distinguished its slogans from those of feudalism, did not wholly meet the needs of a Grammar, when considered independently of these urgent polemical requirements. There is an analogous difficulty about Korzybski. The "sanity" which is his primary concern is essentially *personal, social and political.* But the "science" in terms of which he interprets it is essentially the science of physics and physiology.

Though Korzybski is always on the track of basic truths, he approaches them through a kind of vocabulary which seems to work better as a Rhetoric than as a Grammar. Since he regularly seeks to translate the problems of action into terms of motion, and since science as so conceived is usually equated with "reality" itself, his explanations in such terms draw upon strongly formed attitudes in us. Hence his doctrine, as so expressed, may have a magically "curative" value, in helping one to convert misgivings into a sense of "knowing."

Korzybski is psychologically acute. Reading his remarks about the "unspeakable level," one gets glimpses into an almost mystical cult of silence. He would systematically sharpen our awareness of that silent moment from which we may derive a truer knowledge, in transcending the level of automatic verbalizations that hide reality behind a film of traditional misnaming. And the moment of delay which he would interpose between the Stimulus and the Response seems to derive its pattern from a sense of that situation wherein, when a person has been thinking hard and long about something, in purely internal dialogue, words addressed to him by another seem to happen twice, as though there were a first hearing and a second hearing, the words being heard first by an outer self, who heard them as words, and then by an inner self who heard them as meanings.

What bothers me always is the conviction that Korzybski is continually being driven by the nature of his keen intuition, to grope beyond the borders of his terminology. He needs a systematic concern with *dialectic.* Indeed, his very key concept, the "consciousness of abstracting," is a haphazardly rediscovered aspect of Neo-Platonism. As such it calls for expansion into a *consciousness of dialectic* in general (a consciousness that would be manifest not merely in a general policy or attitude of skepticism as regards language, but by a *detailed* analysis of linguistic aptitudes and embarrassments). As things now stand, for instance, there is nothing to mitigate our embarrassment on being warned against "two-valued orientations" in the same enterprise that places itself in a two-valued alignment of "Aristotelian" vs. "Non-Aristotelian," or in his distinction between what goes on "inside the skin" and what goes on "outside the skin," or in his flat opposing of "verbal" and "unspeakable" levels.

There is not to this day, nor is there likely to be, a Korzybskian analysis of poetic forms. Nor could a satisfactory one possibly be made without engrafting upon his doctrines a new and alien set of terms and methods. For "semantics" is essentially *scientist,* an approach to language in terms of *knowledge,* whereas poetic forms are kinds of *action.* However, the very incompleteness of his terminology readily allows for the addition of dramatist elements, should any disciple care to pick them up elsewhere and henceforth proclaim them in the name of Korzybskian "semantics." [8]

But whatever may be the shortcomings of Korzybski's "semantics" as a way into the analysis of linguistic forms, any one would be cheating himself who failed to recognize the importance of Korzybski's concern with the abstractive process inherent in even the most concrete of words. His doctrine of the delayed action, as based on the "consciousness of abstracting," involves the fact that any term for an object puts the object in a *class* of similar objects. This logical fact shows in the psychological realm as a situation wherein we see the individual chair not simply as an individual but in terms of its nature as one object in a family of objects.

Thus, we ordinarily sit down in one chair or another, indifferently, assuming that chairs as a class are things to be sat on. But one of Korzybski's greatest triumphs is due to the fact that he does not thus

[8] In brief, the Korzybskian "semantics" is essentially a study of dialectic which is greatly truncated by reason of the fact that it did not formally and systematically recognize its dialectical nature. All enterprises are dialectical which would cure us through the medium of words—and all the more so if their words would cure by training us in the distrust of words. A truly "scientific" cure *ab extra* would be such as corrected a false idea by a drug, glandular operation, and the like. But purely linguistic operations, such as those involved in the use of the "structural differential," are wholly dialectical.

The "structural differential" itself is, to be sure, a mechanical device; but it is merely the kind that *illustrates* a mental process, like Kurt Lewin's "topological" methods for picturing mental states in terms of abstract designs. It illustrates quite graphically *one* dialectical process, the process involving different orders or degrees of abstraction. Mead deals with another, equally important; the seeing of one position in terms of another. Korzybski's favorite words "linguistics" and "semantics" are themselves but other words for dialectic. Indeed, we might define them as "dialectic rediscovered in terms of contemporary science" (which is to say, dialectic rediscovered in terms that constantly hamper the study of dialectic).

consider chairs generically. Being conscious of abstracting, he knows that when we interpret this particular bundle of sense impressions as a "chair," we are considering it not in its particularity, but in terms of an abstraction of "high order." He knows that the abstraction "chair," fails to distinguish between a sturdy chair and a frail chair. And he tells how, in his programmatic awareness that "chair" is an abstraction, on one occasion he sat down on a particular chair with his usual attitude of *delayed* action. And when it turned out to be a frail chair (as the Aristotelians might say, a chair having frailness as one of its "accidents") though it collapsed, the wary savant did not collapse with it; and so he survived to tell the tale, that we might profit from his experience. And so, recalling what we have said about the tragedy of learning: by participation in the Korzybski *mathema,* through the medium of a delayed *poiema* we may avoid a disconcerting *pathema.*

As we have by now become accustomed to expect, the Korzybski concept of "action" itself ranges indeterminately over the areas of both purely physiological movement and critical consciousness, an ambiguity that becomes more unforgivable in proportion as one's terminology of motives aims to be scientistically formed. He follows the usual dialectic pattern whereby he can divide response into both physiological and mental moments, while at the same time admonishing that such dualism must be discounted as a mere convenience of discourse, the reality being a *tertium quid* that has something of both the mental and the physiological, the dialectical conversion of "body" and "mind" into "body-mind" (or in Korzybski's version: the "neuro-semantic").

There are at least three moments here; and if you would pause to examine his position closely at any one of them, you are open to "refutation" insofar as he can jump to one of the other moments and from its point of vantage discover that you are off the subject. But insofar as we can reduce the concept of "delayed action" to its purely physiological moment, note that it must be the very *opposite* of a delay. There must be some particular physiological configuration, some special balance of nerves, muscles, endocrines, and the like, that is the equivalent, in the realm of motion, to this "attitude" of delay in the realm of consciousness, or action proper. Thus, ironically, Korzybski is trying to induce in his patients or students not a "delayed" response, but an unusually *prompt* one. The very split second one becomes aware of a situation, one must remind oneself about the need for "consciousness of abstracting." And he must practice this, until he has firmly established this response in himself, making it almost automatically prompt with him. From the standpoint of action, in the full sense of the term, such a state might properly be considered as a delay—but as regards the bodily *motions,* we must remember that a state of delayed *action* cannot be a corresponding state of delayed *motion.*

In sum, the *action* is delayed precisely because one has trained the body to undergo certain physiological *motions* of a sort designed to forestall the kind of motions ordinarily following such a stimulus when it is received uncritically. The body during the state of delay does not cease to exist. The mental *attitude* of arrest must have some corresponding bodily *posture.* The very delay of action is thus maintained by motions, since the *attitude* of criticism, or delay, or "consciousness of abstracting" must be matched by its own peculiar *physiological* configuration. There is at least as much neural motion going on in the body that hesitates before sitting down as in the body that sits down without hesitation. Mentally to look before one leaps has its equivalent in internal bodily motions quite as leaping does. So we must remember, in hoping for a body-mind (or motion-action, or "neuro-semantic") vocabulary, that the "delay" as regards the norms of action is simply another kind of *promptness,* as regards the norms of motion.

All told, the attitude or incipient act is a region of ambiguous possibilities, as is well indicated in the Latin grammars, where "inceptive" verbs (like *calesco,* grow warm; *irascor,* get angry) are also called "inchoatives," while "inchoate" in turn means "beginning," "partially but not fully in existence," "incomplete," and is now often used as though the writer thought it a kind of metathesis for "chaotic."

Thus, the notion of the attitude as an incipient or delayed action would seem to be a special application of the concept of "potentiality," which in Aristotle's use of the dramatist Grammar was the reciprocal of "actuality." We have tried to show that the attitude is essentially ambiguous, as an attitude of sympathy may either lead to an act of sympathy or may serve as substitute for an act of sympathy. It is thus "potentially" two different kinds of act. In the traditional Aristotelian usage, potentiality is to actuality as the possibility of doing something is to the actual doing of it, or as the unformed is to the formed. In the *Metaphysics,* IX, 8, he says: "Every potency is at one and the same time a potency of the opposite." That which is "capable of being may either be or not be." The term thus shares somewhat the paradox of substance, since the hot is the "potentially" cold. And Aristotle situates the principle of evil in matter not in the sense that matter is essentially evil, but in the sense that it is the realm of potentiality: in being potentially good, matter is by the same token potentially bad. The scientific concept of potential energy lacks the degree of ambiguity one encounters in the potential as applied to the realm of living beings in general and human beings in particular.

The realm of the incipient, or attitudinal, is the realm of "symbolic action" par excellence; for symbolic action has the same ambiguous potentialities of action (when tested by the norms of overt, practical action). Here is the area of thought wherein actual conflicts can be transcended, with results sometimes fatal, sometimes felicitous. But the study of its manifestations will vow us, at every step, to the study of that "attitudinal action" which we have called the dramatistic, but which might also be called the dialectical. We prefer to call it dramatistic because dialectic itself has repeatedly lost tract of its dramatistic origins, when thinkers lay all their stress upon the attempt to decide whether it leads to true knowledge, or when they have so rigidified its forms in some particular disposition of terms (or dogmas) that the underlying liquidity of its Grammar becomes concealed.

Also, in recalling that Mr. Richards speaks of incipient or *imaginal* action, we are reminded that *images* can have the force of attitudes. Hence, when analyzing the structure of a lyric (a form in which there is no act in the full dramatic sense) we may look for a lyric analogue of plot in the progression or development of the poem's imagery. A dramatic or narrative work, for instance, might affect the transubstantiation of a character by tracing his course to and from the abyss, the abyss itself being the realm of transition between pre-abyss and post-abyss identities. A lyric poem might get the same effect by a sequence of stanzas having a different quality of imagery at beginning, middle, and end, with the imagery of the middle section being in some way abysmal. Thus, Shelley's five-stanza "Ode to the West Wind" begins with imagery of that which drives:

> O wild West Wind, thou breath of Autumn's being,
> Thou, from whose unseen presence the leaves dead
> Are driven . . .

In stanza five the poem dwells upon imagery merging the driving and the driven:

> Make me thy lyre, even as the forest is:
> What if my leaves are falling like its own!
> The tumult of thy mighty harmonies
>
> Will take from both a deep, autumnal tone,
> Sweet though in sadness. Be thou, Spirit fierce,
> My spirit! Be thou me, impetuous one!
>
> Drive my dead thoughts over the universe
> Like withered leaves to quicken a new birth!

And the transition involving this idealistic progress towards identification of individual self with universal spirit takes place in stanza three, through abysmal imagery of *submergence*. Here the poet meditates upon the ways in which vegetation at the bottom of the sea responds to the agitations on the surface:

> Thou
> For whose path the Atlantic's level powers
> Cleave themselves into chasms, while far below
> The sea-blooms and the oozy woods which wear
> The sapless foliage of the ocean, know
>
> Thy voice, and suddenly grow gray with fear,
> And tremble and despoil themselves: oh, hear!

Through the medium of his sensitive plant, as here submerged, he has added to the West Wind the character necessary for his final identification with it as Spirit. Actives and passives become one. An ingredient of *sympathy* is unquestionably implicit in this imagery of submerged vegetation. But it so happens that the poet also, in a footnote, makes it explicit:

> The phenomenon alluded to at the conclusion of the third stanza is well known to naturalists. The vegetation at the bottom of the sea, of rivers, and of lakes, sympathizes with that of the land in the change of seasons, and is consequently influenced by the winds which announce it.

The final couplet, idealizing the autumn wind as introduction to the season that leads into spring, is presumably the exhilarating result of the transcendent resolution, which encourages the poet to speculate futuristically: "If Winter comes, can Spring be far behind?"

As regards the analysis of poetic forms, the wavering distinction between the attitude as preparation for action and the attitude as substitution for action, involves a similarly wavering distinction between the dramatic and the lyrical. If Aristotle's world is essentially a dramatic one, his God (as a pure act identical with perfect rest) is essentially lyrical. From the dramatic point of view, the moment of arrest that characterizes the attitude is a kind of "pre-act." But the lyrical attitude is rather the kind of rest that is the summation or culmination of action, transcending overt action by *symbolically* encompassing its end.

In drama there is the intense internal debate prior to the moment of decision. Upon the outcome of this debate depends the course of history. But from the lyric point of view, the state of arrest is itself an end-product, a resolution of previous action rather than a preparation for subsequent action (though of course while life is still in progress any culminating stage is but *pro tempore,* and can also be the beginning of a new development).

Mr. Houston Peterson hit upon the happy idea of assembling in an anthology (*The Lonely Debate*) some typical moments of the dramatic arrest. He notes, for instance, what dire events in *Julius Caesar* "are all foreshadowed by that hushed moment in Brutus' garden, when he broods over the waning liberties of Rome," deciding "It must be by his death." And he observes how the tragic destiny that inexorably unfolds in *Macbeth* is decided not with Duncan's murder, "but in that terrifying soliloquy of the first act":

> If it were done when 'tis done, then 'twere well
> It were done quickly.

Here is the moment when the "potential" in the Aristotelian sense of something that may become either this or that is converted into the potential in the mystical or mechanistic sense of the predestined or pre-formed (as today's decisions are potentially tomorrow's fatalities, as the suicide who has leapt from the bridge is already potentially dead, or as the German proverb, at once mystical and realistic, puts it: *Wer A sagt, muss B sagen*). Yet the very isolating of such momentous soliloquies, and their publication somewhat like a book of lyrics, makes us realize all the more clearly how essentially different they are from lyrics. In fact, we might call them the depiction of such personal situations as *most acutely need* resolution in the lyric state, but drive to action precisely because such resolution is missing.

In contrast with such intense moments of pre-action, recall Wordsworth's sonnet "Composed upon Westminster Bridge." Here we find the perfect lyric mood, marked by the state of arrest in its *culminative* aspect. Here the very process of transition is made motionless: for the imagery is that of a *crossing,* but the crossing just *is,* since the poet stands meditative upon a bridge that by its nature crosses motionlessly from one bank to the other:

> Earth has not anything to show more fair:
> Dull would be he of soul who could pass by
> A sight so touching in its majesty:
> This City now doth, like a garment, wear
> The beauty of the morning; silent, bare
> Ships, towers, domes, theatres, and temples lie
> Open unto the fields, and to the sky;
> All bright and glittering in the smokeless air.
> Never did sun more beautifully steep
> In his first splendour, valley, rock, or hill;
> Ne'er saw I, never felt, a calm so deep!
> The river glideth at his own sweet will:
> Dear God! the very houses seem asleep;
> And all that mighty heart is lying still!

The imagery is of morning, so there is incipience. But it is not the incipience of the internal debate, arrested at the moment of indecision prior to a decision from which grievous consequences are inevitably to follow. Nor is it a retrospective summary. It just *is,* a state of mind that has come to rest by reason of its summarizing nature. It encompasses. We are concerned not with its potentialities, but with it as an end in itself. It has conveyed a *moment of stasis* (we are aware of the pun at the roots of this expression). It envisions such rest as might be a ground, a beginning and end, of all action.[9]

---

[9] For further applications of the dramatist perspective to lyric forms, the reader is referred to the three essays in the Appendix: "Symbolic Action in a Poem by Keats," "The Problem of the Intrinsic (as reflected in the Neo-Aristotelian School)," and "Motives and Motifs in the Poetry of Marianne Moore," two of which essays were once an integral part of this book in an earlier draft, but were edited somewhat to fit them for magazine publication. Hence, there is in them

Considering *Hamlet* in the light of the ambiguity we have observed in the concept of delayed action, might we not say that the play derives much poignancy from Hamlet's way of transforming the very preparations for action into devices for postponing action? Thus the precautionary steps he takes, in his effort to establish the murderer's guilt beyond question, while they are designed to assist his act of vengeance, threaten to interfere with vengeance. Here Shakespeare nearly dissolved the identity of drama, removing it from the realm of action to a realm of pre-action that would amount to no action. He here stands at the very opposite extreme to that of O'Neill at the close of *Mourning Becomes Electra*. For O'Neill threatens to dissolve drama into behaviorism, as Lavinia ceases to be an agent in becoming a merely automatic Response to a Stimulus; but Shakespeare threatens to dissolve drama into an *excess* of scruples, in making the internal debate not merely the originating motive of the action, but its permanent motif.

Moving into the realm of Rhetoric, we may note how legislatures regularly adopt the "Hamletic" strategy as a way to avoid embarrassing decisions. For if you would forestall final vote on a measure, and would do so in the best "scientific" spirit, you need but appoint a committee empowered to find more facts on the subject. This same Hamletic device (Hamlet being the first great liberal) comes pleasantly to the aid of all savants who would busy themselves in behalf of social betterment without hurting susceptibilities. In keeping with the nature of their specialties, they can gather more data and still more, to aid us in the making of wise decisions. And when the matter has been documented beyond a doubt, they may go on and document it beyond the shadow of a doubt. Assuredly, there will be something for them to do as long as the subsidies last; for no decision in the world's history was ever made on the basis of all the "necessary facts," nor ever will be.

Realist Family and Nominalist Aggregate

We have selected Korzybski's references to the "consciousness of abstracting" as the most important aspect of his doctrine. From the standpoint of dramatistic generation, however, we doubt whether his

---

some repetition of matters already covered. However, such matters are usually given a somewhat different application in the essays; hence it seemed advisable to leave the text in its present form.

treatment of abstraction is Grammatical enough. He does well in showing that even an apparently concrete word like "table" abstracts and classifies, since it applies to a vast aggregate of possible objects, each different in its particularities from all others of its class. And a word like "furniture" would be a still higher level of abstraction, since it would also include chairs, beds, desks, etc. We might next advance to some such word as "conveniences" or "commodities," and might even arrive at some classification as broad as "things" or "objects," and finally "being."

Korzybski's method here is characteristically scientist and nominalist. It begins with *individual things* as the realities with which language has to deal—and it treats classification as a process of abstraction. According to the Baldwin dictionary, nominalism is "the doctrine that universals have no objective existence or validity." In its extreme form, nominalism holds that universals "are only names (*nomina, flatus vocis*)." That is, they are sheer "creations of language for purposes of convenient communication." The realist Grammar works the other way round: It begins with a *tribal* concept, and treats individuals as participants in this common substance, or element (whereas Korzybski stresses above all else the need for a "non-elemental" approach to language). The realistic pattern thus fitted well with the clan origins of Greek democracy and with the familial patterns of thought in Western feudalism. As we have suggested elsewhere, realism treats individuals as members of a group, whereas nominalism treats groups as aggregates of individuals. Hence our proposal to treat nominalism as linguistically individualistic or atomistic. For whereas realism treats generic terms as names for *real* substances, nominalism treats them as merely conveniences of language. Occam's nominalism, for instance, is distinguished by "the positive assertion that specific individualities, differentiated in themselves, are the real."

Korzybski helps to show how the conveniences of linguistic classification can become drastic inconveniences, leading to such morbid "semantic reactions" as race prejudice whereby many individuals greatly different from one another are lumped together as though their characters were *substantially* the same. Korzybski is continually stressing the need of index figures, to remind us that our word "chair" is a generalizing term for chair$_1$, chair$_2$, chair$_3$, etc. Plato, on the other hand, would treat the perfect idea of a chair as the reality, and would consider individual chairs as imperfectly participating in this essence common to all chairs.

As we have pointed out, in the act there is a *creative* or *generative* feature. It is thus clear that, if one thinks of the world itself as either the result of enactment (Plato) or itself a process of enactment (Aristotle), one begins with an act-genus-generation tie-up which can indicate why, on the Grammatical level, traditional realism favors the term, *act*. One can get the point in a rough way by using in a neutral sense our expression, "acts of God," as it is applied to natural calamities. If all natural events and objects were called "acts of God" (as expressions of the divine intention) we should thus have a world in which act, form, and generation mutually involved one another, since each genus would carry out one line of generation, or actualization. Aristotle got the same relation between genus and act in his uncreated world by his principle of the entelechy, which represented the striving of each thing to be perfectly the *kind* of thing it was.

One should also note that whereas the scientist beginning with "the object" explains abstraction, generalization, classification as a process having to do with *nouns,* a dramatist stress upon act suggests an origin in *verbs*. Words like "run," "go," "do," are likewise abstract and general. No action word refers to just this action and no other. One regularly uses nouns, pronouns, and demonstratives that do thus particularize. Every proper name is of this nature. But verbs are always abstract and generic. And we do well to remember, when trying to generate philosophic methods dramatistically, that a key word of traditional realism was *being* or *essence,* which was no demonstrative noun, but a *verbal* noun, the most abstract and general form of the most abstract and general act.

As to how a thing's *essence* or *quiddity* can become identical with its principle of *action,* let us look at it thus: There is an expression, "He has a way with him," suggesting that the man possesses some quality or aptitude peculiarly his own. Would not this be the very principle of his character, in short his very essence, if we could but define it? Thus Shakespeare "has a way with him"—and this way would be his literary style; and insofar as we can describe it accurately we are describing the essence of Shakespeare as a poet.

And so it is with generic words like "animality" and "rationality" (*animalitas* as the character of man's genus, *rationalitas* as the character of his species). The "whatness" that they name is not merely that of tribal substance; it is also a *way* (that is, a kind of *action*). Rationality is a *way;* as Santayana would say, it is a "life" of reason. Thus, rational*ity,* as the "essence" of man, is tribal, formal, and an act. (It is formal because it is the guiding principle of such acts as individuate its nature.)

When the ramifications of the term act are developed thus from within, I think we can get a much sounder understanding of the thought-structure than if we approach it purely in terms of "levels of generalization." Indeed, as we pointed out previously, of the four terms, the generic, the genetic, the genitive, and the general, the fourth takes us farthest from the *tribal* patterns in such thinking. Hence, an approach to the generic in terms of the generalized may serve the ends of a polemic analysis conducted from without; but it cannot enable us to "anticipate" the realistic structure by studying the Grammatical principles of its generation.

The *Doctor Subtilis,* Duns Scotus, whose thinking was so ingenious that he was for long accused of all the doctrines against which he contended, stands in an interesting place with relation to the nominalist disintegration of scholastic realism. On its surface, his stress upon the "thisness" (*haecceitas*) of a thing is nominalistic. But Scotus arrives at his concept of thisness by retaining the familial pattern typical of scholasticism. Nominalism was antithetical to the tribal derivation of individuals. Scotus, on the other hand, retains the concept of the tribal, but extends its application in such a way that the individual can be treated as a genus.

Si loquamur realiter, humanitas quae est in Socrate non est humanitas quae est in Platone. That is, if animal is the genus, and mankind the species, Scotus would contend that Socrates has a different "humanity" than Plato. So, to locate the essence of Socrates, we must go a step further, and recognize that it resides in a special *"socratitas."* Our previous exegesis of the essence or quiddity as a "way" should indicate how this thinking differs from straight nominalism. Insofar as a man's acts are characteristic of him, for instance, they are *substantially* related to one another. And the discerning portrait painter might even be able to make us feel how the "accidents" of the man's appearance share in this substantial relationship.

What of contemporary "scientific realism?" Sometimes the term is used, like naturalism, euphemistically for materialism, in referring to ways of thought that stress the motivational importance of scenic factors, in a scene of narrowed circumference. Sometimes it might better be placed as an aspect of pragmatism, in its stress upon science as a means of social adjustment. Sometimes it applies to the field of rhetoric, where it refers to the unmasking of false idealizations (usually a materialist trend, though also at times it may rather be idealism turned against itself). Sometimes, as where it applies to the field of jurisprudence, it combines all these features with a definite sense of the *need* for a stress upon the term act (not merely as a term but as a term from which a whole set of terms would be systematically derived). For the realm of social relations automatically brings up this requirement, though the norms of physicalist science continually encumber efforts in this direction.

As for nominalism, it is "anti-social" only in the purely *Grammatical* sense which we have indicated. That is, if carried out consistently, it obliterates all notions of consubstantiality, however defined, hence obliterating the Grammatical basis of social community. Grammatically, it leaves us with a world of individuals, united only by monetary symbols and the deceptions of an idealistic rhetoric. In practice, nominalists usually temper their philosophies by an humanitarian afterthought advocating "joint action" for some social aim or other.

Human nature being what it is, men can be relied upon to feel themselves consubstantial with enterprises of one sort or another, even though (as with the followers of Korzybski) it be an enterprise devoted to the systematic elimination of the category of substance. Nominalism still enjoys somewhat the privilege it enjoyed in the Middle Ages, when the very firmness of tribal ways allowed for a wide margin of latitude in non-tribal patterns of speculation. The vocabulary of personal and political relations is still dramatistically infused, at least in a piecemeal way, however greatly the *systematic disposition* of such terms may have been impaired by the radical changes in the conditions of living. The powers that now most suggestively strike men's fancy are not in the vital order (of generation); they are in the technological order (of mechanical production). Yet technology itself is an embodiment of essentially human motives. And thus in it there are preserved, though "ungrammatically," the vestiges of a vital grammar, reflecting at least the quality of action defined in Santayana's concept of "animal faith."

Further Remarks on Act and Potency

We must be on guard in these pages lest our zeal in behalf of "dramatism" trick us into taking on more obligations than we need assume for the purposes of this study. We are asserting that dramatist coordinates provide the most direct way into the understanding of linguistic forms. But we are not vowed to uphold any one traditional application of such a grammar. Our appreciation of Aristotle is itself un-Aristotelian; our remarks about Aquinas would not satisfy a Thomist. And so, the pages of this section on Act are not to be read as an argument for any one traditional application of the dramatist grammar, but simply as a review, from the dramatist standpoint, of grammatical principles involved in the attributing of motives. It considers typical dialectical resources that have been used systematically in the past. And because man is essentially in the order of generation, we believe that these same principles will underlie the linguistic forms of the future, though they may be broken into fragments and concealed from view by approaches in terms of knowledge, learning, technological power, conditioning, and the like.

All such scientist approaches have great admonitory value. They provide us with incongruous perspectives that enable us to see mankind from many angles, each of which in its way adds a new "hark ye" to the lore of human relations. But they are all extrinsic, nonsubstantial approaches—and as such are not suited to define man's essentially dramatic nature. They heckle so superbly that many in the audience come to mistake the heckling for the address.

Modern science asks how acts are motivated; but Aristotelian science tells how motions are activated, thus featuring the very term that would now be eliminated. Platonism had left the subject of motivation in the "tribal" stage. In effect Plato treated the genus as the generator of its members (or, as stated in medieval terms, the Platonist universal was *ante rem*). However, the relation of tribal ancestor to individual offspring was transcendent. The individual members of the family existed on earth, in the world of appearances; the pure form or "idea" of the family identity had its eternal being in heaven. The individual members here imperfectly partook of the pure essence there; and in embodying the principles of their form they were enactments in the sense that their motive was intrinsic to their kind. Such transcendent realism differed from Aristotle's more "scientific" brand in that Plato placed the locus of motivation with the heavenly family identity, whereas the Aristotelian "entelechy" resided in the things of sensory experience. "Actuality," says Aristotle, "is prior both to potency and to every principle of change."

Don't forget, however, that Plato equated the divine with the abstract, apparently because both transcend the realm of the senses. Hence, nearly everything that this greatest of dialecticians says of "heaven" can be profitably read as a statement about *language*. And that man cheats himself who avoids Plato because of a preference for purely secular thought. Even the doctrine of the heavenly "archetypes" is sound enough, if read as a statement about the relationship between class names and names for the individuals thus classified by a common essence. And Plato's account of the approach to "divinity" by the processes of dialectic generalizing, particularizing, and transcendence reveals in all thoroughness the abstractive nature of language. This is in contrast with the mere fragment of linguistic analysis which Korzybski would expand into a whole universe of discourse. Korzybski's contribution, we have said, resides in his having said "alas!" to an aspect of linguistic transcendence that Plato considers edifying. But one may doubt whether even this helpful admonition could survive a serious consideration of the Platonist dialectic as a whole.

In one sense, we might call Aristotle's metaphysics of motivation more dialectical than Plato's. Plato used dialectic as a method leading towards the discovery of truth. The dialectic was a means; the truth (knowledge of the Good) was its end. Aristotle finally dropped the dramatic form of the Platonic dialogue. He isolated method as a separate field, in his analysis of formal logic. And he dropped the process of conversational give and take about which Plato organized the stages of an exposition (and which, as we shall show in the last section of this book, was designed to produce a form wherein the end transcended the beginning). This way of development through the coöperative competition of divergent voices was dropped by Aristotle; but he attributed a dialectical structure to the very nature of the universe. He did this by so revising the Platonist conception of the "forms" in their relation to "matter" that the pair went through a series of transpositions. Thus, the forms were conceived as arranged in a hierarchy of being, with the "form" of beings at each level constituting the "matter" of beings at the next higher level. This series was thought to ascend until you arrived at "pure form," the motionless prime mover that moves all else not by being itself moved, but by being loved, the object of desire.

We might state this form-matter relation in terms of the action-motion pair by saying that each order of being constituted the conditions of motion involved in the action of the next higher order. Human action, for instance, depends upon animal motion; animal action depends upon vegetative motion; vegetative action depends upon physical motion. Ordinarily in these pages, however, we have not used the terms in this particular dialectical way, but have confined "action" to the level of human rationality. The inducement to use the terms thus dialectically comes from the need to distinguish animal locomotion from lower orders of motivation, such as physical motion and vegetative growth. Whereupon, we get purely biological action, as with Santayana's "animal faith."

The Aristotelian concept of the pure act as the final cause of all motion possesses possibilities of reversal. The motions *toward* it might be interpreted as motions *derived from* it (that is, final cause might be equated with efficient cause), particularly when Aristotle's God had been taken over by theologians who restored the usual *generative* principle to the concept of divinity. Subsequently, considering God as both a source and a purpose, mystics distinguished alternate moments, with the creation as an *egressus* from God followed by a *regressus* back to God; and then, having thus taken the two motives apart, the mystic could propose that they be conceived as joined together again, the possibilities of reversal in the Aristotelian concept thus being converted explicitly into an oxymoron. Aquinas unites the two directions (God as source and God as purpose) when he says that God is present in things: (1) after the manner of an efficient cause (but "equivocally," as "in the sun is the likeness of whatever is generated by the sun's power"); (2) as the object of an operation is in the operator.

On a purely contextual basis, we could arrive at Aristotle's "unmoved mover" simply by the generalizing of "motion." For the "motionless" would be all that was left to serve as the dialectical counterpart, or "ground," of a concept so comprehensive. No, that is not the only recourse here. Another was to use the macrocosm-microcosm pattern, considering *universal* motion as the ground of *particular* motions. The whole would thus be the ground of the parts; and the parts would synecdochically (by the *omnia ubique* formula) share the nature of the whole.

Another opportunity here has already been touched upon: the kind of ground one gets when considering "matter" as a "substrate" (*hypokeimenon,* the placed-beneath, or "subject"), possessing potentialities that may be variously actualized. Both members of the potentiality-actuality pair, it will be recalled, are tinged by the paradox of substance. Not only does God as pure act take the grammatical form of a *passive* (in being the object of desire). There is a similar reversal of voice implicit in the fact that matter (possessing, in Windelband's phrase, "an impulse to be formed") is characterized as *potency.*

What passivity ever possessed more "active" a name? In its passive role, matter undergoes the shaping activity of form. Yet it partially resists the efforts to shape it. A seed may either grow or rot; in this sense its potentialities are of an either-or sort. But a radish seed possesses solely the potentialities of a radish; and in this sense, its potentialities are foreordained, being related to its actualities as the implicit to the explicit.

The earlier notions of *rationes seminales* were constructed in accordance with the same proportion (implicit is to explicit as potential is to actual). Some mystics similarly viewed the world pantheistically as a development from a *Deus implicitus* to a *Deus explicitus* (nature being God explicit, or God made manifest).

Similarly Leibniz's monads were "possibilities" conceived after the analogy of seeds (and in accordance with a theory of "pre-formation" that thought of seeds as containing, in miniature involution, all the traits that would later evolve into the full-sized plant). Thus "the present is big with the future, the future might be read in the past." And before the soul has clear and distinct ideas, it possesses them "innately" and "virtually." Looking at this pattern in the light of modern psychology, we could rephrase it: "The unconscious is virtually (potentially) the conscious."

The pattern underlies the thinking of the early criminologist, Lombroso. Lombroso had attempted to establish a correlation between criminality and physical traits. For this purpose, he assembled statistics on the measurements of Italian prisoners. Later, he found that many non-criminals exhibited the same traits as he had discovered in his measurements of criminals. He avoided embarrassment by deciding that the non-criminals possessing these same traits were "criminaloid." That is to say, they were found to possess the special inclinations toward crime, though with proper treatment and good fortune these "criminaloid" types might live orderly lives and die at a ripe old age without having committed the crimes prognosticated by their bodies. Despite their good records, he might have called them "substantially" or "potentially" criminals. The same embarrassment was met by legal theorists who situated in *all* men the "potentialities" for committing crime. (Quite true, and if we made it a crime to breathe tomorrow, only a relatively small portion of today's population would manage to remain law-abiding.)

In any case, one could not dismiss this Grammatical point as merely "academic." For the potentiality-actuality pattern is at the bottom of all "scientific" attempts at "prediction" and "control." Lenin, as a "scientific" revolutionary, was involved in this same pattern when trying to decide just what were the sure marks of a revolutionary situation. It is at the bottom of sampling procedures, as with polls of public opinion. And it is implicit in the planning of sales campaigns and the like.

Another variant of the potential figures in the term "tendency." And the social sciences would be cramped fatally if forced to forego this term, or its equivalent. Yet it has that same ambiguity we have noted in the terms, "potential" and "substantial." When we decide, for instance, that a certain group "tends" toward a certain way of acting, we are not embarrassed if this "tendency" remains unactualized. For a mere tendency to do something is also, by the same token, a tendency *not* to do it. Similarly, we may note a "disposition," "predisposition," or "inclination" towards a certain kind of action, without deciding whether such leanings will or will not reach overt expression.

As an interesting instance of such tactics, one might consider the economic theory of Frank Hyneman Knight, propounded in his book, *The Ethics of Competition*. His theory is based upon what I might call an economist's equivalent for the city of God. That is, he begins with the concept of a perfect economic world, obeying ideal market relationships, which in his case are conceived as pure individualistic competition. He is, of course, quite aware that the market in our imperfect world of actuality does not obey the laws of his ideal market, which he sets up as both a technical aid to the description of the actual market and as an ethical norm (a direction towards which he would have the market "tend"). And insofar as the market of actuality does not obey these ideals of pure competition (which notion of purity we should call the "god term" for his economics), he saves the day by noting that it "tends" to.

Next, he observes that "the 'economic' man [as per his theory of ideal competition] is not a social man, and the ideal market dealings of theory are not social relations." And it is the properties of men as social beings (their "imperfections," as judged from the standpoint of the perfect world of ideal competition) that serve to convert the "tendency" of exchange to follow the laws of the ideal market into a "tendency" *not* to follow them.

The author reveals for us another such Janus-term by noting the function of the concept of *"caeteris paribus."* For you may say that A's behavior will reproduce that of B, "all other things being equal," yet you need not be embarrassed if it doesn't, because "all other things never are equal." Hence, the concept of *"caeteris paribus"* matches "tendency" as a locational device. (*"Mutatis mutandis"* would be another.) "All other things being equal," men would behave in accordance with a uniform set of economic laws—but since all other things are never equal, said economic laws cannot serve as adequate for the description of even exclusively economic phenomena. And in the search for the complicating factors, factors that make the *tendency towards* the ideal market synonymous with a *tendency away from* the ideal market, the author abandons economic considerations for sociological ones. His book thus becomes in effect a kind of "conversion" from an economic perspective to a sociological one—which, in this case, since the economic pattern was an "ideal" one and the sociological pattern breaks the symmetry of this ideal, would seem to symbolize, attenuatedly indeed, a Hans Castorp descent from the "magic mountain" to the "flatlands."

We can readily see the difference between the potentiality of "tendencies" and the kind of potentiality imputed in theories of strict determinism, predestination, or the "historically inevitable." The concept of the inevitable "substantially" merges the permanent and the changing, since it accounts for the flux of events by some underlying principle that prevails always. It says in effect not simply that the future *will be,* but that it *is,* since it is *implicit* in the structure of the present. And any group claiming to represent the "inevitable" course of events, as the proletariat in the Marxist view of capitalism's "inevitable" development towards socialism, shares in this substantiality.

The present ease of printing, which makes it almost a necessary condition of the publishing trade that readers turn avidly from one novel to another, without pause for rereading, has led to a corresponding set of esthetic values. Hence the overemphasis upon the element of *surprise* as a factor in esthetic appeal, for "suspense" is now usually conceived in terms of "surprise," despite the fact that one can feel "suspense" in hearing a piece of music with which one is perfectly familiar; and Greek audiences underwent "suspense" when witnessing dramas whose plots were traditional. But suspense is formally more substantial than mere uncertainty of outcome, even when one has "identified himself" with the characters of the fiction. There is a fundamental difference between art on the one hand and competitive sports and games of chance on the other. For we would resent the thought that the outcome of a game might have been settled in advance by collusion among the players. And we would be just as resentful if the outcome of a play depended simply on the toss of a coin or on a last-minute decision of the actors. Even when the ending of a play has been changed, we are satisfied only if the new ending is felt to grow "inevitably" out of the preceding action (though some audiences may be more exacting than others in their notions of the law here).

Admittedly, writers are now able to depend strongly upon the reader's ignorance of a plot's outcome, and to shape their stories accordingly. Cheap production makes it possible to produce literature hygienically, "to be used once and thrown away." But while this condition itself has been made possible by the advance of science, one is wrong when, as is usual today, he tends to explain the essentials of such plots' appeal in scientist terms (as he does when viewing suspense largely in terms of the reader's ignorance).

When we consider both historical and poetic development at once, however, each can throw light upon the other. And taken together, they enable us to see that historic "inevitability" is but the obverse side of dramatic "suspense." For the appeal of both resides in the kind of *substantiality* that comes of *formally* relating all incidents to *one* organizing principle that prevails throughout the diversity of detail. Insofar as either history or the work of art obeys a guiding principle of development, the nature of the motivation at any one point is "substantially" the same as at any other point. The ending is implicit in the beginning. And so, all the changing details are infused by an "eternal now." [10]

Modern views of "probability" fall puzzlingly across this distinction between the "inevitability" kind of potentiality and the "tendency" kind. Sometimes the theory seems to involve assumptions of strict determinism. That is, the outcome is already in the cards, but we don't "know enough" to read the signs correctly, hence must work in an area of probabilities. Probability here would be epistemological rather than ontological. It would be situated not in the nature of things, but in the defects of our instruments. One may estimate the chances of drawing a full house at poker, for instance, and treat this as a statement about his chances of drawing such a hand on the next deal. But if the cards

[10] The concept of "inevitability" may arise in another way, somewhat akin to this, but sufficiently different to consider it as a special route. Consider those speculations on chance, genius, and historical law which Tolstoy has written at the end of *War and Peace*. Naturally, an author who had written a work in which he commanded so many destinies would feel strongly the sense of a divine principle guiding the totality of historical development. Such a feeling would be but the equivalent, in cosmological terms, of his artistic method. Tolstoy points out that, the farther we move from an historical event, the less "freedom" do we see in it, and the more "inevitability." "Freewill is content," he says; "necessity is form." And insofar as we see history in formal terms, the many diversities of individual choice merge into the inevitabilities of a vast movement. He similarly observes that the total absence of freewill equals death. And however something might have been done before it was done, once it is done it is inevitable.

Does not this suggest that we arise to a concept of "inevitability" by seeing present or future things in terms of the *past?* For once something *has been,* it can *now* no longer *have been* any different *then.* The thought suggests a strange paradox whereby Marxism, so strongly *futuristic* in its promises, may ground a sense of *present* substantiality on a way of transcendence derived from a vision that sees in terms of the past. Such would not be an alternative to the "poetic fatalism" we have discussed above. It would simply suggest the possibility of more "thanatoptic" ingredients in our thinking than we usually detect.

We can place this origin for the sense of inevitability more dramatistically by noting that fatalism can be derived from drama since the outcome of the play is known to have been decided before the play begins.

have already been shuffled, this is a purely epistemological computation. Ontologically, his full house is or is not implicit in the order of the cards.

Sometimes probability is taken as a statement about the very substance of the universe itself, which is then thought to face its own future as tentatively as a market operator faces his. Metaphysically, one may legitimately hold to this view. But I have never been able to see how it can logically be said to have been established on a physical basis by the "Heisenberg principle." One may well take it for granted that statements about the nature of the world's substance can never be established any more firmly by instruments than they can by words. At least, since instruments themselves are so fundamentally implicated in language, deriving both their formation and their interpretation from this source, one might well expect in advance that they would be as beset by ultimate dialectical embarrassments as language itself. For though they contrive to eliminate pressures that beset language on the Rhetorical and Symbolic level, they are profoundly Grammatical. And as such, they cannot be expected to get us past the paradoxes of substance.

We might glimpse the full paradox in stating the Heisenberg principle thus: A margin of *indeterminacy* is *inevitable* in measurement. That the determination of a particle's speed would interfere with the determination of its position and *vice versa* seems simply an ultimate refinement, in precision instruments, of the old paradox considered by Zeno, just as in mathematics there is, finally, the principle of discreteness pitted against the principle of continuity. And in any event, even when proclaiming that indeterminacy is inevitably intrinsic to our instruments, there is no logical necessity to conclude from this that the indeterminacy is intrinsic to nature itself. One may hold such a metaphysical view if he prefers. Or one may say that, by the rules of physics, a physicist is not allowed to assume any greater degree of stability than his partially unstable instruments themselves are able to record or verify, though we should not mistake a convention of physics for a statement about ontology. Looking at the matter from the dramatist point of view, we should expect instruments of precision not to avoid the paradox of substance, but to confront it more precisely.

It is not easy to know just when one is deriving potentialities from actualities and the reverse. Thus, in his history of medieval philosophy

Bréhier cites the scholastic proportion: existence is to essence as act is to potency. This alignment would make "essence" synonymous with "matter," if we sought to maintain a strict matter-potentiality equation.

Aristotle, in selecting pure actuality as his God term, resolutely sought to maintain the same pattern throughout, in placing actuality as prior to potentiality. Sometimes he maintained the pattern in a temporal sense, deriving the seed from the mature plant rather than the plant from the seed. Thus "one actuality always precedes another in time right back to the actuality of the eternal prime mover." (*Metaphysics,* IX, 8.) But his theory of the entelechy allowed him to introduce another kind of priority, namely the "principle" involved in a given form. A stage that *follows* another in time may be *prior* "in form and substantiality." That is, man is "prior" to boy because man has already attained its complete form whereas boy has not. Everything that comes into existence moves towards an end. This end is the principle of its existence; and it comes into existence for the sake of this end. This state of completion is its full actuality, and "it is for the sake of this that the potency is acquired." Thus, even with relation to geometry, where we might tend to say that all geometrical propositions exist "potentially" in the geometrical figures, Aristotle reverses the emphasis, stressing rather the fact that these potentialities are discovered by the geometer's activities:

> The potentially existing constructions are discovered by being brought to actuality; the reason is that the geometer's thinking is an actuality; so that the potency proceeds from an actuality; and therefore it is by making constructions that people come to know them (though the single actuality is later in generation than the corresponding potency).

In Greek this mode of thought is aided by the fact that the word for "perfect" is *teleios* (which is also defined as "final," "complete," "completed," "having the attributes of an end"). Hence, we can understand why the prime mover, as "end" of action, should be the "most perfect" being (in Latin, the *ens perfectissimum*). The Greek for "adult" is *teleios aner,* that is, "completed man"—yet the attribute is the same that Greek theologians apply to God, so that a word meaning the "finished" can come to characterize the "infinite." Since an action contains some ingredient of purpose, or end, Aristotle uses the term "entelechy" ("having its end within itself") as synonym for "actuality." Since he classes growth as one species of motion, a being that attains its full development has attained its "end" (whereat one need not decide whether the "end" here is an *aim* or a mere *limit*). As for made things, *poiema* has the same ambiguity, in referring either to a "deed, doing, action, act" or to "anything made or done, a work, piece of workmanship, poetical work, poem"—so that we can look for the "perfection" of the work in the principles of its construction, as embodied in its actual form. The *generic* factor here resides in the fact that the aim is to give the work the form proper to its kind.

Before closing this chapter, let us note how the ratios look, in the light of our discussion. We originally said that the five terms allowed for ten ratios; but we also noted that the ratios could be reversed, as either a certain kind of scene may call for its corresponding kind of agent, or a certain agent may call for its corresponding kind of scene, etc. The list of possible combinations would thereby be expanded to twenty. And the members of each pair would then be related as potential to actual. Thus, a mode of thought in keeping with the scene-agent ratio would situate in the scene certain potentialities that were said to be actualized in the agent. And conversely, the agent-scene ratio would situate in the agent potentialities actualized in the scene. And so with the other ratios.

Otherwise stated: A ratio is a formula indicating a transition from one term to another. Such a relation necessarily possesses the ambiguities of the potential, in that the second term is a medium different from the first. For the nature of the mediated necessarily differs from the nature of the immediate, as a translation must differ from its original, the embodiment of an ideal must differ from the ideal, and a god incarnate would differ from that god as pure spirit.

Psychology of Action

Terms such as "action" and "passion" are, of course, hardly more than chapter-heads, still to be given specific content. Or they are gerundives, indicating that certain blanks on a questionnaire are "to be filled out" according to certain prescribed rules. As we have seen in the case of Spinoza, for instance, "action" and "passion" are but names for bins into which one sorts various kinds of particulars, Spinoza's alignment of the "affections" differing somewhat from that to which any other philosopher would subscribe.

But just as there are relationships among individuals within a State, so there are relationships among States; and similarly, the Grammatical forms can be considered in their relations to one another, over and above the relations prevailing among the many different particulars that may be subsumed under them. A dramatist, for instance, might select any two ethical motives (say: fear and honor), and enact them in the image of particular characters under particular conditions. But the form of the enactment in its *total development* could be *summed up* as the interrelations and transformation of active and passive principles.

A character in a play will not often specifically use the dramatist Grammar. St. Thomas in Eliot's *Murder in the Cathedral* is an exception, owing to Eliot's interest in Dante and theology. Thomas specifically meditates upon human motives in terms of "action" and "passion." [11] Similarly, in *The Dry Salvages,* Eliot specifically considers the action-motion relation, when contrasting supernatural motivation with a state of affairs

[11] The design of the turning wheel that forever turns and is forever still, which Eliot takes as the image for his equating of action and passion, may recall our remarks on "inevitability." If the "dead centre" of the turning wheel were the unchanging substance of the self, then we could explain how the wheel could forever turn and be forever still, since the transformations would all partake of one underlying quality. They would possess what Emerson calls the "tyrannizing unity" of man's "constitution," the principle which man seeks in nature and attains in art. Emerson celebrates it zestfully in the same essay (on *Nature*) in which he wrote:

> Herein is especially apprehended the unity of Nature—the unity in variety—which meets us everywhere. All the endless variety of things make an identical impression. Xenophanes complained in his old age, that, looking where he would, all things hastened back to Unity. He was weary of seeing the same entity in the tedious variety of forms.

The full discussion of the subject belongs rather in the study of symbolic, but since we are trying to indicate, where the opportunity offers, how the different fields overlap, we may note here how "high orders of abstraction," when *personalized,* can become replicas of the "unchanging self," hence a delight insofar as one is pleased with oneself, and a bondage insofar as one would be reborn.

Where action were otherwise movement
Of that which is only moved
And has in it no source of movement—
Driven by daemonic, chthonic
Powers,

though the motion here does not remain the neutral kind considered by science, but becomes rather a kind of sinister passion. Usually, the Grammar is left implicit, as when Lear calls himself "more sinned against than sinning," a complex bit of grammar indeed, particularly when we consider the ingredients of passion in the concept of "sinning," that here has the active form.

The Japanese propagandists explicitly used the action-passion grammar when explaining to their people the steady American advances in the Pacific. The Japanese were told they were not to think of the Japanese forces as passively suffering attack, but as actively drawing the enemy closer, so that the eventual counterblow might be more effective. On reading this, one immediately saw the grammatical principle at the basis of German propaganda under conditions of defeat. When they were being pursued across North Africa from the East, for instance, it was explained that their armies were rapidly "advancing Westward." And their retreats in Russia were described as the use of "space as a weapon." Here, on the Rhetorical level, we find the underlying Grammar of the situation implicitly recognized in its explicit stylistic denial.

The examination of the particular way in which any particular writer of imaginative literature exemplifies the grammatical principles would require individual analysis on the Symbolic level. The purposes of this present book, however, require us rather to consider the dialectical resources of terms at a high level of abstraction, such resources as one utilizes when pitting a term like "action in general" against a term like "passion in general."

In discussing the *poiema, pathema, mathema* series, we have noted how you can draw out the grammar into a temporal succession: The action organizes the resistant factors, which call forth the passion; and the moment of transcendence arises when the sufferer (who had originally seen things in unenlightened terms) is enabled to see in more comprehensive terms, modified by his suffering.

Or action and passion may be made simultaneous equivalents, as with the theory of Christian martyrdom, wherein the act of self-sacrifice is identical with the sufferance. In *Murder in the Cathedral,* Eliot shows us this identification arising as a result of the *mathema.* Or rather, the Saint has first suffered temptation *(pathema);* he has detected and resisted this temptation *(poiema);* and the understanding *(mathema)* derived from the trial equips him for martyrdom (which is a new level of action-passion in one). Similarly, we have seen in Spinoza how *mathema* ("adequate ideas") can transform passion into action.

And we should recall here how the Gods, considered as motives, are *par excellence* instances of the dramatist grammar, since they are an active vocabulary for the naming of mental processes and "mechanisms." In proportion as men's sense of *tribal* identity is uppermost, a supernatural vocabulary of motives (either divine or Satanic) is felt adequate. Guilt is a tribal judgment; hence one is being quite "realistic" in attributing remorse to the action of Furies. For they are gods, which is to say, they are tribal motives. And they have external existence (in contrast, for instance, with an individual's sensations). But in proportion as the sense of tribal identity gives way to the sense of individual identity, this "realistic" vocabulary of motives becomes tautological. The sense of guilt is located in the individual; and in explaining it as caused by the Furies one is duplicating the motive. Both "guilt" and "pursuit by the Furies" designate the same condition.

After several centuries of individualism, this development is reversed, as psychologists idealistically begin with the "ego" and treat the tribal motives in terms of a "super-ego." The tribal element is thus reaffirmed (as likewise with Jung's concept of the "collective unconscious"), though the resultant view of psychological mechanisms has necessarily dropped the sense of the human mind as a battleground of supernatural powers. But whereas the grammar of action becomes modified, it remains with us, partly as a mere survival from earlier vocabularies, partly as evidence of man's essential dramatism.

The concept of the "ruling passion" is an instance of a dramatist motivation not directly theological though it was strongly ethical, and showed many vestiges of the Christian pattern. It is at bottom almost an oxymoron, or at least a conceit, as were we to speak of someone's "dominant subjection," or his "sovereign bondage," or his "most commanding weakness."

In *One Mighty Torrent, the Drama of Biography,* Edgar Johnson reviews and discusses this "fascinating theory of the 'ruling passion' " in seventeenth-century biography, a theory that he derives particularly from Tacitus and Theophrastus. Such biographies, he says, were constructed

> upon a deductive scheme of what was consistent for such and such a type to be like, rather than upon detailed observation of what a man was in fact like. Each person, so ran the theory, had one ruling passion, with all the others grouped like vassals round and swaying to its imperious motions.

In *Every Man out of his Humour,* Ben Jonson had already given the term "humour" a similar application. First he observes that the word was originally scenic, referring to a liquid. Next, that there are liquids in the body ("choler, melancholy, phlegm and blood") which are called humours. Here too the usage would fall within our concept of the scenic. Next he explains that the word is metaphorically extended to designate states of mind corresponding to the disposition of the four liquids in the body:

> It may, by metaphor, apply itself
> Unto the general disposition;
> As when some one peculiar quality
> Doth so possess a man that it doth draw
> All his effects, his spirits and his powers,
> In their confluxion all to run one way,—
> This may be truly said to be a humour.

One might choose to see in the passage an adumbration of behaviorism, though only if, at the same time, one recognizes that Jonson's interests are in the opposite direction. He would translate the concept from a materialistic to a dramatist significance. For Jonson's notion of the humour involves a particular kind of dramatic form. The prologue to *Every Man in his Humour* said that comedy deals "with human follies, not with crimes." The dedication of *Volpone* says that "the office of a comic poet" is "to imitate justice." And Jonson carries out the pattern by showing human passions (in this case, "human follies") as inner motives leading to outer actions that in turn lead to the suffering of punishment, a form of plot that Volpone sums up by saying:

> What a rare punishment
> Is avarice to itself!

We have already considered Hegel's variant, in his *Philosophy of History,* where Absolute Spirit is said to *act* by using the blind *passions* of individual men as its medium (a "world-historical individual" thus being one who, in consciously following the lead of merely personal interests and ambitions, unconsciously furthers the designs of the Universal Dialectic).

Much of the action-passion grammar is to be spotted, in liberal writings, beneath references to "freedom" and its opposite. When Aristotle speaks of metaphysics as a liberal art, he conceives of its liberality in contrast with the usefulness or serviceableness of a slave. "As the man is free, we say, who exists for his own sake and not for another's, so we pursue this as the only free science, for it alone exists for its own sake." (I, 2.)   And in Book III, Chapter 2, he celebrates it as the "most architectonic and authoritative" science, so authoritative that "the other sciences, like slave-women, may not even contradict it."

"Freedom," as a dialectical term, may be conceived in opposition to *slavery.* Or it may be conceived rather in opposition to *authority.* There is an important psychological distinction between them.   Aristotle, in here speaking of freedom, speaks in the role of one who considers himself in the class of free men, in contrast with the class of slaves.   He does not conceive of freedom in dialectical opposition to authority; his attitude rather is that of a participant in the authoritative structure.   His trade was that of the intellect, in which resided the powers of human action and virtue (through control over the enslaving passions).   Aristotle's freedom was not that of protest.   It was not negativistic or revolutionary.

But modern freedom, as the slogan of an upstart middle class, was polemic, propagandistic, a doctrine of partial slaves in partial revolt, as with its stress upon service and utility.   In proportion as the social values of this rising class became the norm, the original upstart aspect of modern libertarianism was transferred to socialism and anarchism. The propagandistic ingredient in works like *Pilgrim's Progress* and *Robinson Crusoe* (and in general, the novel of middle class *sentiment*) could be dropped. For the development of business had so circumscribed the concepts of practical or moral utility within monetary limits, that the original religious and moralistic vocabulary of bourgeois apologetics became more and more like a sheer Rhetorical evasion of the Grammatical realities. Art now became "useless," a "free play of the imagination," as per the Bourgeois-Bohemian dichotomy. Except among social reformers and revolutionaries, propaganda art was *categorically* decried, for the liberal critic usually insisted that he was against not just "Leftist" propaganda, but *all* propaganda. He was able to hold this position until the recent war against Fascism, when one by one the "pure" artists came forth with some kind of work in which an anti-Nazi or anti-Fascist position was consciously embedded in the very form and style. For it had become too undeniably obvious that political actions and passions are a major aspect of "reality" as now constituted. Where motives are vigorously actual, there are the themes of art.

One can readily become so involved in such controversies on their own terms, that one neglects to place them in terms of their underlying grammatical principles. What is needed is not that we place ourselves "above" the controversies. Rather, we should place ourselves *within* them, by an understanding of their essential grammar. And this result can be attained, according to the present theory, by seeking for vestiges of the dramatistic in modern liberal terminologies that do not directly abide by this Grammar, *concealed beneath synonyms*. Originally, as we saw in Spinoza, the synonyms were explicit. Later, the Grammatical side of the equations is dropped or slighted—and we may thereupon be led to think that modern theories of motives are operating on principles different from those of the earlier Grammar, whereas they are merely different ways of exploiting the same dialectical resources. But for purposes of classification, one must have categories that include all kinds of motivational doctrines. And if such ways of classification are to be substantial, they must name generative principles which the various species have in common. For this reason we would cling as long as possible to the traces of the action-passion alignment; and at the point where we must relinquish it, we would deal with the shift in terms of the action-motion disproportion.

Thus, when considering the vocabulary of that essentially liberal psychology, psychoanalysis, we would look for the common underlying Grammar by classing "frustration," "fixation," "complex," and the like as species of passion; and "adjustment," or "normality" as equivalents of action. "Sublimation" would equal transcendence, and "repression" or "inhibition" would represent a new dialectic of "reason" as the *hegemonikon,* stated in quizzical terms whereas formerly it was stated in terms unambiguously favorable. We do not thereby ask that modern psychology abandon its terms for terms more apparently "Grammatical." Rather, we should ourselves apply such exegesis. For only in this way can we see the true significance of whatever changes may have been introduced into the newer terminologies of motives. It is by such forms designed for bringing out continuities in psychological terminology that we can best locate the *discontinuities,* and thereby be able to know just how religions and secular, ancient and modern, psychologies do square with one another.

As regards normal psychology, McDougall's stress upon the "sentiments" would seem, from this point of view, to require broad placement as another study of "incipient action." For this reason it merits more attention, at least *in principle,* than it now usually gets (having been displaced by psychologies more exclusively scientist in their concerns, as with experiments in perception and learning).

On the other hand, most modern works have departed far from a direct relation to the dramatist grammar. One can see "action" readily enough behind a word like "freedom"; it is more attenuated when we come to "adjustment" (in fact, as we have observed, this term can signify passivity, or sheer motion); we can discern the lineaments of potentiality, or incipient action, in attitudes, images, and sentiments. But often one does best to begin one's analysis the other way round, simply looking for the key terms in a work, inquiring how they are related to one another, and waiting for the dramatist forms to force themselves upon the attention, letting the matter lie in abeyance while one charts the given terms just as they are, on their face. Summarization, characterization, and placement is the general aim. The "tendency" is to summarize, characterize, and place in dramatist terms. But the search for such underlying forms must not lead to a neglect of terminological tactics peculiar to the given work. A particular poem, for instance, might be organized about a single image, variously ramified, as theme with variations. It would be enough to discern these developments in themselves, without regard for the possible significance of the image as "incipient action" or "incipient passion." And only when examining the images of the writer's work in its entirety might we come to see the full significance of this image as a symbolic act. (The subject has been considered at some length in our *Philosophy of Literary Form*. We also intend to consider many other aspects of it in our volume on the Symbolic of Motives.)

Considered solely in terms of political power, an "act" would be possible only to a ruler, or to a ruling class. Or, as applied by analogy to the psychology of the individual, an act would be possible only to the part of the soul that enjoyed a corresponding status of authority. At least, that seems to be the ratio at the basis of that *hegemonikon* which the Stoics located in the reason, thus linking the idea of private rule with the idea of public rule by equating reason with authority. Recalling what we have previously said about the nature of modern liberalism, we can grasp the significance of the Stoic's reason-authority equation by comparing it with the partial shattering of that equation in Rousseau.

Rousseau proposed to ground Emile's education in a respect for the "necessity in things" rather than deference to the "caprices" and "authority" of other men. Dependence on things, he said, is the "work of nature." But dependence on men is the "work of society." Dependence on things, "being non-moral, does no injury to liberty." But dependence on men "gives rise to every kind of vice," as "master and slave corrupt each other." It is obvious now how Rousseau's partial dissociating of reason and authority pointed towards the French Revolution. And looking further back, in the light of Rousseau's naturalism, and still on the Rhetorical level, can we not discern the anti-authoritarian implications in Spinoza's naturalism? It was not merely a position to be considered in itself. It was a *counter*-position (as Spinoza, of course, himself made explicit in his political views disagreeing with Hobbes).[12]

---

[12] In studying the nature of linguistic action, one must always be on guard for evidence of Rhetorical action embedded in Grammar. A pure scenic approach

As the reason acts, and the body moves, so authorities could act by adopting policies to be carried out by others (who moved as slaves, servants, or assistants). Thus, eventually a "ruling class" (in accordance with the properties of its status) could become transformed from a class that "does" to a class that "does not." It is the development we considered earlier with relation to the actus-status pair. Acts require properties of status; and the "substantiality" of such properties can be inherited independently of the act which was originally their generating principle.

We have already seen how Stoicism led into the Christian paradox, the "revolutionary" transvaluation whereby suffering (the passive) could be treated as an *act* (accounts of martyrdom, for instance, being termed either "passionals" or "acts"). We find this change emerging in Stoicism, with its emphasis upon the moral value of sufferance, and its great humanitarian sympathy with slavery—indeed, its tendency to dwell upon the ways in which all men are slaves and servants (to their appetites, emotions, errors, or to natural or political necessities). Christianity offered a doctrine whereby the subjects were persons, and in their passion were capable not merely of motion, but of action. It permitted one in a way to "will" his subjection—and in so doing it gave him a "substantial" freedom, a "pure" freedom. By the ambiguity of substance, or the paradox of purity, it could call a man free precisely because he was enslaved. And in calling him "substantially" free, in effect it invited him to make himself so in actuality (inviting him to translate his "essential" freedom into its "existential" counterpart, or to proceed from the "form" of freedom to its "materialization"). And by *universalizing* the concept of servitude (so that all

---

errs in stressing this relation at the expense of formal analysis. But one must watch lest the scenic excess lead to the opposite excess, that would eliminate extrinsic reference entirely. Let's remember that, in the long conversation of history, few statements are made simply "in themselves." They are *answers* to other statements. And this function is a part of their intrinsic form. Recently, reading the autobiography of St. Teresa, I was struck by her account of her efforts to establish a complete distrust of herself. Recalling pious exhortations to "put one's faith in God," I suddenly realized that this had been a *dialectical* injunction, as opposition to those who put their faith in *any* human being. In other words, the injunction had not originally meant simply that one should rely upon God; it implied also whom one should *not* rely on. Of a sudden, then, I saw Rousseau's statement in a line of transformations, having St. Teresa's position at one end, and Emerson's cult of "self-reliance" at the other.

men "served," all men "obeyed," all were "patient," as Christians doing the work of the Lord), it could also include the realistic, Aristotelian concept of the free person. For if *all* men are slaves, or better, *servants,* it would be as true to say that *no* men are slaves, "substantially." Hence all would merit a respect for themselves as persons; and it would be wrong to treat men merely as objects of use. Men's servitude to God, law, and other men would be dependent upon a *voluntary* submission to their divinely appointed status. Such a way would make of submission an act and not a mere sufferance. Or better, it made submission an act because sufferance itself was considered an act.

In proportion as the servitude took the form of private enterprise, it endowed the "servants" with material powers. The "passivity" thus did, in the most obvious sense, become active, since ambitions netted results. The "freedom" of universal Christian "servitude," thus in time became transformed into a condition of action, even revolutionary action, particularly since the ideals of *private* wealth could be Rhetorically stated as the ideal of a Christlike *poor* Church.

All told we have, as motivational patterns which psychologies more or less patently realistic might exemplify: the action-passion and actus-status pairs, the action-motion ambiguity, and the potential. These can be variously *individuated* in specific terminologies (as with different schools of psychology, religious or secular, or in the one-time motivational structures of particular biographies, histories, reports, poems, plays, and narrative fictions). Obviously the Grammatical principles here considered can merely suggest the broad categories by reference to which any particular vocabulary of motives would be classed. Such realistic reclamation would enable us to class "ethical" and "scientifically neutral" psychologies together with terms that can be applied to all such terminologies of motives. In brief, all psychologies can, without violence to their subject matter, be approached dramatistically, as vocabularies concerned with the kinds and conditions of action and passion.

Even the most extreme behaviorism would belong here. We refer not only to its dramatistic placement in terms of a narrowed circumference that reduces action to motion. We refer also to the behaviorist concept of "transference." According to this concept, the conditioned response to an object or situation of a certain quality may be transferred to other objects or situations felt to be of the same quality. But this process involves the interpretation and *classification* of signs; and when this is capable of modification by purely linguistic means, as with human beings, it opens up a field of investigation that takes one far beyond the "conditioned reflex" in its simplicity. But though it involves kinds of transcendence and symbolic action that could not be treated in such terms, the need of richer terms can be shown to exist simply by a strict analysis of the elements subsumed under the concept of "transference" itself. For it introduces problems of classification and reclassification that could readily lead to the equating of "adequate" classifications with "action" and the equating of "inadequate" classifications with "passion" (though the two be concealed beneath terms like "adjustment" and "maladjustment").

But one other Grammatical resource of action need be considered briefly, and we can turn to our remaining terms, Purpose and Agency.

In Book I, Chapters 6 and 7 of his *Physics*, we find Aristotle trying to decide "whether the basic principles of nature are two or three or some greater number." As we read on, we see that the matter is purely dialectical, involving the question whether we should reduce nature to a pair of opposites, related as hot and cold, increase and decrease, active and passive, or should postulate a "third something underlying them." He does not make a final choice, being content to observe that, from one point of view, a third term is needed, to serve as the mediating ground of the opposites. But from another point of view, only two are needed, since we can account for change by considering one of the opposites as present or absent; and in this case we should need only it and the underlying principle. As for the underlying substratum itself, we can understand it by analogy:

> It is to any particular and existent substance what bronze is to a completed statue, wood to a bed, and still unformed materials to the objects fashioned from them.

In brief, it is the principle of potentiality which we have already considered.

Looking at this issue from the standpoint of the Grammatical voices, we see Aristotle here asking whether the *active* and *passive* are enough, or whether we may also require a *middle* voice in our Grammar of motives. As a matter of fact, in the Indo-European family of languages, the passive voice is a late development. Originally there were but the active and middle (or reflexive) forms, and the passive developed out of the middle. (In Greek, the conjugations of middle and passive are alike in many tenses.) Prior to its development, passive ideas were expressed actively, but reflexively, in treating the action as directed by the self upon the self. Passive forms probably indicate a high degree of development from actus to status, with a corresponding increase in the sense of mental states.

Once such a development has taken place, however, as it did with the complex vocabulary of sensibility and scruples accumulated by Christianity, the scene is set for "post-passive" kinds of active and reflexive. Writers like Caldwell and Hemingway, for instance, can be sparse in their recital, contenting themselves largely with purely behavioristic narrative, precisely because readers can be relied upon to supply the scruples of themselves. The apparent harshness is thus but a sophisticated variant of sensitivity, perhaps even sentimentality, for the expression of emotions is sentimental in proportion as it is inexact.

But the reflexive, as a mediate relationship, moves us rather in the direction of means; accordingly, it will be considered again when we look at the term, Agency. We have now considered the big three, scene, agent, and act. We shall now consider the remaining two, Agency and Purpose, that draw together in the means-ends relationship. And following that, we shall consider our category of categories, dialectic.

IV

AGENCY AND PURPOSE

The Philosophy of Means

UNDER Pragmatism, in the Baldwin dictionary, we read: "This term is applied by Kant to the species of hypothetical imperative . . . which prescribes the means necessary to the attainment of happiness." In accordance with our thesis, we here seize upon the reference to *means,* since we hold that Pragmatist philosophies are generated by the featuring of the term, Agency. We can discern this genius most readily in the very title, *Instrumentalism,* which John Dewey chooses to characterize his variant of the pragmatist doctrine. Similarly William James explicitly asserts that Pragmatism is "a method only." And adapting Peirce's notion that beliefs are rules for action, he says that "theories thus become instruments," thereby stressing the practical nature of theory, whereas Aristotle had come close to putting theory and practice in dialectical opposition to each other. James classed his pragmatism with nominalism in its appeal to particulars, with utilitarianism in its emphasis upon the practical, and with positivism in its "disdain for verbal solutions, useless questions and metaphysical abstractions."

In one sense, there must be as many "pragmatisms" as there are philosophies. That is, each philosophy announces some view of human ends, and will require a corresponding doctrine of means. In this sense, we might ask wherein "Stoic pragmatism" would differ from "Epicurean," "Platonist," or "Kantian" pragmatisms, etc. But modern science is *par excellence* an accumulation of new agencies (means, instruments, methods). And this locus of new power, in striking men's fancy, has called forth "philosophies of science" that would raise agency to first place among our five terms.

William James, in his book on *Pragmatism,* quotes Papini, who likens the pragmatist stress to the corridor in a hotel. Each room of the hotel may house a guest whose personal interests and philosophic views differ from those of the guests in the other rooms. But all guests use the corridor in common. Pragmatism would thus be a principle of mediation that all philosophies have in common, quite as the instructions for operating a machine are the same for liberal, Fascist, or Communist.

There is a sense, of course, in which this is not so. Two men, performing the same *motions* side by side, might be said to be performing different *acts*, in proportion as they differed in their attitudes toward their work. We might realistically call it one kind of act to run an elevator under a system of private ownership, and another kind of act to run that same elevator, by exactly the same routines, under a system of communal ownership.

Aristotle's concern with logic as the instrument (*organon*) of human reason is "incipiently" pragmatist. But we have already noted that his representative position in a slave culture led to a slighting of agency as we think of it, after the intervening centuries of Christian servitude, business service, and the utility of applied science. We saw how agency failed to attain full rank as a locus of motivation in Aristotle's list of causes (material, efficient, formal, and final). In fact, from the standpoint of the pentad, we might well situate the source of the "non-Aristotelian" element in modern science in the fact that it makes uppermost the very domain of motivation that Aristotle subordinated.

In Aristotle's classification of cause, either a first mover (person, agent) or a last mover (implement, tool, agency) can be classed as an efficient cause. And means are considered in terms of ends. But once you play down the concept of final cause (as modern science does), the distinction between agent and agency becomes sharp. Also, there is a reversal of causal ancestry—and whereas means were treated in terms of ends, ends become treated in terms of means. John Dewey, for instance, lays great stress upon the fact that the formulation of an end may serve as a means of adjustment. And our entire curriculum of vocational training is an instance of agency as ancestor. Thus, because there are cars, some men learn to become automobile mechanics, their conception of a life purpose ·deriving from the nature of the instrument which they would service. Money, as we have pointed out previously, here figures as the medium that can supply a kind of "absolute purpose" over and above the motives peculiar to each class of instrument.

According to James, the pragmatist evaluates a doctrine by its "consequences," by what it is "good for," by "the difference it will make to you and me," or by its "function," or by asking whether it "works satisfactorily." Having extended Peirce's secular doctrines to include religious utility, he even asks what "menial services" men can require of God. Also, with a disastrous felicity that his opponents were quick to seize upon, he said that the pragmatist looks for the "cash value" of an idea. And if we allow that James was here borrowing a trope from the language of pure capitalism, we see how faithfully the figure retains the stress upon agency, in using a mode of thought according to which a thing's value is tested by its economic usefulness, as tested in turn by its marketability (that is, its function as a means in satisfying desires).

Now that modern pragmatism has flourished long enough to show a curve of development, we can see the incipient pragmatism in Emerson's idealism. His early book, *Nature*, is particularly relevant in this respect, since he is inquiring into the "uses" of Nature. The whole matter is approached much as with the "moral pragmatism" we previously noted in Stoicism:

> Whoever considers the final cause of the world will discern a multitude of uses that enter as parts into that result. They all admit of being thrown into one of the following classes: Commodity, Beauty, Language, and Discipline.

Here, obviously, agency has not yet become the ancestral term, but is seen in terms of universal purpose. Emerson does not even mean by "commodity" quite what the word has come to mean in business English. Here he ranks "all those advantages which our senses owe to nature." He notes how the things of nature "serve" in nature's "ministry to man," and how by the useful arts men serve one another. Later, in the *Over-Soul*, he was to represent the Protestant idealization of the secular by affirming that the world of everyday experience "is one wide judicial investigation of character." Throughout his work, he struggles to see high moral principles behind men's economic acts. And he places modern inventions in this pattern of an idealized utility:

> The poor man hath cities, ships, canals, bridges, built for him. He goes to the post-office, and the human race run on his errands; to the

book-shop, and the human race read and write of all that happens
for him; to the court-house, and nations repair his wrongs. He sets
his house upon the road, and the human race go forth every morning, and shovel out the snow, and cut a path for him.

And characteristically, he ends his brief discussion of "commodities"
with the "general remark, that this mercenary benefit is one which
has respect to a farther good. A man is fed, not that he may eat,
but that he may work."

In the love of Beauty, "a nobler want of man is served." Emerson
discusses language as "a third use which Nature subserves to man."
And by the Discipline of Nature he considers the ways in which we
can derive moral improvement from our dealings with the "sensible
objects" of Nature, by "perceiving the analogy that marries Matter and
Mind." Property too, with its "filial systems of debt and credit," performs this moralizing service: "Debt, grinding debt, whose iron face
the widow, the orphan, and the sons of genius fear and hate—debt,
which consumes so much time, which so cripples and disheartens a
great spirit with cares that seem so base, is a preceptor whose lessons
cannot be foregone, and is needed most by those who suffer from it
most." Nature disciplines the will, for "Nature is thoroughly mediate.
It is made to serve." In accordance with this idealizing of agency, we
are told that the ethical character

> so penetrates the bone and marrow of nature, as to seem the end for
> which it was made. Whatever private purpose is answered by an
> member or part, this is its public and universal function, and is never
> omitted. Nothing in nature is exhausted in its first use. When a
> thing has served an end to the uttermost, it is wholly new for an
> ulterior service. In God, every end is converted into a new means.
> Thus, the use of commodity, regarded by itself, is mean and squalid.
> But it is to the mind an education in the doctrine of Use, namely,
> that a thing is good only so far as it serves.

Whether nature has a real existence, or is but a form of thought, he
says, "It is alike useful and alike venerable to me." And imagination
he defines as "the use which the Reason makes of the material world."

We have cited enough to show that in Emerson secular agency is a
function of divine purpose. Obviously, only if we narrow the circumference, by dropping the concept of final cause, could we get to

the true pragmatist stress upon agency as the ancestral term. If we re-place Emerson's transcendentalism and James's personalism with Dewey's and Mead's biologism (as in *Experience and Nature* and *Philosophy of the Act*) we find a transitional device that can help us to get farther along in the course from purpose to agency pure and simple. This is in the concept of biologic functioning. That is, the bodily organs are means toward ends; each, insofar as it is functioning properly, carries out the kind of "purpose" for which it is designed; and it serves a use in furthering the survival of the organism. At this level, agencies can be considered without reference to final causes in the theological or personalistic senses; yet in such a view there is no strict *opposition* to purpose. Insofar as the instrumentations of biolog-ical adjustment are stressed, we have the pragmatist stress upon agency, while allowing for such a level of "action" as we noted in San-tayana's concept of "animal faith."

By this interpretation, pragmatism pure and simple would not be reached until we come to P. W. Bridgman's "operationalism," as de-scribed in his *Logic of Modern Physics*. For here we come to a com-plete treatment of meaning in terms of laboratory instruments. What-ever may have been the purposes of a man who designs such agencies, they themselves are totally without purpose, even in the ambiguously biological sense of the term. We would hardly say that the mercury in the thermometer rises on hot days "in order to" assist the thermom-eter in the struggle for life, or "in order to" avoid certain discom-fitures that it might experience if it did not decide to rise, or even "in order to record the temperature." We treat it purely and simply as an instrument, or agency, that has no intrinsic interest in recording the temperature.

Bridgman has written many studies on the compressibility of gases to high pressure, pressure coefficients of resistance, compressibility of metals as a function of pressure and temperature, the effect of pres-sure on the rigidity of metals, the effect of pressure on the thermal conductivity of metals, the effect of pressure on viscosity of various liquids, the effect of tension on the electrical resistance of certain ab-normal metals—and so on. Obviously, such investigations required a vast battery of meters, gauges, rules, tubes, and sundry other items of laboratory equipment, with strict observance of the procedures or operations involved in their use. Here is *par excellence* a realm of *agencies*. And as philosophers old style would usually pay a tribute to their calling by conceiving of God in ways that, whatever they might tell us about the character of God, told us a lot about the character of the philosophy, so Bridgman pays a tribute to his calling by conceiving of meaning in the strict sense suggested to him by his intensive concern with these agencies. His concern is with the meaning of means.

There are clear adumbrations of this strict position even in James. But Bridgman exemplifies it to perfection, in making a concept synonymous with the corresponding set of operations. A concept of temperature would thus be equated with the actual operations by which one recorded temperature. And strictly speaking, he says, one would have as many concepts as one had sets of operations. (That is, two ways of recording the same temperature would be two concepts.)

The dramatist may tell us that the world's a stage; the sailor might tell us that we're all afloat; a philosopher, having long thought about thinking, might tell us that God is "thought of thought." And so this savant has done well by his instruments, in telling us that concepts are nonsense except insofar as we can define them in instrumental terms. By contrast, we see the strong dramatist ingredient in Mead's concept of the "other" whose attitudes we dialectically include in the internal dialogue of thought and judgment. And the contrast also indicates how thoroughly the stress upon agency fails to notice the demands of the remaining motivational domains. When Bridgman says, for instance, that two different operations for recording the same condition would "in principle" be two different concepts, he expresses himself by the use of a term ("principle") that is possible only to substantialist thought. And were he to ask himself wherein the similarities of operations end and their differences begin, he would find himself involved in all sorts of purely formal problems for the solution of which there can be no such instruments as exist in his laboratories. Indeed, he might even see the instruments themselves as merely one aspect of dialectic, one voice among the several voices whose competitive coöperation is necessary for the development of mature meanings. And when he writes that the world of laboratory experimentation "is not understandable without some examination of the purpose of physics," we must recognize that he is writing about his *purpose in eliminating the concept of purpose*, a state of linguistic affairs which calls for a kind of analysis not possible to his method. Yet it obviously requires consideration, if we are to take his own book seriously; for it represents the *underlying Grammar* of his argument.

Though our laboratory instruments may transcend human purpose, they exist only as the result of human purpose. And we might even say that they can perform satisfactorily without purpose only because they have purpose imbedded in their structure and design. An instrument like a thermometer has its purpose so thoroughly built into its very nature, that it can do its work without purpose, merely by continuing to be itself.

The Range of Pragmatism

Conditions

In philosophers like Aquinas, the concept of "conditions" is highly formal in nature. Kant's "transcendentalism" was the first step towards a more purely historical concept of conditions. For though Kant's conditions were highly generalized, they were distinguished from those of formal logic in being exclusively the conditions of *experience*. (And the condition of conditions, you will recall, was the *unconditioned* realm lying beyond the reach of experience.) Fichte brought us a step nearer to a more particularized notion of conditions in treating the Ego as spiritual source, and the Non-Ego as its material incarnation. This amounts to its translation into a structure of natural conditions.

The movement towards particularization was carried a step further in Hegel, as he traces the particulars of history, but sees them following internal principles of development. It is quite to our purposes that Hegel called the utterance (*Äusserung*) of this internal principle a *mediation* (*Vermittlung*): the expression of itself in a *medium* (a mode of thought which suggests from another angle why idealism is a precursor of pragmatism).

Marx reversed Hegel by treating material, or economic conditions, as formative of spirit (as against the Hegelian genealogy that begins with spirit as source and ground). We have here gone from "God" to "matter" as the condition of consciousness. And the Hegelian pattern of transcendence could be applied by Marxists to account for the development of "higher" forms from "lower" in accordance with the notion that changes in quantity call forth corresponding changes in quality, as at those critical points where a rise in the temperature of water changes it from solid to liquid, and from liquid to gas. But there was a pronounced sense of form pervading Marx's view of history. It was not "pragmatist."

The "Facts"

Essentially pragmatist history enters, I think, with the concept of the "documentary" as the historiographer's ideal. For the documentary facts are the medium with which the historian works; and insofar as he tries to write "pure document," he is placing the major stress upon the medium itself. In this sense such historiography would be a featuring of agency. Avoiding problems of causal ancestry, it would simply record whatever historical events are known to have occurred together.

Lying about the edges of this ideal, there are of course the demands of our other terms. For the historian must in some way seek to characterize, summarize, and place the period with which he is concerned. And in his presentation of an historical era, he is guided by more or less clearly formed notions of its essence (as a character in itself, or as a character in contrast with the character of other times, or as a stage in some historical development). But insofar as he professes to carry out his program, such wider claims of definition must make themselves felt surreptitiously. He must give us essences while disclaiming any such purpose.

Two Principles of Truth in James

Looking again at James from the standpoint of what we have been saying about the concept of "conditions," we find in him a conflict of dramatist and positivist ideals, as revealed in the notion of truth. Kant, while granting that theological meanings could not be proved, had tried to save them negatively by showing that they could not be disproved. Thorough-going positivism, with which James has expressed affinities, would equate meaning with verifiability, hence asserting that a statement capable of neither proof nor disproof is "meaningless."

At the bottom of James's pragmatism seems to lie the Grammatical fact that human acts are not "verifiable" in the way that purely scenic statements are. The "proof" of a human act is in the *doing*. God's acts, however, are different. Insofar as God's acts are the Creation, his actions can be equated with natural events. Hence, as *acts* they are out-and-out *scenic*. And if we say that the island of Manhattan is on the West Coast, we can test the statement by trying to act on the basis of it.

But when you narrow the circumference to humanistic scope, you get two kinds of situation. What A does "from within" as an act, B sees "from without" as an event (that is, a scene). The distinction however is complicated by the fact that A can dialectically consider his own act in terms of B, thus to some extent looking upon it from without; and B can to some extent respond to A's behavior from within, so that it is not felt merely scenically, as a set of signs, but is vicariously *participated in* (or "incipiently imitated") as an *act*.

James's pragmatism, with its stress upon the act of belief, stands midway between the ethical or dramatist sense of act and the positivistist-scientist reduction of the act to terms of sheer events (a behavioristically observed scene). And this midway position is fittingly manifested in terms of *agency*, the function that is essentially *mediatory*. And this concept of agency contains within itself the ambiguity of the two verifications: (1) The verification of an act by an act, as believing is the test of belief: (2) the verification of an act-less *scenic* statement by an act framed in accordance with the scenic statement, as one can test a map by following it in the charting of one's course.

Symbolic of Agency

Instruments are "essentially" human, since they are the products of human design. And in this respect, the pragmatist featuring of agency seems well equipped to retain a personal ingredient in its circumference of motives. But as regards the functioning of Agency on the Symbolic level, we are advised to be on the look-out for a personal principle of another order, stemming from the fact that the human being, in the stage of infancy, formatively experiences a realm of personal utility in the person of the mother. The combination of planning and usefulness that characterizes maternal care apparently suggests the view of "Mother Nature" that we considered in the Hellenistic philosophies and in the incipient pragmatism of Emerson. One might well look for similar motives in James, owing to the devotional ingredient in his brand of pragmatism, for the reference to the "menial services" of our Protector would apply more aptly to maternal attentions than to God.

As we move into more professedly secular varieties of pragmatism, such motivations become more tenuous and dubious. Bridgman, it is true, speaks of the scientist's devotion to his "facts" as something "religious." But though the expression offers grounds for a "hunch," it proves nothing in itself. Perhaps we should have to know what figures or images fleetingly suggest themselves to him when he is at work in his laboratory, or what quality runs through the haphazard reference to his experiments in his conversation, before we could claim that there are "parental" motivations of one kind or another in his morality of science. Yet it is possible that an examination of his writings, undertaken on the purely Symbolic level, might in itself be enough to reveal some such structure.

As regards the Grammatical relation between Agency and Purpose: when translated into sexual terms, it presents an opportunity, on the Symbolic level, for involvement in the relation between the maternal woman and the erotic woman. In coming to sexual maturity, and preparing psychologically to seek a mate, the male during the period of courtship turns from the maternal woman (the principle of utility) to the erotic woman (the principle of purpose, in the form of the *desired*). Insofar as the feminine principle retains maternal aspects, courtship involves symbolic incest; hence, the principle of erotic purpose must "transcend" the principle of maternal utility. A dissociation in the attitude towards woman becomes necessary.

All sorts of possibilities suggest themselves here, particularly when one adds other factors, as when the "pure" poetry of the Art for Art's Sake sort is equated with the sexual, leading to a cult of purely "decorative" women. Obviously, the maternal-erotic dilemma is not solved normally until the woman as wife becomes "useful" on a new level, not directly to the husband (who, by his purpose as wage-earner, has himself become useful, though impersonally), but in her ministering personally to their joint product, the family.

The systematic consideration of such possibilities belongs rather in the Symbolic of Motives. Suffice it here to note that such speculations indicate Symbolic motives behind the thinking of that crabbed old bachelor, Jeremy Bentham, who propounded the philosophy of Utilitarianism, and who visited upon himself a kind of Symbolic castration in his plans for a "neutral" scientific vocabulary for avoiding the "censorious" terms of rhetoric and poetry. His utilitarian theory of language reduces purpose to agency by seeking for the *interests* that correspond to *ideals* (another word for the purposive). And despite his programmatic dislike and distrust of metaphor, in his *Table of the Springs of Action* he calls such idealizing words "eulogistic coverings" or "fig-leaves." All told, his intellectual situation, as with other great Bachelors of Capitalist Liberalism, would seem to be that of one who, arriving at that stage of maturity where the dissociation between the maternal woman and the erotic woman must be confronted, developed a philosophy of utility that could deflect erotic purpose into terms (themselves transformed) of maternal agency. The principle of the erotic could be capitalistically translated, as a rationale of utilitarian enterprise.

And we might well recall that Rousseau begins Emile's education with stress upon the test of usefulness, which he equates with the state of nature prior to society (a perfect parallel to the state of childhood prior to rational awareness of abstract social factors beyond the orbit of the personal). If such usefulness were a "mother principle," we could understand why he himself fell in love with maternal women, even explicitly recognizing this motive in his affair with Madame de Warens, as noted by Matthew Josephson in his *Jean-Jacques Rousseau*, p. 74:

> He found himself for the first time in the arms of a woman, a woman whom he adored. An overwhelming sadness and faintness poisoned the charm of the moment. "Twice, or thrice, as I pressed her passionately to me, I flooded her breast with my tears. *It was as if I were committing incest.*"

Behind the pure Grammar of his educational principle, then, we could discern the pattern of his romances, built about the cataclysmic step from the state of innocence to the state of erotic awakening (when the taboos directed towards the woman as mother become transformed into purpose directed toward the "new" woman).

Stendhal's hero begins similarly with attachment to maternal women, who remain mothers even in their adulterous relations with the hero. In pure capitalism, the transformation from woman-as-agency to woman-as-purpose is effected through the medium of *money* as pur-

pose (money being one kind of "potency"). But the "fires" of Brû-
lard could not thus transcendently burn, owing to the esthetic distrust
of the money motive in the era of *Napoléon le petit* when *enrichissez-
vous* was the slogan for the non-esthetic bourgeois.

In pure poetry, perhaps the most magnificent instance of a merging of
the maternal and erotic principles (sexual equivalents of agency and
purpose) is in Baudelaire's sonnet *La Géante*. Here the disproportion
in size between mother and child is idealized as a relation between
queen and cat, giantess and poet, mountain and hamlet. The conceit
is "evil" because the ratio is maintained in amatory imagery suggesting the attitude of a lover towards his mistress.

On the Symbolic level, there is also the more obvious correspondence,
as revealed in the folk puns that refer to the sex organs themselves as
instruments, such as tools and weapons. These puns provide bridges
that can variously link love, war, and work, thereby greatly complicating the relations between filial and parental principles.

Purposive Agencies of Applied Science

But though Rhetorical and Symbolic factors can surreptitiously re-
enforce the appeal of Agency, its prestige derives first from the Grammatical fact that it covers the area of applied science, the area of new
power. This relation alone is enough to account for its featuring.
And since the requirements of such science favor the elimination of
Purpose, or final cause, the means-ends relation provokes a shift to
the term nearest of kin, which can supply the *functions* of purpose
even when the term is formally omitted as a locus of motives. Since
agents act through the medium of motion, the reduction of action to
motion can be treated as reduction to Agency, Pragmatism having the
advantage over Materialism that *tools* are more "purposive" than *impersonal backgrounds* are, so that the Pragmatist emphasis can more
conveniently straddle the action-motion ambiguity.

And of course, the close connection between technological diversification and the monetary motive reminds us that the medium of money
also contributes to Pragmatist thinking, quite as James's reference to
the "cash-value" of ideas suggested. The ambiguities of personal
action and impersonal motion are here too, as with that typical capitalist agency, the stock-market, where the speculative *acts* of the individual trades add up statistically to a *movement* of prices. Such statis-

tical results would themselves be analyzable in terms of *adjustment* rather than *purpose*. Yet this impersonal effect of personal acts in the aggregate, is readily felt not nominalistically, but as the action of a corporate entity. In the financial columns, for instance, we read of a broker who, commenting on the market of that day, said: "It very frankly acts as if it wanted to have an old-fashioned reaction but is afraid to carry it out."

Once Agency has been brought to the fore, the other terms readily accommodate themselves to its rule. Scenic materials become means which the organism employs in the process of growth and adaptation. The organism itself is a confluence of means, each part being at the service of the other parts. Reason becomes a means of adjustment. Empiricism can conform to the genius of Agency, in that the senses play a *mediatory* role, as we likewise come upon the mediatory in reducing everything to *relations*, thus completing the development from Substance to Subject to sheer correlation. Indeed, we seem to be confronting a principle of entropy, as with the second law of thermodynamics, with the distinctions of the various philosophic schools levelling off towards their "heat-death" in Pragmatism (which would be but another way of saying what James had in mind when borrowing Papini's figure of the corridor).

Ends

In the Baldwin dictionary we are told that Mysticism embraces "those forms of speculative and religious thought which profess to attain an immediate apprehension of the divine essence or the ultimate ground of existence." And: "Penetrated by the thought of the ultimate of all experience, and impatient of even a seeming separation from the creative source of things, mysticism succumbs to a species of metaphysical fascination." For it develops an ideal of passive contemplation "in which the distinctions of individuality disappear, and the finite spirit achieves, as it were, utter union or identity with the Being of beings."

Such references to "the divine essence," "the creative source," and "the Being of beings" indicate why we would equate Mysticism with the featuring of our term, Purpose. Often the element of unity *per se* is treated as the essence of mysticism. We should contend, however, that not mere unity, but unity of the individual with some *cosmic or universal purpose* is the mark of mysticism. One realizes this most readily when recalling that scientific philosophies which propose to eliminate "vitalism," "voluntarism," "spiritualism," "animism," "occult powers" and the like from their accounts of motivation regularly herald their attainments as the elimination of "mysticism" and "teleology" (the metaphysician's word for Purpose, or final cause).

Or we may establish the connection between Mysticism and Purpose sociologically by noting that although individual mystics may arise at any period of history, mystical philosophies appear as a general social manifestation in times of great skepticism or confusion about the nature of human purpose. They are a mark of transition, flourishing when one set of public presuppositions about the *ends* of life has become weakened or disorganized, and no new public structure, of sufficient depth and scope to be satisfying, has yet taken its place. Thus, precisely at such times of general hesitancy, the mystic can compensate for his own particular doubts about human purpose by submerging himself in some vision of a *universal,* or *absolute* or *transcendent* purpose, with which he would identify himself. In his chapter on "The Sick Soul" (*The Varieties of Religious Experience*) William James refers to Tolstoy's account of the drought preceding his rebirth. In this period of dire questioning, Tolstoy asked himself: "Is there in life any purpose which the inevitable death awaiting me does not undo and destroy?"

Our investigation promptly becomes complicated, however, by the fact, in accordance with the paradox of substance, that a purpose as thus conceived is so "pure" as to be much the same as no purpose at all, so far as everyday standards are concerned. Just as the mystic oxymoron conceives of a black radiance, a bitter sweetness, a learned ignorance (*docta ignorantia*), etc., so the mystic's "free" union with the All-Purpose becomes much the same as a *compulsion.* Such considerations explain why the psychology of mysticism is close to the psychology of neurosis. For the neurotic's God can be a disguised replica of his compulsion; and in communing with his God, he may by an unconscious subterfuge be but abandoning himself to his own weakness thus stylistically glorified. Also, in identifying the individual with the *All,* Mysticism often makes it hard for us to decide whether the Purpose is essentially collective or nominalist—though on the sociological level we can distinguish between the mystic who lives individualistically and the mystic who serves as the founder or organizer of a monastic order.

The fact that, in mysticism, Purpose is made absolute, always complicates matters by requiring us to lose purpose at the very moment when we find it. For as we have already noted, doctrines of absolute purpose lead into doctrines of mechanism, since the perfect regularity of nature (such as a thoroughly mechanical universe would exemplify) could be taken to indicate the "design" of its Creator.

All told, of the five terms, Purpose has become the one most susceptible of dissolution. At least, so far as its formal recognition is concerned. But once we know the logic of its transformations, we can discern its implicit survival; for the demands of dramatism being the demands of human nature itself, it is hard for man, by merely taking thought, to subtract the dramatist cubits from his stature. Implicit in the concepts of act and agent there is the concept of purpose. It is likewise implicit in agency, since tools and methods are for a purpose—and one of the great reasons for the appeal of pragmatism today, when the materialist-behaviorist reduction of scene has eliminated purpose, may reside in the fact that it retains ingredients of purpose in the very Grammatical function that is often taken as substitute for it. (It is a substitute; but we are suggesting that part of its capacity for such work resides in the implicit retention of what it is often said explicitly to reject.)

One feels this ambiguity particularly when considering the "Something for Itself's Sake" pattern of motivation so characteristic of modern specialization, the pattern that attains its highest level of generality in the "pure" motive of money. Though money is intrinsically a medium, or agency, in banking, gambling, and the "profit motive" generally it becomes translated into purpose, thus giving rise to what the Technocrat Harold Loeb once called the "mysticism" of money.

Similarly, in the esthetic field, doctrines of Art for Art's Sake would seem to fluctuate between the Pragmatic and the Mystical, though we may need some further distinctions here. Since art is a medium, the Art for Art's Sake formula would embody the grammatical form: Agency its own Purpose. One might call pragmatist such doctrines of art as those which hold that art is a means of biological assistance to man, in making for a better adjustment to conditions. Or the use of applied art (such as the "tendentious" art of political propaganda or commercial advertising) could be called pragmatic. But a pragmatist doctrine of art in a deeper sense would be one that applied in the esthetic field the same *form* of thought as had been applied to other activities. Hence, if specialization in the industrial field is considered pragmatic, then by the same token artistic specialization would be pragmatic. Yet such stress upon the medium for its own sake might have no "use-value," except when (as with the *ars gratia artis* of the Hollywood movies) it serves to attract paying customers, and so is indirectly "useful" in "making work" for a vast army of performers, producers, promoters, distributors, and the like. This last sense of the term would bring us before the dilemma we have been considering: whether to call Art for Art's Sake a pragmatist featuring of Agency or a mystic featuring of Purpose.

In any case, we should be on guard against taking the formula itself too seriously. When we look to see how it "behaves" in particular art products, we shall find that it involves the solution, on the Symbolic level, of many complex problems that could not profitably be discussed in terms so broad as either Agency or Purpose. And on the other hand, even when one adopts a rudimentary pragmatist view of art, as in advertising or propaganda, he has but moved the Agency-Purpose ambiguity a step farther along: for we then have to decide whether the financial or political structure which such applied art serves is to be classed as Agency or Purpose. Thus with the Hitlerite cult of the State: was it crass pragmatism (in using the philosophy of the State purely as a rhetoric for inducing the people to acquiesce in the designs of an élite) or crude mysticism (in genuinely looking upon the power and domination of the State as the ultimate end of social life)?

Perhaps, in view of the fact that the term Purpose is so especially susceptible to dissolution, we should be particularly on the look-out for its covert retention even on occasions where it is overtly eliminated. Thus, I once heard a child of five ask: "What are the hills for?" Hearing such a question today, we spontaneously translate it from teleological to evolutionary terms, so that the child is taught to ask instead: "How do the hills come to be?" But may the teleological intent survive vestigially, beneath the evolutionary style of expression? We have heard much of "repression" in recent decades. May there also

be a kind of "Grammatical repression," as we learn to express ourselves in non-teleological forms, while the experience of purpose is at
the very roots of knowledge: for the first sort of thing a child learns is
that way (indeterminately knowledge and action) whereby its random
sounds and random motions are transformed into the purposive. And
as we later learn to superimpose non-purposive forms of thought, to
what extent might the purposive survive?

It is a difficult problem. On the Rhetorical level, we can discount
language behavioristically by comparing what is said with what is
done. But where we are analyzing language intrinsically, we have
only its own appearances to go by. Hence, we must take an expression at its face value, until its own operations give us cause to do otherwise, by revealing some "perturbation" that can only be explained on
the assumption of some hidden gravitational pull. Meanwhile, we
may recall that we surprised teleological expressions in Darwin, forc-
ing their way through his evolutionism, when he was discussing beauty
as sexual incitement. This indicates at least that the evolutionary
thinking was not quite perfected in this high priest of evolutionism,
so that its symmetry could be impaired when he was on a subject so essentially purposive as the erotic.

At least, even when we would take terms at their face value, we may
at least be admonished always to be on the look-out for those points in
a writer's system at which he fails in his pretensions to outlaw the purposive. When the pentadic functions are so essentially ambiguous,
there is always the possibility that one term may be doing service for
another.

We have noted, for instance, how there is a point at which Mysticism
and Materialism become indistinguishable. Both involve a narrowing of motivational circumference. Materialism accomplishes this by
a deliberate elimination of purpose as a term (except for the fact that
the materialist is quite willing to tell you his purpose for eliminating
purpose). Mysticism arrives at somewhat the same result unintention-
ally, in making purpose absolute, and thereby in effect transforming it
into a fatality. Ironically, motivational schemes that would feature it
less may allow it more.

Modifications of Purpose

Purpose in Aristotle

As against the Mystic absolutism, perhaps the most realistic synonym for purpose is the Aristotelian "happiness" (*eudaimonia*). It stands at a level of generalization next beneath Purpose itself. As Aristotle says in Book I, section 5 of the *Rhetoric*: "Men, individually and in common, nearly all have some aim, in the attainment of which they choose or avoid certain things. This aim, briefly stated, is happiness and its component parts." His whole treatment of the "common places" (or typical hopes, fears, and values upon which the orator draws in seeking to affect his audience) takes shape about this motive. Thus, after listing the components of happiness (such as noble birth, children, wealth, good reputation, good physical condition, influential friends), he next observes that the concern of the deliberative orator is with the expedient. For men deliberate "not about the end, but about the means to the end." And since "the expedient is the good," he next proceeds to enumerate men's notions of the expedient and the good in general, as beliefs to which the orator must appeal if he would be persuasive. The purposive is consistently stressed; he defines the good as "whatever is desirable for its own sake, or for the sake of which we choose something else." And further along: "An end is a good." Next he considers the virtues, having defined virtue generally as "a faculty of providing and preserving good things." And so he proceeds to categorize pleasant and unpleasant things, and just and unjust actions, the entire structure of inducements and deterrents deriving its logic from the fact that it successively breaks down the concept of human aim or end into its components, and thence into the various means that men rightly or wrongly think help or hinder the attainment of this end.

The analysis is anything but "mystical." Indeed, it is wholly realistic, involving the usual Aristotelian concern with action, as when he refers human actions to seven causes (*aitia*): chance, nature, compulsion, habit, reason, anger, and desire—showing how these commonplaces likewise offer resources for the orator to exploit, or in his selection of metaphor, antithesis, and actualization (we might call it "personalization") as the major stylistic devices of the orator. And often his accounts of human character (as with the traits typical of youth and old age) are so dramatistic as to be purely and simply the recipes for *dramatis personae:* the emboldened youngster, and the timid crotchety oldster, with middle age in the mean between these two extremes. We must certainly give due consideration to the fact that the presence of a strongly purposive *ingredient* in the discussion of human motives is not in itself mystical. On the contrary, it is as realistic as the vocabulary of proverbs. Only when purpose becomes *total* does it fit our prescription for mysticism.

Instruments are considered by Aristotle in teleological terms, as their form is said to be derived from the end desired by their users. With living things, the purpose is said to be immanent in their nature, the plant seeking the life proper to vegetation, the animal adding to the vegetative the life of sensation and appetition, while atop these levels of motives, and including them, is the life of reason and moral action that characterizes man and the human community. Accordingly, his *Politics* is constructed about the purposive, as he asserts that every community is formed for the sake of some good, and that the State, as the most comprehensive community, must aim at the highest good.

Similarly, the *Nichomachean Ethics* begins:

> Every art and every inquiry, and likewise every act and purpose, is thought to aim at some good; hence the good has rightly been called that at which all things aim.

Platonist and Neo-Platonist Purpose

This equating of "good" and "purpose" comes nearer to mysticism in Plato, since he likewise equates the Good with the One. And the Neo-Platonists brought this element to the complete stage of the mystic oxymoron, in their dialectic of the Upward Way, as with Plotinus (*Enneads:* Book I, Tractate 3): "Our journey is to the Good, to the Primal-Principle." The Upward Way is much what Korzybski would call a development to higher and higher levels of generalization, or abstraction, until one comes to the principle of Unity (or the "First"). Then the course is reversed: unity is resolved again into particulars. But the particulars, as considered in the descent, are now infused with the spirit of the "First" at which one arrived in the ascent. In one sense, the First is beyond all merely human comprehension, except in the stage of mystic transcendence. But at other times the Neo-

Platonists permit it to be called the Absolute Good, as the nearest approximation possible to human discourse. From the standpoint of our Grammar, we need but consider it as the absolutizing of the concept of purpose, such a First being a principle of Unity quite as a great variety of things otherwise discordant is promptly brought into unity once they are all felt to serve a common purpose.

Physiology of Mysticism

In *Permanence and Change*, speculating on the purely physiological responses involved in the mystic trance, I suggested that:

> the mystic's state of passivity may be a kind of "assertion *in vacuo*," as were all the conflicting nervous impulses to be called into play at once. For instance, since a muscle is moved by the stimulation of a nerve, any *directed* movement such as a practical act would require, would involve the repression of some other nervous impulse. But if the nerves could be stimulated without the accompaniment of muscular movement, even conflicting nervous impulses could proclaim themselves simultaneously. It is at least a possibility that the pronounced sense of unity to which mystics habitually testify involves in the neurological plane some such condition of "pure action," wherein a kind of dissociation between impulse and movement is established, and all the conflicting kinds of nervous impulse may "glow" at once since they do not lead to overt muscular response. Such a possibility would explain why we could choose either the words *pure action* or *total passivity* to describe the state. And it would explain why the sense of attainment that goes with it would be both complete and non-combative, suggesting a oneness with the universal texture as thorough as that which the organism must have experienced during its period of "larval feeding" in the womb.

In brief, I carried the notion of "incipient action" to the point of suggesting that the sense of unity might come from the fact that, in their ambiguously "incipient" stage, even contrary nervous impulses could exist simultaneously, without the necessity for one to repress the other. I would now add that this would amount to a kind of "total purpose," in a transcendent state of "pre-motion."

Purposiveness in the Negative

On the level of purely intellectualistic generalization, what we have is a process whereby the particulars of the world are generalized in terms of a universal purpose (the "Good"), the Upward Way being a process *towards* this principle; and once it has been proclaimed as principle, all the particulars of the world can be derived from it as causal ancestor, hence sharing "substantially" in its nature (or, in our terms, having the nature of copartners in a universal purpose).

When we have thus contrived to detect the ingredient of purpose in Unity, or Totality, we begin to understand how there can be a Mystical strain in Spinoza's stress upon Oneness and Allness, despite his programmatic denial of Universal Purpose. And at this point we can add, to our synonyms for Purpose, another major term in philosophy: the *negative*, as in the mystical *via negativa* of "negative theology."

On the simplest dialectical level, the "First Principle" (as the highest level of generalization) must be endowed with negative attributes (as "infinite," "incomprehensible," "unending," "incorporeal," etc.), by its very nature as highest level of generalization. For it is particulars that have all the attributes of sense; and in proportion as our generalizations broaden in scope, they lose this sensory nature. Hence, the "First" would be something beyond the description of all human experience; we could only say that it does *not* have color, it does *not* have weight, it does *not* have size or shape, etc.

Spinoza, you will recall, proposed at this point to turn things around, treating Universal Substance as the positive, and considering determinate things, the objects of our experience, (the Modes) as the *negation* of this. Hence, his formula that all determination is negation. Accordingly, the applying of negative terms to God does not indicate that God Himself is negative, but only that the human imagination is unable to transcend the limitations of the senses.

In Bergson's semi-pragmatist, semi-mystical *Creative Evolution* there is a discussion of the negative that can be adapted well to our present speculations. As he states it, it is more scientist than it need be. It *should* be dramatist—and we shall make it over dramatistically. Scientistically, Bergson notes that a negative statement, such as "the ground is not damp," really implies some *positive* condition. The ground isn't in a merely negative state of not being damp; actually it is in some positive state, for instance, dry. In the world of nature, there are no negative conditions, but only positive conditions. The only way whereby one can *not be* at one place is for one to *be* at some other place.

The negative, Bergson says, is a function of *desire,* or *expectation,* or *interest.* If I expect an apple, and you give me an orange, then the thing you have given me is *not* an apple. If I want it to be 32 degrees Fahrenheit, and it actually and positively is some other temperature, I may express this state of affairs by saying that it is *not* 32 degrees; but the description of the real condition, aside from my personal interests in the matter, would involve rather the statement as to what the temperature actually is.

I think this is an extremely suggestive notion. And it fits in with a speculation in Coleridge's *Logic,* where Coleridge explains the turning of the head as a sign of negation by suggesting that the gesture arises as with a child which, expecting to be fed one thing, is fed another, and so turns away to avoid the spoon. I think the explanation is at least true "in principle," and where a people has a different gesture to indicate the negative, as I am told the Finns do, I would look for a somewhat different Grammar of the negative, as I believe the Finns have.

The dramatistic revision I would make in Bergson's speculations is to suggest that the origin of the negative should not be sought in such purely *informational* situations. Coleridge's example comes closer, since it involves an *action.* And so I should expect that the negative would originally be the negative of the Decalogue, not an "it is not," but a "thou shalt not," in brief, a *moral* function rather than a *semantic* function. The negative would thus arise in some such usage as this: for the positive, kill; for the negative, kill, at your peril. It would thus in its origin not have the force of a negative at all, but of some *deterrent* positive state. The suggestion is buttressed by the fact that in both Greek and Latin, verbs suggesting fear, apprehension, misgivings, and the like, require negative forms for the positive state. That is, a form like "I fear he will not come" (*vereor ne veniat*) would mean "I fear *lest* he come." And to mean "I fear he will not come," one would have to say, "I fear he will not not-come" (*vereor ne non veniat*). And in accordance with our usual genealogy, we should expect the original *active* meanings *later* to become transformed for purely informational usages.

Of course, from one point of view, we need not try to uphold so much here. It would seem to be enough if one observes that the concept of the One (=good) supplies a principle of purpose which, as highest generalization, would require statement in negative terms. But we hold that such a genealogy does not do quite well enough by the *act*, which is so closely related to the ethical. And we have pointed out that, as against a mere pattern of ever widening generalizations, there is also a kind of abstraction got through the terms for action itself, as verbs are abstract at their very start. (One can make up proper nouns; and demonstrative pronouns like "this" and "that" can be made to serve the same particularizing function; but who ever heard of a "proper verb"?)

And so we are trying to suggest that "negative theology" begins in conceptions of fear and apprehension that lie deeper than the purely "semantic" negative, which is "gnostically" superimposed upon the earlier forms (though the great stress upon the problem of evil in Gnosticism itself reveals the close connection between this abstract "science" and the level of motives prior to the domestication of the negative as an instrument of intellectualistic dialectic). The equating of the "Good" with Purpose is already a step away from this more fearsome religion. And we are still farther off, once the negative has taken its place as a semantic short-cut for stating situations in terms of our interests rather than stating on each occasion what the situation is positively—and one will appreciate what a convenience this is, if one tries to decide just what any situation is positively, except for the answer to simple questions like temperature when one is looking at a reliable thermometer.

However, though we have here extended our speculations beyond demonstration, we believe this much at least has been established: That the negative of negative theology is another variant of our term, Purpose. And since "the unconditioned" is synonymous with "the condition of conditions," we may often likewise expect to find a subtly transformed Purpose lurking behind concepts of "Totality" or "allness" (which are but other expressions for the Unity which we have already related to Purpose).

Unity and the Reflexive

As for the experience of mystic unity: note that communion is a *unification*. Such a feeling of unity implies the transcending of a *disunity*. Thus, in considering the *psychology* of mysticism, we find ourselves trying to chart a fluctuant situation in which merger and division keep changing places. And we are continually encountering aspects of the reflexive, as with works like Melville's *Pierre,* where the mystical pattern is expressed in the imagery of incest and self-abuse. Similarly, William James cites one Xenos Clark, who reported an anaesthetic revelation in which he seemed always just about to catch up with himself, so that, if he were but a fraction of a second sooner, he could have kissed his own lips.

The condition described by Xenos Clark might be accounted for neurologically if we assume that the action of the drug intensified the moment of dissociation between the "higher" brain centres and the "lower" vegetative functions so that the "delayed reaction" between the two levels of experience can itself become an experience, whereupon there would be two selves, separated by an appreciable instant. And I believe that the sense of "eternal recurrence" (or its simpler form, the feeling that "this has happened before") has been explained in such fashion.

But there are more purely Grammatical factors operating here likewise. In the case of a communion with nature, for instance, such an experience can take place only insofar as nature is in some way felt to be a replica of the self, a mighty self repeated in vast transmogrification, so that a doubling of personality is essential to the situation, as with the doubling of motives we already noted in idioms using the gods as terms for motives. And in accordance with the Spinozist pun on sequence, whereby we can translate a temporal priority into logical terms or a logical priority into terms of historical succession, an *essential* duplication could be conceived as a *temporal* duplication. Hence, as with Nietzsche's moment of ecstatic communion with nature, the translation of this feeling into its cosmic replica would yield the doctrine of eternal recurrence.

Or we might state the matter another way: If the structure of language is essentially human, then a poet or thinker, having gone from the non-linguistic to its replica in linguistic terms, might finally discover in the essence of language, but this time *through* language, the non-linguistic point of origin. And this too would involve a doubling. To be specific: I have suggested, in *Attitudes Toward History,* that the pattern of the wheel forever turning (in Eliot's *Murder in the Cathedral*) duplicates the pattern of Eliot's constant transformation of poet into critic and critic back into poet. And by this interpretation the "dead centre" of this wheel is forever still, because it duplicates the permanent aspect of the self underlying these changes.

In *Little Gidding,* this moment of arrest, necessarily but touched upon in the drama, is lyrically contemplated. The four elements are dialectically opposed to the fifth essence, spirit, as fire to Fire. The Midwinter spring in terms of which the Spirit is introduced, is a kind of *transition made permanent.* Or perhaps we might call it the "essence" of transition in the Santayana sense, a character that in itself would just *be* (an intersection of the timeless moment, at once the mind, England, and nowhere, scenically "never and always").

Shelley's poetry suggests a simpler genesis for the sense of eternal recurrence. In "Alastor," for instance, the poet first wanders on foot. Next, the trancelike state of this "passive being" is repeated, with intensification, as he is carried by a boat through further miraculous regions. Then he comes upon a stream, which he addresses:

> O stream!
> Whose source is inaccessibly profound,
> Whither do thy mysterious waters tend?
> Thou imagest my life.

Whereupon, he follows the course of this stream.

It is not hard to see why such a poet should come upon the doctrine of eternal recurrence. If one takes the imagery in its particulars, merely going from point to point along its course, there is no basic recurrence. But as soon as one considers the *quality* behind the imagery, these passive journeyings are seen to be recurrent. Indeed, the journey along the river of one's own life is perhaps a "journey within a journey," as with the song within a song of Coleridge's "Kubla Khan," or Poe's vision of life as a "Dream Within a Dream," or Ezekiel's vision of the wheel within a wheel. No wonder that such a poet would come upon the doctrine of eternal recurrence (a doctrine the reflexive nature of which is further revealed, in Shelley's case, by his preference for the imagery of incest, which in familial terms involves the communing of the self with a self of the same substance, hence a union of the self with the self).

Mysticism and Idealism: The Self

As we go from Purpose to Unity, and from Unity to Self, we see how Mysticism and Idealism reinforce each other. For Self is, of course, directly under the sign of Agent. But it has the same universalized quality, making it a super-self or non-self, that we noticed in the mystic paradox whereby absolute purpose becomes transformed into necessity. Thus in his chapter on Mysticism, James quotes John Addington Symonds' account of a mystical experience:

> It consisted in a gradual but swiftly progressive obliteration of space, time, sensation, and the multitudinous factors of experience which seem to qualify what we are pleased to call our Self. In proportion as these conditions of ordinary consciousness were subtracted, the sense of an underlying or essential consciousness acquired intensity. At last nothing remained but a pure, absolute, abstract Self. The universe became without form and void of content. But Self persisted.

Reading the passage, we see the Mystical ingredients behind the Kantian system, which is rooted in a similar abstract consciousness (the absolute "I think," or "synthetic unity of apperception"), and which includes as essential to the system the concept of teleology revealed through mechanism. We glimpse the relation to that abstract, anonymous person who is the wanderer of Shelley's poems. Indeed, we might well take the vague journeyings as but the verbal equivalent of a universalized first person pronoun. The kind of super-person thus envisaged *beyond* language but *through* language may be *generically* human rather than *individually* human insofar as language is a *collective* product and the capacity of complex symbolic action is distinctive of the human race. Hence, the Self we encounter at the outer limits of language would be a *transcendent* Self, an individual "collectively redeemed" by being apprehended through a medium itself essentially collective. (The matter is further complicated, however, by the fact that the individual himself is largely a function of this collective medium.)

Images and the "Demonic Trinity"

Images may lead to mystical transcendence of the person in generalizing the concept of role to the point where the realistic or dramatistic notion of people in situations retreats behind the pure lyric of imagistic succession. Here we come upon a kind of "pure" personality to match the absence of role that is characteristic of freedom when complete in either leisure or unemployment.

As for images generally, there is no way of knowing in advance what images may be expected to possess a great degree of purposiveness. In the last analysis, our decisions must wait until we have made a detailed analysis of the equational structure in the particular work. But some images more clearly indicate such possibilities. Thus our expressions "vocation" or "calling" derive from the imagery of a voice calling within. Or one would be justified in looking for the essentially purposive in Meredith where he speaks of certain thoughts as being to the thinker like the striking of a bell. Or the imagery, when half asleep, of a door opening or shutting seems to indicate that one can experience different levels of purpose, felt as we feel the differences of purpose in the different rooms of a house. Or change of scene may indicate purpose in indicating change of motive—and so generally with change of associations or associates. Or imagery of knocking may, as admonitory, indicate an obverse kind of purpose: the deterrent, as similarly with imagery of evil eye. Drought and rainfall, famine and plenty, hunger and feast may contain a dialectic of the purposive. All scapegoats are purposive, in aiming at self-purification by the unburdening of one's sins ritualistically, with the goat as charismatic, as the chosen vessel of iniquity, whereby one can have the experience of punishing in an alienated form the evil which one would otherwise be forced to recognize within.

I believe that I once clearly saw, in a child of eight, an instance of the way in which a purpose on the purely bodily level was first expressed in somewhat transcedent terms, in social and moralistic imagery. He told how he had had a dream of urinating, but had awakened just in time to prevent the potential or incipient action of the dream from attaining its literal translation into the actualities of motion. (Need I say: that isn't exactly how he worded it?) As he was talking, the memory of another dream occurred to him: a dream that he was having a month off from school. When I asked about the order of the dreams, he said the dream of urination had interrupted the dream of the vacation from school. He did not himself use this punning word "vacation"; but even so, is it not obvious that the consciousness of the bodily purpose was first imaged in the morally transcendent guise of a release from the controls of the schoolroom, an image of control natural to his level of experience?

The substantial nature of imagery may often produce an unintended burlesque of substance, in drawing upon the ambiguities of the cloacal, where there are united, in a "demonic trinity," the three principles of the erotic, urinary, and excremental. It is thus with the linking of time, the stream of consciousness, and the river—and with Hopkins' humbled vision of himself as "soft sift/ in an hourglass," following his wreck in saying yes "at lightning and lashed rod." Images from the cloacal sources are basic to the "thinking of the body"; and we may expect their privy nature to complicate the capitalist rationale of private property, where matters of monetary income are prominent among the *pudenda,* the bodily and the financial private thus both participating in the mystically secret. The thoroughness and accuracy of mysticism requires that these basic resistances figure in the reckoning. Is not the Hopkins poem built, for instance, about the transcendence that is got in a poetic transformation that takes us from an ambiguous surrender at "lightning and lashed rod" to a clear haven in the divine "lightning and love" (the reference to bodily wreckage in the first phrase having become translated into the incorporeal security of the second)? The relation between imagery and the "thinking of the body" impinges upon neurosis or psychogenic illness in proportion as the correlation between symbolic action and actual motion becomes total, not stopping with the *incipient* bodily agitations which the behaviorist notes as the condition of thought and which were revealed for Richards while reading of the centipede.

We have already considered why the erotic principle is to be considered as purposive. With the other two principles that compose the "demonic trinity" (with its burlesque of "negative theology") the relation is less clear, though their nature as inevitable bodily compulsions would fit them for this role; and the imagery of pollution by which the mystic frequently expresses the sense of drought (as with Eliot's *"Merdes" in the Cathedral,* an *ecclesia super cloacam*) suggests that mystic thoroughness ultimately involves the recognition of the fundamental tabus at the very moment of their transcendence.

Furthermore, in accordance with the cloacal ambiguities, we should be entitled to expect situations where the image of one member in this trinity may serve vicariously for either of the others. Thus, the imagery of rain might on analysis disclose that, besides its function as a transcendent translation of release (as physiologically conceived in terms of urination) it also had the connotations of erotic purposiveness. Of course, one may learn, on a purely social level, that moisture assists the germination of seeds; and the emotional effects of such knowledge may be considered enough in themselves to account for a poet's equating of rain with fertility. But in considering the Grammatical potentialities along the lines of either behaviorism or Yeats's concern with the "thinking of the body," we come upon the possibilities of a more purely internal route of associations. And in accordance with the logic of this route, rain could do imagistic service for erotic purpose in being a transcendent image of release as fundamentally conceived in terms of urination; and urination in turn would be one with the erotic member of the cloacal (demonic, privy) trinity, hence could do service for erotic purposiveness. Similarly, the "excremental" nature of invective or vilification would allow for a translation of erotic purpose from "love" into "war" (whereupon one writer may "commune" with another in the roundabout way of choosing him as specially favored opponent, antipathetically loading him with verbal offal rather than sympathetically showering him with the garlands of fertility).

Silence and the Hunt

Another purely biological motive involved in mysticism derives from the fact that at the very centre of mobility is the purpose of the hunt. Hence the imagery of the desired as that for which we "hunger," so that the quest for prey can become transformed into the erotic quest. Elsewhere (in *The Philosophy of Literary Form*) we have analyzed the opening speech of the Duke in *Twelfth Night* as a subtle instance of such body-thinking, ending on the pun of "hart" and "heart," as objects of the Duke's quest. And in *Emile* Rousseau reflects the same double motivation when advising the hunt as one stage in Emile's education just prior to his concern with a sexual quest. It is designed to delay this very condition into which it ambiguously leads. So thoroughly is our sense of purpose grounded in the expectation of food, that prolonged conditions of frustration may readily lead to digestive disorders, as with disappointments in business or love.

These biological considerations should also suggest why the mystic *silence* has its roots in the purposive. For in the quest one is naturally silent, be it as the animal stalking its quarry or as the thinker meditating upon an idea. Thus, even the utterance of the question begins in the silence of the quest. And we glimpse the profounder motives behind the Socratic questioning, where the essentially *purposive* is transformed into the liberally *problematic*. And so in *Hamlet,* whose bepuzzlement lapses back into silence ("the rest is silence"), following a dissociation in the development of the plot as a whole whereby Fortinbras takes over the role of outward quest, in the forthrightness of his role as warrior.

All told, we may note three aspects of the ineffable. First there is the "unspeakable level" to which Korzybski is referring when he would point to things themselves in an attitude of silence, as possessing attributes not present in their names. Tribes which have rites of "desanctification" reveal, in my opinion, the first "mystical" appreciation of this principle. For the need to "desanctify" the world is essentially but an appreciation of the fact that all things possess powers (and sanctity, divinity, or mana are terms for the designating of such powers). And the rites of desanctification are designed to mitigate the intensity of these powers, as things would otherwise be like highly charged electric wires without insulation.

Though we usually take such rites as perfect examples of "word magic," I am trying to suggest that word magic is but the failure to carry through the original insight. By this notion, word magic has its origins, paradoxically, not in a naïve belief in the power of words, but in man's first systematic *distrust* of words. It began with the sense of the *ineffable*. But there were no opportunities to study the subject, or even to write down one's speculations for others to examine. Hence, the insight was easily lost, and deteriorated into magic, particularly as men's sense of the ineffable could gradually come to be exploited by the use of charms, so that the original "classless" quest could be transformed into the quest for class privilege. Whereupon we got the development of a priestly caste, which by word magic obtained goods for itself and for the nobility with which it became allied.

There is also the ineffability of the visceral processes. No sensation can be described to someone who has not experienced a similar sensation. One cannot describe sight to a man born blind. But a further step enters here, when these processes themselves, having participated in the formation of language, are suddenly discovered to have had a *formative* effect upon language, and what we had taken as purely "rational" statements are seen to retain traces of bodily functioning. If "beauty," for instance, has habitually been considered wholly alien to the "cloacal," one may be quite horrified at the sudden perception of the cloacal beneath concerns that one had thought transcendent. The fear that often leads to mystical conversions often derives, I think, from sudden perceptions of this sort; and it can be quite disastrous if the insight occurs prior to the development of the critical method which makes a less agitated contemplation of the problem possible. A writer like Freud deserves the eternal respect of mankind because of the profound imaginativeness and methodical skill by which he widened our powers of such meditation.

A third stage involves what I might call the ineffability of linguistic relations themselves. Any level of conscious explications becomes in a sense but a new level of implications. And there thus comes a point where, lacking the protections of method, one must go no farther. Nor is there any good reason why one should, since the methods of linguistic skepticism have been developed far enough to ground the principles of wonder, resignation, tolerance, and sympathy which are necessary for sound human relations—and what we now most need is to perfect and simplify the ways of admonition, so that men may cease to persecute one another under the promptings of demonic ambition that arise in turn from distortions and misconceptions of purpose. With a few more terms in his vocabulary of motives, for instance, the rabid advocate of racial intolerance could become a mild one; and the mild one would not feel the need to be thus intolerant at all. And so human thought may be directed towards "the purification of war," not perhaps in the hope that war can be eliminated from any organism that, like man, has the motives of combat in his very essence, but in the sense that war can be refined to the point where it would be much more peaceful than the conditions we would now call peace.

The Mystic "Moment"

One more aspect of purpose should be added to our list. We have discussed purpose as equatable with Unity, and as a First. The two may often be the same, yet they are not quite the same. And by noting the distinction between them we can throw some light upon the Grammar of the mystic "moment," the stage of revelation after which all is felt to be different.

Riding in an elevator, has one not sometimes got the feeling that a given floor is a different floor when passed on the way up than when passed again on the way down? At such moments a number, like *ten,* becomes a slovenly misnomer; for it means both *nine plus one* and *eleven minus one,* yet the tenth floor is not the "same experience" when approached from above as it is when approached from below. And if, of course, some important incident had taken place between the time you ascended in the elevator and the time one descended again, you would feel all the more strongly that *eleven minus one* differed essentially from *nine plus one.* One would proceed from a different "first" than the other.

As translated into terms of capitalist climbing, there is a place in a movie when Jimmy Durante, in the role of an actor in difficulties, is slighted by another actor who thinks himself slated for success. Jimmy admonishes: You had better be nice to people you pass on the way up; for you may pass them again on the way down.

And so it is with the dialectical principle of the Upward Way. Beginning with the particulars of the world, and with whatever principle of meaning they are already felt to possess, it proceeds by stages until some level of generalization is reached that one did not originally envisage, whereupon the particulars of the world itself look different, as seen in terms of this "higher vision." The process itself is ordinary enough. If you had read novels year after year, for instance, approaching each in itself, for whatever entertainment it might afford you, you might next begin to notice that they fell into types or classes. This would be a new level of generalization; and thereafter, when you turned to another book, instead of seeing it simply in itself, you would see it partly at least in terms of your classifications ("detective story," or "historical novel," or "propaganda novel," etc.). Your view of novels would thus be modified to the extent that your system of generalizations provided you with a new "principle" (that is, "First") for judging or classing them.

The dialectic of the "Upward Way" would carry this process to completion, by extending one's level of generalization to the point of an "Absolute First," and thereafter considering particulars as pervaded with the spirit of this principle. It is the *Grammar* of rebirth, which involves a moment wherein some motivating principle is experienced that had not been experienced before. Usually, this dialectic resource takes the form of a generalization carried to the point of some metaphor or image, after which all particulars are seen in terms of it. Our discussion of Perspective in *Permanence and Change* illustrates many aspects of the method.

In *The Past Recovered,* where Proust is writing of the various moments in his life that all had the same quality (being all in effect *one* moment, in deriving from the same principle) he says that these many occasions in essence one were like a peacock's tail spread out. And the *purposive* aspect of the motivation is revealed, as he continues:

> I drew enjoyment, not only from these colours, but from a whole moment of my life which had brought them into being and had no doubt been an aspiration towards them.

Experience itself becomes mystical when some accidental event happens to be "representative" of the individual, as when a sequence of circumstances follows exactly the pattern desired by him. Hence the mysticism of gambling, where it is hoped that one's "pure purpose" in the pursuit of money will be in perfect communion with the inexorable decrees of fate. It has been suggested that Dostoevsky's sense of guilt had its origin in the fact that he had secretly desired the death of his father, and so was in a sense a vicarious participant in his father's murder. Since his father's murder took place as the result of causes wholly outside the orbit of Dostoevsky's real actions, it would be wholly an accident so far as the son was concerned. But if the psychoanalytic speculation is correct, the father's death would be a "representative" accident so far as the son was concerned. Similarly, the witches in *Macbeth* were representative of Macbeth's inner temptations, and so were a uniting of internal and external motives, since they were also the embodiment of universal fatality. Criminality, as so conceived, is thus mystical in effecting a mock communion of the criminal with the cosmic motives.

In *Crime and Punishment,* Raskolnikov's murder of the two wretched women is mystical since it is a kind of "absolute" act, conceived independently of its conditions. That is, it was not Raskolnikov's intention simply to kill and rob an old woman. This literal act was "representative" of much deeper motives, conceived absolutely. The nearest he comes to describing the ineffable purpose is in his thoughts on Napoleon and the cult of power. He apparently seeks the essence of power, that is, another variant of pure purpose. So that the murder would be representative; and even if he had been another Napoleon, his career would but have been representative of an underlying essential purpose, as with Napoleon's "communion" with fate in his role as a "man of destiny." Raskolnikov struggles to see the absolute "purity" of his crime over and above the revolting conditions of its actuality. He tries to retain his vision of it as an *ideal* transcending any and all material conditions. And perhaps the most startling burlesque of the communion between inner and outer is conveyed by the contrasting of two situations: his listening, outside the door, to the sounds within just prior to the murder; and his listening inside to the sounds without, just after the murder. An intolerable internality has been imposed upon him by the representative moment of the crime itself.

Crime produces a kind of "oneness with the universe" in leading to a sense of universal persecution whereby all that happens has direct reference to the criminal. There is no "impersonality" in the environment; everything is charged with possibilities. And though this is in one sense a painful condition, it is obviously so full that one can understand why men become habitual criminals, once they have come to conceive of living in these terms. Much of the world that would be otherwise neutral is charged with personal reference, thereby having much the quality that Aristotle asks of a dramatic plot, as when he says in the *Poetics:*

> Even matters of chance seem most marvellous if there is an appearance of design in them; as for instance the man who had been responsible for the death of Mitys was killed by Mitys' statue, which fell on him while he was witnessing a public spectacle. Such incidents seem to have a special significance.

And for the criminal, the whole world is thus purposive, so that the experience of criminal guilt in a sense restores the teleological view lost by evolutionism: Every next person may turn out to be the one who knows of his offence or is in pursuit of him. Conversely, a sense of guilt may lead to crime as its representation; and by such translation, a sense of persecution that might otherwise verge upon the hallucinatory can be made thoroughly real and actual.

Hence, as a kind of fragmentary mysticism, there is a tendency to interpret transgression as the moment that expresses a man's "true self," while his better ways are considered as mere "sublimations" of untoward impulses. The thought suggests that even the writings of our debunkers might be trailed back to an original source in mysticism (though usually we can assume a directer genealogy, with debunking as a state of disillusionment resulting from an oversimplified desire to locate purpose in the Unity of the Good).

Mysticism of Means

The "moment" is related to what follows as the implicit is to the explicit, as the order of cards after the shuffle is to their distribution after the deal, as the seed is to the sprout, and the sprout is to the blossom, and the blossom is to the descendant seed. It is the pattern of thought in the mystic doctrine of the relation between the *deus implicitus* and the *deus explicitus* (as with the pantheistic vision of a god whose unfoldment is the world).

There is thus a pragmatist kind of mysticism in Aldous Huxley's doctrine that impure acts must follow from impure means. For the over-stress upon *purpose* leads readily into an overly pointed consideration of all policies in terms of means and ends alone. That is, the terms scene, act, and agent fall away, as we talk simply of purposes and the agencies proper to these purposes. And as an introduction implicitly contains the developments that follow from it, so a stress upon the means, as introduction implicitly containing the end, gives us in effect the relation between means and ends that we noted in the mystic doctrine of the relation between *deus implicitus* and *deus explicitus*. The means would thus, in a sense, be the ancestor of the end. Hence the quality of the end would be implicit in the quality of the means. Hence, only if the means were "pure" in substance, could the result be "pure."

Huxley relies upon such patterns as an argument for pacifism, holding that only by peaceful means can we get peace. The logical conclusion of this doctrine would seem to be that peace as an end is either impossible or unnecessary. For if we could get peace by peaceful means we'd have peace already; and if we couldn't get it by means somewhat short of peace, then there would be no use in our attempting to get it at all.

All means are necessarily "impure." For besides the properties in them that fit them for the particular use to which they are put, they have other properties (properties that would fit them for other possible uses, including hostile uses). And their identity in themselves (as against their identity from the standpoint of some particular use) thus makes them ambiguous from the standpoint of their possible consequences. That is, there is no one end exclusively implicit in them. And thus, from the standpoint of any given end, they are "impure." And we act by a progressive purification of them.

Indeed, from the "dramatistic" standpoint, it would seem wrong to speak of ends as resulting from means. Or rather, we should be reminded that this is a very truncated statement of the case, which would require us to consider the resources and obstacles of scene and agents, while seeking to formulate a whole *hierarchy* of purposes. Agencies being related to purposes somewhat as motion is related to action, a statement when confined to terms of means and end eliminates "act" as a special locus of motives by treating the act simply as means to an end. In a dramatist perspective, where the connotations of "to act" strategically overlap upon the connotations of "to be," action is not merely a *means of doing* but a *way of being*. And a way of being is substantival, not instrumental.

The distinction is ethically of great importance, as a man may deliberately choose a less "efficient" *means* for doing something because it is "his way" (if he is concerned not merely for the successful outcome of the given operation, but also for its performance in keeping with his "character," or norms of his being). In a society like ours, where the pragmatist vocabulary is current, he will probably justify his resistance on the grounds that the rejected method "will not work." But his tests of its successful working covertly include the requirement that it fit his concepts of individual and tribal identity.

Thus, in objecting to socialism, we in America often pragmatically reduced our criticism to the assertion that it "wouldn't work." And when Russia was invaded by the Hitlerite armies, many of us expected that Russia would collapse within a few weeks. But after the quality of Russian resistance had given a stupendous example of socialism's "workability," our rhetoric shifted to the use of Grammatical ingredients more idealist and realist. We decided that, while socialism could apparently "work" in Russia, it is not the "American way."

The more insistently one presses upon such a view, however, the more it tends to become pure mysticism. The "American way" is offered purely and simply as a *purpose*, our *business pragmatism* having thus been transformed into a mystical nationalism. This purpose will be expressed (*äussert, vermittelt*) through one's communion with his country's economic plant—a participation that will in turn be mediated in terms of money, the pure purpose essential to our culture insofar as it is a capitalist culture. We are admonished, however, that in this imperfect world, no man can be moved by this pure motive alone, but must alloy it with the pre-capitalist, non-capitalist, and post-capitalist concerns that, in their totality, compose his nature as a person.

To illustrate purity of purpose in Christian terms, we may take Thomas à Kempis' *Imitation of Christ,* which represents in a thorough form the dialectic of the Upward Way as transformed into the discipline of Christian monasticism. "In all things behold the end," it is written in the first book—and since the following or imitating of Christ, as the principle of purpose, is equated with "the contemning of the world" as the means toward this end, the typical Christian paradoxes follow: "learn now to die to the world that thou mayst begin to live with Christ"; "the profit of adversity"; to "suffer benignly"; "to be a fool for Christ." The steps are not towards higher levels of generalization, but towards the "innerness of Jesu," a stage attained in the third book, which treats "of inward conversation," "of the inward speaking of Christ unto a soul," where the biological inwardness of the quest has been transcended by linguistic utterance; and this form of socialization becomes in turn transcended by its transformation into internal dialogue, which in its turn is externalized, though with the mark of its internality strong upon it.

Rationalism and the Verbal Medium

Three meanings for rationalism are given in the Baldwin dictionary. It is the theory (1) "that everything in religion is to be rationally explained or else rejected"; (2) "that reason is an independent source of knowledge," and has a "higher authority" than sense-perception: (3) that "certain elementary concepts are to be sought," and "all the remaining content of philosophy is to be derived, in a deductive way, from these fundamental notions."

All three of these positions, you will note, contain the same *methodological* stress. And so the three great exponents of modern rationalism, Descartes, Spinoza, and Leibniz, offered respectively a *Discourse on Method,* an *Ethics* presented *more geometrico* after the analogy of

Euclidean demonstration, and "the idea of a universal logic and language" which should be to philosophy what the calculus was to physics. And whereas these earlier rationalists said that the world is rational, Hegel went as much farther in that direction as is possible by saying that the world is Reason.

In its stress upon method, rationalism stands as a forerunner to pragmatism. But the two become dialectically opposed insofar as empiricism became the opponent of rationalism, and pragmatism has aligned itself with empiricism. Here we seem to have contradicted ourselves in two successive sentences. But I think that by adding a few distinctions we can get matters placed satisfactorily enough.

Pragmatism, like empiricism, was particularly opposed to the Leibnizian procedure whereby, beginning with a few fundamental principles, one could spin a vast metaphysical web, in the way that mathematicians can erect highly complex mathematical systems. Leibniz himself being a great mathematician, one can understand why he would apply to words a method that was to prove so fertile in mathematics. But its application to mathematics could lead to idealizations that assist empiricist research, whereas its application to words led to idealizations that transcended materialist testing, and could in fact become sheer word-spinning.

In such procedures, we might say, the end is implicit in the beginning; all conclusions are foregone conclusions, once we have selected our ancestral principles. And whatever may be the relation between past, present, and future in the world itself, Leibniz certainly characterized the ideal of his own writings about the world in saying that the present summed up the past and implicitly contained the future. That is, he was making an accurate statement about the progression of terms in his own books. Rationalism, as so conceived, clearly reveals its affinities with dramatic structure, as it likewise did in its familial stress upon substance and derivation. And by having its answers in advance, rationalism was felt to injure the development of scientific inquiry.

The issue can never be quite clear, because rationalists themselves have progressively contributed to the critique of rationalism, and did much to establish forms of thought (particularly as regards deference to traditional authority) that aided the cause of scientific induction. And the most empirical of scientists depends, in the last analysis, upon the canons of rationality in organizing and interpreting his experiments.

The issue is made clearer, I think, if we consider Santayana's equating of mathematics and dialectic on the grounds that both exemplify the principle of internal development whereby one can begin with a few basic principles and use them to spin a system out of itself. This would lead us to consider all rationalism as essentially dialectical. But we should consider pragmatism and empiricism as likewise instances of the dialectical. And we should distinguish between the typically rationalist dialectic and the typically empiricist dialectic by noting that each features voices neglected by the other.

From the dialectical point of view, for instance, there is nothing "anti-rationalist" in the empiricist position. In accordance with something so thoroughly rationalist or dialectical as the scene-act ratio, we might well expect new experimental conditions to reveal new kinds of behavior. The framing of experiments becomes the translating of our questions into terms that permit inanimate conditions to give intelligible answers. In strict accordance with dialectical principles, we may expect that the laws we discover will "transcend" previous laws, in proportion as the new conditions differ from previous conditions. And *furthermore*, as a corrective on empiricism, we shall be reminded that *our instruments are but structures of terms, and hence must be expected to manifest the nature of terms.* That is, we must always be admonished to remember, not that an experiment flatly and simply reveals *reality*, but rather that it *reveals only such reality as is capable of being revealed by this particular kind of terminology.*

We consider the present venture rationalistic in this dialectical sense. We believe that an explicit approach to language as a dialectical structure admonishes us both what to look for and what to look out for, as regards the ways of symbolic action (and no statement about motives can ever be anything other than symbolic action). The project is also rationalist in seeking, by a rationale of language, to chart methodically the "non-rational" and "irrational" aspects of language (here following that kind of rationalism so superbly developed by a great modern dialectician, Sigmund Freud).

So, either rationalistically or dialectically, we have been spinning five terms into a book, by making their implications explicit. Our analysis itself is empiricist in that it must recognize the respects in which every linguistic structure is a "new thing." It is empiricist in that it must approach experimentally the ultimate problem of the relation between symbolic action and practical conduct. Yet it never permits us to forget that empiricism does not transcend the limitations of vocabulary, but is an especially poignant illustration of such limitations.

Aiming always at reduction, it must admonish continually against the dangers of reduction. Aiming at reduction in a capitalist economy, it must pay particular attention to the rationalism of money. For money provides the reduced circumference of rationality that distinguishes the state of modern enlightenment. It affords a position in terms of which we can transcend the earlier, more personalistic or dramatistic vocabularies of motivation. Yet we can dialectically adopt the terms of these other positions to aid us in seeing beyond the structure of monetary motivations which we might otherwise tend to interpret, not as a *kind* of reality, but as "reality" itself.

But however impersonal may be the relations brought about by the high development of a monetary economy, money itself in its role as a medium or agency contains the humanistic or the personalistic ingredients that we have discerned at the very source of agency. The "inhumanity" of finance, like the "inhumanity" of factory speed-up or technological war, is a peculiarly human invention. Money is essentially "humanitarian," its parable in this respect being the coin tossed to the leper; for it possesses that humanitarian ambiguity whereby one can, through financial charity, give aid to those whom one could not possibly bring oneself to touch in directly personal ministrations. It possesses thus the ambiguity of the attitude, the incipient act.

Putting together what we have said about delayed action, mystic purpose, and the representative moment, may we not see in the withholding (or "postponed consumption") of capitalist investment, the dialectical "moment" of delay translated into capitalist terms, and so drawn out into a long history? Or conversely, since one who invests his money in a title accepts a symbolic instrument in lieu of material goods or services, we could call it an "incipient act" of consumption; and the experience of investment could be said to find in the theory of the delayed or incipient action its corresponding "representative moment."

In its role as symbolic action, investment contrived remarkably to merge principles that must usually be antagonistic to each other: the principles of sacrifice and acquisition. For one denies himself to the extent that he does not consume his bounty in the present, but transforms it into purely promissory, futuristic titles. But we should always remember that this view of money is a much better fit for one stage of capitalism than it is for another. It is particularly serviceable when the economic situation calls for the upbuilding of the primary economic plant, the mills, mines, railroads, and the like which, in their stage of formation, bring denials rather than satisfactions to wide areas of the population. It is a stage of upbuilding that once prevailed during the Puritan upbuilding of capitalism. And we have witnessed it again in the last twenty years of Russia, where the people necessarily acquired little for themselves as individual consumers, while expending their efforts upon the national structure of production, transportation, and defense. But insofar as the basic economic plant is developed, the need becomes rather for consumption than for postponed consumption (though consumption for military purposes rather than consumption of "consumer goods" can postpone the obligations of this condition, which has previously proved so embarrassing to the manipulations of capitalist symbolism).

It is hard to know just what has taken place, in proportion as the motives of guilt and retribution attained "enlightened" secular translation in terms of debt, credit, wages, profit, and the like. The rise of psychoanalysis is, however, clear evidence in itself that men are unequal to the monetary vocabulary of motives in its purity, but can use it only as one might mark his course by a thread through a labyrinth. Even at times when religious symbolism flourished, the basic processes of human psychology were often stated in monetary terms. But in proportion as the monetary terms have become the central vocabulary of motives, not figurative, but public "reality" itself, we may have to read the earlier religious monetary metaphors in a different spirit, using them now rather as passages that indicate to us the possible "overtones" of money which the rationale of accountancy itself must leave out of account. That is, we may find earlier statements where religious concepts of guilt and redemption were explicitly expressed in monetary terms; and we may now examine these for the light they throw upon the patterns of guilt and redemption that may be unexpressed but implicit in our present "rationalist" use of the terms for monetary motivation.

Consider, for instance, the resonance of this citation from St. Ambrose, which we found in a Catholic Catechism:

> The devil had reduced the human race to a perpetual captivity, a cruel usury laid on a guilty inheritance whose debt-burdened progenitor had transmitted it to his posterity by a succession drained by usury. The Lord Jesus came; He offered His own death as a ransom for the death of all; He shed His own Blood for the blood of all.

The complexity of ways in which money, property, the familial, the universal, and the vicarious are interwoven in this passage, with an underlying pre-monetary psychology of personal barter, suggests a whole thesaurus of subtleties in human relationship. Do we not see, here united in a religious view of atonement, the two strands that eventually became dissociated into the rationale of accountancy on the one hand, and on the other the psychoanalytic study of "irrational" guilt?

Revolutionaries often think that their particular revolutions (such as those of capitalism or socialism, or the counter-revolutions that would restore dictators ruling in the name of the Church) can omit one or another aspect of our motivational complexity. The other possibility is that men are "Catholic," "Protestant," and "Scientist," all three in one, though historical conditions at one time or another in their history may induce them to stress one at the expense of the other two. Or, as regards the Big Three in their most abstract forms, men conceive of their world primarily in a dialectic composed of three voices: "Catholic" act, "Protestant" agent, "Scientist" scene. And lying across the three, indeterminately Agent or Purpose, are the various kinds of moneys, or counters, or *symbols* of wealth that have, in the changing situations of history, simultaneously performed both socializing and individualizing functions, and have contributed their terms as voices in the total dialectic by which we develop our vision of reality. In its teleological nature as means and end, money is a direction that greatly multiplies the ways of indirection.

In closing, note that the psychoanalytic concept of *repression* is the *reciprocal* of purpose. If purpose is the cameo, repression is the intaglio. It is a kind of "negative purpose." Consider our notion that the religious vocabulary of motives splits into the material of accountancy on the "rational" side and the material of psychoanalysis on the "irrational" side. Recall also our remarks on negative theology as purposive, centering dramatistically in the God of "thou shalt not." And recall that the "dying life" of the *Imitation* is that of a purpose got by transforming the prohibitions against wordly aims, so negating the negativity of the Commandments as to make them into a positive purpose. Recall also our suggestion that Korzybski recognizes the same principle of transcendence as is found in Plato, except that Plato would say "good" where Korzybski would say "alas!" Do not all these parts all fit together? For "repression" would be "purpose" rephrased in terms of post-Christian liberalism (the liberalism of the "freedman" rather than the liberalism of the ruler). And psychoanalysis would be a secular variant of negative theology, though with an important reversal of attitude whereby the elations of the "dying life" may be looked upon as manifestations of a "death impulse," rather than as a transcending of the worldly. For all the talk of "mechanism" in the Freudian psychology, we may see its underlying dramatistic nature. And we may note that the Freudian system is as fully organized about the concept of the purposive as Aristotle, though adding momentously to our understanding of the dialectic laws whereby the purposive can become moralistically transformed into its negation, with corresponding "sublimations" and "compulsions."

Means and Ends of This Grammar

Our five terms are "transcendental" rather than formal (and are to this extent Kantian) in being categories which human thought necessarily exemplifies. Instead of calling them the necessary "forms of experience," however, we should call them the necessary "forms of *talk about* experience." For our concern is primarily with the analysis of *language* rather than with the analysis of *"reality."* Language being essentially human, we would view human relations in terms of the linguistic instrument. Not mere "consciousness of abstracting," but *consciousness of linguistic action generally,* is needed if men are to temper the absurd ambitions that have their source in faulty terminologies. Only by such means can we hope to bring ourselves to be content with humbler satisfactions, looking upon the cult of empire as a sickness, be that empire either political or financial.

Not that we should avoid the problems of "global" order. On the contrary, we must turn precisely in the direction of a neo-Stoic cosmopolitanism, with ideals of tolerance and resignation to the bureaucratic requirements implicit in the structure of modern industry and commerce. The only alternatives are fanaticism and dissipation. By fanaticism I mean the effort to impose one doctrine of motives abruptly upon a world composed of many different motivational situations. By dissipation I mean the isolationist tendency to surrender, as one finds the issues of world adjustment so complex that he merely turns to the satisfactions nearest at hand, living morally and intellectually from hand to mouth, buying as much as one can buy with as much as one can earn, or selling as much as one can sell, or in general taking whatever opportunities of gratification or advancement happen to present themselves and letting all else take care of itself.

This temptation is always with us, partly because sound common sense admonishes that we should not burden ourselves with problems beyond our powers, partly because this piecemeal approach to life represents to an extent the very attitude of humility that we should seek to cultivate, and partly because it is our inheritance from the days when we were taught that the conditions of the market automatically solved the problems of social welfare, if we but put ourselves wholly and trustingly in the market's hands, as though its workings were a kind of automatic Providence invented by man at God's instigation, so that men could turn from Him to it when seeking motivational guidance.

But do we not rather need both an *attitude* and a *method* of wider scope? The attitude itself would be grounded in the systematic development of the method. The method would involve the explicit study of language as the "critical moment" at which human motives take form, since a linguistic factor at every point in human experience complicates and to some extent transcends the purely biological aspects of motivation. The attitude would be mildly that of "hypochondriasis," a kind of "cultural valetudinarianism," which recognizes that the school of ideas is divisible into both a gymnastic of ideas and a clinic of ideas, and which would assist health by aiming always at the first without forgetting the claims of the second. It would rate men's ability individually and collectively to "keep in trim" as immeasurably higher than the naively perverted religiosity that characterizes our devotion to the ways and means of acquisition.

It would find human foibles a theme for constant contemplation. But it would not make the mistake of thinking that the lore of human foibles stops with the depicting of different personal types in fictions. There is also the *categorized* lore of human foibles, as we find it expressed in proverbs or in moral philosophy. Generalizations about human ways are as essentially humanistic as is the depicting of some particular person acting in some particular way; and they are needed to complete the act of humanistic contemplation. And all this comes to a head in the contemplation of men's linguistic foibles, which can so drastically transform their ways of life.

Remember always that no modern instrument could have been invented, or could be produced, without the use of a vast linguistic complexity. A traffic signal seems very simple, but its production, distribution, and operation requires a set of interlocking linguistic acts that would require a century to trace in their particularity. If we are not to be lost in such a maze of particulars, we must build from the essential humanity of dramatist or dialectic lore in general, considering it as central to the contemplation of the human tragi-comedy.

This work (which would have as its motto *Ad Bellum Purificandum,* or Towards the Purification of War) is constructed on the belief that, whereas an *attitude* of humanistic contemplation is in itself more important by far than any *method,* only by method could it be given the body necessary for its existence even as an attitude. We would thus hold at least that an elaborate analysis of linguistic foibles is justified "in principle." Indeed, the study of linguistic action is but beginning. And we must be on our guard lest the great need for an *attitude* of linguistic skepticism allow us to be content with too hasty a "policy" as regards the nature of language itself. This is too serious a matter for such "dissipatory" approaches to the subject as we find among the contemporary "debunkers." And even serious approaches are invalidated when formed in keeping with the ideals of an uncriticized scientism, which is *too evasive of the dramatistic to make even an adequate preparatory description* of linguistic forms. To contemplate our subject, we must have a terministic equipment that lends itself to such contemplation. Otherwise one has a *principle of aversion* implicit in the very nature of his investigation, as if one hoped to see accurately by partially averting one's gaze. There may be true and false transcendences in language. Or for the sake of the argument, if you will, they are all false. But in any case they *are* transcendences. And we must begin by taking some delight in the contemplation of them as such. By the use of dialectical resources, we shape the versions of human motives that have so greatly much to do with our individual actions and our relations to one another.

Questions of motivation come to a head in questions of substantiation and transubstantiation. And so, in Part III of this book, we shall deal with the dialectic of these two processes. We shall take as our text for substantiation, the theory of Constitutions. And we shall consider transubstantiation as the representative moment of dialectic in general.

PART THREE

ON DIALECTIC

for our patriotic selection. We dared commend ourselves: "Let the reader grant this in our favor: that in featuring the Constitution as the model for our idiom, we shall have grounded a book On Human Relations upon the very Constitution of our country—and what social philosophy could be more thorough in its patriotism?" It should be enough to note that I treated the anecdote as containing implicitly what the analysis would draw out explicitly—for insofar as one really did form his terms consistently about some "case" he considered typical of his subject, the level of the analysis could rise no higher than the level of the terms. But certain broad considerations underlying the problem of selection should be mentioned, since they cast more light on the motivational grammar.

The Two Circles

First, we rejected "metonymic" anecdotes. That is, considering no tions of mind-body parallelism, according to which a given state in consciousness has its corresponding physical state, we rejected the tactics of pure behaviorism which would treat the realm of consciousness in purely physicalist terms. Rather, we held that the relation between these two "parallel" realms should be considered as that between two concentric circles, one of them having a much wider orbit than the other ("consciousness," that is, being related to "matter" as the larger of two concentric circles is related to the smaller).

It is the design one should always have in mind when considering the dialectic of Coleridge. Thus, for him, "understanding" would be a narrower term than "reason": it would in fact be but an aspect of reason, one of its idioms (as "logical argumentation," let us say, would be but a restricted form of "wisdom," or as "technology" or "laboratory method" would be narrower than "science," or as "routine" would be narrower than "method"). In Chapter XXII of the *Biographia,* Coleridge himself uses the figure, observing that "truth and prudence may be imagined as concentric circles."

Obviously, in accordance with our previous remarks on the nature of dialectical counterparts, two realms thus related (as concentric circles greatly differing in circumference) could be treated as being either in apposition or in opposition (as either consistent or compensatory counterparts)—and in Coleridge you will find a shifting between the two usages, though as a general rule his idealistic preferences lead him to treat the smaller circle as a misrepresentation of the larger. We likewise hold that an anecdote, to be truly representative, must be synecdochic rather than metonymic; or, in other words, it must be a *part for the whole* rather than a *reduction of the mental to the physical*. (For more on the distinction between metonymic reduction and synecdochic representation the reader is referred to our article on "The Four Master Tropes," in the appendix of this book.) Thus, if our theme were "communication," we should seek to form our terms about some typical instance of communication, rather than selecting some purely physical mode, as a highway system or telegraphic network.

Terminal as Anecdote

Since we were looking for an anecdote where relations "grandly converge," we did actually consider, as a metonymic anecdote which we set up to be discarded in favor of the Constitution, the example of a railway terminal. The name, "Grand Central," may have secretly moved us to hit upon the expression "grandly converge." And in meditating upon a *terminal* we were certainly quite close to the problem of *terms*. Indeed, this is no mere matter of puns. For instance, we once witnessed, in the most obvious physicalist sense, a representation of walking got by the use of six terms (*termini,* terminals). Six different wires, recording pressures at six different spots on the underside of the foot, were connected with an electrical contrivance that made a graph of these pressures as they were modified in the process of walking. Thus, the "representation" of walking (or more accurately in this case, the "reduction" of walking) as it showed on the graph depended entirely upon the selection of these "terms" and the logic of their interrelationship. Select different "terms" (a different number of them, or differently distributed so that they terminate at different points) and you get a correspondingly different record of the walking process itself. Indeed, judged as a "representation" of walking, the graph derived from the six electric *termini* was a pretty dismal one; however, it was serviceable enough as a purely pragmatic "reduction" of walking, made for comparative purposes (i.e., for comparing the graphs of different gaits, as thus reduced). And though such reductions would have little value as representations of walking, in the sense that Rodin's *Man Walking* might, or even in the sense of Duchamps' *Nude Descending a Staircase*, they might serve well for diagnosing different types of illness or temperament as revealed by different types of gait.

A railway terminal, as our basic anecdote, would have had some value as parable, in reminding us to include dialectical complexities. For with such an example before us, we quickly recognize that great mobility here requires great fixity, since traffic must be coördinated, and this coördination is got by such relatively motionless things as routes, schedules, continuity of personnel, bookkeeping routines and filing systems—while all these set ways would in turn depend upon set ways (the schedules upon the standardizations of the calendar, the personnel upon familistic institutions, and the symbols of accountancy upon a distinct educational pattern). And though much of a man's participation in the patterns of exchange may not be intrinsically interesting, he may find it reasonable to spend his life at such work because of the money it brings him, money in turn found reasonable because of the many organizations whereby the general set of promises, implicit in the money, may be redeemed—quite as, when you drop a coin in one particular kind of slot machine, it will according to its kind yield you certain goods.

All such considerations quickly invite us to develop a highly ramified vocabulary (which would be quite complex, even if we insisted, as materialists, upon deriving all the phenomena of the wider circle, or "ideological superstructure," from the narrower circle, or "economic substructure," as its causal ancestor). But the one great technical advantage of physicalist reduction, its readily observable form, would be lacking, since we are so soon carried beyond the acts of physical routing and exchange. Thus, the clarity of the metonymy would be gone, as we vaguely glimpse an interwovenness of traditions, needs, and expectancies that could not be located in the idiom of our chosen anecdote at all, but would simply lie outside its orbit, and could only be treated bluntly as "complicating factors" (or as "epicycles," to employ the term that Ptolemaic astronomers used for the planetary movements that could not be located integrally until the system of Copernicus).

Representativeness of Total War

And holding that the same sort of objection would apply to all metonymic reductions, we turned to inquire whether we could find "some
representative public enactment, to which all members of a given
social body variously but commonly subscribe." We required something representative synecdochically (as a part that can stand for the
whole). Nor could atomistic reductions serve, for it is the strategy of
atomism to reduce the complex to the simple, and the simple cannot
be properly said to represent the complex. We wanted a representative part in the sense that the expression about the eyes and mouth
of a man could not be called either the totality of the man or the
"atomic building-blocks" of which he is constructed, and yet may be
said to sum up what he stands for. In primitive communities, for instance, we might have found such a moment of convergence in tribal
festivals that were felt by all of the participants to have an integral
bearing upon the welfare of the tribe. Such would be totemic rites,
symbolic enactments proclaiming group identity, designed to aid success in hunt and war, fertility of crops and women, the exorcising of
evil—group modes of invocation and thanksgiving. Obviously, an anecdote of this sort would directly bear upon many elements beyond
the materials and conditions of the economic, yet the economic ingredient could not be denied as an important aspect of the total recipe.
In the Christian tradition at its heyday, before industrialism had so
greatly increased the kinds and number of commodities and the impersonality of their production (stimulating the revolution from intimate, familistic thought in terms of gift and sacrifice, to a more abstract
and "enlightened" thought in terms of buying and selling) we might
have looked for the focus of public enactment in the communion service.

Unfortunately, in the modern state, with its great diversity of interests
and opinions, due to the dispersion of technological and commercial enterprise, the act that comes closest to the totality of tribal festivals and
the agape is the act of war. But modern war ("total war") itself is so
complex, that we could hardly use it as our representative anecdote until
we had selected some moment within war to serve in turn as repre-

sentative of war. "Modern war in general" would be unwieldy as an anecdote, since it is more of a *confusion* than a *form*.

Our scruples about the tactics of beginnings suggested a still more serious objection. For if we took war as an anecdote, then in obeying the genius of this anecdote and shaping an idiom accordingly, we should be proclaiming war as the essence of human relations. And that choice is too drastic to be taken unless absolutely necessary. Of course, we might take it as our start, with the intention of promptly asserting our independence by abandoning it. But in that case, it would not really be our representative anecdote at all.

However, we couldn't triumph so easily. There may be the most admirable of scruples behind the selection of war as key anecdote. For one thing, if it is the culminative we want, we must grant that war draws things to a head as thoroughly as a suppurating abscess, and is usually, like revolution, the dramatic moment of explosion after an infinity of minute preparatory charges. Being a crisis, it helps criticism. And we must grant the proportion of war in all forms of theoretical or practical enterprises. In fact, when Heraclitus offered "Strife" and "War" as synonyms for his Universal Fire (proclaiming it the causal ancestor and magistrate, "father and king," of all things), was he not but saying, in a forceful way, that history is "dialectical," developing by the give and take of combat? And his very words for War and Strife survive as words for the dialectic in its more agonistic aspects: "polemic" and "eristic."

When Heraclitus proclaimed that "everything flows," he offered an over-all paradigmatic anecdote in terms of which, as a title, all human histories could be grouped. His dictum was a dramatic way of saying: "The principal or ancestral term needed for the characterization of experience is 'change'." His fluent "fire" was itself a kind of irreducible substrate (we could call it the *permanence* of change), an unchanging title or essence for classifying under a single head all kinds of physical combustion, sentimental warmth, emotional fieriness, and logical glow. And when he also tells us that his essential fire is a kind of universal currency or medium whereby "all things are changed for fire and fire for all things as goods for gold and gold for goods," we may recall our passing comments on the relation between doctrinal and monetary currencies; and we may wonder whether, in thus interpreting money in terms of its *mediatory* properties rather than its *competitive* properties, his conception of an essential "fire" like money might also have had, among its motivational attributes, that of celebrating the life of trade.

Such thoughts might justify us in looking for the militarist core in all historic converse, even during times of peace. Whereupon, we had all the more reason for featuring war as an idiom of reduction, in such times, when war was necessarily at the height of a thinker's fashion; and even while our country was still supposedly at peace, we had thousands and thousands of prisoners held in concentration camps (permanent ones: made of granite and steel, like vaults; i.e., our prisons).[13]

The Constitution and the Admonitory

Accordingly, there is a second sense in which war might figure as our introductory. When there is much preparation being made *for* war, we might at least aim to prepare with equal zest *against* it. And war would be as much our idiom in the second case as in the first, except that in the second case war would not be used primarily as a *constitutive* anecdote but rather an an *admonitory* anecdote. That is, an anecdote shaped about war would be designed not so much for stating what mankind *substantially is* as for emphatically pointing out what mankind is *in danger of becoming*.

Where war is used as a constitutive anecdote, the characteristic pattern of thinking would be (with the shadings and transitions omitted): "The universe is substantially war; hence the acts of men, being qualified by the quality of the universal scene, are substantially war; this gamut of war ranges from its attenuated form, in business competition and forensic, to its 'pure' expression in hunt, rape, rapine, and battle."

An attenuated variant of the idiom runs thus: "Men have developed from a competitive situation in nature; hence they are naturally competitive; but their essential competitiveness may, by various economic and/or psychological transformations, be sublimated into coöperation."

[13] This passage was originally written before our country was at war. "Concentration camps" here refers figuratively to our "normal" prison population in peace times.

It is an enlightened survival from the recipe of original sin, after having lost many of the ingredients that modified the notion of original sin. But it does have a certain medicinal kind of humanitarianism, as it contends, in effect: "If we begin by saying the very worst thing possible about mankind, we shall have grounds for expecting something better." For if you call all men crooks, you may look for a margin of honesty, insofar as men must fall short of the ideal state of perfect crookedness.

It is often difficult to tell whether this humanitarian pattern is constitutive or admonitory. Where it is constitutive, we repeat that it should not be accepted unless no better idiom could be found. Thus, the reader may for the time being accept it, since we have admittedly not as yet offered a satisfactory alternative. But where it is admonitory, we should note two objections: (1) whatever its serviceability as an idiom of reduction for purposes of moralistic pamphleteering, it cannot be considered as representative, since it has not been concerned with the central problem of representation, and an anecdote about *what one may become* is hardly the most direct way of discussing *what one is*. And (2) it may be doubted whether a purely admonitory idiom can serve even the deterrent role for which it is designed; for it creates nothing but the image of the enemy, and if men are to make themselves over in the image of the imagery, what other call but that of the enemy is there for them to answer?

Thus, many doctrines of "progress," while unable despite their futuristic cast to locate our substance now in terms of any future substance beyond a vague commingling of euphoria, anaesthesia, and euthanasia, were zestful in building up an admonitory image of our warlike past. This they got by tracing our causal ancestry back to mechanism, accident, and the Jungle (the Jungle in turn being conceived in the idiom of our pure competition—an overemphasis that any inspection of the ecological balances in nature might have dispelled, had it not been that our ecologists themselves were trying to ground a few simple theories of small business not merely in the Constitution of the United States but in the very Constitution of the Universe). But all told, we observe the paradox that these doctrines of progress contributed their part to usher *in* precisely the gloom they thought they were ushering *out*. For the only substance represented with any fullness in their statements was that of the warlike past—and so, what we were admonished *against* was just about the only tangible thing there for us to *be*.

Peace: Constitutive or Directive?

The idiom most thoroughly bound to the militaristic starting-point, however, is the one that might seem to be freest of it: pacifism, where the admonition against the threat of absolute *warlike* substance is replaced by the exhortation towards the promise of absolute peacelike substance. An ideal of peace is reasonable enough as a directive, counter to the presence or imminence of war. But the whole matter is over too soon, if we would attempt to treat purely pacifistic coördinates as an idiom of reduction for the location and representation of actual human relations in history. You may, if you will, imagine a spectrum with absolute war at one end and absolute peace at the other, and with all acts in time considered to be lying somewhere along the intervening series of gradations, according to the varying proportions of the two ingredients. But this alone would be too thorough a mode of reduction to represent the many colors of action as they are realistically experienced. The hortatory idiom, like the admonitory idiom, is too *futuristic* for the representation of what secularly *is*. It does nobly what the investor does ignobly, who cannot see a thing in terms of what it yields him as he looks at it, but can see it only in terms of what it might yield him later. In the investor's case, this is of course a financially profitable way of being ungrateful.

And it is mildly so in the case of all futurists, except the Great Futurist, which is a special case, as we were there given a monument, a Great Pacifist Manifesto necessary as commemorative source, a thing stylistically beautiful for what it *is* and not, like a formula, solely for what use it may be put to. Also, the potential, the ideal future, was there proclaimed to be *the very substance of the present* (the Kingdom of Heaven *is* within you)—so that, from the most exactingly visionary point of view, this was not a mere exhortation about what *might be*, but a statement about what *now is* (a statement which, if not lie or irony, is possible only to an author essentially and exceptionally peaceful).

The ideal future was "within," and *now*—the present itself was thus substantially the future; so the Great Pacifist Manifesto was not purely hortatory futurism, as with the pacifist who would consider peace as a *directive for existence* rather than as *mandatory for being.* In Christ's poetry, peace was a substance, *the* substance—and only insofar as one was consubstantial with it was he truly alive. But in the ordinary brands of pacifism, peace is but an ideal, a general direction towards which one should incline when plotting a course—and as evidence that it is not a statement about what *substantially is,* recall that it could be added to any number of statements about substance, thus:

Men are essentially fools
  or
Men are essentially crooks
  or
Men are essentially automata   But let's
  or   have peace
Men are essentially fighters
  or
Men are essentially (suit yourself)

"Peace" here is not an integral-part-of; it is an annex-to. The two statements are not related as axiom and corollary, they are merely juxtaposed like the planks in a political platform.

Futurism: Religious and Secular

In a sense, the doctrine of the Great Futurism had so absorbed futurism that it was much less futuristic than the typical secular variants of the doctrine: all those ways, in the pragmatism and Puritanism of science and business, whereby one *clothes onself* in the severe promises of future yield, *donning* the idealizations of what one would like to be, *dressing up* in the symbols of lien and bond (we mean: *"investing"*). And we must watch this distinction between the directive and the substantial, since there are very fatal moments in human decision that radically alter our notions of purpose precisely because the role of the future is allowed to usurp the role of the present—an illicit substitution that takes place when the ideal is treated as the substantial, or the directive is treated as the mandatory, or the quantity of promises in the wage is treated as a scale to rate the rationality of the act (the last being a particularly crucial moment for industrial capitalism, which

requires the expenditure of tremendous effort on work that is intrinsically worthless, and hence would be totally irrational except as tested
futuristically, by the promissory nature of pay-day).

We might bring out the contrast in doctrinal tactics between religious
futurism and secular futurism thus: Whereas both would merge present
and future, religious futurism does so by reducing the future to the
present, whereas secular futurism reduces the present to the future.
That is, the religious tactic says: Find what now *is* within you, and you
have found what will be. The secular tactic says: Find what will bring
you promises, and you have found what is worth doing now. Seeing
the future in terms of the present, as against seeing the present in terms
of the future, has at least this one advantage: that the present *forever is,*
whereas the future *forever is not.* The ontological style of religion, as
contrasted with the futuristic (admonitory of hortatory) style of
naturalism and business, also had the advantage, from the formal point
of view, that it did not require one to tack on a humanitarian annex to
a scene essentially lacking in personal attributes. In the naturalist
strategy, to a bill proclaiming the *what is* to be essentially of one sort,
there had to be added a rider legislating that the *what might be* was of
essentially a contrary sort. And the greater the indebtedness proclaimed in the bill, the greater was the compensatory inflation in the
promissory rider. For without this double-entry system of bookkeeping that countered the malign impersonality of nature with the benign
impersonality of institutionalized philanthropy (maintained by "dead
hand"), men who had once been of equal worth in the eyes of God
would but become of equal worthlessness in the eyelessness of God-
lessness.

We can, of course, but speculate vaguely as to just how this mode of
thought was carried through. (That is, to what extent the ontological
statement was itself futuristic, stylistically rephrasing the optative
"would that it were so" in the mood of the indicative "It *is* so".) For
our immediate inheritance contains several centuries of strongly
futuristic thought, developed by the anti-religious, anti-aesthetic, anti-
ritualistic pragmatism and utilitarianism of business and technology.
We are now idealists all, investors all (even the most impoverished
among us), capable only of *glimpsing* a philosophy of Being (while we

have gone beyond philosophies of Becoming, into philosophies of the merely About-to-Become, either gerundive or future participle).

To be sure, if those economists are right who contend that the market for long-term investments of private capital is rapidly and permanently dwindling, in proportion as this dwindling progresses the futuristic idiom will come to seem less "natural." For in proportion as financial futurism weakens in the narrower, materialist circle, we may expect a corresponding weakness of futuristic imaginings in the wider, cultural circle. Likewise, the power of the dead hand in permanent bequests to institutions of philanthropic cast will promote such a change, as will also the fixing of a bureaucratic order (as per nepotism in private corporations and permanent employment through civil service in political corporations). In sum: the greatly lowered incidence of futuristic opportunities in the financial realm would alter the nature of the problem to be solved on the cultural level; and a greater stress upon the qualities of the here and now would be the most readily available solution. A major factor operating against this solution, however, should be the extremely fragmentary nature of so many of the occupational acts that go with technological division of labor. The vacational act is now much better rounded than the vocational act, whereby something so material as a means of production would re-enforce the Puritan, utilitarian incentives to class the cult of the present-for-itself as dissipation and distraction. The ontological could be restored to the category of vocation only if "mediation" rather than "utility" were taken as the primary characteristic of vocation. Few vocational acts under technology have this character, which can at most be got "after hours," but to trace the ancestry of one's values from the vacational act would be too much like playing golf *pro bono publico*.

Position Epitomized

Meanwhile, it is important that we try to see around the edges of our customary perspective, if we would understand the part that motivational assumptions play in implicitly or explicitly substantiating human decisions, hence in shaping human relations. And related to this, is a still more important reason: When the restricting of investment proceeds without a corresponding change in men's concept of motives, you must get the aggressive futurism of National-Socialist expansion and (or) the balked futurism of would-be business enterprisers who, deprived of an outlet for their ambitions, and with no other conception of effort to replace these, turn in their disgruntlement to a hatred of Jews, foreigners, Negroes, "isms," etc., as a ritualistic outlet. The reduction of the future to the present may be glimpsed perhaps behind the poet's verdict of posterity. For when he, now suffering neglect, contends that the future will vindicate him, he most assuredly does not mean that his work will later possess some intrinsic quality it now lacks. He means that the recognition of his work in the future is implicit in the quality of the work *now*. And so the present is charged with futurity, as the gun *will* shoot because it *is* loaded.

So, the subject of futurism, introduced as a way of making the necessary distinction between the hortatory-admonitory and the representative, required us to venture into a concern with the relationship between ontology and history. We pointed out that the anecdote of peace, as a statement about ontology (about the nature of Substance, or *Being*), was much less futuristic than much temporal, financial thinking that is a secular variant of it. We said that Christ was not making a purely directive statement: "Let us have peace," but was proclaiming that Peace was identical with Being, and that Being now *is*, and that only insofar as people were peaceful did they actually partake of Being, and that the promissory must be *now, implicit*, "within you" —while we took the futuristic element here to be a kind of temporalist restatement, translating a doctrine about ontological simultaneity into the parables of historical sequence. And we tried to establish this distinction between the ontological and the futuristic because of the fact that men's judgments are based upon assumptions as to what constitutes the scenic background of their acts.

The quality of the situation in which we act qualifies our act—and so, behind a judgment, there lies, explicitly or implicitly, the concept of a constitution that substantiates the judgment. And by trying to distinguish between Peace as a statement about Being, and Peace as a pacifist, humanitarian exhortation (between ontology and futurism) we came upon relations among indicative, imperative, and optative which, we shall try to show later, have much bearing upon the strategies for the substantiating of values. (At the moment it is enough to recall that men induce themselves and others to act by devices that deduce "let us" from "we must" or "we should." And "we must" and "we should" they deduce in turn from "it *is*"—for only by assertions as to how things *are* can we finally substantiate a judgment.)

As for Peace: when Peace is considered as the Universal Substantive, we can find some valid grounds for considering it as basic anecdote for the discussion of Being. For if history is dialectical, and dialectics is "polemic" and "eristic" (with all the various shades along the spectrum of strife and competition), and if even thinkers so secular as the Marxists would hold that history itself dwindles to a benign impotence insofar as the perfect state of Communism is attained (because, in a perfect state of Communism, there would by definition be no social classifications out of which might arise the conflicts necessary to the dialectic *agon*)—thus even the eschatology of revolutionary history would have its ground in an ontology of peace. And, if the dialectic process is "war," then *any permanent statement* about the dialectic process would be "peace." That is, as the stable, the unchanging, a statement *at rest,* it would be the "technical equivalent" of peace. However, I doubt whether we, as warriors tainted with the "original sin" of the fall from Edenic oneness into the dialectical Babel of conflicting interests, could conceive of such peace as any but the peace of the grave, the *"requiescat in pace"* kind of peace. Indeed, we are so "corrupt" that, when we think of a two-termed dialectic, of Peace and War, we cannot think of the relation as that of "Peace and War at peace," but as "The Struggle Between Peace and War" (with peace as something "to be fought for").

In any event, the world as we know it, the world in history, cannot be described in its particularities by an idiom of peace. Though we may, ideally, convert the dialectic into a chart of the dialectic (replacing a development by a calculus), we are actually in a world at war—a world at combat—and even a calculus must be developed with the dialectics of participation by "the enemy"—hence the representative anecdote must contain militaristic ingredients. It may not be an anecdote of peace—but it may be an anecdote giving us the purification of war.

Men's conception of motive, we have said, is integrally related to their conception of substance. Hence, to deal with problems of motive is to deal with problems of substance. And a thing's substance is that whereof it is constituted. Hence, a concern with substance is a concern with the problems of constitutionality. And where questions of constitutionality are central, could we do better than select the subject of a Constitution and its typical resources as the anecdote about which to shape our terms? Particularly in keeping with out conviction that human relations are at every turn affected by the nature of verbal dialectic, we should welcome so "substantival" an anecdote. And as for its relation to the broadest of all oppositions, such as war and peace, the many and the one, the dialectic of historical change and the calculus of fixed coördinates, the survival of the Constitutional titles or clauses through radical reconstructions of the national situation will give us testimony about the nature of unity and division that serves pretty much as the over-all category for everything, and certainly for human relations.

Imagistic and Conceptual Summaries

Since, however, we had gone from the choice of the Constitution as introductory anecdote to a pre-introduction justifying this choice, and since the draft of the "pre-introduction" was written, in actual fact, later than the draft of the section that was to follow it, we became very self-conscious about the relation between beginnings and endings. A beginning, we observed, should "implicitly contain" its ending—and an ending should be the explicit culmination of all that had flowed from the beginning. But also, there was some kind of almost mystic reversibility here, and the hint of an infinite regress that made us wonder whether we might need a pre-pre-introduction, itself preceded by an introduction, etc. Uneasily, as we found ourselves following the pattern of Coleridge in retracing the course of his Brook, we stated the matter thus:

New sentences, inserted as preparatory to the opening sentence, would have to be preceded in turn by preparations—a process that would require one to write a book backwards, by going on and on, adding one beginning before another, as though the book had been elicited by a relentless cross-examiner, thus:

Q. And why did you begin with this?
A: For such-and-such reason, that logically preceded it.
Q: And why was this reason logically prior?
A. For such-and-such other reason, logically prior to that—etc.

And were you explicitly to write a book in the Q-A form, you would soon find that this pretense of *retracing* your steps, of *going back* to the step-before-the-step-before-the-step, etc., really had all the qualities of a *going forward,* of a *building up,* not like the uncovering of prior assumptions but like the discovering of new conclusions, or "principles." If the book were then written in exactly this same order, the attempt to arrive at the "logically prior" would take such form that the "logically prior" would be the "temporally final."

About this time, reading Richard Wright's *Native Son,* I made some observations very relevant to these quandaries. I noticed that there were *two kinds* of epitomizing in the novel, one imagistic and the other conceptual. That is, the story opens with Bigger's killing of the rat as it comes from behind the wall, an episode that symbolically represents or foreshadows the course of the plot (as Bigger's rebirth will be attained through the killing of the "rat" within himself). But as the story comes to a close we have the summation by lawyer Max, a doctrinal account of Bigger's situation. And this, I realized, was a culmination of the book in the sense that an essayist's last chapter might recapitulate in brief the argument of his whole book.

There was, then, the imagistic source out of which the story flowed; and there was the conceptual summation in which it concluded. There was an "introductory anecdote" and there were final ideological affirmations which might, to intensify our sense of reversibility here, be called a set of "principles" (i.e., "beginnings").

Genetically, however, this statement of the case would not be enough. It is enough *ontologically* (i.e., as a statement about the structure of the book as it stands). But in an article, *How Bigger Was Born,* Wright states that the opening episode was one of the *last* things he added to the book (in other words, he himself, in the course of working through the logic of Bigger's development, *finally* came upon the episodic imagery that would sum Bigger up, or implicitly "name his number"). And as for the conceptual material, the social philosophy which Max propounds, we are told in the same article that the novel was originally of purely narrative cast, a murder story, and that the social (sociological and socialist) interpretations were woven into it afterwards. (Our own version of the matter would be, of course, that the author, after the symbolic committing of the offences through his imaginative identification with Bigger, had thus ritualistically "transcended" the offenses, arriving thereby at a different state, on the critical level, which he then worked back into the book in terms of concept, or doctrine. His role as Marxist critic transcended his role as Negro novelist.)

Five Basic Terms as Beginnings

But while we were thus pondering about the vagaries whereby beginnings and endings may become so indistinguishable (precisely the vagary that must have prompted Aristotle to give us his concept of "final cause" as "prime mover"), we found our pre-pre-introduction actually taking shape. And this we found in the selection of our pentad, as a "final" set of terms that seemed to cluster about our thoughts about the Constitution as an "enactment." (A similar saliency we had found in Maitland's reference to the first British Parliament as being less a "body" than an "act.") And since we had already, in other writings, equated "dramatic" and dialectical," our decision to feature the five terms was accompanied automatically by our decision to use dramatic anecdotes as introductory illustration, with the material on "the Constitutional Wish" assigned to a position as wind-up.

As for the five terms themselves, we found that they needed nothing to proceed them (thus, our uneasy forebodings as to the need for an infinite regress of introductions were suddenly cleared up). They could, in themselves, be stated as a beginning of the "Let there be—and there was" sort. And their justification could *follow,* as one noted their place in the "collective revelation" of common usage, and showed the range of their applicability.

But though *terms* are thus, we now feel, the proper starting point for a presentation, we should still want always to have it borne in mind, particularly in our era, when scientific experiment has so greatly caught our fancy, that the featuring of some particular scientific experiment as crucial is an anecdote implicitly dictating the selection of a terminology. And often, in being startled by the fact that the given experiment is "true," we forget to ask ourselves whether the anecdote is also sufficiently *representative* of our particular subject for it to yield representative terms.

Meanings of "Constitution"

To convey our view of Constitutions, let us now begin, dutifully, by recalling the ordinary dictionary usages:

1. The act or process of constituting; the action of enacting, establishing, or appointing; enactment; establishment; formation.

2. The state of being; that form of being, or structure and connection of parts, which constitutes and characterizes a system or body; natural condition; structure; texture; conformation.

3. The aggregate of all one's inherited physical qualities; the aggregate of the vital powers of an individual, with reference to ability to endure hardship, resist disease, etc.

4. The aggregate of mental qualities; temperament.

5. The fundamental, organic law or principles of government of a nation, state, society, or other organized body of men, embodied in written documents, or implied in the institutions and usages of the country or society; also, a written instrument embodying such organic law, and laying down fundamental rules and principles for the conduct of affairs.

6. An authoritative ordinance, regulation or enactment; especially, one made by a Roman emperor, or one affecting ecclesiastical doctrine or discipline.

Obviously in this list we are dealing with a word that has to do with matters of substance and motive (as one should always consider likely, when a member of the Stance Family is involved). And just as obviously, the word covers all five terms of our pentad. A legal constitution is an *act* or body of acts (or enactments), done by *agents* (such as rulers, magistrates, or other representative persons), and designed (*purpose*) to serve as a motivational ground (*scene*) of subsequent actions, it being thus an instrument (*agency*) for the shaping of human relations.

We shall, of course, focus our attention upon the legal applications of the word. But we cite the other usages to make it apparent that, as is typical of the Stance Family, it readily branches into a whole universe of terms. And in particular we hope that, by recalling this wide range of usages, we shall by comparison not seem to be interpreting the notion of a Constitution too broadly in the much narrower list of instances we treat under this head.

The dictionary itself, after the fifth usage (we are quoting from Webster's Revised Unabridged), pauses to remind us:

> In England the Constitution is unwritten, and may be modified from time to time by act of Parliament. In the United States a constitution cannot ordinarily be modified, except through such processes as the constitution itself ordains.

And behind this distinction we may glimpse two relations between law and custom: first, law as the mere codification of custom (a relation such as we detect in the expression, "That sort of thing just isn't done," which would construct a precept for the future by obedience to the past as already constituted); and second, law as innovative, as a device for the transformation of customs. In a given instance, of course, it is difficult to decide exactly which of these functions, the conservative or the innovative, a given legal enactment or judicial decision is performing. For when a new situation arises, the treatment of it in terms of past fictions may often have a very radical effect, whereas a corresponding adoption of new coördinates would have made for a temperance of response that in the end would have perpetuated the old ways longer. For instance, the revolutionary changes in the living conditions of America since the adoption of the Constitution were mostly the work of men who hired expensive legal talent to get their *innovations* sanctioned in the name of *tradition*.

A constitution is a *substance*—and as such, it is a set of *motives*. There are constitutions of a purely natural sort, such as geographical and physiological properties, that act motivationally upon us. We are affected by one another's mental constitutions, or temperaments. A given complex of customs and values, from which similar customs and values are deduced, is a constitution. And we may, within limits, arbitrarily set up new constitutions, legal substances designed to serve as motives for the shaping or transforming of behavior.

Even in the case of the British Constitution, which is an undefined accumulation of customs, laws, and judicial interpretations, certain charters formulated along the way stand out with greater prominence, as featured acts, more thoroughly culminative or representative or critical than the general body, such as the Magna Carta wrested from King John in the early thirteenth century, the Petition of Right at the beginning of the seventeenth century, and at the close of the century the Bill of Rights confirming the results of Cromwell's Revolution. As for the United States, the Declaration of Independence is as typical of constitutional tactics as is the Constitution itself, in proclaiming a common substance, or motivational basis, for the rebellious colonies.

At an earlier time, when the style of secular law was closer to that of religious law, and the notion of legal precedent was interwoven with the anecdotes of past living, either historical or legendary, the Old Testament and the Talmud were an accumulated Constitution, and the Mosaic code a representative feature. The New Testament would figure here as a new act, a Constitution that, whatever its continuity with the traditions from which it emerged, had the quality of a discontinuity (as a son, encountering influences alien to his father, might continue the father's training in ways that were, in the father's eyes, an alienation)—and a representative feature, a summarizing or culminating moment, would be the Sermon on the Mount.

However, we must not take on too many burdens. For present purposes, we need merely note that the law of pagan Rome, whatever religious qualities it may have had for Stoic administrators, with their attitude towards the state as a religious body, was felt by the Christians as an alien act, not *their* representative act; and the secular-religious dissociation was not merged again until the triumph of Christianity as a state religion under Constantine (a merger in which Augustine played a major role stylistically). Over the centuries, this theocratic re-association was again gradually dissociated, with faith and knowledge changing their relationship, step by step, from that of complementary counterparts to that of antagonist counterparts.

The typical political platform may be thought of as a kind of flimsy and ephemeral constitution, a set of motivations slung together for the needs of the moment. For the most part, political platforms are best analyzed on the rhetorical level, as they are quite careless grammatically. Also, there is a form, the political tract, which has the properties of both constitutions and platforms. In upholding or attacking some political or social philosophy, which is treated with some degree of thoroughness and complexity, the political tract will necessarily, in the course of its exposition, propound a theory of social action (of substance and motivation) that justifies us in classing such works as constitutional variants.

In fact, it was in the attempt to review two books of this sort that we first found ourselves confronting what we consider the typical properties of constitutions. The books are *Poetry and Anarchism*, by Herbert Read, and *Marxism: An Autopsy*, by H. B. Parkes. And perhaps the handiest way to lead us into the kind of analysis we would develop here, is to explain the problems we encountered in the course of trying to chart the structures of these books.

Technical Immunity of "Anarchism" as Ideal

In considering the Read book, we found ourselves confronting the following situation: The author began by a claim of immunity. He said that he would assert certain social ideals, of anarchistic cast; he would, he said, put these forward as a "vision." And he insisted that his critics, in examining this vision, were not entitled to reject it on the ground of its "impracticality," since practicality is not the proper test of visions.

The "vision," it seemed as we progressed with the reading, had a great many aspects that contradicted one another. We were sure that, in order to enjoy some of the promises proclaimed in the author's vision of ideal anarchy, you would have to forego others. Yet we did not see how we could legitimately raise objections on this score, for we had to admit that the author was justified in his claim that a "vision" was immune to such tests. One might even, in one's "vision," quite properly include among his batch of ideals, or promises, a clause to the effect that in this hypothetical world of pure intention, or pure futurity, all contradictions would be reconciled. And that would be a very noble ideal, an ideal well worth holding. To be sure, it would not be "practicable"—but ideals are never practicable; indeed, they are *by definition* something that you don't attain; they are merely *directions* in which you aim. (You can't hit "North," for instance, though you may hit a target placed to the north of you.)

As for contradictions, we had to admit that each ideal is like a sovereign state, proclaiming and maintaining its identity independently of other sovereign states. And we conceded that, ideal anarchy being by definition a state of affairs in which the lion and the lamb shall lie together, implicit in the very nature of such a project there is an un-written clause to the effect that in this realm all contradictions are to be reconciled; hence it would simply be irrelevant to concern oneself with contradictions at all. For ideal anarchy is, like Christ's vision, the vision of a world in which contradictions merge. Anarchy, as the ultimate extreme of individualism, would be a state of absolute conti-nuity approached through a state of absolute discontinuity.

The thought of Christ's vision reminded us that there is a test applicable to visions: the test of moral grandeur and stylistic felicity. And we began to evaluate Mr. Read's vision on this count, comparing and contrasting it with some of the Great Manifestoes, such as the Decalogue, The Sermon on the Mount, the various proclamations of rights in the British Constitution, the Declaration of Independence, and the vigorously muscular "pre-Constitution" that Marx and Engels laid down for Communism (a document that is, to be sure, explicitly con-cerned with tests of practicability, but would not figure from this point of view if treated as a "vision").

"Anarcho-Syndicalism"—the Ideal Organized

However, while we were grudgingly and laboriously changing our terms of analysis to the kind deemed proper for the appreciation of a "vision," we began to notice a new development in Mr. Read's book. The subject became modified. And instead of merely enunciating a vision of ideal anarchy, the author went on to propose the kind of social and political organization by which this ideal could be embodied. In this rebirth, the subject fittingly transformed its name, being no longer merely "anarchism," but "anarcho-*syndicalism.*"

When we confronted this new, hyphenated term, we realized that the second member of the pair was of a different order than the first member. For only the first member was "ideal," thus enjoying the immunity to questions of practicability that goes with the ideal, or heavenly. The second was a "worldly" term; and thus, like all worldly terms, it dealt with a realm to which tests of practicability do very rigorously apply. The term, "Anarchism," we might say, is the Sermon on the Mount stage in Mr. Read's church; but with the term, "syndicalism," he moves into the epistolary, Pauline realm of organ-izational problems, involving elections, membership drives, finances, and the like. If we think of the hyphenated terms as "counterparts," we find them related as "soul" and "body." And though, in the realm of the soul, the lion and the lamb may lie down together, in the realm of the body the lion either eats the lamb or starves. We know, in brief, that the realm of the body is the realm of "contradictions." Hence, as soon as Mr. Read endowed his vision with a body, he sacrificed his claims that his book should be considered purely on the ideal level.

In sum, in "anarchism" we have an *ideal* term, in "syndicalism" we have a *practical* term—and what we can treat in the former realm as ideal mergers, we must consider in the latter realm as practical contradictions. In the former realm, no compromise is necessary. In the latter realm you encounter the necessity to compromise at every turn. For not only must you, in the process of embodying some one ideal, frustrate the embodiment of some other ideal that points in a different direction; but also, in the mere act of embodying any ideal at all, you are "translating" it into another and "inferior" idiom—and this "translation" may, as per the *"traduttore traditore"* formula, be treated as either a "copy" or a "betrayal" of the original.

This is not the place in which to discuss all the important deployments of Mr. Read's book. By our interpretation, the hyphenated term, "anarcho-syndicalism" is an oxymoron. The first member refers to a spiritual state that is *free of organizational hazards* through being *free of organization,* and the second member refers to the *kind of social organization* through which this happy state would be attained. Hence, all told, the hyphenated pair would, by our way of thinking, add up to something like "disorganized organization."

The Anarcho-Syndicalist "Constitution"

The transformations that the argument undergoes make it difficult to chart the dialectical alignments briefly. But we might try conveying the general quality of Mr. Read's approach. While granting that "form, pattern, and order are essential aspects of existence," he holds that "in themselves they are the attributes of death." This would seem to give us a dialectic of Being vs. Having-Become, with the "unformed" or "to be formed" as "life" and the "formed" as "death." And when he says that "In order to create it is necessary to destroy; and the agent of destruction in society is the poet," we find "destruction," usually a "death" word, redeemed as a bringer of life (an equation typical of Futurism, but "re-Christianized"; for though the Futurists celebrate war and cruelty, Mr. Read celebrates his destructiveness differently, saying: "Peace is anarchy").

The basic pattern of the book involves the equating of poetry, anarchism, syndicalism, in opposition to such institutional structures as church, business, the state, and parties of professional politicians. He would have a world related not authoritatively, as father and sons, but in the true equality of brotherhood. And he would define the anarchist as the "man who, in his manhood, dares to resist the authority of the father," including here the rejection of the leader principle which involves "a blind unconscious identification of the leader and the father." (This rejection, and the destruction of institutional structures interwoven with the parental symbolism would, presumably, be done peacefully. At least, this would be the "ideal." Poetry is here viewed in terms of the "permanent revolution," minus the political application which Trotsky gave to the term. But for our purposes, the crucial moments in the book are to be seen in the difference between the author's handling of the relation between "poetry" and "business" and his handling of the relation between "imagination" and "reason."

We are told that "the doctrinaire civilizations which are forced on the world—capitalist, fascist and marxist—by their very structure and principles exclude the values in which and for which the poet lives." And in considering the suicide of the revolutionary Russian poet, Mayakovsky, he writes of poetic development thus:

> The essential process is that of a seed falling on fertile ground, germinating and growing and in due course reaching maturity. Now just as certainly as the flower and the fruit are implicit in the single seed, so the genius of a poet or painter is contained within the individual. The soil must be favourable, the plant must be nourished; it will be distorted by winds and by accidental injuries. But the growth is unique, the configuration unique, the fruit unique. All apples are very much alike, but no two are exactly the same. But that is not the point: a genius is the tree which has produced the unknown fruit, the golden apples of Hesperides. But Mayakovsky was a tree which one year was expected to produce plums of a uniform size and appearance; a few years later apples; and finally cucumbers. No wonder that he finally broke down under such an unnatural strain!

To ask that a poet become anything so naked as a cucumber tree is, I admit, to place him under a terrific strain. Mayakovsky himself, we might recall, left a suicide note in which he referred to a "Love boat smashed against mores," and on this point Mr. Read writes:

> Obviously there was a love affair, but to our surprise there were also the *mores*—the social conventions against which this love-boat smashed. Mayakovsky was in a special sense the poet of the Revolution: he celebrated its triumph and its progressive achievements in verse which had all the urgency and vitality of the event. But he was to perish by his own hand like any miserable in-grown subjectivist of bourgeois capitalism. The Revolution had evidently not created an atmosphere of intellectual confidence and moral freedom.

One may, of course, put many interpretations upon this event. One may note that the kind of mentality best adapted to flourish at the most liquid stages of a Revolution is hardly likely to be equally adapted to the later period of greater crystallization and organization. And one may wonder whether Mr. Read is not asking more of life than it can give in his assumption that a Revolution should not go through various stages and finally settle into some kind of relatively fixed organizational pattern, with its *mores* (though I have been told that, in this particular case, even the husband of the woman with whom Mayakovsky was in love condoned their affair, since he was a close friend of the poet and a great admirer of his verses, but the poet suffered because of his conflicting attachments to both the friend and the wife).

In any event, we have been quoting to indicate that Mr. Read treats poetry and the world's business as in *opposition* (and by poetry, he means not merely a poetic *attitude,* but the actual *body* of the work done by producing poets). But when he discusses reason and imagination, he treats them as "balancing" each other (even going so far, in fact, as to speak of the "rule of reason," which seems to us the smuggling of a highly incongruous term into an anarchistic project—for if you allow of anarchist "rule," I should think you would by the same token bring back state and *mores,* hence also fathers and leaders). Or, to quote once more:

> I balance anarchism with surrealism, reason with romanticism, the understanding with the imagination, function with freedom. Happiness, peace, contentment—these are all one and are due to the per-

fection of the balance. We may speak of these things in dialectical terms—terms of contradiction, negation, synthesis—the meaning is the same. The world's unhappiness is caused by men who incline so much in one direction that they upset this balance, destroy the synthesis. The very delicacy and subtlety of the equilibrium is of its essence; for joy is only promised to those who strive to achieve it, and who, having achieved it, hold it lightly poised.

To draw this all together: we note that the first pair, poetry and business, confronting one another in the practical world, are conceived as in *conflict,* whereas these other pairs confront each other as in *equilibrium.* (Indeed, in a more rigorously conducted argument, we might even be able to hammer the alignments into such symmetrical shape that "imagination" would be the idealistic equivalent of "poetry" and "reason" the idealistic equivalent of structure, organization, rational order, methods of accountancy and proof, etc., in short, the equivalent of "rule," which is to say, "authority.") And it was this distinction, as a development implicit in Mr. Read's hyphenated term, that struck us as particularly relevant to the tactics of Constitutions. A constitution may, for instance, propound a set of generalized rights or duties, and all these may be considered as a grand promissory unity, a *panspermia* in which they all exist together in perfect peace and amity. Yet when, in the realm of the practical, a given case comes before the courts, you promptly find that this *merger* or *balance* or *equilibrium* among the Constitutional clauses becomes transformed into a *conflict* among the clauses—and to satisfy the promise contained in one clause, you must forego the promise contained in another.

A New Constitution for Laissez-faire

With Mr. Parkes's book, we found this distinction between the ideal and the practical taking a variant form. His book is an argument against Marxism, undertaken from the position of a modified *laissez-faire.* Mr. Parkes did not present his material as a "vision," hence we were at no point called upon to consider it without regard for matters of contradiction. But when we tried to make a diagram of the alignments, so as to know just where the battle was being fought, we found a situation as follows:

First, we noticed that the concept of *laissez-faire* underwent an important alteration, as the author distinguished between "negative" and "positive" *laissez-faire.* "According to the doctrines of eighteenth-century liberalism the functions of the state were negative; it must maintain order by preventing individuals from injuring each other. For the state to issue positive commands, dictating to individuals what they must do, was tyranny." And the author would now have us give to *laissez-faire* this positive emphasis, though in a modified form. To get the pattern underlying this concept, let us define "negative" *laissez-faire* as "hands-off." Then "positive" *laissez-faire* would be "hands off, with a measure of hands-on." (This interpretation is, of course, offered without consulting the author.) Obviously, we have here, phrased as a distinction between positive and negative, an ambiguity of the "potential" or "substantial" sort; hence, proposals of a distinctly hands-on sort can be recommended in the name of hands-off. Under the head of positive liberalism, for instance, Mr. Parkes proposes that the concept of property rights should be extended to include the property rights of every worker in his job. It is a proposal I have myself subscribed to (in *Attitudes Toward History*); but it never occurred to me that such a *universalizing* of the concept of property rights, assured by government interference, could be treated under the head of *laissez-faire,* or "hands-off." As indeed it could not, without flat misnomer, if the author had not proposed his transitional term, "positive" *laissez-faire,* which we, in order to make its form apparent, would call "hands-off *à la* hands-on." The author's purpose, he says, is to reform the practice of capitalism, "not to abandon the principles." And since he would thus preserve the same *substance,* it is understandable that he might strive to retain the same *name* for that substance (or rather, its same *good* name, as tested by the criteria of the liberalism to which his book is addressed).

A Spectrum of Terms Between "Freedom" and "Capitalism"

In attempting to clarify the alignment of the author's key terms, we found a spectrum of such terms, ranging in a graded series from "freedom" on the pure, heavenly, idealistic side, to "capitalism" on the impure, worldly, practical side. The major members of this series seemed to be arranged in a delicately differentiated set of modulations, thus:

On one side, we have freedom, against which there is nothing to be said. It is the ideal term. On the other side, we have the practical, or organizational term, capitalism, against which the author frequently says almost as much as the Marxists (perhaps even more, since the Marxist dialectic requires that capitalism be saluted as a necessary and beneficial stage in the cultural sequence, relatively "progressive" in its destruction of feudalism, and relatively "reactionary" only in its resistance to modern socialism). The major terms intervening between these two are: humanism, *laissez-faire,* free market, the price system (i.e., money), and industrialism. Thus the whole series would be:

> freedom
> humanism
> *laissez-faire*
> free market
> price system (money)
> industrialism
> capitalism

Let us examine these terms by first considering their resources without reference to the actual uses to which the author might put them.

"Freedom," you will note, is the "God" term, since God alone is conceivable as *wholly* free. "Freedom," as the dialectical counterpart of "necessity," may be treated as either in *opposition to* "necessity" or in *apposition with* "necessity." Or, if you divide "necessity" into two terms, one impersonal ("law") and the other personal ("authority" or "dictatorship"), you could treat "freedom" as in apposition with some kind of natural law and in opposition to some kind of leadership or bureaucratic control. For instance, freedom could be in apposition with the laws of the "natural" workings of the free market in goods or ideas, and in opposition to dictatorial or monopolistic interference with such "spontaneous" adjustments. The early liberal slogan calling for a "government by laws rather than a government by men" is an off-shoot of this distinction.

Next adjoining "freedom" comes "humanism." The human is the area of the "substantially" free. Accordingly, "humanism" may be treated as a philosophic attitude that retains the God-term ambiguously. It is a stepping-down of the God-term, a confinement to a narrower circumference, a translation into an idiom that may be treated either as having retained something of the pure original or having lost it by reason of defects in the material (defects which, according to the theological doctrines that shaped the development of Western humanism, were themselves an outgrowth of freedom, since the defects were derived from the fall of man, and man had fallen because his "substantial" freedom had also included the possibility that he could carry freedom to excess).

The next adjoining term, *laissez-faire*, restricts our circumference still further. Indeed, we are here in a marginal area ambiguously covering both the ideal and the organizational. As a principle, ("live and let live") the term is quite ideal. Yet it also refers to various institutional devices for translating the perfection of this ideal into the more or less imperfect world of practical approximations. We could obviously, without violating the orthodox resources of the term, slip back and forth between these two quite different meanings; and conversely, we could treat a given approximation (or deviation) either as a "betrayal" of the ideal or as the retention of the ideal "substantially."

As we move to the next adjoining term, "free market," we are brought more definitely into the purely organizational area. Not wholly, to be sure, for the epithet, "free," is a bridge that can lead us back to heavenly or Edenic origins, though these origins are quite eliminated from the companion term "market." "Free market" is, just ever so faintly, an oxymoron, as would become clearer if we stopped to realize that at the very basis of the concept is the notion of a *labor* market, i.e., a market where men's ability to work for others is bought and sold. A slave market is also a market in which man's ability to work for others is bought and sold. And where a free labor market is the general economic scene in which men must economically act, it is obvious that the *ability* to sell one's services (or one's partial servitudes) is also synonymous with the *need* to sell one's services. Now, a need is not "freedom," but "necessity," and a necessity not *from within* but *from without*. A necessity *from within* can be equated with freedom, as Spinoza contended, since in accordance with necessity so conceived one "must" follow the laws of his own internal development, which would equal freedom, as per Mr. Read's poetic tree prior to the time when political leaders demanded that it give forth cucumbers. But a necessity *from without* is compulsion. And when a need to sell one's services is *imposed upon* one, the market to this extent would be not a "free" market, but a "slave" market.

However, at this point let us look at the next adjoining term, "money" (or, in Mr. Parkes' preferred equivalent, the "price system"). And let us note that, by the introduction of money as motive, the "substantial" freedom is retained. For once man has learned to transcend the material aspect of goods and services by perceiving them in terms of the money motive, then the criterion of the market has become a "second nature" with him. The market motive is then not merely scenic; it is not felt as an alien and outward compulsion (as it is felt, for instance, by members of a primitive African tribe who are forced, by the hut tax, to abandon their non-monetary tribal economy and to solicit work on the white man's plantations in order to get the cash which the requirements of the new economic scene impose upon them). The market motive is also "personal," a spontaneous rationale of conduct *within* the agent. Thus, the medium of money translates the labor market from a "slave" market into a "free" market.

The next adjoining word on our list is "industrialism"—and then, finally, "capitalism." These are terms for subjects wholly in the practical realm, hence terms which, in all strictness, should be treated ambivalently, or ironically, from the ethical, or evaluative point of view, as their placement in "this imperfect world" should endow them with qualities good, bad, and indifferent. In Western history, it is impossible to deal with one of these terms without implying the other.

But we should note that behind "industrialism" (and behind capitalist accountancy) lies another key term, "science," which we should also have included in our list, but which we omitted because of an awkwardness in assigning it a place in the series. For though "industrialism," as "applied science," is a worldly, organizational term, there is behind it "pure science," which carries us directly back to our God-term. For "science," as the study and discovery of "laws," is directly concerned with "necessity," and "necessity" is as divine as "freedom," being its reflex. Though "applied science" may lack the spiritual attributes of "pure science," as a member of the same family it may retain these qualities "substantially"; and its devices and routines compose a material body that is always there to help us appreciate the vast amount of intelligence and imaginativeness ("free" attributes) that lie behind the formulation and utilization of scientific laws (somewhat as religious dogma, which is sometimes said to conceal religious insight behind its rigidities and formalisms, may on the other hand be said to preserve a firm structure of forms that maintains the continuous possibility of true understanding, since everything is there in the semi-darkness, laid out in perfect formation, and it will gleam the moment a sudden light is thrown upon it).

Strategic Choice of Circumference for "Freedom"

We refer the reader to Mr. Parkes's book, if he would decide in detail just how the author chooses to exploit these resources. Our primary interest here is not in giving a full report of the book, but in considering the grammatical relations inherent in the key terms which the author selects as the coördinates for his calculus of human relations. So we shall here attempt to treat only of the aspects that bear most directly on Constitutional tactics.

Though noting that the humanist valuation of freedom is related historically to theological doctrine, Mr. Parkes simply takes this value as part of the socially given, considering it sufficiently well grounded through being grounded in a great and representative tradition. He might also have derived his value from purely naturalistic motivations (that is: an organism that lives by locomotion must desire conditions that allow a primitive "freedom of motion"; and in the evaluations of human speech, this strong preference would be fittingly conceptualized as "love of freedom-in-general," a standard that would be the ideal counterpart of the practical interests). But had he deduced his value from either the theological or the naturalistic circumference, he could not so easily have carried out his tactical aim to present "freedom" and the "free market" as synonymous. For there is no "market" in either heaven or the state of nature—hence, if freedom were ancestrally situated in either of these sources, we could treat the free market as but one idiom among many for translating the "ideal" into practical equivalents. And even if we asserted that it is, by and large, the best idiom, no one could claim by the same token that it is the best idiom for every occasion—for no idiom enjoys such categorical and universal supremacy.

Mr. Parkes avoids these embarrassments by beginning with a social circumference, a traditional cult of freedom which has become a part of our second nature. And since another tradition, the monetary motivation or rationale of pricing, has become a part of our second nature, he thus has, all woven together and supporting one another: freedom, quantitative or monetary pricing, and the controlling laws of the free market (which cease to be a "free" government by law, and become instead a tyrannical government by men, insofar as private monopolies or public dictatorships usurp the legal function of control).

In discussing the free market, Mr. Parkes neglects to treat the ways in which the conception of the free market involved the conception of a free *labor* market. We can't know why he made this omission; but we can note that, having made it, he has a less difficult job in presenting his own proposals in the name of *laissez-faire*. For if a worker would be guaranteed property rights in his job, there must be a vigorous governmental interference and control in the administrative policies of private business—and such "positive" *laissez-faire* would seem more of a misnomer if we were forced to realize that it was designed to "preserve the principles" of the free market by destroying the free market at a most strategic point, the free *labor* market.

Money as "God Term"

In the stress he places upon the price system, or monetary motivation, as a device for rationalizing the structure and trends of the free market, we probably come upon the crucial moment in his concept of substance. Money would be, in the technical sense, his "God term." For a God term designates the ultimate motivation, or substance, of a Constitutional frame. And as we have previously noted how the ambiguities of substance cause extrinsic and intrinsic motivation to merge, we note that when men respond to the laws of the market and its price system as second nature, the qualities of the *scene* are thereby *internal* to the *agent*. Thus, a migration of workers moving from one scene to another in response to a hope of better wages would, however great the social dislocations it produced, be motivated by "free will," in contrast with a transference of population decreed by a dictator or some central planning agency. There are, of course, more complex notions of freedom than this (notions according to which such a migration would be treated as hardly more than a compulsion), but they would not figure here. The slogan here would seem to be: Where one can volunteer, there one is free.

Another indication that this is his "God term" is in the fact that, in the name of the freedom got by the workings of the market, he strongly attacks the rival Marxist God, or substance, "inevitability." Thinking along Spinozistic lines, Marx had arrived at the divine word, "freedom," through its divine counterpart, "necessity." Science is "free" in discovering the "laws" of nature—hence the Marxist formula: "freedom is the knowledge of necessity." Men innovate, or act, but according to law. A class, in "fulfilling its historic destiny," is "free" inasmuch as it is doing what it *wants* to do; that is, in its internal motivation it fulfills the role imposed upon it *ab extra* by the scene and by its place in the total dialectic. But only the proletariat enjoys a freedom uncontaminated by illusion; in its enslavement it is, like the person of the early Christian slave, "substantially" free, for nothing but the truth can set it free, whereas other classes must protect their interests by a partial avoidance of the truth, inasmuch as they enjoy their rights at the expense of others. The proletariat, as *primus inter pares,* is "substantially" free because it can, or must, both represent itself and be the representative vessel or logical culmination of the total dialectic. This is the doctrine, as I understand it, though I am aware that many a Marxist would complain at the theological tone I have given to my summary. But I think I can thus make it apparent why I feel justified in saying that Mr. Parkes attacks the doctrine as a rival God, representing in its grounds for the destruction of the market a causal ancestry directly opposed to Mr. Parkes's doctrines of motivation.

"Principles" and "Reform"

Mr. Parkes's other major proposal to preserve the principles by reforming the practice would aim at a spot as strategic as the free labor market. For he would also end the free money market. (We are using "free" in the traditional *laissez-faire* sense: free of government interference.) Here too, while showing the traditional liberal distrust of strong central government, he somewhat incongruously calls for a strengthening of government authority to "force down the rate of interest to the appropriate economic level."

"It is improbable," he says, "that this can be accomplished by any means short of direct government control of the banking system." And when proposing to alter the conception of property rights by extending them to cover the property rights of a worker in his job, he had acknowledged that such changes would be "revolutionary in their implications." Thus, he would drastically change the traditional conception of the free market at its two most vital spots: the labor market and the money market. And he can presumably feel justified in presenting this program as the reform of capitalist practice rather than the abandonment of its principles by reason of an ambiguity lurking in the notion of "reform." If we say that a sinner "reforms," we mean that he simply gives up his sins and returns to the traditional norms of action. In this sense, a monopolistic capitalist would "reform" if he gave up the exploitation of his monopoly and abided by the traditional "principles" of free competition. But if one calls it a "reform" to change these principles themselves, introducing government control at the two most consequential spots in the structure (spots so strategic that a whole new set of implications would follow from the change), is not one rather using "reform" in the sense of "transform"? And a transformation is a change in substance or principle, a qualitative shift in the nature of motivation. The old motivation could then be said to be "substantially" retained only in the rhetorical sense, as when we say that something is "substantially so" because it is *not* so.

Constitutions and the Opponent

Constitutions are agonistic instruments. They involve an enemy, implicitly or explicitly. We may glimpse their mere beginnings, for instance, in the rites whereby a new sovereign, on his accession to authority, swore an oath promising to obey and enforce the traditional tribal laws, or customs. This implied the inimical possibility that the sovereign might do otherwise. Later, men began to exact more specific promises of their sovereigns, promises that were directed against possible abuses of authority which they would anticipate and forestall. Out of this arose written charters or grants, containing explicit assurances against unwanted eventualities of one sort or another. In all such projects, the attempt is made, by verbal or symbolic means, to establish a motivational fixity of some sort, in opposition to something that is thought liable to endanger this fixity.

In *The Philosophy of Literary Form,* footnote on pp. 109-111, we try to show how shifts of authority, from the Crown to representative government, and thence to modern monopolies, dialectically affected the interpretation of the promises, or principles, in the United States Constitution. Similarly, Mr. Parkes is being quite "Constitutional" in setting up his theory of motivation by reference to an opponent motivation. For what a Constitution would do primarily is to *substantiate an ought* (to base a statement as to *what should be* upon a statement as to *what is*). And in our "agonistic" world, such substantiation derives point and poignancy by contrast with notions as to what should not be.

Logically, of course, we should go from substance to command; but in *proposing* a Constitution we reverse this process, going from command to substance, and thereby trying to so frame the statement of substance that it implies or contains the command (which can then be "deduced" from it by judicial interpreters). Thus, in an article on "The Development of Logical Empiricism," by Lewis S. Feuer (*Science and Society,* Summer 1941), in which the author traces the development of neo-positivist theory through various "slogans" in response to shifts in the scene of world politics (giving us a picture of these austere philosophers veering under situational pressures as with the "party lines" of political factions), we glimpse the "constitutional logic" of substantiation operating:

> With the spread of fascism, however, logical empiricism became an article for export. A new slogan now tended to supersede "physicalism," the slogan "the unity of science." Although opinions differed as to the logical meaning of this expression, there was no disagreement that it was the goal of empiricism. Sociologically speaking, the import of the slogan was the "unity of the intellectual class." Confronted by the anxieties of insecurity, the empiricist proposed that scientists join together in their culture-circle and gather collective solace from their closed ranks. Coöperation with the labor movement was not a meaningful alternative within the bourgeois perspective. The "unity" of science was not, however, without economic consequences, for it conveyed the ethical imperative that universities abroad should provide jobs for the scholars who were leaving their native lands. It was at this juncture that the mating of logical positivism with American pragmatism took place. The child of the union was, after some deliberation, provided with the less sectarian name,—"logical empiricism."

Here we see a new "ought" substantiated by a group of thinkers most of whom would abandon the category of "substance" completely and would confine themselves solely to the tactics of "pointing" and "description."

In Mr. Parkes's case, the use of Marxism as the dialectical competitor coöperating in the pronouncements of his Constitution (or structure of motivation) points up quite readily for us the relation between ideals and practices. For he may thereby contrast the perfections of capitalism's other-worldliness (the ideals of pure *laissez-faire*) with the imperfections of the Marxist world (the organizational aspects of Marxist parties and the problems of Russia during the interregnum of dictatorship). Or, otherwise put: Where he by his criteria finds a Communist practice wrong, he may say that *the error derives from the principle;* but where he finds a capitalist practice wrong he may say that *the error derives from a departure from the principle.* This may, if you insist, be the case. But the issue could be intelligently discussed only from a perspective with coördinates beyond those of either the Marxist "inevitability" or the *laissez-faire* "freedom"—and such a perspective would frustrate Mr. Parkes's purposes, since it would be an alternative to the perspective of *laissez-faire* which he would celebrate.

As for the shift between the ideal and the organizational, like the shift between Mr. Read's visionary anarchism and his organizational syndicalism, we can cite a passage from *The Friend,* Essay IV, where Coleridge notes a similar pattern. He is discussing Edmund Burke, who considered policies in terms of "principles" and "expediency" (holding that a policy should be so framed as to embody permanent "principles," but should take the realities of a given temporal situation into account). Coleridge writes:

> Let me not be misunderstood. I do not mean that this great man supported different principles in different areas of his political life. On the contrary, no man was ever more like himself. From his first published speech on the American colonies to his last posthumous tracts, we see the same man, the same doctrines, the same uniform wisdom of practical counsels, the same reasoning and the same prejudices against all abstract grounds, against all deduction of practice from theory. The inconsistency to which I allude, is of a different kind: it is the want of congruity in the principles appealed to in different parts of the same work; it is an apparent versatility of the

principle with the occasion. If his opponents are theorists, then everything is to be founded on prudence, on mere calculations of expediency; and every man is represented as acting according to the state of his own immediate self-interest. Are his opponents calculators? Then calculation itself is represented as a sort of crime. God has given us feelings, and we are to obey them;—and the most absurd prejudices become venerable, to which these feelings have given consecration.

All told, what are we trying to get at here? We have been considering "ideals" or Constitutional "principles" much as we previously considered "attitudes." That is, as terms bearing upon motivation, they contain the ambiguities of the "substantial" and "potential." Both the Read book and the Parkes book, by propounding "constitutions" in the name of freedom, themselves enjoy maximum freedom of argument, hence were chosen by us as particularly challenging to analysis. The search for alignments in the Parkes book led us into a less clearcut outline than that of the Read book, which was organized in keeping with the like genius of the term, "anarcho-syndicalism." But we have tried to show how, despite the variants, a similar form prevails here, as the author confronts the "evils" of Marxism with the "virtues" of capitalism ("virtues" which are not situated in "capitalism" *per se;* indeed, capitalism is said to have sinned against them; but the other terms are repositories of these virtues, so that we can retain by reference to the repository terms, the principles that are dimmed in terms of capitalist practice). We are not trying to "review" these books. We have been trying to abstract their tactics as "Constitutions."

Constitutions—Addressed by Agents to Agents

Now, a Constitution, as a "substance" (hence, as a structure of motivation) propounds certain desires, commands, or wishes. It is "idealistic," as we use the term, in that such attributes are properties of the term *agent.* Indeed, in actual point of fact, a Constitution is addressed by the first person to the second person. In propounding a Constitution, "I" or "we" say what "you" may or should and may not or should not do. If a Constitution declares a right "inalienable," for instance, it is a document signed by men who said in effect, "Thou shalt not alienate this right."

Two important factors tend to make us forget this idealistic factor in Constitutions, their nature as a document addressed by persons to persons. In the first place, the persons to whom the clauses are addressed must necessarily change with the course of history. In adopting Constitutions, men may impose commands not only upon others (as the signers of our Constitution imposed the principles of alienable property upon the future, and sought to balance them with the principles of "inalienable rights"), but they may also impose commands upon themselves which we could analyze by saying that in their present person they address commands to their future person. Further, a command, when it is subscribed to, may be framed with reference to one kind of sovereignty, but by the nature of language it survives to be interpreted under conditions when there is another kind of sovereignty; hence, in the new situation, the command cannot possibly be addressed as it was originally. Thus, many of the commands in the United States Constitution owe their wording to charters originally wrested from kings ruling by tradition and divine right, yet as they are read today they cannot be so addressed, but must be interpreted as addressed either to a government elected by ballot or to some new kind of sovereignty perpetuated by tradition and lying outside the direct control of the ballot (the great business corporations, for instance).

This vagueness of address helps greatly to make us forget that commands are addressed. They may be addressed "to whom it may concern," which is a cross between "everybody" and "nobody," and so vague an address can seem like no address at all. Moral commands were imposed upon Everyman, but to each as a private individual; hence the Mosaic commands are phrased in the singular. But moral commands fail to strike us as addressed in proportion as we lose a sense of direct communication between God and creature; and this loss, ironically enough, was itself heightened by theological doctrine, as God's commandments were also said to be imprinted in natural law, and natural law was not, like God, a "person," hence could not address us. That is, commands grounded in natural law merged the *what must be* in the *what is*. And thus, whereas an "inalienable" right is really a *gerundive*, a right "not to be alienated," the term assumes the grammar of a much more substantial form, a right "that *cannot* be alienated" (since the "nature of things" would make this "impossible"), a futuristic, idealistic form thus being given the appearance of a scenic, ontological concept, as if it were a statement about "inevitable" structure.

In idealistic individualism, the matter of address could be overlooked by another route. The agent could, as with Mr. Read's "vision," simply propound a list of *wishes,* where the stress upon the will of the visionary ("*I* want such-and-such") could help one forget what his statement implies, ("*You* must do such-and-such if I am to get what I want"). Indeed, in such case, the implied form probably is: "We want such-and-such—i.e., all men of good will want such-and-such—and my statement represents them, as it will represent you also, dear reader, if you agree with me."

Constitution-Behind-the-Constitution

In any case, be one's statement consciously a command or merely some kind of wish in which he hopes others will participate, in having to do with the will of representatives, it is typically under the aegis of our term, agent; yet in laying down the "environment" for future acts, a Constitution is *scenic.* However, no human Constitution can constitute the whole scene, since it itself is an enactment made in a given scene and perpetuated through subsequent variously altered scenes. Since, by reason of the scene-act ratio, the quality of the Constitutional enactment must change *pari passu* with changes in the quality of the scene in which the Constitution is placed, it follows that a complete statement about motivation will require a wider circumference, as with reference to the social, natural, or supernatural environment in general, the "Constitution behind the Constitution."

Actually, however, "positive" law has tried to uphold the fiction that the Constitutional enactment itself is the criterion for judicial interpretations of motive. It would abandon "natural law" or "divine law" as criteria, looking only to the Constitution itself and not to any scientific, metaphysical, or theological doctrines specifying the nature of the "Constitution behind the Constitution" as the ultimate test of a judgment's judiciousness. And since it is simply impossible to so confine the circumference of the scene in which occurs the given act that is to be judged, i.e., since an act in the United States has not merely the United States Constitution as its background, but all sorts of factors originating outside it, the fiction of positive law has generally served to set up the values, traditions, and trends of business as the Constitution-behind-the-Constitution that is to be consulted as criterion. In effect, therefore, the theory of "positive law" has given us courts which are the representatives of business in a mood of mild self-criticism.

Such researches as those of Beard remind us that the Constitution was framed and adopted in a period of reaction; the Revolutionary exaltation of the era in which the Declaration of Independence was enacted had passed; and the time for retraction and consolidation was on. And such expressions of the popular will as found their summation in Shays's Rebellion clearly revealed that, where debtors were in a majority and creditors in a minority, the potential "badness" of popular sovereignty was no mere metaphysical quibble. The Constitution was a capitalist Constitution. "It is a striking feature of American constitutional guaranties," says the *Encyclopaedia of the Social Sciences* (IV, 254) "that with the exception of the Thirteenth Amendment, which protects against peonage, they afford protection only against the possibility of abuse of governmental power and not against the possibility of capitalist exploitation." And not even the Thirteenth Amendment need be excepted here, since exploitation by peonage is more feudal than capitalistic, and this particular command arose in dialectical response to the feudal forms of the Southern plantation system. The irony here is that, with the weakening of the feudal participant in the definition of rights (a weakening of course that got its major blow in the elimination of the Crown as the centre of government and the placing of popular sovereignty in its stead) "rights" that were once asserted in dialectical opposition to feudal authorities would now be asserted in opposition to the authority of the people's government itself.

Shifts in the Locus of the "Representative"

Whereas, in the heyday of feudal thought, the nobility is considered to be the "representative" class (the class in which the society's values culminate) in the course of further social development such "distinction" becomes felt as a "contrast." A "fall" has occurred, and the "representative" part has become the "divisive" part, with an antagonistic part (or rival class) laying claim to greater representativeness, and conceiving of these claims in opposition to the nobility. So long as the nobility still figures as the vessel of sovereignty, rights of the opposing class can be defined with reference to such resistance. But when the nobility is abolished, its function as a dialectical participant in a contrary concept of rights necessarily ends; there is a new scene; and the enactments that derived their significance from the old scene must change accordingly.

Thus, the rights that had been enunciated as *group rights, belonging to "the people" as a class in dialectical opposition to the crown and the crown's administrators as a class,* became the rights of men as *individuals, in dialectical opposition to men as a group.* The Rousseau theory of the relation between the individual and the group had followed the microcosm-macrocosm pattern. The *volonté générale* was the macrocosmic aspect, and individuals were identified as microcosmic participants in this common substance. So long as this common substance was defined with relation to a common *external* enemy (the feudal sovereign whose opposition the people communally shared), it was easy to consider any individual member of the popular antagonist as a consubstantial part of the popular antagonism as a whole. But when the coöperating member in this *agon,* the monarch, had been removed, his vital contribution to the definition of popular essence was gone (for of primary importance in the locating of what one *is,* is the locating of what one is *against*). As a result, we got a different notion of the individual: not the individual as an *integral* part of the popular whole, but the individual as a *divisive* part of the popular whole.

Unheralded, even unnoticed, another "fall" had taken place. And instead of the individual as microcosmic replica of the popular macrocosm, we got the individual *against* the group, men *against* society, business enterprise *against* its own government. And the Court, in keeping with this individualistic perspective, repeatedly nullified the effect of laws passed in strict accordance with the theory of popular sovereignty (i.e., nullified not the laws of a *disobedient* government, as were the legislatures to pass laws in defiance of the majority's wishes, but the laws of an *obedient* government enacting laws that the majority itself favored).

These nullifications were based on reference to the "principles" enacted in the Constitution itself. Hence, what we are trying to do here is to suggest that the nature of "principles" themselves might merit closer study. And we are suggesting that a document, arising at a given period in history, should not be treated (if we are to understand its nature as an *act*) simply as though its "principles" were something eternal, for eternal things do not have a beginning, and these did. We may perhaps rescue universality here—but only by a much more round-about way.

Considering the Constitution, then, as an enactment arising in history, hence a dialectical act, we find something like this: Thrust A (the will of the monarch) had called forth parry A_1 (the "rights" of the people). A document is formed that memorializes or perpetuates this parry. And it survives, in its memorialization, after the role of the opponent whose thrust called forth this parry has been removed. What, then, is the parry in answer to, when in the course of time a new opponent, with his own different style of thrust, has arisen to take the place of the former opponent?

The design can be easily pictured. Imagine a statue of two fencers, the one lunging forward with his sword aimed at the shoulders. And the other fencer raising his sword to deflect the flow. Imagine next that, in the course of historic change, one of this pair is lost. Only the figure of the parrier remains, with his sword obviously raised to ward off a thrust at the shoulders. Imagine next a change to a new form of duelling. And some sculptor portrays this new opponent, a man let us say with a pistol. And now imagine some academician trying to fit the posture of the swordsman's parry to the posture of the man with the gun. Or, if that seems too incongruous, imagine the statue of a swords-man this time thrusting at the groins; and imagine attempting to see in the memorialized parry an *eternal* parry, a *universal* parry, quite as fit to meet the second thrust as it was to meet the first.

The Generalizing of Wishes

There is, however, a sense in which a "principle," even thus arising historically and by partisanship, can be considered eternal or universal. This is so when the principle is raised to a sufficiently high level of generalization. The strategy is then couched in terms sufficiently general to serve as a response to the "human situation" in general.

And even partial or partisan experiences can be "universal" in the sense that all human relations are so, hence such experiences are typical of all men.

If one prays for rain, his prayer is adapted to drought. If one prays for clearing, his prayer is adapted to cloudburst. But if one prays for "welfare" or "security," he has a "higher order" of prayer, prayer at a sufficiently high level of generalization to serve in situations as different as drought, cloudburst, earthquake, pestilence, and debt. Thus, to say of a Constitution (we are quoting a tribute that has been paid to the Constitution of the United States) that "its unchanging provisions are adaped to the infinite variety of the changing conditions of our national life," is to say that it contains some very highly generalized wishes, wishes so generalized that they can be "adapted to" living conditions almost inconceivable to the Founding Fathers who thus so ably wished in our behalf more than a century and a half before our times.

One can thus see "Constitutional" tactics at work grandly, in such a formula as Christianity's golden rule, a prescription so universalized that, like God, it applies to every man uniquely. For every man will conceive in ways peculiar to himself just exactly what he would have done unto him. Hence, this precept can have a precise meaning to him that it could have to no other man. However, if he would obey the rule, he will find that it is like a question to be answered—and since to a general question we can give a general answer, for all the particularities of his notions as to what he would have done unto him, he can conceive of such a policy more broadly, in terms of "justice," or "frankness," or "kindliness," etc. The "principle" itself (it is the *lex talionis* translated from the style of the threat into the style of cajolery) had to be couched in highly generalized form, if Christianity was to qualify as a world religion that would unite under a common cultural constitution the many tribes, with unique rules of conduct, which had been brought into contact by trade and empire. We might think of it as a chapter-head, with each tribe filling out the chapter in details peculiar to the tribe (until in time the body of Christian thought had become comparatively fixed, with a structure of evaluations applicable to the culture as a whole). And similarly with our secular Constitutions, men might lay down a "principle" of liberty (that is, the wish for liberty, or the command, "let there be liberty")—and this would be so generalized a chapterhead that men long afterwards could go on, filling out the chapter differently, interpreting in the light of wholly new situations (new scenes that must give correspondingly new meaning to the clause or slogan or chapterhead, which by the nature of the printed word had long outlasted the scene in which it was enacted, and thus had outlasted the particular opponents who had contributed to its meaning in that scene).

Limits and Powers of a Constitution

There is, of course, a sense in which a human Constitution is an act of supererogation. Imagine, for instance, an Ideal Constitution for Students, that claimed for students the "inalienable right to solve all their problems, whatever these might turn out to be." Obviously, if the student has a problem that he can't solve, he will derive no help from the guaranty in his ideal Constitution. And if he has a problem that he can solve, he needs no Constitutional guaranty. It is in this sense that the right to the "pursuit of happiness" is supererogatory. The "pursuit of happiness," as a motive, is embedded in the Constitution-beneath-the-Constitution—though such a slogan might be of moment in implying the adoption of secular values as against religious values, i.e., a different notion as to what happiness is and how it is to be attained—as were it to be attained, for instance, through a stress upon commercial activity rather than through a stress upon aesthetic or religious practices. Insofar as our Constitution is a Constitution for small business, then in proportion as the conditions favoring such kinds of enterprise drop away, the Constitution willy nilly "abolishes itself." The change of scene makes it inevitable that the enactments become new enactments.

Constitutions are of primary importance in suggesting what co-ordinates one will think by. That is, one cannot "guaranty" a people any rights which future conditions themselves make impracticable; and whatever the limits and resources of liberty in the future may be, if they are there, they need no Constitutional guaranty; but Constitutions are important in singling out certain directives for special attention, and thus in bringing them more clearly to men's consciousness. During the era of the New Deal, for instance, we saw attempts to introduce the "principle" or "directive" of "private economic security without private property" into a Constitution that lacked such a co-ordinate. And it is interesting that this principle of individual security had to be approached through the collectivist coördinates in the document, such as "public emergency" and "national welfare." The socialization of losses, whereby government subsidy had protected private property, became somewhat extended to the point where government subsidy protected private poverty. The state of the population made it necessary; the state of the banking structure made it viable. A capitalist motivation that distributes by money made it reasonable, since only by having the wherewithal to purchase does one stay strictly within the bounds of a money economy.

A Constitution is "binding" upon the future in the sense that it has centered attention upon one calculus of motivation rather than some other; and by thus encouraging men to evaluate their public acts in the chosen terms, it serves in varying degrees to keep them from evaluating such acts in other terms. In this sense we could say that not only Marxist and Fascist calculi of motives, but also all individual and group psychologies, and all naturalistic, metaphysical, and theological theories of motivation, are "un-Constitutional."

Constitutional Tactics of Coleridge's "Pantisocracy" Project

If a man is pushed over a cliff, his descent is not an act; it is a natural event. But if, during his descent, he clutches at something to break his fall, this clutching for a purpose however futile is an act. This substantival (motivational, or "Constitutional") distinction between the human act and the physical event was a basic concern with Coleridge, both in his poetry and in his moral theorizing. He phrased it as a distinction between "motive" and "impulse." If one did exactly as he wished, spontaneously, purely because he so felt, he would be acting from "impulse." If one arrested this spontaneity in any way, he would be acting from "motive." In some contexts Coleridge used "motive" much as Bentham used the word "interest." To write a poem for money, for instance, would be a "motivated" act rather than an "impulsive" one—and the two could be merged only insofar as the poem was written without a single concern with monetary interests but happened to be so constructed that it had a market value.

Coleridge's works show a shifting dialectic with regard to this motive-impulse relationship. At some points, the two are considered after the analogy of our two-circles pattern. Motives, interests, expediencies are treated as the more restricted idiom, but concentric with the wider idiom of impulse. At other points, the two become divisively related, the narrower circle being an antagonist of the wider circle. Judged as a Constitutional wish, his "Pantisocracy" project (an early Utopian enterprise envisioning a Communist colony on the banks of the Susquehannah) was designed to solve the problem by so constructing a society that virtue would be "inevitable." This would be attained, he felt, by the socializing of property, since such "aspheterism" would remove partisan interest as a motive of action.

A solution possibly hysterical is offered in the critical moment of "The Ancient Mariner" where the Mariner impulsively blesses the water-snakes (blessing them "unaware" and proclaiming them beautiful that is, in essence blessable, whereby the command and the obedience would be one—for if one wanted to bless something which was blessable, there would be no problem of virtue). It was a moment that greatly annoyed our great expert in virtue, Irving Babbitt (who held that this could not be a virtuous act because it had no "inner check"). At best, we might say, it could be an innocent act, an Edenic act, an act of oneness—but it could be so only prior to the "fall," and the Ancient Mariner on the contrary is a guilt-laden moralist.

In "Aids to Reflection" we find Coleridge offering in advance his comment on Babbitt's objection, since Coleridge would probably have considered Babbitt's notion of the "inner check" closer to a Stoic position than a Christian one. "The Stoic," Coleridge writes, "attaches the highest honor (or rather attaches honor solely) to the person that acts virtuously in spite of his feelings, or who has raised himself above the conflict by their extinction." But Christianity "instructs us to place small reliance on a virtue that does not begin by bringing the feelings to a conformity with the commands of the conscience. Its especial aim, its characteristic operation, is to moralize the affections. The feelings, that oppose a right act, must be wrong feelings. The act, indeed, whatever the agent's feelings might be, Christianity would command: and under certain circumstances would both command and commend it— commend it as a healthful symptom in a sick patient; and command it, as one of the ways and means of changing the feelings, or displacing them by calling up the opposite."

If Coleridge's "Christian," then, would attain wholeness in his virtuous act ("Faith is a total act of the soul" *The Friend*, Essay XV), he cannot do the good merely because he *ought* to; he must also *want* to. The commanded and the commended must be identical (a difficult merger to coach, as per the formula, *velle non discitur*). If the snakes represented temptation, we should get a secretly subversive solution to the problem of the total act. It would have the *form* of the Christian strategy in translating the *lex talionis* into the golden rule. That is: it would convert a "negative" style into a "positive" style. But beneath this form, it would be furtively diabolical. For it would bless temptation, proclaiming temptation to be substantially blessed, whereby the response to its *com*pulsiveness could become transubstantiated into an *im*pulsiveness. It would be somewhat as though the man, pushed over the cliff, were to make his descent an act by willing that he continue to descend, so that the impulse "from within" would be one with the motive "from without."

However, Coleridge's hope for spontaneous virtue and the total act (a hope basic to both his Pantisocracy project and his radical reconstitution of temptation in "The Ancient Mariner") is obviously an ideal incapable of realization in an imperfect world. The very *wish* for wholeness is derived from partiality—hence could only be attained through the unity of all men with one another and all mankind with the universe. We must aim at congregation by devices making for segregation—*peace* is something we must *fight* for. The more perfect the end, the correspondingly more imperfect the means. If one could get peace by peaceful means, there would be no peace left to get: peace would be here already. We may, it is true, modify the conditions of fighting (forensic competition, for instance, may replace competition by force—but rhetorical sway and logical cogency are dialectical, or agonistic, in that they require the coöperation of an opponent, though this opponent but take the attenuated form of a "problem" to be solved). Some means are so much more "peaceful" than others as to seem, by comparison with them, to be "peacefulness" itself. And we should always seek to select these means farther along towards peace on the peace-war spectrum. It is wrong, however, to consider them as *essentially* peaceful. And there is a real sense in which brute force is less thoroughly militant than poetry or philosophy, since its expression is so crude and superficial, and can only be said to go to the depths of a man because there is a stupid modern habit of thinking that a few easily aroused forms of fury and vengeance constitute the "depths" of mankind. One might with much more justice complain that we today are suffering from a woeful inferiority in the quality of "the enemy." "Evil" has become reduced to brute masses of explosive, with a few rudimentary processes of misrepresentation (got by organized control of the news). By such crass simplifications, people are *emptied* rather than *filled*—and their wars are more like the clashes of automata than the combat of men profoundly locked in a wrestling match that has an infinity of holds.

Constitutions But Partially Representative

But if the total act cannot be attained in a partial world, even in the case of a work enjoying the efficiencies of a private enterprise (as Coleridge's Pantisocracy dream did somewhat and his "Ancient Mariner" still more), it can be still less thoroughly attained in a document attesting to a public act. For it must be representative of a vast and complex social body. So that, even when it was enacted, many men could at best participate in the act vicariously through their representatives as drafters and signatories. While, as research has shown, even at the time, a large proportion of the citizenry did not participate, even thus vicariously.

We should certainly not deny that vicarious enactment is possible. Even an event, caused wholly from without, can be an act, if one wills the event. If a man prognosticates a natural calamity, for instance, and comes to have such a vested interest in his modes of diagnosis as to require the calamity (as vindication of his judgment) he is a vicarious conspirator in the calamity.[14] Or an accident, killing a person one should love but does not, may become representative, and thereby cause feelings of remorse. But though vicarious enactment, through representatives appointed by either vote or destiny, can occur, it can occur for

---

[14] There is a surprising moment, bearing on this, in the movie, *A Man to Remember,* where the audience is greatly gratified at the news that many children are sick and dying of infantile paralysis, so gratified in fact, that, at the performance we saw they broke into applause. The hero had foretold the epidemic, and was in disgrace with the medical authorities for rebelling against their ordinances and taking steps in his community to forestall the outbreak. Hence the audience's impulsive satisfaction on being told that the epidemic had struck the surrounding communities while the children of the hero's community were spared. The calamity vindicated his judgment and his rebellion.

all only insofar as all are united. Even the Declaration of Independence could not be a total act, owing to the large proportion of Tories (many of whom resisted it through an admirable sense of loyalty to the traditional modes of sovereignty). But its dialectic function as a rejoinder to the Crown did make it a representative act for diverse groups unified by the sharing of a single opponent (their consubstantiality thus being defined dialectically, by reference to a contrary term,—totemic communion got if not by a love-feast, by what they ate in common, then at least by a hate-feast, by what they vomited in common—or if the figure seems too extreme, we may think of the king's tea rejected, and of the communal sense implicit in the unified turn to a substitute). But, as we have noted, when the Constitution was drafted, this "second state of Eden" had passed. We call it a second state of Eden, or Eden once removed, because rebellion against the Crown was an act of *division,* hence technically a "fall," but it was a majority division, hence from its own standpoint a unity. But in its very act of abolishing the monarch, it abolished the very term by which it had been unified. And the Constitution was concerned with a new division, the rights of "minorities."

Recently, as we have said, the rise of monopolies has begun to produce a new opponent, thus calling for a corresponding reinterpretation of rights. For a long time the vessels of the business philosophy were felt to be representative of the nation's ways (the *businessmen's* justice served as *everybody's* justice). The business class seemed culminative, as nobility had previously done. However, in proportion as some businesses emerged above the others, it became dubious whether they should be considered as the synecdochic part or as the divisive part. And though the monopolists use all the resources of finance, tradition, and journalistic indoctrination to perpetuate the earlier terminology in accordance with which their role would be interpreted as culminative rather than divisive, their very function as a new form of administration assigns them a crucial role in the dialectical redefinition of Constitutional rights. Only by subsidizing inaccuracy (translating popular education into popular miseducation) can this rising kind of administration henceforth prevent the appreciation of the change that should take place in the concepts of authority and rights.

The rise of monopolies may have one important feature, from the moralistic point of view. Their emerging function as sovereigns provides a stronger incentive for "liberty" to be thought of as a *group* wish, rather than as an *individualistic* wish. And there correspondingly emerges a stronger incentive for the great majority of the people to conceive of their interests collectively in opposition to the economic sovereignty of the monopolists. A Hitler or a Mussolini may be encouraged at such a point, since he centers the collective attitudes in a single person, who can then *appear* culminative while functioning divisively, as a colleague of the monopolists.

Principles of the Conflict Among Principles

We have said enough to make it apparent in what way we would equate "principles" with terms having a volitional element, such as "ideals," "commands," or "wishes." To insert the "principle of equality" into a Constitution is to utter a hope that men may become equal or may continue to be equal. It obviously would proclaim their equality *within* the Constitution as a way of counteracting some kind of inequality *outside* the Constitution (or within the wider circumference of the Constitution-beneath-the-Constitution). "Principles" in this sense are a decreeing of substance, hence a decreeing of motives (and they thereby open the avenues to the ambiguities of substance, whereby those who are called equal "substantially" or "in principle" may be so called because they are not, and new inequalities would be encouraged to develop precisely because the given terminology of motivation introduced a bluntness where a discrimination was needed).

An "ideal" being by definition something that is beyond attainment, and a "wish" referring to a state of affairs that is at least beyond attainment at the time, we can understand why men might salute an actual inequality in the name of "equality in principle." However, we have also called these principles "commands"—and a command, when it is rational, is something capable of being obeyed, or incapable of being disobeyed with impunity. "Commands," as "laws," are more "substantial" than wishes; they say not "would you?" but "you must"; and by this "mandatory" style, so the legal fiction goes, the Constitution, or "Substance," which the Founding Fathers enacted in an act of will, imposes the wishes of the Founders upon the Courts, which must obey them as commands.

Note, however, that there is another meaning of "principle" figuring here, and that much confusion often arises from our failure to make this distinction. A Constitution is but a partial act; the only truly total act would be the act of a Supreme Founding Father who founded the Universal Substance, the Constitution-beneath-the-Constitution, the scene in which the Constitution of 1789 was an enactment, and the motivational circumference of which extends far beyond the motives featured and encouraged by the local calculus that has formally governed our public relations for the last century and a half. And the fact that every single act done within the jurisdictional borders of the United States has involved motives that lie partially within and partially beyond the factors named in the Constitution, gives rise to another use of the term "principles." Here the term refers to the judicial standards developed from the fact that the Constitution, as a necessarily very limited calculus of motives, must be used as the basis of reference, in courts of law, for the judgment of acts more widely or richly motivated.

We have noted, for instance, that ideals, or wishes, need not be consistent with one another. One might, for instance, wish for the right to gamble and one might also wish for security in one's gambling. In themselves, these are contradictory wishes, since gambling by definition involves an element of risk; and if this risk is eliminated, it is not gambling, but a sure thing. Yet one might wish for both dispensations nonetheless. Or, at least, one could enact a document in which both wishes stood side by side. One could even quite consciously work out his calculus of wishes by pitting each wish against a contradictory wish, and by further wishing that these wishes, as contradictory extremes, might counterbalance one another to produce the happy medium. Or one could make up a Constitution as our politicians often make up their political platforms, by deciding how many influential groups there were whose suffrage was needed and introducing planks that would please each group, regardless of their bearing upon the planks introduced to please the other groups—and then all present could sign their names to the lot.

And thus, we could also consider as "principles," the formulae for treating the state of mutuality or contradiction among the ideals or wishes, as revealed by the problem of arriving at judgments in specific practical cases. Thus, in the *volitional* sense, any clause announcing a right or an obligation would be a Constitutional "principle." But in the *necessitarian* sense, any statement would be a "principle" if it signalized a logical or practical conflict between clauses, or defined a procedure for arriving at "Constitutional" judgments despite such conflicts.

Let us consider, for instance, the "principle" (in the second sense) that is implicit in the very name of our nation, which signifies a *plurality* acting as a *unity* (the pattern that is also quite accurately reproduced in the device, *"e pluribus unum"*). As a union of states, we can accent our nation either as "The United *States*" or "The *United* States." The first accent would give us the Jeffersonian stress upon states' rights; the second would give us the Hamiltonian stress upon national federation. "Ideally," as in the name of our country and in the pattern of its thoroughly accurate device, we can have both wishes (or "principles" in the first sense) at once. But practically, a law which grants greater powers to one member of this pair deducts proportionately from the powers of the other member. And we should note this effect as a "principle" in the second sense (not a "wish" but an *inevitable fact* about the relationships between elements in the Constitution as affected by contact with the demands of the Constitution-beneath-the-Constitution). And as an attendant principle in the second sense, we could next note how, as a result of this relationship between the ideal motives of the Constitutional scene and the actual motives of the historical scene, when the ideal merger is converted into the practical division, a Court can sanction a law in the name of plurality (states' rights) or refuse to sanction the same law by judging it in the name of unity (national federation). Or, conversely, the Court could refuse to sanction a law in the name of plurality or could sanction the same law by judging it in the name of unity.

In sum: There are principles in the sense of wishes, and there are principles in the sense of interrelationships among the wishes. Principles as wishes are voluntary or arbitrary, inasmuch as men can meet in conference and decide how many and what kind of wishes they shall subscribe to. But once you have agreed upon a list of wishes, the interrelationships among those wishes are necessary or inevitable. A public right, for instance, "necessarily" implies a private obligation or a private jeopardy; a private right "inevitably" implies a public obligation or a public jeopardy. Confronting such a situation, you could, "of your own free will," draw up a Constitution that merely proclaimed a set of public rights and a set of private rights (or a set of public and private obligations); but in doing so, you would have made it "mandatory" that, in all specific cases, a conflict must arise out of these implications.

Constitution Makes Extra-Constitutionality Mandatory

Judicial theorists often would contend it is the wishes in a Constitution that are mandatory upon the Court. This is in keeping with the genius of the term, "Constitution," as a word for "substance" or "ground" which imposes the quality of its motivation upon all acts enacted within its circumference (the circumference, in such cases being considered coextensive with the span of time in which the Constitution is accepted as the law of the land). But actually, where a Constitution contains a set of wishes more or less at odds with one another, what would really be "mandatory" upon a Court in such circumstances (if this Court is taken to have the right of judicial review of all legislation) would be a "demand" that the Court decide which of the wishes is to be granted and which of the wishes is to be ignored. In other words, where the attempt to carry out the wishes of a Constitution in specific legal cases involves a conflict between Constitutional wishes, what is really mandatory upon the Court is a *new act,* an act of *arbitration,* a partly *voluntary* or *arbitrary* choice decided upon by the Court. Were there no conflict among the wishes proclaimed in a Constitution, it would then obviously be mandatory upon the Court simply to see that its decisions obey the wishes of the document. But where wishes are in conflict (or otherwise put, where the sovereign ideality of the "confluence" or "balance" or "panspermia" of all the wishes must be translated into the idiom of practical *contradictions*) the interrelationships among the wishes impose a new kind of command upon the Court: a command not simply to see that the wishes of the Constitution are fulfilled, but rather to decide which wishes shall be given preference over others.

"Substance" and "motivation" are convertible terms (*Wechselbegriffe*); hence, it is indeed a Constitution of some sort, with its circumference of some sort, that motivates an act in the country where an arbitrarily proclaimed Constitution is the law of the land. But the total motivation of any act (including a Court's act of judgment) must be derived from substance in its total scope, not merely in the restricted range laid down by the document—and it is from this wider area, rather than from the document, that the Court must draw its motivations for arbitrating contradictions within the document.

Indeed, an oration designed to do none other than to celebrate the wisdom and justice of a Constitution would have to go outside the Constitution for reasons. Otherwise, such an oration could be but a tautological restatement of the Constitution itself, not a testimony offering proofs or arguments why the document is good. And if the oration did aim to do more than merely restate, it would be "un-Constitutional" at least in the sense that it was "extra-Constitutional," since it would derive arguments from reference to a wider orbit of motivation, involving some concept of a Constitution-beneath-the-Constitution (as were one to praise the Constitution because of its assistance in helping us to develop modern technology). Similarly, when a Constitution contains a batch of wishes which, as applied to specific practical cases, are found to be variously at odds, were the Court to be as explicit about its motivation as Courts are supposed to be, it would have to formulate a theology, or a metaphysics, or a physics, or at least a philosophy of history as the ground of its decisions. In other words, to be as explicit about its motivations as a Court should be, the Court would have to undermine the very theory of positive law upon which its whole function is based.

There is another very important sense in which Constitutions do have a mandatory effect, however. A written Constitution, which is continually referred to as a basis of decision, is a *calculus* of motives. It is a terminology, or set or coördinates, for the analysis of motives. Thus, when such a vocabulary for the treatment of motives is, by public consent or acquiescence, given far greater authority than any other vocabularly of motivation, oddly enough such a Constitution must, by the very nature of the case, *enforce* a great measure of intellectual tolerance and extra-Constitutional speculation. For by being so obviously restricted or simplified a calculus of motives, it practically *compels* men to put forward alternative calculi, of different focus or wider circumference. In this way, particularly, a positive Constitution "guaranties" freedom of religious belief, as a calculus of wider circumference (explicitly derived from a set of doctrines about the Constitution-beneath-the-Constitution) could not. A religious doctrine of motivation, for instance, could not provide the basis of such tolerance—

for it explicitly refers matters of motivation to pronouncements about substance in the Constitution-beneath (or behind)-the-Constitution, involving substance in terms of the "total" circumference. And whatever substance, or "Constitution," in this wider sense, may be, it *is* "mandatory." Insofar as the "positive" Constitutions in the West have been business Constitutions, thus in effect making the "religion of business" the partially proclaimed and partially unproclaimed circumference of the Constitution-beneath-the-Constitution, positive law here also contributed to religious tolerance, since the perspective of business makes it reasonable for one to tolerate an infidel if he works for low wages or is a good-paying customer. Tolerance fostered by business, however, departs in proportion as the substance of business itself is endangered by untoward developments in the Constitution-beneath-the-Constitution, and by persons or parties who are rightly or wrongly felt to be the vessels or causes of these developments. Hence the businessman distrusts, first of all, the Marxist, since the Marxist substance would replace the business substance. He has no essential objection to Fascism—only his fear that he may not be one of the "insiders" who get the profits of Fascist coördination.

Some Degree of Constitutionality in Every Law

Insofar as a good job of wishing is done in a Constitution (that is, if the document contains an assortment of both public and private rights and obligations) there is one sense in which it becomes almost impossible for a legislature to propose a law in defiance of Constitutional guaranties. The law that frustrates one wish in the Constitution will, by the same token, gratify another. The given law, for instance, may propose confiscatory measures that further restrict the rights of private property; but in so doing it may further the general welfare, or act in a state of national emergency, or make for greater equality, or regulate inter-state commerce; or, at the very least, it may invoke the right of police powers granted to the government.

Imagine, for instance, a recipe of wishes. The recipe calls for an egg, two cups of flour, a level tablespoonful of baking soda, and salt to taste—etc. A legislature proposes a law that falls under the title of eggs. The Court may then either imply its sanction under the title of eggs, or imply its nullification under the title of flour, baking soda, or salt. And even if it is a law that falls under the title of salt, the provision "salt *to taste*" requires a new act of arbitration to decide whether there is too much salt or too little.

Where there is a recipe of wishes, variously related to one another, existing as sovereign states in the ideality and generality of the Constitutional document, but requiring the partial exclusion of one another when they are applied to particular cases, then note that specific measures could not properly be called either Constitutional or un-Constitutional. That is, they would not be wholly and unambiguously one or the other. But in being Constitutional from the standpoint of some one Constitutional principle, they would by the same token be un-Constitutional if considered solely in terms of some opposing principle.

In such a state of affairs, it is obvious that if the Court selects but *one* principle by which to test the legislative measure in question, and considers the matter in terms of this alone, it has simply not confronted the issue. If it wishes to sanction the measure, it can do so in the name of the appropriate wish. If it wishes to nullify the measure, it can do so in the name of a different wish. To say that the decision, under such circumstances, was "mandatory" upon the Court would be to put a "broad interpretation" indeed upon the concept of the mandatory.

In the early years of the Republic, many Judicial decisions were substantiated in the name of the "higher law," which was an idealized way of referring to those aspects of the Ultimate Scene here called the "Constitution-beneath-the-Constitution." However, after a few decades when a sufficient number and *variety* of precedents had been amassed, the Court could ground its choice of "mandatory" decisions in a corresponding choice of precedents, by selecting the particular kind of precedent that best substantiated, or rationalized, the favored decision. Reference to precedent could thus *function* as reference to the extra-Constitutional scene; but in *appearance* such decisions were purely *internal* to the traditions of Constitutional law.

The ironic fact about reference to precedent is that, in a nation whose scenic conditions were changing constantly, one might well expect precedent to count most if used *in reverse*. That is, one might adduce precedents to justify the *opposite* kind of decision now, on the grounds that the scenic conditions are now so different from those when the precedent was established. However, "higher law" and the precedents based upon it referred not to changing material conditions, but to the kind of "immutable scene" that could be idealized and generalized in terms of "eternal truth, equity and justice."

"Essentializing" and "Proportional" Strategies of Interpretation

Constitutional theory has generally swung between "strict constructionists" and "broad constructionists," with the two schools changing places on occasion, (as Jefferson, a strict constructionist, adopted the contrary principle when seeking Constitutional authority for the Louisiana Purchase). But we might make a distinction between the "essentializing" and the "proportional" that would cut across this on the bias. The essentializing strategy would be that of selecting some one clause or other in the Constitution, and judging a measure by reference to it. The proportional strategy would require a more complex procedure, as the Court would test the measure by reference to *all* the wishes in the Constitution. That is, the Court would note that the legislation in question would be wholly irrelevant to certain of the wishes, would wholly gratify one or some, would partially gratify others, and would antagonize the rest. And its judgment would be rationalized with reference to this total recipe. The aim would be to state explicitly a doctrine of *proportions.*

The proportional method would also require explicit reference to a *hierarchy* among the disjunct wishes. To be sure, the wishes, in their pure ideality, are all "sovereign states" or "independent individuals," all of equal importance; but as applied to practical cases some of the wishes must be more important than others. Or some one of them must be more important at one time in history than at another time in history. And since the Constitution itself does not specify priority among the wishes, does not state which among these equals shall be "foremost," then the Court must make these decisions for itself, its judgment being a "new act," so far as the Constitution is concerned. And this act would lie outside the Constitution, being motivated by the Court's views of the Constitution-beneath-the-Constitution (as indeed the Constitution itself justifies, since the notion of a "state of emergency" obviously requires reference to a supporting, extra-Constitutional scene into which the Constitution has survived as an enactment). An explicit rationalization of such a decision would certainly involve a statement as to the Court's grounds of preference among the wishes.

Let us illustrate the difference as it shows through an article by Arthur Krock, "Is There a Way to Dispense with Elections?" (*The New York Times,* September 18, 1941). He writes:

> Some enthusiastic trumpeters for a "truly all-out" rearmament effort have been heard in Washington to propose that the Congressional elections of 1942 be dispensed with. They purport to find executive authority to do this in the war powers of the President, which they contend will be in full operation by November of next year; and legislative authority in Section 4, Article I, of the Constitution to achieve the same result if that method should be preferred, prophesying that the present Supreme Court majority would protect either device.
>
> Their animating idea is that bipartisan Congressional contests will promote further national disunity and paralyze the rearmament program in an even greater degree than was done by the third term campaign of 1940. If, because of the proclaimed "unlimited emergency," the President sees national peril in holding the elections, he should—so argue these zealots—continue the present Congress by executive order or ask the legislators for a law. . . .
>
> This correspondent today consulted several students of the Constitution and the statutes in an effort to discover how the elections could be called off if the Administration so desired. He could not find one who was able to develop a constitutional or statutory base for such a move. But it is interesting to record that several, mentioning Charles Evans Hughes's comment that the Constitution means what the high justices say it means, suggested that if public opinion should be favorable, or the President determine—as Lincoln did concerning habeas corpus—that the emergency required it, made-to-order means could be produced and solemnly called legal.

The issue is reducible to this: Article I of the Constitution specifically provides that members of the House "shall be chosen every second year by the people of the several States" and that Senators shall be elected for a term of six years. Section 4 of Article I permits the States to prescribe the "times, places and manner of holding elections" for Congress unless Congress chooses to alter them, which it may do "at any time." Of these two clauses, every reasonable person would surely select the first as prior, unless he had ulterior motives for doing otherwise. That is, he would take it that the second would not justify the modification of elections to such an extent that it changed the term of tenure stipulated in the first. When we come to the matter of national emergency, however, we confront a much less tenuous problem in priority. There certainly can be situations in which an election would be ill-timed, as regards the welfare of the country—and if such a situation arises, which would be "more Constitutional": should the government fulfil its obligation to hold the elections at the stipulated time, or should it claim its rights to act as best it may in behalf of the general welfare? If the Constitution specifically stated that the clause fixing tenure of office is under all circumstances to be given priority over the clause granting the President extraordinary rights in times of emergency, there would be no question. But since no such hierarchy is specified, the Court's decision must be a new act.

The Constitution itself justifies the President's recourse to extraordinary acts when an extraordinary situation prevails in the Constitution-beneath-the-Constitution (perhaps this is even a supererogatory grant, since the nature of the scene-act ratio would seem to make it "inevitable" that acts be out of the ordinary when the scene is out of the ordinary, as with the fictions of Constitutionality made by many European governments in exile during the Nazi invasion. But in any case, were Congress to pass a law postponing the elections, or were the President to make a proclamation of this sort, by reason of his powers in war time, then the Court would be using the "essentializing" strategy if, for instance, it simply noted that Article I stipulated the terms of tenure and that the measure was "un-Constitutional" because it violated these stipulations. But the Court would be using the "proportional" strategy if it explicitly rationalized its decision by proclaiming a hierarchy among the Constitutional wishes and judging the *"relative* Constitutionality" of the measure accordingly.

We see an attempt to avoid the proportional strategy in the principle that all rights not specifically granted to the federal government are reserved to the States. But the proportional strategy is implicit in the change of policy that came over the Court under the impact of the New Deal. This change amounted to an "interpretative revolution" in the sense that, whereas private rights and States rights had previously enjoyed a higher rating among the hierarchy of wishes, they were now deposed in favor of the wishes granting power to the central government. Or we could state this more analytically by saying that the earlier granting of private rights to public corporations, in accordance with the legal fiction that they were "persons" with the properties of persons, had encouraged the development of these corporations to the point where it resulted in the "depersonalization," or rightlessness and rolelessness and propertylessness, of many citizens as the inevitable dialectical reflex.

The revolution in the Court's hierarchy of judgments was a partial response to the growing tendency to treat the popularly elected government as a "corporation of corporations," and to endow it with a "personality" having rights to match the "personal" rights of the business corporations. Hence the complaints that we were getting "personal government," that we were sacrificing our traditional "government by law" for "government by men," that we were becoming more prone to the "leader principle" in looking to the President as the human person in whom would be vested the increased personalization of the government in its role as the "corporation of corporations." The Court, as finally affected by the New Deal psychology, was more inclined to grant the rights to the government as a person which it had once restricted to private individuals and business corporations as persons.

Now, it is a Judge's role to be judicious; and since the proportional mode of judgment would obviously be more judicious than the essentializing mode, one will find traces of this mode throughout the whole course of Judicial Review. However, there are many factors that have as constantly favored the essentializing mode. For one thing, nineteenth-century thinking is one grand gallery of rival essentializations. The law of parsimony came into its very own; if entities had once been multiplied beyond necessity, it would be truer to say that now they were *reduced* beyond necessity. The increasing complexity, giving rise to a compensatory cult of simplification, made "essentializing" seem the most "natural" mode of thought. "It all boils down to this" . . . etc. —an excellent direction in which to move, but a very bad one if arrived at by shortcuts. Further, the dialectics of the law court itself encourages a Justice to make his decisions in its image. Since attorneys for both plaintiff and defendant spontaneously sharpen and substantiate their antagonism by featuring the particular Constitutional wish that seems most serviceable for their purposes, they supply a dramatic inducement for the Court to decide the issue on the basis of the *particular* wishes the antagonists had isolated as their rules of combat. Also, the natural sympathies of the Judges with one or another trend of material interests would make them lean towards the essentializing strategy, since their own judgment was, after all, itself a plea, requiring justification by Constitutional reference, quite as did the pleas of the barristers. Accordingly, the efficiency of the essentializing method had as much in its favor with them as with the barristers.

You could hardly think of anything less judicious than the patterns of litigation; yet they are precisely the patterns of experience that the Justice confronts during every moment of his office—so we find as a judicial replica of the split between plaintiff and defendant, a split of the Court into majority decision and minority decision, with each "Judicial faction" invited to justify its decision as "effectively" as possible by featuring the wishes that would provide maximum plausibility for that decision. Furthermore, since the Constitutional principles or ideas, by their very nature as generalizations, are expressions which can give no indications as to "where you draw the line" in specific cases, one can show that any measure leads to damnation, by the mere expedient of following out its possible implications.

That is, any one of the Constitutional principles would lead to an absurd state of affairs, if enforced independently of all the other principles that modify it; and similarly any proposed legislative measure may be found to contain ominous implications, if we extrapollate such implications in a straight line, without reference to all the other factors, in law and custom, that would correct or check such a simple development. Columnists, doing the Court's work in advance, have often made themselves highly serviceable in certain quarters by thus essentializing and extrapollating the implications of some measure, which they feature in isolation, without reference to the modifying and corrective factors. It is the method used by all cartoonists to make us laugh; it is a method that can be used by our judges on and off the bench to make us tremble. And since the implications of a new measure are certainly something about which a Court could legitimately concern itself, such resources for the solemn production of "judicial cartoons" are there for pointing up the essentializing mode.

Marshall's Argument for Right of Judicial Review

Let us go back to the decision by Chief Justice Marshall in which the Court's right of review is established. He writes:

> If two laws conflict with each other, the courts must decide on the operations of each. So, if a law be in opposition to the constitution; if both the law and the constitution apply to a particular case, so that the law, disregarding the constitution; or conformable to the constitution, disregarding the law; the court must determine which of these conflicting rules governs the case: this is the very essence of judicial duty. If then, the courts are to regard the constitution, and the constitution is superior to any ordinary act of the legislature, the constitution, and not such ordinary act, must govern the case to which they both apply.

The Justice then proceeds by selecting as a test case, not one of the more generalized wishes, such as the Bill of Rights, the general welfare clause, or the granting of police powers or control of interstate commerce; instead, he selects a thoroughly specific clause, which is not fully representative of the issue:

> There are many other parts of the constitution which serve to illustrate this subject. It is declared, that 'no tax or duty shall be laid on articles exported from any state.' Suppose, a duty on the export of cotton, of tobacco, or of flour; and a suit instituted to recover it. Ought judgment to be rendered in such a case? Ought the judges to close their eyes on the constitution, and only see the law?

The Justice is here discussing precisely the kind of case which, by our approach, would require the use of the "proportional" strategy. For he is establishing the right of the Court to pass upon the "constitutionality" of a legislative measure—and in accordance with our thesis, this should be discussed not in terms of constitutionality or unconstitutionality, but in terms of relative constitutionality. Indeed, by our thesis, there are so many generalized wishes in the Constitution, that it would be very difficult for Congress to pass a law wholly un-Constitutional; for the law in question would probably be in accord with at least *one* clause, particularly if this clause were conceived as existing independently of all the other clauses.

Yet note that there seems no occasion for a "proportional" treatment. Even more, the "essentializing" treatment seems to be the only one appropriate to the issue as so presented. A law establishing an export duty would obviously have direct bearing on a clause prohibiting export duty. Hence, unless the Constitution is amended, a law establishing an export duty would run flatly counter to this particular wish. And the Chief Justice had overwhelming good reason on his side, in such cases, not only to choose the Constitution as the highest public motivation or "supreme law of the land," but what is more relevant to our purposes here, to test the validity of the given law by the essentializing strategy, with reference to the specific relevant clause.

We must recall, however, that the same Justice established precedents of broad interpretation, whereby a clause may be interpreted to cover not merely what it *explicitly* lays claim to cover, but also what, in the Court's opinion, it *implies*. This allowance was necessary, particularly in view of the fact that the pace of the industrial revolution (with all the changing modes of relationship and action that went with it) was producing a constant change of situation; and in proportion as the situational context that gave meaning to a clause at the time of its pronouncement underwent change, an almost infinite procession of new amendments to the Constitution would have been necessary unless the Courts were allowed to interpret according to the "spirit" rather than the "letter." Our own analysis of Constitutional principles as generalized wishes would force us to admit that a *strict* interpretation of "principles" is simply a contradiction in terms.

However, although broad interpretation is inevitable insofar as a wish uttered prior to experience with a given new situation is to be taken as a wish relevant to that situation, the tenth article of the Bill of Rights utters a contrary wish:

> The powers not delegated to the United States by the Constitution, nor prohibited by it to the states, are reserved to the States respectively, or to the people.

To interpret a clause in terms of its "implications" is, if this clause delegates powers to the national government, to interpret it as granting powers that it does not grant. For one can't delegate "implications" to anybody. Nor can one reserve them to anybody. They are "inalienable," though their inalienability is not grounded in the Constitutional substance, but in the substance supporting that substance, in the nature of existence itself (the Constitution-beneath-the-Constitution).

And more ironically still, in the very clause in which rights not delegated to the national government are reserved (i.e., the clause attempting to establish Constitutional grounds for literal interpretation), we find an ambiguity requiring an improvisation on the part of judges: for the phrase, "reserved to the States respectively, or to the people," gives us an "or" that may treat "the States" and "the people" as either in *ap*position or in *op*position. The more idealized a statement is, the broader will be its area of possible relevance; hence the greater its demand for new juridical acts, in deciding what weight shall be laid upon "implications." Otherwise put: in broad interpretation, such as a concern with "implications" involves, it gets down to a matter of "where you draw the line"—and no document that did our willing for us more than a century and a half ago can will the point at which our representatives today shall draw the line.

The point I am trying to make is this:

In order to make the case for Judicial Review as effective as possible, the Chief Justice, in his role as an advocate, selected a case where a new law would be in flat contradiction with a wish in the Constitution. Hence, the only issue was that of a conflict between the Constitution and the new measure. And he could present the Court's rulings as made mandatory upon the Court by the explicit motivations proclaimed in the Constitution. The important omission, from our point of view, is this: the Justice does not here ask what relationships prevail among the generalized wishes, or ideals, in the Constitution itself, and whether they too, when embodied in specific practices, might come in conflict with one another. Instead, he selects a kind of case in which a law clearly either *is* or *is not* Constitutional. And he can present his judgment as one that the Constitution makes mandatory.

However, a broad interpretation, involving a concern with "implications" and a decision as to "where you draw the line," is not "mandatory." It is "free," so far as the Constitution is concerned. It is a new act. Indeed, it is a kind of Constitutional Amendment made by the Court, without waiting for the unwieldy processes of amendment prescribed in the Constitution. And once you recognize that, as regards the more generalized grants and guaranties in the Constitution, (with undefined private rights confronted by undefined public powers), the implications of one clause can be extrapollated to the extent where they encroach upon the implications of another, then you realize that the proportional method, involving a hierarchy among the clauses, is the only one that a Justice could use in the great majority of cases. In brief, the same Justice who established the right of Judicial Review introduced principles of free interpretation that would call for a different kind of Judicial Review than the kind he cites. As an advocate of Judicial Review, he employs the essentializing tactics of a litigant—but once the right was established, the Court found itself constantly facing situations calling for a kind of judiciousness not claimed by the Chief Justice at all. These would require modes of rationalization alien to the patterns of litigation, and based upon the explicit recognition of the Court as a free agent, set free of the "mandatory" by reason of the ambiguities and contradictions arising from the nature of the Constitution itself, as a batch of generalized and variously related wishes.

Constitutional Unity and Political Diversity

The clauses of a Constitution would be "substantially" related insofar as we could show that they develop out of one another, as with the propositions of Euclidean geometry. A common essence would pervade the lot, as something from which all the parts radiated, and it is in this respect that the essentializing strategy of interpretation would be relevant. Thus, it would seem fair to characterize our Constitution as essentially a capitalist Constitution, but one that points beyond capitalism (since there are no limitations whatsoever placed upon the range of wishes that can be covered by amendment).

Theological, metaphysical, or naturalistic terminologies may, with varying degrees of plausibility, appear to embrace the total circumference of motivation. But our capitalist Constitution could not possibly pretend to such thoroughness. Indeed, whereas the theological, metaphysical, or naturalistic constitution is the scene (of varying scope) in which a human act takes place, a political constitution is itself an act. And though such an act, in establishing an arbitrary set of motives, becomes in turn the scene of subsequent acts, this quasi-scenic property does not take away its essential character as an enactment of human wills, an enactment that goes on being reënacted each time its principles are reaffirmed (or goes on being reënacted in effect, as a kind of "act by default," insofar as any who would withhold their active assent do not proclaim an active dissent).

Thus, when we speak of the relation between a Constitution and a Constitution-beneath-the-Constitution, we are really dealing with the relation between a political act and a non-political or extra-political scene. And when the framers of the Constitution (or more accurately, the framers of The Enactment that would be the Basis or Ground of Future Enactments) referred to states of "emergency" that might arise, they were obviously recognizing the fact that a human constitution, in contrast with a constitution laid down by God or nature, could not be total. Scenes might arise of such a sort that the wishes enacted in the document would be irrelevant acts.

There is even a sense in which one might even say that, since the establishment of the Constitution, every single day has been a day of emergency, ranging from very grave emergency to emergencies more or less limited or attenuated. Or in other words, every single day has been a day in which the particularities of the scene required some manner of new decision involving motivational ingredients not treated in the Constitutional calculus.

Just as the patterns of litigation are reproduced in the pattern of minority and majority decision on the part of the Supreme Court, so Constitutional wishes have their replica in Party Promises, often the most disparately assembled Constitutions of all, motivations-for-the-nonce: political platforms. And these platforms, as verbal acts of preparation, have regularly manifested the dual nature of preparations, either in leading towards the promised political act or in serving as prayerful substitute for it. As a Constitution can, by reason of ideality, stylize a conflict of material interests as a diversity of principles or a reciprocation of rights, so a political party will, quite as a matter of course, sling together a platform containing promises for each class of voters. Though the party could carry out some of these promises only by violating other promises, the politicians can be "idealistic" or "visionary" enough during the campaigning stage to play down this stylistic matter, except when discussing the platform of the opposition.

Political coalition (uniting the contingently or accidentally related rather than the integrally or substantially or constitutionally related) is got by two methods of compromise. In the *bloc* system, there are a great many factions, each with a very definite and fairly self-consistent platform, its promises usually too accurately attuned to the interests of some one group of voters for general acceptance by other groups of voters. When there is a great number of factions, no one faction can control a majority of the votes, hence various temporary coalitions among the *blocs* must be formed after the election. And since each group in the coalition must make concessions to the other groups in order to get concessions in return, at this stage the clarity and definiteness of the campaign promises must necessarily give place to what you may call either "intelligent compromise" or "betrayal," as you prefer.

Or you may assemble much bigger parties, as we do in the United States, by platforms that themselves represent a coalition of various factions (usually geographically distinguished). It is customary to ridicule Hitler's 25-point program, by noting how the promises in the various clauses would cancel one another if seriously translated into the realm of practical interests. Yet this was a "coalition" platform such as is quite the norm of United States politics. (Whereat we may recall that the Founders of our nation expected us to have a one-party government, with elections involving primarily the choice of individual administrators. Hence, the whole party structure developed outside the provisions of the Constitution. And Washington's grave misgivings, in his Farewell Address to the nation, reflect simply his disturbance at the rise of the party system which we have since been taught to take as the norm, and even as our glory.)

Behind the various legislative factions in turn, are the lobbies that represent local pressure groups of varying size and strength and that employ varying degrees of publicity and secrecy (with the secrecy usually more candid than the publicity). In these extra-legislative or "pre-legislative" bodies, there is a plurality of interests adding up to a pure babel of fractional and factional motivations so much at odds with one another that Congress as a body cannot possibly yield to them all, though each has its individual Congressmen that would.

How ironically far we are here removed from the "Edenic" state of the Constitutional wishes in their sovereign ideality may be glimpsed in the typical businessmen's convention held at Washington. The businessmen, as a national body, pass a resolution strongly in favor of decreased government expenditure. But, being in the national capital, each member individually, as representative of his local interests, visits his Congressman to urge upon him that he do all in his power to get a larger federal grant for local projects. Thus the businessmen's ideal unitary wish becomes the exact opposite of their divisive practical wishes.

Role of the President

The President, as head of a party hoping for reëlection, seeks to act as the happy resultant of these many contradictory motives. The platform on which he was elected is usually a replica of the Constitution, containing promises for everybody—but since his acts as national executive translate such matters from the realm of ideal "balances" to that of practical "contradictions" where "differing ideals" become "conflicting interests," he finds himself continually confronting a multitude of piecemeal situations at odds with one another. His problem then is, like that of any ruler, to find some unitary principle from which all his major policies may consistently radiate. In brief, his problem is to find for himself and his party a "substance" or "constitution," of varying duration. And a slogan, as motive, serves here, either as an honestly ancestral title from which the specific policies may descend, or as a rhetorical misnomer that gives at least the appearance of substance.

In the person of Franklin Delano Roosevelt, our country surely found the politician most thoroughly and competently at home in such exigencies as we have been considering. It is even conceivable that his illness contributed substantially as an important motive shaping the quality of his understanding, and thence the quality of his acts. For during the period of the attack and the slow recovery, he must have experienced most poignantly and forcibly a distinction between action and motion, since he could act only by proxy, through enlisting the will and movements of others. Thus, even down to the purely physiological level, he must have learned to make peace with a kind of dissociation between impulse and response rarely felt by men whose physical motions are in more spontaneous or naïve relation to their thinking. Hence, it is conceivable that from this dissociation could arise a more patient attitude towards motives outside one's direct control than other men would naturally have. And from this could arise a sharpening of the administrative sense, which is decidedly that of acting by proxy, and utilizing the differences among the agents through whom one acts.

But this would take us beyond grammatical and rhetorical matters, into the areas of symbolic speculation.

And in any case, we should note this: Whatever private motives may have contributed to Roosevelt's sense of tactics, a man in his position who would want to think of himself as in some measure a free agent and not a mere "servant" of either the public or some one class or group among the public, could retain this role only insofar as he had strong opposing groups with which to work. While there are fairly equal weights at both ends of a seesaw, the "candlestick" at the center can swing things this way or that by redistributing his own weight; but if the weights are made greatly unequal, then the candlestick is but "prisoner" to the pull of the heavier weight. It is doubtless for this reason that the President, as an astute political tactician, so often refused to go as far towards the weakening of labor organizations as the general public, under the "education" of the press, seemed willing to have him go. Let labor unions be weakened beyond a certain extent, by either the manufacturing interests or their own internal dissensions, and the President's own ability to act would be impaired, since he needed labor as one of his "reflexes." "Discord" in this sense would be his only means of personal harmony (assuming that harmony requires in some measure freedom of action). Nor is this statement inconsistent with the fact that, in moments of exasperation, he could wish a plague on both the houses.

For here we confront the unity-diversity paradox all over again, as we see that a President who would strive to unify a democratic nation must not unify it too well. That is, if the material situation itself contains vast conflicts of interests, he must keep all the corresponding voices vocal. Yet at the same time he must seek to find some over-all motive, or situation, as would be got in some slogan featuring a common goal or a common enemy. These we had, first, in "The New Deal" motif, and next in "All-Out Aid to the Democracies." The measures for the first were justified on the grounds that the nation was in an emergency like that of war; so were the measures for the second. It was almost as though the metaphorical usage of the first time served as incantatory preparation that brought about the reality the second time.

Political Rhetoric as Secular Prayer

However, we must note some ironies here, due to the nature of political rhetoric as a secular variant of prayer. Imagine that you, as President, were about to put through Congress some measure that would strongly alienate some highly influential class. What would be the most natural way for you to present this matter to the public? Would you not try, as far as is stylistically possible, to soften the effects of the blow? You would try to be as reassuring as possible. Thus you might say: "Really, the proposed measure is not so drastic as it seems. Those men who are so afraid of it should look at things more calmly, and they'll understand how it will actually benefit them in the end. It is really a measure of partial control, done for their own good." And the more drastic the measure is in actuality, the more natural it would be for the politician to present it in a way that would allay fears and resentment.

Imagine, on the other hand, that the public had been clamoring for such a measure, but you as President did not want to be so drastic. In fact, if the measure did what the public wanted it to do, it would alienate some very influential backers of your party. In this case, you would try to put through a more moderate measure—but you would make up the difference stylistically by thundering about its startling scope. One could hardly call this hypocrisy; it is the normally prayerful use of language, to sharpen up the pointless and blunt the too sharply pointed. Hence, when Roosevelt, some years ago, came forth with a mighty blast about the death sentence he was delivering to the holding companies, I took this as evidence on its face that the holding companies were to fare quite favorably. Otherwise, why the blast? For if something so integral to American business was really to be dissolved, I was sure that the President would have done all in his power to soften the blow, since he would naturally not go forth courting more trouble than he would be in for already. To use language consistently in such cases, rather than for stylistic refurbishment, would seem almost like a misuse of language, from the standpoint of its use as a "corrective" instrument. And I think that a mere treatment of such cases in terms of "hypocrisy" would be totally misleading: it would be not judicious, but litigious.

However, this stylistic or rhetorical factor gives rise to many ironies.

The collective emphasis of the early Roosevelt period, for instance, did much to reinvigorate the individualistic trends to which such official ideologists as Tugwell were bidding farewell. This "collectivism" was more like the extension of individualism into new areas, as the federal recognition of unemployment opened new avenues of private career. And even the Tennessee Valley development was designed to be as much a boon to private property and private business as to the nation at large. Indeed, when the Roosevelt administration began, the country was quite prepared for socialization of the banking structure. Even a large proportion of the bankers themselves were willing; for their banks were insolvent, and one thing that our capitalists are always willing to socialize is a loss. Yet it was precisely here that Roosevelt's "collectivism" made its most important contribution to individualism, in that he drew upon the government credit, not to introduce a new collectivistic step (as his ideologists interpreted his moves) but to underwrite the traditional modes of private investment insofar as the changes in the situation itself permitted. And since banking is the very essence of a monetary economy, the whole logic of his administration followed from this act, which really was "constitutive." For in a capitalist economy, a decision about banking is a decision about the very core of motivation, and in its substantiality it is the ancestor of a whole family of policies.

War and Collective Nature of "Sacrifice"

A truly collectivistic movement would have shifted the locus of motivation by changing the concept of wealth. To illustrate our meaning by an extreme example: We have a truly collectivistic motive when a group is content to live in private hovels, while deriving great and enduring satisfaction from the thought that some magnificent public building, such as a church or school, is "theirs." A genuine change from individualism to collectivism as a motive would involve such a shift in the locus and definition of wealth, just as the shift from feudalism to capitalism presented the cult of individual wealth as a demand for a "poor church." When the retreating Russians destroyed their great power dam at Dnieprostroy, an American reporter in seeking to explain for his readers in America the significance of the dam to the people of Russia, said that it was an outstanding landmark such as the

Empire State Building is to New Yorkers. So consistently had the propaganda of our press played down the value of our great public constructions and played up the value of private constructions, in contrast with the stress upon the all-importance of public construction in Russian propaganda, that the reporter was probably right in comparing a public works project there to a private real estate promotion here. Even where the mood is so highly collectivistic as in the Americans' attachment to their local baseball team, we have but a vicarious or symbolic sociality here, since these teams are all privately owned businesses which but have the *mask* of public institutions.

Perhaps the one public institution that is generally spared invidious comparison with private models in the steady propaganda of our press is the military. I have never heard it said that we should let out our wars to private contractors, so far as the recruiting of a fighting force itself is concerned, though of course we are encouraged to find a place for the private contractor at every other stage of equipment and action. I do not think that this is due simply to the fact that a mercenary army would be too expensive. It would obviously be hard to get many men who would face maiming or death in war for a few dollars a month, if their inducement to work were placed on a purely capitalistic basis, as a monetary reward for the private's enterprise. But there is also the fact that, since business had become identified with all the constructive acts in our society, business itself was willing to consider the purely destructive function of "defense" as its dialectical opposite. And as the two-worlds distinction between church and state gradually became replaced by the two-worlds distinction between private business and public business, businessmen were jealously apprehensive whenever government threatened to encroach upon the constructive side of the equation. As a consequence, the press, in propagandizing for business, constantly strove to present any increase in the public debt as a menace to our entire civilization, when such increases were made in order to build up the wealth of the nation as a whole; and it propagandized strenuously against the notion that a government might, like public business itself, keep its books in a way that treated such improvements as new assets to balance the new liabilities—and the press ceased its alarm only when the constructive acts of the government were dropped to a minimum while the expenditures for purely destructive purposes rose fabulously. In brief: the same editorializing which foresaw national disaster when the government was spending billions for economically useful goods lapsed into calm approval when the same government began calling for scores of billions for armaments, which are from the purely economic point of view, as a contribution to the world's total wealth, a dead loss.

Indeed, ironically enough, this same press found it highly edifying to call for greater "sacrifice" on the part of the people; which presumably means that the business class it represents found the idea similarly edifying. Yet, translated into purely monetary equivalents, such "sacrifice" on the part of the people could only mean a lowering of consumption, which is to say a decreased market for the businessmen themselves, insofar as they were engaged in any business but the war business.

However, insofar as they can succeed in changing over their plants for the war business, this particular embarrassment is removed. While, furthermore, once the situation has become thoroughly a war situation, it so permeates the whole scene that many an act formerly an act of peace becomes secondarily an act of war: the growing and transportation of foods, for instance. And now, at last, an important contradiction has been taken out of capitalism, thus:

In capitalism, under normal peace-time conditions, the worker possessed a dual role. As a wage-earner he was feared; at times of strikes he was quite systematically slandered; and the attempt was always made to keep his salary at a minimum. Yet this same man was also a customer. And as a customer, or wage-spender, he was subjected to an incessant campaign of cajolery and flattery. He was given, for a few cents a copy, papers or periodicals that cost as much as thirty or forty cents a copy, all for the purpose of wheedling his attention, or his inattention, in behalf of sellers. On the radio, he was treated to all sorts of blandishments, given more entertainment than a jaded Oriental monarch. And these were his two fabulously different roles: one as an object of great distrust, and even vilification; the other as an object of almost abject courtship.

On the other hand, in proportion as you turn to a war economy, this incongruity drops away. The ideal worker then becomes the one who produces a maximum and consumes a minimum. He no longer needs to be courted as a private consumer, since the public market for war goods takes care of the consumption factor. From then on, a one-direction logic is possible: to shrink the market for consumption goods and proportionately increase the production of destruction goods. From this standpoint, alas! a war economy is quite "rational."

We may now circle back to the matter of collectivism. For note that, although capitalism as a war economy "makes sense" in that the contradiction between the wage-earning and wage-spending role is eliminated, what has happened to your individualist motive? Obviously, when you are asking that individuals produce much more and receive much less, you cannot present this in terms of the individualistic incentive. You must, indeed, present it in terms of "sacrifice." But sacrifice *for what*? Capitalism itself has too thoroughly trained people acquisitively for them to retain in very vigorous form the earlier religious belief in the spiritual value of sacrifice *per se*.

An individual sacrifice must be presented in terms of a public benefit. An individual impoverishment must be presented in terms of public wealth. An individual risk in terms of group security. In other words, for the conditions of a war economy, as for the conditions of warfare itself, we need a *collectivistic* motive, which will be shared by all except the war profiteers and the empire-builders of big business.

To say as much is to realize the magnitude of the problem. The orthodox philosophy of capitalism involves precisely the opposite kind of dialectic. In the capitalist dialectic, as per Adam Smith, individual aggrandizements are made synonymous with public benefits. Though Christians have a record of much turbulent fighting, Christianity is a philosophy of peace. In the Adam Smith vision of peace, people would be too busy amassing things to stop and fight over them. And the more they amassed as individuals, the more this would add up as total wealth for the society as a whole. Here there would be neither need nor room for a concept of individual sacrifice for the collective good— individual and collectivity being in apposition, not opposition.

Yet in a war situation, i.e., under a war motive, you must so alter the dialectic that individual sacrifice equals collective good. A mere "investment psychology" is not enough here. That is, it would not be enough to contend that, by sacrificing now one may hope for rewards later. For one thing, we had been told that even a small increase in the public debt would ruin the future, even though that increase in debt was largely an investment in national welfare and economic resources; what then could we expect of an incomparably larger debt, expended on armaments that could bring us positive economic returns only if we used them to despoil other peoples of their wealth, precisely the kind of Fascist plundering we are supposed to be arming *against?*

Hitler, by his attacks upon democracy, helped give us democracy as a slogan. But "democracy" is not public wealth or public power. It has been one of the ideals, or means, implicated in the amassing of wealth as we have known it in the past. But it cannot serve as a compensation for private loss, since we have been taught that its value resided precisely in the resources it provided for the man of ability to recover from private loss.

As a result, the motive of "All Out Aid to the Democracies" was vague. Insofar as it asked men to undergo personal sacrifice, a compensatory concept of collective wealth was needed. The Fascists and Hitlerites provided this compensatory concept in the promise of booty. That is, when the wars were over and the period of sacrifice ended, all citizens would profit by the resources taken from other peoples. And these resources would be taken by the people as a whole. Our incentive, on the other hand, was the promise of return to an economic order which was already proving unworkable. In a sense, the "democracies" propose a more "reactionary" solution than the Fascists.

In Russia, we see evidence of an almost fanatical will to sacrifice as individuals in behalf of the public good—yet without the Hitlerite motive of booty. We know that this incentive derives from the collectivistic point of view. But in America, our propagandists feared to adopt this motive, even in cynicism, even for purposes of deception. For it was feared that, were the mildly collectivist slogans of the New Deal to be refurbished this time, while reinforced by the collectivist quality of a war situation, their "potentialities" as incantatory imagery inviting us to make things in its image would this time really bring about the end of "business as usual." Accordingly, Roosevelt dropped all policies except those of the "win the war" sort, deeming it enough that, for the time being, the war as grand collectivist consumer solved the problem of our great productivity.

The Dialectics of Federation

We might end this section, by a kind of *aria da capo,* in considering an essay, "The Idea of a Federation," by Denis de Rougemont (*The*

Virginia Quarterly Review, Autumn 1941). The author being Swiss, he considers the possibility of an international federation in the light of Swiss experience "as an inheritor of the oldest federalist tradition—six and a half centuries."

It is the old problem of unity and diversity, as we have discussed it with relation to our own Constitution. And the author would have us work towards a "federalist philosophy" for uniting all the world's sovereign states, while attempting to avoid a "system." For any system, he says, even if it is called federalist,

> is unitary in essence, and therefore anti-federalist. It is so in spirit, and it will therefore be fatally so in its application. The true federalism is the absolute opposite of a system, which is always conceived in the brain and centered about one abstract idea. I should even define federalism as a constant and instinctive refusal to make use of systematic solutions.

A "system," presumably, would require some kind of "educating and organizing hegemony," which is precisely what the idea of a federation must avoid. And as against notions of a systematic *Gleichschaltung,* in a federation differences must be cherished:

> For it is not superficial or partial similarities (language, race, geographical vicinity) which are federated, but essential differences, which reveal themselves as complementary. It should no longer be said: "Let us renounce what sets us apart and underline what forms a bond between us." For it is precisely on the basis of recognized and legitimate differences and diversities that fruitful unions are formed.

And he likens federation to "a marriage, and not an economic, military, and geometrical alignment."

The author here passes over things a bit too swiftly for our purposes. For though we grant that the kind of spiritual or cultural differences he has in mind may be treated as "complementary," we would consider that marriage a feeble one indeed in which the husband and wife were not bound together in a community of economic interests—and where economic interests are at odds, such differences are not "complementary" but "antagonistic." There was perhaps a bit of prestidigitation in thus quickly bracketing the "economic" with the "military" and "geometrical." And owing to this particular distribution of his terms, the author is able to treat the whole subject on somewhat too "spiritual" a plane.

However, the author does very clearly reveal the difference between a federalist dialectic and a centralizing one, each constituted of a distinct political substance. And in one passage much to our purposes, he writes:

> Let us here introduce a new concept: the essential paradox of federalism, which means taking seriously the expression "union in diversity." Unitary or totalitarian systems are easy to conceive and to carry out: it is enough for them to crush opposition. But federalism implies the vitality of a large number of opposing elements and their harmonization. That is the whole problem.
>
> The word "federalism," in Switzerland, has in our day taken on among conservatives the limited and inaccurate meaning of the autonomy of the canton or district and the systematic opposition to central authority. To be a "federalist," in French Switzerland especially, is to reject on principle whatever proceeds from Berne, the capital of the confederation. This amounts to a kind of local nationalism. On the other hand, the German word corresponding to federation—*Bund*—emphasizes only the central union. When we speak of federalism, we ought to mean both the union and the autonomy of the parts that are united; both *one for all* and *all for one,* the two parts of our ancient Helvetian motto.

A good statement of the case, but hardly a "new concept." Rather, we find it well explored by Coleridge—and before him, it was a key emphasis of Leibniz. In an article on Surrealism (New Directions: 1940), we have applied it to Coleridge's distinction between "fancy" and "imagination" thus:

> Coleridge, as a dialectician, knew that there must be a concept of "one" behind a concept of "many," or a concept of "many" behind a concept of "one." Each implies the other. However, a radical difference in stress, or accent, is possible here. You may emphasize unity in *diversity,* or you may emphasize *unity* in diversity. If you emphasize *unity* in diversity, you get the effect that Coleridge called "imagination." If you emphasize the unity in *diversity,* you get what he called "fancy." It was the use he made of the Leibnizian dialectic, of unity and plurality, an idealist dialectic that is with us even in the name of our nation, "The United States," which is to

say, "The Unity of Plurality," or *"e pluribus unum"* (a dialectic that our Supreme Court is also at home with, as it may sanction or discredit a law either from the standpoint of the *nation as a whole* or from the standpoint of *states' rights,* which is to say that it can give either *imaginative* decisions or *fanciful* ones, depending upon whichever of the opposed principles it prefers to use in the given case).

DIALECTIC IN GENERAL

The Transformation of Terms

BY DIALECTICS in the most general sense we mean the employment of the possibilities of linguistic transformation. Or we may mean the study of such possibilities. Though we have often used "dialectic" and "dramatistic" as synonymous, dialectic in the general sense is a word of broader scope, since it includes idioms that are non-dramatistic.

One may study the possibilities of linguistic transformation in general (as with our analysis of the possibilities inherent in the pentad). Or one may study particular instances of linguistic transformation (as with the critic describing the developments in some one work of art).

The use of the pentad as a generating principle somewhat resembles the Kantian transcendentalism in one respect. Kant was concerned with the necessary forms of experience; and similarly the pentadic ratios name forms necessarily exemplified in the imputing of human motives.

As regards the analysis of particular forms: one looks for key terms, one seeks to decide which terms are ancestral and which derivative; and one expects to find terms possessing ambiguities that will bridge the gulf between other terms or otherwise serve as developmental functions. One seeks to characterize the *dis*position and the *trans*position of terms.

For the discussion of dialectic in the most general sense, we shall consider dialectic under three heads:

(1) Merger and division. (There may be a state of merger, or a state of division, or developments from either state to the other.)

(2) The Three Major Pairs: action-passion, mind-body, being-nothing.

(3) Transcendence. (Transcendence likewise may be either a state or a development. Non-representational art, for instance, may be a state of transcendence with respect to representational art, as the

artist thereafter dwells in the contemplation of relatively disem-
bodied forms. But within the fixity of this stage, the particular
things he paints will have development, quite as the lyric, while
arresting some mood or attitude and making it the entire universe
of discourse, yet has progression rather than mere succession.)

Other definitions of dialectic are: reasoning from opinion; the discovery of truth by the give and take of converse and redefinition; the
art of disputation; the processes of "interaction" between the verbal
and the non-verbal; the competition of coöperation or the coöperation
of competition; the spinning of terms out of terms, as the dialectician
proceeds to make explicit the conclusions implicit in key terms or
propositions used as generating principle (the kind of internal development that distinguishes mathematical systems); the internal dialogue
of thought, as with the inward way of Thomas à Kempis, or as with
ratiocination and calculation generally; or any development (in organisms, works of art, stages of history) got by the interplay of various
factors that mutually modify one another, and may be thought of as
voices in a dialogue or roles in a play, with each voice or role in its partiality contributing to the development of the whole; or the placement
of one thought or thing in terms of its opposite; or the progressive or
successive development and reconciliation of opposites; or so putting
questions to nature that nature can give unequivocal answer. An
ever closer approximation to truth by successive redefinition is sometimes offered as the opposite of the dialectical method, or such "spiral-
ing" may very well be taken as the example *par excellence* of dialectic.
All these definitions are variants or special applications of the functions
we shall consider under our three headings.

Merger and Division

In the *Phaedrus,* Socrates describes the principle of merger as "the
comprehension of scattered particulars in one idea." And on the principle of division, he says that the dialectician must learn to carve an
idea at the joints, "not breaking any part as a bad carver might." And
of both principles, in sum:

> I am a great lover of these processes of division and generaliza-
> tion; they help me to speak and think. If I find any man who is

able to see unity and plurality in nature, I follow him, walking in his steps as if he were a god. And those who have this art, I usually call dialecticians.

In evolutionary thought, the simplest instance of the two principles is Spencer's formulation of a progressive development from homogeneity to heterogeneity.

In his section on the Transcendental Dialectic (in the *Critique of Pure Reason*) Kant contrives to turn the merger-division two-ness into a three-ness by introducing a third principle that partakes somewhat of both the others. Merger in its simplicity he calls the principle of genera or "homogeneity." The unity of nature is assumed, he says, in the Occamite law of reduction according to which "principles must not be multiplied beyond necessity (*entia praeter necessitatem non esse multiplicanda*)".

But in contrast with those half-dialecticians who would seek only a rational reduction to unity, he also formulates a counter-principle, the principle of diversity or "specification," admonishing us that varieties must not be reduced without due caution (*entium varietates non temere esse minuendas*). Kant is exemplifying this notion of specification when, in his introduction to the second edition, he writes: "Rather than enlarging the sciences, we merely disfigure them when we lose sight of their respective limits and allow them to merge with one another."

The principle of specification is particularly applicable, as regards the subject of this book, to terminologies of motives that attempt to treat of ethical issues in exclusively non-ethical terms, or of verbal action in terms of non-verbal motion, or of human motives generally in terms of non-human entities, such as the learning processes of lower animals, or the physiology of endocrine secretions, and the like. In brief, we violate the principle of specification when our terms for the examination of one field are got by simple importation from some other field.

Kant's third formula is a principle of "continuity" that, in bridging the opposition of the other two principles, partakes somewhat of both. It leads to what Lovejoy would call the "great chain of being": the principle that the step from kind to kind is by a gradual increase of diversity. As Arthur Lovejoy points out, the scholastic notion of a continuous series of beings, extending without an hiatus from the highest to the lowest forms of life, involves a contradiction. For such complete continuity would not allow for a series of species, but would run them all into one. It would be a gradual slope rather than a succession of specific steps such as we get in a hierarchy of biological classification. And may we not see a similar ambiguity in the third Kantian principle?

When he is discussing what one could call the *dialectics* of mathematics (in *The Handmaiden of the Sciences*), Eric T. Bell notes the shifts between the mathematics of continuity and the mathematics of discreteness. Here in mathematical translation is the merger-division pair, its members still confronting each other as they did in the days when Zeno showed how the dialectic of discrete, ordered points was at odds with the dialectic of continuous motion. Bell notes that in the past, continuity has been the fashion at some times, discreteness at others. And at present, he observes, the two are "inextricably knotted together in one gorgeous confusion." Our present traditional frame of logic, he says, does not permit us "to imagine a third basic pigment, which shall be neither continuous nor discrete." But in reading of this logical dilemma as regards the dialectic of mathematics, can we not at least use it to reveal the *necessary* ambiguity in Kant's third dialectical principle? For is it not a concept which, if translated into an exact mathematical counterpart, would be the *tertium quid* for bringing merger and division together in a formula that is in some respects neither and in some respects both?

In brief, we again confront a variant of the Grammatical need for a third term that will serve as the ground or medium of communication between opposing terms. And whatever logical problems such a third term may give rise to, we are being logical in feeling the need for it. Similarly, we may expect to find such ambiguous or pontificating thirds strongly at work in dialectic on the Rhetorical and Symbolic levels.

The paradox of substance contains something of all three principles. The offspring is "substantially one" with the parent: its history thus being a development from merger (during the Edenic conditions of the foetus in the womb) to division (at the first "biological revolution," experienced by the offspring at the time of parturition; the "birth trauma" due to the bursting of the bonds that has been made necessary by the growth of the foetus to the point where the benign circle of protection, the "enclosed garden," had threatened to become a malign circle of confinement); and its status as offspring of *this* parent rather than *that* keeps it consubstantial with the familial source from which it was derived. So we have here, in another form, the ambiguity of starting points, which may be considered either as the inaugurating moment (the introduction that will contain implicitly all that is to follow explicitly) or as the point abandoned (inasmuch as the offspring becomes a new bundle of motivations peculiar to itself). Or, recalling another formulation: that which was "a part of" the parent has become "apart from" the parent; yet it may, from the familial point of view, still be considered consubstantial with its ancestral source. Seen in this light, metaphysics might be described as an attempt to decide which propositions we should connect with a "therefore," which we should connect with a "however," and which with sheer "and."

Dialectic of the Scapegoat

When we examine the "scapegoat mechanism" in these terms, we find it a very clear example of the three principles. For the scapegoat is "charismatic," a vicar. As such, it is profoundly consubstantial with those who, looking upon it as a chosen vessel, would ritualistically cleanse themselves by loading the burden of their own iniquities upon it. Thus the scapegoat represents the principle of division in that its persecutors would alienate from themselves to it their own uncleanlinesses. For one must remember that a scapegoat cannot be "curative" except insofar as it represents the iniquities of those who would be cured by attacking it. In representing *their* iniquities, it performs the role of vicarious atonement (that is, unification, or merger, granted to those who have alienated their iniquities upon it, and so may be purified through its suffering).

All told, note what we have here: (1) an original state of merger, in that the iniquities are shared by both the iniquitous and their chosen vessel; (2) a principle of division, in that the elements shared in common are being ritualistically alienated; (3) a new principle of merger, this time in the unification of those whose purified identity is defined in dialectical opposition to the sacrificial offering.

Criminals either actual or imaginary may thus serve as scapegoats in a society that "purifies itself" by "moral indignation" in condemning them, though the ritualistic elements operating here are not usually recognized by the indignant. When the attacker chooses for himself the object of attack, it is usually his blood brother; the debunker is much closer to the debunked than others are; Ahab was pursued by the white whale he was pursuing; and Aristotle says that the physician should be a bit sickly himself, to better understand the symptoms of his patients. The same pattern of thought is rephrased by W. H. Auden, with our characteristically modern conversion of the valetudinarian principle from the gymnastic to the clinical: "Every brilliant doctor hides a murderer."

The Christian dialectic of atonement is much more complex than this, hence includes many ingredients that take it beyond the paradigm we are here discussing. Here we are concerned rather with the kind of scapegoat seen in the Hitlerite cult of Anti-Semitism. Here the scapegoat is the "essence" of evil, the *principle* of the discord felt by those who are to be purified by the sacrifice. Note also that the goat, as the principle of evil, would be in effect a kind of "bad parent." For the alienating of iniquities from the self to the scapegoat amounts to a *rebirth* of the self. In brief, it would promise a conversion to a new principle of motivation—and when such a transformation is conceived in terms of the familial or substantial, it amounts to a change of parentage.

We have here introduced another principle (previously considered in these pages): the pun on sequence, which allows for an ambiguous shuttling between concepts of logical priority and concepts of temporal priority. "Essences" or "principles" are among the logically prior, as an essence is logically prior to its accidents, or as a principle is logically prior to the instances of its workings. Hence the ancestral nature of the scapegoat as vessel of vicarious atonement. And by the same token the scapegoat can possess the divinity of a sacrificial king, since gods too are terms for the essence of motivation, as a tribe that regulates its life about the seasonal fluctuations of a river may sum up the whole complex of tribal motivations in the concept of a river god, which would be the "essence" of the tribal adjustments to the stream's behavior and utility.

As an essence of motivation, the scapegoat is a concentration of power, hence may possess the ambiguities of power, which may be for either good or evil until that stage of religious development is reached where power is dissociated into good and evil principles. This stage was more complete in the Manichaean heresy than it is in orthodox Christianity, which sees in Lucifer a fallen *angel,* and which proclaims the divinity in Jesus by a revolutionary redefinition of the figure whom His crucifiers had classed with criminals. In the Christian dialectic of atonement, the vicarious sacrifice Who took upon Himself the burdens of the world thus retains the ambiguities of power only in the sense that He suffered calumny.

The Hitlerite Anti-Semitism as scapegoat principle clearly reveals a related process of dialectic: unification by a foe shared in common. On the purely Grammatical level, this is reducible purely to the *antithetical nature* of "dialectical" terms, like "freedom," "perfection," or the terms for social movements, that derive their significance from their relation to opposite terms. One can best see their nature by contrasting them with terms like "house" or "apple," which require no counter-words like "anti-house" or "un-apple" to define them.

Where the principle of division is frustrated, as it was in Germany after the Allied victories began making it impossible for Hitlerism to assert itself in further expansion as a "master race" conquering the "Semitic" enemy, the discords must again be faced *within*. Hence the mood of self-destruction (called "honor") which led the Nazis to prolong the war even when it was apparent that such prolongation could but add to the sufferings of Germany itself. "Honor" was the name for the fact that, insofar as ritual transference of guilt feelings to the scapegoat is frustrated, motives of self-destruction must come to the fore.

Per Genus et Differentiam

Returning to the two principles in their simplicity, we have them in the traditional scholastic concept of definition *per genus et differentiam,* or in Coleridge's opposing of unity and multeity. The stress upon the principle of division is seen in theories of literary criticism that would attribute the excellence of a work to the respects in which that work is unique. Thus one critic maintained that to characterize the "beauty" in Marlowe we should find wherein his work is distinct from that of other dramatists. And similarly, advocates of esthetic nationalism or regionalism would situate the essence of esthetic motivations in the factors thought peculiar to that nation or region. Yet obviously, Marlowe's greatness also draws upon the effectiveness of esthetic principles that he shares with other great dramatists, (or even with inferior dramatists, for there are necessary principles of drama embodied in the works of both good dramatists and bad, as poet and poetaster may be alike in that they both derive some measure of appeal by exemplifying the rudimentary principles of prosody involved in a sonnet). And the appeal of national or regional art to readers outside the local circumference of motives embodied in its production must obviously involve respects in which the work embodies artistic principles generically.

The excessive cult of the three dramatic unities seems to have derived from an overstress upon the principle of division, or specification. For Aristotle, proceeding to define drama *per genus et differentiam,* in an essay that also originally contained a treatment of the epic, rightly pointed out the stricter canons of unity in drama, as compared with the epic. But later, the section on the epic was lost—and theorists seized upon these specifications without reference to the epic, in dialectical opposition to which they were originally stated. As defined with reference to the epic, the distinction is quite sound. The epic was quite loose in its treatment of the three unities (of time, place, and action), whereas even now the drama is relatively strict. It is by ignoring the generic context of such specifications that the French theorists arrived at such excessive reverence for these canons.

The Scotist stress upon the principle of thisness (*haeccëitas*), the particular way of the individual thing, does not in itself require the nominalist overstress that would see in a thing's uniqueness the totality of its characters. *Haeccëitas* should be thought of rather as the third stage in characterization, as one begins with generic characters, next notes the specific ones, and *only then* determines the respects in which the individual entity is unique. Its character would be a merger of all three.

The principle of merger, on the other hand, is overstressed when our reduction to generalizations causes us to overlook specifications. For there are always ways whereby, in searching for the "essence" of a thing, we can consciously or unconsciously choose to seek either the "specific" essence or the "generic" essence.

Thus we may define man as an animal, or even as a bundle of chemicals, thereby "reducing" our definition to wholly generic terms. Surprisingly, such stress upon *generic* definition of man's essence co-exists today with an equally intensive stress upon man's *specific* essence; but the two methods continue in isolation from each other, so far as conscious method is concerned.

When Aristotle defined man as a rational animal, he defined *per genus et differentiam,* with "animal" designating the generic and "rational" the specific. But note that our vocabularies of technology and finance derive wholly from man's "specific" essence—since money and machinery are *exclusively human* attributes. No such motives exist in nature, outside of human invention. And they provide that withinness-of-withinness or atop-the-atopness that is so characteristic of human thought, as with tools for making tools, money for making money, or Aristotle's view of God as thought of thought. (Similarly, Kant says that only man reads signs *as signs.*)

To see man in terms of money and technology, as when we "efficiently" construct a rationale of human motives about either of these terminologies, is thus in a sense to reduce the subject of motives "perfectionistically." For we treat an *aspect* of human motivation as the very *essence* of human motivation, thereby in effect asking that man's generic essence be reduced to the specific essence. Ironically enough, though we no longer *formally* accept it that man in his specific essence is "rational," we *informally* place much more stress upon the rational than Aristotle did, when we consider human motives in the reduced (scientist) terms of technology or finance alone. And we uncritically recognize the inadequacies of our definition by a compensatory "discovery" of man as "irrational." That is, when the specific essence has been so strictly reduced, the generic essence is rediscovered in terms correspondingly askew. And so, in our shifting between the pure animality or chemicality of man, and the pure pragmaticality of man, we reëncounter, ironically disguised, the traditional mode of definition. But in the dialectical naiveté due to our neglect of the fact that the language of *science* is a *language* of science, we usually fail to recognize that we are but reënacting piecemeal and without method the very ways of definition that we so often reject as "purely verbal."

More Variants of Merger and Division

A recent interesting example of the unity-multeity dialectic is to be seen in Otto Neurath's *Foundations of the Social Sciences,* where he carries the principle of division to such an extent that he speaks not merely of an individual Cromwell, but of a "pluri-Cromwell," and would set over against this extremely nominalist position an "oceanic feeling" that begins with the generic approach (the principle of merger), as when he writes:

> We suggest not starting with the antithesis: living being and the environment (as bio-ecology does), but starting with what may be called a "synusia" composed of men, animals, soil, atmosphere, etc. I am here using the term 'synusia' in analogy with the term 'symbiosis,' and I hope that the old theological use of the word will not mar our argument. . . .

Such a "synusia," he says, "may present a kind of cohesiveness, i.e., continuance of some relations." And this "aggregational program" has its counterpart "in some metaphysical speculations, e.g., in what is called 'Holism' ('Ganzheitslehre,' etc.)."

A more fanciful variant of the merger principle (atop division) occurs in a dialectical exercise by Coleridge, a *Theory of Life,* wherein he simultaneously describes and exemplifies the dialectic process. Discussing the relation between flowers and insects, he writes:

> The insect world, taken at large, appears as an intenser life, that has struggled itself loose and become emancipated from vegetation, *Florae liberti, et libertini!* If for the sake of a moment's relaxation we might indulge a Darwinian flight, though at the risk of provoking a smile, (not, I hope, a frown,) from sober judgment, we might imagine the life of insects an apotheosis of the petals, stamina, and nectaries, round which they flutter, or the stems and pedicles, to which they adhere. Beyond and above this step, Nature seems to act with a sort of free agency, and to have formed the classes from choice and bounty. Had she proceeded no further, yet the whole vegetable, together with the whole insect creation, would have formed within themselves an entire and independent system of Life. All plants have insects, most commonly each genus of vegetables its appropriate genera of insects; and so reciprocally interdependent and necessary to each other are they, that we can almost as little think of vegetation without insects, as of insects without vegetation. Though probably the mere likeness of *shape,* in the *papilio,* and the papilionaceous plants, suggested the idea of the former, as the latter in a state of detachment, to our late poetical and theoretical brother; yet a something, that approaches to a graver plausibility, is given to

this fancy of a flying blossom; when we reflect how many plants depend upon insects for their fructification.

In this notion of insects and flowers as part of a single system (so that the insect is a kind of "flying blossom") the principle of merger is uppermost, though in this essay as a whole the dialectic traces a series of progressive differentiations, with each higher level of existence transcending the next lower level, by including it while at the same time exemplifying a new principle of motivation.

In *Creative Evolution,* Bergson offers a variant that, whatever doubts one may have of it as a description of nature, well illuminates the ambiguities of sympathy and antipathy we have considered with reference to the scapegoat. He is contemplating the fact that the *Ammophila Hirsuta* in attacking the caterpillar in which it is to lay its larva, usually contrives to paralyze the caterpillar without killing it. He suggests that this ability is derived from "a *sympathy* (in the etymological sense of the word)" between the *Ammophila* and its victim. Hence it does not need to acquire, by a process of trial and error, its knowledge how to paralyze without killing. Its sense of the caterpillar's vulnerability comes *from within,* since both the attacker and the victim are parts of the same system (or "duration") so that it knows how to hurt the other somewhat as it might know how to hurt itself. The principle of merger in Bergson is thus regularly localized in his views of instinct and intuition (which is a kind of super-intellectual instinct). And the intellect represents the principle of division, as with his "cinematographical" analogy. According to this analogy, the continuity of motion (or "duration") which we instinctively sense is analyzed by intellectual concepts into a succession of disconnected steps or stages, as the movement of the actors in a motion picture is photographed by a series of stills, with an unphotographed hiatus between each exposure and the next.

Coleridge suggests some purely formal terms for distinguishing varieties of the merger and division principles. Beginning with oneness, or identity, he writes:

> But as little can we conceive the oneness, except as the mid-point producing itself on each side; that is, manifesting itself on two opposite poles. Thus, from identity we derive duality, and from both together we obtain polarity, synthesis, indifference, predominance.

Suppose that we began, for instance, with a concept like "the good." It would subdivide into "good" and "evil," as with "duality". The "polarity" of these terms would reside in the fact that the concept of each involves the other. Their "synthesis" might be found in some "higher level" generalization, like "morality," which unites both. Or it might be got by an act or power ambivalent in its effects. "Indifference" would reside in a ground term "beyond the opposites," as with a non-moral or "extra-moral" or "sub-moral" concept that neutralized both. Or there might be a "predominance" of one over the other.

Perhaps we might also add "succession" (as a history may develop from either term to the other, with a different significance in the two orders). Another variant of succession would be "alternation."

A variant of predominance would be "substitution". We have in mind the dialectical resource whereby, if paired terms are made equal, one of them may come to do service for both, as the Spinozist equating of "God" and "nature" prepared the way for the naturalist dropping of "God" as an unnecessary term. Or when confronting opposed terms, the thinker may see in one of them the essence of the pair, as with Augustine's view that only the good really exists, with evil as a mere deficiency. The position is almost reversed in many modern tendencies to take the dyslogistic term as real and primary, and to see the eulogistic term as illusory and derivative. A case in point is Thurman Arnold's picture of human rationalizations as a pageantry erected above a set of human motivations that are essentially "psychiatric."

The principle of identity itself is perhaps most succinctly illustrated in Jehovah's sentence: "I am that I am." One can see how it immediately suggests possibilities of expansion, since the *am* invites to the discussion of God as a *being,* which term in turn calls for some variant of non-being. Or the Spinozist statement of identity in his definition of substance as *Causa sui,* invites to expansion in terms of cause and caused (freedom and necessity).

Or an identity like the theme of a play is broken down analytically into principles of opposition which in their variants compete and communicate by a neutral ground shared in common. For instance, were we to situate the "identity" of *Othello* in the theme of jealousy, we should immediately find it subdividing, in accordance with the properties of love, into love as the essence of the Othello-Desdemona relation and hate as the essence of the Othello-Iago relation. Iago may be considered "consubstantial" with Othello in that he represents the principles of jealousy implicit in Othello's delight in Desdemona as a private spiritual possession. Iago, to arouse Othello, must talk a language that Othello knows as well as he, a language implicit in the nature of Othello's love as the idealization of his private property in Desdemona. This language is the dialectical opposite of Othello's; but it so thoroughly shares a common ground with Othello's language that its insinuations are never for one moment irrelevant to Othello's thinking. Iago must be cautious in leading Othello to believe them as *true:* but Othello never for a moment doubts them as *values*.

We can grasp the point by contrasting the assumptions behind the entire play with such notions of material and spiritual property as might prevail among the peasants of polyandrous Tibet. Or we could state the matter formally by recalling the dialectic formula quoted by Coleridge: *inter res heterogeneas non datur oppositio,* a notion that he also expresses by observing that *rivales* are opposite banks of the *same* stream. Iago's goatish imagery works upon Othello by suggesting Cassio in his place; and this puts Othello beside himself, in leading him to experience his own relations exclusively from without rather than from within. In the image of Cassio as his successful rival, motives within himself become alienated. The effect is all the more brutal in that, as thus considered only from without, many of the important modifications in the relations between Othello and Desdemona are eliminated—and Othello now sees Desdemona in terms of this greatly reduced idiom, wholly lacking in possibilities of idealization.

The principle of identity, as carried into the realm of discourse, always leads to a localizing in some term which has potentialities of its own. Thus we noted that Jehovah's words, "I am that I am," implicitly contain the equating of God with being. Or one might also have chosen to develop the words idealistically, in the featuring of the "I" as the essence of the identity. The whole matter leads us into the strategic choice between synonymizing and desynonymizing that momentously affects a writer's key terms. For we may stress either the element that two terms have in common or those respects wherein they are distinct. And if they are ancestral terms, different perspectives may be generated from such beginnings, as a slight deflection at the centre may show as a vast one at the circumference.

Thus, to treat two terms as differing in degree is to exemplify the principle of merger (as with Hume's treatment of "impressions" and "ideas" as respectively "more lively" and "less lively" perceptions). And we exemplify the principle of division when treating such pairs as differences in kind (as with Kant's distinction between concepts and ideas). The Hegelian *Insofern* (like Spinoza's *quatenus*) offers a basic resource here—as Hegel says of something white, cubical, and tart that *insofar as* it is white it is not cubical, *insofar as* it is white and cubical it is not tart, etc. "Shakespeare *qua* Englishman" draws the line differently than "Shakespeare *qua* poet"—and such resources permit us to *divide speculatively* the *empirically indivisible*. Thus is made possible the Socratic way of thought whereby the artist *as artist* can be said to be interested only in the perfection of his art; the ruler, *as ruler,* can be said to be interested only in the good of his subjects; and "in what he prescribes, the physician, *insofar as* he is a physician, considers not his own good but the good of the patient; for the physician is also a ruler having the human body as a subject, and is not a mere money-maker." In sum, one's initial act in choosing "where to draw the line" by choosing terms that merge or terms that divide has an anticipatory effect upon one's conclusions.

Eric Bell discusses a similar aspect of dialectic in his remarks on the importance of the way in which the mathematician "sets up" his equations, when confronting the situation that is to be "idealized" in mathematical terms. And in his *Procedures of Empirical Science,* Victor F. Lenzen treats of the same dialectical resource when discussing the "partition between object and observer," as affected by the use of instruments. Citing Bohr, he notes that if one taps an object with a stick held firmly in the hand, "the stick is an apparatus that may be viewed as part of the observer." (Note the term "part of," which here gives us merger.) But if the stick is held loosely, the stick itself becomes the perceived object, "and the partition is between stick and hand." (The stick here is "apart from" the observer.)

There is a card trick that illustrates to perfection the strategic importance of the shifts between the principles of merger and division. Let us say that you hid the Jack of Hearts, and your problem is, by leading questions, to bring your audience to the selection of this card.

The leading questions follow an order of decreasing generalization, and so shift between merger and division. Let us say that the Jack of Hearts is always kept implicit in the various orders of generalization.

Thus, you first ask: "Name the four suits." The answer is: "Spades, clubs, hearts, and diamonds." Then you ask: "Select two of them." If the answer is, say, "Hearts and clubs," your next question is, "Now select one of these." But if the answer had been, say, "spades and clubs," the Jack of Hearts would be excluded. And in that case, you would say instead: "That leaves hearts and diamonds. Now select one of these." Similarly, if hearts are selected, you "merge" with the choice, and proceed: "Now name the four highest cards in that suit." But if diamonds are named, you "divide," saying instead: "That leaves hearts. Now name the four highest hearts." Next you call for a selection of two among the four, again using whichever principle serves to keep the Jack of Hearts implicit in the choice. Then you call for a selection of one. If the Jack is named, you produce it. If the other card is named, you say, "That leaves the Jack," and produce it.

When thinkers shift between their therefore's and their however's, are they not following a like procedure? Or between synonymizings and desynonymizings. Or between distinctions in kind and distinctions in degree.

We previously mentioned (on page 254) Aquinas' distinction between the univocal and the equivocal. An "univocal" derivation of the world from God as its efficient cause would be like that of offspring from parent: an exact reproduction in kind ("as when man reproduces man"). But the relation is "equivocal" as when the work bears the character of the workman (as when "an agent is present to that upon which it acts"). The work, as the effect, "pre-exists virtually in the efficient cause" (the workman). An agent as such is perfect (being actual); but the matter upon which an agent acts is imperfect (being potential). Hence "to pre-exist virtually in the efficient cause is to pre-exist . . . in a more perfect degree." Hence, in such equivocal derivation, God as cause is more "eminent" than the world as effect.

Such a course from God to His Creation can, by our interpretation, collapse into a blunt distinction between the start and the finish—whereupon we confront the paradox of substance, and can say that a world derived "substantially" from God both is and is not like its divine ground. But, of course, the paradox in its simplicity is greatly modified, and even concealed, by the steps that are thus interposed. And in a similar spirit, theologians can shift between "merger" and "division" tactics in choosing on some occasions to reason from human experience to the divine and on other occasions to consider God and man as fundamentally different. To use the former method alone (as with reasoning in formal logic) would lead to pantheism; to use the latter method alone encourages a stress upon "conditions" that, when Occamistically truncated, leads to materialism.

The dialectical principles of merger and division are clearly apparent in any systems of *classification,* be they the formal and explicit classifications of the sciences or the classificatory structure implicit in the "equations" of a poem. Though scientific classification is often considered to possess a kind of non-verbal or extra-verbal "reality," its essentially *dialectical* nature is obvious in Lenzen's remark that "Classification is founded on the similarities between things and events; it is based upon the fact that things are similar in specific respects and dissimilar in others." And as for the classification of "events": though "events" themselves are often said to be "constitutive of reality," we appreciate the essentially dialectical nature of an event when Lenzen lists as examples of events "a flash of lightning, an eclipse of the sun, an earthquake, the birth of a living being," all of which are capable of being carved at many different joints, while we are further told that "In daily life and qualitative science an event may extend through an appreciable duration, but for precision an event is idealized as the occurrence of properties at an instant."

Even so apparently "factual" a matter as correlation depends upon the place at which our concepts draw the line between merger and division; and the dialecticians of mathematics can derive "invariance" as a function of their symbols, though the fruitful use of this dialectical resource is not taken as proof that invariants exist in nature. Whether or not invariants exist in nature, they *do* exist in language, since any generalization that applies to a whole series of transformations is invariant with respect to that series.

The language of poetry has this same classificatory nature, and the analysis of "equations" on the Symbolic level is intended to reveal it; but it is usually left implicit. The concrete vocabulary used in proverbs may conceal from us their essentially *classificatory* nature. But actually, proverbs comprise a moralistic frame of concepts so highly generalized that incidents unlike in every particular circumstance can be classed together under the same proverbial head. Both the king and the peasant, for instance, might have an experience that led each to say,

"One man's meat is another man's poison." This would be the proverbial heading under which each classified his experience. It would be the "invariant" element common to both experiences. Yet the two experiences could be as distinct in their particulars as the differences between their two ways of life.

The thought suggests what we mean by treating imagery as classificatory. For instance, if a book were constructed about action in two contrasted scenes, one featuring imagery of the country and the other imagery of the city, we could treat each of these scenes as the generalization that classified all the details of action taking place in it. Similarly, a man with a tic, as with an eye that twitches when certain things are said, thereby gives us, in a bodily image, the evidences of a classification. For the tic reveals that he feels an emotional element in common among a series of events that, to men with other points of view, would not seem thus closely classifiable together. It testifies to the merger, within the individual psyche, of matters that for others would be divided.

On the Rhetorical level, the merger-division shift draws upon the fact that any *distinction* is liable to sharpening into a *contrast,* and any contrast may be attenuated into the form of a distinction. At the time of French hegemony on the continent of Europe, for instance, French thought placed much stress upon the *universal* aspects of human motivation. The Germans on the other hand got for themselves a kind of "symbolic autonomy" by stressing the *distinctness* of the various cultural strains. It was a kind of art-gallery principle, involving an appreciation of different cultural traditions somewhat as one might appreciate different traditions of painting, or different types of human personality, valuing each for itself, in its cultural sovereignty, without necessarily choosing among them. Yet the position had implicit in it a declaration of independence from French hegemony (stated in terms of "universal" man). And in time it developed into the militance of a cultural *contrast,* as when used to reënforce Nazi expansionism.

Mind-Body, Being-Nothing, and Action-Passion Pairs

The mind-body, being-nothing, and action-passion pairs generalize the first major steps usually taken towards the localizing of identity. That is, the principles of merger and division apply to all thought; the mind-body, being-nothing, and action-passion pairs, singly or in combination, variously overlapping, and variously manipulated, will be found to figure in any statement which embodies the principles of merger and division specifically. Their scope as generalizations is only slightly less broad.

The resources of the mind-body pair are obvious. The members of the pair can be treated as in apposition or in opposition, or as sharing a relation in which one member is primary and the other derivative, or as aspects of an underlying reality that is the ground of both, etc. Since either of the terms can be taken to represent the other, physicalist or idealist reductions are readily available. And Rhetorically, by shifting from one member of the pair to the other, one has the opportunity to "idealize" his own cause while "materializing" that of his opponents.

The being-nothing pair has its most prevalent form in the essence-existence pair, with either member of the pair being capable of selection as the "reality." Thus Plato situates the reality in *being,* the appearance in *existence;* but Santayana's variant of Platonism would situate the *substantial* nature of things in the flux of existence, while "essences" are such characters as existing things share with non-existents. Or in historicist frameworks, the pair may take the form of a distinction between the *becoming* and the *having-become.* Here the vital principle that gives form is equated with becoming; and the formed is equated with the fossilized, as a state of having-become.

The principles of merger and division can readily figure here, as when being is equated with the one, and becoming with the many (though of course the principles of the one and the many may be considered in apposition rather than in opposition, as with the microcosm-macrocosm pattern whereby any part of the universe is taken as representative of the whole (*omnia ubique*). Or we may move into the Eleatic paradoxes, as with the dialectician Zeno, "who has an art of speaking which makes the same things appear to his hearers like and unlike, one and many, at rest and in motion," as Socrates says in the *Phaedrus.*

In any given work, the pairs usually merge and divide in many ways, depending upon the particular interests that set the course for that given work. And once you have localized a form, the requirements of this particularized logic come to the fore. The action-passion pair, for instance, may be localized as the peace-war pair, or as coöperation and competition. Or if the active principle is equated with mind and the passive principle with body, we may find ourselves working rather with a faith-knowledge or act-scene pair. Or action and passion may become indistinguishable, as with a pair like love and war, or the Wagnerian pair, love and death. Theories of psychogenic illness seem to be a commingling of the action-passion and mind-body pairs. The principle of evil is usually equated with division ("Legion"); yet there can also be malign unities, and we know how nations can be unified by resistance to a common enemy.

Reviewing briefly, let us recall that the action-passion pair, as used directly, gives us the resources of actus and status (the agent's status residing in the *properties* that go with his act). And such sub-stance in properties leads us into considerations for linking the Stance family of terms with the Power family. And acts become scenic in that *enactments* survive as *constitutions*.

Theories of the development from implicit (sometimes equated with the "unconscious") to explicit (the "conscious") can be treated as variants of the action-passion terminology, owing to their bearing upon the potentiality-actuality relation. But here obviously we are moving close to the third aspect of our subject: *alloiosis,* transformation, transcendence.

The Socratic Transcendence

We have said that a distinction can become a contrast. This takes place when some part formerly treated synecdochically, as representative of the whole, becomes divisive with reference to the whole of which it was a part. Thus a class that represents the culmination of a society's purposes may, under changing scenic conditions, gradually arrive at the point where its act (and therefore its status) is no longer representative of the new conditions in their totality. The actus and status that were formerly representative thus become antithetical (as with the position of the nobility, which had represented a culmination of the feudal society, but became antithetical to the society of trade except insofar as they adapted themselves to the new conditions, themselves becoming *embourgeoisés*).

In any event, it is obvious that the transformation from the merger of the representative role to the division of the antithetic role represents a change of *principle*. A critical point has been passed; a new quality of motivation has been introduced. The moment of crisis in transcendence involves a new motive discovered en route.

Such an introduction of a new motive may often look like a break in continuity, particularly when it is exemplified in the form of a change in the character of some figure in a fiction. And surprisingly enough, though Jowett devoted so great a portion of his life to the translating and interpreting of Plato, he fails to deal with the nature of transcendence or transformation as embodied in Plato's dialogues. That is, whereas he fully recognizes the Platonic *doctrine* of transcendence, he does not analyze the dialogues themselves as *acts* of transcendence. For not only do they *plead for* transcendence; they are themselves so formed that the end transcends the beginning. Thus, in his Analysis of the *Republic,* Jowett writes:

> Or a more general division into two parts may be adopted; the first (Books I-IV) containing the description of a State framed generally in accordance with Hellenic notions of religion and morality, while in the second (Books V-X) the Hellenic State is transformed into an ideal kingdom of philosophy, of which all other governments are the perversions. These two points of view are really opposed, and the opposition is only veiled by the genius of Plato. The Republic, like the Phaedrus, is an imperfect whole; the higher light of philosophy breaks through the regularity of the Hellenic temple, which at last fades away into the heavens. Whether this imperfection of structure arises from an enlargement of the plan; or from the imperfect reconcilement in the writer's own mind of the struggling elements of thought which are now first brought together by him; or, perhaps, from the composition of the work at different times— are questions, like the similar question about the Iliad and the Odyssey, which are worth asking, but which cannot have a distinct answer.

Similarly, in his Introduction to the *Phaedrus,* Jowett questions "the notion that the work of a great artist like Plato could not fail in unity, and that the unity of a dialogue requires a single subject." He says that the dialogue is not "a style of composition in which the requirement of unity is most stringent." The double titles in several of the dialogues, he says, seem to indicate that Plato made no attempt at a "severer unity." He notes that some dialogues have digressions only remotely connected with the main theme. And:

> The Republic is divided between the search after justice and the construction of the ideal state; the Parmenides between the criticism of the Platonic ideas and of the Eleatic one or being; the Sophist between the detection of the Sophist and the correlation of ideas.

And he concludes that we should not expect to find one idea pervading a whole work, but several, "as the invention of the writer may suggest or his fancy wander." If each dialogue were devoted to the development of a single idea, there would be no controversy "as to whether the Phaedrus treated of love or rhetoric." But "like every great artist he gives unity of form to the different and apparently distracting topics which he brings together." He "works freely," and is not supposed to have worked out a perfect outline before he begins. He "fastens or weaves together the frame of his discourse loosely and imperfectly."

Yet throughout these comments, Jowett was in a sense quite accurate. He has characterized the process of transcendence as it looks from without, rather than as it looks from within. For as seen from without, the change from one level of discourse to another would be a kind of jolt or inconsistency, a somewhat random or opportunistic juxtaposition of partially disrelated subjects. Yet as seen from within, this change of levels would be precisely what the dialogue was designed to trace. For a Platonic dialogue is not formed simply by breaking an idea into its component parts and taking them up in one-two-three order (the purely scholastic aspect in Aristotle's method of exposition). A Platonic dialogue is rather a process of *transformation* whereby the position at the end transcends the position at the start, so that the position at the start can eventually be seen in terms of the new motivation encountered en route.

Considering a dialogue thus, as the development through a series of levels, we find that Jowett's summary of the Phaedrus reveals its structure perfectly, so perfectly that it is hard to see why he could fail to draw the proper conclusions from his own description:

> The subjects of the Phaedrus (exclusive of the short introductory passage about mythology which is suggested by the local tradition) are first the false or conventional art of rhetoric; secondly, love or the inspiration of beauty and knowledge which is described as madness; thirdly, dialectic or the art of composition and division;

fourthly, the true rhetoric, which is based upon dialectic; fifthly, the superiority of the spoken over the written word. The continuous thread which appears and reappears throughout is rhetoric; this is the ground into which the rest of the Dialogue is inlaid. . . . The speech of Lysias, and the first speech of Socrates are examples of the false rhetoric, as the second speech of Socrates is adduced as an instance of the true. But the true rhetoric is based upon dialectic, and dialectic is a sort of inspiration akin to love; they are two aspects of philosophy in which the technicalities of rhetoric are absorbed. Thus the example becomes also the deeper theme of discourse. The true knowledge of things in heaven and earth is based upon enthusiasm or love of the ideas; and the true order of speech or writing proceeds according to them. Love, again, has three degrees: first, of interested love corresponding to the conventionalities of rhetoric; secondly, of disinterested or mad love, fixed on objects of sense and answering, perhaps, to poetry; thirdly, of disinterested love directed towards the unseen, answering to dialectic or the science of the ideas. Lastly, the art of rhetoric in the lower sense is found to rest on a knowledge of the natures and characters of men, which Socrates at the commencement of the Dialogue has described as his own peculiar study.

Does not Jowett's own summary make it apparent that the themes of love, rhetoric, and dialectic are here all parts of a single series? Lysias' speech on love, which is read with naïve admiration by Phaedrus, is trivial. It is built about a conceit, the proposition that Lysias should gain his suit not because he is a lover but because he is a non-lover, and the non-lover will never cause the beloved the many disturbances that a lover would. Socrates lifts the dialogue to a higher level in using the same conceit as Lysias, but developing it with examples of much deeper moral significance. His next speech transcends this in turn, by abandoning the terms which Lysias had set for the discussion. It is an impassioned celebration of love; and it is dialectically matured by systematic subdivision into the kinds of love, and by the matching of Eros with Anteros. When Socrates has finished, he proceeds to point out the superiority of this speech over the other two. He thereby raises the dialogue to a fourth level: the abstract appreciation of the formal principles that had been embodied in his speech. This involves a discussion of dialectic in general—and the last level is reached when Socrates rounds out this discussion by a celebration of the spoken word as superior to the written word.

Why does this round out the whole dialogue? Why is it the ultimate step that in a sense enables us of a sudden to see down, as through
an interior shaft, to the place where we had started, far below, and to
see it now in terms of the place at which we had arrived? I would
interpret the matter thus:

At the opening of the dialogue there had been reference to a "feast
of discourse." We might be content simply to call such an expression
a metaphor, and think no more of the matter. But when we consider
it from the standpoint of the Platonic theories, I think we can see in it
much more than a metaphor. It is not merely a "metaphor." It is a
juncture of two levels. "Feast" is on the level of bodily appetite. Yet
not quite. For the element of *sociality* in a feast introduces an ingredient of motivation beyond that of sheer animal hunger. And
"discourse" completes this pattern of transcendence—for the feast of
words that accompanies the banquet involves bodily appetite in only a
most roundabout way, as one most enjoys his food and digests it best
when his general attitude towards the world is that of a "healthy appetite." We may again recall the modern theories of psychosomatic
medicine that illustrate the principle in reverse, as with the doctrine
that digestive disorders, even to the extent of ulcers, may derive from a
sense of insecurity or disappointment. For in the "thinking of the
body," the primary expectancy is that of food; hence digestive disorders
may well result when mental insecurity is metonymously reduced to
its equivalent in purely physiological terms.

Since love is similarly appetitive, we have a cluster of *food, love,
hunger, enjoyment* experiences functioning at the roots of purpose.
And recalling Plato's *Symposium,* we see a certain deeper justice in
discourses on love on the occasion of a banquet (a pattern which in our
less eloquent society, is often exemplified more modestly by the com-
fortable interchange of ribald jokes).

And so, I propose to interpret the dialogue, not as a sequence of parts
somewhat disrelated to one another and given a tolerable semblance
of unity by the sheer literary tact of the writer; but I would interpret it
as leading, step by step, from the sheer bodily appetite of the "non-
lover" who would possess the beloved without even the rudiments of
sentiment, up to the stage of purely verbal insemination. In brief, the
dialogue is a "way" from sexual intercourse to the Socratic intercourse
of dialectical converse.

We generally use too few terms when interpreting the concept of "Platonic love." Thus, turning to the dictionary, I read that Platonic love is "a pure, spiritual affection, subsisting between persons of opposite sex, unmixed with carnal desires, and regarding the mind only and its excellences;—a species of love for which Plato was a warm advocate." In the first place, there is nothing to be gained by overlooking the fact that Socrates was *not* talking about love "subsisting between persons of the opposite sex." The Athenians' charge against Socrates, as *corruptor juventutis,* involved his relations with young men. It was with these young men that Socrates carried on his dialectic intercourse, with its educational insemination.

And it is the living, *spoken* word that would be the completest form of love, as thus transformed into the corresponding interlockings of verbal interchange. Socrates complains that once a speech is written down, its possibilities of dialectical accommodation are ended. It must present the same wording to all sorts of people. And then he turns to the principle of the seed, embodied in the spoken word of knowledge which has a living soul, as the garden in which it is sown by a skilled husbandman. The garden of letters, he says, exists at its best in this "serious pursuit of the dialectician," who

> finds a congenial soul, and then with knowledge engrafts and sows
> words which are able to help themselves and him who planted them,
> and are not unfruitful, but have in them seeds which may bear fruit
> in other natures, nurtured in other ways—making the seed everlast-
> ing and the possessors happy to the utmost extent of human happi-
> ness.

In his poem "The Mother of God," Yeats startlingly applies the pattern to Christian symbolism, in referring to Mary's conception of the Logos as received "through the hollow of an ear," in keeping with a Byzantine notion as to the way in which the Annunciation, or receiving of the word, took place.

Does not this view give us a deeper insight into the nature of Plato's thought than is got by too pruriently pure an interpretation of Platonic love? We see its relation to the whole theory of abstraction that pervades Platonist thought. We see exactly how the transcendence *begins* in the bodily, and may even *return* to the bodily, though with the difference that new terms have been discovered en route, so that new

principles are introduced.   The third oration is the turning point of the
dialogue.   Following it, the restricted terminology of the first and
second orations is permanently discredited.   But could we also say that
steps four and five similarly discredit the third stage?   I think not.
Socrates has spoken too eloquently in honor of Eros.   And it is left as
a profound motive, by which any one may expect to be moved on occasion.   But along with it, as its purely socialized equivalent, is the
universal converse of dialectic.

There are two acts representative of each situation, though by the
paradox of substance they may readily merge into one, as the "essential"
is one, and thus continually resists the attempt to divide it clearly into a
"good" and a "bad."   And the distinction further tends to be obliterated by the dialectical fact that either of such two extremes is ultimately stated in terms of the other, their differences partaking in a
common ground of indifferences.   But insofar as the separation is
maintained, there would be a representative action and a representative
passion (which latter, in a secular terminology, would amount either
to a representative illness or a representative crime).   The transcending "essence" of a situation would, in brief, tend to manifest the defect
of its qualities, at least as regards heresies which efficiently tracked
down such unwieldy possibilities at a sacrifice of balance.   Thus the
slaying of the ruler is the act representative of the democratic situation.
And "pride" is a kind of "blanket" offense, representative of the human
situation in general.

Biologically, Greek love was an offence, since its fruitfulness would
not be that of tribal progeny.   It was thus the "representative crime" of
the Athenian enlightenment, the practice that corresponded in the
realm of transgression to the pedagogy of Socratic intercourse in the
realm of the transcendent and ideal.

Socrates was thus accused of the "representative" transgression.   And
whatever may have been the realities of the case in the literal sense, the
structure of the *Phaedrus* shows that he was a "corruptor of youth" in
the transcendental sense.   He was thus resigned to the hemlock, since
"impiety" was the "logical conclusion" of his austere philosophy as it
would seem when reduced metonymically to the simplest biological
terms.

Ironically, then, this theorist of transcendence was the victim of a
transcendence transcended.   On this one occasion at least the fellow-

citizens who cast their judgments against him were themselves transcending. For the homosexual love which lay at the basis of their educational system was most fully and nobly represented in the ideals of Socratic intercourse. Hence in selecting Socrates as their victim, they were choosing the thinker who represented the very *essence* of the cultural trends away from tribalism. They could not have been more accurate. Doubtless they were for the most part simple fellows who, insofar as homosexual love attracted them at all, were content with boy favorites, as with the practice of Greek army officers casually but frequently mentioned in Xenophon. But they were sensitive enough to know when they had come upon the very *essence* of such practices. And it resided of course in the Socratic doctrines of transcendence whereby "corruption" was transformed into a "saving of souls," an ambiguity that Mann recovers when the Aschenbach of *Death in Venice* commingles expressions from the *Phaedrus* in his conscientiously corrupt contemplation of young Tadzio. A process that had thus been translated from the bodily to the spiritual, they (the lumbering citizenry) translated back again. In punishing him, they were punishing the biological transgression implicit in their enlightenment itself, which was in every way tending to transcend the thinking proper to them as a tribal integer. He was their properly "representative" victim, their properly chosen vessel. And so thoroughgoing a searcher after essence was bound to feel that their choice of him was "essentially" correct.

In sum: His version of the dialectic, as attested in the *Phaedrus,* had the ambivalence of the potential. It was either a *transcendence* of homosexuality or a transcendence of *homosexuality*. Being in the latter aspect "biologically guilty," it was transgression against the principles of the tribe. It was thus essentially "impious," quite as charged. And in the light of what we have said about the vicarious atonement through the scapegoat, we need not be deterred by the thought that those who judged against him were incipiently implicated in his guilt. Indeed, we assume that this was a contributing motive in their judgment against him.

Thus Socrates died that Plato and Aristotle might live. Out of his death, Plato was enabled to reconstruct a tribal emphasis idealistically atop the enlightened break-down of the tribal culture. The steps from the *Phaedrus* to the *Republic* to the *Laws* form a dialectic series in themselves: the first motivated by a dissolution of the tribal in its traditional, realistic, "pre-enlightened" state; the second reclaiming the tribal concept on a "higher" level, in the form of an idealistically constituted State; the third brought down to the *business* of legislation, almost a Benthamite kind of project.

As for Aristotle, whose work is like a final revision of Plato, adjusting to one another the *conclusions* in which the Socratico-Platonist heuristics had terminated, he too could without strain transcend the original tribal patterns of thought which the Socratic dialectic had "impiously" surpassed. His strangely infertile god, a principle of the *loved* rather than a principle of generation, was in this respect sufficiently non-tribal to serve as the basis of a Hellenistic imperialism that extended far beyond the tribal orbit, though it was finally merged with the tribal deity, Jehovah, in the new more "spiritualized" Christian concept of the tribal, which allowed for the catholic inclusion of all men in one family.

We have spoken of the *Republic,* placing it midway between the *Phaedrus* and the *Laws.* If one examines it from the standpoint of its nature as a "way," I think one will find that it is a process whereby an *economic necessity* is transformed into a *moral purpose.* We begin by observing how injustice develops *pari passu* with the increase of economic specialization. Such occupational diversity, we are told, makes for the break-down of the original tribal homogeneity into a corresponding diversity in ways of living.[15] And by a series of transformations involving the search for an ideal of justice that will prevail over and above the many divergencies, we reach the conclusion that justice resides in each man's readiness to do that for which he is best fitted. Here, you will note, you are back at much the same diversified situation with which you began. The development is now repeated grandly, as you are taken on the Upward Way to a vision of the One (a principle of Unity which, as we observed in our discussion of Purpose, Plato equates with the purposive concept of the Good). And when you return to the world of diversity, you consider it in terms of the new principle encountered en route, whereupon it is viewed in a transcendent light. And what the transcendence amounts to in this case is the addition of moral terms that solve a technical problem

---

[15] Recall our previous remark that the Greek word for "justice" (*dike*) is also the word for "way" in the sense of what we today might call "pattern of life" or "class morality," etc.

(the breakdown of the tribe into a condition of great occupational diversity). The philosopher will devote himself to the welfare of the State, whose diversity is now infused for him with his vision of the One.

In all that we have been saying about transcendence, it is easy to see why Plato, as dialectician, was so attracted to mathematics as a dialectical discipline. For in both the Platonist and neo-Platonist versions of transcendence, the dialectician begins with the particulars of the senses, with the images of imagination—and he subjects these to progressive transformations whereby their sensory diversity is thoroughly lost in generalization, the structure being completed in the vision of the One (which we might call the Title of Titles). When reading accounts of mathematical progress, and of the ways in which images, or metaphors, guided the development of mathematical formulae,[16] we can readily see why mathematics should be treated as an aspect of dialectic.

One might, for instance, conceive of electricity after the analogy of a river, and thereby arrive at formulae for ohms, volts, and amperes, corresponding to the strength, speed, and volume of the current in a river bed. Other aspects of electricity, however, would suggest other metaphors, which in turn acquired corresponding mathematical formulation. And finally, as men began to work with these formulations themselves, complicating them with the help of still other metaphors, or modifying them in terms wholly intrinsic to mathematics, the entire procedure resulted in a body of formulations beneath which lay a whole jumble of disjunct imagery, more bewildering than any mystic's oxymoron or any Surrealist's assemblage of forms from different orders of experience. That is, in effect, a way of carrying out the dialectician's ideal: the use of imagery to transcend imagery.

And surely Faraday's search for a mathematical formula that would reduce all forms of energy to one expression is, in effect, an embodiment of the Platonist movement towards the One, which we would call the Title of Titles. Such a formula would be a perfect "god-term," inas-

---

[16] *Aspects of Scientific Rationalism in the Nineteenth Century,* by George de Santillana, contains a very clear review of the ways in which imagery guided mathematical formulation. Indeed, both this essay and its companion piece, Edgar Zilsel's *Problems of Empiricism* are recommended highly as works that at every point bear succinctly on the subjects considered in this book. And we originally included a section (later omitted for exigencies of space) which attempted a partial translation of these two excellent studies into the language of "dramatism."

much as it had, through a dialectic operation lasting through two thousand years and carried on by many voices, progressed through imagery to the complete transcending of imagery. Still it would not be quite the end, for it would not quite have led through language to the transcending of language, since mathematics is but a special case of language. But as regards the relation between such transcendent use of the principle of merger and its relation to the principle of division, even though we might in a sense say that such a universal reduction as Faraday's would provide the generic formula for all motivation, we should note that any such summarizing term would necessarily be dispensed with, in any statement about specific motivational problems, or even specific mathematical problems. For whatever its value as a generalization about the nature of nature, it would be of no value for particular problems requiring description in particular terms. Or, in the personal realm, it would not be of value for describing the disposition of factors to be considered by a particular person trying to reach a decision about a specific matter of human relations. Only its "spirit" might be present in such instances. In another way, its very nature as a generalization, or summation, or title of titles, would lay it open to the same objection that Galileo raised to the name of God as an explanation of natural causes, since in explaining everything it would explain nothing.

The Temporizing of Essence

Because of the pun whereby the logically prior can be expressed in terms of the temporally prior, and *v.v.,* the ways of transcendence, in aiming at the discovery of *essential* motives, may often take the historicist form of symbolic *regression.* That is, if one is seeking for the "essence" of motives, one can only express such a search in the temporal terms of imaginative literature as a process of "going back." And conversely, one given to retrospect, as Proust in his "remembrance of things past," may conceptualize his concern as a search for "essence."

This double vocabulary for the expression of essence is, I think, a basic factor to be watched continually if one would know how to translate back and forth between logical and temporal vocabularies. And many statements that might otherwise seem worthless, depending upon the kind of language you favor, can be readily reclaimed by such discounting.

In his *Foundations of the Social Sciences,* for instance, Otto Neurath proposes that we should drop the "cause-effect phraseology," and should use instead the "growing-out-of phraseology." That is, instead of saying that certain causes produce certain effects, we should follow the example of some savages who speak of some things as "growing out of" other things, or "arising from" them, or "coming out of" them. Such a change of phraseology would obviously reduce to terms of temporal sequence the parent-offspring relation that we have noted where ancestry is stated in causal terms. "The whole cause-effect phraseology," he says, "seems to be rooted in some older assumptions." ("Rooted in," you will note, is another of his proposed emendations. If we replaced it by an expression like "derived from," we might have a usage which would satisfy both temporalist and essentialist at once, as each could read it in his own way.)

The only way in which I would want to change Mr. Neurath's suggestions would be to interpret them differently. And I would advise one to read carefully this section of his pamphlet for added hints as to the ways in which essentialist and temporalist thought can be convertible. In the light of such speculations consider, for instance, a doctrine like Freud's borrowing of Darwin's theory of the "primal horde," as explained in his *Totem and Taboo,* and in *Group Psychology and the Analysis of the Ego.* If you recall that Darwin's evolutionism vowed him to a wholly historicist vocabulary, you will begin by taking it for granted that Darwin could not possibly state a theory of essence in his characteristic terms except by attributing to this essence some stage of existence in the past. And Freud, in response to the Darwinian vocabulary, would be led to a similar mode of expression. Hence, if you take the theory of the "primal horde" as a statement about *existence* rather than about *essence,* you find it proved or disproved by anthropological research.

Anthropologists seem to have done it quite a lot of damage. There seems to be no evidence that any such "primal horde" ever existed. But if we interpreted the concept as a statement about *essence,* we might find it quite usable despite the anthropologists' discrediting of it. For it may well be that the human relation which the concept of the primal horde designates really is *essential* to some social structures, such as the society of his own day which Freud was studying. Indeed, do we not see Freud himself attempting to rescue the concept as "essentially" true, despite its existential discrediting? Thus he writes in his chapter on "The Group and the Primal Horde":

> In 1912 I took up a conjecture of Darwin's to the effect that the primitive form of human society was that of a horde ruled over despotically by a powerful male. I attempted to show that the fortunes of this horde have left indestructible traces upon the history of human descent; and, especially, that the development of totemism, which comprises in itself the beginnings of religion, morality, and social organization, is concerned with the killing of the chief by violence and the transformation of the paternal horde into a community of brothers. To be sure, this is only a hypothesis, like so many others with which archaeologists endeavour to lighten the darkness of prehistorical times—a 'Just-So Story,' as it was amusingly called by a not unkind critic (Kroeger); but I think it is creditable to such a hypothesis if it proves able to bring coherence and understanding into more and more new regions.

At the end of this citation, we see clearly what the historicist vocabulary here lets Freud in for. His analysis of the patriarchal family convinced him that certain kinds of rivalry and allegiance are essential to it. But to state this belief in historicist terms, he had to assume: (a) that such a condition had existed in its purity in some past era, and (b) that the lineaments of this original extreme form were still observable as more or less attenuated survivals. When the theory was attacked by anthropologists, he still wanted to retain it, and for a good reason: for whatever doubts one might cast upon the pattern of the primal horde as an *existent,* he needed the concept as a term in his description of the family *essence.*

And may we not see the same principle at work, though more subtly, in the Platonist doctrine (as in the *Meno*) that knowledge is innate in us, remembered from a past existence? Might this doctrine be a somewhat "storial" way of saying that there is certain *essential* knowledge, or that there are fixed *principles* of knowledge?

Similarly, the doctrine of "original sin" could be converted from historical terms (i.e., the "historical" terms of legend) to essentialist terms, if we translated it as "essential sin" (that is, man as "essentially a transgressor"). And we could then clearly see Freud dealing with the same "essential" situation, though in non-theological terms, when in his *Reflections* he sees behind the injunction, "Thou shalt not kill," man's lineal descent from a long line of murderers. But murder is not essential to man just in this temporally derivative sense. It is essential in that it is the "logical conclusion" or "reduction to absurdity" of vituperation and invective. This condition exists *now*. Indeed, I felt it when witnessing the genuine dismay that many of Roosevelt's bitter enemies revealed at the news of his death. I recalled the psychoanalytic theory (previously mentioned in these pages) that Dostoevsky had been disastrously unsettled by his father's death, since he had vicariously participated in this death by secretly willing it. And when, reversing our application of time to essence, we recall that magical prophecy aimed to bring about events by solemnly proclaiming that they would come to pass, we might also recall the great "concern" which Roosevelt's opponents at the last election constantly showed about his health. I do not mean that there is a single one of them who would have killed him. I mean simply that his sacrifice was demanded, as the logical conclusion of their own position. His death was "representative" of their antagonistic attitude. And when it came, they were perhaps more deeply shocked than was the case with many of his devoted followers, for whom his spirit would still live on, since for them his death was likewise a resurrection. For his followers his death was a sacrifice ennobling the cause that, thus revivified, would survive him.

Ibsen's *Peer Gynt* offers us an exceptionally good opportunity to observe the workings of the time-essence ambiguity. For here the plot is explicitly concerned with Peer's search for his true self (that is to say, his essence). And since drama necessarily takes the form of "story," the approach to essence is conveyed in temporal, or "storial" terms.

Peer Gynt is the third of the poetic satires that preceded Ibsen's turn to realistic social drama. The first, *Love's Comedy,* attacked the community's insensitivity to the values of individualist, idealist love. The second, *Brand,* ennobles the cause of reform as personalized in a priestly, sacrificial figure. The third satirizes what Ibsen considered characteristic trivialities of the Norwegian character.

But there are important complications. For the paradox of substance operates strongly in Ibsen's plays. Thus, in *The Wild Duck,* Ibsen seems to accept many of the attitudes he most strongly condemned in *An Enemy of the People;* for *The Wild Duck* shows us the reformer from the standpoint of his opponents, quite as *An Enemy of the People* had shown us the opponents from the standpoint of the reformer. There is here a dialectical shift from the voicing of one position to its opposite. Or rather, though both positions are voiced in both plays, the dramatist's sympathies have changed sides, at least within the special conditions of the fiction. And similarly, before Ibsen had finished with the character of *Peer Gynt,* it had greatly transcended its original purely satiric intent. In fact, as we shall show, a close analysis of its imagery will reveal that Peer ends as a replica of the Christ-child.

There seems to run through Ibsen's work an attempt to distinguish, not conceptually but in terms of dramatic action, between an "egoist" and an "individualist." Both in a sense stand alone. But whereas the loneliness of the egoist is selfish, and may thus even take the form of an easy-going sociality, the loneliness of the individualist is that of one who is willing to sacrifice himself for the good of mankind, and who may thus outrage society by *acting alone* in behalf of some *social ideal.* But the distinction is difficult to maintain in its purity, particularly when it is made in terms of action. For egoist and individualist have a neutral ground of attributes shared in common. There are many respects in which these two concepts, even if desynonymized, again become synonymous. Hence one may expect to find ambivalences in Ibsen's portraying of the two types.

The ambiguities responsible for Peer's translation seem to derive in great part from the motives we have been considering with respect to the masculine problem of dissociating the maternal woman from the erotic woman (the problem of distinguishing one's responses to woman as mother from one's responses to woman as the object of courtship). *Peer Gynt* performs a notable role in Ibsen's own development, since it marks the turn from verse to the realistic prose of his problem plays. Where verse and prose become thus motivationally contrasted, we are justified in looking for evidences of precisely such stock-taking as comes with the turn from the maternal to the erotic. For verse, as thus contrasted, is usually set in the familial or "pre-political" cluster of motives (a cluster coadunating the parental, the religious, and the poetic). Hence it in itself may be taken as indicative of a conservative principle lying deeper than the accidental properties of reform which Ibsen may be advocating. A profound inventory is taking place here. And the character whose development must meet these demands is bound to become so laden with ritualistic functions that he is translated far beyond the role of purely social satire.

The ambiguities are complicated by Ibsen's own vocation as a playwright who, in the nature of the case, would possess great aptitude at fabrication, and much responsiveness to the ways of prevarication. Hence, Peer's glibness as a spinner of fantastic tales (a teller of lies that in a deeper sense are true) amounts to a playful idealizing of the playwright's own vocation. And that again would be enough to translate Peer to a "sacrificial" level, as a personal embodiment, however dubiously, of the writer's devotion to his craft. Accordingly, the character as thus finally developed sums up a sufficient complexity of motives to make his very vices attractive, somewhat as with our complex response to the transgressions of Falstaff.

In brief, then, *Peer Gynt* depicts a character in search of his identity. This quest of essence centers in the need to "desynonymize" Peer's responses to the maternal and erotic principles. The desynonymizing is not completed, but instead the erotic woman is idealistically transformed into the maternal woman. Peer's search for essence is thus depicted in terms of a return to the mother. Solveig, who was to be his wife, becomes instead his spiritual mother, replacing his real mother in whose death he had magically participated. Peer is thereby transformed, having found a new principle of motivation. This transformation is expressed in terms of dramatic substance as Peer's grounding in a new parentage. And now, to indicate the major steps in this transformation:

Note that the play begins with Peer as story-teller, inventing tall tales which he tells his mother, to explain his recent absence. But we should take this opening anecdote much more seriously than Peer does, for it wholly symbolizes his situation. Peer is obviously outgrowing his mother's powers to restrain him. Indeed when, a little later, she tries to strike him as if he were still a child, he playfully picks her up and carries her, protesting helplessly. Peer has become too big for the nest. However, the story he tells, to account for his recent absence indicates what form the new motivation has taken. For he tells of having seized a buck reindeer by the horns, of being carried high up on the mountains, of how the buck finally plunges from a cliff towards the water far below, and of how Peer saw in the water the reflection of himself and the buck rising to meet him in his fall.

In sum: breaking free of the earlier, familial identity (going from merger to division), sensing a new purpose as symbolized in the hunt, Peer is carried by the horned buck (a potency). And the mounting and the fall is in its design reflexive, ending as Peer, carried to a fall by this powerful buck, meets the reflection of himself. The pattern incidentally suggests a "problem" at the very centre of Ibsen's individualism; for Peer, in finally dividing from the familial identity with which he had been merged, is here seen to fall into the self. Hence, though Ibsen in his later plays repeatedly seeks for ways in which the individualistic motive can be resocialized (by enlistment in some cause), Peer's story indicates that in its inception it took the pattern of a potency whereby the fall involved encounter with the self. Later the pattern will be repeated in Peer's encounter with the Boyg, who introduces himself as "Myself." The Boyg is so shapeless that when Peer attempts to attack him, there is nowhere to strike, and Peer falls to biting his own arms. As we shall see, this Boyg plays a momentous role in motivating Peer's way of life.

The reindeer theme belongs as essentially to this story as the theme of the two horses belongs to Socrates' talk of love in the *Phaedrus*. It is a power theme, and appears at several important stages in Peer's development. First, when Peer is carried over the cliff to his encounter with the self; next, in Peer's carrying of his mother where, as she struggles helplessly, he plays that he is the Reindeer and she is Peer (whereupon he puts her on the roof, where she is afraid of falling). When he meets Solveig, he likens her to a reindeer that "grows wild when summer's approaching."

There are many women in *Peer Gynt* who appeal to Peer, as it were, in their "pure sexuality." Indeed, the whole thesaurus of amative responses seem to be composed of: the maternal principle, the reflexive; sheer sexual appetite without affection (as when he mounts the hill with another man's bride; when he goes with the three girls who, lacking boys, would play with trolls; and when later, as elderly "prophet," he is the dupe of his transient interest in Anitra)[17]—and finally, Solveig, the one woman he would love with affection. But when Solveig

---

[17] These women, possessing almost the "pure" sexuality of prostitutes, are also close to the reflexive. For their attraction acts upon Peer Gynt's absolute male selfhood, as such an absolute would be expressed in terms of a relation to Woman.

comes to live with him in his newly built forest hut with reindeer horns over the door, he remembers the Boyg's injunction, "Go roundabout." And as Solveig waits to welcome him inside the hut, instead of entering he begins his wanderings.

This is a five-act play. Act III ends appropriately on his mother's death. It is significant timing. Solveig, the one woman whom he could court with affection, has come to live with him. As she calls him, he remembers the Boyg's injunction to go roundabout. If, as we have said, Solveig is to be not simply his beloved, but a new mother-principle, his mother Aase is henceforth superfluous. So Peer's first "roundabout" episode is his return home, where he sits on his sick mother's bed and plays that he is driving her to a party given by Saint Peter in heaven. During the make-believe, she is dying; when he has finished, she is dead. I invite the reader to examine carefully this final scene of the third act, to see whether he can agree with me that Peer has "playfully" participated in her death, thus almost bringing it about, by imitative magic. And in any event, from the standpoint of the development as a whole, if we are right in saying that Solveig is to be the "new mother," Aase becomes superfluous the moment that Solveig enters Peer's cabin to be his woman. And since all the incidents of the plot are but scenic replicas of Peer's own transformations of character, his first "roundabout" approach to Solveig is appropriately his presence at the death of Aase.

Act IV is concerned with Peer's wanderings: the first movement in his search for his essence. Near the end of this act, after he has been deceived by Anitra, he makes an observation much to our purposes. "I have made mistakes," he says; "but it's comforting to realize that my mistakes were the result of the role I had assumed." (He had assumed the role of a prophet.) "It wasn't I myself that made the mistakes." In brief, he is distinguishing between a "scenic" motivation, derived from the *situations* in which he found himself, and such *essential* motivations as an idealist like Ibsen would locate in the Agent, or personality. And then comes the resolve that clearly formulates in temporal terms his search for his essence:

> Suppose I become a travelling scholar, and make a study of past ages? I believe that's the thing for me! I always liked history, and recently I've improved my knowledge. I'll trace the story of mankind. I'll float like a feather on the stream of history. And I'll live

the old days over again, like in a dream. . . . The Past shall be a lock, and I have the key to it. I'll abandon the sordid ways of the present.

Significant timing again: immediately after this resolve, the scene shifts to a hut in a forest in the far north of Norway, where Solveig, now middle-aged, tells us in a song that she still waits for Peer's return.

It is not necessary, for our purposes, to follow all the steps of Peer's return, after the incident where the inmates of an insane asylum (where "each shuts himself in a cask of self") had crowned Peer "the Emperor of Self." But it is worthy of note that, having at one point likened himself to an onion, he peels off the successive layers until nothing is left, whereupon the voice of Solveig is heard. And his encounters with the buttonmoulder, who brings up such embarrassing questions about his lack of identity, are "regressive" in a double sense: both as regards the problem of essence with which they are explicitly concerned, and as regards the fact that Peer, when a child, had pretended to mould buttons (ambiguously tin or gold) with an old casting-ladle.

Peer, through lack of a real self, is to be returned to the buttonmoulder, to be dissolved and recast into a new person. Twice the buttonmoulder has called for him, twice Peer has managed to put him off. And then, with the buttonmoulder waiting for him at the next crossroads, Peer comes upon Solveig, now an elderly woman:

> PEER GYNT. Tell me, then—where was my real self, complete and true—the Peer who bore the stamp of God upon his brow?
> SOLVEIG. In my faith, in my hope and in my love.
> PEER GYNT. What are you saying? It is a riddle that you are speaking now. So speaks a mother of her child.
> SOLVEIG. Ah, yes; and that is what I am; but He who grants a pardon for the sake of a mother's prayers, He is his father. (*A ray of light seems to flash on* PEER GYNT. *He cries out.*)
> PEER GYNT. Mother and wife! You stainless woman! Oh, hide me, hide me in your love! (*Clings to her and buries his face in her lap. There is a long silence. The sun rises.*)

And the curtain descends with Solveig singing a lullaby. The buttonmoulder is again heard saying that he will meet Peer at the next crossroads. But Solveig's lullaby has the last word: "I will rock you to sleep and guard you! Sleep and dream, my dearest boy!"

Has not Peer here at the last found his identity again in the maternal woman? And since he had gone on his wanderings at the very moment when Solveig had first come to his hut, she is the Virgin Mother, who has conceived him as an idea derived from God. He is, in brief, translated to the role of the Christ-child, whose conception was an Annunciation. And his essence resides in merger with this spiritualized maternal grounding, which simultaneously transforms the wife back into a mother and replaces his real mother and his drunken wandering father by a new and ideal parentage.

Despite the vast difference in particulars, we can discern in Proust the same shuttling between temporal and essential terms. And whereas through many volumes the search for essence is novelistically expressed in terms of a prolonged reminiscence, the final volume culminates essayistically in a non-temporal doctrine of essence, as exemplified in the Proustian theory of art. Here one will find many of the typical devices we have considered in these pages. Above all, there is the cult of the moment, with its peculiar synthesizing quality. Moments separated in time are linked outside of time, their community being idealistically grounded in a transcendent self that is neither present nor past, but lies outside of both by reason of its ability to experience the present in terms of the past.

Proust's attentiveness (or in his word, "aspiration") suggests a variant of that "looking forward to looking back" we have elsewhere noted in Shelley. That is, he singles out for appreciative description those moments which he will remember at some later moment. They will not be remembered because they were observed; rather, they were observed because they would be remembered. And their fulfilment as terms for the designation of essence occurs when some later moment is felt to partake of their same quality. His attentiveness at these first encountered is thus the adumbration of an eventual return to them, when later moments are to be defined in terms of them as prototype (a "first edition" for Proust being the particular edition in which he first read any given work).

But we have said enough to illustrate the nature of the time-essence ambiguity as it is reflected on the level of Symbolic. Rhetorically, this ambiguity prepares the way for "temporizing," as a person who is against some policy *absolutely* may assert simply that he is objecting to it *now*. Each time the conditions change, he can rephrase his objections accordingly, by stating them in terms of the new conditions. He thus need never defend his position categorically; and in fact, by thus temporizing he may recruit on a day-to-day basis allies who would be against him if he upheld his position in the absolute. Few men are absolute pacifists, for instance; but nearly all men are against war at any particular time, and the pacifist can get them to *function* as his allies by translating his categorical beliefs into the terms of ever-changing conditions. The search for one constant interest underlying a faction's shifts of policy (as with the doctrine of *Zweck im Recht*) is thus seen to be an attempt at the discernment of an *essential* motive beneath the particular appearances of many *temporized* motives.

Dissolution of Drama

All told, dialectic is concerned with different levels of *grounding*. It may be arrested after but a brief excursion, hardly more than a half-formulated enumeration of the most obvious factors in a situation. But whatever the range of the enterprise, the procedure is in general thus: Encountering some division, we retreat to a level of terms that allow for some kind of merger (as "near" and "far" are merged in the concept of "distance"); then we "return" to the division, now seeing it as pervaded by the spirit of the "One" we had found in our retreat.

Even on the purely Grammatical level, the process can lead to surprising results. In the case of our pentad, for instance, after having stressed the need for the functioning of all five terms in rounded vocabularies of motives, we summed up our position as "dramatistic"— whereupon of a sudden we discovered that our terms had collapsed into a new title that had, as its only logical ground, the "non-dramatistic." Thus we have two kinds of scene: one designating a function *within* the pentad, another designating a function *outside* the pentad; for a term as highly generalized as the "dramatistic" calls for the "non-dramatist" as its sole contextual counterpart. And the fact that one of these usages "transcends" the other may be concealed by the fact that we can refer to either of them by the same word, scene.

What, then, has happened to the genius of our pentad, which has thus dissolved before our very eyes? (Similarly, Korzybski must sometimes wonder what happened to his admonitions against "two-valued orientation," when they are finally summed up as an opposition between "Aristotelian" and "Non-Aristotelian," a "two-valued orientation" if we ever saw one.)

The "dramatistic" itself must have as its context a grounding in the "non-dramatist." The permanent structure of interrelations prevailing within the pentad would be "principles of development" that could not themselves develop (though they could be progressively discovered). So there is a point at which the dramatist perspective, defined in terms of its contextual opposite, must "abolish itself" in the very act of its enunciation. But though this eventuality is inevitable, one must be continually coming upon it, if he would retain an intrinsic appreciation of linguistic structures. A terminology that "begins where others left off" is not in a different order of linguistic resources and embarrassments, though it may contrive to conceal its true nature and conditions until we approach it intrinsically, in dramatistic terms.

The four ways in which drama is dissolved have been considered elsewhere. But it may be appropriate to list them here:

(1) Drama is dissolved by the turn from dramatic *act* to lyric *state*. This is not to be considered a dissolution in the full sense, since *status* is a reciprocal of *actus*.

(2) Drama is dissolved by terminologies that reduced action to motion.

(3) Drama is dissolved by philosophies of "dramatism," as with our present work. We use coördinates derived from the contemplation of drama, yet our use of them is non-dramatic.

(4) Drama is dissolved by philosophies of "super-drama."

By "super-drama" we refer, of course, to the way whereby a monotheistic god, in being treated as a "super-person," becomes "*im*personal." Such impersonality is in effect a dissolution of the person, a dramatistic paradox that makes it readily clear why scholastic theology could prepare the way for the secular terminologies of science.

A Neo-Liberal Ideal

So much for the Grammar of Motives. As we have said, our primary purpose has been to express towards language an *attitude* embodied in a *method*. This attitude is one of linguistic skepticism, which we synonymize with linguistic appreciation, on the grounds that an attitude of methodical quizzicality towards language may best equip us to perceive the full scope of its resourcefulness.

This Grammar is of course designed for reading independently of the Rhetoric and Symbolic. The Rhetoric and Symbolic are required, if one would examine *in detail* the ways in which the Grammatical resources are employed for the purposes of persuasion and self-expression; but the present book has already indicated how these other areas impinge upon the Grammatical and bear upon its logic.

All told, in this project directed "towards the purification of war," the Grammar should assist to this end through encouraging tolerance by speculation. For it deals with a level of motivation which even wholly rival doctrines of motives must share in common; hence it may be addressed to a speculative portion of the mind which men of many different situations may have in common. The Rhetoric, which would study the "competitive use of the coöperative," would be designed to help us take delight in the Human Barnyard, with its addiction to the Scramble, an area that would cause us great unhappiness could we not transcend it by appreciation, classifying and tracing back to their beginnings in Edenic simplicity those linguistic modes of suasion that often seem little better than malice and the lie. And the Symbolic, studying the implicit equations which have so much to do with the shaping of our acts, should enable us to see our own lives as a kind of rough first draft that lends itself at least somewhat to revision, as we may hope at least to temper the extreme rawness of our ambitions, once we become aware of the ways in which we are the victims of our own and one another's magic.

Such, then, are the "moralistic" reasons for the enterprise. They are offered in the firm belief that a kind of "Neo-Stoic resignation" to the needs of industrial expansion is in order. For better or worse, men are set to complete the development of technology, a development that will require such a vast bureaucracy (in both political and commercial administration) as the world has never before encountered. Encountering a "global" situation, to what extent can we avoid the piecemeal response of dissipation (that is content simply to take whatever opportunities are nearest at hand) and the response of fanaticism (that would impose one terminology of motives upon the whole world, regardless of the great dialectic interchange still to be completed)? To what extent can we confront the global situation with an attitude neither local nor imperialistic? Surely, all works of goodwill written in the next decades must aim somehow to avoid these two extremes, seeking a neo-liberal, speculative attitude. To an extent, perhaps, it will be like an attitude of hypochondriasis: the attitude of a patient who makes peace with his symptoms by becoming interested in them. Yes, on the negative side, the "Neo-Stoicism" we advocate would be an attitude of hypochondriasis. But on the positive side it would be an attitude of appreciation. And as regards our particular project, it would seek delight in meditating upon some of the many ingenuities of speech. Linguistic skepticism, in being quizzical, supplies the surest ground for the discernment and appreciation of linguistic resources.

Addendum for the Present Edition

With regard to the Dramatistic pentad (act, scene, agent, agency, purpose), I have found one modification useful for certain kinds of analysis. In accordance with my discussion of "attitudes" (in the section on " 'Incipient' and 'Delayed' Action," pp. 235–47), I have sometimes added the term "attitude" to the above list of five major terms. Thus, one could also speak of a "scene-attitude ratio," or of an "agent-attitude ratio," etc. "Agency" would more strictly designate the "means" (*quibus auxiliis*) employed in an act. And "attitude" would designate the manner (*quo modo*). To build something with a hammer would involve an instrument, or "agency"; to build with diligence would involve an "attitude," a "how."

I have also found that it is sometimes useful to differentiate the ratios by the order of the terms. For instance, by a "scene-act ratio" one would refer to the effect that a scene has upon an act, and by an "act-scene ratio" one would refer to the effect that an act has upon a scene. The Supreme Court would be exemplifying a "scene-act ratio" in deciding that emergency measures are admissible because there is a state of emergency. And we should be exemplifying an "act-scene ratio" in fearing that an arms race may lead to war. At still other times, however, there is merely a state of conformity between scene and act, without any notion of cause and effect. For instance, in Joseph Conrad's novel *Victory* a volcano erupts precisely at the time when the plot attains its maximum degree of agitation. Yet one could not properly say either that the erupting volcano caused the story to erupt, or *vice versa.*

Incidentally, one might note that all the ratios are essentially analogies. That is, by a "scene-act ratio" we mean that the nature of the act is implicit, or analogously present, in the nature of the scene, etc.

APPENDIX

A

SYMBOLIC ACTION IN A POEM
BY KEATS

W<small>E ARE</small> here set to analyze the "Ode on a Grecian Urn" as a viaticum that leads, by a series of transformations, into the oracle, "Beauty is truth, truth beauty." We shall analyze the Ode "dramatistically," in terms of symbolic action.

To consider language as a means of *information* or *knowledge* is to consider it epistemologically, semantically, in terms of "science." To consider it as a mode of *action* is to consider it in terms of "poetry." For a poem is an act, the symbolic act of the poet who made it—an act of such a nature that, in surviving as a structure or object, it enables us as readers to re-enact it.

"Truth" being the essential word of knowledge (science) and "beauty" being the essential word of art or poetry, we might substitute accordingly. The oracle would then assert, "Poetry is science, science poetry." It would be particularly exhilarating to proclaim them one if there were a strong suspicion that they were at odds (as the assertion that "God's in his heaven, all's right with the world" is really a *counter-*assertion to doubts about God's existence and suspicions that much is wrong). It was the dialectical opposition between the "aesthetic" and the "practical," with "poetry" on one side and utility (business and applied science) on the other that was being ecstatically denied. The *relief* in this denial was grounded in the romantic philosophy itself, a philosophy which gave strong recognition to precisely the *contrast* between "beauty" and "truth."

Perhaps we might put it this way: If the oracle were to have been uttered in the first stanza of the poem rather than the last, its phrasing proper to that place would have been: "Beauty is *not* truth, truth *not* beauty." The five stanzas of successive transformation were necessary for the romantic philosophy of a romantic poet to transcend itself (raising its romanticism to a new order, or new dimension). An abolishing of romanticism through romanticism! (To transcend romanticism through romanticism is, when all is over, to restore in one way what is removed in another.)

But to the poem, step by step through the five stanzas.

As a "way in," we begin with the sweeping periodic sentence that, before the stanza is over, has swiftly but imperceptibly been transmuted in quality from the periodic to the breathless, a cross between interrogation and exclamation:

> Thou still unravish'd bride of quietness,
>   Thou foster-child of silence and slow time,
> Sylvan historian, who canst thus express
>   A flowery tale more sweetly than our rhyme:
> What leaf-fring'd legend haunts about thy shape
>   Of deities or mortals, or of both,
>   In Tempe or the dales of Arcady?
> What men or gods are these?   What maidens loth?
>   What mad pursuit?   What struggle to escape?
>   What pipes and timbrels?   What wild ecstasy?

Even the last quick outcries retain somewhat the quality of the periodic structure with which the stanza began.   The final line introduces the subject of "pipes and timbrels," which is developed and then surpassed in Stanza II:

> Heard melodies are sweet, but those unheard
>   Are sweeter; therefore, ye soft pipes, play on;
> Not to the sensual ear, but, more endear'd,
>   Pipe to the spirit ditties of no tone:
> Fair youth, beneath the trees, thou canst not leave
>   Thy song, nor ever can those trees be bare;
>   Bold Lover, never, never canst thou kiss,
> Though winning near the goal—yet, do not grieve;
>   She cannot fade, though thou hast not thy bliss,
>   Forever wilt thou love, and she be fair!

If we had only the first stanza of this Ode, and were speculating upon it from the standpoint of motivation, we could detect there tentative indications of two motivational levels.   For the lines express a doubt whether the figures on the urn are "deities or mortals"—and the motives of gods are of a different order from the motives of men.   This bare hint of such a possibility emerges with something of certainty in the second stanza's development of the "pipes and timbrels" theme. For we explicitly consider a contrast between body and mind (in the contrast between "heard melodies," addressed "to the sensual ear," and "ditties of no tone," addressed "to the spirit").

Also, of course, the notion of inaudible sound brings us into the region of the mystic oxymoron (the term in rhetoric for "the figure in which an epithet of a contrary significance is added to a word: e.g., *cruel kindness; laborious idleness"*). And it clearly suggests a concern with the level of motives-behind-motives, as with the paradox of the prime mover that is itself at rest, being the unmoved ground of all motion and action. Here the poet whose sounds are the richest in our language is meditating upon *absolute* sound, the *essence* of sound, which would be soundless as the prime mover is motionless, or as the "principle" of sweetness would not be sweet, having transcended sweetness, or as the sub-atomic particles of the sun are each, in their isolate purity, said to be devoid of temperature.

Contrast Keats's unheard melodies with those of Shelley:

> Music, when soft voices die,
> Vibrates in the memory—
> Odours, when sweet violets sicken,
> Live within the sense they quicken.
>
> Rose leaves, when the rose is dead,
> Are heaped for the beloved's bed;
> And so thy thoughts, when thou art gone,
> Love itself shall slumber on.

Here the futuristic Shelley is anticipating retrospection; he is looking forward to looking back. The form of thought is naturalistic and temporalistic in terms of *past* and *future*. But the form of thought in Keats is mystical, in terms of an *eternal present*. The Ode is striving to move beyond the region of becoming into the realm of *being*. (This is another way of saying that we are here concerned with two levels of motivation.)

In the last four lines of the second stanza, the state of immediacy is conveyed by a development peculiarly Keatsian. I refer not simply to translation into terms of the erotic, but rather to a quality of *suspension* in the erotic imagery, defining an eternal prolongation of the state just prior to fulfilment—not exactly arrested ecstasy, but rather an arrested pre-ecstasy.[1]

Suppose that we had but this one poem by Keats, and knew nothing of its author or its period, so that we could treat it only in itself, as a series of internal transformations to be studied in their development from a certain point, and without reference to any motives outside the Ode. Under such conditions, I think, we should require no further observations to characterize (from the standpoint of symbolic action) the main argument in the second stanza. We might go on to make an infinity of observations about the details of the stanza; but as regards major deployments we should deem it enough to note that the theme of "pipes and timbrels" is developed by the use of mystic oxymoron, and then surpassed (or given a development-atop-the-development) by the stressing of erotic imagery (that had been ambiguously adumbrated in the references to "maidens loth" and "mad pursuit" of Stanza I). And we could note the quality of *incipience* in this imagery, its state of arrest not at fulfilment, but at the point just prior to fulfilment.

Add, now, our knowledge of the poem's place as an enactment in a particular cultural scene, and we likewise note in this second stanza a variant of the identification between death and sexual love that was so typical of 19th-century romanticism and was to attain its musical monument in the Wagnerian *Liebestod*. On a purely dialectical basis, to die in love would be to be born to love (the lovers dying as individual identities that they might be transformed into a common identity). Adding historical factors, one can note the part that capitalist individualism plays in sharpening this consummation (since a property structure that heightens the sense of individual identity would thus make it more imperiously a "death" for the individual to take on the new identity made by a union of two). We can thus see why the love-death equation would be particularly representative of a romanticism that was the reflex of business.

Fortunately, the relation between private property and the love-death equation is attested on unimpeachable authority, concerning the effect of consumption and consummation in a "mutual flame":

[1] Mr. G. Wilson Knight, in *The Starlit Dome*, refers to "that recurring tendency in Keats to image a poised form, a stillness suggesting motion, what might be called a 'tiptoe' effect."

So between them love did shine,
That the turtle saw his right
Flaming in the phoenix' sight;
Either was the other's mine.

Property was thus appall'd,
That the self was not the same;
Single nature's double name
Neither two nor one was called.

The addition of fire to the equation, with its pun on sexual burning, moves us from purely dialectical considerations into psychological ones. In the lines of Shakespeare, fire is the third term, the ground term for the other two (the synthesis that ends the lovers' roles as thesis and antithesis). Less obviously, the same movement from the purely dialectical to the psychological is implicit in any imagery of a *dying* or a *falling* in common, which when woven with sexual imagery signalizes a "transcendent" sexual consummation. The figure appears in a lover's compliment when Keats writes to Fanny Brawne, thus:

> I never knew before, what such a love as you have made me feel, was; I did not believe in it; my Fancy was afraid of it lest it should burn me up. But if you will fully love me, though there may be some fire, 'twill not be more than we can bear when moistened and bedewed with pleasures.

Our primary concern is to follow the transformations of the poem itself. But to understand its full nature as a symbolic act, we should use whatever knowledge is available. In the case of Keats, not only do we know the place of this poem in his work and its time, but also we have material to guide our speculations as regards correlations between poem and poet. I grant that such speculations interfere with the symmetry of criticism as a game. (Criticism as a game is best to watch, I guess, when one confines himself to the single unit, and reports on its movements like a radio commentator broadcasting the blow-by-blow description of a prizefight.) But linguistic analysis has opened up new possibilities in the correlating of producer and product—and these concerns have such important bearing upon matters of culture and conduct in general that no sheer conventions or ideals of criticism should be allowed to interfere with their development.

From what we know of Keats's illness, with the peculiar inclination to erotic imaginings that accompany its fever (as with the writings of D. H. Lawrence) we can glimpse a particular bodily motive expanding and intensifying the lyric state in Keats's case. Whatever the intense *activity* of his thoughts, there was the material *pathos* of his physical condition. Whatever transformations of mind or body he experienced, his illness was there as a kind of constitutional substrate, whereby all aspects of the illness would be imbued with their derivation from a common ground (the phthisic fever thus being at one with the phthisic chill, for whatever the clear contrast between fever and chill, they are but modes of the same illness, the common underlying substance).

The correlation between the state of agitation in the poems and the physical condition of the poet is made quite clear in the poignant letters Keats wrote during his last illness. In 1819 he complains that he is "scarcely content to write the best verses for the fever they leave behind." And he continues: "I want to compose without this fever." But a few months later he confesses, "I am recommended not even to read poetry, much less write it." Or: "I must say that for 6 Months before I was taken ill I had not passed a tranquil day. Either that gloom overspre[a]d me or I was suffering under some passionate feeling, or if I turn'd to versify that exacerbated the poison of either sensation." Keats was "like a sick eagle looking at the sky," as he wrote of his mortality in a kindred poem, "On Seeing the Elgin Marbles."

But though the poet's body was a *patient,* the poet's mind was an *agent.* Thus, as a practitioner of poetry, he could *use* his fever, even perhaps encouraging, though not deliberately, esthetic habits that, in making for the perfection of his lines, would exact payment in the ravages of his body (somewhat as Hart Crane could write poetry only by modes of living that made for the cessation of his poetry and so led to his dissolution).

Speaking of agents, patients, and action here, we might pause to glance back over the centuries thus: in the Aristotelian grammar of motives, action has its reciprocal in passion, hence *passion* is the property of a *patient.* But by the Christian paradox (which made the martyr's action identical with his passion, as the accounts of the martyrs were called both Acts and Passionals), *patience* is the property of a moral *agent.* And this Christian view, as secularized in the philosophy of romanticism, with its stress upon creativeness, leads us to the possibility of a bodily suffering redeemed by a poetic act.

In the third stanza, the central stanza of the Ode (hence properly the fulcrum of its swing) we see the two motives, the action and the passion, in the process of being separated. The possibility raised in the first stanza (which was dubious whether the level of motives was to be human or divine), and developed in the second stanza (which contrasts the "sensual" and the "spirit"), becomes definitive in Stanza III:

> Ah, happy, happy boughs! that cannot shed
> > Your leaves, nor ever bid the Spring adieu;
> And, happy melodist, unwearied,
> > For ever piping songs for ever new;
> More happy love! more happy, happy love!
> For ever warm and still to be enjoy'd,
> > For ever panting, and for ever young;
> All breathing human passion far above,
> > That leaves a heart high-sorrowful and cloy'd,
> > A burning forehead, and a parching tongue.

The poem as a whole makes permanent, or fixes in a state of arrest, a peculiar agitation. But within this fixity, by the nature of poetry as a progressive medium, there must be development. Hence, the agitation that is maintained throughout (as a mood absolutized so that it fills the entire universe of discourse) will at the same time undergo internal transformations. In the third stanza, these are manifested as a clear division into two distinct and contrasted realms. There is a transcendental fever, which is felicitous, divinely above "all breathing human passion." And this "leaves" the other level, the level of earthly fever, "a burning forehead and a parching tongue." From the bodily fever, which is a passion, and malign, there has split off a spiritual activity, a wholly benign aspect of the total agitation.

Clearly, a movement has been finished. The poem must, if it is well-formed, take a new direction, growing out of and surpassing the curve that has by now been clearly established by the successive stages from "Is there the possibility of two motivational levels?" through "there are two motivational levels" to "the 'active' motivational level 'leaves' the 'passive' level."

Prophesying, with the inestimable advantage that goes with having looked ahead, what should we expect the new direction to be? First, let us survey the situation. Originally, before the two strands of the fever had been definitely drawn apart, the bodily passion could serve as the scene or ground of the spiritual action. But at the end of the third stanza, we abandon the level of bodily passion. The action is "far above" the passion, it "leaves" the fever. What then would this transcendent act require, to complete it?

It would require a scene of the same quality as itself. An act and a scene belong together. The nature of the one must be a fit with the nature of the other. (I like to call this the "scene-act ratio," or "dramatic ratio.") Hence, the act having now transcended its bodily setting, it will require, as its new setting, a transcendent scene. Hence, prophesying *post eventum,* we should ask that, in Stanza IV, the poem *embody* the transcendental act by endowing it with an appropriate scene.

The scene-act ratio involves a law of dramatic consistency whereby the quality of the act shares the quality of the scene in which it is enacted (the synecdochic relation of container and thing contained). Its grandest variant was in supernatural cosmogonies wherein mankind took on the attributes of gods by acting in cosmic scenes that were themselves imbued with the presence of godhead.[2]

Or we may discern the logic of the scene-act ratio behind the old controversy as to whether "God willed the good because it is good," or "the good is good because God willed it." This strictly theological controversy had political implications. But our primary concern here is with the *dramatistic* aspects of this controversy. For you will note that the whole issue centers in the problem of the *grounds* of God's creative act.

Since, from the purely dramatic point of view, every act requires a scene in which it takes place, we may note that one of the doctrines (that "God willed the good because it is good") is more symmetrical than the other. For by it, God's initial act of creation is itself

[2] In an article by Leo Spitzer, *"Milieu* and *Ambiance*: An Essay in Historical Semantics" (September and December 1942 numbers of *Philosophy and Phenomenological Research*), one will find a wealth of material that can be read as illustrative of "dramatic ratio."

given a ground, or scene (the objective existence of goodness, which was so real that God himself did not simply make it up, but acted in conformity with its nature when willing it to be the law of his creation). In the scholastic formulas taken over from Aristotle, God was defined as "pure act" (though this pure act was in turn the ultimate ground or *scene* of human acting and willing). And from the standpoint of purely dramatic symmetry, it would be desirable to have some kind of "scene" even for God. This requirement is met, we are suggesting, in the doctrine that "God willed the good *because* it is good." For this word, "because," in assigning a reason for God's willing, gives us in principle a kind of scene, as we may discern in the pun of our word, "ground," itself, which indeterminately applies to either "place" or "cause."

If even theology thus responded to the pressure for dramatic symmetry by endowing God, as the transcendent act, with a transcendent scene of like quality, we should certainly expect to find analogous tactics in this Ode. For as we have noted that the romantic passion is the secular equivalent of the Christian passion, so we may recall Coleridge's notion that poetic action itself is a "dim analogue of Creation." Keats in his way confronting the same dramatistic requirement that the theologians confronted in theirs, when he has arrived at his transcendent act at the end of Stanza III (that is, when the benign fever has split away from the malign bodily counterpart, as a divorcing of spiritual action from sensual passion), he is ready in the next stanza for the imagining of a scene that would correspond in quality to the quality of the action as so transformed. His fourth stanza will concretize, or "materialize," the act, by dwelling upon its appropriate ground.

> Who are these coming to the sacrifice?
>   To what green altar, O mysterious priest,
>   Lead'st thou that heifer lowing at the skies,
>   And all her silken flanks with garlands drest?
> What little town, by river or sea shore,
>   Or mountain built with peaceful citadel,
>   Is emptied of this folk, this pious morn?
> And, little town, thy streets for evermore
>   Will silent be; and not a soul to tell
>   Why thou art desolate, can e'er return.

It is a vision, as you prefer, of "death" or of "immortality." "Immortality," we might say, is the "good" word for "death," and must necessarily be conceived in terms of death (the necessity that Donne touches upon when he writes, ". . . but thinke that I / Am, by being dead, immortall"). This is why, when discussing the second stanza, I felt justified in speaking of the variations of the love-death equation, though the poem spoke not of love and *death,* but of love *for ever.* We have a deathy-deathless scene as the corresponding ground of our transcendent act. The Urn itself, as with the scene upon it, is not merely an immortal act in our present mortal scene; it was originally an immortal act in a mortal scene quite different. The imagery, of sacrifice, piety, silence, desolation, is that of communication with the immortal or the dead.[3]

Incidentally, we might note that the return to the use of rhetorical questions in the fourth stanza serves well, on a purely technical level, to keep our contact with the mood of the opening stanza, a music that now but vibrates in the memory. Indeed, one even gets the impression that the form of the rhetorical question had never been abandoned; that the poet's questings had been couched as questions throughout. This is tonal felicity at its best, and something much like unheard tonal felicity. For the actual persistence of the rhetorical questions through these stanzas would have been wearisome, whereas their return now gives us

---

[3] In imagery there is no negation, or disjunction. Logically, we can say, "this *or* that," "this, *not* that." In imagery we can but say "this *and* that," "this *with* that," "this-that," etc. Thus, imagistically considered, a commandment cannot be simply a proscription, but is also latently a provocation (a state of affairs that figures in the kind of stylistic scrupulosity and/or curiosity to which Gide's heroes have been particularly sensitive, as "thou shalt not . . ." becomes imaginatively transformed into "what would happen if . . ."). In the light of what we have said about the deathiness of immortality, and the relation between the erotic and the thought of a "dying," perhaps we might be justified in reading the last line of the great "Bright Star!" sonnet as naming states not simply alternative but also synonymous:

> And so live ever—or else swoon to death.

This use of the love-death equation is as startlingly paralleled in a letter to Fanny Brawne:

> I have two luxuries to brood over in my walks, your loveliness and the hour of my death. O that I could take possession of them both in the same moment.

an inaudible variation, by making us feel that the exclamations in the second and third stanzas had been questions, as the questions in the first stanza had been exclamations.

But though a lyric greatly profits by so strong a sense of continuousness, or perpetuity, I am trying to stress the fact that in the fourth stanza we *come upon* something. Indeed, this fourth stanza is related to the three foregoing stanzas quite as the sestet is related to the octave in Keats's sonnet, "On First Looking Into Chapman's Homer":

> Much have I travell'd in the realms of gold,
>   And many goodly states and kingdoms seen;
>   Round many western islands have I been
> Which bards in fealty to Apollo hold.
> Oft of one wide expanse had I been told
>   That deep-brow'd Homer ruled as his demesne;
>   Yet did I never breathe its pure serene
> Till I heard Chapman speak out loud and bold;
>
> Then felt I like some watcher of the skies
>   When a new planet swims into his ken;
> Or like stout Cortez when with eagle eyes
>   He stared at the Pacific—and all his men
> Look'd at each other with a wild surmise—
>   Silent, upon a peak in Darien.

I am suggesting that, just as the sestet in this sonnet, *comes upon a scene,* so it is with the fourth stanza of the Ode. In both likewise we end on the theme of silence; and is not the Ode's reference to the thing that "not a soul can tell" quite the same in quality as the sonnet's reference to a "wild surmise"?

Thus, with the Urn as viaticum (or rather, with the *poem* as viaticum, and *in the name* of the Urn), having symbolically enacted a kind of act that transcends our mortality, we round out the process by coming to dwell upon the transcendental ground of this act. The dead world of ancient Greece, as immortalized on an Urn surviving from that period, is the vessel of this deathy-deathless ambiguity. And we have gone dialectically from the "human" to the "divine" and thence to the "ground of the divine" (here tracing in poetic imagery the kind of "dramatistic" course we have considered, on the purely conceptual plane, in the theological speculations about the "grounds" for God's creative act). Necessarily, there must be certain inadequacies in the conception of this ground, precisely because of the fact that immortality can only be conceived in terms of death. Hence the reference to the "desolate" in a scene otherwise possessing the benignity of the eternal.

The imagery of pious sacrifice, besides its fitness for such thoughts of departure as when the spiritual act splits from the sensual pathos, suggests also a bond of communication between the levels (because of its immortal character in a mortal scene). And finally, the poem, in the name of the Urn, or under the aegis of the Urn, is such a bond. For we readers, by re-enacting it in the reading, use it as a viaticum to transport us into the quality of the scene which it depicts on its face (the scene containing as a fixity what the poem as act extends into a process). The scene *on* the Urn is really the scene *behind* the Urn; the Urn is literally the ground of this scene, but transcendentally the scene is the ground of the Urn. The Urn contains the scene out of which it arose.

We turn now to the closing stanza:

> O Attic shape! Fair attitude! with brede
> Of marble men and maidens overwrought,
> With forest branches and the trodden weed;
> Thou, silent form, dost tease us out of thought
> As doth eternity: Cold Pastoral!
> When old age shall this generation waste,
>   Thou shalt remain, in midst of other woe
> Than ours, a friend to man, to whom thou say'st,
> 'Beauty is truth, truth beauty,'—that is all
>   Ye know on earth, and all ye need to know.

In the third stanza we were at a moment of heat, emphatically sharing an imagery of loves "panting" and "for ever warm" that was, in the transcendental order, companionate to "a burning forehead, and a parching tongue" in the order of the passions. But in the last stanza, as signalized in the marmorean utterance, "Cold Pastoral!" we have gone from transcendental fever to transcendental chill. Perhaps, were we to complete our exegesis, we should need reference to some physical step from phthisic fever to phthisic chill, that we might detect here a final correlation between bodily passion and mental action. In any event we may note that, the mental action having departed from the bodily passion, the change from fever to chill is not a sufferance. For, as only the *benign* aspects of the fever had been left after the split, so it is a wholly benign chill on which the poem ends.[4]

I wonder whether anyone can read the reference to "brede of marble men and maidens overwrought" without thinking of "breed" for "brede" and "excited" for "overwrought." (Both expressions would thus merge notions of sexuality and craftsmanship, the erotic and the poetic.)   As for the designating of the Urn as an "Attitude," it fits in admirably with our stress upon symbolic action. For an attitude is an arrested, or incipient *act*—not just an *object,* or *thing.*

Yeats, in *A Vision,* speaks of "the diagrams in Law's *Boehme,* where one lifts a paper to discover both the human entrails and the starry heavens." This equating of the deeply without and the deeply within (as also with Kant's famous remark) might well be remembered when we think of the sky that the "watcher" saw in Keats's sonnet. It is an internal sky, attained through meditations induced by the reading of a book. And so the oracle, whereby truth and beauty are proclaimed as one, would seem to derive from a profound inwardness.

Otherwise, without these introductory mysteries, "truth" and "beauty" were at odds. For whereas "beauty" had its fulfilment in romantic poetry, "truth" was coming to have its fulfilment in science, technological accuracy, accountancy, statistics, actuarial tables, and the like. Hence, without benefit of the rites which one enacts in a sympathetic reading of the Ode (rites that remove the discussion to a different level), the enjoyment of "beauty" would involve an esthetic kind of awareness radically in conflict with the kind of awareness deriving from the practical "truth." And as regards the tactics of the poem, this conflict would seem to be solved by "estheticizing" the true rather than by "verifying" the beautiful.

Earlier in our essay, we suggested reading "poetry" for "beauty" and "science" for "truth," with the oracle deriving its *liberating* quality

---

[4] In a letter to Fanny Brawne, Keats touches upon the fever-chill contrast in a passage that also touches upon the love-death equation, though here the chill figures in an untransfigured state:

> I fear that I am too prudent for a dying kind of Lover. Yet, there is a great difference between going off in warm blood like Romeo; and making one's exit like a frog in a frost.

from the fact that it is uttered at a time when the poem has taken us to a level where earthly contradictions do not operate. But we might also, in purely conceptual terms, attain a level where "poetry" and "science" cease to be at odds; namely: by translating the two terms into the "grammar" that lies behind them. That is: we could generalize the term "poetry" by widening it to the point where we could substitute for it the term "act." And we could widen "science" to the point where we could substitute "scene." Thus we have:

"beauty"	equals	"poetry"	equals	"act"
"truth"	equals	"science"	equals	"scene"

We would equate "beauty" with "act," because it is not merely a decorative thing, but an assertion, an affirmative, a creation, hence in the fullest sense an act. And we would equate "truth" or "science" with the "scenic" because science is a knowledge of *what is*—and *all that is* comprises the over-all universal *scene*. Our corresponding transcendence, then, got by "translation" into purely grammatical terms, would be: "Act is scene, scene act." We have got to this point by a kind of purely conceptual transformation that would correspond, I think, to the transformations of imagery leading to the oracle in the Ode.

"Act is scene, scene act." Unfortunately, I must break the symmetry a little. For poetry, as conceived in idealism (romanticism) could not quite be equated with *act,* but rather with *attitude*. For idealistic philosophies, with their stress upon the subjective, place primary stress upon the *agent* (the individual, the ego, the will, etc.). It was medieval scholasticism that placed primary stress upon the *act*. And in the Ode the Urn (which is the vessel or representative of poetry) is called an "attitude," which is not outright an act, but an incipient or arrested act, a *state of mind,* the property of an *agent*. Keats, in calling the Urn an attitude, is *personifying* it. Or we might use the italicizing resources of dialectic by saying that for Keats, beauty (poetry) was not so much "the *act* of an agent" as it was "the act of an *agent.*"

Perhaps we can re-enforce this interpretation by examining kindred strategies in Yeats, whose poetry similarly derives from idealistic, romantic sources. Indeed, as we have noted elsewhere,[5] Yeats's vision of immortality in his Byzantium poems but carries one step further the Keatsian identification with the Grecian Urn:

[5] "On Motivation in Yeats" (*The Southern Review,* Winter 1942).

Once out of nature I shall never take
My bodily form from any natural thing,
But such a form as Grecian goldsmiths make
Of hammered gold and gold enamelling . . .

Here certainly the poet envisions immortality as "esthetically" as Keats. For he will have immortality as a golden bird, a fabricated thing, a work of Grecian goldsmiths. Here we go in the same direction as the "overwrought" Urn, but farther along in that direction.

The ending of Yeats's poem, "Among School Children," helps us to make still clearer the idealistic stress upon agent:

Labour is blossoming or dancing where
The body is not bruised to pleasure soul,
Nor beauty torn out of its own despair,
Nor blear-eyed wisdom out of midnight oil.
O chestnut tree, great rooted blossomer,
Are you the leaf, the blossom or the bole?
O body swayed to music, O brightening glance,
How can we know the dancer from the dance?

Here the chestnut tree (as personified agent) is the ground of unity or continuity for all its scenic manifestations; and with the agent (dancer) is merged the act (dance). True, we seem to have here a commingling of act, scene, and agent, all three. Yet it is the *agent* that is "foremost among the equals." Both Yeats and Keats, of course, were much more "dramatistic" in their thinking than romantic poets generally, who usually center their efforts upon the translation of *scene* into terms of *agent* (as the materialistic science that was the dialectical counterpart of romantic idealism preferred conversely to translate *agent* into terms of *scene,* or in other words, to treat "consciousness" in terms of "matter," the "mental" in terms of the "physical," "people" in terms of "environment").

To review briefly: The poem begins with an ambiguous fever which in the course of the further development is "separated out," splitting into a bodily fever and a spiritual counterpart. The bodily passion is the malign aspect of the fever, the mental action its benign aspect. In the course of the development, the malign passion is transcended and the benign active partner, the intellectual exhilaration, takes over. At the beginning, where the two aspects were ambiguously one, the bodily passion would be the "scene" of the mental action (the "objective symptoms" of the body would be paralleled by the "subjective symptoms" of the mind, the bodily state thus being the other or ground of the mental state). But as the two become separated out, the mental action transcends the bodily passion. It becomes an act in its own right, making discoveries and assertions not grounded in the bodily passion. And this quality of action, in transcending the merely physical symptoms of the fever, would thus require a different ground or scene, one more suited in quality to the quality of the transcendent act.

The transcendent act is concretized, or "materialized," in the vision of the "immortal" scene, the reference in Stanza IV to the original scene of the Urn, the "heavenly" scene of a dead, or immortal, Greece (the scene in which the Urn was originally enacted and which is also fixed on its face). To indicate the internality of this vision, we referred to a passage in Yeats relating the "depths" of the sky without to the depths of the mind within; and we showed a similar pattern in Keats's account of the vision that followed his reading of Chapman's Homer. We suggested that the poet is here coming upon a new internal sky, through identification with the Urn as act, the same sky that he came upon through identification with the enactments of Chapman's translation.

This transcendent scene is the level at which the earthly laws of contradiction no longer prevail. Hence, in the terms of this scene, he can proclaim the unity of truth and beauty (of science and art), a proclamation which he needs to make precisely because here was the basic split responsible for the romantic agitation (in both poetic and philosophic idealism). That is, it was gratifying to have the oracle proclaim the unity of poetry and science because the values of technology and business were causing them to be at odds. And from the perspective of a "higher level" (the perspective of a dead or immortal scene transcending the world of temporal contradictions) the split could be proclaimed once more a unity.

At this point, at this stage of exaltation, the fever has been replaced by chill. But the bodily passion has completely dropped out of account. All is now mental action. Hence, the chill (as in the ecstatic exclamation, "Cold Pastoral!") is proclaimed only in its benign aspect.

We may contrast this discussion with explanations such as a mate-

rialist of the Kretschmer school might offer. I refer to accounts of motivation that might treat disease as cause and poem as effect. In such
accounts, the disease would not be "passive," but wholly active; and
what we have called the mental action would be wholly passive, hardly
more than an epiphenomenon, a mere symptom of the disease quite as
are the fever and the chill themselves. Such accounts would give us
no conception of the essential matter here, the intense linguistic activity.

B

THE PROBLEM OF THE INTRINSIC

(as reflected in the Neo-Aristotelian School)

I

THERE is a *rhetorical* explanation for doctrines proclaiming the eternity of art. We can say that, esthetic standards being transitory, men try to compensate for this changefulness by denying its existence. Then we might fill out this explanation on the rhetorical level by sociological considerations, noting for instance that the doctrine would fit well with a collector's or antiquarian's attitude towards art, and thus with the business of selling art objects to customers in search of sound esthetic investments. And when art is approached from the antiquarian point of view, men may ask so little of it that it can easily meet the requirements. Thus a work that, in its original context, might have seemed "terrifying" or "divine," could at least remain eternally "interesting" or "odd," thereby possessing a kind of permanence as tested by dilettantish criteria. Much esthetic theory stressing the appreciation of "form" would doubtless fall under this head.

Or noting how much of art has been a secularized variant of religious processes, particularly since the rise of the romantic reaction against capitalism and technology, we may offer a *symbolical* interpretation. A doctrine proclaiming the eternity of art would, from the symbolic point of view, be the natural secular analogue of a belief in the eternity of God.

But we may discuss motives on three levels. Besides Rhetoric and Symbolic, there is Grammar. We are on the grammatical level when we begin with the "problem of the intrinsic," as reflected in the attempt to characterize the substance of a work. We are faced with *grammatical* problems when we would consider a given work of art "in itself," in what I believe the scholastics might have called its *aseitas,* or "by-itselfness." Considered "intrinsically," the work is said to embody

465

certain "principles." And these principles are said to reside in the division of the work into its parts, and in the relation of these parts to one another and to the whole.

Even though a work of art were to last but a few moments, being destroyed almost immediately after its production, during its brief physical duration you might deal with it *sub specie aeternitatis,* in terms of timelessness. This you could do by considering solely the relation of its parts to one another and to the whole. And you would thereby be thinking in terms of the "eternal" or "timeless" since the relations prevailing among the parts just are. Each part *is* in a certain relation to the others; and all the parts *are* in certain relations to the whole. You would thus be concerned with a work in terms of its *being*—and being is by definition an "eternal now." (Recall that the Aristotelian word for substance is *ousia,* being. Anything capable of consideration by itself, *kath auto,* would be a substance in this sense: as a man, a tree, a stone.) "Beings" may come and go; but insofar as you treat of something in terms of its *being* (in contrast, for instance, with treatment of it in terms of its genesis), by the sheer technicality of the treatment you are working in terms of the eternal—outside the category of time. (It may possess a kind of "internal time," in the sense that, if it is a work of literature or music, some of its parts may precede others. But such order can be discussed in terms of purely structural relationships. And time in this sense is not the kind of time we have in mind when we consider the work in terms of personality, or class, or epoch, etc.)

In sum, when you consider a thing just as it *is,* with the *being* of one part involved in the *being* of its other parts, and with all the parts derived from the being of the whole considered as a generating principle, there is nothing but a "present tense" involved here, or better, a "tenselessness," even though the thing thus dealt with arises in time and passes with time.

In Aristotle, such a concept of substance or being (*ousia*) was carried to its full metaphysical limits. For he abided by the logic of his terminology to the extent of concluding that the world itself was not created, but was eternal. Every vocabulary has its limits, imposed by the internal logic of its terms; and Aristotle, as a superior thinker, carried his own vocabulary to its limits. And though individual beings came and went, he held that their *genera* (their family identities that contain the principles of their being, as the principles of an equilateral triangle reside in the class of such triangles) had existed and would exist forever.

But, though in Aristotle every individual stone or tree or man, or any other thing capable of treatment as a separate entity, was a being, I think we should be wrong in saying that he treated beings simply in terms of their *individuality*. Rather, he located an individual thing's principle of being in its identity as a member of a *tribe* (his word *genos,* or genus, being originally a word of strong familistic connotations, with the same root as our words "generate" and "generation"). It was the types, or kinds, or classes, or families of natural beings that continued permanently. Hence, the intrinsic principles of a being were not unique, but were variations of principles common to the whole family, or genus, of such beings. The internal principle of motivation, the "entelechy" (or "that which contains its own aim") was the incentive of the thing to attain the kind of perfection proper to the kind of thing it was (a stone's kind of perfection thus being quite different from a tree's, or a man's).

Aquinas in his borrowing from Aristotle retained the Aristotelian stress upon being. But the Christian acceptance of Genesis made it impossible for Aquinas to retain the ultimate implications of this key term. For him, as a Christian, the most important fact about the nature of the world was that we might call a *genetic,* or "historical," or "temporal," fact: its derivation from a divine Creator. Thus the *substance* of things was determined not solely by their nature as beings in themselves; it also involved their place, or grounding, as *creatures* of God in a *creation* of God. And by giving the Aristotelian concept of the genus this "ancestral" emphasis, he engrafted an "extrinsic" principle of substance. Men's abilities and habits were said to be "intrinsic" principles of action —the "extrinsic" motives were God and the Devil.[1]

---

[1] You will note the beginning of an ambiguity here. For an ancestral God is not wholly "extrinsic." A creature who was descended from God and whose substance was grounded in the creative act of God would somehow bear this qualification "within." The logical completion of such thinking, however, would lead to pantheism, as the substance of God would be "within" his creation—and in Aquinas God is expressly classed as an "extrinsic" principle of motivation. From the sociological point of view, we may note that in proportion as the notion of an "extrinsic" God attained its institutional counterpart in the formalistic externalization of religion, the Protestant pietistic stress upon God as a principle "from within" came by reaction to the fore. And at the time when this change was taking place, the meanings of two very strategic terms in philosophy

Spinoza, taking the Aristotelian notion that a being, or substance, is to be considered "in itself" (*id quod per se concipitur*), went on to observe that nothing less than the totality of all that exists can meet this requirement. For any single object in the universe must be "defined" (limited, determined, negated) by the things that surround it. Only when considering the universe as a whole, and in considering the principles of the relations of the universe's parts to this universal whole, would we really be dealing with an "intrinsic" motivation. And when dealing with such individual things as a tree, a man, a stone (which are merely *parts* of the universe), we should have to consider their nature as grounded in a wider context, rather than simply as individuals embodying principles of their own. As Locke was to point out later, though we use the word "substance" to designate properties within a thing, etymologically the word means that which supports or grounds a thing (in brief, not something *inside* it but something *outside* it). And when the most "intrinsic" statement we can make about a thing is a statement not about it in itself but about its place as part of the whole world, have we not just about reversed the meanings of the words "intrinsic" and "extrinsic"?

Paradoxically, the Spinozistic advice to see things *sub specie aeternitatis* was really a splendid introduction into philosophies that would see things in the terms of history. Spinoza, to be sure, considered the universe in terms of *being;* he proposed to treat of the parts in terms of this eternal whole; and when considering *historical* sequence, he proposed to consider it in terms of *logical* sequence (here using one of the profoundest puns in all thought, as one event in history is said to "follow" another the way the conclusion of a syllogism "follows" from the premises). But to treat individuals in terms of a much more inclusive whole is certainly not to consider them "eternally" in the Aristotelian sense, which required that they be treated "in themselves." As soon as you begin treating things in terms of a surrounding context (and a naturalistic context at that) you have laid the way for their treatment temporally, in terms of history. At every important point in Spinoza's doctrines, he had a compensation for such a movement. His history was equated with a timeless logic; his nature was equated with God.

changed places. The terms "subjective" and "objective" (bearing upon the "inner" and the "outer") reversed their meanings; medieval philosophers had called the "objective" what modern philosophers call "subjective" and vice versa.

But when you equate two terms, either can replace the other, which is to say that the equating of two terms prepares the way for eliminating one of them. Hence, Spinoza's equating of naturalistic history and pantheistic being could be developed into a doctrine of naturalistic history pure and simple by merely dropping the theological side of the equation. (Spinoza himself made seminal contributions to the study of religion from the *historicist* point of view.)

In proportion as theological geneticism developed into a purely secular historicism, the notion of a thing's intrinsic substance dissolved into the out-and-out extrinsic, until now many philosophers of science would formally abolish the category of substance. Aquinas had balanced intrinsic and extrinsic motivations by saying that, though God moved all beings, he moved each according to its nature. But modern science is *par excellence* the approach "from without" (the "scenic," "environmentalist," or "situational" approach). It is interested not in what men "are," for instance, "in themselves," but in what respects men are to be treated as animals, in what respects they are to be treated as vegetables, in what respects as minerals, as electro-physical impulses capable of conditioning by material manipulations, as creatures of food, or climate, or geography, etc. Thus, typically, the papers recently reported of a "gerontologist" who was making investigations designed to increase longevity by increasing the "intrinsic resistance" of the body to the processes that make for old age; and he proposed to do this by dosage of the body with various sorts of chemicals. We are not in a position to know what are his chances of success. But we may raise doubts about his terms. Could such extrinsic agencies as chemical dosage properly be expected to *increase* the body's intrinsic resistance? Insofar as it was effective, wouldn't it rather gain its effects by *decreasing* intrinsic resistance (somewhat as we keep warm "scientifically" not by methods that increase our intrinsic resistance to cold, but by improved modes of heating that decrease our resistance to cold).

Indeed, the question as to what a thing is "in itself" is not a scientific question at all (in the purely empiricist sense of the term science), but a philosophical or metaphysical one. Recently, for instance, there appeared a very intelligent book by a contemporary psychiatrist, Dr. Andras Angyal, entitled *Foundations for a Science of Personality*. But opening it, one finds the entire first half of this project for a "science" of personality constructed about the relationships between "organism" and "environment," two terms that in their very nature *dissolve* the concept of personality by *reducing* it to non-personal terms. Strictly speaking, the expression "science of personality" is a contradiction in terms, a "perspective by incongruity." For "personality" (derived from a word referring to a man's role) is a "dramatist" concept, and as such involves philosophical or metaphysical notions of human identity. But a "science" of personality would be evolved by translating matters of personality into terms wholly outside the personal (as the biologistic terms "organism" and "environment" are outside the personal). I do not say that there cannot be a "science" of the personality, for Dr. Angyal's valuable book goes a long way towards showing that there can be. (Or at least it shows that there can be a "scientific terminology" of the personality.) I am trying simply to suggest that such a science will be totally "extrinsic" in its approach, not aiming to consider the philosophic problem of what the personality is "in itself," but perfectly at home in a vocabulary that simply dissolves the person into a non-person.

II

One will quickly realize why we wanted to approach the three essays[2] thus circuitously as we turn now to Mr. Crane's "Prefatory Note," built about his opposition to the method he calls "Coleridgean." In the Coleridgean method, Mr. Crane says, one begins by expounding some general philosophic or metaphysical or psychological frame. Next one treats poetry in general as a representative aspect of this frame. And finally one treats specific poems as individual instances of vessels of poetry. The Coleridgean critic thus employs what we might call a process of narrowing-down. For he begins with the terms that apply to much broader fields of reference than to poetry alone; these are paired with contrary terms (such as "subjective and objective," or "extension and intension"); then other terms, more specific in reference, are added (I think Mr. Ransom's "structure and texture" pair would be an example); and this process is repeated "until, by a series of descending

[2] This article was written as comment on three essays (by the "Neo-Aristotelians," R. S. Crane, Norman Maclean, and Elder Olson) originally published in *The University Review*. Mr. Maclean's was constructed about the analysis of a sonnet by Wordsworth, Mr. Olson's about the analysis of one of the Yeats "Byzantium" poems; and Mr. Crane contributed a general statement on the theory and method exemplified by the two analyses.

proportions, a transition is effected between the universality of the 'principles' and the particularity of the texts."

The poem would thus not be explained in itself, but "as a kind of emblem or exemplar of principles broader in their relevance than poems or any given kind of poems." The conclusions of such inquiry could be related to the texts "only as universal forms or platonic ideas are related to the particulars in the world which are their more or less adequate reflection." There might even be no need to consider the poem as a whole, since representative passages or lines can be also treated as vessels of the abstract qualities which the critic would discover in the particular work. Hence, "Coleridgean" critics are given to talk about "poetry" rather than about "poems"—and they may like to cite passages that can serve as "touchstones" of the qualities they would select as "poetic."

Messrs. Maclean and Olson, on the other hand, "represent a radical departure" from this tradition:

> They are interested in lyrics not as exemplars but as objects; they insist on approaching them as poems of a distinctive kind rather than as receptacles of poetry. . . . The appreciation they wish to make possible is one of which the object is not a universal form or value reflected in the poem but the poem itself in its wholeness and particularly as a structure of mutually appropriate parts.

To attain this "theoretical grasp of the parts of lyrics and of the principles of their unification," Mr. Crane says, we must confine ourselves to "an inductive study of lyrics pursued apart from any a priori assumptions about the nature of poetry in general." And after many more such essays, on many more poems, we may begin to see "what an inductive poetics of the lyric is likely to be." It is a necessary part of Mr. Crane's position, taken in dialectical opposition to the "Coleridgean," that he adopt this excessive stress upon the *inductive*.

If you consider philosophic or critical terminologies as languages, however (languages from which we derive kinds of observation in accordance with the nature of the terms featured in the given philosophic idiom), you find reason to question his claims in advance. For the critic does not by any means begin his observations "from scratch," but has a more or less systematically organized set of terms by which to distinguish and characterize the elements of the poem he would observe.

In this sense, one's observations will not be purely "inductive," even though they derive important modifications from the observing of the given poem. They will also in part (and in particular as to their grammar, or form) be deduced or derived from the nature of the language or terminology which the critic employs. Such languages are developed prior to the individual observation (though one may adopt the well known philosophic subterfuge: "Let us begin simply by considering this object in front of us, just as it is").

If there were only some few "true" things to be said about a poem's structure, and if men of various sorts readily made these same observations independently of one another, one might be justified in considering these observations a matter of "induction." But since so many valid things are to be said, a given vocabulary coaches us to look for certain kinds of things rather than others—and this coaching of observations is a deductive process, insofar as one approaches the poem with a well-formed analytic terminology prior to the given analysis, and derives observations from the nature of this terminology. Hypothetically, one might be perceptive or imaginative enough to transcend any vocabulary, as one might hypothetically add enough "epicycles" and other qualifications to the Ptolemaic system of astronomy to make it do the work now done by the modern system of astro-physics. But under conditions of ordinary experience, such a transcending of vocabulary is decidedly limited. Ordinarily, we see somewhat beyond the limits of our favorite terms—but the bulk of our critical perceptions are but particular applications of these terms. The terms are like "principles," and the particular observations are like the judicial casuistry involved in the application of principles to cases that are always in some respects unique.

Some terminologies contain much richer modes of observation than others. And the "dramatist" nature of the Aristotelian vocabulary could be expected to provide the observer with very rich modes indeed. But one cannot be purely "inductive" in his observation of poems when making these observations through the instrumentality of so highly developed a philosophic language. One owes too much to the language. However, if Mr. Crane admitted that his "inductive" method also contained strongly "deductive" elements, he would have to relinquish the symmetry of his own dramatizing, got by pitting his position in dialectical opposition to the "Coleridgean" mode of derivation.

When considered in a linguistic, or terministic, perspective (the perspective in which we would consider "dramatism"), the apparent distinctness between "inductive" and "deductive" modes of observation and derivation here ceases to exist. Indeed, insofar as the writers do abide by their pretensions, and begin with each analysis anew, their interpretation of the principles by which a given poem is organized is mere "prophecy after the event," which is not a very exacting kind of "induction." Induction must also use generalizations which, in effect, prophesy *before* the event. It should not be merely a casuistry ready to rationalize any case after the case has occurred (a temptation to which Aristotelianism has been prone in the past). It must also risk statements as to *what to expect,* and *why.* Otherwise, such criticism becomes merely a disguised variant of impressionism, a kind of improvisation wherein the critic simply translates the unique imaginative sequence of the poem into a correspondingly unique conceptual equivalent.

III

As for the two long analytic essays by Messrs. Maclean and Olson, I should have to quote or paraphrase nearly every paragraph to convey how ably and discerningly they carry out their project. But as one cannot do justice to a poem in paraphrase, but must follow it from line to line, and from word to word, in its unique order, so these exegetes analyze their poems with a particularity that must be read in its particularity to be appreciated. However, in the course of their analysis, they make generalizations about their method and their conclusions—and we can consider these.

Mr. Maclean takes as his opponent specifically a critic who had based his discussion of a Wordsworth sonnet upon a theory about its reference to the poet's illegitimate daughter. Against this somewhat sorry position, Mr. Maclean says of his own:

> As the unity of a poem arises from the facts that it is divisible into parts and that these parts are harmoniously related, so the obligations resting upon this kind of criticism are twofold: to discover the parts of a poem and to render an account of their relationships.

He convincingly divides the sonnet into three parts, and considers their relation to the whole, in producing a "spiritual and religious translation of the evening." And he does well in making us realize the steps by which this translation progresses, as in his remarks on "the completeness with which the beauty and serenity of the Nun have been transferred to the immensity of the evening." [3]

At this point I must introduce some reference to the line of thought developed in my Grammar. In my analysis of the drama, I try to show how the quality of the scene contains the quality of the act that is enacted on that scene. (Most obvious example: the Shakespearean use of storm or darkness as setting for a sinister bit of action. Hardy's use of background as a source of motivation is an obvious instance of this scene-act ratio in the novel.) This is a "grammatical" principle of much wider application than the drama (hence, open to Mr. Crane's charge of "Coleridgean"). For in the various mythological, theological, metaphysical, and scientific theories of motivation the character we attribute to human action changes according to the character we attribute to the universal scene in which human acts take place. (Contrast, for instance the quality of human acts when placed against a background of struggles among the gods, and the quality of human acts in a behaviorist's background of mechanism and reflexes.) In considering the lyric, where there is no action but where there may be reference to persons (agents), we find that this same relationship may apply between scene and agent. Indeed, it is this scene-agent identification that makes it possible for the poet to convey states of mind (psychological processes) by the use of corresponding scenic imagery. "Dramatistically," therefore, one is invited to observe that this particular

---

[3] I quote the sonnet herewith:

It is a beauteous evening, calm and free,
The holy time is quiet as a Nun
Breathless with adoration; the broad sun
Is sinking down in its tranquillity;
The gentleness of heaven broods o'er the Sea:
Listen! the mighty Being is awake,
And doth with his eternal motion make
A sound like thunder—everlastingly.
Dear Child! dear Girl! that walkest with me here,
If thou appear untouched by solemn thought,
Thy nature is not therefore less divine:
Thou liest in Abraham's bosom all the year;
And worshipp'st at the Temple's inner shrine,
God being with thee when we know it not.

sonnet is constructed quite neatly about this scene-agent ratio. The octave establishes the quality of the scene; then at the beginning of the sestet, we turn to the agent ("Dear Child! dear Girl!"); and we find the quality of the agent so imbued with the divine quality of the scene containing this agent, that she can possess this quality even without knowing it, by the simple fact of having it as her ground.

Also, I would hold that a "dramatistic" placement of the lyric is to be arrived at "deductively" in this sense: one approaches the lyric from the category of *action,* which Aristotle considers the primary element of the drama. And then by dialectic coaching one looks for a form that will have as its primary element the moment of *stasis,* or *rest.* We are admonished, however, to note that there are two concepts of "rest," often confused because we may apply the same word to both. There is rest as the sheer cessation of motion (in the sense that a rolling ball comes to rest); and there is rest as the end of action (end as finish or end as aim), the kind of rest that Aristotle conceived as the *primum mobile* of the world, the ground of motion and action both. It is proper for the physical sciences, we would grant, to treat experience nondramatically, in terms of motion, but things in the realm of the social or human require treatment in terms of action or drama. Or rather, though things in the realm of the human *may* be treated in terms of motion, the result will be statements not about the intrinsic, but about the extrinsic (as per our remarks on an "incongruous" science of the personality).

A treatment of the lyric in terms of action would not by any means require us merely to look for analogies from the drama. On the contrary, the *state of arrest* in which we would situate the essence of the lyric is not analogous to dramatic action at all, but is the dialectical counterpart of action. Consider as an illustration the fourteen Stations of the Cross: The concern with them in the totality of their progression would be dramatic. But the pause at any one of them, and the contemplation and deepening appreciation of its poignancy, in itself, would be lyric.

A typical Wordsworthian sonnet brings out this methodological aspect of the lyric (its special aptitude for conveying a *state* of mind, for erecting a moment into a universe) by selecting such themes as in themselves explicitly refer to the arrest, the pause, the hush. However, this lyric state is to be understood in terms of action, inasmuch as it is to be understood as a state that sums up an action in the form of an attitude.

Thus approached, an attitude is ambiguous in this sense: It may be either an incipient act or the substitute for an act. An attitude of sympathy is incipiently an act, for instance, in that it is the proper emotional preparation for a sympathetic act; or it may be the substitute for an act in that the sympathetic person can let the intent do service for the deed (precisely through doing nothing, one may feel more sympathetic than the person whose mood may be partially distracted by the conditions of action). In either case, an attitude is a state of emotion, or a moment of stasis, in which an act is arrested, summed up, made permanent and total, as with the Grecian Urn which in its summational quality Keats calls a "fair Attitude." [4]

We have here a cluster of closely related words: action, rest (designated in the sonnet by such synonyms as "calm," "quiet," "tranquillity," "gentleness"), motion, attitude or potential action. Mr. Maclean says something much to our purposes here, in his gloss on the word "free" in the first line: "It is a strange word when coupled with 'beauteous' and 'calm.' As endowing the evening with the power to act, it seems at variance with the beauty of tranquillity." The comment enables us to discern that in "free" we find obliquely a reference to potential action. However, our thoughts on the relation between action and the rest that is the end of action would lead us to hold that there is nothing "strange" about this usage. Who would be more "tranquil" than the wholly "free"? For his complete freedom would so thoroughly contain the potentialities of action that there would be no problem to disturb the state of rest.

Nearly every particular observation that Mr. Maclean makes about the sonnet, I could salute and zestfully, if he but gave it the pointedness that would derive from an explicit recognition of the "dramatistic" element in his vocabulary. Thus I would hold that an explicit concern with the scene-agent ratio provides a central statement about the grammatical principles involved in the structure of the poem. Or Mr. Maclean cites a passage from "Lines Composed Above Tintern Abbey":

> . . . that serene and blessed mood
> In which the affections gently lead us on,—

---

[4] Wordsworth's formula, "emotion recollected in tranquillity," could be translated into our terms as "a state of emotion conveyed as a moment of stasis."

Until, the breath of this corporeal frame
And even the motion of our human blood
Almost suspended, we are laid asleep
In body, and become a living soul:
While with an eye made quiet by the power
Of harmony, and the deep power of joy,
We see into the life of things.

And here by the use of an explicitly dramatist perspective we would distinguish between a level of bodily motion ("the motion of our human blood") and a level of mental or spiritual action ("a living soul"). The "power of harmony" here would be another synonym for the rest of "potential action." And the state of arrest is said to be attained when the level of mental action transcends the level of bodily motion. (The "Ode on a Grecian Urn" is constructed about a similar transcendence. Progressively through the stanzas we can watch the poet's fever split into two parts: a bodily passion and a mental action. But in the "Ode" it is a state of agitation that is arrested, to be transformed into its transcendent counterpart.)

IV

It is to be regretted that none of these three writers, in stressing the importance of an analysis which considers the relations of parts to whole, makes any mention of the fact that in Aristotle's treatment of tragedy, there are *two* versions of this relationship. In Chapter 6, Aristotle writes:

> There are six parts consequently of every tragedy, as a whole (that is) of such or such quality, *viz.* a Fable or Plot, Characters, Diction, Thought, Spectacle, and Melody.

But in Chapter 12, he writes:

> The parts of Tragedy to be treated as formative elements in the whole were mentioned in a previous Chapter. From the point of view, however, of its quantity, i. e., the separate sections into which it is divided, a tragedy has the following parts: Prologue, Episode, Exode, and a choral portion, distinguished into Parode and Stasimon.

In any event, it is notable that both these treatments of part-whole relationships apply not only to single tragedies but to tragedies as a *class*. Yet Mr. Maclean says, in conclusion to his article: "To explain the poem . . . in terms of its particular beginning is to explain as exactly as possible its uniqueness, and to distinguish it from other poems by Wordsworth that treat much the same 'theme.'" And likewise Mr. Olson will end his article on a similar remark to the effect that "great art . . . is always in the last analysis *sui generis*." There is, of course, a sense in which every work is unique, since its particular combination of details is never repeated. But is the emphasis upon this fact feasible if one would develop an "Aristotelian" poetics of the lyric, treating lyrics as a class? And a mere concern with one lyric, then another lyric, then another would not yield the kind of observations needed to treat of lyrics as a class. For to treat lyrics as a class, one must examine individual lyrics from the standpoint of their generic attributes. And to do this, one must have terminological prepossessions, prior to the analysis, even before one can select a poem that he considers representative of the lyric. At least, one must have negative or tentative touchstones that enable him roughly to differentiate lyrics as a class from such classes as epic, drama, epigram, etc.

One does not place a form in isolation. The placement of a given form involves the corresponding placement of other forms. Thus *a vocabulary wider in reference than the orbit of the given form is needed for the classifying of that form*. Though the authors would presumably get immunity from such objections by presenting their analyses as mere *preparations* for a poetics of the lyric, we would object that observations confined in their reference to the unique are not classificatory at all.[5]

[5] Mr. Crane reminds us of Coleridge's distinction between "poetry" and "poem," in the *Biographia Literaria*. But perhaps he and his colleagues have been victimized by the "Coleridgean" here: perhaps the distinction between "poetry" and "poem" is not enough. "Poetry" itself may have two different meanings. We may use it as one member of such dialectical pairs as "poetry and science," "poetry and mathematics," "poetry and anarchism," "poetry and politics," "poetry and morals," etc. Or we may use it as a term for poems in a *generic* sense (as Aristotle in his *Poetics* treats of part-whole relationships not by treating of tragedies one by one, in their uniqueness, but generically). So we may need three terms rather than two here: a term for "poetry" (as member of a dialectical pair), and a term for "poem" (this poem, that poem, the next poem),

The point is made still clearer by considering another citation from Mr. Olson:

> The scrutiny of particular poems would thus be the beginning of the critical enterprise; but the principles eventually reached, as disclosed by analysis, would not be rules governing the operations involved in the construction of any further poem, nor would the enumeration of poetic parts and poetic devices suffer extension beyond those objects to which analysis had been turned. . . . Poetic questions would be concerning the poetic structure of a particular work . . . [and] would terminate in a discovery of the parts of a work and of the interrelations through which the parts are parts of a whole.

Now, if the principles of a specific work were so defined that the definition would not apply to "any further poem," would not this also mean that the definition would not apply to any *other* poem? In brief, would not this conception of the relation between parts and whole be so particularized as to make statements about the lyric as a *genus* impossible? And could a critic, aiming at analyses that meet these particularized requirements, go beyond the merely statistical to the generic unless at the same time he happened to be taking some other kind of step not expressly signalized? Surely it is ironic to find Aristotle, who was so long admired and resented as the Prince of Deducers, now serving as Prince of Inducers.

As a matter of fact, there are many passages in Mr. Olson's essay where he profits by going beyond his principle of uniqueness. For he launches into generalizations about the lyric generically that are not at all confined to the particular poem he is analyzing (Yeats's "Sailing to Byzantium," of which by the way he makes what I think is a really superb analysis). These place the lyric as a class with relation to other classes. When he says, for instance, that tragedy, epic, and comedy are "dynamic, for they imitate change," whereas "the kind we have been scrutinizing is static," his concern here with stasis profits by dramatistic reference.

His discussion of the poem itself is thoroughly dramatistic in its choice of vocabulary, being built about distinctions between "action"

---

and a term for "poems" (as a class, with corresponding terms for classes and subclasses).

and "passion," explicitly recognizing the theme as a problem of "regeneration," and treating the whole series of transformations from stanza to stanza as a "dialectic" wherein character is determined "not by its share in an action, but by its role in a drama, not of action, but of thought." Yet, surprisingly, this highly developed vocabulary is employed quite as though it had been forced upon the critic purely by inspection of the given poem—and we are warned against an attempt to find in the lyric "some analogue of plot in the drama and epic." However, imagery, like attitude, has the quality of "incipient action"—and in noting how, in a given poem, it undergoes a series of developments from ambiguous potentiality to clear fulfilment, we should be considering it "dramatistically" without thereby treating it merely as the analogue of dramatic plot.

And let us cite two other statements that are thoroughly *generic,* and as such are derived not from mere observation of the single poem but from the nature of the "dramatist" vocabulary:

> There can be no plot because there can be no incidents; the "events" in a lyric poem are never incidents as such, connected by necessity or probability, but devices for making poetic statements. . . .
>
> Since there is no action, there is no agent, that is, *character,* in the sense in which there are differentiated agents in the drama; rather, the character in the sense in which character may be said to exist here is almost completely universalized. . . .[6]

[6] "Universalized" is a good word here. The poetic "I" that is the ground of a lyric fills the whole universe of discourse.

Mr. Olson's distinction between the dramatic "act" and the lyric "event" opens up interesting possibilities. In the *Philosophy of Literary Form* I had used a similar distinction, but with a quite different application. But by combining Mr. Olson's application with my own, I believe I come a bit closer to glimpsing why the lyric is a better fit with the scientific than the dramatic is. The steps are as follows (first quoting from my summary of the dramatistic perspective, *op. cit.*):

> We have the drama and the scene of the drama. The drama is enacted against a background. . . . The description of the scene is the role of the physical sciences; the description of the drama is the role of the social sciences. . . . The physical sciences are a calculus of events; the social sciences are a calculus of acts. And human affairs being dramatic, the discussion of human affairs becomes dramatic criticism, with more to be learned from study of tropes than from a study of tropisms. . . . The error of the social sciences has usually resided in the attempt to appropriate the scenic calculus for a charting of the act.

V

What, then, is the upshot of our fluctuancy between agreement and disagreement? It is not merely that we would have these authors ply

Now science, as we have observed in the present paper, is "scenic." And since it speaks in terms of motion rather than in terms of action, the typical scientific vocabulary is non-dramatic.

Recall next Yvor Winters' notion of "Pseudo-Reference," one kind of which is "reference to a non-existent plot." As an instance of "pseudo-reference," he cites from "Gerontion":

> To be eaten, to be divided, to be drunk
> Among whispers; by Mr. Silvero
> With caressing hands, at Limoges
> Who walked all night in the next room;
> By Hakagawa, bowing among the Titians;
> By Madame de Tornquist, in the dark room
> Shifting the candles; Fräulein von Kulp
> Who turned in the hall, one hand on the door.

On this Mr. Winters comments:

> Each of these persons is denoted in the performance of an act, and each act, save possibly that of Hakagawa, implies an anterior situation, is a link in a chain of action; even that of Hakagawa implies an anterior and unexplained personality. Yet we have no hint of the nature of the history implied. A feeling is claimed by the poet, the motivation, or meaning, of which is withheld, and of which in all likelihood he has no clearer notion than his readers can have.

In this form which Mr. Winters is considering, do we not see a "watershed moment," the very point at which dramatic "actions" are undergoing a transformation into lyric "events"? Indeed, this would be the way of translating the concept of pseudo-reference into our present terms.

By reason of correspondences between the "objective" and the "subjective" (or what we have called the scene-agent ratio) these "events" (which are more like "scenes" than "acts") convey attitudes, or states of mind, through the use of "objective imagery." The "events" here are "moody," quite as though they were such attitude-purveying imagery as storms, sunsets, or bird sounds. In their nature as imagery, as "scenic," they invite us to *feel* as the situation *is*.

From the standpoint of science, the content of a scene is "knowledge." And knowledge is a *state*. Hence, scientific events and lyric events are both received in the psychological form of *states*. A whole set of such relations would be: science is to the lyric as the impersonal is to the personal, as materialism is to idealism, as scene is to agent, as knowledge is to knower, as the epistemological is to the psychological. (In the "dramatistic" perspective, the primary category is not the epistemological-psychological one of *knowing,* but that of acting.)

their trade under the trade-name of "dramatism" rather than "Aristotle." Mr. Crane gives us a choice between the poem as "exemplar" and the poem as "object"—and as though these alternatives had exhausted the field, he discusses no other. But if we begin by explicitly recognizing the dramatistic nature of the vocabulary, then looking at our pentad (the terms Act, Scene, Agent, Agency, Purpose), we may ask ourselves: "What about the poem considered as an *act?*" Thus, when Mr. Crane says that the poem is to be considered "as a product of purposive activity on the part of its author," we would agree with him, only more intensely than he would want us to.

The treatment of the poem as act would not, by any means, require us to slight the nature of the poem as object. For a poem is a *constitutive* act—and after the act of its composition by a poet who had acted in a particular temporal scene, it survives as an objective structure, capable of being examined in itself, in temporal scenes quite different from the scene of its composition, and by agents quite different from the agent who originally enacted it. The enactment thus remaining as a constitution, we can inquire into the principles by which this constitution is organized.

The poem, as an object, is to be considered in terms of its nature as "finished." That is, it is to be considered in terms of "perfection," as per the stressing of part-whole relationships. These men have done criticism a great service in helping to reaffirm this aspect of criticism, particularly at a time when the state of the sciences has offered so many extrinsic approaches to poetry, which can be considered as the "exemplar" of political exigencies, neurosis, physique, diet, climate, cultural movements, economic classifications, etc. But consideration of it as an act surviving as a constitution would also enable one to consider its intrinsic relations.

The dramatistic perspective, if I may refer to my *Philosophy of Literary Form,* points equally towards a concern with "internal structure" and towards a concern with "act-scene relationships." "Words are aspects of a much wider communicative context, most of which is not verbal at all. Yet words also have a nature peculiarly their own. And when discussing them as modes of action, we must consider *both* this nature as words in themselves *and* the nature they get from the nonverbal scenes that support their acts." But while proposing to consider words "as acts upon a scene," I held that the approach to literature in terms of "linguistic, or symbolic, or literary action" could avoid the excesses of the purely environmental schools "which are usually so eager to trace the relationships between act and scene that they neglect to trace the structure of the act itself."

The explicit treatment of the poem as an act, however, would remind us that it is not enough to consider it solely in terms of its "perfection," or "finishedness," since this conventionalized restriction of our inquiry could not possibly tell us all the important things about its substance. This seems to be particularly the case with the study of lyrics—for often, to grasp the full import of the terms employed in one poem, we must see how these terms are qualified by their use in other poems. That is, the individual lyrics are not to be considered solely as isolated acts, but also as stages or stations of a more comprehensive act. And statements about this more comprehensive act are also statements about the *intrinsic* nature of the enactment in the single poem. I began by speaking of the three fields: Grammar, Rhetoric, and Symbolic. It is perhaps only in the third of these categories that modern criticism has something vitally new to offer the student of literature. And it would be a pity indeed if a dogmatic or formalistic preference for an earlier method interfered with the progress of such inquiry, which promises greatly to increase our knowledge of poetic substance in particular and of human motivation in general. (Nor would it be the first time that the great name of Aristotle had served to stifle fresh inquiry.)

The concern with Symbolic has already been developed to a point where we can see that, as regards the analysis of literary texts at least, it can be more empirical in its methods than is possible to most studies in the human realm. Yet in trying to abide by the neo-Aristotelian ideals for the compartmentalizing of inquiry, one would simply be taking on many encumbrances that interfered with the development of methods proper to the nature of the subject-matter.[7]

[7] To complete the placement of these critics, perhaps we should also have considered the part that the Scotist stress upon the "thisness" (*haeccëitas*) of a thing might have had in shaping their aims. They seem to be encountering in their way what Duns Scotus encountered in his, when he contended that the step from genus to species should be completed by a step from species to individual. And their concern to define the lyric as a *kind* while placing stress upon the unique generating principles of *particular* lyrics seems similarly on the road to nominalism. Or should we say rather that, having encountered the nominalist stress by way of modern empirical science, they would translate it back into scholastic terms?

And always on the look-out for secular analogues to theological doctrine, perhaps we should note that the stress upon the individual poem as *sui generis,* coupled with a search for the principle of the lyric as a *kind,* has somewhat the pattern of Aquinas' doctrine of angels, each of which in his view is both a genus and an individual at the same time.   The search for the intrinsic, demanding in its logical completion a complete divorce of relations with contextual impurities, would seem to require in the end such a view of "pure" or "separate" forms subsisting without admixture of "matter."   That is, the subsistence of the poem must be discussed without reference to any individuating principle drawn from some extrinsic source, which would function as "matter" in being *scenic* to the poem as act.

C

MOTIVES AND MOTIFS IN THE POETRY OF MARIANNE MOORE

IN THIS essay we would characterize the substance of Miss Moore's work as a specific poetic strategy. And we would watch it for insights which the contemplation of it may give us into the ways of poetic and linguistic action generally. For this purpose we shall use both her recently published book, *What Are Years,* and her *Selected Poems,* published in 1935 with an introduction by T. S. Eliot (and including some work reprinted from an earlier volume, *Observations*).

On page 8 of the new book, Miss Moore writes:

> The power of the visible
> is the invisible;

and in keeping with the pattern, when recalling her former title, *Observations,* we might even have been justified in reading it as a deceptively technical synonym for "visions." One observes the visibles—but of the corresponding invisibles, one must be visionary. And while dealing much in things that can be empirically here, the poet reminds us that they may

> dramatize a
> meaning always missed
> by the externalist.

It is, then, a relation between external and internal, or visible and invisible, or background and personality, that her poems characteristically establish. Though her names for things are representative of attitudes, we could not say that the method is Symbolist. The objects exist too fully in their own right for us to treat them merely as objective words for subjects. T. S. Eliot says that her poetry "might be classified as 'descriptive' rather than 'lyrical' or 'dramatic.'" He cites an early poem that "suggests a slight influence of H. D., certainly of H. D.

485

rather than of any other 'Imagist.'" And though asserting that "Miss Moore has no immediate poetic derivations," he seems to locate her work in the general vicinity of imagism, as when he writes:

> The aim of 'imagism,' so far as I understand it, or so far as it had any, was to introduce a peculiar concentration upon something visual, and to set in motion an expanding succession of concentric feelings. Some of Miss Moore's poems—for instance with animal or bird subjects—have a very good spread of association.

I think of William Carlos Williams. For though Williams differs much from Miss Moore in temperament and method, there is an important quality common to their modes of perception. It is what Williams has chosen to call by the trade name of "objectivist."

Symbolism, imagism, and objectivism would obviously merge into one another, since they are recipes all having the same ingredients but in different proportions. In symbolism, the subject is much stronger than the object as an organizing motive. That is, it is *what the images are symbolic of* that shapes their treatment. In imagism, there would ideally be an equality of the two motives, the subjective and objective. But in objectivism, though an object may be chosen for treatment because of its symbolic or subjective reference, once it has been chosen it is to be studied in its own right.

A man might become an electrician, for instance, because of some deep response to electricity as a symbol of power. Yet, once he had become an electrician and thus had converted his response to this subject into an objective knowledge of its laws and properties, he would thereafter treat electricity as he did, not because each of his acts as an electrician would be symbolic like his original choice of occupation, but because such acts were required by the peculiar nature of electricity. Similarly, a poet writing in an "objectivist" idiom might select his subject because of some secret reference or personal significance it has had for him; yet having selected it, he would find that its corresponding object had qualities to be featured and appraised for themselves. And he might pay so much attention to such appraisal that the treatment of the object would in effect "transcend" the motive behind its original singling-out.

Thus, the poem "Four Quartz Crystal Clocks" (in *What Are Years*) begins:

> There are four vibrators, the world's exactest clocks;
>   and these quartz time-pieces that tell
> time intervals to other clocks,
>   these workless clocks work well;
> and all four, independently the
>   same, are there in the cool Bell
>   Laboratory time
>
> vault. Checked by a comparator with Arlington
>   they punctualize . . .   (Etc.)

I think there would be no use in looking for "symbolist" or "imagist" motives behind the reference to the fact that precisely *four* clocks are mentioned here. It is an "objectivist" observation. We read of four, not because the number corresponds, for instance, to the Horsemen of the Apocalypse, but simply because there actually are four of them in the time vault. Similarly, "cool Bell Laboratory time vault" might have outlying suggestions of something like the coolness of a tomb— but primarily one feels that the description is there for purposes of objective statement; and had the nature of the scene itself dictated it, we should be reading of a "hot Bell Laboratory time tower." Though not journalism, it is reporting.

Yet any reader of Miss Moore's verse will quickly acknowledge that this theme, which provides an "objective" opportunity for the insertion of transitions between such words as "exactest," "punctualize," "careful timing," "clear ice," "instruments of truth," and "accuracy," is quite representative of her (and thus "symbolic" in the proportions of imagism). And the secondary level of the theme (its quality as being not the theme of clocks that tell the time, but of clocks that tell the time to clocks that tell the time)—I should consider thoroughly symbolic, as signalizing a concern not merely for the withinness of motives, but for the withinness-of-withinness of motives, the motives behind motives.[1]

---

[1] In passing we might consider a whole series of literary ways from this point of view. Allegory would deal with correspondences on a purely dogmatic, or conceptual basis. In the article on "Vestments," for instance, in the *Encyclopædia Britannica,* we read of various "symbolical interpretations": "(1) the *moralizing school,* the oldest, by which—as in the case of St. Jerome's treatment of the Jewish vestments—the vestments are explained as typical of the virtues proper to those who wear them; (2) the *Christological school, i. e.* that which considered the minister as the representative of Christ and his garments as typical of some aspects of Christ's person or office—*e. g.* the stole is his obedience and servitude for our sakes; (3) the *allegorical school,* which treats the priest as a warrior or champion, who

We can call Miss Moore "objectivist," then, only by taking away the epithet in part. For though many details in her work seem to get there purely out of her attempt to report and judge of a thing's intrinsic qualities, to make us feel its properties as accurately as possible, the fact remains that, after you have read several of her poems, you begin to discern a strict principle of selection motivating her appraisals.

In *Selected Poems,* for instance, consider the poem, "People's Surroundings," that gives us a catalogue of correspondence between various kinds of agents and the scenes related to their roles. The poet is concerned to feature, in a background, the details that are an objective portrait of the person to whose kind of action this background belongs. "A setting must not have the air of being one"—a proscription one can ob-

----

puts on the amice as a helmet, the alb as a breastplate, and so on." A work constructed about the systematic use of any such theories of correspondence would, to our way of thinking, be allegorical. The symbolic would use an objective vocabulary for its suggestion of the subjective, with the subjective motive being organizationally more important than the objective one. The specific literary movement called Symbolism would exemplify this stress to a large extent, but would also gravitate towards Surrealism, which stresses the incongruous and contradictory nature of motives by the use of gargoyles as motifs. Imagism would be "personalistic," in the idealistic sense, in using scenic material as the reflection, or extension of human characters. The "objectivist," though rooted in symbolic and imagist concerns, would move into a plane where the object, originally selected by reason of its subjective reference, is studied in its own right. (The result will be "descriptive" poetry. And it will be "scientific" in the sense that, whereas poetry is a kind of act, the descriptiveness of science is rather the *preparation* for an act, the delayed action of a Hamletic reconnaissance in search of the accurate knowledge necessary for the act. And descriptive poetry falls across the two categories in that it acts by describing the scene preparatory to an act.) Naturalism has a greater stress upon the scenic from the polemic or depreciatory point of view (its quasi-scientific quality as delayed action, or preparation for action, often being revealed in that such literature generally either calls for action in the non-esthetic field or makes one very conscious of the fact that a "solution" is needed but is not being offered). True realism is difficult for us to conceive of, after so long a stretch of monetary idealism (accentuated as surrealism) and its counterpart, technological materialism (accentuated as behaviorism and operationalism), while pragmatic philosophies stress *making* and *doing* and *getting* in a localized way that obscures the realistic stress upon the *act.* The German term, *Realpolitik,* for instance, exemplifies a crude brand of pragmatism that completely misrepresents the realistic motive. The communicative nature of art gives all art a realistic ingredient, but the esthetic philosophies which the modern artist consciously or unconsciously absorbs continually serve to obscure this ingredient rather than to cultivate it.

serve if he makes the setting the extension of those in it. Here are relationships among act, scene, and agent (I use the three terms central
to the philosophy of drama embodied in Henry James's prefaces).
And among these people who move "in their respective places," we
read of

> . . . the acacia-like lady shivering at the touch of a hand,
> lost in a small collision of orchids—
> dyed quicksilver let fall
> to disappear like an obedient chameleon in fifty shades of mauve
>   and amethyst.

Here, with person and ground merged as indistinguishably as in a
pontillist painting by Seurat, the items objectify a tentative mood we
encounter throughout Miss Moore's verses. The lines are like a miniature impression of her work in its entirety. And when, contemplating
a game of bowls, she writes, "I learn that we are precisians, not citizens
of Pompeii arrested in action / as a cross-section of one's correspondence would seem to imply," she here "learns" what she is forever learning, in her contemplation of animals and natural and fabricated things,
as she seeks to isolate, for her appreciation and our own, the "great
amount of poetry in unconscious fastidiousness."

I think appreciation is as strong a motive in her work as it was in the
work of Henry James. "The thing is to lodge somewhere at the heart
of one's complexity an irrepressible *appreciation*," he says in his preface
to *The Spoils of Poynton*. And: "To criticise is to appreciate, to appropriate, to take intellectual possession, to establish in fine a relation with
the criticised thing and make it one's own." It is a kind of private
property available to everyone—and is perhaps the closest secular equivalent to the religious motive of glorification. It is a form of gratitude.
And following out its possibilities, where one might otherwise be
querulous he can instead choose to be precise. This redemption or
transformation of complaint is, I think, essential to the quality of perception in Miss Moore's verse. (Rather, it is an anticipation of complaint: getting there first, it takes up all the room.)

In "Spenser's Ireland" (*What Are Years*), we may glimpse somewhat how this redemption can take place. Beginning in a mood of appreciation almost studious, the poem ends

> The Irish say your trouble is their
> trouble and your
>   joy their joy?   I wish
> I could believe it;
> I am troubled, I'm dissat-
>   isfied, I'm Irish.

Since it is towards this end that the poem is directed, we may assume that from this end it derives the logic of its progression.

Note the general tenor of the other observations: on family, on marriage, on independence and yielding, on the freedom of those "made captive by supreme belief."   There is talk of enchantments, of transformations, of a coat "like Venus' mantle lined with stars . . . the sleeves new from disuse," of such discriminations as we get

> when large dainty
> fingers tremblingly divide the wings
> of the fly.

And there are lines naming birds, and having a verbal music most lovely in its flutter of internal rhymes:

> the guillemot
>   so neat and the hen
> of the heath and the
> linnet spinet-sweet.

All these details could be thought of as contextual to the poem's ending (for, if you single out one moment of a poem, all the other moments automatically become its context).   If, then, we think of the final assertion as the act, we may think of the preceding contextual material as the scene, or background, of this act (a background that somehow contains the same quality as the act, saying implicitly what the act of the final assertion says explicitly).   Viewed thus we see, as the underlying structure of this "description," a poem that, if treated as a lyric, would have somewhat the following argument: "Surrounded with details appropriate to my present mood, with a background of such items as go with matters to do with family, union, independence, I, an Irish girl (while the birds are about—and sweetly) am dissatisfied."

I won't insist that I'm not wrong.   But in any case, that's the way I read it.   And I would discern, behind her "objectivist" study and editorializing, what are essentially the lineaments of a lyric. But where the lyrist might set about to write, "In the moonlight, by the river, on a night like this in Spain," I can think of Miss Moore's distributing these items (discreetly and discretely) among conversational observations about the quality of light in general and moonlight in particular, about rivers mighty and tiny, in mountains, across plains, and emptying into the desert or the sea, about the various qualifications that apply to the transformation from twilight to darkness, in suburbs, or over bays, etc.; and from travel books of Spain we might get some bits that, pieced together, gave us all those elements into which, in her opinion, the given night in Spain should be "broken down."

We might try from another angle by suggesting that Miss Moore makes "because" look like "and." That is, the orthodox lyrist might say, in effect, "I am sad *because* the birds are singing thus." A translation into Miss Moore's objectivist idiom would say in effect: "There are such and such birds—*and* birds sing thus and so—*and* I am sad." The scenic material would presumably be chosen because of its quality as objective replica of the subjective (as observed moments in the scene that correspond to observing moments in the agent). But even where they had been selected because of their bearing upon the plaint, her subsequent attention to them, with appreciation as a motive, would transform the result from a purely psychologistic rhetoric (the traditional romantic device of simply using scenic terms as a vocabulary for the sympathetic naming of personal moods). And the result would be, instead, an appraisal or judgment of many things in and for themselves. They would be encouraged to disclose their traits, not simply that they might exist through the vicarage of words, but that they might reveal their properties as workmanship (workmanship being a trait in which the ethical and the esthetic are one).

What are years? That is, if we were to assemble a thesaurus of all the important qualifications of the term "years" as Miss Moore uses it, what would these qualifications be? I suppose a title is always an assertion because it is a thing—and every thing is positive. Years, we learn by her opening poem of that title, are at least a quality of observation (vision), involving the obligation of courage, of commands laid upon the self to be strong, to see deep and be glad. And years possess the quality of one

> . . . who
> accedes to mortality
> and in his imprisonment, rises
> upon himself as
> the sea in a chasm . . .

Who does this, we are told, "sees deep and is glad." Years are also, by the nature of the case, steps from something to something. And to indicate a curve of development from the earlier volume, we might recall this same theme (of the rising water) as it was treated previously. I refer to a poem, "Sojourn in the Whale," which, beginning on the theme, "Trying to open locked doors with a sword," had likewise talked of Ireland. It is addressed to "you," a "you" who has heard men say: "she will become wise and will be forced to give / in. Compelled by experience, she / will turn back; water seeks its own level." Whereat

> . . . you
> have smiled. 'Water in motion is far
> from level.' You have seen it, when obstacles happened to bar
> the path, rise automatically.

In the earlier poem, the figure was used defensively, even oppositionally. It is a tactic not common in Miss Moore's verse; as against the dialectician's morality of eristic, she shows a more feminine preference for the sheer ostracizing of the enemy, refuting by silence—disagreement implying the respect of intimacy, as in her poem on "Marriage," wittily appraising the "fight to be affectionate," she quotes, "No truth can be fully known until it has been tried by the tooth of disputation."

(When Miss Moore was editor of *The Dial,* her ideal number, as regards the reviews and articles of criticism, would I think have been one in which all good books got long favorable reviews, all middling books got short favorable reviews, and all books deserving of attack were allowed to go without mention. One can imagine how such a norm could be reached either charitably, through stress upon appreciation as motive, or not so charitably, by way of punishment, as when Miss Moore observes in "Spenser's Ireland": "Denunciations do not affect the culprit: nor blows, but it / is torture to him not to be spoken to." We need not decide between these motives in all cases, since they can comfortably work in unison.)

In contrast with the "oppositional" context qualifying the figure of the rising water in the earlier poem, "Sojourn in the Whale," its later variant has a context almost exaltedly positive. And repeating the same pattern (of affirmation in imprisonment) in another figure, the later poem widens the connotations of the years thus:

> . . . The very bird
> grown taller as he sings, steels
> his form straight up. Though he is captive
> his mighty singing
> says satisfaction is a lowly
> thing, how pure a thing is joy.
> This is mortality,
> this is eternity.

The pattern appears more conversationally (*What Are Years*, p. 12) in the suggestion that it must have been a "humorous" workman who made

> this greenish Waterford
> glass weight with the summit curled down toward
> itself as the
> grass grew,

and in "The Monkey Puzzle" (*Selected Poems*) we read

> its tail superimposed upon itself in a complacent half spiral,
> incidentally so witty.

Still, then, trying to discover what are years (or rather, what all are years), we might also recall, in *Selected Poems,* the poem on "The Fish," where the one fish featured as representative of its tribe is observed "opening and shutting itself like / an / injured fan"—in quality not unlike "The Student" of *What Are Years* who

> . . . is too reclusive for
> some things to seem to touch
> him, not because he
> has no feeling but because he has so much.

As the poem of "The Fish" develops, we might say that the theme is transferred "from the organism to the environment"; for we next read

of a chasm through which the water has driven a wedge—and injury is
here too, since

> All
> external
>   marks of abuse are present on this
>   defiant edifice.—

And finally

> Repeated
>   evidence has proved that it can live
>   on what cannot revive
>   its youth.   The sea grows old in it.

A chasm in the sea, then, becomes rather the sea in a chasm.   And
this notable reversal, that takes place in the areas of the "submerged,"
would also seem to be an aspect of "years."   Which would mean that
"years" subsume the synecdochic possibilities whereby those elements
that cluster together can represent one another: here the active can become passive, the environed can become the environment, the container can be interchangeable with the contained.   In possessing such
attributes, "years" are poetry.

We may at this point recall our beginning—the citation concerning
visible and invisible.   In "The Plumet Basilisk" (*Selected Poems*) we
read of this particular lizard that, "king with king,"

> He leaps and meets his
> likeness in the stream.

He is (in the poem it is a quotation)

> 'the ruler of Rivers, Lakes, and Seas,
>   invisible or visible'—

and as scene appropriate to the agent, this basilisk is said to live in a
basilica.   (Another lizard, in the same poem, is said to be "conferring
wings on what it grasps, as the airplant does"; and in "The Jerboa," we
are told of "this small desert rat" that it "honours the sand by assuming
its colour.")   Likewise

> the plumet portrays
> mythology's wish
> to be interchangeably man and fish.

What I am trying to do, in reaching out for these various associations, is to get some comprehensive glimpse of the ways in which the one pervasive quality of motivation is modified and ramified. I am trying, in necessarily tenuous material, to indicate how the avowed relation between the visible and the invisible finds variants, or sophistications, in "objectivist" appreciation; how this appreciation, in an age of much querulousness, serves rather to transcend the querulous (*Selected Poems*, p. 34: "The staff, the bag, the feigned inconsequence / of manner, best bespeak that weapon, self-protectiveness"); and how this same pattern takes form in the theme of submergence, with its interchangeabilities, and so in the theme of water rising on itself. At another point the motive takes as its object the motif of the spinster ("You have been compelled by hags to spin / gold thread from straw," with incidental suggestions of esthetic alchemy, lines that appear in "Sojourn in the Whale," and so link with submergence, Ireland, and the theme of spirited feminine independence, thus relating to kindred subjects in the later poem, "Spenser's Ireland"). I have also suggested that a like quality of imagination is to be found in the intellectual ways of one who selects as his subject not clocks, but clocks for clocks. (To appreciate just what goes on here, one might contrast these contemplative clocks—serene in their role as the motives behind motives—with the ominous clock-faces of Verhaeren, or in the grotesque plays of Edmund Wilson, which no one seems to have read but me.) From these crystal clocks, I could then advance to another variant, as revealed in the treatment of ice and glass. These would, I think, be animated by the same spirit. See for instance (in *Selected Poems*) the study of the glacier as "an octopus of ice":

> this fossil flower concise without a shiver,
> intact when it is cut,
> damned for its sacrosanct remoteness.

"Relentless accuracy is the nature of this octopus / with its capacity for fact"—which would make it a glacier with an objectivist esthetic. And two levels of motive are figured in the splendid concluding vista of

> . . . the hard mountain 'planed by ice and polished by the wind'—
> the white volcano with no weather side;

the lightning flashing at its base,
rain falling in the valleys, and snow falling on the peak—.[2]

We might have managed more easily by simply demarcating several themes, like naming the different ingredients that go to make up a dish. Or as with the planks that are brought together, to make a campaign platform, regardless of their fit with one another. But the relation among the themes of a genuine poetry is not of this sort. It is *substantial*—which is to say that all the branches spread from a single trunk.

I am trying to suggest that, without this initial substantiality, "objectivism" would lead not to the "feigned inconsequence of manner" that Miss Moore has mastered, but to inconsequence pure and simple. But because of this substantiality, the surfaces are derived from depth; indeed, the strict lawfulness in their choice of surfaces is depth. And the objects treated have the property not simply of things, but of volitions. They derive their poignancy as motifs from their relation to the sources of motive. And the relation between observer and observed is not that of news and reporter, but of "conversities" (her word).

In the earlier volume there is a poem, "Black Earth," wherein surprisingly the poet establishes so close an identification with her theme

[2] This is cited from the poem that follows the one on "Marriage," and is in turn followed by "Sea Unicorns and Land Unicorns." The three could be taken together as a triptych that superbly illustrates three stages in the development of one idea. First, we have the subtly averse poem on marriage (done in a spirit of high comedy that portrays marital quarrelings as interrelated somewhat like the steps of a minuet). Then comes the precise yet exalted contemplation of the glacier. And finally a discussion of the unicorn, a legendary solitaire:

> Thus this strange animal with its miraculous elusiveness,
> has come to be unique,
> 'impossible to take alive',
> tamed only by a lady inoffensive like itself—
> as curiously wild and gentle.

And typically, she cites of it that, since lions and unicorns are arch enemies, and "where the one is the other cannot be missing," Sir John Hawkins deduced an abundance of lions in Florida from the presence of unicorns there.

The theme of the lightning that flashes at the base of the glacier is varied in the unicorn poem (in a reference to "the dogs / which are dismayed by the chain lightning / playing at them from its horn"). And it is varied also in a poem on the elephant (still to be discussed) that

> has looked at the electricity and at the earth-
> quake and is still
> here; . . .

as not merely to "observe" it with sympathy and appreciation, but to speak for it. This is one of her rare "I" poems—and in it the elephant sometimes speaks with the challenge and confidence of an Invictus. Beginning on the theme of emergence (coupled with delight in the thought of submergence at will), there is first a celebration of the sturdy skin; then talk of power ("my back is full of the history of power"); and then: "My soul shall never be cut into / by a wooden spear." Next comes mention of the trunk, and of poise. And interwoven with the vigor of assertion, the focal theme is there likewise:

> that tree-trunk without
> roots, accustomed to shout
> its own thoughts to itself . . .

and:

> . . . The I of each is to
> the I of each
> a kind of fretful speech
> which sets a limit on itself; the elephant is
> black earth preceded by a tendril?

I think we can make a point by recalling this earlier poem when, in "Smooth Gnarled Crape Myrtle" (*What Are Years*), the theme of the elephant's trunk appears again, this time but in passing, contextual and "tangential" to the themes of birds, union, loneliness:

> . . . 'joined in
> friendship, crowned by love.'
> An aspect may deceive; as the
> elephant's columbine-tubed trunk
> held waveringly out—
> an at will heavy thing—is
> delicate.

Surely, "an at will heavy thing" is a remarkable find. But one does not make such observation by merely looking at an elephant's trunk. There must have been much to discard. In this instance, we can know something about the omissions, quite as though we had inspected earlier drafts of the poem with their record of revisions. For though a usage in any given poem is a finished thing, and thus brilliant with surface, it becomes in effect but "work in progress" when we align it with kindred usages (emergent, fully developed, or retrospectively condensed) in other poems. And here, by referring to "Black Earth," we can find what lies behind the reference to the elephant's trunk in "Smooth Gnarled Crape Myrtle." We can know it for a fact what kind of connotations must, for the poet, have been implicit in the second, condensed usage. Hence we can appreciate the motives that enabled this trunk to be seen not merely as a *thing,* but as an *act,* representative of the assertion in "Black Earth." And by reviewing the earlier usage we can know the kind of volitional material which, implicit in the later usage, led beyond the perception of the trunk as a thing to this perception of it as an act. At such moments, I should say, out of our idealistic trammels we get a glimpse of realism in its purity.

Or let us look at another instance. Sensitivity in the selection of words resides in the ability, or necessity, to feel behind the given word a history—not a past history, but a future one. Within the word, collapsed into its simultaneous oneness, there is implicit a sequence, a complexity of possible narratives that could be drawn from it. If you would remember what words are in this respect, and how in the simultaneity of a word histories are implicit, recall the old pleasantry of asking someone, "What's an accordion," whereat invariably as he explains he will start pumping a bellows.

Well, among Miss Moore's many poems enunciating aspects of her esthetic credo, or commenting on literary doctrines and methods, there is one, "To a Snail," beginning:

> If 'compression is the first grace of style,'
> you have it. Contractility is a virtue
> as modesty is a virtue.

And this equating of an esthetic value with a moral one is summed up by locating the principle of style "in the curious phenomenon of your occipital horn."

In her poem on the butterfly (*What Are Years,* p. 17), the mood of tentativeness that had been compressed within the term "contractility" reveals its significant narrative equivalents. As befits the tentative, or contractile, it is a poem of jeopardy, tracing a tenuous relationship between a butterfly ("half deity half worm," "last of the elves") and a nymph ("dressed in Wedgewood blue"), with light winds (even a "zephyr") to figure the motives of passion. Were not the course of a butterfly so intrinsically akin to the "inconsequential ease" and "drover-like tenacity" of Miss Moore's own versa-tilities, one might not have much hope for a poem built about this theme (reminiscent of many musical Papillons—perhaps more than a theme, perhaps a set idiom, almost a form). Here, with the minute accuracy of sheerly "objectivist" description, there is a subtle dialectic of giving and receiving, of fascinations and releases—an interchange of delicately shaded attitudes. In this realm, things reached for will evade, but will follow the hand as it recedes.

Through the tracery of flight, there are two striking moments of stasis, each the termination of a course: one when "the butterfly's tobacco-brown unglazed / china eyes and furry countenance confront / the nymph's large eyes"—and the second when, having broken contact with the nymph's "controlled agitated glance," the "fiery tiger-horse" (at rest, but poised against the wind, "chest arching / bravely out") is motivated purely by relation to the zephyr alone. The poem concludes by observing that this "talk" between the animal and the zephyr "was as strange as my grandmother's muff."

I have called it a poem of jeopardy. (When butterfly and nymph confront each other, "It is Goya's scene of the tame magpie faced / by crouching cats.") It is also a poem of coquetry (perhaps our last poem of coquetry, quite as this butterfly was the last of the elves—coquetry now usually being understood as something that comes down like a ton of brick).[3]

---

[3] In the earlier volume there is an epigram-like poem, "To a Steam Roller," that I have always thought very entertaining. It excoriates this sorry, ungainly mechanism as a bungling kind of fellow that, when confronting such discriminations as are the vital purpose of Miss Moore's lines, would "crush all the particles down / into close conformity, and then walk back and forth / on them." We also read there:

> As for butterflies, I can hardly conceive
>   of one's attending upon you, but to question
>   the congruence of the complement is vain, if it exists.

Heretofore I had been content to think of this reference to a butterfly simply as a device for suggesting weight by a contrasting image of lightness. But the role of butterfly as elf conversant to nymph might also suggest the presence of such overtones as contrasting types of masculinity. (This would give us a perfect instance of what Coleridge meant by fancy, which occurs when we discern behind the contrast an element that the contrasted images share in common.)

As for the later poem, where the theme of the butterfly is fully developed, I

The tentativeness, contractility, acquires more purely the theme of jeopardy in "Bird-Witted" (*What Are Years*), reciting the incident of the "three large fledgling mocking-birds," awaiting "their no longer larger mother," while there approaches

> the
> intellectual cautious-
> ly c r e e p ing cat.

If her animals are selected for their "fastidiousness," their fastidiousness itself is an aspect of contractility, of jeopardy. "The Pangolin" (*What Are Years*), a poem which takes us through odd nocturnal journeys to the joyous saluting of the dawn, begins: "Another armoured animal"—and of a sudden you realize that Miss Moore's recondite menagerie is almost a thesaurus of protectivenesses. Thus also, the poem

might now try to make more clearly the point I had in mind with reference to the two moments of stasis. In the opening words ("half deity half worm" and "We all, infant and adult, have / stopped to watch the butterfly") the poem clearly suggests the possibility that it will figure two levels of motivation, a deity being in a different realm of motives than a worm, and the child's quality of perception being critically distinct from the adult's. Examining the two moments of stasis, we find here too the indications of an important difference between them. At the first stasis, elf and nymph confront each other, while "all's a-quiver with significance." But at the final stasis, the conversity is between butterfly and west wind, a directer colloquy (its greater inwardness linking it, in my opinion, with the motive-behind-motive figuration in the theme of clocks-for-clocks). At this second stage, the butterfly is called "historic metamorphoser / and saintly animal"; hence we may take it that the "deity" level of motive prevails at this second stage. The quality of the image in the closing line ("their talk was as strange as my grandmother's muff") would suggest that the deified level is equated with the quality of perception as a child. (The grandmother theme also appears in "Spenser's Ireland," where we are told that "Hindered characters . . . in Irish stories . . . all have grandmothers." Another reason for believing that the second stage of the butterfly poem is also the "motives-behind-motives" stage is offered tenuously by this tie-up with the word "hindered," since the final poem in the book, as we shall know when we come to it, does well by this word in proclaiming a morality of art.)

Another poem, "Virginia Britannia" (*What Are Years*), that seems on the surface almost exclusively descriptive (though there is passing reference to a "fritillary" that "zig-zags") is found to be progressing through scenic details to a similar transcendence. At the last, against sunset, two levels are figured, while the intermediate trees "become with lost identity, part of the ground." The clouds, thus marked off, are then heralded in words suggestive of Wordworth's ode as "to the child an intimation of / what glory is."

in which occur the lines anent visible and invisible, has as its conclusion:

> unsolicitude having swallowed up
> all giant birds but an
> alert gargantuan
> little-winged, magnificently
> speedy running-bird. This one
> remaining rebel
> is the sparrow-camel.

The tentativeness also manifests itself at times in a cult of rarity, a collector's or antiquarian interest in the present, a kind of stylistic tourism. And it may lead to a sheer word play, of graduated sort (a Laforguian delight in showing how the pedantries can be reclaimed for poetry):

> The lemur-student can see
> that the aye-aye is not
>
> an angwan-tíbo, potto, or loris.

Yet mention of the "aepyornis" may suggest the answer we might have given, were we up on such matters, to one who, pencil in hand and with the newspaper folded to make it firmer, had asked, "What's a gigantic bird, found fossil in Madagascar in nine letters?" As for her invention, "invis   ible," I can't see it.

Tonally, the "contractility" reveals itself in the great agility, even restlessness, which Miss Moore imparts to her poetry by assonance, internal rhyme, and her many variants of the run-over line. We should also note those sudden nodules of sound which are scattered throughout her verses, such quick concentrations as "rude root cudgel," "the raised device reversed," "trim trio on the tree-stem," "furled fringed frill," or tonal episodes more sustained and complex, as the lines on the birds in Ireland (already quoted), or the title, "Walking-Sticks and Paper-Weights and Water-Marks," or

> . . . the redbird
> the red-coated musketeer,
> the trumpet-flower, the cavalier,
> the parson, and the
> wild parishioner. A deer-
> track in a church-floor
> brick . . .

One noticeable difference between the later selection and the earlier one is omission of poems on method. In *Selected Poems* there were a great many such. I think for instance of: "Poetry," containing her ingenious conceit, "imaginary gardens with real toads in them"; "Critics and Connoisseurs"; "The Monkeys"; "In the Days of Prismatic Colour"; "Picking and Choosing"; "When I Buy Pictures"; "Novices" (on action in language, and developed in imagery of the sea); "The Past is the Present" ("ecstasy affords / the occasion and expediency determines the form"); and one which propounds a doctrine as its title: "In This Age of Hard Trying, Nonchalance is Good and."

But though methodological pronouncements of this sort have dropped away, in the closing poem on "The Paper Nautilus," the theme does reappear. Yet in an almost startlingly deepened transformation. Here, proclaiming the poet's attachment to the poem, there are likenesses to the maternal attachment to the young. And the themes of bondage and freedom (as with one "hindered to succeed") are fiercely and flashingly merged.

D

FOUR MASTER TROPES

I REFER to metaphor, metonymy, synecdoche, and irony. And my primary concern with them here will be not with their purely figurative usage, but with their rôle in the discovery and description of "the truth." It is an evanescent moment that we shall deal with—for not only does the dividing line between the figurative and literal usages shift, but also the four tropes shade into one another. Give a man but one of them, tell him to exploit its possibilities, and if he is thorough in doing so, he will come upon the other three.

The "literal" or "realistic" applications of the four tropes usually go by a different set of names. Thus:

For *metaphor* we could substitute *perspective;*
For *metonymy* we could substitute *reduction;*
For *synecdoche* we could substitute *representation;*
For *irony* we could substitute *dialectic.*[1]

We must subsequently try to make it clear in what respects we think these substitutions are justifiable. It should, however, be apparent at a glance that, regardless of whether our proposed substitutions are justifiable, considered in themselves they do shade into another, as we have said that the four tropes do. A dialectic, for instance, aims to give us a representation by the use of mutually related or interacting perspectives—and this resultant perspective of perspectives will necessarily be a reduction in the sense that a chart drawn to scale is a reduction of the area charted.

Metaphor is a device for seeing something *in terms of* something else. It brings out the thisness of a that, or the thatness of a this. If we employ the word "character" as a general term for whatever can be thought of as distinct (any thing, pattern, situation, structure, nature, person, object, act, rôle, process, event, etc.,) then we could say that metaphor tells us something about one character as considered from

---

[1] "Dialectic" is here used in the restricted sense. In a broader sense, all the transformations considered in this essay are dialectical.

the point of view of another character. And to consider A from the point of view of B is, of course, to use B as a *perspective* upon A.

It is customary to think that objective reality is dissolved by such relativity of terms as we get through the shifting of perspectives (the perception of one character in terms of many diverse characters). But on the contrary, it is by the approach through a variety of perspectives that we establish a character's reality. If we are in doubt as to what an object is, for instance, we deliberately try to consider it in as many different terms as its nature permits: lifting, smelling, tasting, tapping, holding in different lights, subjecting to different pressures, dividing, matching, contrasting, etc.

Indeed, in keeping with the older theory of realism (what we might call "poetic realism," in contrast with modern "scientific realism") we could say that characters possess *degrees of being* in proportion to the variety of perspectives from which they can with justice be perceived. Thus we could say that plants have "more being" than minerals, animals have more being than plants, and men have more being than animals, because each higher order admits and requires a new dimension of terms not literally relevant to the lower orders.

By deliberate coaching and criticism of the perspective process, characters can be considered tentatively, in terms of other characters, for experimental or heuristic purposes. Examples may be offered at random: for instance, human motivation may, with varying degrees of relevance and reward, be considered in terms of conditioned reflexes, or chemicals, or the class struggles, or the love of God, or neurosis, or pilgrimage, or power, or movements of the planets, or geography, or sun spots, etc. Various kinds of scientific specialists now carry out the implications of one or another of such perspectives with much more perseverance than that with which a 17th Century poet might in one poem pursue the exploitation of a "conceit."

In *Permanence and Change* I have developed at some length the relationship between metaphor and perspective. I there dealt with such perspectives as an "incongruity," because the seeing of something in terms of something else involves the "carrying-over" of a term from one realm into another, a process that necessarily involves varying degrees of incongruity in that the two realms are never identical. But besides the mere desire not to restate this earlier material, there is another reason why we can hurry on to our next pair (metonymy and reduction). For since the four pairs overlap upon one another, we shall be carrying the first pair with us as we proceed.

II

Science, concerned with processes and "processing," is not properly concerned with substance (that is, it is not concerned with "being," as "poetic realism" is). Hence, it need not be concerned with motivation. All it need know is correlation. The limits of science, *qua* science, do not go beyond the statement that, when certain conditions are met, certain new conditions may be expected to follow. It is true that, in the history of the actual development of science, the discovery of such correlations has been regularly guided by philosophies of causation ("substantial" philosophies that were subsequently "discredited" or were so radically redefined as to become in effect totally different philosophies). And it is equally true that the discovery of correlations has been guided by ideational forms developed through theology and governmental law. Such "impurities" will always be detectible *behind* science as the act of given scientists; but science *qua* science is abstracted from them.

Be the world "mind," or "matter," or "both," or "several," you will follow the same procedure in striking a match. It is in this sense that science, *qua* science, is concerned with operations rather than with substances, even though the many inventions to do with the chemistry of a match can be traced back to a source in very explicit beliefs about substances and motivations of nature—and even of the supernatural.

However, as soon as you move into the social realm, involving the relation of man to man, mere *correlation* is not enough. Human relationships must be *substantial,* related by the copulative, the "is" of "being." In contrast with "scientific realism," "poetic realism" is centered in this emphasis. It seeks (except insofar as it is affected by the norms of "scientific realism") to place the motives of action, as with the relation between the seminal (potential) and the growing (actualized). Again and again, there have been attempts to give us a "science of human relations" after the analogy of the natural sciences. But there is a strategic or crucial respect in which this is impossible; namely: there can be no "science" of substance, except insofar as one is willing to call philosophy, metaphysics, or theology "sciences" (and they are not sciences in the sense of the positive scientific departments).

Hence, any attempt to deal with human relationships after the analogy of naturalistic correlations becomes necessarily the *reduction* of some higher or more complex realm of being to the terms of a lower or less complex realm of being. And, recalling that we propose to treat *metonymy* and *reduction* as substitutes for each other, one may realize why we thought it necessary thus to introduce the subject of metonymy.

The basic "strategy" in metonymy is this: to convey some incorporeal or intangible state in terms of the corporeal or tangible. E.g., to speak of "the heart" rather than "the emotions." If you trail language back far enough, of course, you will find that all our terms for "spiritual" states were metonymic in origin. We think of "the emotions," for instance, as applying solely to the realm of consciousness, yet obviously the word is rooted in the most "materialistic" term of all, "motion" (a key strategy in Western materialism has been the reduction of "consciousness" to "motion"). In his *Principles of Literary Criticism,* Richards is being quite "metonymic" in proposing that we speak not of the "emotions" aroused in the reader by the work of art, but the "commotions."

Language develops by metaphorical extension, in borrowing words from the realm of the corporeal, visible, tangible and applying them by analogy to the realm of the incorporeal, invisible, intangible; then in the course of time, the original corporeal reference is forgotten, and only the incorporeal, metaphorical extension survives (often because the very conditions of living that reminded one of the corporeal reference have so altered that the cross reference no longer exists with near the same degree of apparentness in the "objective situation" itself); and finally, poets regain the original relation, in reverse, by a "metaphorical extension" back from the intangible into a tangible equivalent (the first "carrying-over" from the material to the spiritual being compensated by a second "carrying-over" from the spiritual back into the material); and this "archaicizing" device we call "metonymy."

"Metonymy" is a device of "poetic realism"—but its partner, "reduction," is a device of "scientific realism." Here "poetry" and "behaviorism" meet. For the poet spontaneously knows that "beauty *is* as beauty *does*" (that the "state" must be "embodied" in an actualization). He knows that human relations require actions, which are *dramatizations,* and that the essential medium of drama is the posturing, tonalizing body placed in a material scene. He knows that "shame," for instance, is not merely a "state," but a movement of the eye, a color of the cheek, a certain quality of voice and set of the muscles; he knows this as "behavioristically" as the formal scientific behaviorist who would "reduce" the state itself to these corresponding bodily equivalents.

He also knows, however, that these bodily equivalents are but part of the *idiom of expression* involved in the act. They are "figures." They are hardly other than "symbolizations." Hence, for all his "archaicizing" usage here, he is not offering his metonymy as a *substantial* reduction. For in "poetic realism," states of mind as the motives of action are not reducible to materialistic terms. Thus, though there is a sense in which both the poetic behaviorist and the scientific behaviorist are exemplifying the strategy of metonymy (as the poet translates the spiritual into an idiom of material equivalents, and may even select for attention the same bodily responses that the scientist may later seek to measure), the first is using metonymy as a *terminological* reduction whereas the scientific behaviorist offers his reduction as a "real" reduction. (However, he does not do this *qua* scientist, but only by reason of the materialist metaphysics, with its assumptions about substance and motive, that is implicit in his system.)

III

Now, note that a reduction is a *representation*. If I reduce the contours of the United States, for instance, to the terms of a relief map, I have within these limits "represented" the United States. As a mental state is the "representation" of certain material conditions, so we could —reversing the process—say that the material conditions are "representative" of the mental state. That is, if there is some kind of correspondence between what we call the act of perception and what we call the thing perceived, then either of these equivalents can be taken as "representative" of the other. Thus, as reduction (metonymy) overlaps upon metaphor (perspective) so likewise it overlaps upon synecdoche (representation).

For this purpose we consider synecdoche in the usual range of dictionary sense, with such meanings as: part for the whole, whole for the part, container for the contained, sign for the thing signified, material for the thing made (which brings us nearer to metonymy), cause for effect, effect for cause, genus for species, species for genus, etc. All such conversions imply an integral relationship, a relationship of convertibility, between the two terms.

The "noblest synecdoche," the perfect paradigm or prototype for all lesser usages, is found in metaphysical doctrines proclaiming the identity of "microcosm" and "macrocosm." In such doctrines, where the individual is treated as a replica of the universe, and vice versa, we have the ideal synecdoche, since microcosm is related to macrocosm as part to whole, and either the whole can represent the part or the part can represent the whole. (For "represent" here we could substitute "be identified with.") One could thus look through the remotest astronomical distances to the "truth within," or could look within to learn the "truth in all the universe without." Leibniz's monadology is a good instance of the synecdochic on this grand scale. (And "representation" is his word for this synecdochic relationship.)

A similar synecdochic form is present in all theories of political representation, where some part of the social body (either traditionally established, or elected, or coming into authority by revolution) is held to be "representative" of the society as a whole. The pattern is essential to Rousseau's theory of the *volonté générale,* for instance. And though there are many disagreements within a society as to what part should represent the whole and how this representation should be accomplished, in a complex civilization any act of representation automatically implies a synecdochic relationship (insofar as the act is, or is held to be, "truly representative").

Sensory representation is, of course, synecdochic in that the senses abstract certain qualities from some bundle of electro-chemical activities we call, say, a tree, and these qualities (such as size, shape, color, texture, weight, etc.) can be said "truly to represent" a tree. Similarly, artistic representation is synecdochic, in that certain relations within the medium "stand for" corresponding relations outside it. There is also a sense in which the well-formed work of art is internally synecdochic, as the beginning of a drama contains its close or the close sums up the beginning, the parts all thus being consubstantially related. Indeed, one may think what he will of microcosm-macrocosm relationships as they are applied to "society" or "the universe," the fact remains that, as regards such a "universe" as we get in a well-organized work of art, at every point the paradoxes of the synecdochic present themselves to the critic for analysis. Similarly, the realm of psychology (and particularly the psychology of art) requires the use of the synecdochic reversals. Indeed, I would want deliberately to "coach" the concept of the synecdochic by extending it to cover such relations (and their reversals) as: before for after, implicit for explicit, temporal sequence for logical sequence, name for narrative, disease for cure, hero for villain, active for passive. At the opening of *The Ancient Mariner,* for instance, the Albatross is a *gerundive:* its nature when introduced is that of something *to be* murdered, and it implicitly contains the future that is to become explicit. In *Moby Dick,* Ahab as pursuer is pursued; his action is a passion.

Metonymy may be treated as a special application of synecdoche. If, for instance, after the analogy of a correlation between "mind and body" or "consciousness and matter (or motion)" we selected quality and quantity as a "synecdochically related pair," then we might propose to treat as synecdoche the substitution of either quantity for quality or quality for quantity (since either side could be considered as the sign, or symptom, of the other). But only *one* of these, the substitution of quantity for quality, would be a metonymy. We might say that representation (synecdoche) stresses a *relationship* or *connectedness* between two sides of an equation, a connectedness that, like a road, extends in either direction, from quantity to quality or from quality to quantity; but reduction follows along this road in only *one* direction, from quality to quantity.[2]

Now "poetic realism," in contrast with "scientific realism," cannot confine itself to representation in this metonymic, one-direction sense. True, every art, in its nature as a medium, reduces a state of consciousness to a "corresponding" sensory body (so material that it can be reproduced, bought and sold). But the aim of such *embodiment* is to produce in the observer a corresponding state of *consciousness* (that is,

[2] Unfortunately, we must modify this remark somewhat. Reduction, *as per scientific realism,* would be confined to but one direction. Reduction, that is, as the word is now generally used. But originally, "reduction" was used in ways that make it closer rather to the margin of its overlap upon "perspective," as anything considered in terms of anything else could be said to be "reduced"—or "brought back" ("referred")—to it, so that the consideration of art in terms of morality, politics, or religion could have been called "the reduction" of art to morality, or politics, or religion.

the artist proceeds from "mind" to "body" that his representative reduction may induce the audience to proceed from "body" to "mind").
But there is an important difference between representing the quality
of an experience thus and reducing the quality to a quantity. One
might even "represent" the human body in the latter, reductive sense,
by reducing it to ashes and offering a formula for the resultant chemicals. Otto Neurath's "isotypes" (see his *Modern Man in the Making,*
or our review of it, "Quantity and Quality," in the appendix of *The
Philosophy of Literary Form*) are representations in the latter, reductive
sense, in contrast with the kind of representation we get in realistic
portrait-painting.

Our point in going over this old ground is to use it as a way of revealing a tactical error in the attempt to treat of *social* motivations.
We refer to the widespread belief that the mathematico-quantitative
ideal of the physical sciences can and should serve as the ideal of the
"social sciences," a belief that has led, for instance, to the almost fabulous amassing of statistical surveys in the name of "sociology." Or, if
one insisted upon the right to build "sciences" after this model (since
no one could deny that statistics are often revealing) our claim would
be that science in this restricted sense (that explains higher orders by
reduction to lower orders, organic complexities by reduction to atomistic
simplicities, being by reduction to motion, or quality by reduction to
number, etc.) could not *take the place* of metaphysics or religion, but
would have to return to the role of "handmaiden."

Let us get at the point thus: *A terminology of conceptual analysis, if
it is not to lead to misrepresentation, must be constructed in conformity
with a representative anecdote—whereas anecdotes "scientifically" selected for reductive purposes are not representative.* E.g., think of the
scientist who, in seeking an entrance into the analysis of human motivations, selects as his "informative anecdote" for this purpose some
laboratory experiment having to do with the responses of animals. Obviously, such an anecdote has its peculiarly simplificatory ("reductive")
character, or genius—and the scientist who develops his analytic terminology about this anecdote as his informative case must be expected
to have, as a result, a terminology whose character or genius is restricted by the character or genius of the model for the description of
which it is formed. He next proceeds to transfer (to "metaphor") this
terminology to the interpretation of a different order of cases, turning

for instance from animals to infants and from infants to the acts of fully developed adults. And when he has made these steps, applying his terminology to a kind of anecdote so different from the kind about which it was formed, this misapplication of his terminology would not give him a representative interpretation at all, but a mere "debunking." Only insofar as the analyst had not lived up to his claims, only insofar as his terminology for the analysis of a higher order of cases was *not* restricted to the limits proper to the analysis of a lower order of cases, could he hope to discuss the higher order of cases in an adequate set of terms. Otherwise, the genius of his restricted terminology must "drag the interpretation down to their level."

This observation goes for any terminological approach to the analysis of human acts or relationships that is shaped in conformity with an unrepresentative case (or that selects as the "way in" to one's subject an "informative anecdote" belonging in some other order than the case to be considered). For instance, insofar as Alfred Korzybski really does form his terminology for the analysis of meaning in conformity with that contraption of string, plugs, and tin he calls the "Structural Differential," his analysis of meaning is "predestined" to misrepresentation, since the genius of the contraption itself is not a representative example of meaning. It is a "reduction" of meaning, a reduction in the restricted sense of the term, as Thurman Arnold's reduction of social relations into terms of the psychiatric metaphor is reductive.

What then, it may be asked, would be a "representative anecdote?" But that takes us into the fourth pair: irony and dialectic.

IV

A treatment of the irony-dialectic pair will be much easier to follow if we first delay long enough to consider the equatability of "dialectic" with "dramatic."

A human rôle (such as we get in drama) may be summed up in certain slogans, or formulae, or epigrams, or "ideas" that characterize the agent's situation or strategy. The rôle involves properties both intrinsic to the agent and developed with relation to the scene and to other agents. And the "summings-up" ("ideas") similarly possess properties derived both from the agent and from the various factors with which the agent is in relationship.   Where the ideas are in action, we have drama; where the agents are in ideation, we have dialectic.

Obviously, there are elements of "dramatic personality" in dialectic ideation, and elements of dialectic in the mutual influence of dramatic agents in contributing to one another's ideational development. You might state all this another way by saying that you cannot have ideas without persons or persons without ideas. Thus, one might speak of "Socratic irony" as "dramatic," and of "dramatic irony" as "Socratic."

Relativism is got by the fragmentation of either drama or dialectic. That is, if you isolate any one agent in a drama, or any one advocate in a dialogue, and see the whole in terms of his position alone, you have the purely relativistic.   And in relativism there is no irony.   (Indeed, as Cleanth Brooks might say, it is the very absence if irony in relativism that makes it so susceptible to irony.   For relativism sees everything in but one set of terms—and since there are endless other terms in which things could be seen, the irony of the monologue that makes everything in its image would be in this ratio: the greater the *absolutism* of the statements, the greater the *subjectivity* and *relativity* in the position of the agent making the statements.)

Irony arises when one tries, by the interaction of terms upon one another, to produce a *development* which uses all the terms.   Hence, from the standpoint of this total form (this "perspective of perspectives"), none of the participating "sub-perspectives" can be treated as either precisely right or precisely wrong.   They are all voices, or personalities, or positions, integrally affecting one another.   When the dialectic is properly formed, they are the number of characters needed to produce the total development.   Hence, reverting to our suggestion that we might extend the synecdochic pattern to include such reversible pairs as disease-cure, hero-villain, active-passive, we should "ironically" note the function of the disease in "perfecting" the cure, or the function of the cure in "perpetuating" the influences of the disease.   Or we should note that only through an internal and external experiencing of folly could we possess (in our intelligence or imagination) sufficient "characters" for some measure of development beyond folly.

People usually confuse the dialectic with the relativistic.   Noting that the dialectic (or dramatic) explicitly attempts to establish a distinct set of characters, all of which protest variously at odds or on the bias with one another, they think no further.   It is certainly relativistic, for instance, to state that any term (as per metaphor-perspective) can be seen from the point of view of any other term. But insofar as terms are thus encouraged to participate in an orderly parliamentary development, the dialectic of this participation produces (in the observer who considers the whole from the standpoint of the participation of all the terms rather than from the standpoint of any one participant) a "resultant certainty" of a different quality, necessarily ironic, since it requires that all the sub-certainties be considered as neither true nor false, but *contributory* (as were we to think of the resultant certainty or "perspective of perspectives" as a noun, and to think of all the contributory voices as necessary modifiers of that noun).

To be sure, relativism is the constant *temptation* of either dialectic or drama (consider how often, for instance, Shakespeare is called a relativist). And historians for the most part *are relativistic*. But where one considers different historical characters from the standpoint of a total development, one could encourage each character to comment upon the others without thereby sacrificing a perspective upon the lot. This could be got particularly, I think, if historical characters themselves (i.e., periods or cultures treated as "individual persons") were considered never to begin or end, but rather to change in intensity or poignancy. History, in this sense, would be a dialectic of characters in which, for instance, we should never expect to see "feudalism" overthrown by "capitalism" and "capitalism" succeeded by some manner of national or international or non-national or neo-national or post-national socialism—but rather should note elements of all such positions (or "voices") existing always, but attaining greater clarity of expression or imperiousness of proportion of one period than another.

Irony is never Pharisaic, but there is a Pharisaic temptation in irony. To illustrate the point, I should like to cite a passage from a poet and critic who knows a good deal about irony, and who is discussing a poet who knows a good deal about irony—but in this particular instance, I submit, he is wrong. I refer to a passage in which Allen Tate characterizes the seduction scene in *The Waste Land* as "ironic" and the poet's attitude as that of "humility." (I agree that "humility" is the proper partner of irony—but I question whether the passage is ironic enough to embody humility.)

Mr. Tate characterizes irony as "that arrangement of experience, either premeditated by art or accidentally appearing in the affairs of

men, which permits to the spectator an insight superior to that of the
actor." And he continues:

> The seduction scene is the picture of modern and dominating
> man. The arrogance and pride of conquest of the "small house
> agent's clerk" are the badge of science, bumptious practicality, over-
> weening secular faith. The very success of this conquest witnesses its
> aimless character; it succeeds as a wheel succeeds in turning; he can
> only conquer again.
>
> His own failure to understand his position is irony, and the poet's
> insight into it is humility. But for the grace of God, says the poet in
> effect, there go I. There is essentially the poetic attitude, an attitude
> that Eliot has been approaching with increasing purity.

We need not try to decide whether or not the poet was justified in
feeling "superior" to the clerk. But we may ask how one could *possibly* exemplify an attitude of "humility" by feeling "superior"? There
is, to be sure, a brand of irony, called "romantic irony," that might fit in
with such a pattern—the kind of irony that did, as a matter of fact, arise
as an aesthetic opposition to cultural philistinism, and in which the
artist considered himself *outside of* and *superior to* the rôle he was re-
jecting. And though not "essentially *the* poetic attitude," it is essentially *a* poetic attitude, an attitude exemplified by much romantic art
(a sort of pamphleteering, or external, attitude towards "the enemy").

True irony, however, irony that really does justify the attribute of
"humility," is not "superior" to the enemy. (I might even here rephrase my discussion of Eliot in *Attitudes Toward History* by saying
that Eliot's problem in religion has resided precisely in his attempt to
convert romantic irony into classic irony, really to replace a state of
"superiority" by a state of "humility"—and *Murder in the Cathedral*
is a ritual aimed at precisely such purification of motives.) True irony,
humble irony, is based upon a sense of fundamental kinship with the
enemy, as one *needs* him, is *indebted* to him, is not merely outside him
as an observer but contains him *within,* being consubstantial with him.
This is the irony of Flaubert, when he recognizes that Madame Bovary
is himself. One sees it in Thomas Mann—and in what he once called,
when applying the term to another, "Judas psychology." And there
was, if not the humility of strength, at least a humility of gentle surrender, in Anatole France.

In *The Waste Land,* the poet is not saying "there but for the grace of

God go I." On the contrary, he is, if not thanking God, at least congratulating himself, that he is not like other men, such other men as this petty clerk. If this was "humility," then the Pharisee is Humble Citizen No. 1. With Newton, on the other hand, there was no "superiority" in his exclamation as he observed the criminal. He did not mean that that man was a criminal but he, Newton, thank God, was not; he meant that *he too was a criminal, but that the other man was going to prison for him.* Here was true irony-and-humility, since Newton was simultaneously both outside the criminal and within him.

"Superiority" in the dialectic can arise only in the sense that one may feel the need of *more characters* than the particular foolish characters under consideration. But in one sense he can *never* be superior, for he must realize that he also *needs this particular foolish character as one of the necessary modifiers.* Dialectic irony (or humility) here, we might even say, provides us with a kind of "technical equivalent for the doctrine of original sin." Folly and villainy are integral motives, necessary to wisdom or virtue.[3]

---

[3] I would consider Falstaff a gloriously ironic conception because we are so at one with him in his vices, while he himself embodies his vices in a mode of identification or brotherhood that is all but religious. Falstaff would not simply rob a man, from without. He *identifies himself* with the victim of a theft; he *represents* the victim. He would not crudely steal a purse; rather, he *joins forces* with the owner of the purse—and it is only when the harsh realities of this imperfect world have imposed a brutally divisive clarity upon the situation, that Falstaff is left holding the purse. He produces a new quality, a state of synthesis or merger—and it so happens that, when this synthesis is finally dissociated again into its analytic components (the crudities of the realm of practical property relationships having reduced this state of qualitative merger to a state of quantitative division), the issue as so simplified sums up to the fact that the purse has changed hands. *He* converts "thine" into "ours"—and it is "circumstances over which he has no control" that go to convert this "ours" into a "mine." A mere thief would have directly converted "thine" into "mine." It is the addition of these intermediate steps that makes the vital difference between a mere thief and Falstaff; for it is precisely these intermediate steps that mark him with a conviviality, a sociality, essentially religious—and in this *sympathetic* distortion of religious values resides the irony of his conception.

We might bring out the point sharply by contrasting Falstaff with Tartuffe. Tartuffe, like Falstaff, exploits the coöperative values for competitive ends. He too would convert "thine" into "mine" by putting it through the social alembic of "ours." But the conception of Tartuffe is not ironic, since he is pure hypocrite. He uses the religious values simply as a swindler. Tartuffe's piety, which he uses to gain the confidence of his victims, is a mere deception. Whereas Tartuffe is all competition and merely *simulates* the sentiments of coöperation, Falstaff is

A third temptation of irony is its tendency towards the simplification of literalness. That is: although *all* the characters in a dramatic or dialectic development are necessary qualifiers of the definition, there is usually some one character that enjoys the rôle of *primus inter pares.* For whereas any of the characters may be viewed in terms of any other, this one character may be taken as the summarizing vessel, or synecdochic representative, of the development as a whole. This is the rôle of Socrates in the Platonic dialogue, for instance—and we could similarly call the proletariat the Socrates of the Marxist Symposium of History, as they are not merely equal participants along with the other characters, but also represent the *end* or *logic* of the development as a whole.

This "most representative" character thus has a dual function: one we might call "adjectival" and the other "substantial." The character is "adjectival," as embodying one of the qualifications necessary to the total definition, but is "substantial" as embodying the conclusions of the development as a whole. Irony is sacrificed to "the simplification of literalness" when this duality of rôle is neglected (as it may be neglected by either the reader, the writer, or both). In Marxism as a literally libertarian philosophy, for instance, slavery is "bad," and is so treated in the rhetoric of proletarian emancipation (e.g., "wage slavery"). Yet from the standpoint of the development as a whole, slavery must be treated ironically, as with Engel's formula: "Without the slavery of antiquity, no modern socialism." Utilization of the vanquished by enslavement, he notes, was a great cultural advance over the wasteful practice of slaying the vanquished.

V

Irony, as approached through either drama or dialectic, moves us into the area of "law" and "justice" (the "necessity" or "inevitability" of the *lex talionis*) that involves matters of form in art (as form affects anticipation and fulfilment) and matters of prophecy and prediction in history. There is a level of generalization at which predictions about "inevitable" developments in history are quite justified. We may state

---

genuinely coöperative, sympathetic, a synecdochic part of his victim—but along with such rich gifts of identification, what is to prevent a purse from changing hands?

with confidence, for instance, that what arose in time must fall in time (hence, that any given structure of society must "inevitably" perish). We may make such prophecy more precise, with the help of irony, in saying that the developments that led to the rise will, by the further course of their development, "inevitably" lead to the fall (true irony always, we hold, thus involving an "internal fatality," a principle operating from within, though its logic may also be grounded in the nature of the extrinsic scene, whose properties contribute to the same development).

The point at which different casuistries appear (for fitting these "general laws of inevitability" to the unique cases of history) is the point where one tries to decide exactly what new characters, born of a given prior character, will be the "inevitable" vessels of the prior character's deposition. As an over-all ironic formula here, and one that has the quality of "inevitability," we could lay it down that "what goes forth as A returns as non-A." This is the basic pattern that places the essence of drama and dialectic in the irony of the "peripety," the strategic moment of reversal.

INDEX